Elisabeth Settelmaier

'Adding zest' to science education

Elisabeth Settelmaier

'Adding zest' to science education

Transforming the culture of science classrooms through ethical dilemma story pedagogy

VDM Verlag Dr. Müller

Impressum/Imprint (nur für Deutschland/ only for Germany)

Bibliografische Information der Deutschen Nationalbibliothek: Die Deutsche Nationalbibliothek verzeichnet diese Publikation in der Deutschen Nationalbibliografie; detaillierte bibliografische Daten sind im Internet über http://dnb.d-nb.de abrufbar.

Alle in diesem Buch genannten Marken und Produktnamen unterliegen warenzeichen-, marken- oder patentrechtlichem Schutz bzw. sind Warenzeichen oder eingetragene Warenzeichen der jeweiligen Inhaber. Die Wiedergabe von Marken, Produktnamen, Gebrauchsnamen, Handelsnamen, Warenbezeichnungen u.s.w. in diesem Werk berechtigt auch ohne besondere Kennzeichnung nicht zu der Annahme, dass solche Namen im Sinne der Warenzeichen- und Markenschutzgesetzgebung als frei zu betrachten wären und daher von jedermann benutzt werden dürften.

Coverbild: www.purestockx.com

Verlag: VDM Verlag Dr. Müller Aktiengesellschaft & Co. KG
Dudweiler Landstr. 99, 66123 Saarbrücken, Deutschland
Telefon +49 681 9100-698, Telefax +49 681 9100-988, Email: info@vdm-verlag.de
Zugl.: Perth, Australia; Dissertation Curtin University of Technology, 2003; Originaltitel: Transforming the culture of teaching and learning in science: the promise of moral dilemma stories An interpretive case study;

Herstellung in Deutschland:
Schaltungsdienst Lange o.H.G., Berlin
Books on Demand GmbH, Norderstedt
Reha GmbH, Saarbrücken
Amazon Distribution GmbH, Leipzig
ISBN: 978-3-639-13290-8

Imprint (only for USA, GB)

Bibliographic information published by the Deutsche Nationalbibliothek: The Deutsche Nationalbibliothek lists this publication in the Deutsche Nationalbibliografie; detailed bibliographic data are available in the Internet at http://dnb.d-nb.de.

Any brand names and product names mentioned in this book are subject to trademark, brand or patent protection and are trademarks or registered trademarks of their respective holders. The use of brand names, product names, common names, trade names, product descriptions etc. even without a particular marking in this works is in no way to be construed to mean that such names may be regarded as unrestricted in respect of trademark and brand protection legislation and could thus be used by anyone.

Cover image: www.purestockx.com

Publisher:
VDM Verlag Dr. Müller Aktiengesellschaft & Co. KG
Dudweiler Landstr. 99, 66123 Saarbrücken, Germany
Phone +49 681 9100-698, Fax +49 681 9100-988, Email: info@vdm-publishing.com
Perth, Australia; Dissertation Curtin University of Technology, 2003; Originaltitel: Transforming the culture of teaching and learning in science: the promise of moral dilemma stories An interpretive case study;

Printed in the U.S.A.
Printed in the U.K. by (see last page)
ISBN: 978-3-639-13290-8

Elisabeth Settelmaier

'Adding zest' to science education: Transforming the culture of science classrooms through ethical dilemma story pedagogy

An auto/ethnographic case study

Abstract

It has become a habit of our time to lament about the state of the world and simultaneously profess that there is not really anything we, as individuals, can do about it because there is just too much that needs fixing. In this thesis, I challenge this view on the basis that science teachers in particular are in a unique position to raise students' awareness of problematic issues in relation to the world around them by providing students with necessary knowledge. However, sound knowledge does not equate with a positive attitude, this is why I contend that providing students with factual knowledge might not be enough to enable them to participate in the public discourse on making the world a 'better place' in which to live. Given the pervading influence of science on our daily lives, this discourse necessarily includes a focus on science, scientific research and its uses. However, many science educators traditionally have taught science without addressing ethical questions. I argue that the inclusion of a discourse on ethical science-related issues into science teaching might open an avenue for science educators to offer students opportunity for practising their future engagement in the public discourse about science by learning to reflect critically and collaboratively on their attitudes, beliefs and values.

This thesis presents an interpretive case study, situated in the 7th Moment of Qualitative Research, which investigated the planning and implementation of a specially designed 'Ethics in Science' curriculum, in the context of national curriculum reform in Austria. The 'Ethics in Science' curriculum was implemented in two science classes in a public senior high school in Austria by a biology teacher and a mathematics/physics teacher. The study explored the appropriateness of a science teaching approach that uses dilemma stories as a pedagogical tool for initiating individual reflection and classroom discourse on ethical issues.

The study was designed as a 'bricolage', drawing from ethnography, hermeneutic-phenomenology, feminism and biographical research. Autobiography caused me to engage in critical self-reflection on my own attitudes, beliefs and values, bringing to the fore the relationship between my personal history and my own ethical sensitivities. This was helpful as a 'primer' before engaging students in the act of reflection. The use of multiple methods for data-generation served the purpose of crystallisation. Integral philosophy and critical constructivism were theoretical referents for my research on the teaching and learning. The Theory of Transformative Learning and a perspective on moral learning that combines several types of ethics served as a referent for interpreting the analysis of student learning. I have drawn on the multiple perspectives of the students, teachers and myself as the researcher. It was very important to me to maintain the participants' original voices as often as possible in order to establish 'polyvocality'.

Findings indicate that the teaching approach using dilemmas led to critical thinking, in some cases to critical self-reflection, and seemed to help with initiating a classroom discourse. Overall, it appears that the dilemma teaching approach can promote rational, social and emotional learning. On the teachers' side, this type of teaching seemed to challenge the teachers' existing skills with regard to facilitation and moderation of class discussion and the self-restraint needed to avoid imposing their opinion on students. An issue for the teachers concerned their uncertainty about when to intervene in group-processes.

The data-analysis also led to seemingly contradictory results which I interpreted using a dialectical 'dilemma' framework wherein the synthesis of two contradictory poles serves as a starting point for a higher level of understanding. I identified seven 'pedagogical dilemmas' – pedagogical because they are related to teaching and learning in the context of a dilemma teaching approach, and 'dilemma' because they require a choice on the side of the educator who intends to use a dilemma teaching approach. These pedagogical dilemmas were related to the dilemma stories, the individual reflection phases, the collaborative discourse phases, the ideal frequency of dilemma units, the teachers' skills, so-called problem students, and the time-requirements in relation to the dilemma units.

Acknowledgments

There are no impossible dreams just our limited perception of what is possible (Beth Mende Conny)

It has always been my goal to write a doctoral thesis – one day…! For many years it did not look favourable at all: first being the mother of small children - something I never regretted but also something that does not make academic life easily attainable. In addition, I had to confront personal set-backs, family problems, change of country, change of life-style, change of language and many other things that in the end proved not to be 'real' impediments but rather learning opportunities. I have now reached a stage where I can regard the people I met along my path as people who taught me something – sometimes the hard way. I would like to thank them all for giving me this opportunity.

But of course there are some people who deserve to be mentioned in a special way. I would like to use a somewhat chronological order (if possible!). Thanks to my parents who supported me 'durch dick und dünn' (German: lit. through thick and thin = for better for worse): Ihr habt zwar nicht immer mit mir übereingestimmt in Bezug auf was ich wollte, aber Ihr habt mich auch nie aufgegeben (You did not agree with what I wanted for myself but you also never gave up on me). I would like to say thanks to my brother Gerhard for being such a warm-hearted, helpful and supportive man. Furthermore I would like to thank my children David, Sara, Nikola, and Susanna for being so patient with me during all these years, and for going with me through all the ups and downs along the way.

Very special thanks to Peter – my partner, my mentor, my friend for your ongoing support. I greatly appreciate your intellectual input, your caring attitude, and your loving support. Thanks to Nell my stepdaughter for settling in so well to our new family.

Thanks to Nancy Davis for being a mentor and a very special person. Thanks to Brigitte Begusch, Roswitha Gschweitl, Inge and Reinhard Kaindl, Giselinde Ewaller, Horst Ibetsberger and Ulli Winkler for being good friends despite the distance.

Special thanks to Ingrid Roll, my friend, teacher-colleague, and former supervisor who had an invaluable input into this thesis – I hope you make it too – one day. Special thanks also to Sabine, to the staff and administration and the students of the BG & BRG Klusemannstrasse, Graz – I could not have achieved anything without your support. Furthermore I would like to say thanks to the parents and the education authorities of the Land Steiermark for their support.

Here at the Science and Mathematics Education Centre, I would like to thank Peter Taylor, my supervisor, Stephan Millet and Darrell Fisher, my associate supervisors, for their support. Special thanks to Jaya Earnest, Robyn Chien, Chi-Yan Tsui, Poh Sing Huat and to all the other doctoral and master's students for being good friends and for creating a good student community at SMEC. Thanks to Petrina, Rosalie and Helen also at SMEC.

I would like to thank all the people who have contributed to this thesis in one way or another even if they have not been personally named above.

Table of Contents

List of Tables

List of Figures

Prologue – writing a qualitative thesis

Writing a thesis is like putting together a jigsaw puzzle.
Writing a thesis does not occur in a straight line,
much rather in a circle.

Writing a thesis is like a spiral, spiralling up and down and around,
occasionally branching out to one side,
then finding one's way back .

Writing a thesis is like weaving a wreath,
Consisting of twigs,
nodes and leaves.

Weaving a wreath requires us
To pay attention to the details
as well as to the appearance of the whole.

Writing a thesis requires us to
work on it continuously – adding
to the wreath where it looks a bit thin….

Writing a thesis like
weaving a wreath is never static.

A thesis is the process of knowledge
creation frozen at the time of submission.

(June 2001)

Chapter 1

"Why cover the whole world with leather if you can use a pair of sandals?" – Preparing young people for a (post?)postmodern world.

INTRODUCTION

Shantideva, an eighth-century Indian sage, posed this question to his students trying to make the point that there is no use in trying to change the world if we do not try and change our mind (Naphtali, 2003). Lamenting about the state of the world alone, however, does not change it to the better. I believe that teachers, apart from parents, are in a unique position to contribute actively to preparing students for life. As science teachers, we may wish to enable them to participate in the environmental debate and in the discourse on science as informed members of society. We might even argue that scientific literacy comprises the ability to participate in this discourse. However, teaching that has these goals appears to be rare in Austrian science classrooms. This research study, therefore, explored student and teacher (and researcher) experiences during the month-long 'Ethics in Science' project that was conducted at a secondary high school in Austria in 2000 within the context of a national curriculum reform in 1999. The study, furthermore, explored the suitability of dilemma stories to evoke student engagement in ethical reflection and discourse on ethical problems in relation to science.

Purpose and organisation of the chapter

This introductory chapter is designed to provide an overview of this doctoral thesis by illuminating the background of the interpretive case study, by elaborating on the history of the study and the research problem, by describing the emergent nature of the methodology and research design, by discussing appropriate research and ethical standards, and finally by outlining the overall structure of the thesis. The chapter is organised in two parts:

- <u>Part 1:</u> discusses issues that gave rise to the idea of a curriculum development within science education and illuminates the research problem.
- <u>Part 2:</u> focuses on an overview of research design, the research questions, and the thesis outline.

<u>PART 1</u>: TEACHING ETHICS IN SCIENCE – WHY BOTHER?

In theory

Ethics allows us to ask some very basic questions about human life: How ought we live? What is *good*? What is *bad*? One might say that much of human life involves making decisions regarding these questions. We can say that our ethical understanding and thus our values depend on what our culture values (Nash, 1997). Values also influence our thinking about education.

Our Western culture, as Taylor reminds us, depends on controlling and exploiting nature (Taylor, 1994). This correlates with a technical interest in Habermas' sense (see Appendix 7). This technical interest has repercussions for curriculum planning, as explained by Bowers who points out that the curriculum is always grounded in the taken-for-granted culture of the learner. According to Bowers, whilst schools carry an important role in the socialisation of learners, they also tend to carry a technological worldview based on technical interest (Bowers,

1993). I daresay that uncritical science educators play an important role in the promotion of this technical interest thereby perhaps unintentionally promoting an exploitation of nature. It is here where ethics finds its entryway into the realms of science education.

Traditionally, science has often been taught as if it could and should be value-free (Allchin, 1998, 2001). Allchin explains that many science teachers actually shy away from addressing values because of fear that values are outside of the domain of science (education) or, in the worst case, that values betray the very core of science (2001; p. 193). However, as Nash implies, ultimately every education is moral education (Nash, 1997). This coincides with David Orr's suggestion that all education be regarded as environmental education. Given that we, as science teachers, are ultimately all environmental educators, we might conclude that if all education is environmental education and simultaneously all education is moral education, it is thus reasonable to conclude that environmental education is ultimately moral education. Bowers confirms this conclusion by emphasising that everything taught in schools influences how students understand the human culture/natural environment relationship (Bowers, 1993; Orr, 1992). This conclusion suddenly puts science educators in the first row when it comes to dealing with ethical issues. I would like to argue that the discussion of ethical issues in relation to science, to scientific research and its uses, and to uncritical science-transfer between cultures (Cobern & Aickenhead, 1998) forms part of the discourse on the Nature of Science. I am convinced that it is our task as science teachers to promote students' ability to participate in an informed manner in the public discourse on science. I would like to argue further that this forms part of scientific literacy (McInerney, 1986; Zeidler, 1984).

If we believe Wilson who warns us that the survival of the planet depends on a change of people's attitudes toward the world, then we cannot emphasise enough the importance of schools and of science teachers in particular for the formation of young people's attitudes and values (Wilson, 2002). Teaching ethics in science might therefore be an avenue for contributing to a greater level of responsibility towards our environment and the people in it on the side of our students. Tom Barone explains that, "Teachers are the most faithful members of society. They take as a primary article of faith that they can profoundly influence their students. They believe fiercely and deeply that they can imbue their students with proclivities, tastes, sensibilities, styles of thinking, attitudes, and values, and by doing this, deny the determinism lurking within genes or families" (Barone, 2001a, p. vii). With regards to ethics education, I daresay that it appears that this professional zeal, if it exists, is at least not obvious in many Austrian (science) teachers.

In practice

My experiences with ethics education in Austria started already in 1998 when I was working in Austrian schools. What I experienced supports Allchin's suspicion that teachers in general, not only science teachers for that matter, have ambivalent feelings towards teaching ethics. In my experience, apart from philosophical reasons, many Austrian teachers are not prepared to deal with ethical issues for two particular reasons:

1. The lack of books in German containing evaluated teaching materials.

2. The lack of skills, knowledge and experience (Mehlinger, 1986): teachers suspect that their experience in teaching science does not equip them sufficiently for teaching 'philosophy' and for 'facilitating' a discourse rather than leading it.

And I have to say, the teachers are/were right – back in 1998, there were only insufficient hands-on curriculum materials in German (especially for science education) available to the teachers. Whilst this situation might have improved by now, the overall sceptical attitude towards teaching ethics has not really changed as we can see in the next part of the chapter where I briefly describe my earlier

4

experiences with curriculum development for ethics. The 'roots' of this research thesis go back to the year 1998 when the Curriculum Reform 99 was in its planning stages. The next section of the chapter gives a brief overview of the curriculum reform document and its historical origin (see also Chapter 5).

With hindsight.... – Background of the study

Austrian teachers' 'sceptical' attitude (and perhaps complacency?) <u>was</u> challenged by a major curriculum reform, the Curriculum Reform 99, that was implemented in Austrian schools in early 2000. It explicitly includes ethics in the national Austrian syllabus.

FLASHBACK - AUSTRIA 1998

In 1996, a referendum decided Austria's future: Austria was to become a member of the European Union. The ramifications of this decision were soon to be felt in almost every aspect of life: our beloved currency, the 'Schilling', was to be withdrawn in favour of the Euro in 2002, bananas sold in Austrian supermarkets suddenly had to 'bend' to European standards, Austrians as a nation united to fight for the right to label our foods in Austrian German: the mere thought of buying a jar of jam labelled 'Aprikosenkonfitüre' ('apricot jam' in German German) instead of buying one with the long-established Austrian term 'Marillenmarmelade' ('apricot jam' in Austrian German) sparked national pride and great concern amongst the Austrian people.

Of course, becoming part of the European Union also affected the education system. In an effort to make the Austrian curriculum more compliant with other European curricula, the existing curriculum document dating back to 1986 was to be thoroughly overhauled in the 'Lehrplanreform 99' (German: curriculum reform, see Appendix 6). outcomes based education and assessment were to be introduced, schools were required to declare a vision and to partly design their own curricula according to this vision in exchange for greater autonomy.

One issue of the reform that had major repercussions on this thesis research was the overarching curriculum statement. Because ethics education was included in this, it was thus a mandate for all subjects including, of course, science education (Bundesministerium fur Bildung, 2000). However, teachers at the time complained about a lack of material and competency regarding the teaching of ethics and some presumably hoped that, "This too shall pass!"

Interestingly, it was the Austrian Youth Red Cross who responded to the 'desperate' call of teachers and initiated a project that was to result in the design of ready-to-use curriculum materials for teachers of all subjects in compliance with the Geneva Human Rights Convention (see Chapter 5). At the time, I was part of a research team and was involved in the curriculum design and evaluation. Hopes were high and I experienced the atmosphere as one of imminent positive change for the better.

THE NEW CURRICULUM DOCUMENT

In May 2000, the Curriculum Reform 99 for the lower school level (Years 5-8) was implemented in Austrian schools. However, the explanatory curriculum notes state that the overarching curriculum statement, and thus the mandate to include ethics into the curriculum, applies not only to the lower school levels but extends also to the upper school levels (Years 9-12).

Firmly grounded in Middle European philosophical tradition, the core of the curriculum document is formed by the goal of achieving 'Bildung' for every student. The term 'Bildung' is difficult to translate because the equivalent English term, 'formation', does not include the multitude of additional German meanings related to this term. However, 'Bildung' can tentatively be translated as the 'formation of a whole individual', similar to the idea of 'holistic education' in English speaking countries. 'Bildung' is much more than the total of acquired knowledge. This is why the new curriculum framework explicitly advocates an analysis of values as part of 'Bildung'. This analysis is grounded in the rapid societal change in Europe, in European integration, in globalisation issues, in intercultural exchange, in democracy, in worldviews, and in an incorporation of moral and ethical values which allows the individual to approach ethical dilemmas in an informed manner (Bundesministerium fur Bildung, 2000; Vasquez-Levy, 2002).

The new overarching curriculum statement is not only geared towards the acquisition of knowledge, but also towards the development of self and social competencies, the inclusion of values, as well as the development of the ability to make informed decisions. The new overarching curriculum statement also focuses on the development of key qualifications, such as team-competency and empathy, communication skills, self-security, organisational talent, the development of persistence, the ability to include other people and to convince them of common goals (KU Eichstätt). I found it very interesting also that the curriculum document, despite the secular nature of our modern society, stresses the Religious-Ethical-Philosophical Dimension of 'Bildung' which completes the formation of the 'whole' young person (Bundesministerium fur Bildung, 2000) (see Chapter 5 for a more detailed analysis).

Given that the new curriculum document mandates so clearly the inclusion of ethics education in all subjects and for all levels from Year 5 onwards, and given that it was implemented in 2000, I expected that three years into the implementation and into my doctoral thesis ethics education, by now, would be firmly established - even in science classrooms.

FLASHBACK – AUSTRIA IN DECEMBER 2002

During my recent visit to Austria in November/December 2002 a number of events raised my doubts about whether 'I have been flogging a dead horse with my thesis': conversations with former colleagues and with Ulrike Unterbruner, an associate professor at the University of Salzburg indicated to me that the 'grand' Curriculum Reform 99, the reform that was supposed to 'change everything profoundly', might not have turned out to be much more than 'yet another only mildly successful attempt at changing the Austrian schooling system'. I asked Ulrike, "With regard to the Curriculum Reform 99, how successful would you say it has been or has it been yet another attempt at curriculum change that has disappeared in the unfathomable depths of somebody's desk-drawer?" Laughingly she replied, "Rather the latter, I'm afraid to say! It has not been quite as successful as we would have liked it to be!" (U. Unterbruner, personal communication, November 2002). Ulrike explained to me that many teachers had engaged in professional development courses on teaching ethics primarily because they are contractually obliged to undertake professional development. Yet, she knew of very few science teachers who actively practised this type of teaching in their classrooms. In a more recent email, Ulrike contended that, "I have the impression that ...many senior high school [science] teachers still refuse to accept the Curriculum Reform 99. However, I believe that this might be due to resistance to any kind of change." (U. Unterbruner, personal communication, November 2002).

Thus, despite the apparent failure of the new curriculum reform which formed the basis of this thesis research, I am still happy that I chose this topic. It has broadened my horizons considerably. In summary, we might say that due to the impact of the curriculum reform nothing much has changed so far. It seems to me that a good opportunity for change might have slipped past almost unnoticed. On the one hand, one might be resigned to frustration, on the other hand, one might enhance one's efforts and explore even further options for teaching ethical issues in science classrooms – I have chosen the latter.

Given the apparent widespread indifference and uncertainty of Austrian science educators towards moral education, it is clearly not sufficient to simply identify ethics education in the (science) education objectives of a national syllabus. There is apparently still a high level of uncertainty amongst science-teachers as to whether or not ethics should be part of the science curriculum at all: teachers appear insecure about the legitimacy of sacrificing valuable time which could be used for content-coverage. This uncertainty might be explained in terms of the personal philosophies held by teachers (Connelly & Clandinin, 1988), especially, if we assume that these philosophies are, to a large degree, still quite often based on scientism[1], the traditional enculturation into the science teaching profession. Integrating values into science education also involves confronting values as that part of the science curriculum that is deliberately not being taught - the *null curriculum* (Connelly & Clandinin, 1988).

One could conclude that mandating the integration of the teaching of ethics in a national syllabus is one thing – integrating ethics as part of a teacher's personal curriculum is something very different. Mandates from above do not necessarily help teachers feel better equipped with regard to teaching something that involves uncertainty and accepting potentially many different views if one feels slightly intimidated by this type of thinking. It was one of the goals of this study to better equip teachers by developing materials that teachers could use in their classroom and with a view to providing professional development, if needed. Having elaborated the reasons for developing an ethics curriculum for Austrian science educators, I now turn to the thesis research and to the research problem.

PART 2: OVERVIEW OF THE RESEARCH

Research problem

My thesis research has been grounded in Austrian teachers' needs for curriculum materials and teaching strategies in German in the light of the Curriculum Reform 99. There were insufficient materials available at the time. When I was about to embark on this thesis research and had decided on the topic, I searched the literature on moral education and found that most commonly 'dilemmas' are

---

[1] Scientism holds a materialistic view of the world (Smith, 1992).

suggested as 'the' tool to achieve ethical discourse in a classroom and critical reflection in students since Kohlberg (Kohlberg, 1980, 1984, 1996; Mattox, 1975) trialled dilemmas over thirty years ago. He was using hypothetical dilemma stories to introduce participants to a dilemma situation. As elaborated in Chapter 5, the Austrian Youth Red Cross curriculum development also relied heavily on Kohlberg's dilemmas where students elucidate the reasons for decisions they would have made in a dilemma situation on behalf of the character in the story.

Browsing through the literature on moral education in science classrooms, I have come across several attempts at curriculum development in this area – all of which are in English (e.g., Dawson, 1999; Frazer & Kornhauser, 1986). Whilst Dawson's work was focused on her own science teaching practice, Frazer and Kornhauser's book contains more general suggestions for science ethics classes. A more in-depth literature search revealed that in the literature there seems to be a tacit acceptance that 'dilemmas are best'.

Thus, based on my former experiences with dilemma teaching, I decided to use dilemma stories for the curriculum development. However, I had noticed that there appeared to be a lack of critical appreciation with regard to the suitability of dilemmas as a pedagogical tool for use in moral education. No research seems to ask, "Do they work at all? ...and if yes how well do they work?" especially for those who we should care most about – the students. I have not been able so far to locate an in-depth study that focuses on the experiences of students and the teachers during a dilemma teaching unit. I have therefore formulated the following research problem:

What are the experiences of students and teachers in the teaching and learning about science-related ethical issues in relation to dilemma stories? How suitable a pedagogical tool are dilemma stories when it comes to the implementation of an ethics curriculum in science?

Personal significance

One basic ethical question with regard to any type of research is, "Whose interest does the research serve?" Of course, there is a high degree of self-interest for me given my experiences with the Red Cross Project in 1998 (see Chapter 4). Due to external factors at the time – not being able to do the research I was really interested in, nor doing it in a way that felt 'right' for me - I am grateful now to have had the opportunity to 'do it after all'.

Goals of the Research

Given the research problem, my main goals for this research (outside my own self-interest) have been:

- To formulate a rationale for the use of teaching ethical issues in science education.
- To develop and evaluate teaching materials using dilemma stories within the context of science education.
- To evaluate the suitability of dilemma stories for the use as a pedagogical tool for ethics education.
- To develop a list of suggestions and caveats for practitioners with regard to the use of dilemma stories.

Based on these research goals, I constructed a research design.

The emergent nature of the research

RESEARCH DESIGN

A good research design should reflect the research goals and provide a methodological structure for the research that enables these goals to be achieved.

Due to a lack of awareness of alternatives, my initial research design would have enchanted many post-positivist supervisors: I was planning to have a pretest-intervention-posttest design with 'a little bit of qualitative research' on the side – for 'triangulation' purposes. At this early stage, I was also considering postmodern, constructivist ideas, and I did not have a clue how to implement them in my research.

I was thinking of focusing on one school in Austria and one school in Australia, and on finding enthusiastic teachers (five per school) to support my research. I was prepared to write the dilemma stories for teachers to use in their science classes. I began to prepare a questionnaire based on Kohlberg's categories of moral development, for measuring students' morality before and after the 'intervention'. I thought that I would be able to provide ample evidence that moral learning had occurred. In my application for doctoral candidacy, I still find my:

Initial research questions

- Can Kohlberg's Theory and Kohlberg's approach to moral education, if it is embedded in a constructivist framework and used on a regular basis, despite its flaws, become a valuable tool for teaching moral issues and contribute to value and moral education?

- Using Kohlberg's stages as categories for analysis – are there any significant changes in the students' responses after the repeated use of the method?

- Using Kohlberg's stages as categories for analysis – are there any significant differences in the students' answers in regard to the gender of the participants?

- Can any gender typical communication patterns be identified during the collaborative phase of the teaching approach?

- What are the experiences teachers and students make through the use of this dilemma approach?

- How do teachers describe and experience the ethical basis of their teaching?

- What do the teachers think of this method regarding its practicability, and their own competency and confidence?

However, things changed dramatically: having discovered that I would not be able to gain access easily to Australian schools (teachers appeared sceptical?), I was on my way to Austria to conduct the fieldwork. On my way, I stopped over at the annual conference of the American Educational Research Association (AERA) in New Orleans in 2000. This conference attendance had serious repercussions: I attended a series of sessions of the Moral Education Special Interest Group and was disconcerted to find that most presenters restricted themselves to discussing the statistical finetuning of questionnaires for measuring students' moralities. Suddenly I had a profound insight: "This is not how I want to do my research!" I do not want 'to play God'. Who am I to tell whether people are morally good or bad, better or worse than others?"

'Emerged' research questions

As the result of the New Orleans 2000 experience, I adopted a radically different epistemology of inquiry which resulted in a changed research design and different research questions. At this time, I should emphasise constructivism had already profoundly entered my thinking, and was perhaps a driving force behind this decision.

Since the beginning of my thesis, constructivism and postmodernism – a philosophy that contends that there are no 'grand narratives' that proclaim an absolute truth - had entered my life in a more serious manner. I had a vague idea about constructivism before I started my thesis research. However, I was still intrigued – not so much by the underlying philosophical principles but rather by what constructivist teaching should look like. I had ploughed through the literature on various research methodologies and philosophies, and my thinking about the nature and purpose of educational research had developed further (as a result of both the thesis research and events in my life outside the research). In particular, my epistemological focus had shifted. I found that my focus had moved from wanting to measure students' moralities to assessing the suitability of the teaching materials with regard to the experiences of students and teachers engaged with dilemma stories. Thus, I developed a new set of research questions:

1. What conditions need to be established for engaging students in a dilemma learning situation?

Based on the structure of a 'typical' dilemma teaching unit (see Chapter 5), I was particularly interested in how the different components of a dilemma unit affect students and teachers: the reflection process on the individual level, the reflection and decision-making process on the intersubjective group level that is grounded in discourse, and the story itself. Based on these three aspects of dilemma units, I asked further:

2. How can we ensure appropriateness of curriculum materials with regard to the age of the students?

Through my past experiences with curriculum development for moral education, I had gained the impression that, when a teacher presents those materials, 'free' storytelling is the most suitable tool to convey the message of the story to the students. However, during the Red Cross Project in 1998, I experienced much resistance to this assertion from traditionally minded teacher colleagues who insisted that storytelling was too much of an imposition on teachers and that the handing out of paper-copies was 'just as good'. For this reason, I asked the question:

```
3. Storytelling as a teaching method - Is it a suitable
   tool for introducing students to a dilemma situation?
```

In the traditional dilemma unit, the story is paused at a dilemma situation and students are required to reflect individually on the dilemma problem (see Chapter 5). The goal of this exercise is to 'get them to think'. This leads me to the next question:

```
4. How well are dilemma stories suited to initiate
   'thinking' about a dilemma in the individual student?
```

In a classic dilemma teaching sequence, the individual reflection phase is followed by confrontation with other opinions through dialogue in a group situation (Gschweitl, Mattner-Begusch, Neumayr nee Settelmaier, & Schwetz, 1998). If dilemmas are successful they lead to a discourse and thus potentially to moral learning (in theory). I have, therefore, asked the following question:

```
5. Do dilemma stories have the potential to initiate
   discourse?
```

Another important pedagogical concern was the assessment of this type of learning. As one of the collaborating teachers pointed out to me, "The students won't take it seriously if I don't attach any assessment to it…" ('Irene', personal communication, May 2000). I asked therefore,

```
6. How can we assess this type of learning?
```

However, my focus here was on the question, "How do we know that a student has reflected on the dilemma issue?" rather than, "How do we assess a post-intervention increase in morality?"

Structure of the thesis

My thesis structure has changed dramatically over time. My first attempt looked like this: introduction, literature review, methodology, results, summary and conclusion. My supervisor glanced at it, smiled, and said, "What is a postmodern lady like you doing with a research design like that?" That gave me something to think about - I liked the idea of being 'postmodern', whatever that meant – it flattered my ego, I suppose – so I did not get defensive but tried to 'fix' it. This was the beginning of many re-structurings of my thesis depending on my own stage of development which ranged from total confusion to increasing clarity (?) yet always reflecting my personal development and raised levels of consciousness. Some of my earlier structuring attempts can be re-visited in Appendix 3.

The Buddhist concept of 'being-in-the-moment' has gained importance for my understanding of the world, and I can see it reflected in the thesis: just as I will never step into the same river again, I will never be the same person to write these sentences. Research means development, growth – it is important to note that a thesis reflects only a point in time nothing final. Given the fluid and emergent nature of the research, a number of additional research questions arose from the data which I have explored in the appropriate chapters. In the following section of the chapter, I present the final structure of the thesis (see also Appendix 3):

- Chapter 1: Provides an overview of the background, the research problem and research goals, as well as the research design and research questions, personal and broader significance of the research.

- Chapter 2: Discusses basic methodological issues, such as the philosophical background and additional theoretical referents of the research, the research design and research strategies, as well as research quality standards.

- Chapter 3: Introduces the reader to the research context with regard to the fieldwork location, the research participants and the particularities of the Austrian schooling system.

- Chapter 4: Introduces the reader to the context of the researcher through autobiography. The chapter also contains methodology relevant to autobiographical research.

- Chapter 5: Gives an overview of the Ethics in Science Curriculum in 2000 by discussing theoretical and practical aspects of dilemma units.

- Chapter 6: Is strategically situated before the findings chapters and elucidates fieldwork-related issues and data-analysis. Furthermore, I elaborate on additional literature I had become aware of at that time.

- Chapter 7: Presents findings with regard to the implementation of the Ethics in Science curriculum focusing on the dilemma stories.

- Chapter 8: Investigates students' 'thinking' during individual reflection phases of the dilemma units (see Chapter 5).

- Chapter 9: Presents my insights into students' and teachers' experiences during the discourse phases of the dilemma units.

- Chapter 10: Presents additional findings.

- Chapter 11: In this chapter, I summarise, conclude from the findings, and make suggestions for future research.

Significance of the research

About a year ago, I received an email attachment of the National Association for Research in Science Teaching (NARST) mailing list summarising the results of discussion groups formed by several strands of NARST about 'The Role of Moral Reasoning on Socioscientific Issues and Discourse in Science Education' (D. Zeidler, email correspondence, 2002, see Appendix 13). Apart from lamenting the tradition of teaching science in a *moral vacuum,* the discussion groups also concluded that despite the fact that ethics cannot be separated from science, moral issues continue to be traditionally marginalised in the (presumably USA?) science curriculum. These results coincided with my own experiences in Austria and with the research literature, as discussed earlier. This indicates that there appears to be a need for research in this area.

Given the difficult relationship of values and science education as elaborated earlier, which seems to be also reflected in the rather small number of references with regard to ethical education within science education (e.g. Dawson, 1999; Degenhart, 1986; Frazer & Kornhauser, 1986; Johnston, 1995; Mattox, 1975; Michael, 1986; Patry, 2000; Poole, 1995; Witz, 1996; Zeidler, 1984), and given the lack of appropriate teaching materials in German, as well as the urgent socio-cultural demands on science education, a research thesis exploring the suitability of dilemma stories as a pedagogical tool for the teaching of ethics in science classrooms appears to be a significant contribution to the body of knowledge within the science education community.

REVIEW OF THE CHAPTER

In this introductory chapter, I have developed a rationale for the research that explores the suitability of dilemma stories to invoke ethical reflection and discourse in science classrooms as part of Nature of Science instruction and scientific literacy. Based on the research problem, I have elaborated on the research questions. I have described the emergent nature of the research design and given an overview of the structure of the thesis. I grounded the research in existing literature and discussed the significance of the research for me personally and for the wider science education community.

Chapter 2

Methodology I

The gendered, multiculturally situated researcher approaches the world with a set of ideas, a framework (theory, ontology) that specifies a set of questions (epistemology) that he or she then examines in specific ways (methodology, analysis) (Denzin & Lincoln, 2000b, p. 18).

INTRODUCTION

For reasons of readability, the methodology of this study is distributed in four strategic places throughout the thesis. There are two methodology chapters: Methodology I serves to introduce the reader to the overall methodology of the thesis research including a discussion of the historical development of the methodology. Furthermore, it locates the research within qualitative inquiry in the '7th Moment' and discusses also additional theoretical referents, such as integral philosophy and critical constructivism. I have used a naturalistic approach resulting in an emergent research design (Erlandson, Harris, Skipper, & Allen, 1993) (see Chapter 1). I present my thesis as an interpretive case-study and, in relation to the notion of research as 'bricolage'. I discuss several research methodologies from which I have borrowed individual strategies. Methodology II (Chapter 6) serves to discuss fieldwork-related issues, issues of data-generation and data-analysis, as well as emergent theoretical issues in relation to moral education. It is strategically located before the findings chapters. In addition, Chapter 4 contains a methodological section on autobiographical writing, and Chapter 5 provides a methodological overview of the Ethics in Science curriculum development and the pedagogical aspects of its implementation in this study.

This chapter is organised in four parts:

- In <u>Part 1</u>, I present a historical overview of the development of the research methodology including several methodological crises that stalled my research efforts intermittently.
- In <u>Part 2</u>, I introduce the reader to qualitative research within the 7th Moment. Furthermore, I discuss two additional theoretical referents that have supported the research: integral philosophy which was helpful during data-analysis and interpretation (see Chapter 11), and critical constructivism that informed the teaching and learning side of the curriculum development as well as the research. In addition, I elaborate on writing as inquiry.
- In <u>Part 3</u>, I discuss the quality standards of the research in terms of crystallisation - from many different angles. Furthermore, I present my personal credo as a researcher.
- In <u>Part 4</u>, I elaborate on the ethical standards applicable to my research.

<u>PART 1</u>: HISTORICAL OVERVIEW OF THE DEVELOPMENT OF THE RESEARCH METHODOLOGY

Lily as a learner

Contrary to the beginnings of my research, where I was still flirting with a post-positivist research design, the thesis presents a qualitative interpretive case study, involving a naturalistic approach to the subject matter. This, of course, involved a major shift in my thinking…turning me into a 'border-crosser' between two sub-cultures of the research community (Giroux, 1992). I have tried to illustrate my learning experiences in this vignette drawn from my research journal:

<u>BE(COM)ING A QUALITATIVE RESEARCHER</u>

> So I had left the safe and cosy cradle of quantitative research to embark
> on an adventure tour for a disillusioned ex-natural (mineralogist) scientist:
> *abseiling into unknown territory* - equivalent to having to deal with 'real'
> human beings, *bungee-jumping from a high cliff* - equivalent to having to
> design my own research, *rock-climbing in the Dolomites* - equivalent to
> becoming knowledgeable of several qualitative methodologies and
> theoretical frameworks, in order to practise 'crystallisation', *trekking in*
> *the Himalaya* - equivalent to trying to maintain an ethical commitment with
> all the people involved, and last but not least *high-speed windsurfing* -
> trying not to, despite rapid developments, lose track of my original
> intentions. I have had similar experiences during my research so far, such
> as fear of the unknown, feeling overwhelmed, sometimes feeling just
> great, sometimes highly focused, sometimes erratic, as if having lost
> track of everything.

One of the major changes in my life as a researcher has been to give up the metaphor of a 'truth seeker' in favour of the metaphor of a 'learner' (Tobin & Tippins, 1993). This has not been very difficult for me, as I have always felt uncomfortable in the role of the omniscient scientist. However, the change from quantitative to qualitative research was, in my case, also accompanied by a change from the objective natural sciences – my master's thesis was in mineralogy - to the subjective human sciences, resulting in a profound shift in focus <u>and</u> perspective (see Chapter 4).

Prior to commencing this thesis research, I took up a course in constructivism and consequently read a number of relevant publications on constructivism (e.g., Noddings, 1984; Tobin & Tippins, 1993; von Glasersfeld, 1990, 1995). I also started to read about phenomenology, for example, Moustakas' book on transcendental phenomenology, van Manen's work promoting the use of a pedagogical hermeneutic phenomenology in educational research, and more (e.g., Crotty, 1996; Grumet, 1992; Heidegger, 1962; Holstein & Gubrium, 1994; Moustakas, 1994; van Manen, 1990; West, 1996, Stewart & Mickunas, 1990). I was introduced to Wilber's works which also had a profound impact on my thinking (Wilber, 1995, 1997, 1998, 1999, 2000).

Methodological 'hiccups'

However, the development of my research methodology did not happen without having to overcome obstacles in my thinking. Looking back, I can now distinguish four major 'methodological crises' that I experienced during the planning and implementation phases of the research.

Crisis 1: When I presented my supervisor with the list of my initial research questions he pointed out to me that there was a potential problem with having a post-positivist research design and simultaneously having constructivism as a referent for the teaching and learning part of my research. This was easily fixed by adjusting my research design to a more postmodern methodology. The next issue was not so easily resolved and 'unbalanced' me a bit.

Crisis 2: I was planning to use phenomenology as my primary methodology for the research whilst I planned the Ethics in Science curriculum with constructivism as the main referent. But, as one of my colleagues and my associate supervisor pointed out to me, for philosophical reasons there is a potential problem with using phenomenology and constructivism in the same study. Because I insisted on understanding the intrinsic problems between these two competing referents, I got stuck in this subject area for a while, as I did not want to end up with unsolvable problems towards the end of the study. At this early stage, I felt disillusioned and temporarily quite confused, as each of the two 'philosophies' I had read about offered something good and interesting, but each of them also had its flaws and contradictions and/or they tended to exclude each other potentially.

When I continued reading the literature on methodology, I suddenly found myself confronted with yet another profound question: given that most of the literature on qualitative research is on ethnography, "What am I doing – is it ethnography, or is it phenomenology?"

Crisis 3: Reading further did not really help because much of the literature on ethnography is quite 'obscure' to the novice qualitative researcher, and it seems to presuppose that you already have an understanding of what ethnography is or at least of what it is not. After engaging in conversations with colleagues and other academics, I realised that there appears to be 'some' insecurity about the distinction between ethnography and phenomenology. I heard many different, and sometimes contradictory suggestions. I believe that this would be an ideal topic for a book that would be welcome wholeheartedly by the science education research community.

In my 'despair', I contacted someone who should know: Max van Manen. I asked him 'What am I doing?' – thinking that there was not much to be lost in doing so. He responded and pointed me back to the original focus of the thesis and to the research questions – What is the focus of your research? Are you interested in (i) the description of a sub-culture leading to ethnography or (ii) understanding the meanings participants attach to phenomena or events, leading to a phenomenological study whereby the researcher is primarily interested in the phenomenon? I re-read Max van Manen's book 'Researching Lived Experience' and Brown's commentary on van Manen's impact on the educational research scene, and realised that what I had been doing during the implementation phase was similar to a pedagogical hermeneutic phenomenological study, in van Manen's sense (Brown, 1992) – but then again, it was not. I was primarily interested in the participants' experiences during the curriculum implementation and I wanted to give voice to each of them. I felt that restricting myself to a description of the phenomenon was not what I wanted to do. Thus, the study did not become a 'phenomenological' study.

Crisis 4: After becoming increasingly frustrated with competing methodologies and apparently incommensurable research strategies, I decided to use Frederick Erickson's broadly encompassing anthropological framework for qualitative research - especially for the data-analysis. I decided also to use critical constructivism as a theoretical referent (Kincheloe, 1998; Taylor, 1998) for (i) the research and (ii) the teaching and learning in relation to the curriculum development and implementation because it combines radical constructivism, social constructivism and a critical perspective.

In the following section of the chapter, I introduce the reader to the 'emerged' research methodology.

PART 2: QUALITATIVE RESEARCH IN THE 7TH MOMENT

Qualitative research was born out of a concern to 'understand' the 'other'. It is multimethod in focus, and it involves an interpretive, naturalistic approach to its subject matter, which means that people are studied in their 'natural' settings. Being a situated activity, it locates the observer in the world. Qualitative research involves the studied use and collection of a variety of empirical materials, that describe routine and problematic moments and meanings in individuals' lives, and it deploys a wide range of interconnected interpretive practices (Denzin & Lincoln, 1998, 2000b). According to Denzin and Lincoln (2000), there have been several successive waves of epistemological theorising across 7 moments in qualitative research, starting with the positivist or traditional moment (1900-1950) and culminating in the current 7th Moment of qualitative research, when researchers have learned how to locate themselves in the text and write differently. The 7th Moment is also concerned with moral discourse and the development of sacred textualities (p. 1048) based on a sacred epistemology (quoting Bateson and Reason) that provides us with a non-competitive, non-hierarchical relationship to Nature, earth, and to the larger world (p. 1052). A sacred epistemology is also political inasmuch as it promotes, for example, values of empowerment, care, love, solidarity, community, morally involved observers and civic transformation (p. 1052). The 7th Moment has turned out to be a powerful framework for my thesis research (Lincoln & Denzin, 2000). Lincoln and

Denzin have constructed a solid building, however, I found that the building is still too theoretical – it is not yet very helpful in terms of applicability to the research in practice. This is why I chose integral philosophy and critical constructivism as additional referents because they provide the 'furnishings' of the new house. I discuss these referents later in the chapter (Tobin, 1993).

I chose a qualitative research methodology because I was more interested in 'understanding' phenomena than in 'explaining' them in the manner of traditional objectivistic research approaches. Given the limited scope of the study, I suggest that it be regarded as an interpretive case study.

I adopted the role of an interpretive 'bricoleur' who produces a 'bricolage' - a pieced-together, close-knit set of practices . The bricolage is the result of the bricoleur's method, and is an emergent construction that changes, takes new forms as different tools, methods, and techniques of representation and interpretation are added to the puzzle. It represents the researcher's images, understandings and interpretations of the world or the phenomenon under analysis (Denzin & Lincoln, 2000, pp. 4-6). The concept of a bricolage correlates well with the concept of an emergent research design which takes into consideration the complexity of human settings. A researcher takes with him/her only as much design as s/he thinks is faithful to the context. The researcher recognises the complexity of the context, goes into the setting with only as much design as he or she believes is faithful to the context and…allows structure to build only as his/her understanding of that context and of the respondents' constructions of reality allows the design to emerge (Erlandson et al., 1993, p. 73). In addition, "methodological changes and shifts in constructions are expected products of an emergent design dedicated to increasingly sophisticated constructions" (Guba, 1989, p. 242). I have documented the emergent nature of the constructions throughout the thesis through historical flashbacks and autoethnographic writing. For the same reason, I have also not included a single, discrete literature review that would present the theory as if it had existed in this form from the outset, but instead I have attempted to present specific theory at the time that it became relevant to each phase of the research endeavour. In the next section of the chapter, I introduce the reader to additional theoretical referents that complement Lincoln and Denzin's 7th Moment of qualitative research.

Additional theoretical referents

Integral philosophy has been a framework that has supported my thinking within the 7th Moment from early in the thesis-research. It has been particularly helpful with interpretation of theories that appeared incommensurable as well as during the data-analysis and interpretation phase of the study. Integral philosophy has thus served as an underlying referent.

INTEGRAL PHILOSOPHY AS A 'COSY BEDDING' FOR THE RESEARCH

Given my increasing interest in Eastern philosophies, in Buddhism in particular, I found it increasingly difficult to accept the traditional Western dualistic worldview that was the result of the Enlightenment Era: the world is divided into subjective and objective, inside and outside, science on the one hand, and art, religion and culture on the other (Wilber, 1998). In the past, the criticism of Western dualistic thought had led to the development of phenomenology as a philosophy in response to the hegemony of positivist, scientistic thought: it resulted in the 'design' of the 'Lebenswelt' (life-world) by Husserl and 'Dasein' (Being) by Martin Heidegger. 'Dasein' is inseparable from his/her 'Lebenswelt' - s/he is deeply immersed and cannot stand outside of it (Heidegger, 1962; van Manen, 1990; West, 1996).

I found integral philosophy helpful for overcoming traditional dualistic thinking. Integral philosophy, as suggested by Wilber, can be interpreted as integrative, inclusive, comprehensive and balanced (Wilber, 1997) and aims at bringing to the fore the interconnectedness of apparently incommensurable philosophies. Integral philosophy not only matches the tenets of the 7th Moment, but I believe the two frameworks mutually support each other, as Lincoln and Denzin also envision a 'sacred epistemology' that allows for recognition of the non-competitiveness of epistemologies. Integral philosophy can be regarded as a holistic[2] philosophical post-postmodernist referent. This again sits well with the 7th Moment, as Lincoln and Denzin (quoting Gergen and Gergen) suggest that research in the 7th Moment lies within the realm of the 'post'-post structuralist, 'post'-post modernist period. Gergen and Gergen refer to this period as an 'age of reconstruction' (Gergen & Gergen, 2000; Lincoln & Denzin, 2000). They describe the new age as characterised by the notion that it is not the individual mind that is celebrated but integral connectivity. Throughout the theoretical chapters in the Handbook of Qualitative Research (2000), various authors stress the trend to move away from separateness to connectedness, from exclusivity to inclusion. I believe that integral philosophy might provide the philosophical background that supports these trends because it gives us a tool – integral vision – that allows us to actively integrate that which appears to be mutually exclusive. Integral, for Wilber, means to integrate, to bring together, to join, to link, to embrace (Wilber 1995, 1998, 1999, 2000).

In the West, there is the common belief that if two opposites cannot be united, we try to either control or eliminate the oppositional pole of the bifurcation (Slattery, 1995). An alternative strategy to elimination is integration through dialectics: we attempt to transform both poles of a contradictory set of metaphors into a higher set of understanding where a higher level of synthesis is yet another departure point of a further dialectic seeking an 'ultimate truth' in a Hegelian sense (Slattery, 1995). Integral philosophy uses a dialectic where one integrates dialectical systems by realising that all elements are interrelated and are reflections of the same underlying unity.

Applied to research, the dialectics of integral vision allows for epistemological pluralism and for a unity-in-diversity instead of conformity

---

[2] The term *holistic* is used throughout the thesis in accordance with the definition suggested by the Holistic Education Network of Tasmania (online document, 2001).

(Pallas, 2001; Wilber, 2000). Simmer-Brown (1994) sees relationships being transformed in a pluralistic setting, "…it is the genuine meeting of two people or two traditions, for whom the common ground is unchartered. On such sacred ground, customary assumptions and power plays hold no sway for a time; we open with curiosity to the realities for another person and tradition (p. 100)." She cautions us though that in order to understand pluralism we have to understand what it is not: pluralism does not equate with diversity. Diversity suggests the fact of differences (cultural, religious, philosophical,…). However, pluralism is the response to diversity: it has us engage with the other person or community. Pluralism is a commitment to communicate with and relate to the larger world (Simmer-Brown, 1994). Recognising epistemological pluralism is, in my view, one of the strengths of an integral perspective. Integral philosophy suggests that we have available a range of 'different modes of knowing', each of which discloses a different type of 'world' (see Chapters 6 & 8). The integral approach recognises the 'moments of truth' in each of these knowledge modes, but it rejects attempts to privilege only a single way of knowing, for example, empiricist (scientific) knowledge. Thus, *integral* means that each of the different types of knowing offers some important 'truths' about the world - each representing only a partial truth - and that all types of knowing are equally valid and important. An integral perspective is also not syncretism, where we would try to blend and homogenise differences into a single path. Pluralism respects the differences that reside in the variety of different traditions, without reconciling or integrating those differences into a single path. Unity-in-diversity and epistemological pluralism as proposed by an integral philosophy suggest that we have to learn to live with the ambiguity of difference which, as Simmer-Brown points out, is a "…courageous practice, and engagement with the fact of diversity in our world" (Simmer-Brown, 1994, p. 101).

One of the most commonly asked questions with regard to integral philosophy is, "What makes you think that all this is not an expression of rampant relativism?" I was asked exactly this question when I was presenting a conference paper at the Annual Australasian Research in Education Conference (AARE) in

Fremantle in 2001 (Settelmaier & Taylor, 2001) (see Appendix 14). Simmer-Brown offers an answer, "Pluralism is not relativism. When we encounter difference, or diversity, it is tempting to shrug our shoulders and proclaim, 'there is no truth that can be discovered: all truths are relative.'…The most serious flaw in relativism is its tendency to see commitment of specificity as incompatible with an acceptance of diversity."(Simmer-Brown, 1994, p. 101). The pluralism of integral philosophy suggests not that there are no 'truths' to be discovered – rather the opposite, as mentioned above: there are different 'truths', each is equally valid dependent on appropriate quality criteria, and each contributes to the 'whole' – which can be interpreted as our knowledge of the Truth grows asymptotically by taking into consideration as many of its parts as possible. This seems to coincide well with the notion of a 'bricolage' in qualitative research.

In summary, an integral perspective that is based on integral vision prepares the way for a unity-in-diversity that is grounded in epistemological pluralism and that allows for 'many voices' to be heard, or for true polyvocality, which has been suggested by Gergen and Gergen (2000) as a characteristic of the 7th Moment: "…the view of polyvocal subjects offers a significant means to go beyond the animosities pervading the qualitative arena… [and thus] allows for new forms of research methods to emerge" (Gergen & Gergen, 2000, p. 1037). Each of the many voices has something important to say and to contribute towards an asymptotic growth of knowledge of the whole. In my thesis, I have tried to attend to polyvocality by maintaining participants' voices as often as possible.

In my thesis, an integral perspective is particularly evident in Chapter 6, where I introduce a 'new' theoretical' framework for moral education that can be described as an integral approach, as well as in Chapter 8 where this framework was applied to the analysis. In the final chapter, Chapter 11, I use integral vision also for the 'final' interpretation. For the interested reader, I have attached a paper in the appendix that was presented at the Australian Association for Research in Education in 2001. In this paper, I discussed potential implications of integral philosophy for science education research (Appendix 14). The other theoretical referent that informed the teaching and learning as well as the research was critical constructivism.

CONSTRUCTIVISM AS A THEORETICAL REFERENT

As mentioned earlier in the chapter, constructivism served as a referent for the curriculum planning and implementation, as well as for the research (Tobin & Tippins, 1993). The crucial question is, "Which type of constructivism for what purpose?" My primary goal for using a dilemma approach to teach ethics (is) was to enhance the awareness of students toward dilemmas in and about science and to enable them to confront the widespread belief that science can provide 'absolute truth and knowledge'. Becoming scientifically literate and becoming part of the scientific discourse community was another goal. Students' development of critical thinking guided by the question, "Whose interests are being served?" and involving reflection on the quality of these interests was an 'intended learning outcome'. These goals constitute a critical social perspective.

The dilemma teaching approach, as suggested by Gschweitl et al., (1998), includes phases of individual work (calling for a radical constructivist perspective) alternating with phases of group-work (calling for a social constructivist perspective) (see also Chapter 5). An integral solution to the perspectives 'dilemma' lay in adopting a combination of all three: critical theory, radical and social constructivism. I was very pleased to find that such a type of constructivism already existed within science education.

Critical constructivism

Critical constructivism combines critical theory, radical and social constructivism, and it also adds an ethical component based on an Emancipatory Ethic and an Ethic of Care (Kincheloe, 1998; Taylor, 1998). Critical constructivism is a valuable referent for my research and for the teaching and learning within the Ethics in

Science curriculum for two reasons. First, it highlights that the Ethics in Science curriculum serves an emancipatory interest, especially the deconstruction of distortions, such as a scientistic, objectivistic worldview. Second, it helps us understand that, with an enhanced sense of moral agency, teachers of the Ethics in Science curriculum are concerned with establishing communicative classroom environments in which flourish discourse practices of critical inquiry (Taylor, 1998, p. 1118). These tenets are well aligned with the goals of the Ethics in Science curriculum development and its implementation as well as with the ensuing critical interpretive inquiry.

In addition to adding a critical perspective, the social constructivist component of critical constructivism foregrounds collaborative classroom learning, whilst the radical constructivist component foregrounds individual learning experiences. For the research, the social constructivist component frames the intersubjective constructions that resulted from the interpretive case study. In the following section of the chapter, I discuss the basic tenets of social and radical constructivism which are subsumed by critical constructivism.

Radical constructivism

Radical constructivism can be regarded as the result of further development of Piagetian constructivism. The biological origin of constructivism is still clearly reflected in the basic tenets of radical constructivism as stated by von Glasersfeld:

- Knowledge is not passively received either through the senses or by the way of communication but instead knowledge is actively built up by the cognising subject.
- The function of cognition is adaptive tending towards fit or viability. Cognition serves the subject's organisation of the experiential world, not the discovery of an objective reality (von Glasersfeld, 1990).

Knowledge is therefore constructed for the purpose of enhancing survival through making experience meaningful (Geelan, 1997; von Glasersfeld, 1990, 1995). Von Glasersfeld points out the importance of the concept of <u>viability</u> which means that in order to be retained newly constructed knowledge has to enable the learner to achieve a valued goal (e.g. reduced perturbation).

Critics have accused radical constructivists of promoting rampant relativism, an 'anything goes' philosophy in which one can construct any reality one likes. Von Glaserfeld rejects this accusation as based on a misunderstanding of the concept of viability: the 'real' (objective ontological) world provides us with constraints, with obstacles that shape the viability of our experiences, thus restricting the 'realities' we construct.

In the dilemma approach, a radical constructivist perspective highlights students working individually, trying to make decisions, reflecting on their own values and experiences: being perturbed by the lack of viability of their 'old' strategies, requiring (what Piaget called) assimilation and accommodation, resulting in the construction of 'new' ethical solutions and thus moral learning. "This sounds reasonable for single work situations but what about group-work? How does radical constructivism account for that?", we may ask. Von Glasersfeld explains that radical constructivists recognise the importance of social interaction for knowledge construction, yet as Ernest seems to criticise, "...the construal of other persons is driven by whatever representations best fit the cognising subject's needs and purposes" (Ernest, 1995, p. 475). For this reason, I feel that social constructivism seems to be a much better referent for the rich tapestry of social interaction involved in science teaching and learning, especially in a dilemma approach.

Social Constructivism

Social constructivism emerged out of the perceived limitations of radical constructivism, and is concerned with the contributions of social interactions to

33

the construction of self (Atwater, 1996). This view is derived from the sociology of knowledge, and states that the construction of reality is an intersubjective process: It is socially negotiated between significant others who are able to share meanings and social perspectives of a common life-world (Berger & Luckmann, 1966; Taylor & Campbell-Williams, 1992). Within the dilemma teaching approach, small group-discussions in which students discuss the results of their individual work activities and reflect on their own values and ideas, are the primary arena for moral learning, from a social constructivist perspective. The confrontation of differing ideas and opinions holds the potential to induce a reflection process and perhaps a moral learning process.

There are many different perspectives on social constructivism, particularly with regard to the construction of scientific knowledge. I have chosen to adopt a perspective that is based on Driver et al.'s work, as well as on Vygotsky's concept of the Zone of Proximal Development. Driver et al. regard scientific knowledge as constructed and communicated through the culture and social interactions of science. Learning is seen as a process of enculturation rather than of discovery, where students' everyday representations which are constructed, validated and communicated within everyday culture, stand in potential conflict with the representations of science (Driver, Asoko, Leach, Mortimer, & Scott, 1994). It is this enculturation which, if uncritical, becomes problematic (This is where the critical component is helpful). Vygotsky suggested a perspective that is helpful when investigating group-learning: "The Zone of Proximal Development is the distance between the actual developmental level as determined by independent problem solving and the level of potential development as determined through problem solving under adult guidance or in collaboration with more capable peers" (Vygotsky, 1978, p. 87). Vygotsky therefore suggests that through collaborative learning the individual can increase the level of development due to the positive influence of peers (or the teacher). In the dilemma teaching approach, students compare their individual opinions and try to arrive at a common solution to the problem (see Chapter 5). In the dilemma approach, the teacher serves as a facilitator, a support-person who operates like a 'guide' for the dialogic process, however, it is primarily one's peers with whom individual students interact.

Summarising I can say that, critical constructivism provides a valuable framework for my thesis research because it subsumes radical and social constructivism, and it adds an ethical and a critical perspective to constructivism.

My research as a 'bricolage'

As mentioned earlier in the chapter, a bricolage is like a jigsaw puzzle: a pieced-together, close-knit set of practices. It is an emergent construction, that changes, takes new forms as different tools, methods, and techniques of representation and interpretation are added (Denzin & Lincoln, 2000a). Given that my research aimed to develop curriculum material associated with an Ethics in Science curriculum, and to investigate students' and teachers' experiences during the implementation of the curriculum, I can distinguish two phases of the research. They are characterised by two distinct methodological approaches.

- <u>Phase 1</u>: the curriculum development
- <u>Phase 2</u>: the implementation of the curriculum

<u>PHASE 1</u>: THE CURRICULUM DEVELOPMENT

In Chapter 5, I discuss in detail the methodology of the curriculum development phase of my research. Thus, in this chapter I provide only a broad overview of two aspects of the curriculum development phase:

- The planned teaching and learning experience.
- The development of teaching materials, i.e., dilemma stories.

The overarching referent for both phases with regard to teaching and learning was critical constructivism which I have described in detail earlier in this chapter.

PHASE 2: THE CURRICULUM IMPLEMENTATION

My basic research goal during the implementation phase and afterwards was to understand "…the nature of the experience of learning - so that I can understand better what a particular learning experience is like for the children" (Brown, 1992, p. 50). Brown continues, "This paring to the very essence of the pedagogical experience is only achieved when the basic existential nature of that experience is understood. The result of this understanding is the possibility of a more informed response to that particular pedagogical experience" (Brown, 1992, p. 50).

In order to attain this goal, I opted to use a qualitative research method for science education as suggested by Erickson (Erickson, 1998). Erickson points out that it is especially useful to use qualitative research if we want to obtain detailed information about implementation, to identify the nuances of subjective understanding that motivate various participants in a setting, and to identify and understand change over time. Given that I was interested in all of these issues, his framework proved to be very helpful. In accordance with Erickson's distinction of different levels of qualitative research, I can say that:

- On a fundamental level, I have described the research context including an introduction to the Austrian schooling system and to the school, in particular, demographic data, descriptions of the classrooms, pedagogical 'biographies' of the teachers, etc. (see Chapter 3).
- On a more subtle level, I have included observations and documentation of classroom discourse[3] and of the pedagogy – where appropriate – throughout the section 'Research Findings' (see Chapters 8, 9, 10, 11).

---

[3] Discourse refers to the conduct of immediate social interaction by verbal and nonverbal means (Erickson, 1998)

Erickson explains that it is useful to formulate questions in advance and to think of the kind of evidence one would like to obtain in order to answer these questions (Erickson, 1998). In order to answer my research questions, as outlined in Chapter 1, and in accordance with the traditions of the bricoleur, I borrowed from various methodologies.

- From <u>ethnography</u> I borrowed the concepts of 'participant observation' and 'thick description', especially with regard to describing the research context (see Methodology II).
- From <u>ethnography</u> I borrowed 'autoethnography' to describe my practice as a researcher (see Chapter 4).
- From <u>feminism</u> I borrowed the concepts of 'voice' and 'care' and also the concepts of the 'separate', the 'connected' and the 'constructed' knower (see Methodology II, Chapters 8 & 9)
- From hermeneutic <u>phenomenology</u> I borrowed the concept of 'Lebenswelt' (lifeworld) (Heidegger, 1962).
- From <u>biographical research</u> I borrowed autobiography to bring to the fore my values and biases and to locate myself, as the researcher, as an integral part of the research context. Critical reflection was a crucial component during the writing of the autobiographical parts of the thesis, thus engaging myself in the same reflective process that I wanted students to engage in (see Chapter 4).

I discuss further details of the actual fieldwork and the data analysis in Methodology II (see Chapter 6).

In the following section of the chapter, I present the act of writing as a form of inquiry. This is particularly important as I have used several writing formats throughout the thesis.

Writing as inquiry

As the world and our views of it have changed, so, too, have changed the kinds of texts we hope to have represent us to ourselves (Lincoln, 1997, p. 37)

Given the postmodern nature of the qualitative research design of my thesis, and given that it is a bricolage drawing from different methodologies and data sources, my writing is characterised by a 'blurred genres' approach (Richardson, 1994, 2000). I have avoided the traditional third person scientific writing style that distances the researcher from the research (Cooper, Baturo, & Harris, 1998). One major concern for me, as a naturalistic researcher, was expressed by Richardson (quoted by Erlandson et al., 1993, p. 27), "A continuing puzzle for me is how to do sociological research and how to write it so that the people who teach me about their lives are honoured and empowered, even if they and I see the world differently." Issues of representation have featured largely during my research (see later in the chapter), given that I had to translate the participants' utterances from German into English, which always leaves the chance of some misrepresentation. In order to 'overcome' these problems, I have opted for an experimental writing style that allows me to choose from a variety of representations (Richardson, 1994, 2000): I have used 'realist', 'confessional' , and 'impressionist' tales in the tradition of John Van Maanen (Van Maanen, 1988). I have written narratives of the self by adopting an autoethnographical methodology throughout the thesis (Ellis, 1997; Ellis & Bochner, 2000). In Chapter 4, I have used an autobiographical methodology (Bullough & Pinnegar, 2001; Denzin, 1989). However, I have not been the first science educator to embark on the 'experimental journey': examples include (Afonso, 2002; Roth, 2000; Taylor & Timothy, 2000). Vignettes or anecdotes serve throughout the thesis to illustrate events or ideas in order to compel, to lead the reader to reflect, to involve me personally in the text, to transform by 'moving' the reader (if possible). Chapters 7-10 contain lived experience descriptions (van Manen, 1990). The quality standards of the writing and of the interpretive case study are discussed in the next section.

PART 3: RESEARCH STANDARDS

From triangulation to crystallisation

The move from quantitative to qualitative research has resulted in a shift of thinking with regard to validity claims, not only with regard to my thinking but also to human science research: the old quality criteria of positivistic research do not suffice in this context. Historically, during the crisis of representation in the mid-eighties of the 20th century, when new models of truth, method, and representation were sought, issues such as objectivity, validity, reliability were made problematic.

Qualitative researchers have replaced validity criteria with the concept of verisimilitude, meaning something appears true or real (Adler & Adler, 1994). In order to achieve a high level of verisimilitude, it is important to maintain a multimethod focus. Triangulation is a strategy for ensuring verisimilitude. It is not a tool to replace validation, but an alternative to validation. It is best understood as a strategy that adds rigor, breadth, complexity, richness, and depth to any inquiry (Denzin & Lincoln, 2000), which is especially important for the human sciences, as postmodernists and poststructuralists claim that there is no clear window into the inner life of an individual. There is no single method that can grasp all of the subtle variations in human experience. Therefore there is no alternative to the application of multimethods. However, I personally prefer the post-modern concept of *crystallisation* (Richardson, 2000) – apart from my conviction that 'three angles' are not enough, this idea is also related to my personal history as someone who has studied minerals in detail and who has come to love and admire their beauty and the great variety of shapes, colours, angles (see Figure 1).

Figure 1: Quartz crystal (SiO$_2$)

Laurel Richardson suggests using mixed-genre texts that, like crystals, combine symmetry and substance with an infinite variety of shapes, substances and transmutations. Crystals grow, change and alter - like research projects and researchers.

> *Crystals are prisms that reflect externalities and refract within themselves, creating different colours, patterns, and arrays, casting off in different directions. What we see depends upon our angle of repose (Richardson, 2000, p. 934)*

Quality criteria

In order to judge the quality, researchers have designed criteria to determine what is of value. Whilst positivist research subscribes to validity standards, interpretive research adheres to different standards more suitable to a qualitative research process.

Doing a 'bricolage', which consists of components derived from different methodologies, means that the individual standards of each methodology apply to the bricolage, resulting in a jigsaw-puzzle of standards. The researcher ultimately needs to determine which standards are most applicable to her study.

To determine the overall quality of this interpretive case study, I have chosen to use the 'parallel criteria', as suggested by Guba and Lincoln in their book "Fourth Generation Evaluation". From the Trustworthiness Criteria I have chosen – Credibility, Transferability, Dependability, and Confirmability, and from the Authenticity Criteria, I have chosen the concept of Fairness (Guba & Lincoln, 1989). How does each of these standards apply to my study?

TRUSTWORTHINESS

Trustworthiness criteria have been designed as alternatives to the methodological rigor criteria of positivist research.

Credibility

Its focus is to establish congruence between the constructed realities of respondents and those of the researcher. I have endeavoured to establish credibility through prolonged engagement – spending one month intensively in the research context, and being a former teacher of the school I was able to immerse myself well into the 'local scene'. Furthermore, I engaged in participant observation throughout the fieldwork period and also in peer-debriefing – I took the opportunity to talk to colleagues who were not actual research participants who, however, witnessed the dilemma teaching firsthand as outsiders. They were present because they would normally, outside of the project, have been involved in team-teaching with the participating teachers. I practiced negative case analysis and found only two cases out of twenty interviewees, one of whom clearly changed her mind during the project. I established progressive subjectivity through writing a research journal. Member checks were performed through email and in the form of letters (see Appendix 2). In the next section of the chapter, I discuss the 'crisis of legitimisation' in this study and I elaborate on the difficulties I experienced with my attempts to engage in member-checking.

Crisis of legitimisation

In order to legitimise my knowledge claims, I tried to approach a 'phenomenon' from different sources, as elaborated further in Chapter 6. However, the most 'reliable' method of legitimising one's claims - 'member-checking' - turned out to be a complex and frustrating task. I supplied all participants with preliminary interpretations of the data, asking for comments and pointing out the importance of this process for representation and legitimisation. Yet, despite all efforts, there were few participants who replied to my questions, and only one of the teachers who stayed in regular email-contact. I experienced first-hand the tyranny of distance and the problematic nature of having only conventional mail and email available to stay in contact with participants.

I have tried to address the issue of legitimisation by using a 'language of probability' that brings to the fore the potential ambiguity of interpretations thereby avoiding the expression of epistemic certainty.

Transferability

Transferability focuses on checking the degree of similarity between sending and receiving contexts (Guba & Lincoln, 1989). Whilst the positivist generalisability is an 'absolute' concept, transferability depends on how much the salient conditions overlap. In writing the thesis, I have used the technique of 'thick description' to allow for transferability.

Thick description

I have produced thick description of particular events to ensure that I, as an observer, do not have a privileged voice in the interpretation, although I am aware that in the end all research is interpretive. Thick description enables readers to understand the context of the study and to maintain links between the theory and the context in which it is grounded (Geertz, 1973; Geertz, 1983; Tobin & Tippins, 1993).

Dependability

Dependability is concerned with the 'stability' of the data over time. Contrary to positivist research, methodological 'instability' is an expected result of an emergent research design and thus needs to be well documented. Writing the thesis, I have, wherever applicable, documented the development of the research process or the development of my thinking guided by new insights, etc.

Confirmability

Confirmability focuses on the integrity of the findings. In order to establish confirmability, I have provided copies of the interviews in the appendix and on CD, and interview quotes have been coded allowing them to be traced back to their sources.

AUTHENTICITY CRITERIA

I chose Fairness from the list of Authenticity Criteria. Fairness refers to the extent to which constructions of participants and their underlying value structures are honoured in the inquiry process, meaning that different constructions need to be presented in the research report. I have tried to satisfy the criterion of Fairness by attending to the concept of voice throughout the thesis.

Voice

Research participants have a right to have their voice preserved in an authentic way. With regard to qualitative research, in general, it is the merit of feminism that the issue of the *other's voice* has been problematised: If voice is provided for each individual, different stories will emerge, which does not indicate differences in truth, but rather what was learned from an experience. Michele Fine speaks about the concept of 'Othering' - to speak about the other (1994). Tobin and Tippins inform us that voices are not different views of an accessible reality, rather that views are dependent on the goals of the participants in the study which can be overt or covert (Tobin & Tippins, 1993). Maintaining the voices of the participants is essential for practising an *Ethic of Care* (Noddings, 1984).

Issues of translation and Fairness

In addition, the issue of 'translation' was of major concern for me: having conducted the research in a German-speaking country, all the videos, interviews, emails, etc., were written and spoken in German. In order to minimise the impact of the translation, I performed most of the data-analysis in German, and only translated those quotes from interview-transcripts, videos and emails that I actually used in the thesis. For me as a German native speaker, it is very difficult to determine whether my English translation meets the German meaning in every detail. Even during the last stages of the analysis and writing, there were some changes to the translations because I felt that I might not have expressed exactly what the person seemed to mean. I have to admit that even though I have tried to be as fair as possible with my translations, I cannot exclude the possibility that I might have misinterpreted a participant's comment.

STANDARDS FOR WRITING

Given that in this thesis I use several genres, I decided to use Barone and Eisner's criteria for 'arts-based' research. Barone and Eisner suggest including aesthetics into the quality considerations. Their criteria are geared towards establishing 'verisimilitude' (something that appears true). This measures a text's ability to enrich and illumine its readers. They list several features that characterise arts-based educational inquiry.

I invite the reader to apply these features as criteria to my texts.

- Creation of a virtual (an 'as if') reality.
- Use of contextualised 'everyday' forms of language.
- Presence of ambiguity where meaning is suggested rather than stated.
- Use of expressive language characterised by the use of metaphor.
- Promotion of empathy.
- Personal signature of the writer where the text embodies the author's vision (Barone, 2001b; Barone & Eisner, 1997).

With regard to autobiography, I have discussed the appropriate standards in Chapter 4. Finally, I would like to invite the reader to engage with my very personal methodological credo.

A Researcher's Credo

- I have attempted to approach the inquiry with self-critical awareness.
- I am aware that the choice of procedures adopted by researchers is very much influenced by their personal history, which ultimately results in a thesis being a very personal statement.
- I am also aware that data are not 'collected' but 'constructed' from experience using personal theoretical frameworks that have greatest salience to my goals as an individual conducting the research.
- I believe that it is important to identify one's personal biases, values and beliefs that have most significance for a specific study - in this thesis I have aimed to reach this goal by using autobiography and autoethnography throughout the thesis.
- I have learned that data recorded as 'relevant' by me conform to my personal theories of what is relevant in a particular context. Data creation and interpretation are not separate events, but components of a dialectical process (Tobins & Tippins, 1993).

PART 4: ETHICS DECLARATION

It is a requirement of the Curtin University regulations for doctoral degrees to obtain an ethics clearance at the time of application for candidacy. My ethics declaration at the time was approved and I have aimed throughout the research to maintain high ethical research standards.

The teachers, students and their parents, the school principal, and the local school authorities were informed in writing about the research background, the methodology and their own 'role' in the study. Teachers, students and their parents voluntarily signed letters of consent. The original letters of consent and the information participants received prior to the project are available in

46

Appendix 1. Consent was also obtained regarding the use of video-tapes and photos for research purposes.

The teachers received an introduction to dilemma teaching that enabled them to understand the background of the dilemma teaching approach and enabled them to use the method within their own curriculum.

In order to attend to the authenticity criterion of Fairness, I have attempted to present authentic voices as often as possible through extensive use of verbatim quotes, thus giving 'voice' to the participants. I have engaged in member-checking in order to represent the participants' views as correctly as possible, which included emails, letters, opinion seeking and negotiation of understanding.

Participants have been guaranteed anonymity. None of the participants will be identified and it was made clear that the participants had the right not to answer questions during interviews, and that they may withdraw from the research at any time.

Throughout the research process, I have endeavoured to sustain an Ethic of Care (Noddings, 1984).

Details of the fieldwork, methods of data-generation and of the data-analysis are discussed in Methodology II (see Chapter 7).

Chapter 3

Situating the research

For the naturalistic researcher, the ability to get inside the social context, to share the constructed realities with the stakeholders in that context, and to construct new realities that enhance both the knowledge of the researcher and the knowledge and efficiency of the stakeholders is the essence of research (Erlandson, Harris, Skipper, & Allen, 1993, p. 68)

INTRODUCTION

Figure 2: The 'Uhrturm' (clock-tower) in Graz, Austria

The research was conducted in a public, co-educational, senior high school in urban Graz, the capital of the province of 'Steiermark' (English: Styria) in southern Austria (see Figure 2). I had been familiar with the school for some years before the commencement of the study in my role as a teacher and as a parent of a student. However, my great familiarity with the locality and the Austrian schooling system tends to 'blind' me to the 'needs' of people who come from other than Middle-European contexts.

In this chapter, I would therefore like to introduce the reader to the research context. Given that I cannot expect the reader to be knowledgeable about the Austrian schooling system, I include a description of the particularities of the research locality – the Roseggerschule (Rosegger- School), one of the schools within the Schulverbund Graz West (School Alliance Graz West). Given school alliance's particular status, I also discuss the 'special' position of the Schulerverbund Graz West within the broader context of the Austrian schooling system. Writing this chapter, I had to deal with an ethical dilemma: the school explicitly wanted me to mention the name of the school because they considered it as an 'advertisement' if somebody writes a PhD thesis about them. However, for ethical reasons in order to preserve the anonymity of the participants, I have renamed the particular school but kept the name of the school alliance. I have named the school after Peter Rosegger who is widely considered one of the greatest Austrian writers. His writings capture well what it was like to live in the rural Steiermark in the 19th century. I have also added to the list of references the web-address of a piece of his work in English that I discovered on the World Wide Web (Rosegger, 2003).

Before I launch into the description of the research-context, I would like to invite the reader to join me on a meditation on the fieldwork experience...

FROM OUTER SPACE

Imagine you are looking down on the Earth from outer space, and you can make out Europe from a distance. If you look a bit closer you can see a small country in the heart of Europe: well of course you could not see the outline of this country in the shape of a boot – this is only the case for political maps. If you zoom into the picture even further, you see a city and in this city there is a green field and on this green field you might be able to make out a group of people. If you move close enough to count them, you might find that there are 53 people on the field, but what (on

Earth?) are they doing? From your vantage point out there, it looks as if there are two groups, one has thirty members, the other one has twenty only. They seem to be running around aimlessly on the field, then again sitting in groups, then showing big pieces of paper to other team-members. Maybe they are playing a game? Two people seem to be the referees. If you look closely enough, you can see that the two referees are women, organising the two groups of what looks like teenagers. But there is one other person left. What is she doing there? She is (frantically) moving between the groups, seemingly looking for something, occasionally talking to one of the two 'referees', then again to some of the kids. Obviously she is trying to stay on top of what is happening on the field, but please don't forget she cannot see what you can see from up there – the whole picture. Nevertheless, she is trying hard. On the other hand, she sees things, you cannot see from a distance, so in order to see more of the whole picture she has to move around on the field, collecting tiny puzzle pieces. I can tell you now that this woman is a researcher, trying to collect data from this particular field. The whole set-up might seem to you (up there) to be a random, disoriented, chaotic process but you might also detect some spaces showing order...

This is how I, as a researcher, experienced my 'field' work – chaotic and simultaneously ordered. Sometimes, but only sometimes, I envy you for your privileged position out there and 'curse' the entangled webs of personal involvement which provide (great) insight but also personal bias that is problematic inasmuch as familiarity sometimes breeds blindness. But this is how research works down here on the Earth's surface: as a participant observer I am part of the whole picture - not standing outside, not looking down on it. Dealing with real human beings, not with tiny moving spots. Dealing with emotions, experiences - my own and those of others. Maintaining an open mind and heart seems to be tantamount, or as Antoine de Saint-Exupéry said in his famous book 'Le petit prince' (The Little Prince), "On ne voit bien qu' avec le coeur. L' essentiel est invisible pour les yieux." You only see well with your heart. The essential things are invisible to the eye (de Saint-Exupery, 1995)

Organisation of the Chapter

The chapter is organised in two parts: <u>Part 1</u> focuses on describing the Austrian schooling system, the Schulverbund Graz West, and in particular the Roseggerschule, as the site of the research. For this purpose, I relied on my own experience, conversations and interviews with teachers, and available literature on the school and the school alliance.

Part 2 introduces the research participants through two lenses: my own and the teachers. Part 2 consists of two sections: Section 1 introduces Irene and her class whilst Section 2 focuses on Sandra and her class.

PART 1: LOCATING THE FIELD

Having safely returned to Earth, I would like to invite you now on a journey that brings us back to the small Middle-European country, home to almost eight million inhabitants, famous not only for its history, its music, its mountains and beautiful landscapes, but in recent years unfortunately also for a political development that has resulted in news headlines overseas. The country's name is Österreich, derived from the old German word 'ostarichi' which means '[the land that] reaches to the East'. To speakers of English, it comes under the more familiar name of Austria. Two thirds of the country are characterised by mountainous landscapes, more commonly known as the Eastern Alps. The rest of the country is rather flat or hilly and this is where main cities such as Salzburg, to the north of the Alps, Vienna, situated east of the Alps, and Graz, in the south-east of the country, are located. You have already seen Graz from outer space. It is the capital of the province of the Steiermark. It has always had strong historical connections to the countries east and south of what comprises Austria today: Slovenia, Croatia, Hungary and Italy. This is maybe why Graz (at least) to me has an almost Mediterranean character, especially during summer-time, with street-cafes and many cultural events. Prior to migrating to Australia, I spent almost five years living in Graz. I received much of my professional training there and was lucky enough to work as a *Lehrerin* (teacher) at a school in Graz: the Roseggerschule which forms part of the Schulverbund Graz West. For my thesis, this school has been 'the centre' of my fieldwork, with the collaborating teachers being former colleagues and co-teachers, and some student-participants former students of mine.

Failure to get access to Australian Schools

In my original research proposal (see Chapter 1), I was suggesting not only to visit Austrian but also Australian schools. I intended to 'compare the moralities' of Australian students with Austrian students. I also set out to 'determine cultural difference in the moral responses of students'. Apart from a change in my personal priorities, this plan also failed due the reluctant response of the Australian schools that I approached. It seemed too time-consuming and problematic to get access to schools in Perth, whilst I did not have to struggle with the school in Austria. In addition, as my literature reading proceeded, it became clear to me that if I wanted to engage in a qualitative study, I should rather focus on one school only and forget about the cultural comparison. Now I can say that I am grateful that the original plan did not work out, as this forced me to focus on the one school and to rethink my whole research design.

Why did I choose the Roseggerschule?

When my original plans did not work out, the first school that came to my mind was the Roseggerschule in Graz, which is part of a greater school alliance called the Schulverbund Graz West. It was clear to me from the beginning that I wanted to collaborate with the teachers at the Roseggerschule for various reasons: one was that every teacher within the Schulverbund Graz West is contractually bound to trial innovative practices if appropriate. This, of course, does not mean that every teacher embraces wholeheartedly every new fad that comes along nor that everybody actually gets involved but it offers the possibility for those who want to experiment. In short, the following reasons caused me to choose this location for my fieldwork:

- I was likely to find teachers who would collaborate.
- I knew from experience that the students are used to using alternative methods and are well "trained" with regard to group-work, presenting results, etc.
- I expected minimal resistance from the principal and from the school authorities.
- I was familiar with the school structure and school culture.

First contact with the Schulverbund Graz West

With hindsight, I can say that my first contact with the Schulverbund Graz West can be described as 'unusual' already. At that time, I was looking for a school where I could complete my introductory year, after having finished my master's degree. Coming originally from the north of the Austria, Graz was as foreign to me then as Perth was when I first got to Australia. I did not know anything about the local schools, such as which schools had a good reputation, or which teachers were good to work with. The language spoken is German but many speak a very broad Styrian dialect, which I found hard to understand at the beginning. The Education Department was not very helpful either – a serious looking man, hiding behind his glasses (and his desk) said to me, "For completing the year of induction, <u>you</u> will have to find a teacher with the qualification to supervise novice teachers in science education. I don't have a list of them. You will have to phone up the schools and find a supervisor yourself!"

So I started phoning schools, with the telephone book on my lap. Most schools did have some teachers with the necessary qualification, but none for science. This was a very frustrating experience. Close to giving up, I called the Schulverbund Graz West, the last school on my list, where the secretary told me that they had one lady on their staff, who could supervise me. When I talked to this lady, called Irene, later on the phone, she said, "Are you aware of what you are getting yourself in to?" As I had no clue what she was talking about, I said very bravely, "This [not really knowing what 'this' might be!] ...was the actual reason why I had chosen this particular school!" Silly me, I thought afterwards but, on the other hand, I felt I would have looked stupid had I admitted to not knowing anything about the school. I can freely admit now that her remark remained ambiguous and quite unsettling for me during the weeks before school started in September. However, having gone through twelve years of schooling myself I thought there was hardly anything I could not have anticipated beforehand. I was prepared to become a novice teacher in a typical, traditional Austrian Gymnasium. Little did I know!

In order to understand the great impact the 'unexpected' had on me, I have to introduce the reader to the more traditional Austrian schooling system beforehand.

The traditional Austrian school system

I - like any other Austrian child - entered primary school along with cohorts of kids who were also missing their two front teeth, at the tender age of six. After four years, the first life-determining decision had to be made, between 'Hauptschule' (high school) leading up to year 8, and 'Gymnasium' (grammar school), leading up to year 12 and to the 'Matura' (A-level examinations; Tertiary Entrance Exams), which is essential for entry into tertiary institutions. Needless to say, my parents decided in favour of the Gymnasium which at the time (1974) was reserved for the so-called 'bright' kids. Most other kids of my primary class went on to high school and proceeded from there into apprenticeships. Thus, after four years of primary school, I entered Form 1 (equal to Year 5) of the Gymnasium and left it at the end of Form 8 (equal to Year 12) with a certificate that enabled me to enter university.

In recent years, there has been a change in attitude towards the Gymnasium: more and more parents have felt that their children should rather attend to the 'higher goals in life', thus sending them to the Gymnasium often regardless of the actual capability of their children - leaving high schools increasingly empty. Already, many 'Hauptschulen' have been closed down for lack of students. The reasons are the low reputation of high schools as 'schools for dummies' and the fact that passing the *Matura* followed by a university degree seem to be the preferred options for many parents. After all, they want the best for their children. Many are willing to accept the financial challenge of having to support their children into their twenties. I think that this trend is comparable to the trend towards private school that I have observed here in Australia.

Another reason for choosing a Gymnasium might also be that high school teachers do not hold a university degree but graduate from a Pedagodical Academy (PÄDAK) whilst teachers at a Gymnasium hold at least a master's degree. It appears that some parents think that the university training qualifies teachers better for their classroom practice. In my view, however, this belief is unfair and misguided. High school teachers usually receive a better pedagogical training whilst the training at university is more subject-matter oriented which leaves many novice teachers from university ill-prepared compared to their high school colleagues. With regard to achievement, expectations and demands on the students are much higher at the Gymnasium: students are expected to work independently, with a high level of self-responsibility. At a Hauptschule students generally have more time and less pressure, plus more support as team-teaching is common.

The current situation and ongoing trend has led to an overproduction of university graduates, a development that started at the beginning of the eighties. This is also reflected in the high unemployment-rates of academics, especially pressing amongst teaching graduates and medical graduates.

The Austrian schooling system also differs from other European and overseas countries in its approach to assessment, the organisation of the school year, and the organisation of the class structure. Academic outcomes or achievements are measured on a scale of 1 to 5 (1 represents very good, 2 stands for good, 3 stands for satisfactory, 4 stands for passed, and 5 stands for failed). The school year is divided in two semesters (semester 1 starting in September, finishing at the beginning of February, and semester 2 starting in February, finishing at the beginning of July). At the end of each semester, students receive an outcomes report. The end of the year report determines whether a student has passed a class and therefore can proceed to the next level in September, or whether s/he has to repeat the class. Of course, there are additional exams that allow students under certain circumstances to pass the level after all.

Subject-choices are relatively limited compared to the Australian or US system because the overall goal of Austrian schooling lies in providing students with a sound general knowledge base (Bildung, see Chapter 1) from which they can develop further in more specialised areas at university level. With few exemptions, depending on the type of school, the majority of Austrian students have classes in German, maths, English, history, geography, physics, chemistry, biology. At Gymnasium level most students have at least one other foreign language, in addition to English. Unlike in many English-speaking countries, the same students share a classroom for most of the day because the subject-choices are limited and most students share the majority of subjects. In Austria, it is the teachers who move from one class to the next whilst Austrian students usually stay in their rooms, except for science, art and physical education classes. This is why the concept of 'class community' becomes so important (see also Part 2 of the Chapter). Every class community – we might use the term 'form' from now on – has a form teacher who is responsible for the pastoral care and the administrative necessities in the kids' daily lives. This can be a teacher of any subject. Usually the form teacher and the students remain together for a period of years to warrant continuity.

Why the Schulverbund Graz West is different

When I applied at the Schulverbund Graz West, I had no idea that this was an alliance of trial schools. I had naively presumed that every school in Austria had to fall into one of the two categories of the traditional school system – Hauptschule or Gymnasium - and being trained as a senior high school teacher, it appeared clear where I would end up. In order to convey to the reader what it was like to teach at that school, I would like to present my first impressions of the school in the form of an autobiographical vignette.

Figure 3: Roseggerschule, Graz. Austria

THE ROSEGGERSCHULE - FIRST IMPRESSIONS

When the school year finally started at the beginning of September 1996, I arrived at my new school (see Figure 3). The first person I saw was a woman with long, blond hair, wearing jeans and a jumper. She immediately introduced herself to me and I thought she was very friendly and open-minded. Honestly, I thought she was a secretary. Later I was to learn that she was the school administrator (as I am writing this text now, she is the acting principal of the Roseggerschule). Most of the teachers were wearing casual clothes and I felt a bit 'overdressed', as I had chosen a rather formal outfit perfectly suitable for a traditional school. I spotted some other 'specimens of overdressed' teachers but they were outnumbered by the majority of people who had decided to attend the first general staff meeting of the year in rather informal outfits. I noticed that most of the teachers introduced themselves to me first, before I could, and offered the 'du' [German = you] on this very first occasion which is unusual in professional environments outside the student culture at universities (in German we differentiate between 'du' = 'you' for our friends and relatives, and 'Sie' = 'you' for formal use).

When I thought it was time to introduce myself to my supervising teacher, I asked one of the other teachers where I might find her and she told me," Irene? She is looking after the plants for the whole school. I would search the plants for her!" When I finally discovered her she was watering a palm-tree. I met a lively, blond woman radiating energy and enthusiasm. "Welcome to chaos – you are right in the middle of it!" she said. "What chaos?" I said looking around me - for the time being everything looked like a 'normal' school to me. "Nothing is normal here, forget everything you know about traditional schools – it does not apply to us!" And she was right. I was going to embark on a steep learning curve...

Trialing a new middle school model

A few years ago when Austria still had a Labour government, a trial for a new model school, the *neue Mittelschule* (the new middle school), was introduced: a comprehensive, co-educational school-type for years 5 to 8, comparable to the concept of comprehensive schooling in English speaking contexts. One of the reasons for introducing this school type was to make a smoother transition from the Hauptschule to the Gymnasium, and to allow the *Langsamstarter* ('slow-starters' - kids who need more attention than others while they are young but who are able to get through school quite well in general) to develop maturity at a slower rate. The mainstream Gymnasium does not cater well for these students but instead students there are expected to cope with the high demands made on them or, "They just don't make it!"

The government implemented the new model in several locations, one of which was the Schulverbund Graz West. The Schulverbund Graz West is an alliance of five trial schools, all of which are implementing the middle-school model. In their discussion paper 'Profile of a new middle-school type', Konig, Krepelka, Messner, Schnelzer, Stauchner, and Weinberger (1997) inform us that the Schulverbund rests on five pillars. The Schulverbund Graz West is:

- A new school-type for the middle-school-level.
- A pedagogical reform school-model supporting the individual. learner and supporting students at different levels of achievement.
- An institution of teaching-organization and planning.
- An institution for professional development.
- A support-system for developmental processes.

The pedagogical rationale is based on equal opportunities for every student. Learning is not seen as a cognitive process only. Action-oriented processes are to be enhanced. Group-work, individual learning, self-responsible learning control are supported. Teaching and learning goals are openly structured so that real-life, practice-oriented, student-oriented, and integrated learning become possible. One of the main foci of the curriculum is the teaching of cooperative and communicative competences. Based on insights from learning-psychology, students of a democratic school should be offered action-based, self-responsible and cooperative learning opportunities. The school strives to compensate for social disadvantages (Konig et al., 1997)

For the teachers at the Schulverbund, action-research based professional development is an important focus in their professional lives. Many of them have published their experiences in the form of papers, published in a series in collaboration with the Austrian Ministry of Education (e.g., Bauer, 1993; Bauer, Hofbauer, Kienzl, & Tasch, 1995; Fuchs & Frech, 1995; Hopferwieser, 1994; Messner, 1995; Pelzmann & Schiretz, 1996; Seidl, 1995; Silldorf, 1997).

The professional and pedagogical rationale, in practice, means that the first four years (year 5 to year 8) are conducted in the style of a 'Mittelschule' (middle school). Thus, students who would normally enter high school share a classroom with Gymnasium-level kids. The resulting problems are particularly obvious to teachers who have formerly taught at a mainstream Gymnasium - I will discuss in greater detail later in this chapter. *'Innere Differenzierung'* (internal differentiation) is the magic word used to describe the teaching style that supposedly provides learning opportunities for both fast and slow learners. In order to promote this 'inner differentiation', the teaching is usually conducted by teacher-teams, usually consisting of one Gymnasium-teacher and one high school teacher. This is <u>unusual</u> for Austrian schools. It is also <u>unusual</u> for Austrian schools that some of these teachers, in accordance with the school structure, were required to design their own new curricula long before the Curriculum Reform 99 gave teachers more authority. Before 1999, every school had to comply with the National Austrian Syllabus. For the teachers at the Roseggerschule this meant that they needed to plan curricula without any models to draw from. This has led to the 'invention' of new subjects, such as *ecology*, which is a combination of geography and biology (Pelzmann & Schiretz, 1996)

The upper school level (<u>years 9 to 12</u>) is organised in a way similar to a traditional Gymnasium. The Gymnasium is operating at the location Roseggerschule providing a choice between three branches: a language-oriented branch, a creative-branch promoting art and drama, and a natural sciences branch providing opportunities for laboratory courses and in-depth science study.

For this school to function, it requires a lot of collaboration and team-organisation in areas such as coordination of subject activities, integration and form activities. Staff are organised in form-teams, subject-teams, school-level-teams, language-teams, etc., and some curriculum-development-teams. These structures exist in all participating schools. Additionally, there is a school alliance coordinator who is responsible for all issues concerning the whole school community. The teamwork is supported by a strong professional development program, which tends to be embraced voluntarily by many (though not all) teachers. Teachers are encouraged to trial new teaching approaches and to evaluate and to improve their work – in fact, this is the core of the school's philosophy.

All these 'differences' have made the schools of the Schulverbund Graz West 'unusual', resulting in many different opinions which tend to lie between the two extremes: either you are totally convinced that the Schulverbund Graz West is the way to go, or you simply hate even the idea of it! As a German-teacher at a mainstream Gymnasium in Graz so eloquently elaborated for me, "You at the Roseggerschule, you can't really call your school a Gymnasium – everyone can pass there. Even the greatest dummies!" Or the wife of a university professor who was doubtful as to whether or not, "…students who are high-achievers should never be taught together with low-achievers. That doesn't lead anywhere. I would never enrol my kids there because I want my children to get the best possible education that prepares them for uni later on." Alternatively I heard opinions such as the one by the mother of my son's friend," I think all kids should have a similar chance to get a solid education, without the pressure and stress they exert in other Gymnasiums." In principle it boils down to political stances – a traditionalist, conservative, economic progress-oriented stance versus a left-wing perspective that promotes equal rights to quality education, if you like. In order to provide a more balanced picture, I present some teachers' opinions about 'their school'.

What do teachers think about their school?

I asked several teachers how they saw the Roseggerschule in comparison with the schools they had worked at in the past. Irene responded with a long, "uhhhmmmmmm!" and she took a while to think about the question. "I think I have stopped comparing this school to other schools, a long time ago. I made this mistake during my first year here, but the situation and the demands on me as a teacher have been so different from the outset. My demands on the kids are also very different. The whole concept is different, so I have come to the conclusion that I won't compare this school to another nor do I want to be compared to teachers at other schools. I CANNOT be compared, neither on the basis of content matter nor on the basis of the student population." Asked what she experienced as the most striking difference to other schools, Christine who teaches English and history at the Roseggerschule, replied, "The pressure of responsibility to develop new ideas in a way that students are not the ones being used but the ones who are enabled to benefit." She pointed out that the workload for her increased dramatically. "Teaching is a great challenge at times! "Yet, she also referred to the satisfaction she got out of successes, such as the love of the children and the recognition by the parents. However, she reported competition amongst teachers that apparently caused her problems. Teamwork was less of a challenge for her when she felt she had some responsibility. I found Christine's perceptions of teacher competition very interesting as I had not experienced anything of that kind myself but then again – I was not involved in the 'deeper political levels' of the school. Franz who teaches mathematics at the school reported that the workload sometimes consumed his weekends which did not go down well with his family. Yet this workload could not deter him from applying again to work at the school, if he had to, "I appreciate the freedom. In my old school there was no real recognition of my achievements." How do my experiences of the school range amongst the valued comments of former colleagues?

LILY AS A FORMER TEACHER AT THE ROSEGGERSCHULE

In short – I was thrown in at the deep end – at a point where more experienced teachers were struggling. However, I realise now that this might actually have been an advantage because in addition to my lack of experience I also lacked high expectations. I was prepared to learn - and I had to learn much and fast! When I started teaching at the Roseggerschule (1996), I felt overwhelmed at times by the intensity of responsibilities (though I was teaching only part-time!). I was teaching middle-school classes which meant that I had to meet with my team-colleagues to discuss the daily 'what, who, why and how' of team-teaching for each lesson. Apart from that, I was expected to be present at the weekly form-team meetings where issues regarding integration of subjects, projects concerning the form as a whole, etc., were discussed. Though there was usually a relaxed atmosphere, these meetings were anything but a leisure-activity. Every few weeks there were also faculty meetings.

It is important to stress that the notion of 'faculty' is different from Australia. It does not have the narrow meaning that teachers of a particular subject area 'cling together for better or worse': just the opposite, teachers of all faculties share a staff common room in which they have a desk and cupboard-space. Faculties are rather 'organisational' entities without much impact on teachers' social lives. Isolation from other teachers, to the extent that has been reported to me by Australian university colleagues, is unknown (or at least unlikely). Thus problems with communication between teachers of different subjects are also less common. Looking back now, the meetings, for me, were an avenue for mutual support and friendship apart from work, especially in the form-team. Overall, I have very positive memories of my time as an active staff-member at the Roseggerschule. I would like to add another perspective – experiencing the school from the other side of the fence.

LILY AS A PARENT

My son David spent his two happiest years at school at the Roseggerschule before we migrated to Australia. He had been struggling in a mainstream Gymnasium for three years before I enrolled him there. By that time, he had lost his self-confidence, had become withdrawn and unhappy about school, life and the universe. Within months, the 'loner' and 'potential sociopath' – expressions used by his former form-teacher to describe my son to me! – had become representative of his class, was thriving socially and had also improved academically. He became a much happier person. In my view this is possibly the main achievement of this school: one can argue about academic achievements and grades, one can argue about the unnecessary complexity of the school's organisation, the pros and cons of the middle-school model and much more, but it is hard 'to argue away' the fact that the kids seem to like it there.

Review of Part 1

In Part 1, I have tried to illustrate the particularities of the Austrian schooling system, starting with a description of the traditional schooling system, including issues such as the organisation of the school year, assessment issues, etc., followed by a comparison between the traditional system and the Schulverbund Graz West which is an alliance of trial schools for a 'new' middle-school model. I have described the organisation of the Schulverbund Graz West. In order to put my researcher impressions in perspective, I have also interviewed other teachers, and have drawn on my other roles as a former teacher and former parent at the Roseggerschule which is part of the Schulverbund. I have also tried to outline key-differences between the Austrian schooling system and systems in English speaking countries like Australia, for example, thus hopefully making it easier for the reader to 'enter' the research context almost like an 'insider'.

PART 2: INTRODUCING THE RESEARCH PARTICIPANTS

In this part of the chapter, I would like to introduce the reader to the people who I collaborated with during the research. I try to approach this issue from several perspectives using two lenses: my own and the teachers' perspectives. I am aware that my impressions are biased through my personal experiences. Drawing from different sources and member-checking has helped me to see my views in perspective. This chapter comprises two sections: Section 1 focuses on Irene and her class, followed by <u>Section 2</u> which focuses on my perceptions of Sandra and her class.

Figure 4: The interior of the Roseggerschule

<u>Section 1</u>: Irene and Form 5A

The Roseggerschule is a modern building dating back to the early '90s. Numerous windows allow light to flood the interior of the school, the corridors and stairwells, which are decorated with plants (Irene's babies!) and students' pieces of art (see Figure 12). To me, the most impressive part of the school is the library, a double storey, round building, with a spiral staircase and parquetry floors, and a cone-shaped glass-roof.

On this warm May morning, Irene and I find a quiet spot on the upper floor of the library, while Josef, a biology teacher and Irene's co-teacher, works with the students downstairs. Irene looks down on her class list and asks me, "What do you want to know because there is so much I could tell you!" She speaks like a mother about her Form 5A (equivalent to Year 9).

'FORM 5A' - HOW IRENE SEES IT

We decide that first she should describe her class to me from a demographic point of view. When she speaks, her concern for the kids radiates warmth. She tells me about her students, 12 girls and 18 boys who come from 9 different nations (Macedonia, Ghana, Togo, Austria, Bosnia, Romania, Mongolia, Iran, Hungary), across 3 continents (Europe, Africa, Asia). Between them, they have 9 different first languages (Albanian, Kal, Bosnian/Croatian, Romanian, Mongolian, Persian, Hungarian, German, English, French) and 5 different religions (Roman Catholic, Islam, Greek Orthodox, Buddhist, Lutheran Protestant). Appendix 4 depicts this demographic data. "This is the modern Austria!" I think to myself, looking down on the students. "How much it has changed since I was a child!" Five students are doing year 9 for the second time as they had to repeat the class, all of them are of Austrian origin. The reportedly low level of academic achievement cannot, as one might presume at first sight, be related to the high numbers of foreign students with language difficulties. Just the opposite seems to be the case: some of these foreign students are amongst the best achievers in the class.

Many of the students have had a turbulent past: one child has been a child slave in Africa, another arrived two years ago as an unaccompanied juvenile asylum seeker from Mongolia, without a word of German – now he is able to write German spelling tests without any mistakes and has become one of the best students in the class! Another (half-Austrian) was taken to South Africa by his parents, spent his childhood in slums, before being put on a plane back to Austria, all by himself. In Austria he was put into an orphanage by the local authorities.

Irene also describes the problems she is going through with the authorities on behalf of her students, namely those who have applied for asylum in Austria and are waiting for refugee status. Getting a visa and especially refugee status in Austria these days is a very tedious, often fruitless endeavour, often resulting in expulsion. The exploding refugee numbers in this country have favoured political changes and a shift to the political right. This has led to a recent reform of immigration laws, making it very difficult if not impossible, to stay in Austria on a permanent basis, especially as a newcomer.

'FORM 5A' - HOW OTHER TEACHERS SEE IT

Colleagues describe the class as friendly, collaborative and having a good attitude toward school work. As Josef, a biology teacher, describes them, "Irene's class is really great!" Via email, I also interviewed Walter, a physics teacher, about his impressions of Irene's class (see also Chapter 8). He described the class as one of the 'more pleasant ones' without any major behavioural problems. He said, "Most students have a high level of communicative competence – if I manage to focus this communicative competence on the subject then their achievements are acceptable. Unfortunately this is not often the case." He contended that, "... some students show high levels of intelligence which unfortunately is not always paired with the will to engage themselves." When it came to weaknesses, Walter pointed to the tendency of the whole class to reject tasks that 'smelled of work'. When he eventually gets them to cooperate, with a lot of pressure, this usually results in good outcomes. On the other hand, Walter stressed that <u>the</u> positive feature of this class is their 'tender way of dealing which each other!' Summarising he said, "If I could choose which classes I would drop – this would not be one of them!" (see Appendix 2)

'FORM 5A' – HOW I SAW IT

I wrote this impressionist tale in order to illustrate my experiences when I first met Irene's class.

<u>COLOURS AND SMILES</u>...

A hot day – over thirty degrees – very unusual for an Austrian spring. Humid. Feeling sweaty. Thunderstorms forecast for the afternoon…

Class has already started. Trying not to disturb too much. Opening the door with care. "Colours", I think seeing these kids for the first time – the colours of three continents – and smiles. I recognise some of the faces – former students of mine – they have grown a bit! Not children any longer, almost grown-ups. Even those I do not know (yet) look at me with a friendly smile on their face. Sensing warmth and openness toward me- feeling welcome. I see Irene in her role as their form teacher dealing with administrative issues. She introduces me to the class and informs them about the timetable for the project. One student raises his hand and asks about the use of the video-camera. ……having almost expected this question…..I explain to the class the "why and how" of using video in my research….

Worksheets about Photosynthesis mark the "final" beginning of the biology-lesson. Students are supposed to answer the questions using their books and collaborating in pairs…. Irene introduces each student to me, while we are walking from desk to desk. Great to have this opportunity to talk to the kids personally. Irene really tries to involve each student in a short conversation at least…Those who have known me as their teacher seem keen to find out whether I still recognise them and am able to guess their names, which is easy with some – finding that I remember faces better than names! Walking around in the classroom, I start helping the students with their worksheets. Funny feeling after so many years out of school but works quite well. Somewhere at the back of mind a little voice reminds me of the fact that I love to be a teacher…

I wrote this piece of writing immediately after having met Irene's class. It was a very moving experience for me, especially as I recognised some of my own former students in the class who were obviously pleased to see me again. The class looked peaceful and friendly, the faces bearing witness to recent political developments in my home country: Austria has within the last few years become a multicultural society with all its associated problems. Nevertheless, these kids, some of whom had already gone through hell in their short lives, gave me a warm welcome. Having introduced the students, I would now like to turn to Irene, the teacher. I was particularly interested in finding out the reasons why she wanted to collaborate with me in this research project, but also about her professional history, her biography and her philosophy of teaching.

FINALLY INTRODUCING IRENE

I am aiming at describing her in a way that she can recognise herself when she reads this text. This is the reason why I have chosen to let her speak for herself. I have constructed a 'tale' that is based on an interview that took place in her garden over coffee and cake and which I checked with Irene via email.

A 'summer' afternoon in May

A beautiful garden on the Waltendorferhöhe, one of the classy suburbs of Graz. Looking down on the roofs of the city, the air is so clear. From a far distance we can hear the hustle and bustle of city life. Only bees disturb the peace and quiet of the occasion. A few years ago, I lived down there, in the valley, where "it is all happening", often looking up to the hills in the east of Graz, thinking what it might be like to live up there, where the wealthy people live….
Irene has set the coffee table on the veranda of her father's home, where she spends most of her waking hours. I am starting to relax – jet lag and organisational stress seem so unimportant up here. It is all so far away. We want to talk about Irene's career, her ideas about the Ethics in Science Project, her reflections on her own teaching and much more. I think we have to attribute to the relaxed ambience, the warm weather and maybe my own tiredness that what was planned as an in-depth interview turns out to be an in-depth conversation about highly philosophical life-issues. I start by asking an easy 'warm-up' question:

Lily: Can you tell me a little about your tasks and responsibilities at school?

Irene: (starts laughing) Do I have to tell them all? Ach du liebes Bisschen (~Oh, my God!) – where shall I start? Maybe hierarchically? Well, for the past four years I have been in the position of a deputy principal, which includes duties such as representing the school elsewhere, expelling students from school, dealing with the law, and with the performance of colleagues.....sometimes this includes 'setting a colleague free' if you know what I mean!

Lily: I can imagine. Has it been necessary? (Irene giggles)

Irene: Sometimes people need a little nudge.

Lily: You mentioned the other day that you had responsibilities within the 'science-faculty'?

Irene: Yes, I am the ARGE-group-leader (ARGE = Arbeitsgemeinschaft – working-group, action-group) for the natural sciences at this school. I am responsible for the organisation of meetings, projects, the acquisition of materials, curriculum development, etc. I have to deal with the financial management with regard to materials due to the latest budget-cuts: that is, find and apply tricks for getting money, or materials if you don't have any money...this gets me to one of my other jobs – I am the 'cleaner' of the science department. There are no cleaners for the labs or the resource-room – budget-cuts, you know?

If I am not cleaning or organising then I am operating as a form-teacher, which is quite a task in such a multicultural class I have got. Apart from that, I am a 'normal' biology-teacher, and a 'normal' chemistry-teacher, and a 'normal' physics-teacher.....(she giggles again!) Ah yes, I must not forget – I am the 'garden-gnome' of this school and look after approximately 200 plants and their inhabitants – the aphids (laughing)....

Lily: This is certainly one of your strengths – having a green thumb! Can you think of any others?

Irene: I can see my greatest strength in well-developed communication skills, a relatively high sensitivity toward other people's problems, and in a high level of tolerance. Plus, I think I have a very good time management in place – what do you think - otherwise I could not manage it all!

I think that my abilities are very versatile – I could have chosen all sorts of other professions....

Lily: So why did you choose to become a teacher - a science teacher in particular?

Irene: Well, apart from having had a sound biological understanding of the world from an early age onwards, I have always had a great love for life as such. I grew up in the country. Another factor for my choice was rather accidental: when I was about to enrol for the first time, I entered the enrolment hall at university, saw the queues and chose the shortest queue of course, only to find out that I could enrol only for biology at this counter. The decision was made quickly, as I could not see myself queuing for a few more hours at the other counters...(laughing)

Lily: Wow! That was quick – have you ever regretted this step afterwards?

Irene: No, never! Not once.....

Lily: So when did you decide to go into teaching instead of research?

Irene: Very early, I must say! This decision was clear from a financial point of view - the faster I could finish my studies, the earlier I could earn money. And of course, I come from a family of teachers. The relatives on my father's side have been teachers for many generations, not so on my mother's side but she was a 'pure bred' teacher with all the pedagogical talents you could possibly think of.

Lily: What was the situation like for teachers when you started to teach?

Irene (laughing): Very good. In my case I had a full-time contract at the Gymnasium Gleisdorf and simultaneously I was completing my introductory year at the Oversee-Gymnasium in Graz.

Lily: Times have truly changed. When I finished there was no job to go to and I am still on the waiting list.

Irene: Yes I know it is very depressing. It was very different then - my main problems were that I had not been prepared for the daily teaching practice like 'How to teach about –the cat?' I mean I had learned about 'felidae' at the university but I could not use this at all. Ah yes, and another problem was that this was the time when mini-skirts came into fashion and I had to teach a year 12 class, boys only, with a very traditional introductory supervisor...a major hassle I can tell you!

Lily: So your skirt was obviously too short?

Irene: No, no – well, yes, maybe! But I think the main problem was that I was female and that my male supervisor had the idea that girls should get married, stay at home and look after their husbands....That's why he taught me 'how to swim' – he deliberately put me into difficult situations and had me cope completely by myself – one example – I was supposed to sit-in during one of his lessons but he did not turn up, so I had to teach unprepared. I can tell you, I did learn how to 'swim' then. I think what I learned then was that as a teacher I have to be incredibly flexible!

Lily: In your teaching now - what are the basic learning outcomes you hope to achieve with your teaching?

Irene: Well, good question - unfortunately I am forced to assess the 'famous' knowledge... This is not only a requirement of the education authorities but also of myself: I am convinced that I can neither philosophise nor think in any broader context, if I do not have any basic knowledge. I think that the teaching of 'normal' knowledge is absolutely essential to weave a web of concepts from which one can start any inquiry. It is difficult for the students to think in terms of a web, to realise that things are interconnected. But it works, like last week with my 5A - the kids suddenly realised that if we managed to perform photosynthesis in a laboratory, the oil-sheiks of the Middle East could buzz off altogether...and the kids believe that they can make it - one day in the future! I think that what happened in this case was much more than simple knowledge transfer: they understood that what I am trying to teach them is based on facts, but also that nothing is absolute and thus can be questioned. We need those 'facts' now to build on them later, to continue with our research so that we can understand things better. Not – this is how things are, but let's continue the search and find something new. Only - turn this way – show them some direction!

Lily: What do you think science education can offer to students in terms of personal and human development?

Irene: I can offer a basic understanding of their own body, a positive attitude toward nature, an understanding of the connection between my actions and my products during a lifetime and of changes in the environment and atmosphere that might affect me and my offspring. I believe that this is the core of my teaching. I believe that everyone has a certain character- spectrum and only within this spectrum can I as a teacher 'modify' a person by encouraging certain developments.

Lily: What would you say is the ethical basis of your teaching?

Irene: You mean the core? My goal?

Lily: Yes I suppose so!

Irene: To me the most important goal of teaching and thus the ethical basis of my teaching is to convey respect for life. My own personality is based on this respect for life. Due to my professional training and thus my knowledge, I do see the connections and mutual influences. I can only pass on a view I myself possess. This of course results in a very personal style in my teaching.

Lily: This is true – you do have a very personal style in your teaching. You have served as a great example for me.

Irene: Well....it is my goal to pass on this passion for teaching to my student teachers.

Lily: So.... what is the goal of this project for you [the Ethics in Science Project]?

Irene: I am completely open - I often get involved in situations in which I do not necessarily have a distinct goal. Maybe it's curiosity. Maybe it's due to my flexibility – who knows? Of course there is my ethical stance in everything I do. I accept the challenge of 'How do we approach this? How can we deal with this topic of moral education within science education?' I suppose that my students will not interpret the project as me 'abusing them' in a research project – after all, they will have to study less content matter for their next test, and I believe this arguments goes down well with them...and last but not least: I want to help you with your doctoral dissertation (laughing) – maybe I will have time to do this too, maybe after my retirement.

Lily: Well to me the main goal of moral education is to raise awareness. I mean I am aware that I cannot change the world from one day to the next, but I can contribute a little bit with my work here....

Irene: Yes, you are right. I think moral education is incredibly important. The question though remains for me: is the morality I am modelling here a valid one? You know, for me there are many different 'moralities' and I think this is dependent on your cultural background. To me, morality as a concept is the expression of 'tolerance toward everything', acceptance of others and ...yes, tolerance! Always though within the framework of maintaining life - this is how I see it!

SUMMARY OF SECTION 1

Irene seems to be a science teacher who not only possesses the energy to perform the role of a deputy principal as well as many other roles within the school, she is also a teacher with principles and a vision. She described herself as having good communication skills plus a sensitivity toward other people's problems that involves high levels of tolerance. She regards basic scientific knowledge as a necessity to engage in philosophising and lateral thinking. Her goal is to show students how everything in our environment is connected and thus that our actions influence directly our environment, ourselves, and our offspring. Her vision is to convey to students respect for life, a vision she thinks she can pass on only if she possesses this view herself. Her reasons for engaging in this research project were, apart from trying to help me with my doctoral thesis, curiosity about how we could address ethical issues in science, and the fact that she is aware that there is an ethical stance in everything she is doing. She was adamant that moral education is very important, yet she was unsure whether or not the morality she is modelling in her teaching, which is based on tolerance toward everything and acceptance of others, is a 'valid' form as she is also aware of the cultural dependence of morality.

She was the form teacher of a multicultural class consisting of students with different religions, languages, and a variety of personal experiences and backgrounds, all resulting in an interesting mix. The form was quite big, consisting of 30 students. Irene described to me her struggles when dealing with authorities on behalf of her students. Some students had arrived without their parents whilst others had lived trough traumatic experiences such as slavery, war, and orphanages. Many were still learning how to speak German. Other teachers described her class as communicative, caring but also quite lazy.

This chapter would not be complete without an introduction to the other key-participants. In the next section, I introduce Sandra and her class.

Section 2: Sandra and Form 6A

If catching up with Irene was easy, catching up with Sandra turned out to be much more difficult. Finally, on day two after my arrival, I met her more or less accidentally in the staffroom, and we decided to meet for a coffee in a nearby café to discuss the organisation of the Ethics in Science Project with her class.

MEETING SANDRA

The next day. A café down the street owned by a popular Austrian singer. Sandra is younger than Irene. I have known her rather from a distance, so far, mainly because I did not have anything to do with her directly before, apart from a few conversations on the bus and in the staff room. She reveals to me that she has been the form teacher of the 6A for the second year – the students have been together as one class only for the past two years. The group-dynamics have caused her some problems. Sandra invites me to her maths class next morning, when she wants to introduce me to the 6A…

IMPRESSIONS OF MEETING 'FORM 6A' FOR THE FIRST TIME

I now describe my experiences of first meeting Sandra's class. I have written an impressionist tale about the experience based on my research journal.

THE LOST VOICE

Dominoes – the arrangement of the desks in this classroom reminds me of domino pieces, randomly placed in groups throughout the classroom. I sneak in and find a chair at the back of the class. Some students look at me with curiosity.

Most students don't take any notice at all. They more or less ignore me. I start to draw the arrangement of the desks on a piece of paper, wondering whether there is any meaning to it at all. I can see only six girls, two of whom sit separately from the rest of the class to the right of me on a desk at the back, whilst three other girls occupy seats within the central front group of desks (see Figure 13). One girl shares a desk that is part of an L-shaped small group in the right front corner with a boy. On the left hand side there are two L-shaped desk-clusters, one is further to the front, the other one is set back almost as far as possible, almost touching the rear wall. This class looks like an average Austrian year 10 class – Caucasians only, Austrians only with one exception, as it turns out later.

Sandra comes in and introduces me to the class. She asks me to say a few words, but………what has started as a slight hoarseness last night turns out to be much worse - I have suddenly lost my voice. The students look at me giggling, trying to hold back laughter while I am struggling to get out a few words. "Oh great! What a start!" I think, when I recognise one of my son's best friends amongst the boys of the class. He had to repeat the class last year. This is why he is here. At least one comforting sight! Sandra explains to the kids, how we intend to implement the project. The class seems to be quiet and rather well behaved.

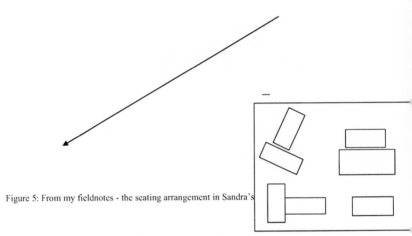

Figure 5: From my fieldnotes - the seating arrangement in Sandra's

When Sandra begins to teach the maths lesson, she announces that she is planning to bring in content from physics as well this morning. Showing some overhead-transparencies, she explains the concept of exponential growth. She speaks with a low voice – sitting at the back of the class, I am finding it a bit hard to grasp everything Sandra says. The students copy examples from the blackboard. Sandra walks around the class between the desks, explaining here, helping there, praising some students' work at the central desks. Conversations everywhere…noise levels rising. One girl, Daniela, finds out that log10 equals 1 – Sandra asks one of the noisy boys, Johnny, at the back of the class, why he thinks this is the case. He is very evasive and then starts to play the clown. The rest of class is laughing at him. Finally one of the girls, Maria, as I learn later, who is sitting at the central desks, calculates an example on the blackboard for the others.

Sandra, standing in a corner of the room, explains the implications of this example. Whilst she is talking, noise-levels rise again, especially at the central desks and the desks on the left. Only one boy, sitting at the left-hand front corner, does not join in: he just sits and stares into the air in front of him…his name is Julian, Sandra explains to me after class. He is always that dreamy.

FORM 6A - HOW SANDRA SEES HER CLASS

The picture Sandra presented of her class was quite different from Irene's class.

This class of 23 students was, with one exception – a boy from former Yugoslavia –

monoculturally Austrian, with 15 boys and eight girls. Some of the students lived in the countryside and commuted every day to school. In 2000, the kids in this form had been together in that composition for one year only. Before that they were attending various schools within the Schulverbund. Sandra pointed out that it was very difficult at the beginning to establish a class community because of the formation of groups that closely stuck together. This was why I included Figure 5 depicting the desk arrangement, illustrating the insular sub-communities in Sandra's class.

Sandra had tried to overcome this problem in the past by organising 'project days', in which she and the students stayed in a hut out bush for a few days. The students had to organise food and other supplies. Sandra felt that the class community had improved since then. Yet the class was still divided into several groups. Apart from a rather quiet group of girls, there was one group in the class consisting of boys and girls that was dominated by two girls, Maria and Ulli. This group tended to assume leadership within the class. Some of the other girls apparently tried hard to get into the 'leading girls group'. There were girls who seemed to have a tendency to anorexia, a fact that worried Sandra and the girls' parents. To some of the girls, it was of great concern not to make fools of themselves in front of the boys. With regard to the boys, there was one boy, Julian,who apparently had a tendency to daydreaming. There was another group of three boys who apparently could not find a basis for communication with the dominant girls in the class. One of them, Johnny, found it hard to fit into the class community. He had friends in his home village. He liked to go to the disco and he drank beer. He had interests that separated him from the rest of the class. Sandra described Johnny as an outsider. She gave me an example, "There was a discussion about raising the levels of achievement in English. As the form teacher, I asked them to line up: people wanting higher achievements on the one side and those who wanted low achievements on the other. About three quarters of the class were standing on the high achiever end, about three to four students somewhere in the middle, whilst Johnny positioned himself at the other end."

Apart from Johnny, Sandra described her class as quite success-oriented, even though there were phases when they were a bit more easy-going. Overall, the students wanted to be successful at school and at uni, and to get a good job, and be successful at it. This was what the discussion about 'raising the achievement levels in English' was all about – the students (!) regarded it as necessary to study English at a higher level in order to be more successful later in life.

My interpretation was that probably not all students had the same goals: I perceived a gap between the high-achievers and those who were less interested in success. It also appeared to me that part of the problem might be that because some of the students lived in the countryside, and their interest and environment were fundamentally different from most of the city-dweller kids, mutual understanding might have been difficult to achieve.

Despite trying hard, I could not get other teachers of this class to participate in an interview, not even via email in order to put my impressions in perspective. I have therefore to rely on my own impressions, field-notes, and interview data with Sandra.

FINALLY INTRODUCING SANDRA

I conducted another interview with Sandra about her reasons for participating in the project, the philosophy behind her teaching, the reasons why she decided to become a mathematics and physics teacher in the first place. For this purpose, we met in a quiet room next to the physics laboratory. After I had finished with Sandra's interview, I continued to interview several students. Later in the day, when I listened to the tape in order to transcribe, I was horrified to find that I had accidently recorded the students' interviews over Sandra's interview. Sandra was helpful enough to spare me another hour of her valuable time to repeat the interview. I found this situation quite embarrassing especially as I was aware that Sandra did not have much time to spare at all. As with Irene, I would like to have Sandra speak for herself in a way that she recognises herself when she reads this. I have thus created the following text in the form of an interview from the second recording. I sent a copy of the interview to Sandra for comments .

TRY AGAIN: INTRODUCING SANDRA

Sandra sits opposite me in a bright, sunlit room. We both try to recall what we had been talking about the day before – reconstructing the earlier interview. We quickly cover yesterday's territory and move on to areas, we had not touched the day before – overall this interview is more in-depth and more open than the previous one. I start to recognise that perhaps it was not too bad after all to lose the recording because the first interview now feels like a warm-up for the second…

Lily: Why did you become a teacher?
Sandra: Actually, I always wanted to study medicine yet towards the end of my schooling I suddenly wanted a job that would allow me to have a family as well as a job. Becoming a teacher seemed the ultimate choice.
Lily: So why did you study physics and maths?
Sandra: The choice of my subjects is closely related to the last four years at school, especially in physics. After year 8, I transferred from the Hauptschule to the Gymnasium. I was always good at maths and physics but coming from the Hauptschule, I was not used to having to be prepared for each subject every day. When my physics teacher asked me some questions during the first few lessons, I got so nervous that I forgot the easiest things. He ridiculed me in front of the whole class. I knew though that I was good at physics. I got very angry at him and wanted to show him that I can do better than that…well, maybe this is why I succeeded in the end: I passed my A-Level exams in physics with distinction and, of course, I went on to study physics afterwards.
Lily: You mentioned yesterday that you have always been very interested in the role of women in physics and technology?

Sandra: Yes, during my studies it became clear to me that hardly any women study physics in order to become scientists. With physics teacher students, it was at least a fifty-fifty distribution. So I started to think about these issues and I approached organisations that deal with this problem.

Lily: Yesterday, you also mentioned some disillusionment about physics in general?

Sandra: Oh yes! Towards the end of my studies it became clear to me that from all the questions I had as a young girl, physics had answered none. This was very frustrating…

Lily: What questions were you thinking of?

Sandra: Well, I cannot think of a concrete example now but I remember, for example, that when I was studying for my master's diploma exam, I went to see my supervisor, and I kept on asking questions about the literature and he responded, "Well because this is the way things are! There is no further explanation to this!" I found this very frustrating! I know now that this is a characteristic of the natural sciences that every time you have reached the end of logical explanations, there is a tendency to refer to natural laws and/or facts that you can prove experimentally but you still continue to pretend that everything can be explained to the very end. This left me very dissatisfied and I asked myself, "What did I study physics for?"

Lily: But in the end you chose to become a physics teacher…

Sandra: Yes, apart from the 'family-question' which I see differently now, I always knew that I wanted a job where I have to deal with people – this was one aspect of why I wanted to study medicine.

Lily: Have you ever regretted becoming a teacher?

Sandra: No, not really. I think it is a great job and I still like to teach my subjects. I mean when I was studying mathematics I wasn't interested at all [in the subject] but somehow I managed to pass successfully although these days it sometimes occurs to me that I might be interested in mathematical science after all…I can see now that this might be a thrilling endeavour.

Lily: Thrilling, in what way?

Sandra: After having stayed away from uni for almost ten years, I find some interest again in maths, especially in some of the more philosophical questions about mathematics. But of course this does not mean that I am sure that I want an academic career – I sort of like it the way it is now!

Lily: From what you have said, I take it that you have always had an interest in the philosophy of science?

Sandra: Yes, this is a very important issue for me.

Lily: What do you think is the philosophical basis of your teaching?

Sandra: I think I regard it of upmost importance to convey to students that they carry responsibility for their actions. I mean, most of these students will end up in professions where they create things, be it in the areas of computer software development or medicine, or in technical areas. What they can learn at school is that they, being part of society, can contribute constructively. This is where it is important to realise that you carry responsibility for your actions, for their consequences.

Lily: Have you tried to implement this principle in your teaching?

Sandra: I have not tried it in mathematics yet, but I am trying to do it in physics. In physics there is not the same 'A-Level-orientedness' as in maths. So far I have tried to include issues such as energy problems, role of your behaviour in public traffic, or, for example, historical questions of how certain scientific achievements have affected worldviews – it is like showing students the importance of approaching such issues from a critical perspective. This is very important to me.

Lily: Why did you engage in this project [the Ethics in Science Project]?

Sandra: First of all, because I have been aware of the dilemma method through the Red Cross Project. Secondly, I am very interested in constructivist approaches to teaching. And thirdly, being a form teacher, I am always looking out for opportunities for personal development…

Lily: Yesterday, we also touched on the issue of ethics and morals and got stuck in values education. Then we discussed the problematic term moral education and its sexual connotations. In the end we agreed to use the term ethics and values education…am I correct?

Sandra: Yes. To me this means education towards responsibility. I believe that a social system cannot function unless every individual takes over responsibility and is able to assess the consequences of one's actions for everybody else. As an example, we have to separate rubbish in the classroom and I have to get them to do it but they don't, and I am finding this very frustrating. Given their level of intelligence, all my students should be capable of separating rubbish yet they don't…I am aware that I will not succeed by telling them or lecturing them – because that would mean that I impose my values onto them. This is one of the reasons why I am interested in how I can approach issues such as this.

SUMMARY OF SECTION 2

Sandra was apparently confronted with problems quite different from Irene's. In her class it was not the problem of multiculturality and the related difficulties but much rather social problems such as the formation of cliques, of non-communication between particular groups, of outsiders, and of dominant girls which seems to me to be a rather rare problem. However, with regard to academic achievement her class appeared largely success-oriented. Despite Sandra's efforts to improve the class community, there were still problems with the cliquey behaviour.

Sandra described to me the challenges she experienced with her high school teacher which ultimately caused her to become a mathematics and physics teacher. However, she also described her frustration about the hypocrisy in the natural sciences to pretend that one can explain everything down to the finest detail. She explained to me that the main reason for her participation in the Ethics in Science Project was her interest in personal development in her role as a form teacher, and also because she wanted her students to understand that their actions will have consequences, and that they, therefore, have a responsibility for their actions.

REVIEW OF THE CHAPTER

I conducted my research at a non-denominational, co-educational, public senior high school in Austria. I was familiar with the context as I had experienced the school in my role as a former teacher, as the parent of a former student, and as a colleague of the participating teachers. The school is part of an alliance of several schools situated in the western suburbs of Graz in Austria.

In Part 1 of the chapter, I tried to illustrate the particularities of the Austrian schooling system, starting with a description of the traditional schooling system, including issues such as the organisation of the school year, assessment issues, etc., followed by a comparison between the traditional system and the Schulverbund Graz West which is an alliance of trial schools for a 'new' middle-school model. I also described the organisation of the Schulverbund Graz West. In order to put my researcher impressions in perspective, I interviewed other teachers and I drew on my other roles as a former teacher and former parent at the Roseggerschule as part of the Schulverbund. I have also tried to outline the differences of the Austrian schooling system from systems in English speaking countries like Australia, for example, thus hopefully making it easier for the reader to 'enter' the research context almost like an 'insider'.

I worked with two teachers and their classes: Irene and 'Form 5A' (Year 9) as well as with Sandra and 'Form 6A' (Year 10). The student population of the two classes consisted of commuters who travelled to school from the country as well as students who lived in the city. From a cultural perspective, I can say that Form 5A was multicultural compared to Form 6A which was, with one exception, monoculturally Austrian. Many students in Irene's class had German as a second language. Whilst Irene's multicultural class seemed to have a well-developed class community, Sandra's monocultural class seemed to struggle with the formation of groups within the class, hampering the development of a good class community. 'Survival-related' goals seemed to dominate the agenda in the multicultural class, whilst academic success seemed to be of greater importance for the Austrian students. Comparing the philosophical background of both teachers, I can say that Irene seems to promote a philosophy of respect for life whilst Sandra seems to stress the importance of reflecting on the consequences of one's actions to her students.

Chapter 4

Mapping the researcher's sensitivities towards her subject(s) – a critical autobiography

One lies more to oneself then to anyone else (Edel, 1984)

"A SMALL STEP FOR A MAN, A GIANT LEAP FOR MANKIND

(NEIL ARMSTRONG)

Cuddled into the black leather TV-chair in my parents' living room, wrapped up in a blanket, I am watching the black and white pictures delivered from the moon's surface into our home in a small Austrian town. I remember having a strange feeling about the fact that some human beings are actually "up there" and are able to look down on "us"...

I was five years old when Neil Armstrong first set foot on the moon. My family had gathered around the television set, my parents, my brothers, their girlfriends... I remember the tension in the room during those last moments before the landing – fear something might go wrong in the very last moment. At last it was certain – the human race had achieved something unique and I remember feeling that I had just witnessed something extraordinary. Pride of what humans can do, pride of what science can help us achieve. I believe that in this very moment the foundations for my interest in science were laid. As a child, I never wanted to become a nurse, a police-woman, least of all a teacher. Marie Curie as an idol was much more like it – funny enough, events and choices made during my later life have turned me into a science teacher and not into a scientist

Later I remember seeing pictures from the Houston control room. My mother pointed out a man to me, tall and blond, amongst the scientists and technicians, "This is Wernher von Braun," she said, "He originally came from Germany and is now one of the great American rocket scientists. He has contributed considerably to this event tonight." I was impressed, to

87

say the least. The fact that he came from a neighbouring country with some cultural and historical commonalities left us with a feeling that we also to some degree shared the glory of the moment...

INTRODUCTION

In this chapter I explore, through the use of autobiography, how my personal history has influenced my research into the teaching of ethical issues within science education. The chapter serves several purposes:

- Exploring the 'emergent' nature of the research in Erickson's sense in relation to my autobiography.
- Reflecting critically on my three roles during the research study as teacher, curriculum developer, and researcher (Erickson, 1989), thus bringing to the fore the reasons for shifting from a still largely postpositivistic original thesis design that was based on an epistemology of critical certainty to a postmodern epistemology of ambiguity.
- Giving an autobiographical overview of events, epiphanies and 'mentors' that have contributed to the developments in my life culminating in this thesis-research.
- Investigating my own hidden biases and interpretive horizons.
- Illustrating my journey through critical self-reflection and assessment of assumptions.
- Relating my personal history and cultural background to particular aspects of my research.

This chapter is organised in two parts:

- <u>Part 1</u> is concerned with discussing the theoretical context of autobiographical method in the social sciences in general and in science education in particular. Autobiographical vignettes interrupt the flow of the theoretical text in order to prepare the reader for Part 2 of the chapter.

- In <u>Part 2,</u> I describe the research I have been involved in, and relate it to autobiographical vignettes in order to illustrate influential events, people, literature, etc., that have led to the development of particular sensitivities. This part is organised around Parker Palmer's (1998) questions 'What? Why? How? and Who?' with regard to the research. The connective tissue between the autobiographical vignettes is provided through interpretive commentary in which I analyse and interpret the stories and offer multiple interpretive possibilities.

PART 1: THEORETICAL BACKGROUND

Writing an autobiography

Laurel Richardson (2000) speaks of 'writing as inquiry' – this is how I experienced the act of writing an autobiography that is both <u>descriptive</u> of the inquiry process and <u>constitutive</u> of it, especially when the act of autobiographical writing stimulates <u>critical reflective thinking</u>. This writing process usually started off with a descriptive account of key issues, and sometimes developed further into reflective thinking, which generated new insights and heightened sensitivities toward those issues. Whilst writing my autobiography, I found that there are different levels of depth when engaging in autobiographical research. There is, I found, always a 'top-layer' of self-knowledge, a layer we have constructed and never really questioned afterwards. However, there are many more layers underneath that we have completely forgotten about. I would like to compare the process to 'peeling an onion' where you pull away layer after layer' and move towards the core of our mostly unconscious biases. When one engages in critical self-reflexivity in combination with the act of writing, other issues that have been hidden from sight come to the surface, and yet others follow. Our hidden biases have an influence on how we conduct our research and interpret results – from this perspective it seems vital to explore one's own history before engaging in qualitative research.

Autobiographical writing results in narratives about our lives. But why, we may ask, is this worth the effort? What might be the intended purpose of writing an autobiographical narrative apart from pure self-indulgence and ego-pampering? Barone (2001) (quoting Bruner) suggests that narratives are designed to do what art does so well, and he continues (quoting Baldwin) that the greatest achievement of art is to lay bare questions that have been hidden by the answers. With regard to autobiography, we might start to question that which seems

90

unquestionable to us, a given fact, something that "has always been there". We might begin to confront what the phenomenologists call the 'natural attitude' about ourselves.

Mezirow explains that when self-reflection is critical, it involves a searching view of the unquestioningly accepted presuppositions. He continues that most of what we have learned about ourselves has not been examined for unconsciously incorporated assumptions (Mezirow, 1991). This process might be of benefit to others. Instead of asking, "Why would anybody be interested in my unimportant life?", we might want to ask, "What experiences, issues, stories, from my life can be of benefit for others? How can this affect my research and my attitude about <u>who</u> I am dealing with as a researcher and what I hear from the participants? What can I learn from getting to know myself better?" This leads to the questions I have asked in my self-study...

The What, the How, the Why and the Who? Questions that have informed the research...

Questions characterise the beginning of Parker Palmer's book (1998), "The Courage to Teach", in which he poses a set of questions. The first, "What do we teach?", turns out to be the most commonly asked question of all with regard to teaching and learning, followed in popularity by, "How do we teach?". Somebody might even ask, "Why?", but only rarely does anybody ask, "Who is the self that teaches?". I would like to use these four questions in the context of this research, in fact, these questions reappear throughout the thesis as signposts of quality control.

1. <u>What</u> is this research about?
2. <u>How</u> do I perform this research?
3. <u>Why</u> do I bother to inquire into a certain topic?
4. <u>Who</u> is the researcher doing this study?

Engaging in critical self-reflection or, in other words, pondering about the implications of these questions on my own research, I realised how closely related to my own autobiography were the answers to the four questions. Denzin and Lincoln recognise this close connection between interpretive research and the researcher's biography by proposing that behind every interpretive study stands the biographically, multiculturally situated researcher. They suggest that

> …*three interconnected, generic activities define the qualitative research process. They go by a variety of labels, including…ontology, epistemology, and methodology. Behind these terms stands the personal biography of the gendered researcher, who speaks from a particular class, racial, cultural, and ethnic community perspective (Denzin & Lincoln, 2000b, p. 18)*

I realised that I, as the researcher, approach the world with a set of ideas, a framework (ontology) that specifies a set of questions (epistemology) that are then examined (methodology) in specific ways. It is thus important to bring to the fore the historical background of this research study. In this thesis, autobiography serves as a tool to put my interpretive research study about teaching ethics in science classrooms using dilemma stories into its biographical, historical context which is especially important for the interpretive act (Roth, 2000).

Autobiography and qualitative science education research

Denzin defines autobiography as a person's life written by oneself or as inscribing and creating a life (Denzin, 1989). Educational autobiographies in teacher education research have gained in importance, as Ken Zeichner (Bullough & Pinnegar, 2001)pointed out in his presidential address to the American Educational Research Association in 1998. Bullough and Pinnegar add that self-study as a method to study our research practice points to a simple truth: to study a practice is simultaneously to study self - a study of self-in-relation to other (Bullough & Pinnegar, 2001). This type of self-study can also lead to the enhancement of personal practical knowledge (Connelly & Clandinin, 1988) and to pedagogical thoughtfulness in one's reader (van Manen, 1990).

In these postmodernist[4] – some say (post)postmodern times (Marcus, 1994), especially if we ground our interpretive work in the Seventh Moment of Qualitative Research, which amongst other issues is concerned with moral discourse (Denzin & Lincoln, 2000a), dealing with one's own biases before interpreting and representing others becomes an important question of research ethics. The crisis of representation has taught us to look critically at attempts to speak authentically of other people's experiences. Many researchers now accept that they are not disinterested but are deeply invested in their studies, personally and profoundly (Bullough & Pinnegar, 2001). Autobiographical research allows us to explore aspects of our interpretive horizons (Roth, 2000) and thus of our biases. Regarding the legitimisation of the research, Lincoln and Denzin emphasise that interpretive inquiry in the Seventh Moment celebrates autoethnography and personal accounts grounded in the striving to understand how others enact and construct meaning in their lives (Denzin & Lincoln, 2000a). Given that our

---

[1]Postmodernism suspects all truth claims of serving particular interests (Richardson, 2000). Relativism is the characteristic philosophical stance (Denzin & Lincoln, 2000a). The core of postmodernism is the doubt that any method or theory, discourse or genre, has a universal and general claim as the 'right' or privileged form of authoritative knowledge.

autobiographies and our scholarly works are deeply integrated – we can therefore draw on our autobiographies to elucidate our knowledge (Roth & Bowen, 2000)

In this thesis, I have used autobiography as well as autoethnography which blend ethnographic research with life writing, and tell us about a culture as well as about lives at the same time (Roth, 2000). The two genres play an increasingly important role in the social sciences as the work of, for example, Ellis and Bochner clearly show (Ellis, 1997; Ellis & Bochner, 2000). Roth explains that, although these two genres have become a central means of critiquing other forms of representing individuals and their culture, their influence in science education remains minimal (Roth, 2000). I agree with Roth that, apart from a special issue of the Journal of Research in Science Education Research (Vol 30(1)) on autobiography, in which researchers such as Roth, Tobin and Eisenhart published autobiographical accounts (Eisenhart, 2000; Roth, 2000; Tobin, 2000), as well as papers by Taylor and Timothy (2000) and Afonso (2002)the widespread recognition of this genre as a methodology suitable for science education research has yet to happen.

I have found that the postpositivist[5] tradition of reporting science education research using a scientific, objectivist, "scholarly" writing style, has made it difficult for alternative genres of scholarly writing to be accepted amongst the majority of the science education research community. Barone reports on authors who (still) fret about the potential contamination through subjectivity of objective findings about the "real world", a soiling to be minimised – a phenomenon I have experienced myself with colleagues. According to Cronbach (quoted by Barone), the primary purpose of (postpositivist) social scientific research is to reduce uncertainty, to seek literal truth (Barone, 2001b). Coming from a science background, I was used to writing in an objectivistic, scientific style – my Master's thesis on the fixation of Cesium isotopes on clay minerals in Alpine soils is a good example.

---

[5] Postpositivism is characterised by critical realism, and a modified dualist/objectivist attitude. External and internal validity, reliability, and objectivity suggest that findings are probably true (Lincoln &Guba, 2000).

On entering qualitative, postmodern, human science, I was stunned by the variety of possible writing styles: Postmodernists in their quest for understanding rather than explaining, have abandoned striving for certain and total knowledge that transcends a fallible, human perspective. Instead, they promote an epistemology of ambiguity whose purpose is the enhancement of meaning rather than the reduction of uncertainty. Despite my background in science, I never experienced problems with uncertainty – dealing with human beings and their subjectivities was not only acceptable to me but the preferable option when it came to research participants.

Poststructuralists believe that every autobiography is a construct for a particular audience. I believe this is true – our shifting self that moves from context to context allows us to do this well. Poststructuralists look at the intention behind the construct – at how the interaction between reader and author re-constructs the writer (Rodriguez, 2000). My intention was not only to find out about the connections of my life history to my research but also to offer to the reader opportunities of identification and perhaps disagreement. Researchers working within a (post)postmodernist tradition. like myself, find themselves confronted with a variety of writing genres, including autobiography, autoethnography, and performance texts, each serving as a tool for better understanding and supporting interpretation of the 'other'. Such experimental texts enable the researcher to 'work the hyphen' (Richardson, 2000), as Michelle Fine calls it (Fine, Weis, Weseen, & Wong, 2000): when the 'self' of the researcher meets the 'other' – the participant's self. Using experimental writing genres within a postmodernist framework offers a possibility of addressing issues of legitimisation and representation in one's research.

Autobiography from the perspective of communication theory

Before coming to Australia in 1998, I was working as an adult educator in the field of communication. I was running seminars on improving communication skills and through this also became familiar with adult education and communication literature. Later in the chapter, I describe how I became an adult educator and how this period of my life relates to my research. One tool that is very commonly used in communication courses is the 'Johari Window', named after its inventors, Joseph Luft and Harry Ingham (Yen, 1999). I have always found it very useful to illustrate very basic principles of communication. In the following I shall discuss how I see the Johari Window related to autobiographical writing.

	What I see in me	What I do not see in me
What you see in me	Public Self	Blind "Spot"
What you do not see in me	Private Self	Unknown Self

Figure 6: The Johari Window (Augsburg College, n. d.; Jarvis, n. d.; Yen, 1999)

THE WINDOW PANES

In Figure 10, the Public Self represents free and open exchange of information between me and others: this quadrant represents what is known to me and to you. The Private Self represents what, for one reason or another, stays hidden from others but is known to me. Fear and insecurity are inhibiting factors. The Blind Spot is that part of ourselves that we are not consciously aware of but which is well known to others. (Invited) feedback helps to reduce the size of this quadrant: the smaller the Blind Spot the more we know about how others see us. The last of the quadrants represents the Unknown Self standing for what affects me below the surface of awareness thereby influencing my behaviours and motifs. Influences might include unknown resources and traits. Learning opportunities and exchange of feedback may allow for these influences to surface and be opened – but only if I want to! If we change the size of one of the quadrants through learning experiences, the sizes of the other quadrants will change accordingly. Communication is generally better if the Public Self quadrant is large.

With regard to the Johari Model, autobiography might lead to a decrease in size of the unknown sector and thereby contribute to a growth in the Public Self quadrant. I believe that autobiography and the involved critical reflexivity and introspection can contribute to bringing some of the contents of the Unknown Self to our awareness through offering insights and learning opportunities (Augsburg College, n. d.; Jarvis, n. d.) potentially leading to transformative learning (Mezirow, 1991).

Organisation of an autobiography

Autobiographies need to be organised around particular foci: Norman Denzin, in his book, 'Interpretive Biography', examines different types of organisation of biographies and autobiographies (Denzin, 1989). There can either be a chronological order, from birth to death, or alternatively from death back to birth. Or, less common, there can be no chronological order at all. In this chapter, autobiographical stories or vignettes are organised around 'nodal moments' (Bullough & Pinnegar, 2001), epiphanies or turning points (Denzin, 1989), and 'mentors who evoked us' (Palmer, 1998). One aspect that lends itself as a focus to our attention is the researcher's sensitivities towards her subject(s) which are characterised by a heightened awareness toward a certain knowledge area. The purpose of the chapter lies in the exploration of my sensitivities with regard to the research:

- What were the driving forces that led me to take up a study on the teaching of ethics in science education?
- How did "the subject find me" - why did I choose a particular research topic?
- What were the incidents – the nodal moments - leading to the research?
- Who were the people that influenced me along the way (my mentors)?
- In what way has my upbringing and my own school education influenced my research and my attitude toward science education?

The Role of Sensitivities

Sensitivities are what makes us more perceptive towards certain phenomena than to others. Sensitivities are part of the legacy of evolution, Skolimowski informs us in his book, 'The Participatory Mind'. Quoting Pierre Teilhard de Chardin, he explains that evolution is a process of augmentation of consciousness: after new insight is absorbed, the growing consciousness is expressed and articulated by the acquisition of new sensitivities. Sensitivities are therefore articulators of the growing consciousness (Skolimowski, 1994). Being sensitive toward ethical dilemmas, I believe, represents the growing consciousness and awareness of my history and culture as I develop as a human being. I can clearly trace back my interest in ethical dilemmas to my personal history and to certain formative events.

In the following section, I relate my research into the teaching of ethical issues to my biographical background, I discuss methodological aspects of writing autobiographically, and I also include issues of quality control in self-studies.

Critical voices and autobiography

Despite the reasons that speak for the use of autobiography, there are critical voices, questioning the legitimacy of the autobiographical enterprise as scientific. Can autobiography ever be rigorous? How can we make sure that we do not only indulge in solipsism and/or narcissism (Hargreaves, Earl, & Schmidt, 2002)? Does autobiography as a form of arts-based, fictional writing not open the door for scientific dilettantism – research for the pleasure or benefit of the researcher only? Can autobiography ever be an acceptable form of thesis writing? In the following section, I try to answer this question by consulting the literature on autobiographical research.

How to read an autobiography – quality guidelines

A number of researchers have suggested guidelines and quality standards for narrative and self-studies in particular. I would like to draw from Barone (2001) as well as from Bullough and Pinnegar (2001). Barone and Eisner listed qualities that turn a narrative into an arts-based text. They suggest that the language should be expressive and contextualised. The text should create a virtual reality and present an aesthetic form. It should carry the author's signature and, above all, it should show a degree of textual ambiguity (Barone, 2001b; Barone & Eisner, 1997).

Bullough and Pinnegar ask the most crucial question of all: When does self-study ever become research? Answering their own question, they explain that history and biography need to be joined, "...When the issue confronted by the self is shown to have relationship to and bearing on the context and ethos of a time, the self-study moves to research (p. 15)." In order to answer the famous "so what?" question about the significance of the work that "wise" readers tend to ask, they emphasise that there must be a balance in evidence not only in what data have been gathered and presented but in how they have been analysed, in how they have been brought together in conversation. Ultimately the aim of self-study research is moral, to gain understanding necessary to make that interaction - between the researcher's self and others, who share a commitment to the development and nurturance of the young - increasingly educative (Bullough & Pinnegar, 2001).

According to Bullough and Pinnegar, self-studies should 'ring true' and enable connection, and the author's voice should appear (Bullough & Pinnegar, 2001). This brings in the notion of what (Adler & Adler, 1994) refer to as 'verisimilitude'. The stories should promote insight and interpretation. History should be engaged forthrightly and the author should take an honest stand. A good self-study should be a good read, and attend to nodal moments of our biographies, thereby enabling the reader to gain insight or understanding into the self. Good autobiography should reveal a lively conscience and balanced sense of self-importance, tell a recognisable story, portray character development, give place to the dynamic struggle of living life whole, and offer new perspectives. The plot of the autobiography is a series of events deliberately arranged so as to reveal their dramatic, thematic, and emotional significance. Similar to fiction, a good autobiography tries to reproduce the emotional impact of the experience in order to move the reader.

Our autobiographies as learners in childhood, adolescence, and young adulthood frame our approach to teaching at the start of our careers, and they frequently exert an influence that lasts a lifetime " (Barone, 2001a, p. 50). Given this life-long influence, and drawing from Parker Palmer's work, we might want to ask the question, "Who is the self that does the research?" This leads to Part 2 of the chapter…

PART 2: THE WHAT, THE WHY, THE HOW AND THE WHO?

As an introduction to Part 2, I would like to tell a story of 'how it all began'. This vignette introduces the reader to the environment I grew up in. In the second part of the chapter, I attempt to connect my biography, my history, and my research, thereby putting "personal struggle into the context and ethos of time" in order for my stories to become part of the research (Bullough & Pinnegar, 2001).

HOW IT ALL BEGAN?

Looking back I can see that some influences during the early stages of my life have probably made me very sensitive to ethical dilemma situations. One influential dilemma has to do with my birthplace: My father used to be a medical doctor before his retirement. He worked in medical research in Vienna, in the Netherlands, and in Britain, for many years before he gave up this academic career and became the senior-anaesthesist at the local hospital in a semi-rural town in Upper Austria. My parents decided to move from Vienna to Braunau am Inn, a small but beautiful, medieval town of architectural splendour, only a few years before I was born.

This decision presented me with the dubious pleasure of sharing my birthplace with Adolf Hitler, a fact that indeed was to be of some importance for my personal development later. It involves being confronted with a terrible past at an early age, as well as being "equated" with the Nazis of 60 years ago, no matter what your personal political stance really is. Many people overseas tend to identify Nazi with German or, even worse, Austrian, due largely to a lack of historical knowledge, I believe. The dilemma with Braunau for me was that, on the one hand, I love the place, I still have my parents and friends there. I like the people. I love the river Inn, its quiet hidden arms, the relatively intact ecosystems along the river, the bird and beaver colonies, the river-woods that offered us (as children in the 60s and 70s) a great adventure playground . But times have changed: Braunau is a border town within the European Union. In 2002 the river-woods are no longer safe for children to play in: they have become a different type of 'playground' - illegal immigrants trying to cross the river into Germany play hide-and-seek with border patrols which are supposed to prevent 'illegals' from 'infiltrating' the German border. But this is a different story, reflecting the modern Austria...

The peacefulness and sleepiness of the small town is deceptive: Braunau's historical background tends to relate us to a terrible, incomprehensible past, even though Braunau's most notorious ex-citizen spent only the first two years of his life there. However, regardless of how old Adolf was when he left, or how much political indoctrination he received whilst living here, to uncritical and unknowing overseas spectators Braunau's reputation has been tainted for all times. However, the inhabitants of this small town do not really want to be seen in relation to this particular past. There is a strong spirit of political awareness about the past, as especially this web-page shows clearly http://www.hrb.at/ . This political awareness was especially obvious when a granite boulder was to be set up in front of Hitler's birthplace as a monument against Nazism, carrying the words, "Für Frieden, Freiheit und Demokratie – nie wieder Faschismus. Millionen Tote mahnen. [6]The population of Braunau was split because a great number of people rejected the project, but not as might be presumed because they opposed the monument, as such, or because they thought that Nazism was such great a thing, but much rather out of fear that Braunau could become a pilgrimage-site for Neo-Nazis or other war-tourists from all over the world. Others saw it as a clear sign: Braunau is declaring its

---

[6] German = For peace, freedom, and democracy. Fascism never again! Millions of victims remind us!

> standpoint openly. Yet others, especially the elderly, thought the past
> should best be left alone and not be touched, "Let's be glad it's all over!"

Reading this story the reader might ask, "What is the reason that she is telling us this story?" Some might think, "She comes from a guilt-ridden society and now she is trying to take on the national guilt as her own". Others might say, "She is just trying to whitewash what cannot be whitewashed in order to make herself feel better." Perhaps a little of both of these perspectives underpins my motives, yet the main purpose for telling this story of my home town and my upbringing is that, from an early age, I have had a sensitivity towards ethical dilemmas. Autobiographical analysis has shown to me that the idea of my thesis project topic goes back a long way to my childhood, a connection that had not been obvious to me before.

Organisation and purpose of Part 2

Part 2 contains several autobiographical vignettes that illustrate nodal moments and people of influence. The connective tissue between them is the interpretive commentary of myself in terms of how and why I think a certain story is related to my research. The interpretive commentary was based on journal notes, as well as on dialogues between my partner and I. These dialogues have been of great importance inasmuch as my partner's questions have repeatedly forced me to go back to my texts and clarify, go deeper in the analysis, to move from a descriptive to a critical reflexive perspective. It happened on several occasions that suddenly I had a very 'moving' insight – some of these insights were very significant. I believe that I might never have engaged in this type of analysis had it not been for autobiographical analysis. Part 2 is organised in four sections that explore Palmer's questions: Section 1 illustrates the 'What', Section 2 the 'Why", Section 3 the "How' and Section 4 the 'Who'. In the following section of the chapter, I would like to answer the first question by describing how the <u>what</u> of my research relates to my autobiography.

Section 1 - The 'What': An interpretive case study on a teaching approach to moral education in science classrooms

Chapter 1 of this thesis describes in great detail what the research is about. For this reason it may suffice to give a short summary in order to illustrate the 'content side' of the research.

MY DOCTORAL THESIS RESEARCH

My doctoral thesis inquires into the teaching of ethical issues in science classrooms. The research revolves around the use of dilemma stories and a teaching approach to moral education. I was closely involved in the curriculum development for this particular purpose, before moving to Australia. I was writing and evaluating four dilemma stories, and collaborated with two female teachers – a biology and a physics/mathematics teacher. The relationship between the dilemma stories and my autobiography became obvious when the teachers presented me with the planned curricula and I tried to write stories that fitted those curricula. Whilst pondering about different possibilities, certain topics sprang to my mind from the 'depths' of my past, all closely related to dilemmas I had experienced either in my private life or in professional life.

THE AUTOBIOGRAPHICAL BACKGROUND OF THE DILEMMA STORIES

In the following, I present short summaries of the four dilemma stories I wrote for the project. At this point, I would like to direct the reader's attention also to Chapter 5 and Chapter 6 where the dilemma stories play a major role – in Chapter 5, I discuss the curriculum development leading to this research study, and in

Chapters 7, 8, 9 and 10 where I describe the actual implementation phase and the related findings. Only three of the four original stories were evaluated within the project due to unforeseen difficulties during the fieldwork phase as described in Chapter 6. The full text of each dilemma story is available in Appendix 5. I found out, through autobiographical analysis, that each of these stories has a close relationship with my own biography.

The first story is about research ethics, about whether there should be any restrictions to scientific research, and if so, what they might look like. Sandra, who was not only the form teacher but also the mathematics and physics teacher of the Year 10 students, told the story freely within the context of the astrophysics curriculum. At several points throughout the story, questions relating to the moral dilemmas in the story were presented to the students and they were asked to make choices and explain these choices, first by themselves, later in the form of group-work.

The Rocket Dilemma

The story is about a rocket scientist who has a life ideal: he wants to build a rocket that can fly to the moon. As the political situation in his country changes he collaborates with the new totalitarian regime. At some stage, he encounters serious problems in his research that can be resolved only through human experiments on concentration camp prisoners. Later he joins the US space program with the knowledge he has gained in his homeland. His biography is "whitewashed".

You might have guessed whilst reading the story – the man in the story, the researcher, the torturer, was Wernher von Braun, the man I had come to idealise from the moment of the first landing on the moon. This closes the loop I started to draw in the first autobiographical vignette of this chapter. Wernher von Braun might even have been one of my idols when I chose a career in science. You can imagine the shock when the truth about this man was revealed to me during my twenties. The impact of this revelation was strong enough for me to choose him as an example of bad research ethics for one of the dilemma stories I evaluated with the students. Yet, at the time when I was writing the dilemma stories, I was not aware of this connection – it became obvious to me only whilst I was writing my autobiography, and I then looked more closely at the reasons behind why I had chosen to write particular stories. It also became clear to me that the reason why I am actually sitting here right at the moment is that one day, when I was a little girl, I was sitting in my parents' living room in front of the television and watching the first landing of astronauts on the moon… it was then that my love for science was awakened. It was through this autobiographical writing that my moral sensitivities regarding research and research ethics were sharpened, due largely to the big disappointment I experienced when my idol turned out to be different from what I wanted him to be.

The second story is about the value of life, and asks the question: Why do we not attach the same value to life in all living beings? If asked the obvious question, "Do you think life should be protected?", almost everybody would respond, "Yes, of course!". Yet, in real life, we do not treat every life-form with the same level of respect. This story is meant to make students reflect on the value of life in general. It was trialled with Year 9 students and presented by their teacher, Irene, as part of the Year 9 Biology/Botany curriculum.

Peter's Tree

> When Peter is born his parents plant a tree in commemoration of the occasion. Over the years, the boy develops a "close" relationship to his tree. Years later, the parents decide to buy a campervan and the tree has to go – Peter is devastated that his "birth-tree" is to be cut down and raises the question why we treat plants differently to animals although they are living beings too, and why do we attach so much value onto a car.

This is a true story and happened to my ex-partner. It might be difficult to understand how an adult man can have such a strong relationship to a plant but he did: he fell into a deep crisis and felt seriously uprooted. For me, this was a time of reflecting a lot about the different values we attach to animals and to plants. I reflected on how I would decide in a situation like this and what I would do if I were my ex-partner's parents. I witnessed the decision-making process and experienced the involved dilemmas first hand. At first sight the story looks very simple – almost too simplistic as Irene, the teacher, feared in the first place. I believed, though, that the story had a lot of potential because of my former experiences. As it turned out, as described in greater detail in Chapter 9, the dilemmas were powerful enough to make some students reflect and engage in a heated discussion.

The third story is about one of my favourite ecosystems – the rainforest. As mentioned earlier, Irene had suggested writing a story that would fit in with the topic botany and/or the rainforest. This story, once again, has to do with research ethics, but it also includes questions of uncritical culture transfer and exploitation of natural resources in Third World countries by the so-called 'developed' nations.

The Rainforest Dilemma

> *A young female researcher is chosen by her employer, a pharmaceutical company, to accompany a senior researcher on his travel to the Brazilian rainforest to find a remedy for a disease affecting a growing number of people in her home country. Shortly before she leaves on the journey she falls ill with a serious influenza. Fearing for her job in case she does not go, she travels anyway. The villagers are very helpful and support the researchers with their knowledge. One plant sample proves to be useful, yet the "imported" influenza and the construction works for the new pharmaceutical facility in the rainforest village prove detrimental for the locals...*

Whilst I was studying for my master of science education degree, I was engaged with the Austrian version of 'Oxfam', a Non-Government Organisation that focuses on fair-trading and issues of development in so-called 'underdeveloped' countries. This story is based on a journal article I read at that time which left an enormous impression on me as I had never really thought about the consequences of uncritical culture and, last but not least, of science transfer, where scientific knowledge and cultural values are uncritically exported from the so-called developed world and imported into the so-called developing world: well-meaning, yet totally oblivious to potential consequences. I started to see that the great vision of "scientists as the saviours of the world" does not always work out well and can actually be detrimental for some people and their cultures. I think that it was then that I became interested in issues of cultural sensitivity with regard to the transfer of scientific knowledge and cultural values. The story itself is very complex, and I was a bit frightened it might be too complex, but Irene thought it would be fine with her Year nine students provided we simplified its storyline. This is described also in greater detail in Chapter 7. As it turned out, the students found it very complicated and much preferred the tree dilemma because of its simplicity.

The fourth story was written for the Year ten students in Sandra's class and was intended to be part of the maths curriculum about 'growth', using population growth as an example. Due to circumstances beyond my control (see Chapter 6) the story was never 'put into action'. I mention it at this point only for purposes of completeness and to show its relationship to my personal history.

Naiame's Children

> *As part of a population control program, a young English nurse comes to an African country where she encounters Naiame who has two wives and eight children. Given the high infant mortality, it is very likely that not all of the children will grow up into adulthood. Naiame has many children because due to the lack of superannuation opportunities and because it raises his status in the village. The young nurse is confronted with needs so different from home. She experiences the dilemma of trying to solve a global problem by trying to impose foreign values on a society.*

This story has its background in a course titled 'Gen-ethics' that I attended the University of Graz in Austria and which dealt with issues such as eugenics, genetically modified crops and, last but not least, population control. We learned about the downsides of population control, about how it can be used to serve particular political interests. One example that was shown on television is a project from Peru that had indigenous mountain tribes that are on the brink of extinction undergoing a widespread sterilisation program. My purpose for choosing this topic for my research was to raise students' awareness about unethical, politically grounded abuse of power under the pretence of dealing with global problems and of course Sandra's suggestion to write a story to match 'her' topic of mathematical growth.

Given that not only the choice of my thesis topic but also the choice of topics of the dilemma stories is closely related to my former experiences, it becomes very obvious that I have a vital interest in this type of research. It occurs to me that, at this point, there is an almost natural flow from the "What?" to the "Why?"...

Section 2 - The 'Why'

ON THE SURFACE

Again, I have engaged in many levels of autobiographical analysis about the issue of why. On the surface, the reason for me engaging in moral education within science teaching seems obvious: before moving to Australia, I was involved in the research project initiated by the Austrian Youth Red Cross where I was involved in the development of the teaching approach, in the writing of dilemma stories, in the evaluation process, and in the writing process leading to the publication of a book that was distributed to Austrian schools. However, our relationship with the initiators of the project was not always easy...

ONE HUNDRED INFALLIBLE WAYS TO MAKE YOURSELF UNHAPPY (IN PAUL WATZLAWICK' S SENSE!)

It was the task of the small research team under the guidance of Prof. Schwetz of the Pedagogical Academy in Graz to develop curriculum materials suitable for all subjects and ready-to-use. The dilemma stories were written by the members of the research team, using real-life topics (Gschweitl et al., 1998). Yet the collaboration with the Youth Red Cross was a sobering experience: the meetings we had with representatives of the organisation were all too often frustrating, as our "employers" had a tendency to change their minds about contracts, story topics, styles and numbers of pages, not to mention potential payment, from meeting to meeting. This pattern culminated at a meeting at the headquarters in Vienna where we were supposed to present our work to the Board of Executives of the Austrian Youth Red Cross.

We felt great that day. We also felt that our stories were good - after all we had tried them out in either school classes or with groups of students to whom we were teaching discussion skills. Well, suffice to say, the meeting did not turn out as great as the day started. I was told with regard to my story, for example, that there was no such thing as a 'life-ideal' and that asking teachers to tell the stories freely was too much of

> an authoritative demand to place on them. My colleagues received even
> harsher criticisms.
>
> We had written the stories from our hearts. My colleagues and I
> left this session demoralised as we had planned an interactive dilemma-
> unit to not only present one of our stories, but also to give a hands-on
> impression of how things were going to work. As this initial attempt did
> not go down too well we subsequently wrote for the Youth Red Cross
> publication very simple stories with no contentious issues, and we were
> surprised that they were published without problem. This was good, on
> the one hand, because we did get some stories published; on the other
> hand, these were not the stories we cherished.

Needless to say, I came away from this experience with a feeling of great
dissatisfaction. For quite some time, I regarded with great displeasure the project,
the book, and everything to do with dilemma stories. Yet one day, around the time
that I seriously started to consider engaging in a doctoral thesis, my previous
work regained importance. I realised that science education is a 'fruitful' area of
research into moral education. Of course, I wanted to include all the changes to the
dilemma approach I had wanted to include during the Red Cross Project and was
not 'allowed' to do so.

Reflecting on ethical issues in science brought me back to the time when I
was studying at the university of Salzburg in Austria for my Masters degree. For
me, the reason to study science in the first place was to "contribute something to
create a better world." I was primarily enrolled in a science degree in genetics and
decided half way through my studies to change over to science education.
Thinking about the reasons for doing so brought to the surface two issues that I
found very disturbing at the time.

PROFESSOR CZERNY'S RATS

> The girl is wearing a white coat – she is crying. She is sitting in the
> cafeteria of the natural sciences building at the University of Salzburg in
> Austria. I have known her for a while because we have done a few lab-
> courses together. Whilst I am yet undecided as to whether or not to
> become a scientist or a teacher, she has decided to go down the career

> path of a geneticist. She tells me sobbingly that she cannot stand the experiment she has to perform for her thesis: She must inject a thick syringe into the liver of a live rat in order to obtain a tissue sample - of ten lab rats only two have survived. When she showed great concern about this to her supervisor, he told her off angrily that she should not be a 'whimp', "….if a rat dies, so what, take another one, and if that one dies as well, …well take another one…", and "..if you cannot handle this then you should find yourself a different profession!" She was totally beside herself and was questioning her choice of studies altogether.

This incident showed me the 'ugly', the unattractive, the unethical side of scientific research. A second "nodal point" in my academic career saw me working as a research assistant in the government of Salzburg's radiation laboratory situated at the University of Salzburg. I have to mention that this was during the aftermath of the Cernobyl accident in 1986, and the lab was still concerned with measuring radiation levels of soils, food, milk, etc.

MY TIME AT THE RADIATION LAB

> It was my duty to prepare food and soil samples for measurement, then to perform the measurement and to add the data to a databank. As part of my contract, I was not supposed to tell any 'unauthorised' person about the outcomes of the measurements. It just so happened that, one day, I measured a sample of milk that had been drawn from a farmer whose farm is situated opposite my parents' holiday house, and this is where we often buy our fresh milk from. The measurement showed a high level of radiation, so high that that milk had to necessarily be "diluted" with less contaminated milk from other areas. Now the dilemma for me was clear – shall I comply with my work contract or shall I tell my parents that they are facing a potential health risk by consuming the "oh so healthy milk straight from the farmer's cow?" I have to admit that I decided to inform my parents, yet when I spoke to my boss about this dilemma he said that people are not supposed to know details, "They might panic!" Well I did anyway.

After these events and with a certain degree of disillusionment about scientific research as a career, especially with the ethics of the research, I decided to contribute to a better world through teaching its children and becoming a teacher.

At that time of my life, I became a member of several Non Government Organisations, for example, Greenpeace, Global 2000, a fair-trade NGO and, last but not least, Amnesty International. For years to come I was a fervent letter writer and supported urgent actions in favour of prisoners who had been imprisoned because of their beliefs or political convictions. Autobiographical analysis has helped me to recognise that my vision to contribute to a better world, and all my social activities, were grounded in the work of a "mentor who influenced me deeply".

'BRAUNAU? ISN'T THAT THE PLACE WHERE YOU KNOW WHO WAS BORN?" OR ERICH MY GERMAN TEACHER

When I was a teenager, the source of my literary and 'philosophical impulses' was my German teacher, Erich. He was a German, history, and philosophy teacher. One might say, he never only teaches German or history or philosophy; he always combines all three of his subjects, which results in an 'exciting' mixture of: Who wrote what, and why? What were the historical circumstances of this text? What was the philosophical background at this time and of this author? He presents his subject in a way that you, as a student, live "through" the text.

One day, I think it was during Year 10, he told us about the 'moral purpose' of his teaching (this is at least how I remember it). "As I teach German in, of all places, Hitler's birthplace – I see it as my foremost duty to educate my students towards being critical thinkers. First of all, don't believe what anyone tells you without checking first, then think about it and then speak up! Be especially wary of any so-called 'authorities', whoever they might be. Make up your own mind. Be yourselves and be aware that democracy is a fragile thing carried only by those who 'live it'."

Bearing this background in mind, we read all sorts of literature (not only German literature of course) and, over time, we became very much aware of critical issues, because Erich would tirelessly show up uncritical tendencies in our essays. At that time, I thought he was too critical sometimes but I enjoyed the challenge of actually having to think before sitting down and writing an essay. I am convinced now that the 'tragic' coincidence that Hitler was born in Braunau, like most of us were, contributed considerably to making us much more aware of possible ethical and political dangers. Erich made it quite clear that being uncritical leaves your mind open for influences of all kinds, which is especially dangerous for adolescents, who are developing their personality and belief systems. The only remedy against this is to have an opinion that you should be able to defend. I think now that Braunau, due to its past, is one of the few places in the world where you can find many (at least amongst the younger generation) people who critically reflect on both the past AND on the modern society!

My generation grew up facing a terrible incomprehensible past. "How could anyone do such things?" For us, this meant that we were living together with people who had been alive at the time of World War II, who had some kind of relationship to us (family members, neighbours, etc.) and who had played some sort of a role during this specific time. People who, like me, were born in this beautiful little Gothic town will always have to struggle more than other people with the legacy of the past. "You come from where? Braunau? Isn't that the place where you know who was born?" Yes sure, but I was born there too just like several thousand other people before and after me. But, I suppose I might not have become who I am if I had been born and grown up somewhere else. I am still very grateful for the gift of Erich's teaching.

Section 3 - The 'How''

Whilst I was reading literature on dilemma stories and moral education, somebody asked me, "Why dilemmas? What makes you think they work?". I pondered this question for quite a while, and suddenly I realised that there had been an incident in my past during my active time as a teacher that had made me sensitive to the use of dilemmas in teaching.

HOW I CAME TO TEACH DILEMMAS…

I got my first impression of the potential usefulness of dilemma stories while I was team-teaching *Ecology* (a subject that tries to integrate geography and biology, compare Chapter 3) together with my colleague Gerhard in a Year 7 class. He and I had planned to address issues of mass tourism in alpine regions from a biological as well as from an economic perspective. Yet, the class turned out very differently to what we had planned, primarily through the unexpected initiative of my colleague.

> Whilst I was teaching from a biological point of view, he suddenly
> interrupted me and started to bring in an economic perspective in a quite
> contestatory manner. It took me a while to discover that he was doing
> this on purpose and I engaged in the dialogue that unfolded as an
> unplanned dilemma approach. Yet it worked out fabulously well: the
> students started to join in the discussion, they took sides, some became
> very serious in their attempts to convince 'the other side'.

After the lesson, Gerhard and I were exhausted because this unplanned staging of
a role-play had used up a lot of energy, but we agreed that this was a wonderful
way to introduce students to two different perspectives on the same phenomenon,
without necessarily privileging one. I realised how useful a teaching approach
using dilemmas might be to illustrate ambiguous, potentially contentious issues.
At a deeper level of analysis, it became clear why using dilemmas seems so
natural to me. It lies in the fact that I took part in an adult educator course which
deeply influenced my teaching style, my pedagogy, and my attitude toward
learners.

BECOMING AN ADULT EDUCATOR

> Being a teacher in Austria does not necessarily mean that you end up with
> a job – the truth is rather that there is a high unemployment rate
> amongst teachers, particularly amongst science teachers. My contract at
> the Roseggerschule ran out and I had to find other opportunities to make
> myself useful. One of these opportunities was a year-long course in adult
> education that turned me into a communication facilitator and prepared
> me for the task to not only facilitate learning in large groups of people,
> but also to teach basics, such as presentation skills, discussion skills to
> adults as well as to students. In addition to this course, which actually
> taught me how to teach well, I gained new insights into areas such as NLP
> (Neuro Linguistic Programming), speech and voice training, meditation and
> other interesting topics. Adults are very different to teach – they stand
> up for themselves and demand respect. Dilemma-games are widely used in
> communication courses in order to improve collaboration between
> participants, to exchange ideas and, last but not least, to induce self-
> reflective practice. In the years following this training course, I worked

> as an independent communication and education consultant in Graz in
> Austria.

I understand now that the teaching of large groups, in particular, led to a teaching style very much in accordance with constructivist principles. 'Lecturing' was to be kept to a minimum, student activities had to include phases of working by themselves as well as exchange of opinions: learning from each other was emphasised. I also know now that the teaching used in the adult education pedagogy I was introduced to during this course was based on radical and social constructivism, though the terms were never mentioned. In Chapter 5, I discuss in greater detail the theoretical background of the curriculum development.

All of this played an important role when, during my doctoral research, I had to choose a methodology for the research. Constructivism as a theoretical framework seemed 'natural' to me – after all I had been using "constructivist teaching approaches" unknowingly in my teaching for years. Two other aspects that have strongly influenced the 'how' of the research are that, first, I used to teach at the school where I completed my fieldwork and, second, I am the mother of a former student at that school. Given these experiences, it was very easy for me to gain access to the school, as well as to understand the structure, organisation and curriculum of the school. These aspects lead to:

Section 4 - The Who

On the surface, when I asked myself the question, "Who is the researcher doing the research?" I might have responded: I am a white, middle-class, Catholic, Middle-European, female researcher with South-Eastern-European (Austrian, Croatian, Czech, Hungarian) family heritage, with German as a first language and several other languages, such as Croatian floating around the household, with a Catholic father and a Protestant mother, and in recent years with a growing interest in spirituality, human consciousness development, integral philosophy, and yoga. But of course, this covers only a small proportion of who I really am, after all I am the mother of four, and the partner of….and the colleague of…and a friend of…and much more.

I might add that I am a science teacher and an adult educator with a vision – a vision to contribute to a better world. My vision, which is grounded in my past, and my past itself, has driven me to take on research into ethical dilemmas. The vision itself has changed over time: I want to support students in their quest to become critical self-determined citizens and consumers. Mentors, certain turning points along the way, have contributed in the shaping of this path. The following text has been drawn from my journal and forms a piece of phenomenological writing in van Manen's tradition (van Manen, 1990) The phenomenon in question was 'Being in a dilemma situation'.

DILEMMAS EXPERIENCED FIRST HAND

Since I started this dissertation-project, my life has been subject to many ethical dilemmas, some of which were very difficult to resolve. It has been as though Neale Donald Walsch's words, "You teach what you have to learn!", had to come true in my own life (Walsch, 1998). On the 21st of August 2000, after having gone through a major personal crisis which had been the result of a marriage break-up, I took some time out to reflect on my life and I asked myself, "What does it actually mean to me, Lily, to be in a dilemma situation?"

BEING IN A DILEMMA SITUATION: FROM MY DIARY 21. 8. 2000

I know that I have to make a decision but there is also the fear that I might make a wrong decision. Helplessness – is one of the first emotions that come up when I think about the dilemmas I have been in. I feel cornered, with no escape. I feel challenged to the extreme and under enormous pressure. I am trying to find guidelines on "How have I decided in similar situations before in my life?". I revisit my own values, which have their roots mainly in my childhood and adolescence upbringing,

117

reassess those values, often only to find out that they have either lost their meaning for me, or that they are unsuitable for the current situation because there simply has not been a similar situation like this before. It is very scary to make this decision with no 'real ' guidelines. Sometimes I can find public, commonly shared values and guidelines, but they do not 'feel good' *or* 'feel right' for me. Then there is also some degree of anger as to "Why do I have to make this decision at all?", and an unwillingness to engage in a decision-making process. I find that time is an important factor - "How much time do I have of making this decision?" - The less time the greater the pressure. The pressure on me is enhanced if the decision involves other people, especially those close to me, like my children or my partner. Trying to describe what I feel in my body, I experience a tight feeling around my heart and my throat, as if being suffocated by the necessity to make a decision. My thoughts are racing, many possibilities come up, disappear, reappear, thoughts going in circles. I feel restless. Insomnia - with all its related problems. I have repeatedly revisited similar situations in my memory, checked all possibilities and values, yet there is still the fear that I might have overlooked another possibility that would allow me to decide more easily.

Having written this text helped me enormously, later in the research (Chapters 7-11) with the interpretation of students' interview-comments regarding the dilemma situation itself, especially with descriptions about how the students felt in the dilemma situation. Having gone through the emotional upheavals involved in ethical dilemmas myself, I was able to accept and understand what students reported to me about their feelings and thoughts. I think, reflecting on my own experiences of dilemma situations made me more humble towards the students, and I could identify with their accounts on the common basis of being human.

REVIEW AND IMPLICATIONS OF THE CHAPTER

What have I learned from writing an autobiography?

Autobiographical writing involved not only critical reflection on my past but also critical reflection on my practice as a researcher and curriculum developer. I believe that much of what I have learned through the autobiographical study can be grounded in the Theory of Transformative Learning (Mezirow, 1991). For transformative learning to occur, we, as teachers or researchers, need to engage in a critically reflective process during which we examine our assumptions through different lenses, one of which can be an autobiographical lens (Brookfield, 1995). Mezirow explains that, through critical self-examination and assessment of assumptions, we can change our perspectives of how we see ourselves and our environment.

Revisiting Parker Palmer's questions, I would like to summarise the chapter using 'his' questions again:

- <u>What</u> was my research about and how is the what of my research related to my autobiography? Autobiographical writing illustrated the close relationship between my biographical background and my interest in ethics, science, and the teaching of ethics within science education. It also revealed the relationship between the topics of the dilemma stories and my personal history. However, the self I have been describing in this chapter has continued to develop – it is not the same as it was at the beginning of the research. I explore the implications of this insight further in the last chapter where I speculate on how the what would change if 'I could do it all over again': how would I – given the new insights I have gained through the research - try to ensure, for example, age-appropriateness of the dilemma story.

- <u>Why</u> did I perform the research? It has become clear to me that my past experiences have raised my sensitivities towards ethical dilemmas: Certain events and developments in my past have resulted in my conviction that controversial issues in and around science should be addressed in a critical manner in the science classroom. The emergent significance of the topic culminated in the curriculum development and ultimately in this study.

- <u>How</u> did I perform the research? Autobiography has led to a much clearer understanding of how my sensitivities have affected and continue to affect my research. The writing process helped me to elucidate my culturally situated values and how my life-world values ultimately influenced the 'emergence' of the research design (see Chapter 1). Autobiographical inquiry allowed me to bring the resulting expanded awareness of the researcher's meaning perspective to the interpretive act, especially at the point of representing the other, thereby enabling an epistemology of ambiguity to shape the analysis (see also Chapters 7-11). An example is the move away from my epistemological predisposition to making judgements about (measuring) students' moral development towards an interest in understanding (interpreting) their learning experiences (see also Chapters 1, 5, 9, and particularly Chapters 10 and 11). As mentioned earlier, the researcher's self has changed through all the insights gained during the research – as with the what, this would also have implications for the how – if I had the chance to 'do it all over again' how would I do it differently? In Chapter 11, I try to find an answer to this question.

- <u>Who</u> is the Self doing the research? - Autobiographical writing (with a critical reflexive intent) involved me in an exploration of my own interpretive horizons. Exploring my identity (Palmer, 1998) through critical reflective practice (Brookfield, 1995) has led not only to enhanced awareness of my personal practical knowledge as a teacher and a researcher (Connelly & Clandinin, 1988) but has also led to a perspective transformation (Mezirow, 1991) – through this research has become a journey of personal development for me and potentially also for my audience.

Chapter 5

The 'planned' Ethics in Science curriculum

Curriculum is intensely historical, political, racial, gendered, phenomenological, autobiographical, aesthetic, theological, and international....Curriculum is an extraordinarily complicated conversation (Pinar, Reynolds, Slattery, & Taubman, 1995/1996).

INTRODUCTION

The development of a curriculum for a month-long Ethics in Science Project formed the basis of this thesis research. The curriculum was planned with teachers of, and implemented at, the Roseggerschule in Graz (Austria) (see Chapter 3). The ensuing interpretive case study of students' and teachers' experiences was based on the implementation of this curriculum.

This chapter serves several purposes: given that I expect the audience of this study to come primarily from a background in science education, I believe it might be helpful to the reader to provide a brief description of the dilemma teaching approach and an overview of the historical development of the Ethics in Science curriculum, tracking changes in the theoretical framework undergirding the curriculum development that resulted as increasingly sophisticated constructions emerged over time (Guba & Lincoln, 1989). In addition, I regard it as important to provide an analysis of the 'new' Austrian curriculum document that formed the basis of the development of the Ethics-in Science Curriculum. The chapter is therefore organised in <u>three</u> parts:

- <u>Part 1</u>: The historical context of the curriculum development
- <u>Part 2</u>: The Austrian Curriculum Reform 99 and its implications for ethics within science education
- <u>Part 3</u>: Teaching and Learning within the dilemma approach – the practical aspects

The development of an Ethics in Science Curriculum formed the core of this thesis. Given that the term 'Curriculum' means different things to different people, I explore the meanings of the term curriculum in the next section of the chapter before I embark on the journey through the curriculum development.

The meaning of curriculum

Schubert, along with Connelly and Clandinin, list many perspectives on curriculum which I had never thought of before I commenced this thesis research, and they suggest we regard curriculum as a 'field' (Connelly & Clandinin, 1988; Schubert, 1986).

As a 'border-crosser' between the German-speaking Austria and the English-speaking Australia, I am constantly confronted with the problem of translations as well as cultural differences. Often words have a similar meaning on the surface, however, when one looks more closely one often discovers slight but important differences in meaning. 'Curriculum' is one of those terms. The most common English interpretation of the Latin word 'curriculum', which literally means 'little run or little race', is that of a 'plan for learning' (Van den Akker, 1998). The German word for curriculum (and/or syllabus) is 'Lehrplan' which literally means 'plan for teaching' (German: lehren = to teach). Although 'Lehrplan' in the Middle European context outlines the prescribed content for teaching it is seen as an authoritative selection from cultural traditions that becomes educative only as it is interpreted and given life by the teachers (Hudson, 2002). Hudson explains that within the German tradition the teacher possesses 'relative pedagogical autonomy' which means that the teacher can choose from the given framework, based on his/her professional autonomy. Teacher control by the curriculum as in the US context or in Australia is unknown (Hudson, 2002). It is also worth mentioning that Austria has university entry exams (Matura) that are designed by the individual teacher and are not administered on a national scale. Germany, on the other hand, has a similar system (Numerus Clausus) to Australia's TEE exams (Tertiary Entrance Examinations) – students have to meet a particular benchmark with their exam scores to get into their preferred courses. In Austria, a student can study everything as long as s/he passes the 'Matura' at the end of Year 12 which, in my view, takes a lot of pressure off the teachers and gives them more pedagogical freedom – however, many Austrian teachers do not seem to realise how much freedom they actually have – perhaps because of lack of comparison?

It is interesting to note that the two translations of curriculum - as a 'plan for teaching' and as a 'plan for learning' - represent two diametrically different perspectives of the same phenomenon: With 'plan for teaching' one assumes the position of the teacher facing the students – thereby focusing on the teacher - whilst with 'plan for learning' one assumes the position of the student facing the teacher thus focusing on the student. One could therefore conclude that in the German-speaking context, the focus on curriculum development is on 'how do we improve the teaching?' whilst in the English-speaking context the focus appears to be on 'how do we improve student learning?'. However, I believe that both perspectives ultimately share a vital interest in improving both, but the starting points might be different.

In this study, I use the term curriculum in its German meaning – as a 'plan for teaching' because this is what it meant to me when I first engaged in the curriculum development. This leads me to the next section of the chapter in which

I give an overview of the historical development of the Ethics in Science Curriculum.

PART 1: HISTORICAL CONTEXT OF THE CURRICULUM DEVELOPMENT

The Red Cross Project in retrospective

In 1998, when the new curriculum framework was about to be implemented, many Austrian teachers voiced concerns about the dilemma of how to teach 'moral issues' without appropriate methodologies, materials and pedagogical competency, whilst being required to teach ethics by the new curriculum framework. Given this background, the Austrian Youth Red Cross initiated a study addressing how to improve moral and values education in Austrian classrooms (Gschweitl et al., 1998). I was a member of the research team, and consequently was directly involved in the initial planning, implementation and evaluation stages of the project. We wrote dilemma stories, trialled them and incorporated our experiences into a new planning circle very much in the tradition of action research. The result of our efforts was a teaching approach based on Kohlberg's theory of moral development using dilemma stories within a constructivist (in a very general sense) learning environment.

The use of dilemma stories in the study can be traced back to one of the pioneers of moral development research and moral education, Lawrence Kohlberg, who developed a cognitive-developmental theory of moral development consisting of three levels and six stages, each determined on the basis of moral reasoning and judgement (Kohlberg, 1984, 1996). Kohlberg's theory is an elaboration of Piaget's work who studied children at play and concluded that morality can be considered as a developmental process (Piaget, 1977). According to Piaget, moral development is the result of interpersonal interactions through which individuals

125

work out resolutions that are deemed fair (Nucci, n.d.). To Kohlberg, each of the levels represents a fundamental shift in the socio-moral perspective of an individual. Kohlberg had developed a Stage Theory of Moral Development (Kohlberg, 1980, 1984, 1996) outlined in Table 1.

Table 1: Kohlberg's stages of moral development (Kramer, n.d.)

Preconventional Level	Stage 1	Punishment & Obedience Orientation
	Stage 2	Instrumental Relativist Orientation
Conventional Level	Stage 3	Good boy-nice girl Orientation
	Stage 4	Law & Order Orientation
Postconventional Level	Stage 5	Social Contract Legalistic Orientation
	Stage 6	Universal Ethical Principle Orientation

According to Kohlberg, the child can develop from judging the goodness or badness of a human action based on its consequences (Stage 1), to the highest level of moral development in which right is determined by the decision of conscience in accord with self-chosen ethical principles that appeal to logical comprehensiveness, universality, and consistency (Stage 6) (Kramer, n.d.). The confrontation of a person with a moral dilemma leads to a cognitive disequilibrium and subsequently to a learning process (Kohlberg, 1984, 1996). Later, Kohlberg added four basic principles to his theory:

- An individual can be at only one stage at a certain time.
- An individual can develop only from one stage to the next (regression is impossible!).
- Each higher stage is more complex (and therefore indicates a higher level of moral development) than the previous stage;
- The six stages are universal and therefore independent of the cultural environment;

As I learned in due course of reviewing literature for my dissertation, it was these principles that led to most of the criticism of Kohlberg's work, which I discuss later in the chapter.

KOHLBERG'S THEORY IN PRACTICE

Kohlberg established several 'Just Community' schools in the United States where he trialled his ideas. Unfortunately his project was not very successful (HGSE News, 2002). In Germany, Brambring, Dobbelstein-Osthoff, Heckrath, Reinhart and Stiel (1991) described their experiences with a 'Just Community' approach in Soest, a town in the state of Nordrhein-Westfalen. They describe how dilemmas can be taught and how the teacher who becomes a facilitator moderates the process rather than giving theoretical input. They also describe the different stages involved in a dilemma unit, ranging from the presentation of a story to a whole-group discussion. During the pilot study, we found this report very helpful.

Apart from Brambring et al. (1991), we pulled together suggestions from several other 'dilemma approaches' that were drawing on Kohlberg's work (Lind, 1987; Oser & Althof, 1992). We made changes where we thought they were appropriate, and implemented the adapted version(s) in schools. In our role as independent communication facilitators, we also trialled them with participants in our communication courses because we thought that the teaching of dilemmas lends itself very well to the teaching of argumentation, collaboration, reflexivity, and conflict resolution (see Chapter 4 & 9).

During the implementation phase, we experimented with group sizes. We trialled different seating arrangements, such as rows and circles, and considered whether the teacher should be standing at the front or alternatively be seated amongst the students. We also experimented with different ways of presenting group results, such as preparing transparencies, posters, or simply telling about experiences. We were doing the teaching and we (mutually) evaluated different possibilities by giving each other feedback. The teachers were 'only' in the role of observers. Overall, this model worked out very well especially in terms of saving time – we did not have to introduce somebody else into the teaching approach, so that I may say now: it was fast but exclusive! Our experiences and insights became part of the introductory theory chapter of the book "Gibt es nur einen Weg?" (Gschweitl et al., 1998)

At the end of the evaluation period, we felt well equipped to present the national committee of the Austrian Youth Red Cross with our results. However, as described in the autobiographical vignette in Chapter 4, our employers had their own ideas regardless of the results of the evaluation and the suggestions we had come up with. For example, one contentious point was that, in the evaluation paper, we had suggested the dilemma stories be told freely, if possible. The reaction from the 'pedagogical' panel was that it was "…too much of an imposition on teachers to ask them to tell the stories" (see Chapter 10).

For the research team there was a clear dilemma that I could not fully understand then but which I understand much better now: There was a clash between different paradigms – (post)positivism versus constructivism. Whilst there was a clearly formulated demand by our employers, the Austrian Youth Red Cross, that the dilemma approach be consistent with constructivism, there was implicitly yet another demand, "Whatever you do, do not ask the teachers to change their teaching." I believe now that the reason for many problems was this gap between theory and practice: constructivism was to be included because it was the 'rising star' on the paradigm sky and it sounded wonderful (in theory). When it came to the practical side, it became more obvious that our views of teaching and learning were incongruent, perhaps even incommensurable, with the ideas of the pedagogical panel in terms of what was meant by good teaching practice.

With regard to Kohlberg's stages of moral development and his theory, our Red Cross project team at the time regarded them as valuable categories that provided the researcher and the teacher using this method with valuable information about the concepts a student is holding at a particular time regarding a particular issue. I believe Kohlberg's theory was chosen during the Red Cross Project because it seemed to be well aligned with constructivism which was a paradigm growing in importance at the time. Herbert Schwetz, the co-ordinator of the research team, who is a mathematics teacher educator in Graz, Austria, and who has a strong background in constructivism, introduced us to von Glasersfeld's and Watzlawick's work (von Glaserfeld, 1990, von Glasersfeld, 1995; Watzlawick, 1984). The idea that students in dilemma situations construct values and virtues, themselves, appealed to us. Most of us had gone through (partly gruelling) years of religious education that strongly resembled indoctrination. It was clear to us that teaching in the traditional sense, with the teacher 'preaching' to the students what is good or bad, does not work. Kohlberg had also rejected the traditional view that teachers can teach virtues through example and through direct communication primarily because he found a lack of consensus on what virtues are to be taught. This had been an issue for the teachers in this study as well as I discuss in Chapter 3. Instead of arbitrarily imposing certain values on students, Kohlberg thought teachers should rather focus on the different stages of moral development (Nucci, n.d.). Summarising, I can say that the theoretical framework of the Red Cross project was grounded in Kohlberg's theory of moral development and radical constructivism (see Chapter 2) as a theory for moral learning.

The publication of the Youth Red Cross book with the title, "Gibt es nur einen Weg: Informations- und Unterrichtsmaterialien zur Friedenserziehung und Konfliktarbeit im Sinne der Genfer Abkommen und des Humanitären Völkerrechts" (German: Is there only one way: Information and curriculum materials for peace education and conflict work in the sense of the Geneva Convention and the Charter of Human Rights) marked the end of the Red Cross Project, and I have to admit that for quite a while I wanted to hear about neither the Red Cross nor about moral dilemmas. I migrated to Australia and found out about a doctoral program at Curtin University, and whilst I was pondering on a possible thesis topic, the 1998 Youth Red Cross Project rose in my consciousness again and I realised that I might be able to build on my former experiences and perhaps 'do it better this time'. I, therefore, decided to use the teaching approach as developed, evaluated and documented in Gschweitl et al., 1998), refine it and apply it to science education. Yet at the beginning, it was still unclear what exactly I wanted to use it for. Science education was my own subject area and I felt that there were many controversial issues that lent themselves to dilemma stories. However, first I engaged in a thorough literature review on moral education (e.g., Arbuthnot & Faust, 1981; Blake, 1994; Brady, 1974; Damon, 1978; DeVries & Zan, 1994; Edwards & Ramsey, 1986; Fraenkel, 1977; Hawley, 1974; Hawley & Hawley, 1975; Hersh, Miller, & Fielding, 1980; Hersh, Pritchard Paolitto, & Reimer, 1979; Hill, 1973, 1993, 1996; Jones, 1976; Kirschenbaum, 1976; Lemin, Potts, & Welsford, 1994; Lind, Hartmann, & Wakenhut, 1985; McPhail, 1982; Munsey, 1980; Musgrave, 1978; Pack, 1991; Perry, 1970; Peters, 1981; Power, Higgins, & Kohlberg, 1989; Presno & Presno, 1980; Purpel, 1989; Purpel & Kevin, 1976; Straughan, 1982; Taylor, 1975; Torney-Purta & Hahn, 1988; Wilson, 1972).

1999: A new beginning

Re-reading the literature on moral education and expanding my readings beyond Kohlberg, I realised that Kohlberg's theory was regarded as highly problematic by some researchers: Kohlberg's theory had become the focus of feminist critique, primarily through the work of Carol Gilligan who criticised Kohlberg's work as biased against women. She suggested an 'Ethic of Care' that did not, contrary to Kohlberg's view, represent a lower stage of morality than men's 'Ethic of Justice' (Gilligan, 1982; Gilligan, Ward, Taylor, & Bardige, 1988). In contrast to Kohlberg's dilemmas, which were hypothetical in their nature, Gilligan preferred to draw from participants' lives (Tronto, 1994). She also developed a three-level model with six stages that is grounded in an increasing level of care, of differentiation of the self and the other, and a growing understanding of the dynamics of social interactions (Gilligan et al., 1988; Hofmann, 1998). Nevertheless, Gilligan's work also became the target of criticism by, for example, Tronto and Hoff Sommers (Hoff Sommers, 2000; Tronto, 1994). The focus of their criticism is primarily about the one-sidedness of Gilligan's approach:

- There are men and boys who also have a caring and empathic attitude – caring is therefore not exclusively a characteristic of females (see also Chapter 7 & 11).

Kohlberg based his theories on male students (only), Gilligan, in principle, did the same by working with females only. Hoff Sommers in particular, in her article 'The War Against Boys', argues against the inherent hostility against males in Gilligan's theory.

MOVING AWAY FROM KOHLBERG AND GILLIGAN

Now there was a dilemma for me! Finding that Kohlberg was problematic and that Gilligan's theory also had its flaws, I chose to adopt a critical stance towards both theories. Kohlberg became unacceptable to me because of his underlying bias against women, and Gilligan became problematic because of her claim that an Ethic of Care is intrinsically female (only).

Where to from here, I asked myself? At that time, I had already planned the curriculum in accordance with Gschweitl et al. (1998). This curriculum, however, was largely based on Kohlberg's work, however, I did use critical constructivism as a referent for teaching and learning. I did not have the time to develop yet another curriculum because I had to be in Austria in May 2000 in order to implement the Ethics in Science curriculum (i.e. the fieldwork of this interpretive case study). However, I continued to look for more suitable alternatives after my return and during the data-analysis by continuing my literature search (e.g., Daleo, 1996; Halstead & McLaughlin, 1999; Halstead & Taylor, 1996; Haydon, 1997; Haynes, 1998; Ingall, 1997; Sharma, 1999a, 1999b; Smith & Standish, 1997).

The results of this search are presented in Chapter 6. In the following part of this chapter, I introduce the reader to the reasons for developing an ethics curriculum for science education.

PART 2: THE CURRICULUM REFORM 99 AND ITS IMPLICATIONS FOR SCIENCE EDUCATION

As described earlier in Chapter 1, the changing global society has made necessary changes to the education system and thus changes to the national curriculum frameworks of many countries, for example, Western Australia (Curriculum Council, 1998; Gribble, Rennie, Tyson, Milne, & Speering, 2000) or in South Africa (Gevisser & Morris, n.d.). When Austria joined the European Union new challenges and requirements needed to be met by the Austrian schooling system (Kirste, 2001; Pädagogisches Institut Tirol). The result was a completely revised curriculum framework, the 'Lehrplanreform 99' (Curriculum Reform 99) for the lower level of secondary schools that is now at the stage of implementation.

Several years before the Austrian Curriculum Reform took place, Bastian (1991) in the renowned German education journal 'Pädagogik' demanded values-education in the spirit of Enlightenment that is based on democracy. I have to admit that his article influenced me deeply during the development of the Ethics in Science Curriculum. Bastian elaborated that children, adolescents and adults must be capable of judgement, conflict-solving and achieving consensus. The ability to express one's own interests, to accept the interests of others and to establish a balance of all interests (e.g., accepting the existence of conflicts and working out compromises) must be seen as key-characteristics of a democracy that is based on participation and autonomy. Self-determination is to be regarded as a premise of codetermination. But a focus on the self cannot be enough: the ability to adopt different perspectives has to be practised. Finally, he suggested that the enhancement of self-esteem can replace self-defence because only self-confident

132

people can deal without angst with foreigners, with competition and with stress (Bastian, 1991). It appears to me that the new curriculum framework tries to incorporate many of Bastian's suggestions.

The new overarching curriculum statement is geared towards the development of self and social competencies, and focuses on the development of key qualifications and on an incorporation of moral and ethical values into the curriculum, and it applies also to the upper school level. In Chapter 1, I introduced the concept of 'Bildung' and discussed its central role within the Middle-European education system(s). I briefly summarised how the new Austrian curriculum document sets out to meet the 'new' requirements of 'Bildung', and I discussed the overarching curriculum statement and its implications for the teaching and learning of ethics (see also Appendix 6). In the next section of the chapter, I would like to present a brief overview of the analysis of the new curriculum document with regard to the teaching of ethics in science education.

An analysis of the curriculum document in relation to the Ethics-in-Science Curriculum

Part 1 of the curriculum document states that (i) the curriculum is divided into five 'Bildungsbereiche' (areas of 'Bildung') and that (ii) the 'Religious-Ethical-Philosophical Dimension of Bildung' forms the foundation of integration and of collaboration between the different 'Bildungsbereiche'. The five 'Bildungsbereiche' are: language and communication, humans and society, nature and technology, creativity, health and movement. Science education, I would like to argue, covers all of these areas, even the area of creativity because it is defined as 'giving students opportunities to connect creativity and affective experiences with cognitive insights as a way of developing intellectual abilities which can also be achieved in science classrooms' (Bundesministerium fur Bildung, 2000, pp. 1-9).

In addition, Part 1 of the curriculum document describes the 'allgemeines Bildungsziel' (general goal of 'Bildung') which can be translated as the overarching curriculum statement. It outlines the guiding concepts that are applicable to all subjects, and that are based on an analysis of society and values which includes the topics: rapid societal change, European integration, globalisation, intercultural recognition, democracy and self-determination, world-views and life-ideas, an engagement with ethical and moral values as well as with questions about the sense of life, new technologies, the orientations of science and the lifeworld. Mutual acceptance and respect, as well as the ability to deal with communicative and collaborative tasks later in life are important learning outcomes. The curriculum document states very clearly that the teaching and learning ought to promote these values democracy, solidarity, tolerance, peace, justice, equality, and environmental awareness. Content-specific and values-dependent decision-making as well as the ability to take over social responsibility form part of democratic communication and co-determination opportunities (p. 2).

Content-specific and values-dependent decision-making forms the core of the Ethics in Science Curriculum. Preparing students for active participation in public discourse on science in an informed manner is a goal of the Ethics in Science curriculum that is also related to the promotion of democracy. Many theorists, such as Dewey (1944) and more recently Henderson (2001) and Marples (1999) have argued that the preparation of students for democracy is an overarching curriculum goal regardless of the subject area. Dewey argued that democracy is a moral way of life – enabling students to participate in and contribute to democracy in their countries thus becomes a moral enterprise. Applied to science education, this means that promoting emancipated, scientifically literate citizens who are able to understand and contribute to the discourse in and about science, is our contribution to democracy in our role as science teachers.

The curriculum document states, furthermore, that the ability to engage in critical reflection and to 'think' individually ought to be promoted (p. 1). This is yet another core-issue within the Ethics in Science curriculum – promoting individual and critical reflection (see Chapter 8). With regard to the 'acquisition' of knowledge, the curriculum document points out that students ought to be encouraged to critically assess available knowledge. This demand is well aligned with the goal of establishing a critical consciousness amongst students and teachers that I want to promote in the Ethics in Science curriculum which is based on Paolo Freire's concept of 'conscientisation' that he characterises as an overcoming of a naïve state of consciousness and the insertion of a person into a demythologised reality (Freire, 1998). The issue of myths in science (education) has been critically analysed (e.g., Milne & Taylor, 1998; Pitt, 1990; Tobin & McRobbie, 1996). Within an Ethics in Science curriculum, addressing ethically contentious issues in science and allowing for a dialogue to happen is therefore also aimed at supporting students in becoming aware of the myths in and around science and promoting their conscientisation in Freire's sense.

Furthermore, the overarching curriculum document cautions that learning should not be restricted to content-knowledge but extended to the development of social and self-competencies such as gaining knowledge about one's strengths and weaknesses, the ability to engage in new situations, the ability to co-operate with others but also to develop the initiative if needed, and the ability to participate in the design of school and out-of-school social life (Bundesministerium fur Bildung, 2000). The Ministry for Education concludes that the 'promotion of these abilities should prepare students for situations in which knowledge and experience gained through rote learning is insufficient and where other solutions have to be actively developed (p. 3). All of the above learning outcomes form part of the learning outcomes of the Ethics in Science curriculum where social co-operation and learning about the self is promoted through (i) individual reflection and (ii) group-discourse – I describe the details later in the chapter.

Given that the overarching curriculum statement applies to <u>all</u> subjects, I argue that the inclusion of ethics education into science education is clearly mandated by the new curriculum document (p. 4) because (i) it forms the foundation of the 'Bildungsbereiche' (thus including all subjects) and (ii) it offers opportunities to cover the mandated learning outcomes of the overarching curriculum statement, as outlined above. I believe that on the basis of the overarching curriculum statement, the Ethics in Science curriculum is well warranted and therefore well aligned with the new Austrian curriculum document.

However, there appears to be resistance against the inclusion of ethical and sociological issues into science education. In Australia, Dawson has argued against the inclusion of citizenship-education into science education on the basis that it "…would place unrealistic demands on science education" (Dawson, 2000). In my experience, some Austrian science teachers have also argued that there is no 'room' in the science curriculum to include ethics as well because the curriculum already is 'too crowded'. Nevertheless, the new Austrian curriculum document states otherwise: with regard to the actual planning of the teaching and learning,

Part 3 of the document emphasises the existence of a 'core-curriculum' – those contents that ought to be taught (about 2/3 of the curriculum of a year) – and the existence of an 'area of extension' which allows the teacher to design one third of his/her curriculum freely. I would like to argue that this extra 'third' could be used for including ethics education which would then allow Austrian science educators to fulfil the official mandate to include the 'Religious-Ethical-Philosophical Dimension of Bildung' in addition to covering the 'content' (Bundesministerium fur Bildung, 2000).

According to the curriculum document, science educators have an obligation to educate students towards participation in a critical discourse about science thus preparing them for their later adult and professional lives. Students ought to be able to make informed decisions about science-related issues which, in my view, goes hand-in-hand with what Skovsmose (1994) called 'Erziehung zur Mündigkeit' (education towards majority and/or responsibility) which forms part of 'Bildung'. 'Mündigkeit'[7], however, has a double-meaning: First, the term relates to legal theory referring to a person obtaining full age and therefore adult's rights and responsibilities in society – the person has the legal right to speak for himself/herself and to vote. However, in German there is a second meaning that refers to a person's capacity to speak for oneself. In this way 'Mündigkeit' becomes a component of critical citizenship. A person with 'Mündigkeit' shows the capacity to take well-balanced decisions.

Especially in the German speaking context, given the historical background, it is vital to educate for 'Mündigkeit' and not to educate followers. The prime goal is to prevent another 'Auschwitz' (Skovsmose, pp. 40-41). Wilber (1997) has argued that Auschwitz was made possible by the achievements of modern science, "You cannot seriously attempt genocide with bow and arrow; but you can attempt it with steel and coal, combustions engines and gas chambers, machine guns and atomic bombs" (p. 75). He argues further that the problem does not lie with

---

[7] 'Mündigkeit' is derived from the German noun 'Mund' = mouth. It can be literally translated as the ability to use one's mouth.

advanced technologies but rather with the irrational use of them. This is where ethics enters the picture – in my opinion, students ought to understand that neither science nor its products are value-free (e.g., Allchin, 1998; Hempel, 1998; Kieffer, 1977; McMullin, 1998; Patry, 2000; Poole, 1995).

Thus, apart from a mandate by the Austrian Education Ministry, there are also reasons from within science and science education that call for an inclusion of ethics-education into science education: as I discussed in Chapter 1, the notion of a value-free science is promoted by scientism and is (still) very powerful in science classrooms[8]. In 1984, Zeidler explained that, the development of students as rational beings who are capable of making informed judgments about policy with respect to science and society, has been regarded as a major goal of science education for many years (Zeidler, 1984). However, I daresay that in 2003 the field of science education still promotes 'desert conditions' for moral education and for open discourse on scientific research, and thus not much has changed since 1984. However, there have been initiatives by individual authors to call for an increased inclusion of values into science education (Allchin, 1999a, 1999b; Lacey, 1999). Yet, as Eisner and Connelly argue values are a part of the hidden curriculum and thus are omnipresent in all classrooms (Connelly & Clandinin, 1988; Eisner, 1979; Feinberg & Soltis, 1985) – an issue that ought not to be overlooked.

Given that I regard education towards 'Mündigkeit' , towards self- and codetermination and towards critical citizenship as integral parts of any type of education (e.g., Cross & Fensham, 2000; Parker, Ninomiya, & Cogan, 1999; Torres, 2002), my personal goals for the Ethics in Science curriculum development were to develop a curriculum that was engaging, promoting various opportunities for learning, and complementing existing science education curricula. I chose a dilemma approach to teaching ethics because I believed that it can potentially enhance the awareness of students toward dilemmas in and about science, and to confront the widespread belief that science can provide 'absolute truth and

---

[8] scientism presents a radical materialist perspective on science and is (still) very powerful in science classrooms

knowledge'. Becoming scientifically literate and (Cobern, 2000; Good & Shymansky, 2001), at the same time, becoming part of the scientific discourse community was another important learning outcome, in my view, thereby enabling students to engage in critical thinking guided by the question, "Whose interests are being served?", in a Habermasian sense (see Appendix 7).

The traditional science curriculum serves, in my opinion, primarily a technical interest by controlling and managing the environment (Lacey, 1999). I can also see a practical interest involved (with some teachers) that serves the understanding of our environment grounded in the fundamental need of humans to live in and to interact with our natural environment which is a concern of environmental ethics and of education towards sustainability (Bowers, 2002; Wheeler & Bijur, 2000). Yet neither of the above interests alone will ensure that the fundamental interest in young people becoming autonomous and responsible adults is served (Grundy, 1987). The curriculum metaphors that can be applied here are 'curriculum as cultural reproduction' that is, curriculum propagated by uncritical science teachers who unknowingly promote a culture of scientism, and 'curriculum as societal reconstruction', which sits well with an emancipatory interest and that includes an ideology critique geared towards an uncritical propagation of the status quo (Schubert, 1986; P. C. Taylor & Campbell-Williams, 1992).

Summarising, I can thus say that the inclusion of ethics into science education may not only serve the purpose of contributing to scientific literacy but also may promote students' abilities to participate in democracy and the conscientisation process in Freire's sense. The inclusion of an ethics curriculum into the science curriculum can potentially enrich the existing curricula and contribute to a shift in curriculum metaphors: from a dominant metaphor of 'curriculum as cultural reproduction' to 'curriculum as an agenda for social reconstruction' (Schubert, 1986). In the next section of the chapter, I introduce the reader to the dilemma approach as suggested by Gschweitl et al. (1998) which was

139

used as the basis for the Ethics in Science curriculum after minor changes and refinements.

PART 3: TEACHING AND LEARNING WITHIN THE DILEMMA APPROACH – THE PRACTICAL ASPECTS

Given that the most commonly used tool in moral education is the presentation of a dilemma story during which students are required to determine and justify which actions an actor in the story should take (Nucci, n.d.), I have focused my research deliberately on the teaching and learning involved in and resulting from the use of dilemma stories.

In this part of the chapter, I would like to discuss the <u>What</u>, and the <u>How</u> in relation to the Ethics in Science curriculum development, drawing also on my contribution to the book "Neue Wege der Werteerziehung" (Gschweitl et al., 1998).

The <u>What</u> – The dilemma stories

Dilemma-stories are not just 'stories'. They represent a genre and are characterised by ethical dilemma situations. The purpose of telling dilemma stories within moral education is to introduce students to a moral dilemma situation in which choices have to be made by the characters in the story. The language of the stories is kept simple in order to allow for ample associations. Dilemma-stories are (usually) open-ended. Typically a dilemma-story is presented in several parts, interrupted by several dilemma-situations. Most dilemma-stories contain several dilemmas with a main dilemma towards the end of the teaching unit. However, there are variations as to how these dilemma stories can be presented – in my thesis research I used and 'refined' the teaching approach suggested by Gschweitl et al. (1998). The topics of the dilemma stories were chosen to fit in with the curriculum that the science teacher was teaching at the time of the Ethics in Science Project (for the full text versions of the dilemma stories, see Appendix 5).

CO-CREATING DILEMMA STORIES

I wanted the dilemma-stories to have direct relevance to the science curriculum that was being taught at the time that I arrived at the school, so that the teachers would not need to make too many 'artificial' changes to their teaching, but rather be able to offer additional perspectives on what would have been taught anyway. In order to achieve this, it was important to collaborate closely with the teachers about their plans for that time of the year, for a particular class and subject.

This turned out to be very difficult, as both teachers pointed out the high degree of flexibility in their science curricula. So we started negotiating whether or not it was possible to teach certain topics that lent themselves to dilemma-stories at particular periods of time. When I had finished a story in German, I sent it to the teachers and to two friends of mine, both German teachers in Austria, asking for their additional feedback. Then I translated the text into English and passed it on to my thesis research supervisor and friends here in Australia. Of course, it was the teachers who had the greatest input here – after all it was their classes. I would like to illustrate the teachers' input with an example from an email exchange with Irene (26.1.2000):

> *1) In principle, I like all your proposed topics. I am not sure yet as to how useful it is to involve the students in the choice of dilemma-topics. Either I decide for them or I offer them to choose after a short introduction to the project. 2) What sort of topics appeal to fifteen-year old kids? 3) Is it advisable to point out the value of the lives of people of Third World countries in this multicultural class I have got? After all some students actually come from there! Or should we ask these questions particularly because these students are in my class? (see Appendix 2)*

Irene's comments highlighted to me the importance of addressing the question, "How do we ensure age-appropriateness of the topics?" This became one of my research questions (see also Chapter 1, 8, 11). However, this was also when I realised that the implementation of the dilemma approach might bring to the fore 'emergent' questions of ethics for the teacher, such as, "Is it ethical to ask certain questions which might be culturally insensitive?" or as I discovered during the analysis of the data, "Is it good, ethical teaching practice to require students to perform tasks that they perhaps are not really prepared to do?" (see Chapter 10).

The How

During a dilemma unit, students are confronted with one or more dilemma questions that are designed to initiate a cognitive disequilibrium and thus a reflective process. Students are consequently asked to identify with the character in the story having the dilemma, and to reflect individually on how they would solve the problem in his/her place. The individual reflection phase is followed by dialogue: students are asked to exchange their views with colleagues. Eventually this teaching approach culminates in a whole-class discussion. There are alternating phases where participants work individually or in groups (see Figure 7).

ORGANISATION OF A DILEMMA-UNIT

In the following, I give a brief overview of a dilemma unit:

Step 1: Introduction to the dilemma-story
The teacher tries to tell the story as freely as possible until the story reaches the first dilemma-situation.

Step 2: Interrupting the story and asking questions
Dilemma stories in the approach suggested by Gschweitl et al. (1998) contain two types of questions: 'warm-up' questions that prepare the students for engagement with the story and dilemma questions that contain the actual dilemma-problem.

The teacher reads the questions out aloud. S/he points out that it is of great importance to give an explanation as to <u>why</u> one has chosen a particular solution.

Step 3: Working on the questions
During the first dilemma-interruption each participant works individually at first. The results are then discussed in pairs and, depending on the available time, presented to the whole class. During the second dilemma-interruption each participant works individually at first, then the results are discussed in small groups of three students, and so on. Results can be presented to the whole class after each group-collaboration, depending on the available time. At the end of a dilemma-story, there is usually a final dilemma-situation during which each participant works (again) individually at first. The results are discussed within small groups, and are then used to prepare a poster that is presented to the whole class. Following the poster-presentation, the teacher initiates a plenary discussion. As dilemma-stories are (usually) open-ended, there is (usually) no final solution. During the Red Cross Project, we found that the arrangement of the seating can have a great effect on the communication and discourse-processes. Breaking up the 'everyday' seating and rearranging the chairs (without any tables) in the form of a circle contributes substantially to enhanced engagement in the discourse.

THE ROLE OF THE TEACHER

Within a dilemma approach, teachers have a new role within the teaching and learning environment that is well-aligned with constructivism's tenets: the traditional teaching style that was focused on the teacher as a lecturer has been replaced by a new social teaching-style which focuses on the teacher as a moderator/facilitator. During class discourse phases, the teacher tries to make connections between the contributions of the discourse but does not influence directly the content of the discourse. It is the teacher's task to give voice to all participants and to create a climate in which all opinions are valued equally. There are no 'right' or 'wrong' contributions in the sense that a student is being evaluated on the basis of his/her utterances. It requires teacher moderation skills to play unacceptable answers back to the whole class for comments. However, it has to be noted that the teacher is primarily responsible for the discourse-processes within the group, not for the content. Using dilemma-stories *sensu* Kohlberg, within value- and moral- education, the teacher's role is to activate reflexivity, to guide group-processes and to provide for everyone to express his/her own opinion without fear through establishing feedback rules. The major goal for the teacher is to 'guide everyone deeply into the dilemma-situation so that the story speaks directly to the person and becomes a personal concern' (Gschweitl et al., 1998)

Summarising, I can say that each step of a dilemma-story-unit consists of the following phases, whereby each phase represents a potential starting-point for social and moral learning: storytelling, dilemma-situations, asking questions, individual reflection, collaboration with others, presentation of results, plenary discussion (see Figure 7).

REVIEW OF THE CHAPTER

In the first part of the chapter, I gave an overview of the historical development of the dilemma teaching approach and its theoretical background. I discussed how the curriculum development during the Red Cross Project was based on Kohlberg's work and on radical constructivism. Furthermore, I elaborated on how, through additional reading, my theoretical horizon expanded, leading to theoretical crisis the 'solution' of which I discuss in Chapter 6. In Part 2 of the chapter, I presented an analysis of the 'new' Austrian Curriculum document that was the result of the Curriculum Reform 99. I discussed this document with regard to the Ethics in Science curriculum development. In Part 3, I gave an overview of the practical pedagogical aspects of the Ethics in Science curriculum, providing the structure of 'typical' dilemma unit, and discussing the role of the teacher.

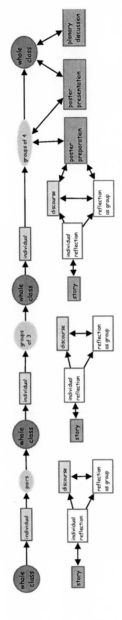

Figure 7: 'Activities during a 'typical' dilemma unit' (as suggested by Gschweitl et al, 1998)

Chapter 6

Methodology II

Analysis is a bit like taking apart puzzles and reassembling them – however, puzzles cannot be completed if pieces are missing, warped, or broken (Le Compte, 2000, p. 146)

INTRODUCTION

The purpose of this methodology chapter is to provide the reader with an overview of the fieldwork, the research-strategies, the data-sources and storage, and the data-analysis. I have also added 'new theory' that emerged whilst doing the data-analysis and thus influenced my way of interpreting the findings. I have strategically placed this chapter at the beginning of the findings section, in order to discuss the relevant methodology and theory when it is needed. The chapter is organised in five parts: fieldwork, research-strategies, data-sources and –storage, data-analysis, additional theory. In the following part of the chapter, I discuss issues related to the fieldwork.

PART 1: THE FIELDWORK MAY/JUNE 2000

This part is written as an autoethnographic account (see Chapters 2, and 4) and contains two sections:

- <u>Section 1</u> describes the fieldwork preparation phase of the research
- <u>Section 2</u> describes the initial phase of fieldwork.

<u>Section 1</u>: Sowing the seeds or how I prepared the fieldwork

I started this project by contacting my former supervising teacher, colleague and friend, Irene, informing her about the project and asking whether she had any interest in collaborating, knowing that she suffers chronically from a lack of time. The time of project preparation was characterised by several phases and events, some of which were troublesome, others surprisingly smooth.

NO PROBLEMS GAINING ENTRY TO THE SCHOOL AND FINDING PARTICIPATING TEACHERS

Irene responded in the form of an email– "Ich bin begeistert über dein Dissthema. Werde dich unterstützen, wie es in meiner Macht steht [I am really enthustiastic about your thesis topic. I will try to support you wherever I can!]." (see Appendix 2). Irene passed my research proposal on to the other science teachers in the school. I received four positive responses. Two biology teachers, Irene and Theresia, and two physics teachers, Sandra and Walter. I was more than impressed by the warm welcome of my ideas. For example, Sandra's first response was (4.1.2000): "Danke für die ausführliche Information zu deinem Forschungsvorhaben! Das klingt sehr spannend und ich freue mich schon darauf [Thanks for the detailed information about your research project! Sounds thrilling and I am very much looking forward to participating] (see Appendix 2). The time after these interactions was characterised by what have called *developing and maintaining relationships* (or rather the problems with it) and *decision about sampling* (Cohen, Manion, & Morrison, 2000).

PROBLEMS WITH "KEEPING" PARTICIPATING TEACHERS

A few weeks later, the impressive number of four had shrunk to two. Walter, despite showing initial interest, never contacted me after that. Theresia was worried initially about the additional workload, yet expressed serious interest in an email to me (28.1.2000): "Ich habe die Post gelesen, die du Irene geschickt hast. Du hast meine Bedenken zerstreut. Ich bin gerne bereit mitzuarbeiten und werde meine Einverständniserklärung Irene......geben. Genauere Information hätte ich noch gerne wegen des Tagebuchs![I have read the letter, you sent to Irene. You have eliminated my worries. I would like to collaborate with you and will pass my letter of consent on to Irene, I would like more detailed information about the journal though!] (see Appendix 2). I responded by explaining why it would be helpful if teachers kept a journal during the process as requested, nevertheless she stopped all contact after this. Looking back and re-reading my journal entries, it became obvious to me that the sudden "loss of interest" of these two colleagues affected me more than I would have admitted officially at that time (journal entry: 16. 5. 2000).

Theresia, a very (!) engaged biology-teacher had promised to collaborate with me because she felt it was very important to deal with ethical issues in her science teaching, according to the first email she had sent to me. Her interest seemed to abate as soon as I had asked the teachers to write a journal regarding their role as a teacher and a learner within this project about moral education. I received an email that expressed her fears about the use of the journal in my research. I responded by explaining to her about the 'hows and whys' regarding the use of journals. She replied to me, saying that she felt reassured by what I had told her yet after this email she stopped the correspondence altogether.

For some naïve reason, I thought that she would explain her reasons for her silent withdrawal to me, when I would get to Austria – instead I found that she seemed to 'avoid' me - might be a personal impression only. I have tried to talk to her – just talk, not to accuse her or make her feel guilty, but because I am interested in the reasons, why she suddenly decided not to collaborate. So far she has always produced reasons why she can't possibly talk to me 'right now'! Well then…be it! With Walter, the physics teacher, it is even worse: Walter, who conveyed to Ingrid obvious enthusiasm about participating in the project, never responded to my emails at all. After a while I gave up the illusion that he might still get involved. When I met him here, he did not even pretend, that he had no time – he simply does not mention the project at all!

But maybe I just feel disappointed because I think that as a co-researcher I would have handled the situation differently - I would have tried to explain the reasons why I could not or would not participate. I will finally have to accept that different people handle the situations differently – sounds so clear from a rational point of view – still a source of disappointment from the emotional point of view.

So, I was left with two teachers – Irene, who apart from all her additional duties in and around the school teaches biology, physics and chemistry, and Sandra who teaches physics and mathematics. Well I thought, this is not too bad after all – after reducing my focus to one school on one continent, focusing on two teachers instead of four might be just the right set-up – each teacher with one class, each class with two dilemma-units.

BLISS AND CONSTANT SOURCE OF TROUBLE: THE USE OF NEW INFORMATION TECHNOLOGY AS A MEANS OF SUSTAINING CONTACT

During the months leading up to my trip to Austria to do my fieldwork, I stayed in email contact with both of them, more regularly with Irene. Recurring email and server problems had to be overcome. Messages such as one from Irene (31. 5. 99), "Just sent you 900 words but this monster does not like me. All our servers are out of order. I am sorry that you receive this response so late…." (see Appendix 2). Or on the 29.1.2000 she wrote, "Hi, this information technology confronts me daily with never ending surprises and challenges: how can I pass your information on to Theresia – her email account does not work – the printer does not work, transfer onto a floppy disc was impossible. I need a professional! Please H-E-L-P!" (see Appendix 2).

Despite all these hiccups with the new technology, I was able to pass my ideas on to the teachers and receive valuable feedback from them, which was of great importance, at the time when I was writing the dilemma-stories.

CO-CREATING DILEMMA STORIES

In Chapter 5, I discussed the co-creation of the dilemma stories in detail, however, I mention this part of the research in this section only for reasons of completeness – after all it formed a vital part of the preparation phase of the fieldwork (see Chapter 5 and Appendix 2).

CONTACTING PARTICIPANTS, THEIR PARENTS, AND SCHOOL AUTHORITIES AND ADDRESSING ETHICAL ISSUES IN PRACTICE

One advantage of the email contact was, that I could send information materials about the project to the two teachers, who then distributed it to the principal, the students, the parents, and other interested teachers. This allowed me to organise access to the school from a distance, by informing school authorities and participants, months before the fieldwork actually started. From an ethical perspective this meant that every participant received detailed information about what was involved in the research. Students returned a letter of consent which had been signed by their parents and themselves. Teachers signed for themselves. The principal and the school authorities were informed and the principal returned a written note of consent to me. Everyone was reassured that anonymity was guaranteed and that the video-data, audio-data and written notes would be used for research purposes only. None of the participants objected except for one parent who refused that her child be shown on video in public – this is the reason why I cannot add a CD with the videos to the thesis – I cannot make sure that the girl is not on the videos. When the research actually started, I reminded the students that they had the possibility of leaving the project any time they wanted to.

When I finally left Australia to fly to the United States to the AERA and NARST conferences in 2000, and then on to Austria to start up my fieldwork, I felt well prepared and could not think of anything, that I had forgotten to check. Well, maybe there was nothing to be checked or overlooked at that time after all. It is only at the "real beginning" that you realise where your omissions have been lying...

Section 2: The real beginning or "You reap what you sow..."

I arrived in Vienna on the 7th of May 2000 and continued to Graz the next morning to catch up with Irene, who had kept the day free for me. This allowed us to get started with the organisation of the project in her class shortly after my arrival and after having said hello to everyone I knew. We set up a preliminary timeframe for the project. Irene was very keen on getting Sandra involved as soon as possible, to work as a team, so to speak, but as it soon turned out – due to different teaching duties (and other private duties!) it proved impossible to get both together in one place at any time during the project. So I arranged to meet Irene later in the day in the library, where she was team-teaching with another teacher, who had promised to take over the teaching load for this day, so that we two could discuss issues about Irene's class in a quiet corner of the room. Irene gave me valuable demographic information which I have included in Chapter 3.

Meeting Sandra provided me with a challenge during our first meeting already. We met in a café and my goal was to discuss the organisation of the Ethics in Science Project. I quickly browsed through 'my' plans and introduced her to my ideas about the project, about how and when we should implement the two dilemma units I had prepared. However, she interrupted me, saying, "Well, actually I have to tell you right away that I have also applied to attend a seminar at the same time you said you were coming. Yesterday, I received the OK and I am really keen on going, so we have to take into consideration that I will be gone for a whole week!"

I had not really expected to be the centre of the universe for those two teachers whilst we were collaborating on the research, however, I had expected that Sandra would make time for the project. I have to admit I was stunned and I did not really know how to respond to this. My plan had been worked out in detail, checked with her beforehand on email, and now suddenly I found myself confronted with the possibility of working with her and her class for one to two weeks less. I had only four weeks available to me, and I had carefully mapped everything out. I felt that the ceiling of my organisational edifice was caving in. When and how should we implement two dilemma-units, in only three weeks time, and when should I interview the students and Sandra and….and….and….so many questions - chaos, panic! Nevertheless I managed to come up with an emergency research design in which I decided that I would use only <u>one</u> dilemma in Sandra's class.

This was how the fieldwork started, and I realised that not even good and long preparation can prevent 'disasters' from happening. Given that the fieldwork consists largely of trying to find answers to our research questions by applying various research methods in the field, I discuss the research strategies in the following section.

PART 2: RESEARCH-STRATEGIES

Participant observation

I observed both classes as a participant-observer over a period of the month (the duration of the Ethics in Science Project), not only during the science lessons but also during other subject-lessons as long as the teacher agreed. Erlandson et al. (quoting Marshall & Rossman) inform us that, "…observations can be defined as the 'systematic description of events, behaviours, and artefacts chosen for the study" (Erlandson et al., 1993, p. 94). In qualitative research, participant observation is used because it is less intrusive to the 'natural environment' than other types of data-generating methods. By adopting the role of a participant observer over an extended period of time, I could develop friendly and informal relationships with most of the observed participants (one exception which I describe on several occasions during the findings chapters). I was also able to discern some behavioural patterns that helped me make sense of the findings, in Chapter 10 in particular (Cohen et al., 2000).

Taking field-notes

Recording classroom observations in the form of field-notes was a challenging endeavour to me because I was trying to be constantly vigilant in order not to miss out on 'anything important'. My scribbled, hand-written notes (both German and English) were typed as soon as I returned 'home' every night. A summary of my field-notes can been seen in Appendix 8 ('Tales of the Field') which I sent as an email attachment to my supervisor to keep him up-to-date about my research. During the actual dilemma units, I used video-taping (as long as the camera was working) as an additional back-up.

Interviewing

Much has been written about interviewing – for me the most helpful texts were "InterVsiews" (Kvale, 1996) and "The interview" (Fontana & Frey, 2000). "Asking questions and getting answers is a much harder task than it may seem at first" (Fontana & Frey, 2000). This is how I experienced some of my interviews (with one girl in particular) as described during the findings chapters. I conducted semi-structured interviews (see Appendix 9) and semi-structured focus-group interviews with the students (see Appendix 9). For the single interviews, I chose five students from each class, partly randomly or partly based on their performance during the dilemma units. In addition to the single interviews, I interviewed five students from each class in a focus-group interview where I asked each students to respond to my question individually at first, and then the students had the opportunity to engage in a discourse about the questions and answers. From Irene's class, I interviewed Fatima, Emma, Gregor, Alex, Damian and Melinda during the single interviews. For the group interview, I spoke with Attila, Imelda, Anna, and Susan. From Sandra's class, I interviewed Maria, Ulli, Manuel, Paul, and Daniela. For the group interview, I spoke with Clarissa, Stephanie, Thomas, Markus, and Andreas. In addition, I interviewed both the teachers, during semi-structured interviews as well as during unstructured feedback-sessions immediately after the dilemma units.

Videotaping and audio-taping

The school provided me with a video-camera, however, this was not without problems. On several occasions when I had booked the camera, it was simply not available because somebody else had 'just taken' it. Or a recurring problem was the charging of the battery – I charged up the battery after use, however, on several occasions when I wanted to use it somebody else had used it in the meantime without re-charging. Or one occasion, it was impossible to focus the video-camera – a problem that miraculously disappeared later in the day. However, despite these problems I was able to make good use of the videotapes, as back-ups of the field-notes. In addition, they proved helpful to recollect classroom interactions, body-language of participants, the tone of the voices, the mood of the speakers, interruptions, the speed of talk, who was communicating with whom, what was being said, pauses and silences, etc. (Cohen et al., 2000). With the audio-recordings I was less than successful during the dilemma units: I had planned to record group-conversations whilst the students were working on the dilemma questions, however, either the background noise levels were too high, or the students spoke with such low voices, and/or stopped talking to each other altogether until I removed the audio-recorder. Eventually, I gave up and used the recorder for the interviews only.

Transcription and translation of the interviews and videotapes

All the interviews and videotapes were in German. However, the transcription had to be done in Australia and given that, the number of professional transcribers who speak Austrian German fluently enough to follow the conversations is rather limited, I had to do the transcriptions myself – not to speak of the translations during the data-analysis. This was a very time-consuming activity and kept me busy for several months. Following Lemke's advice that it is better to transcribe as much as possible, I transcribed the complete interviews as well as the complete videos (Lemke, 1990). I was grateful for this advice later during the analysis phase.

PART 3: DATA-SOURCES AND –STORAGE

Data Sources

This range of research-strategies provided me with an abundance of data derived from various data sources ranging from:

- students' written notes as part of their learning portfolio
- my field-notes gathered during participant observation in the classroom
- video-tapes and audio-tapes
- individual interviews with students and teachers
- group interviews with students
- feedback sessions with the teachers immediately after the teaching experience

- conversations with non-participating teachers who were present at the time of implementation.

Data Storage

All raw data (including data stored on audio- and video-tapes, diskettes, CDs) collected during this study will be kept in a safe place at the Science and Mathematics Education Centre at Curtin University for five years. The field notes, students' notes, and the questionnaires will be stored for five years and then destroyed. Teachers' journals remained with the teachers. Students' portfolios remained with the students – I obtained photocopies with their consent.

PART 4: DATA-ANALYSIS

Erickson reminds that research actually means to seek again (and again, and again) – recursively. When I commenced the analysis, I was not sure where to start, thus I started with the obvious – the interviews. At that time I was still unsure whether I was doing phenomenology, ethnography or any other interpretive research. However, my initial analysis of the interviews was in line with the Van Kaam Method of analysis of phenomenological data (Moustakas, 1994). In this type of analysis, initially every utterance has the same value. Only after themes emerge, the researcher starts to eliminate data that do not pertain to the phenomenon. With hindsight and knowing that I was not really doing phenomenology, I think I should have started with the analysis of the field-notes and the videos. This is supported by Erickson when he says, "… data-analysis proceeds, when hunches about patterns that were developed on the basis of field-notes are cross-checked and confirmed by reference to interview data" (Erickson, 1998, p. 1159). However, given that I was looking for nothing in particular, my search through the interviews felt overwhelming. I overcame this problem by learning how to use the computer-software package QSR NVivo which has been designed with qualitative researchers in mind. However, at the time there were no courses available but I needed quick results, so I taught myself how to use the program. The following vignette from my research journal illustrates my initial struggle as well as my little successes. I wrote this piece whilst I was struggling through the learning process by having a Word-document open in the background and writing in it as often as something happened – or not!

FROM THE DIARY OF AN NVivo LEARNER

9.15am: I loved the colours of the Demo Version – that's why I chose it!
Watching the demo movies
NO problems importing the interviews
Problems!!! – what problems – problems everywhere:
Saving a project.
Coding the texts.
What on earth is a node?
How can I organise my nodes?
Tons of free nodes.
Doing it by trial and error and consulting the manual. Moving to and fro
between the keyboard and the manual.
Finally organising my nodes into tree nodes.
But what are node and document links? Check manual......unintelligible
language!
Too many nodes – need to reduce but how?
I have not yet managed to merge two nodes which are similar, so that the
information does not get lost....
I cannot even open the 'merge' window in the node explorer – frustration!
Ok I have managed to do that – you have one node in the clipboard,
highlight one on the left pane and go to merge. I can then delete the
redundant node (hopefully!)
Just managed to reorganise my nodes......uffzi! But what is a set? Maybe
this could help me a bit.....
I made it, I made it – it works: I have finally seen through the mystery of
sets of nodes and they were exactly what I was looking for: now I have
got five sets of nodes: learning experience, self and others, time, space,
and evaluation and I am able to produce coding reports for each set now,
which is much more user-friendly!
There is a pattern developing – I have an idea and a need. I try to find
intuitively what I am looking for - especially problematic if I do not even
know what exactly I am looking for and what it might look like. Sometimes
I find a solution just like that, on other occasions it is very frustrating
because everything I try fails and the manual does not get me further
either.....like in a hermeneutic circle I am moving between the big picture
and the detail, intuition and theoretical knowledge....
Eventually I succeed, combining both.
By now I have been able to organise my coding quite nicely!
7pm: I have printed out coding reports for each set and checked them
carefully, moving between original text and the print-out. Desperate need
for re-organising the codes: too much double coding, too much

repetition!!!!! Checking the text I find that some codes which are in the text do not appear in the report, so it is necessary after all to check the coding report for completeness!

This vignette (hopefully) illustrates that it was not easy to (i) learn how to categorise qualitative data and simultaneously (ii) learn how to use a computer-program without any help because nobody else in the department was using it at that time. However, I managed to distinguish several basic categories or themes:

- Utterances that were related to the Self
- Utterances that were related to the interactions between Self and others
- Utterances that were related to the dilemma stories
- Utterances that were related to external factors influencing the dilemma experiences such as time, space etc.

I analysed every interview, fine-tuned categories – adding new ones and deleting redundant ones. I printed a coding report from each interview which included the paragraph number of each quote – a 'director's cut' of the QSR NVivo projects can be viewed on CD containing categories before the fine-tuning that happened during the writing process.

After analysing the interviews, I transcribed the videos and compared these transcripts with my field-notes. From this several patterns emerged, such as patterns of social interactions and patterns of pedagogical significance. By that time, I had adopted Erickson's qualitative research method which is characterised by a process through which the researcher reflexively generates questions and assertions on the basis of evidence based on analytic induction (Erickson, 1998).

The writing process was the next major step of analysis for me. Analysis occurred during the writing of Chapters 7 to 10 of which the topics were largely based on the research questions. Chapter 10, on the other hand, was based on the emergent themes from the interview analysis. I then cross-checked patterns from the video-analysis and field-note analysis with student and teacher interviews. As it turned out, there were no major differences between the focus-group interviews

and the single students interviews. This is why I used only the individual
interview-data in the report and used the focus-group interview data only as a
back-up.

In case of doubt, I tried to contact the research participants on email –
unfortunately more often than not they did not respond. This problem was
especially difficult with Sandra – Irene helped me wherever she could. I indicated
in the text of the findings chapters (Chapters 7, 8, 9, 10), where I tried to get
feedback from participants.

Figure 8 illustrates the data-analysis/interpretation process through the
'movement' of the arrows.

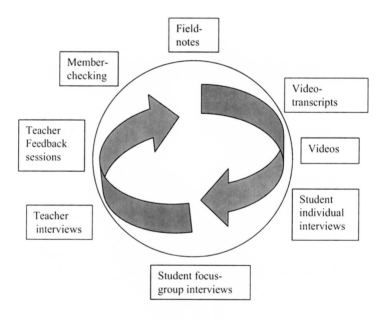

Figure 8: The data-analysis and interpretation process during Lily's thesis research

Erickson informs us that in participant-observer research the data-analysis is largely a matter of post-hoc decision making, "Analysis consists in recursive review of information sources with a question in mind, ...deciding progressively which information bits to attend to further" (Erickson, 1998, p. 1162). The data-analysis process was thus characterised by cross-checking that was moving backwards and forwards in circular motion in order to find evidence (compare Figure 8 & 9) – the researcher alternatively contemplates the whole circle and its parts thus following a hermeneutic circle (Packer & Addison, 1989). However, as indicated in Figure 8, I am not thinking of a 'vicious circle' in Nietzsche's sense (Klossowski, 1997) but rather that with every 'round' we gain new insights and a higher level of understanding in Gadamer's and Heidegger's sense (Gadamer, 1984, pp. 265-267; Heidegger, 1962, p. 153). In Figure 9, I present a 'map' I designed after 'finishing' the data-analysis of the student interviews in order to get an idea about emerging themes. However, this was not the end of the data-analysis: I searched all data-sources repeatedly. Erickson reminds us that there is still the question of generalisation – to what extent was a particular phenomenon represented within the setting (Erickson, 1998). I tried to attend to this question by mentioning in the text whether the extent of the representation. I also deliberately looked for discrepant cases – cases that did not fit the picture.

It was a rewarding process to see patterns emerge from the data that helped me to gain new insights and to understand better the actors in the research context. I have learned much and in Erickson's words, "Analytic induction, when successful, teaches us fresh insights – something we could not have known before we started our inquiry" (Erickson, 1998, p. 1167).

Towards the end of the chapter, I would like to introduce briefly a new theory that was helpful to me during the analysis.

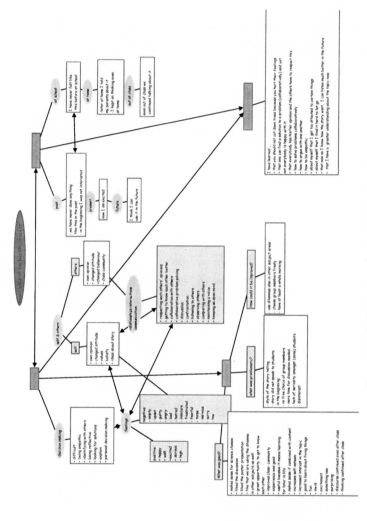

Figure 9: 'Map' of themes emerging from initial coding of student interviews

PART 5: THEORY SUPPORTING THE DATA-ANALYSIS

In Chapter 2, I explored the advantages of dialectical thinking, which has fascinated me ever since. I returned to Kohlberg and Gilligans' work and tried to apply a dialectical perspective on these frameworks. At that time I came across a book that turned out to be very influential for me in my quest for a dialectical framework for moral development, and ethical decision-making: Felicity Haynes book 'The Ethical School'. Her theory is based on the 'Borromean Knot' of Ethics.

The 'Borromean Knot of Ethics'

Haynes has 'borrowed' the metaphor from Lacan who called it the 'Borromean Knot' – a set of interlocking rings that falls apart when one of the rings is cut (compare Figure 10). Haynes' motivation to use this metaphor sounds truly integral in Wilber's sense: "What the Borromean Knot emphasises is the fall from privilege of any of the rings that constitute the knot (Haynes, 1998). For Haynes neither Kohlberg's view of an Ethic of Fairness (sometimes called Ethic of Justice, e.g. (Tronto, 1994), nor Gilligans' Ethic of Care, not an ethic of consequences should be privileged. She merges Kohlberg's view on ethics representing a (rather) masculine, subjective view of ethics that is based on the Principle of Consistency, with the rather objective view of an ethics based on the Principle of Consequences, and with the intersubjective, (rather) feminine, perspective of an ethic based on the Principle of Care.

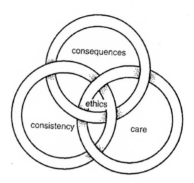

Figure 10: The Borromean Know of Ethics after Lacan (Haynes, 1998)

This model expresses three ethical principles:

Principle of Consistency: Subjective aspect of ethics – practice is regarded as intentional. Ethical action is deliberate, chosen, shaped and made justifiable by the coherence of internalised rules, meaning and values (Kohlberg)

Principle of Consequence: Objective aspect of ethics – practice is regarded as externalised in terms of causes and consequences. It focuses on what can be observed and agreed upon based on scientific or measurable aspects of morality. Teleological view focused on the goals. Actions are assessed with regard to whether or not the goals have been achieved.

Principle of Care: involves a broad web of relationships. It is holistic and responsive making of reciprocal connections in order to help others in a special act of receptivity (Haynes, 1998).

Haynes presents us with a paradox: She argues that the strength of the consistency and of the consequentialist perspective is to provide an impartial and distanced form of cognitive accountability meaning that in some situations these types are the better 'ethics' to choose. On the other hand, this narrow focus on the cognitive is also their limiting factor: Kohlberg's framework failed because of its lack of empathy. This is where an Ethic of Care is needed, an ethic that promotes connection and responsibility. Yet neither consistency, consequences, nor care, taken individually, provide an adequate foundation for ethical decisions but jointly they constitute the base for ethical decision-making (p. 26). Haynes argues further that an ethic of care is not superior to the consistency or consequence aspects – they are all necessary components of a dialogical and relational process of moral growth (p. 25). For moral growth and maturity it takes the form of an evolving spiral in which there is no prior value or end point (Haynes, 1998).

I found that Haynes model not only merges Gilligans', Kohlberg's, and the consequentialist viewpoints, it also overcomes the traditional dualisms between subjectivism and objectivism, very much in alignment with an integral philosophy as suggested by Wilber. To use Haynes 'Borromean Knot of Ethics' allows me to use the tool of dialectics to 'create' an Integral Ethics-in-Science Curriculum that uses critical constructivism as the theory for moral learning thereby including a critical, transformative perspective geared toward social reconstruction in terms of supporting students to grow up to become responsible, autonomous, democratic citizens, who are able to practice an ethic of consistency, able to evaluate consequences of their actions, and practice empathy and care in their lives.

Ways of knowing

A theory that goes almost hand in hand with Haynes dialectical perspective is another feminist work that looked into the ways women construct knowledge. Belenky, Clinchy, Goldberger and Tarule (1997) discovered that the women they interviewed had different ways of making meaning – similar but not identical. On the one hand, the focus was on understanding others, on the other hand, the focus was on knowledge. Belenky et al. (1997) explain the difference between understanding and knowing: 'understanding' has a similar meaning to the

German word 'kennen' which implies a personal acquaintance with an object which involves some level of intimacy and equality between self and the object, whilst 'knowledge' has a similar meaning to the German word 'wissen' which implies a separation from the object and mastery over it (compare the German word 'Wissenschaft' = something that creates knowledge; equivalent but more inclusive than the English word 'science').

Women who made meaning by understanding had a tendency to view a situation from a perspective that entails acceptance and precludes evaluation (evaluation implies that the object is at a distance and oneself it in a higher position), and quantifies a response to the object that should remain qualitative – Belenky at al. (1997) call women who make meaning in this way 'connected knowers' and their basic question is, "What is something/somebody trying to say to me?" Connected knowing builds upon the subjectivist presumption that personal experience is the most trustworthy source of knowledge thus connected knowers develop procedures for gaining access to other people's knowledge. At the core of these procedures lies the ability to show empathy.

Women who make meaning through applying standards to evaluate the situation, who rely on impersonal rules and whose focus is on knowledge are called 'separate knowers' because they create a distance between the object of their evaluation and themselves. Belenky et al. (1997, p. 101) contend that, "These women might almost be men". The hallmark of separate knowing is critical thinking which is characterised through the 'doubting game' which involves 'putting something on trial to see whether it is wanting or not. Separate knowers thus tend to immediately 'look what its wrong' with something. Belenky et al. (1997) explain that separate knowing is in a way the opposite of subjective knowing: whilst subjectivists think everybody is right, separate knowers think, everybody is wrong.

When women integrate both of these perspectives they become 'constructed knowers': reclaiming the self by attempting to integrate knowledge they felt intuitively was personally important with knowledge they had learned

167

from others. They weave together rational and the emotive thoughts and integrate subjective and objective knowledge. Rather than extricating the self in the acquisition of knowledge, these women used themselves in rising to a new way of thinking (p. 134-135). Women view all knowledge as contextual and experience themselves as creator of knowledge, and value both subjective and objective strategies for knowing. I believe, that going back to Wilber's integral philosophy, the constructed knower could also be called an 'integral' knower because s/he is able to engage in dialectical thinking and to embrace both subjective and objective views of the world. This perspective is a major step from the separate knower for whom thinking and feeling are incommensurable, and also from the connected knower who thinks primarily in emotive terms.

Belenky et al. (1997) also discovered a relationship between the types of knowing and ethical decision-making. They explain that it appears that separate knowers have a tendency towards an ethic of Justice whilst connected knowers have a tendency towards an Ethic of Care.

They also stress that separate and connected knowing are not gender-specific but may be gender-related, meaning that more women seem to have a tendency towards connected knowing and thus to an ethic of Care than men whilst more men tend towards separate knowing and an Ethic of Justice (Belenky et al, 1997, p. 102).

During the data-analysis, the three types of knowing were helpful to identify types of ethical reasoning – as I was not interested in the 'quantity' of morality, I was rather focusing on the quality. I did not go and specifically look for examples of the three types of knowing, I rather pointed it out in the text when I recognised a particular type during the analysis.

Theory of Transformative Learning

Marylin Ferguson, " Each of us guards a door to transformation that can only be opened from the inside. We cannot open the door of others, neither through argumentation nor through appealing to emotions" (Birkenbihl, 1997, p. 480).

I found that much of the moral education literature is focused on "How can we change people more effectively!" And with children, "How can we ensure they develop in the 'right' directions." These attitudes towards moral education presume (i) that we, as teachers, can actively change students behaviour and character and (ii) that we, as teachers, know what is best. I have to admit, the dilemma unit as designed by Gschweitl et al. (1998) is no exception. Despite the good intention, we all had, we somehow presumed we could perhaps 'turn the little switch in a student's brain' and make him/her a better person. Findings this perspective increasingly unattainable, I was pleased to discovered the Theory of Transformative Learning which was developed by Mezirow, at the time of the data-analysis. It occurred to me that this theory offers a powerful framework for the type of learning we, as teachers, would (really) like to happen during a dilemma unit or as a consequence of it – which is a 'change' inside the person's thinking. Transformative learning appears to be a widely used concept within adult education, however, I believe that it has much to offer to the education of adolescents as well, particularly for moral education. Mezirow combined critical theory and constructivism - thus again producing a type of critical constructivism (Imel, 1998). "Transformative learning occurs when, through critical self-reflection, an individual revises old or develops new assumptions, beliefs, or ways of seeing the world" (Cranton, 1994, p. 4) (see Figure 11).

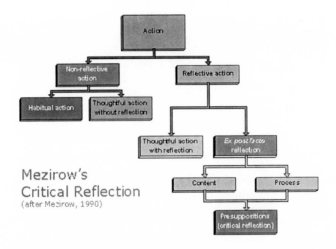

Figure 11: Critical reflection after Mezirow (Atherton, 2002)

Given that change of assumptions, beliefs, values and worldviews is a learning goal in the Ethics of Science curriculum, I chose this as the theoretical framework for 'moral' learning because it seems to explain the type of learning we are aiming at, and it subsumes critical constructivism which I had chosen as a framework for learning earlier in the thesis (compare Chapter 2). The advantage of this referent is that it puts the responsibility for moral development into the student's hand. However, the teacher does not become redundant much rather s/her tries to create opportunities for critical reflection.

REVIEW OF THE CHAPTER

In Section 1, I described how I planned the fieldwork, including the difficulties encountered along the way, culminating in an account of the first meeting with each teacher which was the actual starting point of the fieldwork. In Section 2, I browsed through the research-strategies that helped me finding answers to my research questions. In section 3, I describe the data-sources and how the data were stored after the data analysis. In Section 4, I describe my initial struggle with the interpretive data-analysis including my steep learning curve with regard to a data-analysis program. In Section 5, I have added theory that was not available to me earlier in the thesis but that became very influential during the data-analysis, such as Haynes' Borromean Knot of Ethics, women's ways of knowing, and the Theory of Transformative learning.

Chapter 7

Engaging students in a dilemma learning situation: the promise of dilemma stories

In our efforts to share our love of this beauty and truth we label as science or history, we need to ask: What distinguishes the workings of story from the giving of information? When I speak of story, I am thinking of a 'way' in which content is expressed. This 'story way' could find various forms such as personal anecdote, current event, history, folktale, legend, fable, parable, discourse of scientific fact, fairy tale or myth. Some of these forms are recognisable as story, yet some interpreters will object to including history or science on this list. History and science, the will insist, are information – by which they mean facts.…doesn't science tell a story? A story that is continually changing as 'new facts' are uncovered and old ones discarded? When people use the word 'information', do they mean giving the scientific story in a particular way that distinguishes it from the 'story way' and therefore must be dry, lifeless and unrelated to a whole? (Strauss, 1996, p.3)

INTRODUCTION

The Enlightenment Era resulted in the separation of science, art and religion into three distinctly 'different' cultural value spheres: science set out to find the truth, art set out to 'express' the self, and religion regarded itself as the guardian of morals. Whilst each of the three cultural value-spheres could flourish independently – which was beneficial for progress – a profound 'suspicion' remained between the supporters of either value-sphere. Science, for example, therefore should be neither related to arts nor to religion (Wilber, 1997, 1998). This can be a problem if one wants to use 'stories' as part of science education. The 'purists' of this worldview which is called scientism and which I have described in earlier chapters (1,2 & 5) would probably adamantly argue that there is no room in

172

science education for fiction which is equated to invented truths whilst science should only present 'discovered' truths. Without wanting to go down that path of argument much further, I would like to point out that due to the remnants of scientism even progressive teachers, like the ones I collaborated with, 'struggled' with the idea of storytelling as a legitimate part of science education.

In this study, the teachers were required to tell dilemma-stories which both teachers reportedly experienced as a 'bit of a challenge' in the beginning. Irene, on the other hand, realised during the Ethics in Science project that she was using stories all the time in her teaching and that they formed an integral part of her curriculum. However, in my experience I have found that many science teachers felt 'intimidated' by the act of storytelling as if it was something alien to the profession. Susan Strauss who is a professional storyteller within the science (education) context tells the story about an incident where somebody said to her, "We should hire you to teach our school teachers how to tell stories. I think it is a very new technique." She replied, "Actually, it is very old...and it is not a technique" (Strauss, 1996, p. 2). Apparently in this 'information-age' we have lost the ability to tell stories or to recognize that we are telling any.

Dilemma stories

In ethics education, dilemma stories are used for introducing students into a dilemma experience. Dilemma stories as a genre are characterised by ethical dilemma situations. Their purpose is to get students to reflect on the dilemma(s) in the story and to provide a starting point for discussion. However, 'dilemma stories' mean different things to different people and are used in a variety of ways (see Chapter 5). Dilemmas can be presented in different forms:

- They can provide a short summary of a problematic situation accompanied by examples.

- They can be presented in the form of a film (e.g. 'Sophie's Choice').
- Role-play
- They can be more elaborate stories containing several dilemma situations where a character in the story is required to make a decision (see Appendix 5), e.g. Kohlberg's Heinz dilemma.

Dilemma stories can be implemented in different ways:

- They can be distributed for individual students to read.
- They can be told freely.
- They can form the basis of a whole teaching approach where the teacher tells the story freely, and there is a range of class and individual activities at different stages as the story unfolds.

It was in the last sense that dilemma stories were implemented within this project where the teaching and learning within the ethics unit rotated around the dilemma stories (see Figure 7 in Chapter 5). The stories were told freely by the teachers to their students and were the starting points for discourse and individual reflection. The purpose of telling these dilemma stories was to introduce students to a moral dilemma situation in which choices were required to be made on behalf of the characters in the story. The flow of the stories was purposefully interrupted as each dilemma situation arose. Students were asked to identify with the character in the story having the dilemma, and to reflect on how they would have solved the problem in his/her place. Then students were asked to exchange their views with colleagues. Eventually this teaching approach culminated in a whole-class discussion. Phases of individual work alternated with phases of group-work. This approach was intended to provide opportunities for individual reflection and for 'moral' discourse within groups or amongst the whole class (see Figure 7. and view the dilemma stories in this project in Appendix 5)

Organisation and purpose of the chapter

The chapter aims at answering the following research questions: <u>How well are dilemma stories suited to introduce students to controversial issues (dilemmas)? How can we ensure appropriateness of curriculum materials with regard to the age of the students?</u> The third related question about storytelling as a teaching method is discussed in detail in Chapter 11. In this chapter, I have drawn on four perspectives to explore the suitability of dilemma units for engaging students in a dilemma experience: my own experiences at the time of the fieldwork (in my role as a participant observer), my view now at the time of writing, and the teachers' and students' perspectives after the actual dilemma teaching experience. These perspectives mirror also the different stages of analysis that occurred during the fieldwork, during the subsequent 'data analysis' stage, and during the final writing up stage (compare also Chapter 6, Methodology II). Retrospective member checking often proved difficult given the tyranny of distance, email-related problems, family and personal disasters here and there (see Chapter 2). I have attempted to indicate in the text where I had problems with backing up my data further.

The chapter is organised in three parts, each part representing one of the three dilemma units implemented during the Ethics in Science project:

- <u>Part 1</u> examines the introduction of the <u>Tree Dilemma</u> in Irene's 5A class with her Year 9 students as part of the Botany curriculum.
- <u>Part 2</u> focuses on the introduction of the <u>Rainforest Dilemma</u> in Irene's 5A class with her Year 9 students as part of the Bacteria/Botany curriculum.
- <u>Part 3</u> explores the introduction of the <u>Rocket Dilemma</u> in Sandra's 6A class with her Year 10 students as part of the Astrophysics curriculum.

The three parts portray the dilemma units in 'chronological' order in which they were taught. Each part covers the introduction of a dilemma story up to the first dilemma situation because after the first dilemma questions the focus of the dilemma unit shifts from storytelling towards individual reflection and discourse. Each part is written in narrative form comprising verbatim quotes from classroom interactions and extracts of interviews, extracts of my fieldwork journal and subsequent interpretive commentary. Each of the four perspectives is illustrated by a different font: Helvetica is used for the participant observer's/researcher's voice at the time of the fieldwork. Book Antiqua characterises the chapter narrator's voice (e.g., above). *Monotype Corsiva is used for direct speech during classroom observations.* Courier is used for students' post hoc commentaries and Tahoma illustrates teachers' post hoc commentaries and conversations. Arial Narrow represents my interpretive commentary at the present moment of writing and is also used for summaries and reviews. I have tried to make the text more readable by using headings (in appropriate places) that indicate the 'voice' that is speaking. Verbatim interview quotes are referenced as follows: initial of the pseudonym of the interviewee, followed by reference number and paragraph number (e.g., F23p2) to allow for the audit trail. An example of a coded interview transcripts can be seen in Appendix 10 and on the CD.

From the analysis arose three major themes that seem to require our attention if we want to use dilemma units for the purpose of teaching ethics: curriculum issues (e.g., lifeworld appropriate content of the dilemma stories), and organisational issues (e.g., timetabling for continuity of learning) which are discussed in detail in a later part of the chapter and in Chapter 11. Teaching issues (e.g., reading versus free storytelling) are discussed in Chapter 11.

PART 1: THE TREE DILEMMA (15. 5. 2000)

Introduction to the story

The Tree Dilemma is about a man whose 'birth-tree' is about to be cut down in favour of a campervan his parents bought (see Appendix 5 for full text). He rejects this plan and tries to save his tree. However, the man is faced with a decision as to whether he wants to cut down the tree himself or leave this task to professional tree-loppers. The ultimate question is: do plants have the same right to life as animals or humans? Why do we attach different value to plant lives on the one hand, and animal or human lives on the other?

The day before - Preparation of a dilemma unit

After visiting her class on several occasions Irene and I meet in what 'insiders' call the "dungeons" of the Roseggerschule, and which are referred to by 'outsiders' as the biology lab, in order to finalise the organisation of the first dilemma unit in Irene's class. She tells me that she has convinced the Catholic religious education teacher that it would be greatly appreciated if we could use his lesson too because we will need more time than one single period of fifty minutes. In exchange, she has promised him that he will become our 'camera-man' and that he will video the first unit in order not to get bored. He has been very supportive of the ethics project from the beginning and has told me that he is curious and wants to see "how things work out in practice".

Irene expresses concerns that the students might not take the project seriously if she does not attach some form of assessment to it. So we decide that students must produce a portfolio containing their written notes, their reflections, their ideas regarding the project, and a timesheet in which they have to write dates and events - Irene promises to produce the timesheet later that night. We re-read the story and discuss issues regarding the teaching of dilemma stories. Irene fears that the story might be too "simplistic", too trivial for some students and that some might 'freak out'. I do not share her concerns and try to point out to her that dilemma stories should be simple in order to allow for associations. I also tell her about my experiences with trialling earlier versions of this story on several occasions with students and adults. Later that evening, I am still unsure as to whether or not I have managed to convince her that the story might be on the right level for the kids but, on the other hand, I am not really worried because I know her as a good story teller – she always tells stories in her teaching. So what can possibly go wrong?

Day 1: Admin (is trivia)

8am in the classroom that is used by Irene's 5A class – every Austrian class has their own classroom in which they spend most of their day – it is the teachers who commute between classes (see Chapter 3). It is a fairly small classroom for such a big class. I have the impression that the students just about fit in there. I am starting to wonder how we are going to arrange the chairs in a circle for the storytelling and later for the discussion – there is very little room. Irene enters the classroom and starts off with administrative issues and the minutiae involved in being a form teacher, checking absences and asking for parents' notes. Time passes and not much happens in terms of the dilemma unit. The administrative process takes about fifteen minutes and I am starting to feel a bit nervous about time limitations. Although the religious education teacher has volunteered to give up his lesson time for this project, we have only two fifty minute periods available. I feel we are losing precious time. Finally…

It is now twenty minutes into the unit – suddenly a knock at the door - three students enter and apologise for being late. Irene circulates a timesheet, and explains the nature of the portfolio that is to be produced for assessment purposes. Students form a circle. Irene explains how the timesheets are to be filled in, in order to provide a clear timeline of activities for students and some information for the parents at home.

At last after 30 minutes Irene starts to tell the story…

THE STORYTELLING

1. *Irene: I am going to confront you with a problem and I would like to ask for your opinion. Actually, it is an acquaintance of mine who has a problem and he has a difficult decision to make. Yet this problem has a lot to do with myself - I will*

178

have to make a similar decision very soon. As you all know, decisions are easier made this way. This is why many opinions might be helpful for me.

Irene has seated herself on one of the desks that has been pushed towards the wall so that she can overlook the student' seated in a semi-circle in front of her…

2. *Irene: A friend of mine has a problem, and it all started when he was born. His parents received a little spruce in a pot as a 'birth tree' for the baby and as you can imagine, the tree did not stay in the pot for long but was planted in the front garden very soon. This tree has grown over time and the boy was told that this tree was 'his' tree and that the two belonged together because they were born together. Of course, as you all know, if the tree was already in a pot this means that it was born before my friend in fact when it germinated from the seed…*
3. *One boy adds: But they have been growing up together!*
4. *Irene: Yes, exactly! A relationship has formed over the past 33 years – this is how old my friend, we call him Peter, is now…Let's think about what this tree – apart from growing bigger and more beautiful – what this tree has done for the people he was 'living with'. This tree has done things for the family some of which are obvious whilst others are not. It has absorbed carbon-dioxide and produced oxygen, it has produced glucose and subsequently starch…It has grown many, many needles each of which is able to absorb a lot of dust and dirt out of the air, thereby cleaning the air for the family nearby…every spring it has grown healthy young shoots which then have grown into mighty branches over time. This is basically how plants grow.…but what else was the tree doing for the people?*
5. *Alois responds: They never have to buy a Christmas tree because they already have a big one in the garden!*

Everybody laughs at this joke. I notice that Irene at this point tries to relate the story to the curriculum content of botany.

6. *Irene (laughing): Yes, you are right, this is another aspect of having a big spruce in the front garden – one might decorate it with electric candles perhaps…(pause)*
7. *Let's get back to what else the tree was doing for its family – you can imagine, when a tree grows, it grows strong roots and these roots fixate the soil which was especially important in this case as the front garden is situated on a slope and needs to be firmly held in place by the roots of plants. Now it is about 12-15m high – it has long and strong branches, deep green needles. Even the dog Ricky appreciates the branches as it can hide underneath. The bark of the tree serves as Ricky's brush when he has an itchy back. But apart from the dog there is also a turtle named Max…"*
8. *Alois interrupts: Of course, a turtle named Max!*

Alois' comment makes me wonder whether it is not so much the story itself but the style of storytelling that is perhaps too 'childlike' for 15 year olds? On the other hand, I have experienced Alois in other lessons as well with other teachers, and this behaviour matches my other observations.

> 9. *Irene (ignoring Alois' comment): Apart from the wonderful scents, the lovely green colour, it also provided a nesting ground especially during spring when many birds choose the tree as a perch to perform their concerts. You can imagine that sometimes it got a bit too much for Peter, my friend, because there was such a noise. So you can see the tree has had a lot of value for the family, some they were aware of, others they were oblivious too. Anyway, this was only the introductory story, the problem I mentioned before is like that now....*

She is telling the story freely although I am getting the impression that maybe she is trying a bit too hard. She sounds very different from when she normally tells stories which flow easily and convey a lot of her personality. Somehow this is not the case this morning! I am thinking to myself – can she be nervous? To me it sounds as if she is telling a story to little children…yet I notice again that Irene repeatedly tries to link the story to biological content knowledge. I feel that she is doing this quite skilfully.

Looking around the classroom, I notice that some students seemingly ignore the story altogether and continue to talk to each other. Eventually even these conversations ebb away and most people seem to listen, others seem to drift off to dreamland, such as Fatima. After a while, some students start to make comments on the story, some of which sound quite cynical to me. Alois and Alex in particular. They seem to regard the 'story time' rather as a joke. I feel some tension rising in me – have I really underestimated the effect of the 'problem-students'? – although Irene had forewarned me!

STUDENT COMMENTARY ON THE BEGINNING OF THE DILEMMA UNIT

I chose Fatima, originally from Iran, as an interview-partner because she appeared to be one of those students who showed a remarkable change throughout the dilemma unit: in the beginning she did not seem to be very interested – more focused on her friends or drifting off whilst later she participated in a very (!) engaged manner. It was interesting to me to find out what had happened for her during the dilemma unit. In my first interview with her, Fatima commented on Irene's storytelling-style, "*Mrs Rock told the story in a 'funny' way in the beginning* [pause]*...it is fun to learn like that... uhmm...*" (F36p43&p7). I had the impression she was hesitating as if looking for the right words. Later she added, "*It was told like in an animation*" (F40p10). I interpreted Fatima's statement as supporting my impression – something felt 'artificial'.

RESEARCHER COMMENTARY IN 2003

However, because I had failed to recognise this issue as potentially important at the time of the interviews, I did not check this observation with other students. Despite my efforts to contact students on email, I did not receive back any feedback on this matter after the fieldwork was finished.

STUDENT COMMENTARY (CONTINUED)

Fatima related her problems at the beginning of the dilemma unit also to a lack of interest, "*Honestly, in the beginning I thought it was really stupid (F23p2). I don't know, perhaps I just wasn't interested (F5p7)... Well, it started already with Peter and there is a tree. It simply wasn't so interesting*" (F6p10)... I *believe I was the only one who was not very interested in the beginning*" (F8p43), Fatima continued, "*Whilst I was listening, in the beginning, I was constantly checking my watch and thinking, 'My God, when is this lesson over!'*" (F30p7). Unfortunately, she was not the only one who lacked enthusiasm in the beginning. Melinda, for example, whom I interviewed because Irene had suggested that Melinda was a highly critical student, reported a similar experience, "*During the first period on Monday morning I had very different ideas*

181

of what it [the dilemma unit] was going to be… when I first heard the story about the spruce and so, I thought, 'Oh well!' But now in the end everything has turned out quite OK!" (Me21p13) She added, "It was very good if only it had been a different story, something that is more interesting for students of our age but that still fits in with the curriculum. If it had been a different story I would have preferred that!" (Me22p19)

RESEARCHER COMMENTARY 2003

Fatima's and Melinda comments indicate to me that there were problems, at least initially, that were partly to do with the style of the storytelling as well as with a lack of interest in the topic of the story itself that might not have been appropriate enough for the age-group despite all efforts from me and from Irene during the preparation phase. Irene had been apprehensive about the simplicity of the story beforehand, a hunch that turned out to be correct at least during the beginning of the unit. However, as my observations and Fatima's comment indicate, the style of the storytelling might have contributed to the problem of disinterest in the story.

Had I stopped the analysis at that stage, I would have been quite depressed about the apparent 'failure' of the project. However, my observations and some interviews indicated that students' attitudes changed during the dilemma unit. It was therefore interesting to me why Alex, for example, changed his attitude over time. He was not the only one – Fatima and Emma, Melinda, Gregor and other students were other examples. I asked myself: Was it because students were not used to storytelling in science classes in the beginning (this would have been a teaching-related issue)? Or was it because of a sudden twist in the storyline that made the story more age-appropriate (this would have been a curriculum related issue)? Or was it that some unforeseen event in the classroom raised students' interest? With these questions in mind I continued the analysis of the data…

Reading student interview comments and reviewing my own field-notes and the classroom videos, I have the impression that initially Irene was trying too hard – it was as if storytelling, which was something she always did intuitively and very well, suddenly had become alien to her. I was wondering why and I asked Irene how she had experienced those first moments of the dilemma unit…

IRENE'S COMMENTARY ABOUT THE BEGINNING OF THE DILEMMA UNIT

"I was initially very sceptical about the simplicity of the story – to tell it in a way that they listen to me – you know I cannot take it for granted that they listen to me at this age for much longer – however, I feel they did listen after all" (I-FS1p13). It seems that Irene's initial concerns almost became a self-fulfilling prophecy until she suddenly 'let go of the handbrake' and became much more her usual self again. This comes across in the video as a different storytelling-style – more lively and less like 'talking to little children'.

MEANWHILE BACK IN THE CLASSROOM…

"Oh my God, I think, this story is too trivial for this class!" In my mind I am already constructing an emergency plan. I am finding it hard to stand back and not interfere with the teaching. I would like to speed things up a bit but I have to accept that this is Irene's class and it is her style of telling the story (but do I really recognise her style?). I am starting to think that this dilemma might not work out well at all.

> 10. *Irene: Peter is now, as I mentioned before over thirty years old, the other children have also left the house and the parents now have the luxury of being able to do what they would like to do. Well, they have always wanted to buy a campervan. So they have browsed the campervan shops in town, and finally they have made a careful decision and bought a campervan. They are really looking forward to going travelling now! So they buy this van which was not cheap, I have to mention, drive it home proudly, drive through the garden entrance, Oh no!! The campervan is too long – its rear end points out onto the road, far enough to endanger cars driving past. OK they realise, this does not work. The tree is in the way! Let's cut down the tree…*

Looking around now, I feel that most of the students are listening attentively. What has happened? I realise that Irene has suddenly changed her style of storytelling –

she is much more herself again. Has she noticed that the students did not appreciate her earlier storytelling style?

RESEARCHER COMMENTARY 2003

Irene changed her storytelling style, however there was probably more that had changed. It was the story itself – suddenly there was a problem, a dilemma that started to emerge that had not been obvious in the beginning. Suddenly students' attention seemed to have risen: perhaps it was this twist in the story, in addition to the change of the storytelling style, that contributed to an apparent change in students' attention.

BACK IN THE CLASSROOM – 'TAMING' SO-CALLED 'PROBLEM STUDENTS'

I wonder if the students also have recognised the changed conditions because suddenly they seem to listen more carefully except for one student, Alois, who continuously tries to get Irene's attention. He is one of the students Irene had identified to me beforehand as a problem-student. However I presume he has different reasons that lie perhaps outside of the classroom altogether.

> 11. *Irene:* *…and Peter's parents trying to be generous call him on the phone, tell him that they have bought a campervan. He is quite happy for them and asks about the details. "But", they continue, "the campervan is too long and your tree is in the way – unfortunately it has to go. We thought we let you know because after all it is your tree and…" In this moment, Peter is shocked! He realises his tree has to go and in connection with this, I have a question now which I would like you to answer for me…*
> 12. *Alois:* *Umm, Mrs. Rock, I have an alternative solution!*
> 13. *Irene:* *That's nice Alois! But let's wait and see what my questions are!*

It is interesting for me to see how Irene manages these disturbances – with great patience and yet determination. Irene obviously has no intention of allowing Alois to dominate the scene. She recognises his comments and tries to redirect his attention (see Chapter 9). Finally, Irene leaves her 'perch' and walks towards the blackboard turning her back to the students.

RESEARCHER COMMENTARY 2003

Given Alex' and Alois' behaviour, I had the choice (dilemma?) of interviewing Alex or Alois – ultimately I decided to interview Alex for the following reason: despite being one of the 'problem students' initially' his behaviour changed dramatically in due course of the dilemma unit. Alois' behaviour remained 'disruptive', although as we can see in Chapter 10, his comments actually indirectly contributed to keeping the discussion going which can be regarded as a positive outcome. When asked what was happening for Alex during the first part of the dilemma unit, he summarised, "*In the beginning we did not take the story seriously*" (A15p15). When I asked why this had been the case, he said, "*Because I was only interested in having fun.*" This supported Irene's earlier concerns regarding those students. I asked her about how she had experienced that situation.

TEACHER COMMENTARY ON 'PROBLEM STUDENTS'

She explained to me that one of her main concerns and main reasons for her initial 'tension' was related to the so-called 'problem students' in the class, "My basic idea was...I was concerned that one or more students might freak out – but overall I think, I did quite well" (I-FS1p204). Irene was right – there was a potential problem with the so-called 'problem students', especially Alex and Alois, who could have undermined all her efforts. However, Irene problematised her own attitude towards those students, "For me there was a weak point from the start namely that I was thinking about who might lose it and who might freak out... and there was primarily Alex who came to my mind....and of course Alois." (I-FS1p139-153)

RESEARCHER COMMENTARY 2003

I have to admit that I had not taken the issue of 'problem-students' seriously enough. These students could have ransacked everything with their behaviour. However, it did not happen for two reasons, I think: one was because Alex swapped sides and became a mainstream-discussant and, two, because Irene was able to sustain control over Alois for most of the time. Irene was also right to notice that it worked out quite well in the end. Thus, for me, the 'development' of those two students during the dilemma units turned out to be worthwhile further investigation.

BACK IN THE CLASSROOM: TELLING A STORY FROM THE HEART – A TURNING POINT

As the end of the class draws near and the students start to pack their bags, Irene suddenly starts to tell a very personal story...something we had not planned beforehand... The next few moments turned out to be of great importance for the whole project and left me with a lasting impression that I would like to describe in a brief vignette taken from my research journal.

GRANDMA'S TREE

"I have a similar problem at home", Irene said, "I have a tree in my garden that was planted when my grandmother was born in 1894 and now my neighbour has decided that he has enormous problems with it!" Students who were already packing up their bags suddenly stop – everyone is standing, nobody is sitting, everybody looks intently at Irene. Everybody is listening while she is telling a story from her life. One can feel the tension in the air, "I have always problems with this monster of a tree now. It always drops dry branches on my vegie-patch – then I really tell it off! In the meantime it has grown so big and so strong – it is simply gigantic – a wonderful piece of a tree! But I do not want it cut down although we have been considering this solution for a while."

I add, "Think about it for a moment: what we are talking about here is not only about a plant that needs to be cut – given that plants are living beings as we are, and I think we agree on that – this is a question of life and death!" Suddenly there is a change in atmosphere again – students look touched, some even shocked.

Fatima covers her mouth with her hand and breathes in sharply, "You're right. Oh my God, this is terrible. Plants really are living beings just as well!" Imelda, addressing Irene, adds, "But you don't have to cut it all down. It is enough to prune the lower branches (an opinion I have heard her mention before in class!). Concern is mirrored on the students' faces. Nobody makes stupid remarks – silent reflection – silence. Irene breaks the silence and says, „But of course nobody in our family really thinks about cutting down this tree after all this tree is like a piece of my grandmother. It is just as if she was still with us...." Murmuring in the class.

I add, "Until next time, please take the time and reflect on the reasons why we attach different value to the lives of plants compared with animals. If your tree is sick most people would say – let's cut it down. If your cat is sick – do you throw her out of the window because of that? No, you will take her to the vet, won't you?"

Irene and I met immediately after the unit to discuss our experiences. We were both still under the impression of those last few moments in class. The following dialogue was taken from the transcript of I-FS1 (Feedback Session 1 with Irene).

CONVERSATION WITH IRENE AFTER THE FIRST PART OF THE TREE-DILEMMA

<u>Irene</u>: What I also noticed was towards the end that they started to engage with the issues! Because I contributed this personal story, perhaps, about our ancient tree – a number of them immediately responded to that and came up with possible solutions to my problem. (I-FS1p13)

<u>Lily</u>: This was a clear turning point for me – suddenly everybody was quiet and looked at you! (I-FS1p15) Whilst before that – somebody was definitely talking somewhere. (I-FS1p19)

<u>Irene</u>: Yes or made an unnecessary commentary...and I am convinced they will come back to that next time – with some new ideas. Although I have to admit that with our tree I really get annoyed occasionally because of the branches everywhere in vegetable beds. I keep on telling it [the tree] off. (I-FS1p21-22)

<u>Lily</u>: The question is now what to do with this insight – we have seen that telling a personal story induces great personal involvement - in the students also. I wonder whether or not it would be better to do this right at the beginning of a dilemma unit (I-FS1p24).

<u>Irene</u>: Yes, I mean I mentioned briefly in the introduction that this is a personal story which although not my own, still affects me somehow. Of course I also know

that none in our family would voluntarily cut down our old tree/ It shall live its life to the end. It still represents our grandmother, so to speak. (I-FS1p26)

RESEARCHER COMMENTARY 2003

We both agreed that during that conversation the telling of this personal story had added considerably to the effect of the other story, and that it should perhaps have been told at the beginning of the dilemma unit. It had also offered an opportunity to present 'the' underlying dilemma question as to why different values are attached to plant lives versus animal or human lives embedded in Irene's personal story. As mentioned before, I sensed that the story changed the atmosphere in the room and it touched me personally to see that the 'dilemma was suddenly written all over people's faces'.

STUDENT COMMENTARY

In the student interviews I focused on asking why they finally got interested in the story, and most student responses revolved around the question regarding the different values of animal and plant lives. I asked Fatima during her interview what had happened to her that made her interested. She said, "It was funny – in the beginning I felt quite happy but then suddenly… it was as if I had to contract myself internally – I have never had a similar feeling like that at school before. Suddenly I realised… the longer I listened to that story – well OK it is about a tree…but actually it is about much more, it is about something really big… (Fp50) She added, "…when the question was then whether or not you would cut the tree yourself – I realised I could not do it!" (Fp53). Emma, Fatima's friend from Bosnia, supported Fatima's statement, "I realised I would feel very sorry. I could not do it …really difficult… after all it is not 'only' a tree or so…I have learned that it is important to attach higher value to certain things…" (E27p39-42). I was also interested what the African students in Irene's class had to say, so I interviewed Damian from Ghana (Africa). However, the interview turned out to be very difficult because neither Damian's English nor his German were sufficient to keep a conversation going – the analysis afterwards also proved quite tedious. Damian told me during his interview in English[9], "We should know that living things are like human beings – trees, animals – they are like human beings. If we do something bad against them it seems we do something bad against a human being! (Dm1p92). Finally, I asked Alex, one of the 'problem students' what it was that finally got him interested. He replied, "When the last question was, for example, what is the difference between cutting down a tree and killing an animal – this was interesting for me. This was when I started to respond properly!"

However, not all students could see the dilemma as a dilemma: Melinda, for example, who had complained about the story-topic earlier, pointed out that, "...well I don't think that the tree really 'dies' or so!...I cannot see how one could feel so close to a tree!" (Me27p64&70)

RESEARCHER COMMENTARY 2003

It seems that the first part of the story that served as an introduction to the 'underlying' dilemma was not very well received by the students for reasons that apparently include a lack of interest in the topic, a lack of willingness to engage in the learning process and the teacher's storytelling style. However, it was the telling of a personal story and consequently the presentation of the 'underlying' dilemma that seemed to have provoked students' thinking. This indicates that whilst the story itself perhaps was experienced as too simplistic by some, the dilemma itself seems to have been age-appropriate because it engaged some students. Melinda, on the other hand, apparently did not understand the dilemma as such.

---

[4] The original quote is in English. I have deliberately not made any corrections.

189

Summary of the Tree Dilemma

Looking at the data now, I can summarise that the first part of the tree-dilemma session was characterised by Irene 'struggling' with the storytelling-style, not knowing how to tell the story so that students would listen. She was also apprehensive regarding the apparent 'simplicity' of the dilemma story. The students might have sensed her discomfort, which Fatima expressed as 'told like in an animation'. The introductory story apparently was not well received which was also reflected in students' behaviour through high noise-levels, unproductive commentaries, and a reported lack of interest. However, a turning point seems to have been Irene's personal story in combination with the presentation of the 'underlying' dilemma that seems to have evoked personal involvement in the students as documented in Chapters 8 and 9. This, on the other hand, seemingly resulted in an increased focus and increased personal engagement for some students.

Another issue that crystallised for me was that of the so-called problem students. Alex and Alois could have created chaos during the dilemma unit. However, whilst Alex chose to participate in a productive manner. Alois did not but he was closely supervised by the teacher.

From a pedagogical point of view, I also found that instructions were not given clearly enough which caused delays and confusion on the student side.

PART 2: RAINFOREST DILEMMA (22. 5. 2000)

Introduction to the story

This dilemma story is about a young female scientist who is sent to the Amazon Rainforest to find a cure for a mysterious disease that has caused many casualties in the so-called developed world (see Appendix 5 for full text). With the help of local indigenous tribes she and her research-partner find a plant that provides a cure. However, the drug needs to be manufactured without delay after the harvest of the plant which means that the necessary infrastructure has to be built in the middle of the rainforest, thereby affecting the locals lives. In addition to that, the young researcher has infected the locals with a type of influenza that proves to be fatal for many of them. The underlying dilemma questions are: Is it warranted to affect negatively some people's lives (in this case the local tribes) if it is for the common good of all (in this case) the Western world? Does searching for cures for 'our' Western diseases justify that we potentially transfer 'our' germs to other areas of the world where people might not be immune to them?

During the 'co-creation' of the story, Irene and I had simplified considerably earlier versions until we had reached a level where Irene thought that it was still a complex story but that it could work. The rainforest is Irene's special area of interest – she is very knowledgeable about rainforests. She has travelled extensively these regions of the world and brings with her a wealth of personal experiences, especially about the Brazilian rainforest. After the first story had turned out quite well in the end, we were both enthusiastic about getting started on the second story.

In the library

Full of enthusiasm, I enter the school for the 1st period on Monday morning. The first surprise – many students are absent, especially students of denominations other than Catholic. Normally, this would be a free period for non-Catholic students who comprise a large proportion of Irene's class. Irene appears to be furious, saying that she had told them last week they must come to school on Monday morning because the religious education teacher has again swapped a lesson with her and because this is part of the 'Ethics in Science' Project. She asks those present whether or not there might have been a misunderstanding. The students claim not to know…

After the usual ritual of registering absentees, Irene introduces the new dilemma. She is very involved and radiates enthusiasm, perhaps because she has travelled this part of the world herself and has some very similar first-hand experiences.

But the students seem to be half asleep (or bored?). I find this difficult to determine from observation only. Compared to last week, the class is quiet - some students look like 'zombies' – I wonder whether the decision to implement

Dilemma 2 on a Monday morning has been a bad one. Even those students who were full of praise for Dilemma 1 in their last interviews look tired.

Irene speaks about the symptoms of the deadly disease in the story and she compares the symptoms to those of Multiple Sclerosis (MS). A student, Susan, tells a story about an auntie who is suffering from Multiple Sclerosis. In reply to Susan's story, Irene tells the story of a nephew who showed early signs of MS at the age of 28. In the story, the virus X12 causes MS like symptoms within a very short time. As with the first dilemma, Irene includes biological content knowledge in her teaching. This seems to work well. Students respond with examples. However, they are very (perhaps too?) quiet this time. Even Alois tries to cooperate a little bit better – but he is still the noisiest student of all.

After the end of the first period, a number of other students arrive claiming they had been unaware that they were required to come to the first period. Irene checks the absences again and finds that there is still a number of students apparently 'sick'. She looks annoyed because she feels, as I discover later, that some students apparently think that 'if it is not content that is being taught they do not need to go to school'. For those who have come late she summarises what the story was about. I look around and there is no apparent change in the students' demeanour. They still look tired and/or bored. Some students look almost overwhelmed.

I am starting to ask myself: Can it be that the story is too complex this time? Perhaps it is only suitable for an older age group?

However, undeterred Irene races through the dilemma story. She seems determined to finish much faster this time...I notice that the group-work works better. They are faster than last time but I have the impression they are less involved. After the first dilemma situation, Irene continues the storytelling. She explains that the pharmaceutical company for whom the young researcher works tries to establish a production plant amidst the rainforest. Manuel interrupts Irene and asks...

Manuel: Does this pay off for the company at all to put so much effort into this project?

Irene explains briefly that if a company manages to produce a medicine against a disease, and they are the first ones to claim a monopoly, then everyone who wants the medicine has to pay them 'big dollars'. The bell rings. We have not finished (again!) and Irene announces that the dilemma unit will be continued on Thursday in the first period. Nevertheless, some students, like Manuel, have asked questions, and this indicates to me that they might after all be reflecting on the story.

RESEARCHER COMMENTARY 2000

Later that day, I was reflecting on my overall impressions during this dilemma unit. I wrote in my journal: "…it appears that there is a coincidence between the early hour on a Monday morning and the overall apathy of the students. Thinking back one week, I recall that the first two units of Dilemma 1 were also not very fruitful, compared with the later sessions. However, I have come to believe that the storyline of this story may be also too complex for this age-group: some students looked slightly overwhelmed. Perhaps a combination of tiredness and/or inappropriateness of the dilemma story? It seems to me that the students did not engage as well as last time in social interactions. The noise levels were continuously low, which is nice for disciplinary reasons, but which also indicates to me that there might not have been as much discourse going on amongst the students as I would have liked. Another question arising from the observations is whether or not the overall timing of the second dilemma might have been inappropriate – perhaps the two dilemmas should have been taught with greater time-interval between for the students to fully 'digest' the first dilemma? However, Irene seems to have had a different impression of the situation, as I discovered when she and I met for a feedback session.

TEACHER COMMENTARY ON THE SECOND DILEMMA UNIT

The following dialogue was taken from the feedback session I-FB3-2000.

Lily: How did you experience the teaching this time?
Irene: It was much better firstly because the students were more focused - they already knew what was expected of them. This was the reason why much of the

social conversations during class did not happen this time. The more complex the questions, the quieter they became, I have noticed ...I have the impression that they did engage much better with the story this time. They also listened much better to my directions which tells me that this story was much more age-appropriate - this is how I interpret this!

Lily: I have noticed that you told the story freely and that you included a lot of personal stories. Did you plan that beforehand or did it just happen like that?

Irene: After having had the experience last time that they listen to me better if I tell personal stories, and I have also made this experience on other occasions during my teaching practice, I deliberately tried to make a connection between my trips to Brazil, my time as a student when I really wanted to become a parasitologist – I was advised not to go ahead with this at the time, being a woman, and so...at that time they would not have accepted you in parasitology as a woman although it would really have interested me (FS3p7). This is why I could add in so much more because of my own personal experiences of how the locals do something to using the resources of the environment...and of course, I should not forget to tell that, I was living on a station that belonged to the Church and there was a hospital where they treated severely burnt patients with remedies derived from rainforest-plants, without antibiotics or water-bed - this was a very good memory. Of course all this makes it much easier (FS3p9).

Irene was full of ideas and energy.

Lily: Overall you have the feeling that it worked out better this time than last time?

Irene: Yes, I do! It isn't that it didn't work well last time but they were much faster this time and they were clearly better prepared to engage with the content – that was nice!...It [the fact that the storytelling works well] supports my way of teaching in general because I always include stories in my teaching and I have them discuss [issues].

RESEARCHER COMMENTARY 2003

Re-reading the transcript of this feedback session and my journal entry, I realised that I had actually forgotten to ask Irene the crucial question about whether she had also noticed that the students looked overwhelmed in class or at least very tired or whether this had been only my impression. However, Irene appeared full of enthusiasm about how well everything had worked out this time, which now indicates to me that she might have been oblivious to my observation at least at the time. This was quite understandable, from her perspective: The rainforest was Irene's arena - it was her special topic! This was how she was teaching it – full of glee. I wonder whether she had simply presumed that because the topic was of special interest to her, it was also of interest to her students? I remember that Irene had concerns during the planning phase of the project about the level of complexity of the topic for her "darlings". However, she appeared quite confident that she could handle the difficulty of the storyline this time...

Intrigued by the apparent difference between my impression and Irene's, I tried to interview students. However, I was not successful. During and after the Rainforest Dilemma, it became difficult to interview Irene's students because they were either too busy or otherwise engaged (or burned out?) – I could not get hold of more than two students (Fatima and Melinda) for very short follow-up interviews. Unfortunately, Melinda's interview was not recorded on tape due to problems with the tape-recorder. From what I recall Melinda said that she liked the second dilemma unit better because she already knew what was expected of her. However, she had experienced the second story as more difficult than the first one. Email member checking has so far been unsuccessful with the students. I have therefore included Fatima's comments although I am aware that without further back up it might just express the opinion of a single person and I have added Melinda's comments from my memory.

STUDENT COMMENTARY

Fatima expressed concerns regarding difficulty of the Rainforest Dilemma story, "The second story was much harder to understand...and somehow it was clear to me that I could not do it anyway - like go to a foreign country and bring diseases." (FIIp18&23) She added, "I only had negative impressions – even when students said their opinions – they were negative most of the time. In the first story we tried to arrive at a solution – this time we simply could not find any. It was so difficult to find a solution in this story.(FIIp16)...The first story was much more interesting than the second one – the first one was exciting whilst the second one was something rather ordinary.(FIIp4) ...The first story made me sad...with the second one, there was really nothing" (FIIp12). Finally, she even gave an evaluation as to what she had learned, "I have learned much more from the first story than from the second." (FIIp27)

RESEARCHER COMMENTARY 2003

Fatima's comment highlights a major difficulty with regard to writing dilemma stories and curriculum material for teaching ethics: I had attempted to ensure age-appropriateness through relying on the teachers' knowledge of their classes. However, thinking back to our discussions about the apparent simplicity of Dilemma 1, I realised that this strategy does not necessarily work well: when Irene thought the story about the tree was too simplistic for her students the dilemma turned out to be right for some students at least. When she thought the complex story about her area of interest was complex but suitable, it seemed to be much too difficult at least for one student. Obviously, not even Irene's familiarity with her class could completely rule out these problems. When I discovered the discrepancy between Fatima's experiences and Irene's, I again tried to get in touch with the students in order to clarify my observations regarding the apparent difficulty with the second story. Unfortunately I did not receive any feedback from the students. However, Irene responded in an email.

TEACHER COMMENTARY 2003

Over the years, Irene had changed her mind. She wrote, "I believe that the topic [of the second story] was too extensive and it was too complex for the know-how of the students despite my efforts." She pointed out the necessity of better preparing students with regard to science content for a dilemma topic. " ....I also believe that there should have been more time between the two dilemma units. This would have been helpful, I think. Like this, the teaching approach was repeated which was good for my organisation but which also led to boredom on the students' side [Email 11. 3. 2003]

RESEARCHER COMMENTARY 2003

Both of these recent comments support my overall impressions. However, Irene added yet another dimension: the dimension of the relationship between subject matter and the dilemma stories. She argues that for the stories to be understood, students need to have a basic understanding of the science content. I agree to some degree: content coverage is necessary for basic understanding of the problem, yet the primary focus of the dilemma units need not be on content coverage but on ethical learning within the context of science learning. However, I admit that during the preparation phase of this project we did not pay enough attention to this detail. We tried to ensure that the stories fitted into the curriculum but we did not make sure that the necessary science content for complex stories had been taught beforehand.

BACK IN THE BIOLOGY LAB: 1ST PERIOD THURSDAY MORNING

Part 2 of the Rainforest Dilemma: Once again, we have to struggle against the early hour: the students look sleepy (again!) and it takes Irene the best part of this period to get students to work on their task which is to collaborate on designing a poster in order to present it to the class. She hands out poster-materials and walks from group to group, offering advice or just checking that they are working. One group still does not work properly. Finally, after Irene has explained the task several times, the group becomes a little bit more active – and Irene slightly more annoyed.

Irene tells about some of her own personal experiences in the rainforest. She tells the story of the transport of a huge crane into a remote area in the Brazilian rainforest, an event she had witnessed. She explains further that the background of her story was that there were a few endemic plants had been discovered in this particular area and someone wanted to explore them.

RESEARCHER COMMENTARY 2003

Timetabling seemed to be working against us as most of our class periods coincided with first periods, which was especially bad on Monday mornings when students appeared to be very absent-minded. However, Irene managed to maintain students' attention through the personal stories she occasionally allowed to flow into the main dilemma story. On several occasions, she also drew on biological subject matter thus seamlessly combining science teaching with ethics teachings. Her storytelling style was strikingly different from the first part of the first dilemma unit! However, from a pedagogical point of view, there seemed to be a problem with 'group-work' inasmuch as Irene needed to reprimand the same group again and again in order to keep them on task.

BACK IN THE BIOLOGY LAB

Finally, presentation time. A group mounts the 'stage': Imelda. Melinda, Karin and Jakob. They have not started when there is yet another interruption: The bell for the end of the period rings and we still have not finished. I am starting to feel desperate because of the discontinuity of the whole dilemma unit. If the students feel half as exhausted by the long drawn-out unit as I do, then I fully understand that they are not too enthusiastic. Irene has one more science period this morning – the 6th period!!! Thinking of the 6th period - in my experience, it is often characterised by students who are tired from the long morning (in Austrian schools there is no long lunch-break!), and I am not optimistic that the situation will improve dramatically then.

RESEARCHER COMMENTARY 2003

The tyranny of timetabling again - I had obviously completely misjudged in my planning the long (!) duration of each of the units and consequently the constant interruptions because of awkward timetabling. I had taught dilemma units before even with big classes of thirty students. However, I had never taken longer than two hours. I am unsure as to why the units during the Ethics in Science Project, especially in Irene's class, took so long. It might have been due to the fact that many of her students are not German native speakers and thus took longer to understand the story, the questions and tasks, and to formulate their responses. Another reason might have been that I, having been trained as a communication facilitator, approach group-process differently and in a more goal-oriented and time-conscious manner. For example, if we need to finish within a particular timeframe, the unit needs to be adjusted accordingly. Perhaps I automatically expected teachers to practice the same time-awareness. However, as this was not the case, the dilemma units were interrupted too often which seriously affected the flow of the stories and perhaps also affected student engagement.

A FEW HOURS LATER - IN THE LIBRARY (AGAIN!)

This is our third attempt to finish the second dilemma unit! However, it starts off with yet another delay. Irene makes many administrative announcements in her role as a form teacher. Finally, she has the remainder of the posters presented and initiates the plenary discussion by introducing the fourth and last dilemma situation.

> *Irene: Locals ask the two researchers: Why has nobody bothered to ask us whether the plants can be taken from our rainforest? But as a researcher you are powerless.*

In this context, Irene explains the higher politics of globalisation. She does this in a very simple and seemingly intelligible manner. This leads over to the plenary discussion (which is discussed in Chapter 10). Finally, the students seem to wake up a little bit. I believe, this could be because they like discussions.

Researcher commentary 2003

It seemed obvious that the students enjoyed discussions. I discuss this matter in greater detail in Chapter 10, however, it seems worthwhile mentioning here that Irene's class of sleepy Year 9s suddenly was resurrected by the prospect of a discussion. This is, I believe, an important observation from a pedagogical point of view.

Summary of the Rainforest Dilemma 2003

In the first dilemma unit, we had the situation that the teacher thought the story was too simplistic and taught it accordingly. However, the students apparently liked it in the end and evidence shows that at least some experienced the dilemma as a dilemma. With the second story, at least Fatima, and from my memory Melinda preferred the first to the second story which they regarded as too difficult. Fatima claimed not to feel engaged and seemed to not really see the dilemma(s) in the story, which indicates to me that the story was probably not age appropriate for her. My classroom observations during the second dilemma unit indicate that students appeared less involved and 'tired'. Reasons for this could be the short interval between the two dilemma units and/or that the story was to complex for the age group. Irene, the teacher, supports these possible explanations, and added another one – students might have been overwhelmed because their knowledge base was not sufficient -which points towards the need for better preparation of students prior to dilemma units.

The results have repercussions for curriculum planners: In one case, the teacher (perhaps) would not have chosen a 'too simplistic' story that seemed to have worked out well in the end, whilst in the other case, the teacher enthusiastically taught a story that probably was far too complex for students. So how, we may ask, do we ensure age appropriateness and appropriateness of complexity with regard to the content of dilemma stories? How, if not through the teachers' knowledge and experience, can we ensure that a dilemma is a dilemma for both the teacher and the students? What criteria should we choose to judge our materials?

The second dilemma concluded the Ethics in Science project in Irene's class. The third dilemma unit was the Rocket Dilemma in Sandra's 6A class (Year 10) – I was looking forward to seeing how Sandra would handle the 'new' teaching style given that she did not at all consider herself a storyteller. During the analysis stage of the research, Sandra's dilemma unit served a crystallisation purpose. I asked myself: Did the same phenomena as I described earlier in the chapter, also occur in Sandra's class?

PART 3: ROCKET DILEMMA (25.5.2000)

Introduction to the story

The Rocket Dilemma is a story about research ethics and how far scientific research should be allowed to go? A young rocket-researcher finds himself confronted with a number of dilemmas such as collaboration with a totalitarian regime or flight, human experiments or failure of the research (see Appendix 5 for full text). His knowledge makes him very valuable especially for nations striving for dominance in space. For this reason, his biography is whitewashed in his later life which makes him acceptable to our modern society. This story has a real life background – the biography of Wernher von Braun, a famous rocket scientist, who had been involved in unethical research involving concentration camp prisoners during the Nazi Regime in Germany. Given that almost all of the students in Sandra's class were of Austrian origin and thus had grown up in post-war Austria like me, I was interested in the level of critical awareness these young people brought with them. As I mentioned in Chapter 4, all Austrian students learn about history at school - it is regarded as part of general 'Bildung'- which meant for me that I could 'expect' basic knowledge about that period of Austrian history.

Part 3 of the chapter takes us further into the third dilemma unit than the two previous parts, namely to the beginning of the plenary discussion where a personal story told by Sandra, the teacher, marked a turning point (as in Irene's class when she told the story about her grandmother's tree).

In the library

When I arrive at the beginning of the lesson, the students are already sitting in a circle. Sandra has seated herself in the circle. Unlike Irene, who often chose a 'perch-like' seat above the students, Sandra has chosen to be on the same level. She addresses the class:

Sandra: For the first time in my life, I am going to be a storyteller. Ms Settelmaier has written a story for us. We have decided that the story comes across better if told freely. The title of the story is "The journey to the Moon" and it is based on a true story. Perhaps some of you will recognise the characters in the story. You certainly know the pictures of the first moon-landing and Neil Armstrong stepping on the moon's surface saying those famous words, "A small step for a man, a giant step for mankind." Humans have long held the dream to land eventually on the moon....

Sandra continues the story about Herbert, his childhood and how the bedtime stories his mother read to him informed his wish to build a rocket. Her voice sounds a bit monotonous to me yet the students sit quietly and listen attentively. Maria, who has been described to me beforehand as very politically active, listens with arms crossed, legs stretched out and toes pointing to the ceiling. "Being defensive!", my inner voice points out to me – during my training as a communication consultant we also learned to interpret body-language, but we also learned not to over-interpret particular clues. I quickly decide therefore to interpret her posture as perhaps merely habitual. I have chosen to observe her and a few other students. Johnny is another one: Johnny and his friend hide behind their hats and chat quietly without making much noise. He stares at the floor in front of him. I am amazed at how well he has developed the art of having a conversation yet appearing to be listening to the teacher.

Sandra tells about the time when the regime of Herbert's country changes and concentration camps are established, people are reportedly being deported and killed.

Sandra: Many leave the country, most have to stay because they simply cannot afford to leave. Many prefer not to believe the rumours. "This can't be true, not in our country!" They say. After a while when the economy gets a boost people think that, "The regime is not as bad as we thought. The economy has become better and new jobs have been created. Professor Schubert, the leader of Herbert's research team, has to migrate as well. The team is left behind leaderless. Herbert has a meeting with a government official who makes it clear to him that he is offered Schubert's job as team-leader. Herbert and his friend Andreas have to make a decision whether or not they will stay in this country given the rumours about human rights abuse. At this point I would like to interrupt the story. Could you please take a moment and reflect on whether you – if you were Herbert – would accept the government's offer or leave the country?

The students reflect individually at first and then go together in pairs which is discussed in greater detail in Chapter 8 and Chapter 9. After the first dilemma situation, Sandra continues the story.

> *Sandra: Both Herbert and his friend Andreas stay on, and find support from the government. Problems during the research cause them to take longer than expected. The government official confronts them with the government's plan to go to war and the need to build rockets suitable for war…*

Sandra talks about concentration-camp prisoners and how they have been (ab)used as "material" – she talks about perpetrators 'getting used' to being confronted with abuse, pain and suffering.

RESEARCHER COMMENTARY 2003

This issue touches a very difficult part of the shared history of post-war Austrians – we live with an incomprehensible past. I believe that students, provided the Austrian curriculum has had some positive outcomes, should have some awareness of it. Sandra had mentioned to me beforehand that especially Maria was very politically active which made her very interesting for my research (see also Chapters 8 & 9).

BACK TO THE STORYTELLING

Sandra describes how Herbert eventually uses people for human experiments because, she explains, he is obsessed with the wish to build a rocket that can fly to the moon and transport people. The human experiments yield many 'useful' results.

> *Sandra: Last dilemma… Think about Herbert's dream, think about the moon-landing and the price that had to be paid. Think also about other problems with science – especially about the abuse of scientific knowledge, example given, in genetics research. The question is now – how far should science [scientific research] be allowed to go? Is it OK to sacrifice a few for the good of many?*

This final comment sparks off some muttering in the audience. "Finally!", I think, "there are some unsolicited discussions!" Unfortunately, these 'discussions' coincide with the end of the two periods that were available to us. Sandra announces that the dilemma will be finished on Thursday.

RESEARCHER COMMENTARY 2003

There it was again – the torturous two-period limit that had dominated and affected the first two dilemma units in Irene's class! Once again we had to interrupt the dilemma unit – although not purposefully in this case!

RESEARCHER COMMENTARY 2000

From my journal: …"OK, OK. Now it is finally clear to me that my stories are too long – at least for the length of periods we normally have available!" [which is 50 minutes] They are much rather designed for a whole afternoon or a whole morning… Yet, looking back at my experiences with Irene's class, I can say now that Sandra's class has come much further in the dilemma unit than did the other class after two periods [Sandra's class reached the poster preparation phase!]. I gather that the 'slowness' of Irene's 5A class has greatly contributed to the discontinuity of the dilemma units. But of course I can also see that the dilemma stories I have written are too long for use with school classes in the current school environment. This is something to think about in the future.

RESEARCHER COMMENTARY 2003

After analysing the video of Sandra's class, I realised that my earlier observations appeared to be correct – Irene's class needed much more time and support to get organised whilst Sandra's students, on the other hand, appeared to be more on task. They seemed to understand questions immediately, and they followed instructions immediately. This has led me to believe that language problems might have been responsible for the delay in Irene's class. Part of the social interactions in her class might have been related to clarification of tasks and questions in order to understand what the students were required to do. With regard to the teaching of the dilemma unit, Sandra appeared quite self-confident although she had admittedly been frightened of the storytelling. The only sign that might have indicated some nervousness was that she speaking with a very low voice – one had to listen very carefully to hear what she was saying.

TEACHER COMMENTARY

In a feedback session after the first part of the unit, Sandra openly admitted to some stage-freight regarding the dilemma unit: "I was stressed in the beginning..." I reassured her that I hardly noticed and asked, "How did you experience the 'new' teaching style?"

Sandra responded: "I was lost for words in between..." She informed me that the students had come up with an organ donor story – which I had missed completely – that unbalanced her a bit. She added, "I thought this was really drifting too far from the subject....although it was me who originally started this discussion." She admitted to being unsure as to when to intervene.

RESEARCHER COMMENTARY 2003

Despite looking very confident, even Sandra apparently experienced some difficulties teaching a dilemma unit: when the discourse drifted in a direction she had not anticipated, she apparently felt lost. Although she mastered the group-organisation quite well, she still felt unsure as to when intervention was needed and how it was to be done.

STUDENT COMMENTARY ABOUT THE STORY

When I asked students what they liked about the dilemma unit Daniela immediately responded, "Actually everything. First of all, the story itself." (D20p5) Ulli seemed to support this view, by saying, "I was thinking that this really is an interesting topic because it is about humans and about how humans really are." (U6p64) Julian was one of those students who demonstrated historical awareness by indicating that he was intrigued to find out about the 'real story' behind the dilemma story, "It wasn't mentioned that it was about Wernher von Braun, but I knew who it was about and I also had a vague idea about who the other people were...and by the way it was pretty clear that we were dealing with the Nazi Era." (J8p73)

RESEARCHER COMMENTARY 2003

All three comments indicate to me that these students found something in the story that 'spoke to them' and made them reflect on the story. For these students, it appears that the dilemma story presented them with a recognisable age-appropriate dilemma.

STUDENT COMMENTARY CONTINUED

Yet for some (again!) this was apparently not the case, particularly for Maria, "I liked it, if only it had been a different story, something that speaks more to our age group but still fits well with the curriculum. If the story had been different I would have preferred that!" (M22p20). Also Paul found it difficult to identify with the dilemma because his interests are different from the character in the story, "It is very difficult to think oneself into the situation because from the outside you're not really in the situation and you can hardly experience the feelings because I don't want to fly to the moon, so I cannot talk about this easily. But there are certainly other issues that would interest me." (P8p34)

SUMMARY OF THE ROCKET DILEMMA

As with Irene's class, some students in this class seemingly did not experience the dilemma in the story as a dilemma, whilst others did. However, I believe that it is these students, those who we cannot reach, that should be of special concern for curriculum planners. This raises the question again as to how, when designing the stories, we can ensure that a dilemma is a dilemma for everybody in a class?

REVIEW OF THE CHAPTER

In this chapter, I explored the conditions the question whether or not dilemma stories are suitable to introduce students to controversial issues. I discussed examples from the 'Ethics in Science' project bringing together teachers', students' and my own perspectives. Overall, students seem to have regarded the dilemma stories as a suitable way of introducing them to a dilemma by promoting identification with the story characters and their situations, imagination, emotions, and raising students' attention levels. However, students also raised issues such as a disinterest in the topic, a too high level of complexity of the storyline, lack of age-appropriateness of the stories.

This led me to the exploration of the question, "How do we ensure age appropriateness of the dilemma stories?" or in other words, "How do we ensure that a dilemma story provides an ethical dilemma for all participants?" To me, this has highlighted that this is probably one of the most crucial problems of the dilemma approach. During the curriculum planning stage, I tried to address the issue by relying on Irene's and Sandra's familiarity with their classes. However, the two dilemma units in Irene's class have illustrated a dilemma with dilemmas: sometimes a teacher regards a dilemma as a dilemma that does not engage the students, whilst sometimes students experience a clear dilemma where the teacher thinks it might be too simplistic. Good knowledge of a class (only) does not seem to provide a good enough answer to this problem because Irene is a very engaged form-teacher who takes high personal interest in getting to know 'her kids'. This indicates to me that when we develop curriculum materials for teaching ethics in science classrooms, regardless of how careful we are planning and how well we try to meet the requirements for an age-group and for the current curriculum of a class, there seems to remain a possibility that we simply cannot meet 'everybody's taste'.

In both classes, the dilemma teaching and learning was suffering from too many interruptions due to unfortunate time-tabling as well as (perhaps) too long stories. In the future I would thus cut back on the length of the stories and attempt to achieve better time-tabling such a whole a morning or afternoon in order to be able to finish a dilemma unit in one go.

Comparing the two <u>teachers as storytellers</u>, both teachers did their best to tell the stories. Obviously they were 'better' storytellers when they could identify with the story (like Irene in her fist dilemma unit). Given that Sandra had been quite apprehensive with regard to storytelling beforehand, she appeared quite confident in her role as a storyteller. She even added a very personal story that once again did not fail to leave an impression.

Chapter 8

Reflecting individually

In the beginning, I wasn't really reflecting on the dilemma, I was primarily responding to the questions but the longer I kept thinking about it and talking about it the more I started thinking about it and then it occurred to me that it was actually very difficult to make a decision (P5p30).

INTRODUCTION

Dilemma units are designed to promote reflective thinking which is mirrored in the organisation around alternating phases of individual reflection and group discourse. The idea behind it is that when a student is confronted with a dilemma situation s/he will use reflection to solve the problem (see Mezirow, 1991). As mentioned in Chapter 5, the intent behind 'my' dilemma curriculum was emancipatory and transformative – I wanted to provide students with the skill to participate in the public discourse about science and simultaneously introduce them to critical reflection as a means of personal transformation. I hoped to engage them in a process of '(re)assessment of their uncritically accepted assumptions' in order to raise their ethical awareness.

However, when educators say, "We want students to 'think' about a controversial issue or a dilemma", they often mean different things: Thinking, reasoning, reflecting, reflecting critically, thinking critically – all these terms are being used in the (moral) educational literature, often interchangeably. Whilst the term 'critical thinking' is primarily used for education of children and adolescents, it appears the term 'critical reflection' is used primarily by adult educators.

209

Given this blur of meanings, I felt that before I embarked on further analysis of the data, particularly with regard to what I had termed 'individual reflection' (see Chapter 5), I needed to clarify for myself what I was actually looking at. This is why I explored the terminology and some of the theory at the beginning of this chapter. However, as in Chapter 8, most of the data-analysis preceded the analysis of the theoretical literature on the topic. The themes emerged before I consulted the literature. The analysis was therefore largely data-driven rather than theory-driven. Nevertheless, whilst I was writing up the findings, I consulted the literature in order to make sense of my findings.

In the context of moral education, Kohlberg thought that 'moral reasoning' illuminates why certain decisions have been made (Kohlberg, 1984, 1996). He used moral reasoning to determine the 'stage of moral development'. He presumed that the moral reasoning of people classified as members of the later stages of his theory of moral development involved 'reasoning better' than those at earlier stages. Kohlberg based his theory on the measuring of people's morality levels derived from the analysis of moral reasoning (see Chapter 5). Velasquez informs us: ethicians tend to evaluate moral reasoning on the basis of logic, accuracy, completeness, relevance of the argument and the consistency of moral standards (Velasquez, 1998). Moral reasoning, as a form of critical thinking, is what numerous teaching approaches to moral education seem to promote (Brownfield, 1986; Porter & Taylor, 1972). Critical thinking is generally characterised by elements such as interpretation, analysis, evaluation, inferences, explanation, self-regulation, comparison, classification, sequencing, cause/effect, patterning, webbing, analogies, deductive and inductive reasoning and many more. Critical thinking seems to be thinking that assesses itself, and also making reasoned judgments. Bloom developed a taxonomy of learning objectives in which he distinguished cognitive, affective and psychomotor domains (Anderson & Krathwohl, 2001). According to Bloom's taxonomy, critical thinking is thought to develop along the six levels in the cognitive domain of knowledge, comprehension, application, analysis, synthesis, and evaluation. Critical thinking

210

is also thought of as a left-brain activity, and critical learning apparently takes place when students are required to perform in the analysis-evaluation range, something that is often referred to as 'good thinking' (Facione, 1996; LaGrange College Education Department, n.d.; Lamb, 2001; Walker, 1997). A search on the World Wide Web made me realise how much material is available on this topic, much of it geared towards teachers of children. Critical thinking, according to Bailin (2002), is apparently one of the goals of science education.

Moral reasoning in Kohlberg's sense seems to focus primarily on critical thinking which promotes impartiality. This was disputed by feminists, such as Carol Gilligan, who favoured a caring focus. Based on my findings in this chapter, I support Gilligan's critique in that I believe that a focus on critical thinking alone does not allow us to see the full picture of what I would like to call 'individual reflection'.

Borchers (quoting John Dewey) explains that decision-making requires reflective thinking which he defines as a careful, systematic approach to a problem (Borchers, 1999a). The term reflection has been defined as thinking for an extended period of time by linking recent experiences to earlier ones. This type of thinking may involve looking at commonalities, differences and interrelations beyond their superficial elements (Clark, n.d.). Mezirow tells us that we can reflect on three different foci: on problem-solving, on understanding others, and on the self (Mezirow, 1991). When this type of thinking involves also a critical dimension, then it may include assumption analysis, contextual awareness, imaginative speculation and reflective scepticism. In other words, critical reflection seems to be a process of analysing, reconsidering and questioning experiences with a focus on the self within a broader context. Thus learning by critical reflection tends to involve creating new understandings by making conscious the social, political, economic, and ethical assumptions constraining or supporting one's action in a specific context (Reid, Buckland, Clarke, & Mackay, 2000; Stein, 2000). However, as we might expect, critical reflection itself is not an uncontested concept. According to Stephen Brookfield it has four competing meanings: an ideology

211

critique, a psychoanalytical and psychotherapeutical strategy, a process through which we become more skilful in argument analysis, a means to construct and deconstruct our own experiences and meanings in a pragmatist constructivist sense (Brookfield, 2000). Mezirow, in Transformative Learning Theory, promotes the first and second views. Brookfield explains that for reflection to be critical it needs to contain some ideology critique.

"Ideology critique – for science students? Now that sounds a bit over the top! ", we might say. However, if we interpret ideology as a set of values, beliefs, myths, explanations and justifications that appear self-evidently true and morally desirable (Brookfield, 2000) then I believe it is justifiable to involve ideology critique when one of the tasks of science education is to prepare students for a public discourse about science, its uses and the influences of scientism.

Which of the three – critical thinking, reflective thinking, reflection and/or critical reflection – did I focus on during the preliminary process of analysis? I have to admit to none, in particular. Given that the purpose of my study was not to measure the extent of these types of thinking, I did not check the data with a view to finding, for example, evidence of critical thinking. It was rather a process that went hand-in-hand with the later interpretation of the data corpus (Erickson, 1998): whilst I was writing interpretive researcher commentaries (in 2003), I often realised that a particular statement might be an example of critical thinking or critical reflection. Earlier, at the time when I was designing the Ethics in Science curriculum I used the term 'individual reflection'. Given the blurr of types of thinking, I have decided to maintain the term individual reflection in this chapter. In case, I want to illustrate particular examples of critical thinking, reflection, or critical reflection, I have specified this in the text.

Of course the question remains as to how do we know that students really engaged in reflection? What can be regarded as evidence that they have been thinking about the problem and about problem-solving? In this study, I tried to approach this question from several angles: classroom observation, students' statements in class following an individual reflection phase, students' written comments taken from their portfolios, teacher comments and students' comments during interviews. With regard to the written notes I focused on those students who I interviewed.

Purpose and organisation of the chapter

This chapter aims at answering the following research questions: <u>Do dilemmas stand up to what they promise which is to induce a moral reasoning process that forms the basis of potential moral learning? If yes, how did students experience the individual reflection phases of the dilemma unit</u>? What was it like for students to engage in a reflection process during a dilemma unit? What were the characteristics of this experience? First we need to clarify several terms and concepts in relation to 'thinking' within a dilemma unit. What were the experienced problems and obstacles that need to be overcome in order to improve the teaching approach by optimising conditions for learning?

Given that the development of critical reflection, as part of the 'thinking' spectrum, appears to be time-dependent, I have organised this chapter (and the next) along a timeline. As it is impossible within the limitations of a thesis to present all the situations where moral reflection potentially occurred, that is all the individual reflection phases, I have chosen three situations during which reflection was intended to occur:

- <u>Part 1</u> explores the conditions for individual reflection by investigating classroom interactions and individual reflective thinking following the initial 'warm-up' dilemma questions. These questions were designed to prepare the students for more difficult dilemma questions towards the end of the unit.
- <u>Part 2</u> investigates individual student reflection towards the end of the dilemma unit before students entered into the final plenary discussion round.

By this time, we may expect that they had had enough time to engage with the story and its dilemmas.

- Part 3 explores whether students continued to reflect after the official end of the dilemma unit, as well as how students experienced the reflection phase as such.

For crystallisation purposes, I have contrasted Irene's class with Sandra's class wherever possible. Data sources during this phase of the research were classroom observations, video-tapes, student interview data, teacher interview data, and individual students' written notes that formed part of their assessment portfolio.

As in Chapter 8, I have used different fonts to identify the different voices and lenses used to explore this phenomenon: Book Antiqua was used for the thesis narrator's voice whilst HELVETICA was used for the participant observer's voice at the time of the fieldwork in 2000. Arial Narrow was used for researcher commentaries in 2003 and reviews. *Book Antiqua Italics* was used for direct speech during classroom observations. Courier was used for students' post hoc commentaries and Tahoma illustrates teachers' post hoc perspectives. To avoid confusion for the reader the voices are labelled throughout the chapter. As in Chapter 7, verbatim interview quotes are referenced as follows: initial of the pseudonym of the interviewee, followed by reference number and paragraph number (e.g., F23p2) to allow for the audit trail.

PART 1: INDIVIDUAL REFLECTION DURING THE FIRST DILEMMA SITUATION

Part 1 is organised in two sections: Section 1 explores the first dilemma situation during the Tree Dilemma in Irene's class; Section 2 focuses on the first dilemma question of the Rocket Dilemma in Sandra's class. The purpose of Part 1 is to investigate students' thinking during the initial individual reflection phase in which the purpose was to 'prepare' students' thinking for more difficult questions later in the dilemma unit.

Section 1: The Tree Dilemma in Irene's class

During the first part of the dilemma unit, I had the impression that Irene's initial storytelling style did not help to get the story across very well (see Chapter 8).

When Irene finally puts a transparency on the overhead projector and confronts the students with the first dilemma situation, I feel relieved. Whilst she is explaining the students' task, she hands out copies of the instructions to be distributed amongst the students which leads to yet another distraction – students appear more focused on getting hold of a copy than on what Irene is explaining. Irene asks the dilemma question and asks students to reflect on the solution individually at first! She reads from the transparency.

> *Irene: Imagine you are Peter and you are trying to convince your parents not to cut down your tree. Which arguments would you use? Explain your arguments!*

However, instead of quiet 'contemplation' conversations flare up throughout the classroom. This is not what we wanted them to do – they are not supposed to collaborate yet. Irene trying to focus them on the task, says, "There will be opportunity to compare your ideas later! For now, we want you to work individually!" Some students try to comply and find space for themselves where they can work individually, however, this proves difficult because of the limited space in the classroom. Others use this opportunity for yet another chat and/or do not really seem to know what they are supposed to do. Some students, such as Fatima, frantically look around at what others are writing – she looks lost. Yet others concentrate on fastidiously sticking the instructions on their worksheet – I am asking myself whether they are just trying to win time in order to figure out what they are supposed to do? Overall, the number of students who really seem to work individually appears limited, and there are discussions throughout the classroom. I wonder whether the instructions are not clear enough because some students apparently do not know what to do and therefore have to consult a neighbour. On the one hand, perhaps the manner of giving instructions needs adjusting or they are simply not willing to comply. Irene reminds them to be quiet and to work individually.

Irene tells them, "*You know what you have to do, there is no problem whatsoever!*" Alois turns around from his desk and asks, "*Mrs Rock, what do we have to do?*", totally ignoring what Irene just said. Irene reminds Alois that she has explained the task already several times. To me it looks as if Alois (one of the so-called 'problem-students' in the class) uses the situation for engaging Irene in a conversation and getting her attention.

One of the African students, Damian, who still has some language difficulties asks Irene again about what he is supposed to do. These interactions with individuals seem to distract Irene's attention from the rest of the class, and the noise levels rise again - too high for my taste. For me, it is difficult to distinguish which students are working individually and which are not. I feel that some intervention is needed to keep students on task.

I walk across the room to Irene who is standing on the other side of the classroom and remind her that it is vital that the students work individually in the beginning. "*What shall we do?*" Irene asks shrugging her shoulders and looking slightly desperately at the merrily chatting groups. I suggest that one strategy for getting the situation under control could be to cut short individual reflection time and have the students go together in pairs earlier than planned in order to discuss the outcomes of their 'single' reflection exercise. I can see that these students are apparently not used to thinking individually, at least not in a class situation...

CONVERSATION WITH IRENE AFTER THE FIRST DILEMMA UNIT

Irene: ...and what I also heard...I don't even want to make decision!...and another one said, 'I have to obey my parents in any case'! and again another student said that 'I can't make a decision if the tree and the campervan belong to my parents'...so there was this money question!...Again and again I have heard this hierarchical thinking, 'Only the parents can decide!'...

Lily: ...And then I wrote [in my notes]– the students are not really working individually when they are supposed to! These 'premature' discussions have cost us a lot of time!

Irene: Yes exactly this was where we lost time!

Lily: This was why we did not finish and why we have to spend yet another period on the dilemma unit! (I-FS1p37&113-117)

RESEARCHER COMMENTARY 2003

Irene's comments were very interesting – somebody had said to Irene that they did not want to make a decision because they felt somewhat powerless and they had to do whatever their parents wanted them to do. Others argued that if the tree and the campervan belong to the parents, then there is nothing THEY can decide. This power-through-money-thinking might explain, at least for some of the students, why they did not fully engage. For some students, it appears that they found it hard to identify with an adult character perhaps because this was beyond their own experiences or perhaps because it is the parents who have the money.

The question remained – did the dilemma story induce the students to reflect on the dilemma? Did they 'think' about it? In order to get an insight into their thinking I looked at their portfolios and at their responses to the first 'warm up' question: If you were Peter how would you try to convince your parents not to cut down the tree? This is followed by student comments drawn from interviews.

EXTRACTS FROM STUDENT PORTFOLIOS

When I studied student portfolios (see Appendix 12), I concentrated on students who I interviewed. Fatima who had reportedly struggled with disinterest in the beginning of the dilemma unit, argued: "I would say to my parents, 'firstly, you can park the campervan somewhere else, and secondly, the tree was born with me and nobody has the right to take it away from me. This is my tree and nobody has the

217

right to take it away without my consent. I love my tree more than anything and this is why I do not want that anything happens to it. I would try and find a different parking spot for the campervan."

RESEARCHER COMMENTARY 2003

Despite her professed disinterest (see Chapter 7) she was trying after all to find arguments against the cutting of the tree. Her arguments involved issues of connectedness to the tree (born with me; love the tree; don't want anything to happen to it) (Belenky et al., 1997) as well as arguments involving justice (rejecting somebody else's right to cut down her tree). It seems clear that she was not valuing the campervan more than the tree.

Emma was Fatima's friend and she was seated next to Fatima for most of the first part of the dilemma unit. The video shows some 'collaboration' between the two. This is why I almost expected an identical result in their written notes. However, to my surprise not all her arguments were identical. When Emma argued, "The tree is something like a brother or a sister – after all the tree has grown up with him. What would happen to all the animals – they would lose their habitats!" she added a new perspective that had not appeared in Fatima's text, demonstrating connectedness (brother , sister) and concerns for the animals. "The campervan could be parked somewhere else, e.g., with other people or so. I would try to find a parking area for the campervan." These last two arguments appear to have been derived by collaboration with Fatima.

RESEARCHER COMMENTARY 2003

It seems quite likely that Fatima and Emma collaborated, however, each of them had her own ideas as well. Thus it seems to indicate that they apparently did reflect individually on the issues.

Damian, from Africa, once again surprised me with his response. It is very different from most answers given by his Austrian colleagues. He 'speaks' directly to his parents: "Why do you want to cut down the tree that I have known for 33 years. ..you know every time when I come home there is nobody but me and the tree. If you cut it down then I will be home alone forever. It is my friend and even like my brother. If you cut it I will be very lonely – please don't cut it... What would happen to the living space of many animals [in the tree]."

RESEARCHER COMMENTARY 2003

Damian argues on an emotional level evoking his parents' feelings for him by pointing out to the parents how lonely he has been and how the tree has become 'like a brother' who has comforted him. Furthermore he, like Emma, reminds the parents of the consequences for the animals living in and around the tree. His comments seem to express connectedness and concern for others (Belenky et al., 1997).

Gregor did not write much, however, his portfolio shows the marks of his struggle: several attempts at answering the question had been crossed out. His first attempt looked like this, "I would build a parking area. I would cut down the tree and with the wood..." (unfinished sentence). The final version of the answer looked like this: "I would build a parking area, leave the tree – Peter has grown up with the tree."

RESEARCHER COMMENTARY 2003

He apparently did not know what to say in this situation thereby indicating that he was in a 'disequilibrium' of some kind. Building a parking area appeared in both attempts. More interesting is the first crossed out sentence indicating that he was considering that the tree would be cut, and he was about to suggest what he would do with the wood. Does this illustrate an inner dilemma? Does it express a feeling of powerlessness? For some reason, however, he decided that he wanted to argue for the life of the tree on the basis of the connectedness between Peter and the tree.

Like Damian, Melinda chose direct speech to her parents to answer the question, "If you cut down the tree, then a piece of myself is missing. I feel connected with the tree. You cannot simply cut down a tree because of a campervan. Park the campervan somewhere else, where shall all the animals go? You don't really have to cut down the whole tree – cutting off a few branches might be enough."

RESEARCHER COMMENTARY 2003

Melinda uses the term 'connected' to express how she would argue about this issue with her parents: 'a piece of myself is missing'. This could be interpreted as an expression of connectedness between the girl and the tree. She is confronting the parents by appealing to the different values of a tree and a campervan and it appears that she holds the tree dearer than the campervan. She also expressed some concern about the animals living on the tree, as did Damian and Emma. The student portfolios indicate that despite some collaboration, there was individual reflection on the 'warm-up' question. In Mezirow's sense, it was primarily reflection on problem solving. One interesting aspect regarding the written notes is that some students used a first person narrative style whilst others restricted themselves to third person arguments. I wonder if this is related to the degree to which students identified with the character in the story? We might interpret the use of first person narrative as a strong identification with the person who students are making a decision for. Looking at the quality of the reflection, it appears that student thinking at this stage was largely reflective (only) without the critical component that involves reconsidering one's assumptions. On the other hand, the warm-up question was not designed to foster critical reflection but to prepare for it. The above responses indicate, however, that students analysed the dilemma situation and tried to find a solution. This could be regarded as evidence of critical thinking. In the following section, I explore what the students said about their experiences during the initial reflection phase of the dilemma unit.

STUDENT COMMENTARY

Referring to my field-notes, where I had noted that Fatima looked frantic in the beginning, I interviewed Fatima about this, and she replied, "In the beginning, I was really nervous when we had to write down notes. I was asking around, 'What are you writing? What are you writing?' But it did not really help me in any way because everybody had her own opinion!" (Fp62). Fatima added, "I also found it very difficult when we had to write down our opinion (F15p23). It was so difficult and I could not think of anything. I thought I have to make, God knows, what a decision here…"

Emma pointed out that, "I always have to think before I make a decision. I think it was worthwhile to be confronted with this." (E2p36) However, she also contended that, "It was really difficult to think oneself into the situation! I was thinking perhaps I decide differently now than I would if I had to make the decision [in reality]"(E3p36)

RESEARCHER COMMENTARY 2003

Fatima reports the difficulty she experienced when she had to write about her opinion. Consulting others seemed to be not helpful either. Emma's reported difficulty of identification with the story character might be related to her use of third person arguments. This seems to support my earlier assumption that students who experienced identification as difficult probably used third person arguments whilst students who identified easily with the story character used a first person narrative. Both students assessed their own thinking and in Emma's case, displayed a sceptical stance towards future decisions. This may count as critical thinking.

Emma's suspicions regarding future decision making were also supported by Gregor who pointed out that a decision made now might be different from a decision in the actual situation, "If I got in the same situation as Peter I would find it difficult to cope. It does not really matter whether or not we have done this [dilemma] now – It would still be my decision. It won't help me then just because I have done this [the dilemma unit] now!" (G2p63) Gregor elaborated further on the difficulty of the decision-making, "Some questions were really difficult and some were very easy, for example, finding a solution for whether or not the tree should be cut down or not was difficult – there one had to think for a long time. Not so in the case of, for example, what to do with the tree once it has been cut down – I could think of something quickly." (G15p33)

RESEARCHER COMMENTARY 2003

This last comment is very interesting in relation to Gregor's written notes where crossed out sentences seem to express his inner struggle. This comment seems to illustrate his thinking at the time. Save the tree or not? What to do with the wood, if the tree gets chopped down? Gregor appears to have clearly been involved in a reflection process that included problem-solving as well as an analysis–evaluation process, which is typical of critical thinking.

Emma expressed concerns regarding the authenticity of the content of student notes, "The issue with writing down your own opinion... so that everybody really writes down their own opinion. Well, perhaps not everybody dares to do this. Perhaps it would be better if opinions were written down anonymously because then people might actually write down their personal opinions." (E27p9)

RESEARCHER COMMENTARY 2003

This last comment was quite disconcerting for me as it potentially questions the general authenticity of student written notes. Given that, within the dilemma approach, the individual reflection phase is regarded as a crucial phase for potential moral learning, there seems to be a fundamental issue! Emma mentioned fear as a potential underlying reason – however, Irene mentioned very clearly that it was the effort displayed in the written notes that would be assessed not the content. Fear of assessment therefore could not really have been the culprit – or could it?

The brief overview of student comments indicates that students seemed to be reflecting despite several problems related to the initial reflection phase, including (i) the difficulty of the task of decision-making and identification with the story-characters, and as Fatima pointed out, (ii) a lack of focus or disorientation. Irene reported a student who was unwilling to make a decision at all, and others who apparently considered themselves too powerless to make a decision, thus (iii) expressing a lack of agency. Perhaps some of these issues can be related to the novelty of the task of individual reflection, a factor that can be identified in some students' interview comments. On the other hand, if decision-making is not really part of the students' lifeworld because it is foreign concept in their lives with their parents, we might, at least initially, overwhelm them with the task. There is also some evidence that critical thinking occurred in the form of analysis, evaluation and inferences.

On the teachers' side, teaching a dilemma unit requires many (partly new?) skills. Apart from the skill of storytelling, which I discussed in the previous chapter, giving clear, unambiguous instructions seems to be of upmost importance if students are to settle down quickly for the reflection phase and no valuable time is to be lost. As we can see in this first example of Irene's first dilemma unit, instructions need to be given in a way that other sources of distraction, such as the distribution of photocopies whilst giving instructions, and engaging in conversations with individual students before 'order' has been re-established, are minimised.

In the following section, I explore further the issue of values regarding the relationship between students and their parents, as expressed in some students' comments. I am aware that some of the following comments pertain to the end of the dilemma unit, however, I believe that the content of the statements fits in following the above section.

ADDITIONAL STUDENT COMMENTARY

When I asked Damian, from Africa, what he had learned from the dilemma unit, he said, "[I have learned] that one should not simply cut down trees and sometimes one has to accept the opinions of the parents." (Da2p63&69) I have to admit I was quite surprised at this learning outcome for Damian so I asked further, "Why do you think it was difficult for Peter to accept Peter's parents' decision [to cut down the tree]?" Damian replied, "Well the parents of Peter...they have given life to him, and Peter sometimes has to accept his parents. This shows respect for the parents because they would say, 'You are a bad child'." Later he reinforced, "I believe we have to respect our parents!" (Da3p75)

Melinda, an Austrian student, who according to Irene was going through an adolescence crisis at the time, argued quite differently from Damian, "I would like others to accept my opinions and that something means a lot to me. They should not only think, 'We don't like this and we don't care, we want to get rid of it because if these are people who love me and [they know that] something is precious to me, then they should accept that I don't want this [thing] to go." (Me27p73).

RESEARCHER COMMENTARY 2003

I was stunned by Damian's response because I was quite sure that most students, like Melinda, would have taken a typical adolescent stance and opposed their parents. Damian, however, seemed to have found his own cultural values reinforced. Unlike many Western kids, he apparently believed that it is necessary to pay respect to one's parents whilst Melinda seemed to argue that if her parents loved her it was up to them to pay respect to her. Apparently Damian had not yet been fully enculturated into the Western culture. However, as Irene mentioned before, there were also some Austrian students who felt they had little or no agency at home. Whilst the modern Austrian culture certainly promotes agency, there remains traces of quite traditional values where children are expected to obey. To me, Damian's and Melinda's comments illustrate how our own cultural values can shape moral learning. What we 'get out of it' seems to depend on 'where we start from'.

Ruggiero tells us that the above phenomenon can be related to the Principle of Cultural Relativity which states that a culture's values, rituals, and customs reflect its geography, history, and socioeconomic circumstances. It also seems to be a very complex and partly controversial principle, as Ruggiero points out, "...hasty or facile comparison of other cultures with one's own culture tends to thwart scholarly analysis and produce shallow or erroneous conclusions." (Ruggiero, 1997). I have thus decided to not overinterpret my observation but to suggest my interpretation as one possibility.

SUMMARY OF SECTION 1: THE TREE DILEMMA IN IRENE'S CLASS

With regard to the conditions for individual reflection, it appears that there was a 'methodological blur' in terms of which pedagogical methods were used to give the instructions: it might have been better to use either the overhead-projector or pass out photocopies with the instructions instead of trying both at the same time. Some students might not have been able to fully concentrate on either of the demands made by the teacher: look at the screen and/or try and get hold of a photocopy. Whilst Irene allowed herself to get distracted by engaging in conversations with Alois and with Damian leading, noise levels increased in the class. It might have been better to establish good working conditions for everybody in the class before responding to individual requirements.

The optimal conditions for individual work could not really be met in the small classroom – if students wanted more privacy there was nowhere to go. Some students might not have been interested in the story as was indicated in Chapter 7, whilst some students might have felt overwhelmed by the 'new' task and therefore sought support from their colleagues. This might have been due to language difficulties as in the case of Damian or because decision-making is at odds with experiences in their own lifeworld due to a lack of agency. With regard to classroom interactions, 'caring' for each other seemed to be a characteristic feature of this class, as interviews with other teachers show. The emphasis of this class as a whole might have been on 'communion' instead of agency (Belenky et al., 1997; Wilber, 1997). One student reported fear as a potential reason for inauthenticity of student comments. Student portfolio notes seem to show that despite some collaboration, individual reflection happened. Students' suggestions ranged from finding a different parking spot to a 'plea' to the parents not to cut down the 'brother and friend'. One student's work sample indicates that he was apparently finding it difficult to make a decision. There seems to have been a cultural difference in values regarding parent-child relationship between Austrian students and African students.

In the following section of the chapter, I change my 'angle on the crystal' again and report on classroom observations in Sandra's class. Sandra, having had the advantage of learning about Irene's initial difficulties with giving instructions clearly, did not use an overhead projector and had prepared photocopies (only) of the dilemma questions.

Section 2: The Rocket Dilemma in Sandra's class

At the end of the first part of the story, Sandra gets up and hands out worksheets. She restricts herself to waiting until the process of distribution is finished. No chaos – no noise. The students sit quietly and work. I am surprised at just how quiet they are, how focused, although it is difficult to judge from the facial expressions whether they are being attentive and fully concentrating. Only the group around Johnny is involved in chatter. I do not think they are getting much work done. During these first few activities the difference between Irene's and Sandra's classes becomes very obvious to me: Sandra's students are very task-oriented. Most of them received the task and started working on it without discussions. Sandra finally asks the students to come together in pairs and without having to be asked again, students find a partner and start the new task.

RESEARCHER COMMENTARY 2003

The way students approached the individual reflection activity was strikingly different in the two classes: Contrary to Irene's class, there was no observable chaos in Sandra's class, when students were first asked to reflect individually on the dilemma questions. This might have been related to Sandra's approach to introducing the task as well as to language issues, as already indicated in Chapter 7. Given that most of the class are 'native' Austrians, they are less likely to have language-related problems (see Chapter 4). It is also likely that the majority of Sandra's students spent most of their secondary schooling (Year 5 onwards) at the Roseggerschule or within the Schulverbund

(School Alliance) Graz West. This might indicate that they have been well enculturated into the school's innovative approaches to teaching and learning. Irene's class, on the other hand, consisted of a colourful multicultural mixture of local children, refugees and asylum seekers (compare Chapter 4) with quite different problems. Many of these children were settling into the Austrian culture and were still getting used to the school-culture.

I believe that it makes sense to presume that the conditions for individual reflection were very different for these two groups of students, and that this might have been reflected in their classroom interactions and in the way they approached individual reflection. Gerold, the physics teacher of Irene's class, pointed out that for him the most salient characteristic of Irene's class was that the students cared for each other and supported each other (compare Chapter 4). Could it be that the 'caring attitude' went so far that 'individual learning' soon became a collaborative affair? Sandra, on the other hand, complained about a lack of community in her class (compare Chapter 4). Students working well individually and quietly are every teacher's delight, however, could it be that Sandra's students were more on-task because voluntary collaboration was not really on their agenda? One might argue, with Wilber, that Irene's students as a class might have reflected a more 'feminine' stance geared towards 'communion' whilst Sandra's students overall seemed to display a greater tendency towards agency (Wilber, 1997).

In the following section, I present Sandra's students' comments about how they experienced the initial individual reflection phase.

STUDENT COMMENTARY

Identification with the story characters appears not to have been a major problem, as Ulli explained to me in her interview, "I was reflecting on the story, what if I had been there, what would I have done?" (U7p64) Her statement illuminates students' identification with the characters in the story.

Daniela, my former student, gave an eloquent and detailed account of how she approached the individual reflection task, "First I tried to think myself into the situation and then I checked, what is going to happen in the future, whether I would do this? And whether

227

or not I would accept the government's offer – How it would turn out in the future or how would it affect the future if I did not accept. I took the better decision, what I thought would be the right one" (D7p17). Daniela added that she took the task very seriously, "If you make a decision you cannot really take it back. If I make a decision now and then find out that it was wrong, that I should have made a different one…then I can't just take it back. It is a weird feeling if you know that you can do something wrong." (D22p25) Ulli supported Daniela's statements by saying, "A dilemma for me is a great challenge. Either you make the right or the wrong decision. Even if you have made the wrong decision, it is important, because we are dealing here with very personal issues." (U29p31)

Paul illuminated a potentially problematic issue regarding the reflection phase, "In the beginning, I wasn't really reflecting on the dilemma, I was primarily responding to the questions but the longer I kept thinking about it and talking about it, the more I started to think about it and then it occurred to me that all that is actually very difficult to decide" (P5p30). Whilst Paul referred to his own 'inauthenticity' at the beginning of the dilemma unit, Julian suspected a more widespread problem with inauthenticity, "With some people, I knew that they would not write down what they were really thinking… I mean of course I cannot know what they are thinking – what I imagined they were thinking [pause] but I still believe they would not write down their real thoughts. However, I was surprised at what they did write down." He added with a broad grin, "In a negative as well as in a positive sense! … If someone has an opinion he will bring it in [to the discussion] and if he doesn't, then he will just write down something anyway!" (J7p33)

228

RESEARCHER COMMENTARY 2003

The questions remains, "Why did some students apparently not respond authentically? Why would students be fearful of writing down their personal thoughts?" I wonder if this problem has occurred to other curriculum planners interested in moral learning. Velasquez tells us that, "The moral standards involved in a person's moral reasoning must be consistent" (Velasquez, 1998). However, the above findings seem to indicate to me that whilst a person is inauthentic in her presentation of her moral reasoning (and thus of her standards), her authentic standards might still be consistent - in other words, we just do not know whether she is in/authentic unless we consult different sources (interview data, portfolio-notes, etc). I wonder therefore, how useful it is to put so much emphasis on the evaluation of moral reasoning and thus of moral standards to the point of putting people into categories of increasing levels of morality, if we cannot be certain that this person is a 'trustworthy' source.

Taking this thought further, is there not a great dilemma for curriculum planners using a dilemma approach given the importance that is placed on moral reasoning and individual reflection in classic dilemma approaches? Why should we engage in this practice if students perhaps only 'write down something', or 'write what they think the teacher wants to hear' or perhaps 'do not write what they think because of fear that the others in the class might not like it'?

To add to my conundrum, Julian explained that a major difficulty for him with regard to individual reflection was that, "I really had to think hard whether or not something was my opinion with all these people around me (J14p25)...what counts as my opinion because after all it was my opinion what I think and what I personally find important and I wanted to present it the way I see it." (J22p25)

RESEARCHER COMMENTARY 2003

Julian added a new perspective – he felt distracted by the presence of other people around him whilst he was trying to reflect on the dilemma question. Perhaps Julian was really asking, "How shall I reflect individually when I am in a group situation?", meaning, "I find it distracting!" Perhaps, on the other hand, he simply wasn't used to reflecting next to other people. This supports my earlier assumptions that voluntary collaboration perhaps did not form part of Sandra's class' lifeworld.

With regard to thinking, all the above student comments indicate that critical thinking was involved: Daniela's detailed assessment of her own decision-making as well as the sceptical comments by Paul and Julian. Critical self-assessment might have occurred in Pauls' and in Ulli's case where both started to reflect on themselves in the dilemma situation.

It seems that, contrary to many students in Irene's class, identification with the story characters was not a real problem for Ulli but rather formed the basis from which she conducted inquiries into her own assumptions. Daniela described in detail how she moved back and forth between different aspects of her thinking, her values and beliefs in order to make a right decision, weighing up consequences of potential decisions. Ulli's and Daniela's statements appear to provide good evidence of critical reflection where students engaged in the process of reassessing their 'old' assumptions in order to make a decision.

The fear of making a 'wrong' decision was an interesting phenomenon. Given that the dilemma unit is (despite all efforts) an artificial facility for practising decision-making without fear of wrong decisions, some students apparently identified so well that they subjectively experienced pressure associated with making a 'right' decision. An alternative interpretation is that students might have experienced (or imagined) peer pressure, "What if I make a silly decision – people in my class (or my teacher ?) might find my response ridiculous?" This might to some extent explain why some students perhaps chose to answer the questions inauthentically (see also Chapter 10).

In his book 'Thinking Critically About Ethical Issues', Ruggiero discusses the role of the majority view as the basis for deciding moral values (Ruggiero, 1997). This made me wonder if some students were inauthentic in their 'thinking' because they were unsure about the majority view at that time: at the beginning of the dilemma unit they could not have known what the majority would think about the issues in question. Perhaps students of that age-group depend so strongly on the opinion of the peer-group that it might cause them to 'just say something' in order to 'be on the safe side'?

STUDENT COMMENTARY

After the dilemma unit, Julian offered a supporting comment by saying, "It was interesting to hear what the other [people] think and one could compare...and also what you are thinking. Your own moral ideas and how this sits with the rest of society, with this class community in this case." (J20p5) For Julian it was apparently important to compare his own opinions with his colleagues.

RESEARCHER COMMENTARY 2003

Summarising we might say that the small selection of student opinions from Sandra's class indicates that the perceived difficulties were quite different from Irene's class. Sandra's students did not mention a lack of agency nor did they indicate that they had problems understanding what they were required to do. Their problems appeared to be rather related to the dilemma decision-making process itself and to exterior circumstances, such as in Julian's case. There is evidence that critical thinking and reflection occurred in both classes, for example, as analysis and evaluation of the situations, and as a sceptical attitude.

EXTRACTS FROM STUDENTS' PORTFOLIOS

The dilemma question was: "Imagine you are Herbert – would you accept the government's offer? In what way would the rumours regarding torture and prison camps influence your decision?"

Daniela wrote, "I would accept the government's offer because then I could continue with my 'hobby' but only as long as the professor would be my colleague. Apart from that, I would be much too scared of prison camps to let that influence my decision."

Maria: I would work for every regime unless it is a right-wing regime or a Nazi-regime. As I know now that what were rumours at the time turned out to be true, I find it difficult to imagine whether or not I would have believed them. But I think that, in any case, I would have found some truth in it and this insight would have reinforced my decision not to work for that regime.

Ulli: I would accept...which I don't believe... I would try to find out the truth about those rumours. If I found that they were true, I would pack my stuff and follow Professor Schubert and continue my work with him. If the rumours turned out to be true we would leave the country and we would continue our work somewhere else.

Paul: No, because I think I could not live with the fact that the government I work for tortures other people and even kills them. No, we hate the Nazis because they are inhumane and we despise violence. In other countries there are certainly also people interested [in our work]

Julian: I would not accept it [the job-offer] because the rumours cannot be rumours only if even Professor Schubert emigrates. I would not support this government, not even for my dream.

RESEARCHER COMMENTARY 2003

Except for Daniela, all students said they would not cooperate with a right-wing government. Daniela's argument that she was too scared of prison-camps to let that influence her decision is very difficult to interpret because by saying that she was too scared she admits that she would have been influenced in her decision-making. Maria argued interestingly that she found it difficult to make a decision as she did not know the 'truth' behind the rumours from her present-day vantage point. Ulli was quite pragmatic – accept yes, but make sure to find out the truth behind the rumours, whilst Julian 'used' the authority of Professor Schubert as reason enough to decide to emigrate. However, only Ulli's and Daniela's argument indicate that they might have engaged with the question on a deeper personal level (critical reflection) whilst Maria and Paul seemingly could not 'enter' the situation in the past whilst still displaying critical thinking in terms of analysis and evaluation of the situation.

SUMMARY OF SECTION 2: THE ROCKET DILEMMA IN SANDRA'S CLASS

As in Irene's class some students, such as Paul and Julian, commented on the apparent inauthenticity of student comments. Their statements provide us with some insider views regarding the authenticity of the written notes: Paul's comment also shed some light on the potential 'inauthenticity' of student comments when he stressed that in the beginning he was answering questions automatically until he realised there was more thinking required. Reading through these comments, I realised that, for a teacher, it is almost impossible to eliminate 'inauthenticity' from students' notes because observation alone by the teacher does not seem to prevent students from faking answers – for whatever reasons. What, I asked myself further, is the value then of using students' written notes for assessment purposes or, as in Kohlberg's case, for measuring somebody's morality levels, if some just 'make up something' to make the teacher happy, or write something they think is expected of them? Is it not that the potential inauthenticity of individual reflection represents potentially a profound dilemma within the dilemma approach? Student portfolio notes showed apparently different levels of engagement with the dilemma: whilst some students indicated that they were reflecting on a personal, critical level (critical reflection) others seemed to have remained at an exterior critical thinking level only.

Review of Part 1: Individual reflection during the first dilemma situation

The individual reflection phase at the beginning of the first dilemma unit in Irene's class was largely characterised by chaotic individual collaboration because of a 'methodological blur' in terms of which pedagogical methods were used to give the instructions to the students. Good working conditions were not established due to the small classroom, noise-levels and the teacher allowing herself to get distracted by individual conversations. In contrast, there were clear instructions by the teacher in Sandra's class and therefore no need to repeat any of the instructions. In Irene's class, possible reasons for the lack of student cooperation might include: disinterest in the story, feeling overwhelmed by a 'new' task, language-difficulties, or a lack of agency because decision-making is at odds with the experiences in the students' own lifeworld. Classroom interactions were focused on caring for each other. In Sandra's class, however, there was little interaction amongst students. Individual students appeared very task-oriented. The overall impression I had of this class was of a group of strong individualists. In Irene's class, a caring attitude appeared obvious during classroom interactions and it also seemed to be mirrored in some of the student comments that expressed 'connection with the tree' (see also Chapters 3, 8 & 9). Portfolio-notes displayed evidence of individual reflection despite some collaboration. The comparison between an African and an Austrian student statement pointed to the Principle of Cultural Relativity: there seems to have been a cultural difference in values regarding parent-child relationship between Austrian students and African students. Sandra's class was almost uni-cultural with no language difficulties involved – this might also have contributed to the smooth running of the dilemma unit. If smooth is best – this was the class! Some student statements and the (lack of) classroom interactions seem to express a tendency towards agency in Sandra's class. Several students reported potential inauthenticity of student comments: fear of making a wrong decision was one of the possible reasons mentioned. Student portfolio notes seem to show different levels of engagement with the dilemma: whilst some student commentaries indicated that they were reflecting on a personal, critical level (critical reflection) others seemed to have remained at a rather exterior critical thinking level. This leads me to the question of whether we are looking at examples of a developmental process? Could it be that the ability to think critically develops before the ability to reflect critically and that some (perhaps most) students at age of 15-16 are not able to engage in critical reflection? The ability to engage in individual reflection might therefore be age- and maturity dependent.

PART 2: INDIVIDUAL REFLECTION DURING THE FINAL DILEMMA SITUATION

Part 2 is organised in 2 sections: Section 1 explores the final dilemma situation during the Tree Dilemma in Irene's class; Section 2 focuses on the final dilemma question of the Rocket Dilemma in Sandra's class. The purpose of Part 2 is to investigate students' individual reflection during the final individual reflection phase before students collaborated on the production of posters and before the final plenary discussion.

<u>Section 1</u>: The Tree Dilemma in Irene's class

After summarising what was happening during the last two dilemma units, Irene then continues the storytelling and confronts the students with the second dilemma:

> *<u>Irene</u>: Peter's parents offer him to cut down the tree himself. What would you do if you were Peter? Would you cut it down or not? And please do not forget to explain why! How do you deal with the situation? Your own ideas, YOUR OWN opinions...*

Irene discusses rules of discourse with the students, given that we had spotted some problems last time, especially with regard to listening to other opinions, and allowing others to finish what they have to say. In the meantime, I distribute copies of the instructions regarding the third dilemma situation.

The students are meant to glue the instructions into their portfolio and to write down their ideas underneath. The students seem much more relaxed this time. I feel more relaxed too especially as the students seem to know what they are required to do. Irene does not have to use up much time or energy to explain what is required or to restore order. Pleasant chatter from the desks, occasional laughter which eventually ebbs away – they all seem to work now and to focus on the task. No silly comments from anyone, no protests. Irene and I move from table to table. With regard to the implementation, I feel that the dilemma approach is working out well at the moment.

> *<u>Irene</u> reinforces: Why would you cut the tree down, or why wouldn't you? The <u>why</u> is important!*

CONVERSATION WITH IRENE AFTER THE FINAL PART OF THE DILEMMA UNIT

Lily: How did you think the second part of this dilemma unit worked out? How did you go...?

235

Irene: I would say, in my view, the second part was much faster...and it gained in intensity."(I-FS2p22-23, 2000)

RESEARCHER COMMENTARY 2003

Irene's comment supported my own impression during the second part of the dilemma unit quite well – the students were working faster. They appeared to be better focused on the task. I believe that students might have been faster because they already knew what to expect and what was expected of them. This indicates that, perhaps, with repetition students can gain the necessary skills to become more efficient dilemma learners.

EXTRACTS FROM STUDENT PORTFOLIOS

Melinda: I would not cut down the tree myself because I would feel guilty that I have cut the tree.

Emma: I would never do that. For me, it is not the point who is cutting the tree but that it gets cut down at all. The fact that it is to be cut at all!

Gregor: I would only cut the tree myself if I first ...[cannot read the writing] the animals because they need the shade. I would build a garden-bench from the wood of the tree.

Damian: This tree is an oxygen-supplier, living-space for animals, shade-provider. If I cut it down, it would be a sin because I would destroy the living-space of the animals and because I have hurt the tree who is alive as well. I would not cut it down!

Fatima: No, I would never cut my own tree – I have grown up with the tree and, apart from that, I have told many secrets about my life to the tree.

RESEARCHER COMMENTARY 2003

The portfolios revealed that students would not cut down the tree, except for Gregor who said he would do it under particular circumstances. Melinda argued, for example, that she would feel guilty. Damian said he would 'commit a sin' because the tree was a living being too. All comments expressed 'connectedness', pointing to a caring attitude. All comments, except for Gregor's, indicate that students were reflecting on their own values, which can be interpreted as critical reflection. However, Gregor's statement points toward critical thinking. In order to arrive at these statements, all students must have analysed and evaluated the situation whilst only some reflected on their own values. Can we presume, therefore, that in order to engage in critical reflection we need to practice critical thinking beforehand? It seems that when engaging in critical thinking one does not necessarily also engage in critical reflection.

STUDENT INTERVIEW COMMENTS

Fatima explained that this dilemma question caused some inner turmoil for her, "…it is not so easy even if it's just a tree – no really, this wasn't easy! It was difficult to think what would I do? And when we had to write down our opinion – I found it so difficult – if I were Peter, what would I have done?" (F17p23) She added, "Exactly where the question was, 'Would you cut it yourself?' I mean, I could never do that! (F28p56). It was not very nice. I had to think long and hard but I still could not find an answer because I would not even let anybody else near [the tree]. I could not do it myself! Certainly not. I am absolutely sure – because if I have lived with a tree for 33 or 35 years – would it not be 'mein Ein und Alles' [German: my one and all] ? (F51p56). Emma argued along a similar line, "I thought I would feel very sorry. I could not do it. Really difficult because it is not just a tree or so…I know that I always get

too attached to things and then I find it difficult to give
something away." (E6p39)

Gregor apparently experienced this decision as very difficult also, "I
would not have allowed this to happen, that the tree gets cut
down. This is a tree that was planted at my birth and it is
therefore my tree. If I am 'ein Leib und eine Seele' [German:
'a body and a soul' = inseparable) then it is as if somebody amputated
my finger" (G24p39)

Melinda made some interesting comments, "Well I don't really
think that the tree dies or so I could not really identify
with Peter that well. It is clear for me that you cannot
always get what you want. There is always something you find
disturbing...(Me16 &17p68) I cannot really imagine that I am so
close to a tree...!" (Me 26p70).

Damian was unhappy about the decision because, "Peter has known
the tree with the tree for 33 years and suddenly the parents
say, we have to cut the tree and it hurts him to cut the tree
(Da4p14)...yes, one should not simply cut away trees. One hurts
their feelings. One does not see their feelings but the trees
inside...how shall I say this...when you cut trees you hurt them!
(Da11p6)...the tree really was his best friend!" (Da2p53)

RESEARCHER COMMENTARY 2003

To me, there is a 'noticeable development' with regard to the depth of students' thinking when I
compare student comments at the beginning of the unit with later in the unit. It seems to me that the
comments have gained in 'reflective depth'. All interviewed students but one reported about the
difficulty of the decision. Especially Fatima's comment illustrates quite well the inner disequilibrium
she apparently went through. In Emma's and Fatima's cases, we can notice self-assessment
exploring assumptions which I would like to interpret as critical reflection. Damian's statement about

the feelings of the tree is also quite remarkable to me. I believe it can be interpreted as profound respect towards living beings.

However, Melinda admitted that she could not really identify with the story character and, after all, she did not really believe that the tree was dying – now this was very interesting because, going back a few pages, she did profess a close connection to the tree and she did try to find a solution in favour of the tree. In her written comments she said that she would feel 'guilty'. So how can we interpret this apparent change of mind? Could it be that she was 'faking compassion' in the first place or could it be that during the interview she was contesting me as a potential authority person and pretending to have a different opinion from what she actually wrote down? Which of the statements reflects her true opinion? When was she being authentic? Given that we cannot find out from her because all my attempts to get hold of her for member-checking purposes have failed so far, let's presume that she was honest in the first place, but there remains a possibility that parts of her opinions are inauthentic.

SUMMARY OF SECTION 1: THE TREE DILEMMA IN IRENE'S CLASS

Compared to the earlier reflection phase in Irene's class, the later one was characterised by less chaos and better conditions for individual reflection. Students reported the difficulty of the task of reflecting and decision-making during this phase. During the interview, one of the students said the exact opposite of what she had written in her written-notes. This can be interpreted as opposition to the interviewer or alternatively as evidence that some students really 'faked it all.' The student-portfolio notes displayed a caring attitude and indicate that some students engaged in critical reflection. It seems that critical thinking may be necessary for engaging in critical reflection, however, critical thinking does may not necessarily result in critical reflection.

Section 2: The Rocket Dilemma in Sandra's class

Sandra talks about concentration-camp prisoners and how they have been (ab)used as "material" – she talks about perpetrators 'getting used' to being confronted with abuse, pain and suffering. This issue touches a very difficult part of the shared history of post-war Austrians – we all have to live with an incomprehensible past, and I believe that these students, provided the Austrian curriculum has some positive outcomes, already have some awareness of it. Sandra describes how Herbert eventually uses people for human experiments because, she explains, he is obsessed with the wish to build a rocket that can fly to the moon and transport people. The human experiments yield many useful results.

> *Sandra: Last dilemma… Think about Herbert's dream, think about the moon-landing and the price that had to be paid. Think also about other problems with science – especially about the abuse of scientific knowledge, example given, in genetics research. The question is now – how far should science [scientific research] be allowed to go? Is it OK to sacrifice a few for the good of many?*

This final comment sparks off some muttering in the audience. "Finally!" I think, "There are some unsolicited discussions!" I am very happy about this development because this indicates to me that the dilemma questions can set off discourse and social interactions, even in a class that apparently displays so few spontaneous, social interactions.

RESEARCHER COMMENTARY 2003

It was very interesting for me to notice that this last dilemma question apparently sparked off some discussions in the class. Perhaps, they were more ready to deal with the issues or the questions just touched something in them. However, the video shows that the students soon settled down and continued to work in a focused manner, even though there were more interactions between them. In the following section, I present some of the written notes.

EXTRACTS FROM STUDENT PORTFOLIOS

Sandra had written the following question on the photocopy:
"Think of Herbert and his dream and the price that had to be paid…How many scientists have great plans – to manipulate the human genetic code, to 'beam' objects somewhere else, to perform nuclear fusion, for example:

240

a. How far should scientific research be allowed to go?
b. Is it appropriate under particular circumstances that some (in Herbert's case prisoners) are sacrificed for the benefit of all mankind? Why? Explain your answer!

Daniela: I think that all that should happen on a voluntary basis only and not like in Herbert's case with prisoners who have to pay for scientific progress. Every human being should be able to decide for him/herself whether or not s/he wants to collaborate because life is every person's right!

Maria: a) I believe that scientific research needs extreme situations to some degree but I believe also that it is possible to have great achievements without, for example, war-related intentions. I believe though that it is legitimate, in general, that a small group of people suffers for scientific progress.
b) [this could be] people who are fond of the idea [to be sacrificed for the rest of humanity] or people who don't experience their life as worthwhile. Example: I know that I am terminally ill so I offer my body for use in experiments.

Ulli: a)[scientific research should be allowed to go] so far as long as nobody must die for it unless s/he wants to die for science.
b) No, not if they have to die involuntarily. Nobody should have to die for the benefit of all humanity because the [person] who dies is also part of this humanity. Nobody should be sacrificed for anybody else.

Paul: a) as long as they [the researchers] don't harm anybody (also no torture of animals]

b) No, based on this reason anybody could get killed, not only prisoners. Apart from that, prisoners are also human beings and thus have a right to live.

Julian: a) never so far that people get killed in any way. Nor should animals or other living beings be slaughtered for scientific research.
b) No, because one human being should not be allowed to determine the death of another.

RESEARCHER COMMENTARY 2003

There was great unanimity amongst four of the five students that people should not be sacrificed against their will for the benefit of scientific research or for the good of all humanity. Everybody has a right to live. There was also the idea that people should have a choice whether or not they want to offer themselves for experiments that might turn out to be fatal. Only Maria defended the 'special' position of scientific research: if it is for the good of scientific progress it can under particular circumstances be warranted to sacrifice a few members of society. She also brings up the suggestion that some people might actually voluntarily suffer because their life isn't worthwhile or because they are terminally ill. These comments express a view that might be interpreted as Utilitarianism which is a strand of moral philosophy. As a form of Consequentialism, it judges the goodness of an action in terms of its outcomes (Goodin, 1993; Haynes, 1998; Pettit, 1993). Without trying to be judgmental here, I have to admit that I started to worry about Maria who had professed that she wanted to study genetics after school, and who apparently thought it was ok for science to 'use' people if it was for the good of all (see also Chapter 10)!

In the following section of the chapter, I explore student comments during interviews. Interviews with Sandra's students brought to fore a variety of topics students apparently reflected on. The students were quite expressive and partly displayed great depth of thinking.

STUDENT INTERVIEW COMMENTS

<u>Identification with victim and 'potential' perpetrators</u>

When I asked students later, how they had experienced this reflection phase, Ulli spoke about putting herself in the victims' shoes, "To reflect on how it would be if I was the one who was subjected to those experiments without my approval (U22p5)." I found it quite remarkable that she did this without prompting by the teacher.

Paul, as I indicated earlier, became aware that there was a problem with trying to uncritically apply our current circumstances to the past, thereby being judgmental about our forefathers, "I think it [the dilemma unit] was good because I mean you do get to think because I mean, it is hard to judge but you get to reflect because, for example, I would have thought that I would almost certainly have continued with my work in that situation because in that situation, I would not have thought that far, because now, in our situation we already know what happened with the Nazis. Because if you were working [then], you did not really know, I mean it wasn't like the whole population of Germany was aware of what was really going on. This is why I believe I would have continued to work (P10p5). ...you don't know enough. It is always easier to talk [now] after something is over" (P11p74).

RESEARCHER COMMENTARY 2003

Ulli's comment fits well with what Mezirow (1990) called reflection on the self. I found Paul's comments to be very brave because they do not exactly mirror the official politically correct voice. He identified with those people who were alive during the Nazi Era and who might have become potential perpetrators, like Herbert in the story. Most other students chose to decide on the basis of their (now) safe and free environment, and basically repeated the chorus of official public opinion, "We would never have done this!" , thereby positioning themselves on the higher moral ground. Paul was criticising that. He admitted that under the circumstances at the time, he might have collaborated although he clearly states that NOW, with all the information people have now about that time, information that was not readily available to our grandfathers or grandmothers, he would not do it.

Paul even has an explanation for his colleagues' tendency to adopt the higher moral ground, "The main problem might be that one does not easily admit to oneself that one would decide in a particular way in a particular situation. It is, of course, difficult to think oneself into the situation and you just don't know how you really would have decided in the past (P13p72)." Paul also has no illusions about his colleagues' apparent 'delusion', "The interesting thing was what the others said, for example, that they would never continue but I think that more than half of them would certainly have continued. It is only that they are not aware of this now (P24p9)."

RESEARCHER COMMENTARY 2003

This is, in my opinion, a very important insight for any young Austrian (or any young person for that matter) – to not simply and un-self-critically adopt a higher moral ground and mimic the official politically correct version without knowing what it was really like then but to try and study the past carefully, learn from it and make sure that it will not happen again.

As Paul summarised, "I don't know for sure how I would have decided at the time" (P25p86).

RESEARCHER COMMENTARY 2003

Paul, as mentioned above, was concerned with decisions made under different circumstances. Critical reflection apparently led to some insights into the context-boundedness of decisions, the historicity if you like. Paul's observations of others might have set off a reflection process during which he was clearly assessing taken-for-granted assumptions and was trying to find a solution and explanations for himself. As Mezirow informs us, reflective learning involves the (re)assessment of assumptions. It becomes transformative when assumptions are found to be distorting, inauthentic or otherwise invalid (Mezirow, 1991). I believe that Paul's comments are a good example of this process.

Reflection on responsibility of the decision-maker

Daniela explained to me what was important for her during the decision-making process "...especially looking at what might happen in the future - if I make a decision, this can be a life changing decision (D14p41)." I asked her whether she felt that, through the decision-making, she had a responsibility for her actions with regard to the future, which she agreed to. Given this responsibility, "It was very difficult because there is always the possibility for a mistake and to make a right decision - it is a funny feeling somehow to make a decision (D21p21)."

RESEARCHER COMMENTARY 2003

It was interesting for me to find that some students are aware of the responsibility everybody has for their own actions. Daniela's comment is a good example of critical thinking in terms of exploring alternatives, consequences, and analysing the situation.

Identification with others

When I asked students after the dilemma about how they experienced the reflection phase, many described 'identifying with a person in a dilemma situation' as one of the most difficult parts. The process was characterised by interest as well as by frustration for those who could not really identify. For me this was interesting because the ability to identify with the other is often regarded as a characteristic of emotional intelligence (see Chapter 11).

Daniela defined identification with others for me, "To think oneself into the situation and make decisions for somebody and the check what the person has really done, [to find] the differences between the character in the story and oneself." (D6p5) Ulli described it like this, "It was interesting because you think yourself into a situation – this can be a different situation as well, not only from the story because in your life there is always a tendency for dilemmas to come up. If I have to think myself into it and I have to assess the advantages and the disadvantages – you somehow learn from this (U8p28)." She added, "… if you continue to do research you destroy human lives or you leave and have to start a new life, or you stay and live with your bad conscience." (U29p31).

RESEARCHER COMMENTARY 2003

Ulli herself states that she believes that it is the assessment of advantages and disadvantages that can lead to learning. She displays critical thinking in the form of analysing alternatives and evaluating the effort, as well as critical reflection through relating the assessment process to her self. Daniela compared herself with the story character and explored similarities and differences. Whilst this includes critical thinking as well (recognising patterns), it points also strongly towards critical reflection – learning about oneself, reflecting on one's self.

Paul who had demonstrated a high level of critical reflection argued that, "It is very difficult to think oneself into the situation because from the outside you're not really in the situation and you can hardly experience the feelings because I don't want to fly to the moon, so I cannot talk about this easily. But there are certainly other issues that would interest me (P8p34)." He added, "I think I cannot think myself into the situation, I don't know what the situation is really like when your family is in danger, and so I think you cannot imagine what it is really like. Perhaps you have a house and a family – one cannot imagine what it's like...(P9p82)."

Maria supported Paul's concerns, "It was very difficult for me to identify with this person or the situation but there are, in my opinion, always several ways and which one I would have chosen, I don't know. I have really chosen the one that I think I would have taken." (M6p53)

RESEARCHER COMMENTARY 2003

Maria, like Paul, expressed difficulties in identifying with the story (characters). We might conclude from Ulli's and Paul's contrasting comments that critical reflection is perhaps not necessarily bound to being able to identify with a story character because it seems to occur in both instances. Perhaps being unable to identify can also lead to a disequilibrium that 'draws' a person into critical reflection on a dilemma.

SUMMARY OF SECTION 2: THE ROCKET DILEMMA IN SANDRA'S CLASS

The final dilemma questions provoked unsolicited communication between Sandra's students, however, they soon returned to their work. Student-portfolio notes indicate that most students would reject scientific research based on involuntary human sacrifices. Most students argued that participation in experiments should be strictly voluntary. However, one student argued that it might be ok if it served scientific progress or if the life of the person was not worthwhile. Her thinking might be interpreted as that of a 'separate knower'. Students seem to have reflected on and assessed their values, which points towards critical reflection. Several themes emerged from the interview data: identification with the victim and the perpetrators, reflection on the responsibility of the decision-maker, identification with others.

Review of Part 2: Individual reflection during the final dilemma situation

Compared to the earlier reflection phase in Irene's class, the later one was characterised by less chaos. The final dilemma question 'provoked' Sandra's students, for the first time, to engage in unsolicited communication. Students in Irene's class reported difficulty with the task of individual reflection and decision-making during this phase. During the interview, one of Irene's students said the exact opposite of what she had written in her written-notes. This can be interpreted as opposition to the interviewer or alternatively as evidence that some students really 'faked it all.' In Irene's class, the student-portfolio notes displayed a caring attitude and indicated that some students engaged in critical reflection. In Sandra's class there was one girl, in particular, who expressed a separate way of knowing. In both classes there were examples of critical thinking and sometimes of critical reflection. It seems that critical thinking is necessary to engage in critical reflection, however, critical thinking does not always result in critical reflection. Individual reflection appears to encompass all of these modes of thinking.

Chapter 9

When self meets other:

Collaborative decision-making

Irene: in my opinion... this part [of the dilemma unit]... *resulted in what I had hoped for: an intensive engagement with the matter and, something I normally can't stand, when everybody is talking over everybody else, but in principle this was still organized... and this was what we had in mind, at least I did, that they confront each other and seriously defend their opinions (I-FS2p22-23)*

INTRODUCTION

Dilemma units, as suggested by Gschweitl et al. (1998), are characterised by alternating phases of individual reflection and collaborative work (Gschweitl, et al., 1998). Students are required to discuss their individual 'decisions' and the 'justifications' of those decisions with their colleagues; in pairs, at first, then in groups of three, four, etc. (sees Figure 7 and Chapter 5). The underlying idea is to engage students in a discourse about the dilemma questions.

The dilemma approach used in this research was the refined version of a teaching approach that was developed during the Red Cross Project (Gschweitl et al., 1998). The approach was originally based on the work of Kohlberg, and Lind, Oser and Althof (who are also Neo-Kohlbergians). Given the influence the Kohlberg framework still exerts in Europe, it makes sense to explore how moral discussions were originally seen within the Kohlberg paradigm. Thus after analysing the data, I returned to the literature on moral education in an attempt to compare my findings with previous work. Kohlberg and his associates had emphasised the importance of moral discussions, and literature on this topic abounds, particularly in the quantitative research field. I was therefore interested in examining the results of other studies and comparing them with my own 'qualitative' findings.

For introductory purposes, to make the reader's interaction with the text easier, and to illustrate the differences between the original Kohlbergian paradigm and 'my curriculum', I give a brief overview of the existing literature on moral discussion within the Kohlberg framework. Beyer informs us that, "Moral discussions consist of a purposeful conversation about moral issues" (Beyer, 1978). According to Berkowitz, moral discussions form a core ingredient of moral education. He elaborates further that it was Kohlberg's student, Moshe Blatt, who explored the use of discussions in moral education and who, in collaboration with Kohlberg, Turiel and Rest, postulated four basic assumptions: (i) the '+1 convention': exposure to reasoning one stage higher (= one of Kohlberg's stages of moral development) results in moral development, (ii) interactions of students at a variety of stages is important for moral education to be effective, (iii) teacher facilitation is essential, and (iv) cognitive conflict is a necessary condition (Berkowitz, 1985). From this Kohlbergian perspective, the goal of moral discussions should be to help students move from one stage of moral reasoning to the next (Beyer, 1978). Silver (1976) elaborated in detail on what a moral discussion within a Kohlbergian framework should look like. He contended that the process of discussing values should avoid moralising. Furthermore, the student should be accepted by the teacher without condemnation, ridicule, etc. The discussion should encourage expression of individuality, and the teacher should also try to maintain a classroom atmosphere conducive to open discussion and exercise care that it does not become unbalanced. Students should be taught to accept the thoughts of others. Each individual should have a right to 'pass'. The teacher should rarely force anyone to participate (Silver, 1976). In case the teacher is still able to remember all the 'should's', s/he should also monitor every single student's stage of moral development so that s/he can prompt a student's comment with a question that promotes thinking at the next higher stage of moral reasoning (i.e., the '+1 convention') (Berkowitz, 1985). All that amidst the turmoil of a heated debate! There are more 'shoulds' that I will <u>not</u> include in this context, however, Silver's text provides even more prescriptions for teachers but without providing an empirical background for his claims. Based on my own experience, I would like to suggest that the practice of this theory appears to be impractical for classroom teachers, as Brambring et al. have also noted (1991).

In the context of this thesis, I prefer to regard a moral discussion in Nash's sense as a 'postmodern dialectic conversation'. Nash's "moral conversation' is inspired by Hans-Georg Gadamer's work (Nash, 1997). Gadamer regarded dialectic as a nonmanipulative, undominated conversation that resists in advance presumptions of what counts as good and true (Gadamer, 1984). In my view, the teacher serves as a support person during small group discussions and as a facilitator and moderator of the plenary discussions. However, s/he <u>should</u> not worry too much about stages of moral development but rather focus on the classroom interactions and the discussions (Gschweitl et al., 1998).

In this chapter, I am not so much interested in what the moral discussion <u>should</u> have looked like according to a pre-established framework but rather what it <u>did</u> look like to me in the context of the two classes I observed. I was interested in the following questions:

- What happened during the dilemma units in Irene's class and in Sandra's class with regard to discourse?
- What was the quality of the discourse and of the discussion?
- How did the students and the teachers experience the discourse phases of the dilemma units?

Before I embark on the 'tour back to the classroom', I regard it as important to bring to the fore a personal bias with regard to the interpretation of the data.

Given that I have been trained as a communication consultant and facilitator, one of my interpretive horizons is derived from communication theory and practice.

From a communication theory point of view, I think it is important to mention several basic assumptions with regard to 'groups' and interpersonal communication. Interpersonal communication serves primarily two purposes: to gain information about others and to give information about us. This leads to an exchange of content and relationship messages at the same time, including a variety of verbal and non verbal cues (Borchers, 1999d). In this chapter, we are looking at two types of interpersonal communication: <u>small group communication</u> and <u>large group communication</u>, known as <u>discussion</u>. According to Borchers, a <u>small group</u> is defined by the number of participants. It should have at least three (and no more than twelve to fifteen) members. The size of small groups allows participants to communicate freely with all other members of the group. This is not possible in larger groups where a moderator – in our case the teacher - is needed. Groups develop norms about discussion and leadership. Group members develop roles that affect the interactions of the whole group. This is usually referred to as group-dynamics. Furthermore to count as a group, the members must have a common purpose and collaborate to achieve a common goal. This goal holds a group together through conflict and tension (Borchers, 1999e).

When I observe group-interactions I do so not only in my role as a science educator but also as a communication facilitator, thereby monitoring group dynamics. I have therefore included this perspective in my interpretations.

Purpose and organisation of the chapter

This chapter aims at answering the following research question: <u>Do dilemma stories have the potential to initiate 'discourse' that may lead to moral learning?</u> I attempted to answer this question by drawing from different data sources, such as: classroom observations, video-tapes, student interview data, teacher interview data, and posters produced by groups of students. I made several attempts to record the conversations of individual groups whilst engaging in discourse on dilemma questions, however, I failed to obtain usable audio-recordings. The background noise levels were much too high making students' voices were unrecognisable. Therefore, I abandoned the idea to include recorded group-discourse, except those episodes that I recorded through my field-notes or that can be reconstructed from the videos. For crystallisation purposes, I have contrasted Irene's class with Sandra's class wherever possible.

As in Chapter 8, I have used different fonts to identify the different voices and lenses used to explore this phenomenon: Book Antiqua was used for the narrators voice whilst HELVETICA was used for the participant observer's voice at the time of the fieldwork in 2000. Arial Narrow was used for researcher commentaries in 2003, summaries and reviews. *Monotype Corsiva* was used for direct speech during classroom observations. Courier was used for students' post hoc commentaries and Tahoma illustrates teachers' post hoc perspectives. As in Chapter 7 and 8, verbatim interview quotes are referenced as follows: initial of the pseudonym of the interviewee, followed by reference number and paragraph number (e.g., F23p2) to allow for the audit trail. The chapter is organised in two parts:

- Part 1 explores the phenomenon of 'moral discussion' in Irene's class
- Part 2 focuses on Sandra's class.

Each part of the chapter consists of three sections each presenting examples of discussion-phases in the course of the dilemma units:

- Section1 presents the poster-preparation in small groups.
- Section 2 examines the poster presentations where the small groups interacted with the rest of the class.
- Section 3 investigates the plenary discussion.

PART 1: IRENE'S TREE DILEMMA

Section 1: Poster preparation in Irene's class

During a meeting following the first part of the dilemma unit, Irene and I had discussed the organisation of groups. We had analysed the course of the unit and discovered that group organisation was a crucial issue that determined the amount of time 'lost'. This time, Irene had developed a 'sophisticated' system for mixing students.

Irene has organised groups of five. She has compiled a list of names beforehand in order to avoid delays.

1. *Irene (reads out from the list): Manuel, Alois, ...*
2. *Manuel: Oh no!*

He does not look impressed, rather a bit frustrated. I believe Irene has purposefully put Alois and Manuel in one group because Manuel was one of the students who had expressed his annoyance with Alois' comments repeatedly.

3. *Irene: ...Fatima, Igor, Imelda*
4. *Various students: Can we please swap...?*

But Irene does not allow any discussions about group comfigurations. Students seem to realise that it is useless trying to discuss the unavoidable and swap seats. Each group has received a large piece of paper and marker-pens. I notice that the organisation of groups works much better this time. Irene introduces the task...

5. *Irene: Same questions. Exchange your views and prepare a poster which you will present to all the others!*
6. *Various students: Oh no!*

Obviously, they do not like presentations. I observe a group of five students (Attila, Emma, Melinda, Eva and Susan) working on their poster. A few comments are already written there. This part of the dilemma unit should initiate social interactions through an exchange of ideas as well as through the creative activity of designing a poster. In this group, the collaboration seems to work very well...

7. *Emma: Well I don' know how we shall write this...*
8. *Susan: But this is easy, first you write that you would not do it because you could not say "Good Bye" to your tree, and then you write that you would do it because then you could say "Good Bye" to your tree. Makes sense?*
9. *Emma: Well, yes and no...*
10. *Emily from the other table leans over: But shouldn't we write about why we would cut it down ourselves if we had to?*

Melinda shrugs her shoulders – I am unsure why: is it because she does not know what to do or is it because she does not understand Emily's question? However, I notice (once again) that collaboration in this class extends beyond the immediate group. Irene notices that help is needed with Emily's group. She comes to their desk and talks to the students, reading and paraphrasing their poster. She adds...

11. *Irene: What is missing here, are a few comments about how you have come to these solutions – how you were talking to each other!*

COMMUNICATION FACILITATOR COMMENTARY 2003

By mixing groups together randomly, Irene had mixed together students who first had to negotiate group dynamics such as roles within the groups. Poole (quoted by Borchers) developed a model of group development, arguing that group development is often more complicated than generally assumed: groups jump back and forth between three tracks: task, topic and relation (Borchers, 1999c). When teachers engage their classes in collaborative work, they need to be aware that all these processes are happening whilst students are expected to work on the task. In the group of Manuel and Alois, one could almost expect conflict from the outset, given the complicated nature of their relationship, as indicated in Chapters 8 and 9. Fatima describes, later in this chapter, the conflict-laden communication in their group. However, in the other example, the group of Emma,

Susan and Emily, I observed a group that was trying to achieve a compromise – obviously they had failed to arrive at a consensus and had decided not to push it any further.

TEACHER COMMENTARY

<u>Irene:</u> What I really liked was that they did not necessarily find a consensus in their groups but that they were still talking intensively about the issues. They interacted very strongly. From my observations I would like to add that I think that it was better to organise the groups using their names.

RESEARCHER AND COMMUNICATION FACILITATOR COMMENTARY 2003

Irene had developed a sophisticated strategy of connecting student names to numbers and then randomly (or sometimes not so randomly) mixing the groups together.

BACK TO IRENE

<u>Irene:</u> The group organization, I think, works best the way I did it: each student gets a number – you say these students belong together and 'basta' [Italian for...] – that's it! I noticed that sometimes the usual pairs got together. There were some [students] who approached me and said, 'I am still with such and such...' I think that they understood what it was all about. After that they did not really want to [go together with their friends any longer]." (I-FS2p119-125)

RESEARCHER AND COMMUNICATION FACILITATOR COMMENTARY 2003

I am not so sure about Irene's last comment because there were a number of complaints. However, given that I experienced problems with the audio-recordings it was invaluable to me to have Irene's 'professional' observations available about how the group discourse worked out. She witnessed lively discourse in the groups, as did I. And as Bruffee explains so aptly, "Closely monitoring students small group discussion is self-defeating" (Bruffee, 1993). I had exactly this experience – either the students lowered their voices to inaudible muttering or they stopped the conversation until I moved on to a different table. Whatever I tried to get a 'closer insider view', I was unsuccessful. However, with regard to the group organization, Irene's system at least on the surface seemed to work.

In the following part of the section, I explore students' experiences of the group discourse. Apparently not all students were happy about Irene's organization strategy.

STUDENT COMMENTARY

Apart from criticising the topic of the dilemma story, Melinda also criticised the constellation of the groups and the poster presentations. In relation to the groups she said, " If we had been able to choose our own group - that would have been much better. I think that it is more fun if you can be together with people you like than with those you don't like." (Me7&8p6)

However, confrontation of one's own opinion with the opinions of others is the main purpose of involving students in a group discourse situation. In some cases, these confrontations led to arguments, as in Fatima's group, "It was very difficult for me because we had several arguments. This is normally never the case - it was very hefty." (F45p26) She continued, "Some said, 'Why are you arguing - it is only about a tree!' But [then] we just started arguing again." (F73p26) Damian also reported conflicts, "Yes, there were [problems], it was difficult to come to a solution in our group." I asked him further, "...but you tried?" "...to find a solution? Yes!" "But this did not work out?" "No, this did not work out." (Da9p35-41)

Emma, Fatima's best friend found that, "Some people had very different opinions to mine and somehow I was starting to think, 'Ok this is what he says, maybe I should take a closer look at this?' This is not as bad an opinion as I thought –

257

one continues to reflect upon it." (E1p18) Emma also pointed out that for her there was no problem with group-work because, "In the group, I feel free enough to express my own opinion." (E10p15)

Alex who regarded himself apparently as a 'class clown' experienced the group-work like that, "Most of the time the others were just laughing about my responses but in the end we arrived at an agreement – because I was taking it seriously then." (A13p38-39) He was aware that because <u>he</u> did not take it seriously in the beginning the group could not arrive at a common solution. Alex added, "Apart from me, [they] all had the same opinion – but I always added 'my mustard' [to add one's mustard (literally) = seinen Senf dazugeben; Austrian German slang ~ to add unsolicited 'ideas or opinions']" (A16p42).

Comparing opinions sometimes had broader social ramifications and led to Fatima's insight that her friend does not always subscribe to the same ideas. " Sometimes it [the group-work] was surprising and disappointing at the same time. When I think now that my best friend had a different opinion to me although I have known her for so long, and I know this may sound ridiculous but I was disappointed that she wrote, she would cut down the tree. Then I was really surprised and I thought, 'Hey this can't be!'. " (F76p28) This 'shocking' insight led Fatima to reflect critically on the situation and on her own thinking, "...when I was at home there were several moments when I thought, 'Why doesn't she have the same [opinion] I have?' I mean I didn't ask her about it but I am still thinking about it…I mean it is clear that not everybody has the same opinion but you are starting to ask yourself, why? Perhaps this person has a good reason for this but I myself did not find this reason…" (F2p34). Fatima found out that comparing with others was of limited help for developing her own opinion, "It wasn't very helpful either because everybody had their own opinion." (F60p62) With regard to the discussions within the small groups,

Gregor said, "In our case, there were some animated discussions and on the poster. We then wrote down all the different opinions because we could not come to a common solution." (G17p42) Later he added, "If we had done all that individually, we would never have discovered that there are so many different opinions. Only the teacher would know about that and nobody else in the class. You never find so many reasons yourself because you never hear an opposite opinion." (G12p51)

RESEARCHER AND COMMUNICATION FACILITATOR COMMENTARY 2003

I have to admit that I had almost expected negative reactions from the students regarding Irene's group-organisation scheme. There had been complaints during the dilemma unit already, so I presume that Melinda was not the only student who found this issue disturbing. One reason for the dislike of the 'artificial' groups might have been that students were required to re-negotiate their social roles which of course requires more effort than with people you know well. Observations and student interviews indicate that there was a lot of conflict in some groups and different ways of conflict resolution: some groups chose to compromise others found a consensus, yet others continued to disagree. Damian's comment, for example, portrays a group that showed perseverance yet could not arrive at a common solution – so they decided to accept the different opinions (compromise). There were intense discussions in Fatima's group also that required some conflict resolution, however, her comments indicate that they did not arrive at a common solution of a kind. Given that conflict resolution is necessary to achieve the common goal, it involves social skills: the group discourse in a dilemma unit seems to provide ample opportunities to practice interpersonal communication skills, such as negotiation, listening to others, and learning to find compromises. Emma gives us an idea of how conflict resolution worked for her: she apparently tried to approach different opinions from an open-minded perspective. We can interpret her role in her group as that of the 'gatekeeper' – a person who keeps the communication channels open (Borchers, 1999f). Emma also explained that the confrontation made her reflect on her own opinion, which suggests engagement in critical reflection. Alex indicated that he was aware that he was responsible in the beginning for the problems in his group. This seems to indicate that he also reflected critically on his own role which might have been the role of the 'recognition seeker' – a person who calls attention to himself (Borchers, 1999f).

Fatima's insight into the difference in opinions also highlights that critical reflection can potentially follow confrontation with other opinions. This fits well with the definition of critical reflection by Mezirow who said that we re-assess our own assumptions when we have found them to be constrained in some way (Mezirow, 1991). In Fatima's case, it seems that the 'shocking' surprise that her best friend did not share all opinions with her 'awakened' her and caused her to reflect critically on her own thinking (e.g., 'why didn't I find that reason?'). Gregor raised an interesting issue by pointing out that it is normally only the teacher who knows about the variety of different opinions in a class. Perhaps it is because students do not often exchange opinions in this way or perhaps because some opinions dominate others?

SUMMARY OF SECTION 1

Irene had organised the groups, and there were some protests from the students about the group configurations. From the outside, the groups appeared to be collaborating well. However, Melinda expressed her dismay about the group configurations in her interview. Fatima and Damian described the conflicts in their groups and how they solved them. Alex identified himself as the reason for the problems in his group at arriving at a solution. Gregor elaborated on the multitude of opinions in a class and that normally only the teacher knows about it. Fatima's sudden insight that she does not always share the same opinions with her friend caused her to reflect critically on her own thinking and on the relationship with her friend. Overall, it seems that the confrontation of individual opinions during the group-work phase caused some of the students (Fatima, Emma, Alex) to reflect critically on their own assumptions which can be interpreted as critical reflection in Mezirow's sense. This can potentially lead to transformative learning and thus perhaps to moral learning. From a communication facilitator perspective, I found that Irene's group-compositions led to some conflict-prone groupings such as Alois, Manuel, Igor, Fatima, and Imelda in one group. The other group around Emma and Susan demonstrated a compromise approach by acknowledging different perspectives without forcing the issue of a consensus. Some of the problems might be related to group dynamics at the beginning of the collaboration with people one does not know well. However, conflict is not negative in itself but it is actually necessary if we want to encourage mutual challenging and the cancellation of unshared biases and presuppositions which again is necessary to induce critical reflection. A certain degree of heterogeneity of groups is therefore an essential component of the social set-up of small group discussions. Groups that are too homogenous tend to succumb to 'groupthink' because there is not enough articulated dissent or resistance (Bruffee, 1993; Mezirow, 1991). There are examples of this type of group in Sandra's class as described later in the chapter. I therefore assume that conflict is welcome and necessary, however, it is up to the teacher to decide when to intervene and to decide when this conflict is getting out of hand.

Section 2: Poster presentation in Irene's class

Irene has organised sticky tape, which allows each group to stick their poster to the wall for everyone to see. (Transcripts and translations of the posters can be viewed in Appendix 11 and on the CD). I am very much looking forward to this stage because this is where usually much of the social interaction happens and where the individual opinion is most likely to be confronted. Group C is the first group to mount the stage. Irene reads their poster and summarises:

12. *Irene: OK so you would cut down the tree yourselves?*
13. *Emily: Uhmm... We could not reach an agreement!*
14. *Alex: If it absolutely had to be done I would do it myself because I would not want anybody else to do it and I would keep a little piece of the crown so that the turtle has something to hide under and as a keepsake.*

Comments from the audience regarding the turtle. Noise levels rise, they are talking over each other. Irene reminds them of the rules of discourse, such as listening to others, allowing other people to finish their sentences, allowing for different opinions, no swearing, etc. She tells them furthermore that there will be a discussion at the end of the unit where they can express their thoughts in greater detail.

15. *Alex adds: If I cut the tree myself I can relive what the tree and I have gone through together.*
16. *Irene: Yes, this is of course a possibility!*
17. *Emily: I would not cut down the tree because I cannot imagine that if someone feels so closely connected to a tree... that he could cut it down.*
18. *Irene: Why not, do you think?*
19. *Adam (calling out from the audience): Because he does not want to appear like a murderer – of the tree that is!*

RESEARCHER AND COMMUNICATION FACILITATOR COMMENTARY

Adam raised an interesting issue, 'feeling like a murderer' or 'feeling guilty' indicates that this is how he might feel in the situation therefore suggesting identification with the person in the story. As one can only feel like a murderer if one has acknowledged the status of plants as living beings with the 'right to live' this indicates that Adam might have understood this concept. He argued with a view to the consequences of the action (Ethic of Consequences) whilst Emily seemed to argue rather in terms of connectedness and care, for example, "If you are really connected to your tree you will not cut it." This not only suggests 'connected knowing' but also an Ethic of Care. Alex seemed to be willing to minimise harm by doing it himself, thereby suggesting a caring attitude that, nevertheless, was characterised by succumbing to outside pressure. In this example of discourse, students argue from the viewpoints of 'connected knowers' implying an Ethic of Care, while others apply an Ethic of Consequences (Belenky et al., 1998).

POSTER PRESENTATION CONTINUED

Figure 12: Students presenting their poster

The next group presents their poster. Group D consists of Manuel, Alois, Fatima, Igor and Imelda. Irene summarises the issues raised on the poster and points out that it seems as though each of them had made a comment but they had not managed to find a common solution. The students agree. Given the group

262

configuration, I imagine that the discussion was not easy as there had been clashes previously between Manuel and Alois regarding Alois' unproductive comments that apparently angered Manuel.

> 20. *Fatima: I would never cut down the tree myself because I have grown up with it and have confided many secrets in it.*
> 21. *Alois (with a stoic expression on his face): I would probably cut it myself!*

Irene chuckles …I think it is the 'probably' that sounds quite funny considering Alois' comments during the last unit where he made it so clear that he would even 'blow up' the tree if necessary.

> 22. *Imelda: I would also cut it down myself because I would not want others to cut my tree.*
> 23. *Manuel: I think that if the parents have planted the tree they are responsible for destroying it.*
> 24. *Irene: Ah, so you think, because the parents have given life to the tree they have the right to take it away?*
> 25. *Alex (from the audience): What does that mean – you cannot shoot your child if you don't like it anymore?*
> 26. *Manuel: No, I think it is their business to sort this out.*

Muttering in the audience. I am not sure whether everyone understands what Manuel really means. I think that he regards it as unfair of Peter's parents to burden all the responsibility on him. The students around me try to make sense of what he has said and start discussing the issue amongst each other.

RESEARCHER AND COMMUNICATION FACILITATOR COMMENTARY 2003

Manuel's comments are interesting inasmuch as he promotes a view that appears to be quite principled – if the parents have caused the problem they need to solve it. He apparently does not emphasise relationships as Imelda seems to do. He appears to have analysed the situation critically and concluded that it is the parents' business. His comment can be interpreted as that of a separate knower (critical thinking) and the ethic he seems to promote can be interpreted as an Ethic of Consistency (Belenky, et al., 1997; Haynes, 1998). Alex, however, seems to have reflected on the issue of why we treat plants differently from animals. This also matches some of his comments presented in Chapter 7. and in Chapter 10. To me, this part of the dilemma unit worked well, the poster-presentation provoked comments by other students and supposedly also a reflection process on other people's opinions, which was reflected in the discussions that flared up every now and then. Irene handled this situation very well in my view. She led the process by asking questions, and she reacted to group processes and to comments from the audience.

ALOIS AGAIN

27. *Igor (summarises a common negotiated group-statement): We would not manage to kill the tree because it is a part of us!*
28. *Alois: I would therefore suggest blowing up the tree!*
29. *Irene: You and your 'blow-up' comments! But I can see that you* [as a group] *have taken my comment about the quality of your discourse seriously – you have written down that you have had a lively discussion, yet have not arrived at a common solution.*

RESEARCHER AND COMMUNICATION FACILITATOR COMMENTARY 2003

Whilst Igor presented a group-statement that seems to express connectedness, Alois tried to undermine the situation by making yet another 'silly' comment. This was the first time Irene actually directly reacted to it but not for long. She did not give him her attention longer than the duration of one sentence, immediately moving back to the issue of the metadiscourse. This seems to have been a good way of dealing with Alois: recognising his presence, however, not allowing him to take over. From a communication facilitator perspective, Alois apparently played several roles within the class: The role of an 'aggressor' with his class mates – someone who attacks other group members - and the role of a 'recognition seeker' especially in his dealings with Irene. Later in the chapter, we will also see him in the role of an 'energiser', especially during the plenary discussion – a person who stimulates the group to a higher level of activity (Borchers, 1999f). Given Alois' impact on the class interactions, the reader might wonder why I did not interview him – I considered interviewing either Alois or Alex at the time and I decided for Alex. One might argue that this decision was wrong, however, retrospectively I believe that talking to Alex, who experienced the dilemma units as worthwhile, was valuable.

TEACHER COMMENTARY 2003

Irene: Alois, the blond guy who was sitting close to Alex for most of the time. Handsome fellow but occasionally he drops these weird comments, always slightly militaristic. I have to say though that he virtually fled the military academy...
Lily: He what?
Irene: He was supposed to attend the military academy in Wiener Neustadt, according to his parents' wishes. He did, however...
Lily: Is that a secondary school at all?
Irene: Yes, it is a gymnasium, a military gymnasium (see Chapter 3). See, I forgot to mention that [to you] but this really came out immediately, did it not?
Lily: You are right! Probably this is how they solve problems in his home: Solution to the problem? – "Let's blow it up!" (I-FS1p143-153)

RESEARCHER AND COMMUNICATION FACILITATOR COMMENTARY 2003

I have to admit I was surprised by what Irene had told me about Alois. I had interpreted his behaviour as that of a child that simply seeks attention all the time through provocative comments. I also thought he might be allowed to perhaps watch violent movies at home, however, his lifestory about his problems at home, having to flee from a school he did not like, made me see him differently and more in perspective. It just pointed out to me once again how important it is to study the context of the students before putting them into categories. Alois is a problematic student in Irene's class – no doubt about that – but it was also important to know why he might be like that.

STUDENT COMMENTARY

Emma found it apparently difficult to cope with Alois' arguments. She considered them simply silly, "[I was not angry] …often only when somebody came up with a stupid argument, like the whole 'blowing up business' but they don't take it seriously really,… [then I asked myself] 'why?' . " (E24p33)) On the one hand, Melina pointed out, "I did not like the group work and I did not like the poster presentations." (Me6p6) On the other hand, she promoted an open-minded approach to other people as long as they fully accepted her own opinion, "Everybody has their own opinion…and others have to deal with this because everybody has their own opinion which has to be respected by others."(Me10p59) Fatima reported that the classroom discourse during the poster presentation challenged her, "Some said, 'one can simply cut down the tree' but I don't know, I had a different opinion." (F63p26). ..Everybody was saying something different (F64p26). ..I mean, it is clear; everybody has a different opinion (F65p34)...Some thought it is only a tree but even if it's only a tree, it is not that easy." (F66p23)

Whilst some students seemed to experience the discussion in the groups primarily as a challenge, Gregor found something positive in the poster-preparation phase. He said, "If we had done all this individually only and just handed in our portfolios, it would never have come out that there are so many different opinions." (G12p51)

RESEARCHER AND COMMUNICATION FACILITATOR COMMENTARY 2003

There had been some concerns when students heard initially that they were required to present their posters to the rest of the class. In my experience as a communication facilitator in Austria, I have often met students who felt too embarrassed to present in public. Speaking or presenting in public is not something that is widely promoted in Austrian schools. I have noticed a great difference in this regard with Australian schools – here in Australia students are often required from an early age onwards to perform in public which I think helps them to feel more secure 'on stage'. I interpret Melinda's comment therefore as grounded in (hidden) cultural values – humility is a characteristic tacitly promoted in Austria. Somebody who acts in the limelight is often regarded with suspicion or as a show-off. Melinda's comment supports what she said in Chapter 8 about her belief that parents should always respect their children's wishes. Emma and Fatima described how some comments challenged them profoundly. Gregor, on the other hand, seemed to have understood the potential benefits of the classroom discourse by recognising the variety of opinions. Fatima described the situation where many different opinions collided and she found herself caught in the middle. Confronted by opinions she did not really like, she reflected on her own.

SUMMARY OF SECTION 2

Summarising, I can say that this phase of the dilemma worked out very well. The poster presentation phase required students to present the results of their small groups discussions to the plenary forum of the class. The presentations and the ensuing discussion showed evidence of consensus, compromise and unresolved conflict whereby a decision to disagree counts as consensus also (Bruffee, 1993). In some cases groups were eager to defend their positions against comments from the audience, an observation Bruffee (1993) has made also. In some situations when the discourse about the posters almost escalated into a plenary discussion, Irene managed to restore order by acknowledging students' ideas and simultaneously pointing towards the discussion at the end of the dilemma unit. Irene excelled in this phase in her teacher-role by recognising student thoughts and concerns through paraphrasing and asking questions about the appropriateness of her interpretations. She welcomed and encouraged dissent from the audience presuming that this might engage students further.

Student commentaries indicated that some students felt intimidated by the poster presentation. This could be a cultural problem as Austrian schools do not often promote presentations in public. Although teachers increasingly try to incorporate public speech and public presentations into their curriculum, the underlying 'anticipation' is still there amongst the students. Other students commented on the difficulty of coping with 'silly' remarks, such as Alois' blowing up comments. One student in particular pointed out that the public discourse illuminated for him the multitude of different opinions that existed previously unknown to him. Fatima reported that the collision of different opinions caused her to reflect on the issues in greater depth. It offered an opportunity for discourse between students in the audience, students as presenters and the teacher. Students showed evidence of having engaged in moral reflection on the dilemma questions. Discourse on the posters was initiated by re-visiting the group-discourse that led to the poster preparation. Given the problematic nature of my audio-recordings, Irene's idea of introducing a metadiscourse with the students about the process of producing the poster proved to be very helpful. Students apparently felt safe enough to make potentially 'unsafe' comments. Their arguments included statements that pointed towards an Ethic of Consistency, an Ethic of Care and an Ethic of Consequences. Some students appeared to be 'connected knowers' whilst others seem to demonstrate a tendency towards critical thinking which is the hallmark of 'separate knowing' (Belenky et al., 1997; Haynes, 1998). There was evidence that the discourse initiated critical reflection in some students. Summarising, we can say that the discourse may have resulted in critical thinking and critical reflection for some students. Overall, the poster presentation phase provided an opportunity for discourse and social interaction amongst students as presenters, students in the audience, and the teacher.

Section 3: Plenary discussion in Irene's class

Irene continues the storytelling. She tells the students that Peter realised that he could not save his tree so he cut it down himself. Some students appear to be disappointed by the outcome of the story, others look even sad. There is mumbling that indicates that some are dissatisfied with the ending of the story – they might have preferred a happy conclusion.

Irene presents them with the final dilemma question, "<u>Do you think that Peter has done the right thing by cutting down the tree by himself?</u>" She asks them to add the instruction-slip to their portfolio and reflect on the question. Irene asks the students to form a circle and explains that we will now enter a new phase, the plenary discussion. She explains the term plenary and reminds them again of the discussion rules. She summarises the results of the poster-session, pointing out that there were obviously two groups of opinions: one group that was for the cutting of the tree and others who were against this course of action.

> 30. *Irene (repeating the final dilemma question): Thinking about all that… what can we say now – did Peter do the right thing by cutting down the tree?*
> 31. *Manuel (sounding annoyed): I think there would have been many other solutions….*
> 32. *Emma: I think that it is superfluous now to ask whether he has done the right or the wrong thing because obviously he has already done it. It is not the question of a decision-making process any longer.*
> 33. *Irene: Do I understand you correctly, you think that it is better to have made <u>one</u> decision – even if it turns out to be a wrong one - than none at all?*
> 34. *Emma: Yes, exactly!*

I feel that Emma, Imelda and Manuel are disappointed about the finality of the situation, and that nothing can be changed.

> 35. *Susan: I think that every person needs to decide [for him/herself] what he or she thinks about his/her own decision because it depends on how I feel [one feels] about it. I might be unhappy about my own decision, asking, "Why did I cut down that tree?" And somebody else might come along and say, "Thank God, she has cut down that tree!*
> 36. *Fatima: Yet, the question remains – was the decision the right one?*

RESEARCHER AND COMMUNICATION FACILITATOR COMMENTARY 2003

Apparently, Susan realised that two people can have different values and she seemed to have understood that feelings are involved when we think about discussions we have had. Fatima's comment, on the other hand, indicated that she seemed to have accepted that, although there might be an acceptance of different values, one should still ask questions about the rightness or wrongness of an action. To me, these are signs of (beginning?) ethical awareness that, to me, include becoming more aware of the consequences of one's actions and of one's responsibilities.

BACK TO THE DISCUSSION

Irene moves on to the next question: <u>Was it fair towards the tree to cut it down?</u>

37. *Manuel: Absolutely not – the tree has accompanied him, has comforted him and so on, and Peter has never done anything in exchange...*
38. *Amelia: I think that nobody should take away the life of any living being - be it a human or a plant.*
39. *Imelda: I do not think that the tree, if it knew about what the parents had said before, it would be mad about Peter cutting it down.*
40. *Alex: I think it is better that Peter cut it down himself*
41. *Manuel: Yes but what if you have a cat and the cat falls sick and have to put it down – I would not do it myself?*
42. *Irene: Yes but please consider that tree is not an animal – does this make a difference?*

Hefty discussion and screaming matches follow. Irene reminds them once again of the discourse rules but it seems obvious that, on this occasion, the noise is related rather to being fully involved than trying to disturb.

RESEARCHER AND COMMUNICATION FACILITATOR COMMENTARY 2003

Manuel argued that it was unfair towards the tree because Peter had only taken but not given anything back – this is consistent with what Manuel had said earlier, representing an Ethic of Consistency. Amelia recognised the right to life for every living being, regardless of whether it is a plant or an animal or a human. I interpret her comment as that of a connected knower promoting an all-inclusive view of care. Imelda, on the other hand, seemed to have projected a human image on the tree assuming that the tree could think like a human being. Interesting also is the discussion between Alex and Manuel: whilst Alex wanted to minimise the bad consequences for the tree, Manuel was principally against the cutting of the tree, comparing this act to putting down a sick cat.

CLASSROOM DISCOURSE CONTINUED

Irene seems to feel a need to re-establish some order so that students can voice their opinions. She does this by acknowledging their involvement.

43. *Irene:* I am very impressed about the multitude of arguments you are throwing at each other but could we please do this in a more orderly manner so that we can actually understand what is being said!
44. *Susan:* I think that the main difference is feelings – animals just have more feelings than plants!
45. *Manuel:* I too believe that humans love animals better than plants because they can show love for humans!...they can express feelings.
46. *Irene:* Plants have been shown to express feelings too when listening to Mozart they virtually hugged the loudspeakers so obviously they do react to vibrations and stuff but not as quickly as we do.

RESEARCHER AND COMMUNICATION FACILITATOR COMMENTARY 2003

From my experience, the above scene is one of the rare events in science classrooms where the students and their teacher discuss 'feelings.' I find it remarkable that, through the discussion and the classroom discourse, students arrived at the core of the issue by themselves: humans feel closer to animals because they can show affection, whilst plants do not seem to 'live' because we rarely notice their movements – their world and their reality is just much slower. It was not the teacher who taught this to the students – it was a student who pointed it out to the other students. I dare to speculate that this insight might have had a thought-provoking effect on some students, especially coming from a colleague. Could it be that dilemma discussions actually promote emotional intelligence (Goleman, 1997)? I discuss this question in further detail in Chapter 11. Irene, as the moderator, had directed the discussion in that direction but primarily through questions. She apparently tried to accept the students' views, and she even managed to relate them to biological knowledge.

ALOIS AS A DRIVING FORCE OF THE DISCUSSION

47. *Alois:* Mrs Rock, Mrs Rock I would like to say something
48. *Alex:* Yes something about blowing up again, isn't it?
49. *Alois:* Hey, Alex what's wrong with you? What is it with you and 'blowing up' things?

RESEARCHER AND COMMUNICATION FACILITATOR COMMENTARY 2003

This scene was very interesting for me because Alex and Alois sometimes mutually reinforced each other in the classroom when they were bored and wanted to entertain themselves. In this case, Alex was involved in the discussion and was seemingly annoyed by Alois' 'explosive' comments. However, Alois did not simply put up with Alex's remark, but immediately reflected it back to its source. Alois, on the other hand, seemed annoyed with those students who showed concern for plants' and animals' lives or simply with those who took the dilemma unit seriously.

Alois launches a counter-attack…

> 50. *Alois: I bet you if you walk across a meadow and step on a few plants you don't give a toss about it. When you have your Wiener Schnitzel or your pork roast on your plate, you won't lament about animals. What is this?*

Indicating his colleagues might be hypocritical does not go down too well with his colleagues. Uproar in the classroom. Discussions flare up across the room. Hands fly up in the air. Many want to comment on Alois' argument. One of the African students, Youssi, even stands up to draw Irene's attention to him. Now, the atmosphere is explosive – 'tension is in the air!' Youssi argues that living beings sometimes must make sacrifices for other living beings.

RESEARCHER AND COMMUNICATION FACILITATOR COMMENTARY 2003

This comment could be interpreted as representing a Consequentialist Ethics view, a Utilitarian stance to be more precise: sometimes it is better to sacrifice a few if it benefits the majority. Alois played several roles in this scene: the role of the 'aggressor', the role of the 'energiser' and, I would say, he also played the devil's advocate. Through his provocative comments, he was driving the discussion and Irene was busily trying not to lose leadership. Her role during the discussion was that of a 'referee' – non-judgmental and not directly involved in the content side of the discussion.

BACK TO THE DISCUSSION

Alois' comment results again in hefty discussions amongst students. Irene tries to control the situation, by relating Youssi's comment to biological content knowledge. This strategy seems to work quite well.

> 51. *Irene: I would like to add – from what we have learned about plants so far – if I walk across a meadow and I step upon a plant – I might hurt it or damage it but is it necessarily dead?*

Some students shake their heads in reply...

> 52. *Irene: Well, can we then compare this situation at all with our spruce* [the tree]*? Is it not certain that the spruce will be dead after it is cut down? Yes, of course!*
> 53. *Imelda: I think plants should have the same right to live as animals!*

Again, many students want to be heard. Manuel has had enough of waiting, gets on his skateboard and skates to the middle of the room to be heard. It is fascinating to watch this scenario unfolding!

> 54. *Manuel: Mrs. Rock, but isn't it the normal course of nature that we must eat and therefore we must kill plants?*
> 55. *Alex: And with animals – even animals eat and kill animals. Ever thought about that? Is that murder?*
> 56. *Susan: No, it is only murder if one does not make use of the killed living being.*
> 57. *Irene: I would like to add from a biological point of view that plants could be regarded as natural resources. In most cases, we do not actually kill the plant but use only parts of it whilst with animals we need to kill them to be able to eat them. This is actually a reason why Buddhists do not eat meat. They are very careful not to harm other living beings. In general, we can say that not many people think much about plants and plants' rights and we should ask ourselves, "Why?"*
> 58. *Imelda (looking sad): Because plants do not scream and they do not cry!"*

Different views are clashing, voices rising; some students are standing up on their chairs to be seen. Josef, Irene's co-teacher, observes all this with a fascinated look on his face, "Hey, this works really well!" At this moment, the bell rings and finalises Dilemma 1. The students continue the discussion, ignoring the bell. Irene has to ask them to leave the library because other students might need the room. Irene looks exhausted and collapses in a chair.

RESEARCHER AND COMMUNICATION FACILITATOR COMMENTARY 2003

This final discussion was characterised by students trying hard to make their point and with Irene, in her role as a referee, trying to keep the situation under control by acknowledging the different opinions and linking them to content matter. She kept the discussion going by asking provocative questions. Alois, who usually excelled by disturbing the classroom discourse, in this case, promoted it through his controversial statements, which he brought forth fearlessly. The students appeared very engaged and raised issues about the influence of feelings when attaching value to an 'object'. The students themselves worked out that it is probably due to the lack of communication between plants and humans that we feel detached from plants and rather attached to animals. The issue of a lack of observable emotions was also discussed. It was also the students who raised the question of killing for the sake of survival – is this a right thing or not? If my goal was to engage students in a reflection process on moral issues, then I daresay it appears to have worked out. Statements of students included arguments that represented an Ethic of Care, an Ethic of Consistency and an Ethic of Consequences.

In the following part of the section, I would like to explore further the experiences of the teacher with this discourse-based teaching style.

TEACHER COMMENTARY

Irene: My God! This was really demanding!
Josef (her co-teacher, who was observing the discussion replies): Yes, but it worked so well, it was worth it!

In a feedback meeting shortly after the plenary discussion I asked Irene:

Lily: How did you go with the moderation of the discussion?

Irene: Of course, the moderation was enormously energy consuming – to calm them down again! [To deal with] the noise level costs me incredible energy which is potentially related to my age, perhaps..., but I always managed to calm them down again, so it wasn't really a problem. ...[however], I could feel it. It gave me great pleasure. It was interesting to observe. Still, it is not easy to moderate, not when you have pro-opinions clashing with contra-opinions. To give them the opportunity to confront each other and simultaneously help them to find common ground again – this was relatively exhausting! (I-FS2p31-32)

Lily: You said last time that you experienced holding back your own opinion without judging as a great challenge. How did you go this time?

Irene: I still tried not to make valuing statements. What I experienced profoundly was...that sometimes there were comments that simply showed incorrect know-how and basic knowledge – I cannot simply cut off the crown and re-plant it. This was when I felt obliged to intervene (I-FS2p34-35).

Lily: How did you deal with answers that were diametrically opposed to your own opinion?

Irene: Well, I mean you really have to shut up – sometimes I really had to bite my tongue! Especially in order not to interfere with an unfolding argumentation the students themselves might discover. Being the moderator this was the last thing I wanted! I mean if somebody had asked me about my own opinion then I could have told him but nobody asked me – they were too busy with their own opinions. Thus it doesn't matter at all! (I-FS2p37-41)

Lily: As a moderator it usually is helpful - if one gets an unacceptable response - to immediately play it back to the group and let them handle it for you...

Irene: Yes, that sounds right....like, 'what do you think about this'...or I tried to do it like that, 'Did I understand you correctly - is this how it was for you?' or 'Let me summarise...'

Lily: Yes, exactly! (I-FS2p43-53)

RESEARCHER AND COMMUNICATION FACILITATOR COMMENTARY

Irene proved very skilled at moderating the discussion without being openly judgemental towards students' opinions. She managed to overcome difficult situations by relating the discussion back to biology content as well as by playing controversial statements back to the group. I have the feeling it worked out quite well in terms of engaging students in reflection and in dialogue. I have to admit that, at the beginning, I was not very convinced that this unit would lead to such animated discussions. Thanks to discussants such as Alex, Daniel, and Alois with his provocative comments, but also to several girls, such as Imelda, Fatima, Emma and Susan, the discussion developed into a lively, animated, and for some students quite passionate event. The meetings with the teachers following the dilemma units, as with the example above, served to reflect on the course of the dilemma unit and plan for improvements. Dissent was openly welcomed by Irene and even encouraged. She did not try to get Alois, as the 'lone dissenter', in line. Instead, she left it to the class to deal with his provocations. As Bruffee puts it, "Wise teachers trust the negotiating process over time ... to bring dissenters within the boundaries of what is currently regarded as acceptable (Bruffee, 1993). Thus, the fear of using collaborative learning because of losing 'problem-students' appears unfounded – provided that the problem-student's perspective does not represent the class norm.

Having explored the teacher's experiences with moderating the discourse phases, I now turn to students and their impressions.

STUDENT COMMENTARY

Emma described the emotional roller coaster involved in the confrontation with other opinions, "When we started the discussion, things got pretty intense and I felt angry. If somebody came up with a counter argument I was thinking, 'What shall I say now?' This really involved feelings – there were always ups and downs, it was never the same." (E22p30)

Fatima found it quite difficult to deal with some of the other opinions, "Sometimes I could not even listen [to other opinions]"(F74p26).

Listening to others was not the only problem she experienced, "I raised my hand very often but I found it difficult to make myself heard." (F21p37). Thus, making herself heard or maintaining a voice presented Fatima with yet another challenge. She indicated also that she was worried about the potentiality of having an opinion that is unique, "...If you say it is ten against ten…but what if I am the one with a completely different opinion" (F46p37). And she added, "Everybody has an opinion and even if it is sometimes not that important, it is still difficult to maintain a voice." (F22p37)

However, for Emma there was a clear advantage of having the opportunity to practice this type of discourse at school, "I think it is much better to be confronted in the safe environment of a circle than unprepared in real life." (E9p48). For Gregor, the discussion meant being confronted with people who apparently have an open mind and with others who seem to be less willing to change their mind. He said, "I think, some [students] were very stubborn and with those you cannot discuss [an issue] very well [with them] because they don't see anything, but others who are more open-minded with those you can discuss much better with because they can accept other opinions." (G18p15). However, Gregor appreciated about the discussion phase that, "...you could hear other people's opinions and I also liked that we discussed these." (G14p6) I asked Gregor, "When you say, this is an opportunity to hear other people's opinions, do you mean this is not the case normally?" He responded, "Yes, but not through discussing it with the whole class - this is much better." (G5p9). "You not only hear the opinions of your group members but also of the whole class. You get a different impression..."(G10p6).

RESEARCHER AND COMMUNICATION FACILITATOR COMMENTARY 2003

Emma's comments seem to show very well how intimately connected was the rational discourse in the discussion with emotionality. She also summarised quite well what it was like for her to be in that dilemma situation whilst being confronted with many competing ideas – what shall I do? What shall I say? - and the emotions that come with these reflection processes. In Fatima's case, it was more about being fearful about the possibility that one might become an outsider if one voices a different opinion. Might this be the answer to the question raised earlier with regard to Emma's comment that students often do not dare speak their opinion? Fatima's comment indirectly supported Emma's suspicion – there might be some students who think that their opinion is not important and fail to maintain a voice. Gregor's comment seemed to indicate that he believed he might be able to change other students' opinions. Gregor's comment indicates that even though group work already exposes a student to other ideas the effect of a plenary discussion is yet stronger. This can be interpreted as what Vygotsky termed the Zone of Proximal Devlopment: I may be ready to understand more as a group member than I would be able to understand by myself alone (Bruffee, 1993). Gregor also appreciated that other opinions were also discussed and not simply presented.

This is an interesting comment because it indicates that discussion might be an avenue for teachers to involve so-called problem students for whom this learning style seems to speak.

SUMMARY OF SECTION 3

The plenary discussion phase in Irene's class turned out to be an animated and passionate event in which one student even used his skateboard to make himself seen and heard. Some students had apparently realised that there are always a number of different values and opinions involved. Fatima suggested that one needs to question in any case whether an action was right or wrong, thereby suggesting a growing ethical awareness. Issues of the right of life for plants, animals and humans were discussed. Furthermore, students also explored why humans tend to attach a lower value to a plant's life and they worked out that it had something to do with being able to show emotions and affection for humans that determined our attitude towards plants. I was impressed by the results of this discussion especially as Irene's 'biological' input was minimal – it was the student interactions and discourse that had them arrive at these quite fundamental insights. Alois who resisted joining in with the mainstream opinions operated as the 'devil's advocate' and provoked his colleagues through his statements. His colleagues attempts to get him in line provided enough 'fuel' to keep the discussion going.

Review of Part 1

Irene had organised the groups for the <u>poster-preparation phase</u>. As expected, there were some protests from the students about the group-composition. However from the outside, the groups appeared to be collaborating well. On the other hand, Melinda expressed her dismay about the group-constellations in her interview. The exchange of opinions apparently led to conflict as described by Fatima and Damian. They also described how they tried to solve these conflicts. Alex identified himself as the reason for the problems in his group arriving at a solution. Gregor elaborated on the multitude of opinions in a class and that normally only the teacher knows about it, whilst for Fatima the confrontation led to the sudden insight that she does not always share the same opinions with her friend. This seemed to have caused her to reflect critically on her own thinking. Overall, it seemed that the confrontation of individual opinions during the small-group discussion phase caused some of the students (Fatima, Emma, Alex) to reflect critically on their own assumptions, in Mezirow's sense. This can potentially lead to transformative learning and thus perhaps to moral learning.

The <u>poster presentation</u> resulted in discourse between the presenters, the audience and the teacher – some comments were contested by the audience. The discussion was passionate and students appeared to be involved. Alois, one of the so-called problem students, kept the discussion going through provocative comments. Some students described their emotional involvement in the process. Irene excelled in this phase in her teacher-role by recognising student thoughts and concerns through paraphrasing and asking questions about the appropriateness of her interpretations. In some situations when the discourse about the posters almost escalated into a plenary discussion, she managed to restore order by acknowledging students' ideas, and simultaneously pointing towards the discussion at the end of the dilemma unit. Some student comments indicated that students felt intimidated by the poster presentation. This could be a cultural problem as Austrian schools do not often promote presentations in public. Although teachers increasingly try to incorporate public speech and public presentations into their curriculum, the underlying 'anticipation' is still there amongst the students. Other students commented on the difficulty of coping with 'silly' remarks, such as Alois' 'blowing up' comments. One student in particular pointed out that the discourse during the poster presentation phase illuminated the multitude of different opinions that existed unbeknown to him. Summarising, I can say that this phase of the dilemma worked out very well. It offered an opportunity for discourse between students in the audience, students as presenters and the teacher. Students showed evidence of having engaged in reflection on the dilemma questions. Discourse on the posters was initiated by re-visiting the group-discourse that led to the poster preparation. Given the problematic nature of my audio-recordings, Irene's idea to introducing a metadiscourse with the students about the process of producing the poster proved to be very helpful. The poster presentation phase thus provided an opportunity for discourse and social interaction amongst students as presenters, students in the audience, and the teacher.

I approached the findings through three analytical lenses: (i) three types of ethics (consistency, care and consequences) as suggested by Haynes (1998), (ii) the concept of the connected, the separate and the constructed knower as suggested by Belenky et al. (1997). (iii) two types of student thinking (critical thinking, reflection, critical reflection) as described in Chapter 9. Students' arguments included statements that pointed towards an Ethic of Consistency, an Ethic of Care and an Ethic of Consequences. Some students appeared to be connected knowers whilst others seemed to demonstrate a tendency towards critical thinking which is the hallmark of separate knowing (Belenky et al., 1997; Haynes, 1998). There was evidence that the discourse initiated critical reflection in some students. Summarising we can say that the discourse resulted in critical thinking, and critical reflection. Student comments apparently gave evidence of the existence of separate knowers and connected knowers who argued for different types of ethics: ethics of care, consistency and consequences.

The plenary discussion phase in Irene's class was a passionate event during which students discussed issues of the right to life for plants, animals and humans. Furthermore, students also explored why humans tend to attach a lower value to a plant's life and they worked out that it had something to do with being able to show emotions and affection for humans that determines our attitude towards plants. As Irene's 'biological' input was minimal, it was through the student interactions and discourse that they arrived at these quite fundamental insights. Alois operated as the 'devil's advocate' provoking his colleagues.

Irene found it difficult, at times, to hold back her opinion. She moderated the discussion very well using questions and paraphrasing to direct the course of the discussion. She experienced this type of teaching as demanding though rewarding. She also had to remind herself not to make valuing comments to students.

We may therefore summarise that it appears that conflict as the result of heterogenous group compositions can serve as the driving force for critical thinking, critical reflection and therefore potentially, for moral learning. Thus, in dilemma teaching conflict in small group discussions can be expected and perhaps should be promoted, but it is up to the teacher to decide when the conflict is getting out of hand. This requires the teacher to be aware of the group dynamics, especially at the beginning of the collaboration.

PART 2: SANDRA'S ROCKET DILEMMA

Section 1: Preparing and presenting posters

Sandra profited from Irene's previous experiences and planned the organization of the groups well in advance. The organisation of the groups worked well - however, some groups found it difficult to communicate at all.

ULLI AND JOHNNY: CONFRONTATION

Sandra organised groups of four and five: The students are partly seated around tables, others occupy the floor. Sandra has distributed large pieces of paper and marker-pens. Again, most students work in a very focused manner. Sandra hardly ever has to reprimand anyone. Suddenly, amidst the peace and quiet, we can hear loud voices: Ulli and Johnny. Ulli seems very excited – she screams at Johnny and we can gather that she does not accept his opinion. Sandra tries to mediate. The following story is drawn from my research journal and backed up by video-analysis:

Loud argument from the stage of the library. It is obvious that there is a problem with one of Johnny's opinions. Sandra, at first, tries to sort out the problem by arguing that every opinion counts as an opinion, that there is no right or wrong answer. Johnny, "*Tell this to those guys*" pointing with his head towards Julian and Ulli. A fourth girl, Susanna, is sitting about three metres away from the rest of the group – she seems to try not to get involved at all whilst Julian is attempting to mediate. Ulli refuses to have Johnny's comments on the poster. We learn that he has argued that he thinks that people waiting for their execution could be used for human experiments because their life was as good as over anyway. Ulli, on the other hand, argues that this cannot be accepted on the poster. "*Only over my dead body,*" she exclaims passionately.

Sandra finally realises that what is going on might be part of an important learning process so she leaves them to deal with the situation themselves. Julian tries an interesting strategy – he takes on the role of a mediator and interprets to the two opponents what the other person 'really' means. It is very interesting to watch and to listen to.

ULLI'S COMMENTARY

In some cases, comparison led directly to a conflict-situation as in the case of Ulli's group. She explained, "We tried to… the three of us who were of the same opinion, …to put everything into one sentence, so that everybody could express their opinion. The problem was Johnny who thought that it was OK to use somebody who is waiting for his execution for human experiments." (U 24p17) Ulli added, "[Our collaboration] worked well apart from the fact that the group did not work well because Johnny more or less saw the whole things as a joke and he was making fun of those in prison cells, to use them for experiments" (U31p5) This attitude resulted in the clash between Ulli and Johnny, "If you're in a group that thinks realistically and not only nonsense then it is certainly not too bad, but, like in my case,…it just didn't work! We were three for and one against!" (U32p13)

Ulli described how she approached the conflict resolution, "I first try to explain my own point of view and if I still don't understand why somebody is thinking in a particular way, if I don't find out why he has this opinion, then I try to add-in new aspects in order to convince him of a different perspective." (U25p21)

RESEARCHER AND COMMUNICATION FACILITATOR COMMENTARY 2003

What Ulli is describing here sounds not so much like conflict resolution but like an attempt at manipulating Johnny into changing his mind. She did not mention that the discussion made her reflect on her own views for a moment. The problem in this group was obviously that the viewpoints of some group members were diametrically opposed – not only slightly different. The values were apparently too different to be ignored. It was interesting to watch the group's conflict resolution: Ulli's 'conflict-resolution scheme' seemed to contain three main components – clarifying her own position, trying to find out about the other person's position and his/her reasons for it, and then trying to convince the other person of her own opinion if she does not like what she hears. When this did not work, Julian came to the rescue by trying to mediate – unsuccessfully as we witnessed in class. Ulli's comments, on the other hand, verify what I witnessed during the poster preparation phase: she tried to convince Johnny and simultaneously rejected his opinion. One important issue that should not be forgotten at this point is what Sandra had told me about her class before the project started, as described in Chapter 3. The group dynamics in Sandra's class were quite difficult with two girls dominating the scene: Maria and Ulli. These two girls apparently determined who was 'in' and who was 'out'. Johnny according to Sandra, was definitely 'out' because he did not share their values. He appeared content about his role as an outsider in the class – he had his own interests including drinking beer with friends and riding a motorbike which apparently was unacceptable to the girls. I think that one should keep this background of self-chosen non-communication in mind when we interpret the conflict between these two students. I presume there was much more going on under the surface than we could detect from the outside. Given that Johnny steadfastly refused to be interviewed by me, I had to rely on Ulli's interpretations of the event backed up by Julian's perspective.

It was also very interesting to find out why she reacted so emotionally to Johnny…

"Angry – I was angry that someone talks so carelessly about human lives as if this person did not count for anything. I think, the generation before me [they cannot change what they did]…we can still change things but when some of us talk like

283

that, …like they don't care at all, then I get very angry
about this." (U13p24)

However, the argument during the dilemma unit was not the end of the debate.

THE AFTERPLAY

Despite her anger, Ulli apparently kept somewhat of an open mind. She told me that Johnny came to see her the next day and informed her that he had changed his mind. Referring to Johnny's changed attitude, she said, "I was really touched when he [Johnny] approached me the next day and said that he had changed his mind (U16p64)." She also explained to me the reasons for her heated reaction the other day.

ULLI'S REASONS

"When others talk about human lives, just making fun, so that someone in an executions cell can be used for human experiments, then I cannot accept this!" (U12p21). She even went further, "When I am absolutely opposed to something then I will not integrate this" (U 24p17). Was there a lack of tolerance noticeable in her comments?, I asked myself. Although, for Ulli it was clear that her efforts to convince Johnny were (at least partly) fruitful, "But this then caused Johnny to change his mind about this issue" (U14p5)

WHAT HAS ULLI LEARNED FROM THE CONFLICT?

Ulli showed some self-awareness when asked what she thought she had learned from the unit, "…that I listen to different opinions, respect them and not to draw premature conclusions has always been clear to me – on a trial basis so to speak, like trying in the dilemma units to do the right thing..." (U26p45) Apparently, Ulli was aware of what she still had to learn but, as she said, "on a trial basis" – it was not yet the real thing, or was it?

Summarising the group work situation, Ulli said, "Reflecting individually was better than in the group because I don't really like group work as such because I would much rather rely on myself and like to do things on my own." (U20p13) Ulli admitted to being more of an individualist when it came to collaborative learning. I wonder how much her individualist attitude contributed to the argument? Or was it the class history which we do not know much about?

ANOTHER GROUP MEMBER'S VIEWPOINT

A different view on the same issue came from Julian who tried to mediate between Ulli and Johnny in the conflict situation, "In our group, the opinions were very overlapping except for Johnny who immediately cut himself off..." He had also noticed Johnny's change in opinion, "He had a different opinion on Friday" (J23p41). I asked Julian whether he was referring to the "discussion" between Ulli and Johnny. He replied, "Yes, they [Ulli and Johnny] don't really get along well." He elaborated further, "Johnny, in the following, adapted his opinion to ours. He came down from his high horse, so to speak, and stopped presenting it in such a drastic way, a little bit different. In this form, even Ulli could accept it, his opinion." Julian interestingly enough interpreted Johnny's behaviour as condescending and extreme. He contended, "But there were conflicts all the time" (J24p49).

RESEARCHER AND COMMUNICATION FACILITATOR COMMENTARY 2003

Ulli's argument with Johnny provided a good insight into how group-work can go wrong. If you have strong individuals such as Ulli, who apparently find it difficult to accept other opinions, and Johnny, who despite the opposition stood to his opinion, conflict-resolution from the outside is needed. Obviously, Julian's attempts were not overly successful. Given the history of the group dynamics in that class, it might not have been a good idea to 'lock' Ulli and Johnny together in a group, however, perhaps they both needed that conflict to tentatively start reflecting critically on themselves as evidenced by Ulli's later comments and Johnny's partial change of mind. Using Benne and Sheat's framework for identifying roles in groups (Borchers, 1999c), one could argue that Johnny might have been playing the role of a 'blocker' - somebody who deliberately resists movement by the group. Ulli's stance, on the other hand, could be interpreted as the role of the 'dominator' because she was unwilling to accept Johnny's opinion and she apparently asserted control over the group by trying to manipulate him through persuasion. This is in accordance with Sandra's descriptions of her class earlier, describing dominant behaviour of Ulli. Julian could be regarded as the 'harmoniser' who tried to mediate differences between group members (Borchers, 1999f). I believe, however, that the argument in this group would have been reason enough to intervene as a teacher. Seeing that the group did not work well, the teacher could have nominated an independent leader, for example, somebody whose role it is to moderate the group's interactions on a small scale. Julian might have been a good candidate but he lacked authority in the group. This could have come from the outside through intervention by Sandra.

OTHER STUDENT COMMENTARIES IN RELATION TO THE GROUP WORK

One major focus of the group-work was for students to compare their individual ideas with those of others. Julian told me that, "We could compare a little bit what the others are thinking and what we ourselves are thinking (J3p5)." And he elaborated further, "Your own moral values and how this fits with society at large – our class community in this case." (J4p5) He apparently valued the opportunity to compare his opinion with others on the grounds of evaluating how he stands with his opinion in comparison with the rest of the class.

Maria gave an account of how her group went about comparing opinions, "First some people spoke about their opinions then others spoke about theirs and in the end we tried to find a solution" (M13p37). She added, "Sure, [we always have to] compare, I think that you always have to compare opinions. It is difficult though with, for example, person X to talk about it because I am aware that it is not important to him!" I asked further, "Do you find this disturbing?" "Oh, Yes", came the immediate reply. "Has a person actually had a different opinion than you would have expected?" I asked. I was surprised to hear her answer, "No!" (M7p69)

Julian, on the other hand, explained that the comparison of opinions led him to try to remember some of the other comments because he thought they were valuable, "I really liked what Ulli and Gudrun had (J5p53)…the others in my group had something similar to me...overall there were some really good opinions throughout the class that I tried to keep in mind (J10p53)." Julian overall seemed to have appreciated the opportunity for comparison whilst for Maria this was apparently not an issue.

Maria seemed concerned about the group-constellation, "I think that, for example, with people who I absolutely hate, who I don't get along with, I do not work well with automatically" (M24p43). "There were different groups – it was very informative and simply fun with people who I accept and respect, [it was] fun to talk about their opinions, more fun than with people who I can't stand" (M3p9) Apparently, Maria distinguishes clearly between the ones "she likes" and the ones "she does not respect". This sits well with her earlier comments. She points out the "pointlessness" of group-work, "Because these are issues we have to deal with anyway and not like this in groups especially in 'organised' groups, where we don't know each other, we don't like each other and together somehow…because if we want to talk, we do that anyway!" (M4p9) Maria seemingly restricts the number of 'respectable' people and dismisses the necessity of discussing issues in 'organised' groups. However, her comments support my earlier observations that Sandra's class has some difficult group dynamics. I asked Maria, "Was the group composition a factor influencing your wellbeing or a factor influencing your dislike?" She agreed, "Yes, because the result is very different in this case" (M15p63-65)

RESEARCHER AND COMMUNICATION FACILITATOR COMMENTARY 2003

Maria made an interesting point here – the result of her work was reportedly dependent on the factor of her well being within a group. This raised several questions for me about group-work: should it be conducted if students are strong individuals and do not like to engage in group-work in general? On the other hand, should students necessarily always be allowed to choose their own group-members in order to avoid conflict? Is it not sometimes the conflict that brings about an opportunity to learn from each other, as demonstrated in Ulli's and Johnny's case? I have to admit that Maria's harsh comments about people she does not respect and people she hates were difficult to digest during the interview. Again, her comments seem to identify her as a strong critical thinker and thus as a 'separate knower' and individualistic thinker. The question for me is – should it not be that especially students like Maria should have plenty of opportunity to practice social skills of collaboration even though they might not 'like' it in order to prepare them for later in life when they might have to be part of a team? I also regard it as interesting that Ulli who, according to Sandra, tended to dominate the class interactions together with Maria, found it equally pointless to engage in collaborative learning. In contrast to Maria and Ulli, for Julian group-work was a welcome opportunity to compare where you stand with your own opinions and values. He apparently tried to remember some of the comments because he regarded them as valuable.

BACK TO THE STUDENT COMMENTARY

Group-work was one of the major concerns of many students in Sandra's class a point that was expressed by Ulli, "[I like it] only if I don't have to do something I don't like to do, for example, all that group-work where you have to discuss things - I don't really like

288

to talk about what I think. I think if I don't have to tell
that all the time, how I see something then that's OK."
(U1p47-48) She apparently was not prepared to share her private thoughts with
others. As she had said before, "Reflecting individually was better
than in a group because I don't really like group work as
such because I would much rather rely on myself and like to
do things by myself" (U20p13) She described herself here as an individualist
who liked to work independently.

Another issue to consider is that of 'groupthink' that was brought up by
Paul who suggested that, "I find that in a group one's own opinion
often does not come across because opinions get suppressed if
one is in a group, if there is one in the group who has more
to say. I think that group-leaders often simply force their
own opinions and this does not show then what individual
people are thinking" (P15p22). He added, "We were collaborating
quite well in our group. We really had the same opinion all
along", said Paul, "Although of course you never know whether or
not this was the real opinion." (P3p70)

All these group-related issues also raised the question for me as to where
more potential moral learning was likely to occur – in groups that had differing
opinions with conflict occurring or in groups like the one Daniela was describing,
"Apart from the first question we were all of the same
opinion in our group" (D1p29). I asked her, "How well, do you think, did
the others accept your opinions?" She replied without hesitation, "Yes, they
were [accepted] too." (D12p35-37)

RESEARCHER AND COMMUNICATION FACILITATOR COMMENTARY 2003

It seems that there is a pattern emerging: the two dominant girls, Maria and Ulli, loathed group-work.
Perhaps, it was not only due to the group configuration, as described earlier, that Ulli and Maria
experienced the group work as so difficult but also through their own strongly developed individual

agency? Paul who appeared to be part of the group around Maria and Ulli also criticised group-work. It seems appropriate to question his authenticity in this case – perhaps he was giving in to groupthink himself?

On the other hand, given that teachers have a duty of care towards every student in a class – is it fair towards a student to expose him/her to group-work if s/he is not prepared to engage or to speak about him/herself in public? Are we not actually exerting unwarranted pressure on a person's individuality? Is it not ultimately incommensurable with an Ethic of Care if we insist on all students conforming and participating in a group-work situation that potentially pressures a person? Some might argue that if we don't challenge them and nobody else ever will then they will never learn how to deal with others. True, however, the dilemma remains – if we plan a curriculum that requires students to speak about themselves in public if they are not prepared to do so voluntarily, are we not, as teachers, acting unethically?

Paul was obviously referring to group-processes due to group-dynamics that again might result in 'inauthentic' results of group-collaboration. As teachers, I think we should consider this aspect when examining the results of group-work – the results might actually reflect the thinking of some dominant group leaders or otherwise represent 'groupthink'. According to Borchers (1999c), groupthink refers to faulty decision-making: a group does not consider alternatives and they desire unanimity at the expense of quality decisions.

Daniela's group seemed to be almost too harmonious for my taste – no conflict, always of the same opinion. This groups appears to be too homogenous which may result in a lack of conflicting opinions (Bruffee, 1993). If moral learning is in any way connected to the quality of the discourse we have with others, I wonder how much moral learning was occurring in groups where there was basically not much discourse happening. In my view, Daniela's almost too perfect group is also a potential candidate to be suspected of groupthink.

SUMMARY OF SECTION 1

Sandra's class appeared to inhabited by strong, dominant individuals such as Ulli and Maria. Ulli had seemingly demonstrated an unwillingness to compromise in her conflict with Johnny. Julian's attempts to mediate had no effect. However, the conflict apparently led Johnny to change his extreme positions at least partly and caused Ulli to the at least theoretical insight that she should become more tolerant towards others. Maria, on the other hand, made the result of her work reportedly dependent on the factor of her well being within a group. Perhaps Ulli and Maria experienced the group-work as so difficult because of their own individual agency? In the light of this strong individualism, should the teacher conduct collaborative learning experiences at all if students do not like to engage in group-work in general? On the one hand, is it not the conflict that sometimes brings about an opportunity to learn from each other, as with Ulli and Johnny? On the other hand, if teachers have a duty of care towards every student in a class, is it fair towards a student to expose him/her to group-work? Are we not actually exerting unwarranted pressure on a person's individuality? Questions of fairness, of an Ethic of Care and of our responsibility towards teaching for life seem to clash. I can see several dilemmas here that a teacher or curriculum developer ought to address – perhaps further research in this area is needed?

Other students, such as Julian, experienced the group-work apparently as a welcome opportunity to compare 'where you stand with your own opinions and values'. He apparently even tried to remember some of the comments because he regarded them as valuable. Paul was suggesting that a phenomenon that could be interpreted as 'groupthink' might tinge the results of group-collaborations and 'inauthentic' responses might be the result. Some groups that are almost too harmonious and homogenous, as with Daniela's group, seem to be more prone to groupthink than groups with a lot of conflict. If a group does not experience any conflict, and there is always the same opinion, this could be an alarm sign for the teacher to look more closely into the group dynamics. Again, it is up to the teacher to decide when to intervene and what to do.

Section 2: Poster presentation

Several students come forward and position themselves around the blackboard. I am particularly interested in the next group because I can spot Ulli and Johnny amongst the group members…

> *Ulli: How far should scientific research be allowed to go – well, we were basically all of the same opinion – today, not so last time!*
> *Manuel: Humans should not be involved in scientific experiments – in principle nobody has the right to decide about a person's life.*
> *Sandra: Can you please illustrate for us where you had the conflict last time?*
> *Ulli: Johnny you explain!*
> *Johnny: Well, I was thinking last time that it is better if a few people die of a disease than let's say ten thousand.*

> *Sandra: Have you thought about one disease in particular?*
> *Johnny: No!*
> *Sandra (to Ulli): But you had thought of a particular disease?*
> *Ulli: No, no! My point was that someone is being forced to die for the "good of all". It was the "good of all" that I found so difficult to deal with!*
> *Sandra (to Johnny): So, you thought last time that it was OK to use people under these circumstances?*
> *Johnny: Yes!*
> *Sandra: OK, So what has caused you to change your mind?*
> *Johnny: Well, I have been thinking…if I was one of the victims, I would not like it.*
> *Sandra: Aha, so you changed your mind because you thought if you were one of them you would not like this situation?*
> *Johnny: Yes, exactly!*
> *Sandra: This was the turning point for you. As far as I remember, you also had another argument about prisoners on death row…*
> *Johnny: Yes, and I still stick to that one!*
> *Sandra: Can you please elaborate this argument for us?*
> *Johnny: Well I said that if someone is a prisoner on death row their life is virtually over anyway and they can be used for experiments.*
> *Ulli (adds with an annoyed undertone): Because their life is somewhat worthless anyway…*

Muttering in the audience. I think it is very brave of Johnny to admit so openly to his opinion even though he has had problems with it last time. Apparently, he feels safe enough to do this, which speaks for the 'climate' in the class. With regard to the dilemma approach, I am positively surprised about Johnny's change of mind. He points out that he changed his opinion about sick people as candidates for human experiments because he realised something about himself – that he would not like to be in that situation. He has obviously identified with the situation to the degree that he realised that his idea was not viable under the circumstances and therefore changed his mind. On the other hand, he did not change his mind about the prisoners on death row; perhaps he found it difficult to identify himself with them? I think about interviewing him afterwards, this would be an interesting question – why did he maintain this point of view? In the class around me, discussions flare up and Sandra tries to control the situation…

> *Sandra: Let's accept this argument as it is and wait for the discussion later.*

RESEARCHER AND COMMUNICATION FACILITATOR COMMENTARY 2003

Apparently, the very different opinions stirred up emotions and confrontations of opinions and values. In this group, it seemed that nobody was prepared to hold back their opinion or to allow the others to suppress him/her. I was impressed that Johnny stood to his 'different' opinion as well as that he admitted to his change of opinion.

ANOTHER POSTER

I notice that the comments on this poster are also focused around the consequences of scientific research. Sandra asks again whether or not there are any questions and then calls out the last group: Maria, Roland. This is another group, I have particular interest in because Maria, the politically active girl, is part of it. Maria, Robert, Christine and Leo stick their poster on the blackboard.

> *Maria: We could not find a consensus - this is why we have one 'for' and one 'against' column. The 'for' column says: …*

Christine reads the contra column.

> *Sandra: Aha, I see now - your central theme is human victims of scientific research and your 'for' column says that human victims can speed up scientific research, especially in medical research. However, there is one comment I do not fully understand: The bad luck of one for the benefit of all…how do you mean that?*
> *Roland: Well, if someone loses his life this might benefit all others!*
> *Sandra: Ah I see! There is also a point saying: personal freedom…*
> *Maria: Well the personal freedom to die for science or not to die for science!*
> *Sandra: OK, so you think that personal freedom should not be limited because it would limit scientific research…*

RESEARCHER AND COMMUNICATION FACILITATOR COMMENTARY 2003

I am surprised about how little this group apparently values human life as such – it almost sounds to me as if scientific research to them is more important than an individual life. In their own way, they arrived at a consensus: they decided not to agree which can also count as consensus. Their poster clearly illustrated the divide in the group.

293

STUDENT COMMENTARY

Daniela, referring to the poster-presentations, was apparently experiencing an inner conflict when she was listening other groups "[It was] difficult because I just could not deal with some other opinions, for example, when someone argued that that human sacrifices are necessary then I simply don't understand this, because I think very differently and I find it difficult to accept this." (D2p33)

RESEARCHER AND COMMUNICATION FACILITATOR COMMENTARY 2003

One could interpret Daniela's comment as an expression of an Ethic of Care, as opposed to the Utiliarianist Ethics displayed by her colleagues. She apparently found it difficult to accept that the end justified the means and that therefore it was OK to kill some for the benefit of all. It was interesting to re-visit the Ulli-Johnny argument when their group presented the poster. Sandra asked them about the group discourse and Johnny explained the course of the conflict from his perspective and how he changed his mind. He 'testified' that the discussion had made him think and he had started to identify with the victims, thereby suggesting an engagement in critical reflection. It also crystallised that Ulli was opposing primarily the Utilitarian stance in Johnny's statements. I think that if the result of the confrontation was that both students apparently engaged in critical reflection, at least to some degree, the argument and conflict might have been worthwhile.

SUMMARY OF SECTION 2

The poster-presentation allowed us a deeper insight into the conflict between Ulli and Johnny: both apparently reflected critically following the argument, which led to Ulli's insight that she should become more tolerant, whilst Johnny changed his mind in part. Maria's group was presenting a poster that seemed to promote a view that it was OK to use people for scientific experiments because this sped up scientific research – but only as long as the victims agreed. They promoted a

Utilitarian Ethic that was not acceptable to everybody in the class, as Daniela's comments seemed to indicate.

<u>Section 3</u>: Plenary discussion in Sandra's class

In 'preparation' for the plenary discussion Sandra has planned to show a video about the first landing on the moon, however, the 'technology god' has withdrawn his blessings for the day – the video recorder does not work. In addition, the half-finished posters from last week have gone missing. Sandra is desperate but we have to put up with our bad luck – she asks the students to produce their posters again! As expected, this is not welcome whole-heartedly, and students are slow to get started on their task. Finally, Sandra stands up, turns towards the blackboard and re-reads the statements. Then she turns around towards the class.

> *<u>Sandra</u>: Let's summarise the positions here.*
> - *If scientific research has to involve human victims then these victims should do it voluntarily. This immediately raises the question for me – Who would volunteer for human experiments? Let's discuss this later.*
> - *In addition, another question is – often the negative results of scientific research surface only after a long time like with atomic power plants. In the past, they were often considered as quite harmless. This question involves the use of scientific knowledge – what are the results being used for? Science is often quasi value-free. However, it is not so much the results of scientific research that are problematic but much more so the abuse of those results. One example has to do with atomic energy, for a long time people thought the peaceful use of atomic energy in atomic power plants is OK whilst atomic warfare was considered bad.*
> - *So my question is now – Is it OK to conduct this type of scientific research or should the research itself be limited already?*
> - *One other point that has repeatedly come up was that scientific research is very important because it contributes to progress and progress has given us a high standard of life.*
> - *Moreover, there is still the other issue of people who have sort of "messed up" their life so much that is 'worthless' anyway, Prisoners on death row for example, perhaps they still have hopes and dreams regarding their life – do we have a right to sacrifice them?*
> - *One more question – should animals be used for experiments instead of humans?*

I think that Sandra's summary is a good way of initiating the following plenary discussion but it is obviously not enough: when Sandra sits down and invites students' opinions for the plenary discussion, nothing happens. Up to now, Sandra's moderation skills have been quite good – she has cruised through most of the dilemma unit. The only issue I have noticed so far is that Sandra speaks with a very quiet voice and it is sometimes difficult to understand what she is saying. This contrasts strongly with Irene who uses a loud and clear voice in her teaching all the time.

Sandra: I would like to invite your opinions now!

Figure 13: Students 'engaged' in the plenary discussion

Silence. The bell rings but it does not affect us because we have a double period this time… Waiting….Still, no comments… Sandra reminds them of communication and discourse rules… Silence again… Sandra who has so far led the students very well through the dilemma unit suddenly 'stops' moderating the discussion. She waits for comments from students, much too long for my taste. I do not fully understand why she is waiting so long. She could ask individual students for their opinions to get the discussion going. Eventually, some students voice their opinions [Have they had enough of the pressing silence?] but the discussion 'dies' soon after it has started because Sandra does not ask further questions. This is not going too well I think and I am quite surprised because the dilemma unit so far has worked out relatively well in this class, apart from technical problems and a lack of social interactions.

Finally, Sandra tells a story of her father's suffering with a heart disease. A hospital asked him to participate in an experiment involving a new drug.

> *Sandra: He agreed to participate without talking to his wife, my mother, about it. My mother was shocked afterwards because she was just as much involved! And I keep on asking myself what could possibly have motivated a man with wife and children and a serious disease to participate in this experiment. Anyway – my mother still claims that my father's health deteriorated from that moment onwards, whether or not this is true does not matter but for her it is real and true. Please try to think yourself into a person who is sick and who volunteers for an experiment. What could be the reasons for this? Please consider that his family needs this person!*

Some students appear touched by her story – an observation I have also made in the other class – personal stories seem to do wonders for engaging students. Sandra's story has this effect on her students too,
however, it is not an invigorating effect as Irene's stories had in her class. Some students here seem to have gone into deep reflection. Now there is total silence, which, on the other hand, is fatal for the discussion. Silence. Silence. Silence. The total anticlimax coming from Irene's Tree Dilemma.

Later on, the discussion becomes 'slightly' more animated, primarily through students like Maria, Ulli, David, Daniela and Manfred. Paul occasionally voices an opinion. It seems to me that Sandra has withdrawn completely at this point. "Why?" I ask myself. "Is it perhaps for fear of falling back into a traditional teacher role?" Alternatively, is it perhaps because the memory of her father's story has touched her deeply as well? I decide to ask her about that later.

TEACHER COMMENTARY

<u>Lily</u>: How did you go when you told this personal story?

Sandra: The one about my father? I really cannot imagine what was going on inside of him!

Sandra also had an explanation for the staggering start of the discussion.

<u>Sandra</u>: [I think] that the posters were missing affected their concentration and they had a two hours mathematics test in the morning. I think it was very hard for them, and I also think that the time from Friday until today was too long. I did not think it worked too well today.

I was wondering how students had experienced the discussion.

STUDENT COMMENTARY

Maria said, "[The plenary discussion] was very interesting, partly very surprising." (M7p81) I have to admit I was positively surprised too that Maria had discovered at least one aspect she liked about the dilemma unit. Daniela supported Maria's opinion, "I really liked the discussion round, the ideas and how they came into being and how we were all talking with each other and so..." (D8p5) Whilst Julian said, "I really liked the 'pros and cons'." (J11p53)

RESEARCHER AND COMMUNICATION FACILITATOR COMMENTARY 2003

Whilst the discussion round was one of the focus points in the interviews with students of Irene's class, in Sandra's class only a few students voiced opinions regarding the discussion. I am unsure as to whether this was because the students experienced the discussion as I did, as a 'drag', or because they thought it was nothing worth mentioning. On the other hand, Daniela seemed to be positively surprised that 'they spoke to each other'. I was surprised by that comment but it fits in well with the overall group-dynamics in Sandra's class – perhaps they simply do not usually speak to each other like that? I was even more surprised that Maria who had been quite critical about most of the dilemma unit finally had found something that she could accept.

SUMMARY SECTION 3

Whilst the discussion in Irene's class turned out to be a passionate, noisy event with plenty of participation, the discussion in Sandra's class was slow to start. Firstly, it appeared that Sandra had lost her initiative for a while which might also have been related to the very personal story she told to the students, and secondly there was poor student involvement. Only a handful of students – primarily those who had 'led' the classroom discourse for much of the time – participated in the discussion. Sandra tried only hesitantly to ask questions to keep the discussion going. There were no attempts from her to deliberately ask students who had not contributed anything. This change in teaching style came as a surprise to me because for most of the dilemma unit she had played the role of the moderator well. Now suddenly she gave away her leadership. I presume that the lack in participation in the discussion might be related to the complicated group-dynamics in Sandra's class. Only the dominant students contributed whilst the others remained silent. One reason might be that individual students were not keen on putting themselves into an outsider position by showing dissent to the dominant group. The discussion might have been sped up by deliberately picking out students who had not yet contributed and asking them about their opinions. On the other hand, we should not forget that the students had a mathematics test that morning which might have drained their energies. However, the few students who made comments about the discussion were rather positive which came as a surprise to me.

Review of Part 2

In this part of the chapter, I described the poster preparation phase, the poster presentation phase and the plenary discussion round in Sandra's class as examples of discourse during the dilemma unit. Sandra's class appeared to be dominated by strong individuals such as Ulli and Maria. I chose Ulli's and Johnny's argument as a particular example of how the comparison of individual opinions led to an open conflict that was partly resolved through negotiations. During her conflict with Johnny, Ulli had seemingly demonstrated an unwillingness to compromise. However, the conflict apparently led to some new insights for Johnny and Ulli. The poster-presentation allowed us a deeper insight into the conflict between Ulli and Johnny: both apparently reflected critically following the argument which led to Ulli's insight that she should become more tolerant, whilst Johnny changed his mind in part.

The poster presentation phase was characterised by a number of statements that could be interpreted as Utilitarian Ethics. I was surprised that this viewpoint was largely uncontested by the rest of the class. Maria's group, for example, was presenting a poster that seemed to promote a view that it was OK to use people for scientific experiments because this sped up scientific research – but only as long as the victims agreed.

With regard to the group-work, some students experienced it apparently as a welcome opportunity to compare 'where you stand with your own opinions and values'. Paul indicated that 'groupthink' might tinge the results of group-collaborations and that 'inauthentic' responses might be the result. Some groups that were almost too harmonious and homogenous, as Daniela's group, seemed to be more prone to groupthink than groups with a lot of conflict.

The discussion round was slow and the contributions came from a handful of (dominant) students only. Sandra stopped moderating at this point which resulted in long and painful moments of silence. Sandra did not actively seek to speed up the discussion by measures of asking questions or playing the role of the devil's advocate.

There was some evidence of critical reflection, especially in Ulli's and Johnny's case, however other interviewees, such as Maria, presented themselves as separate knowers who displayed primarily critical thinking (Belenky et al., 1997).

However, in the light of the strong individualism in Sandra's class, should the teacher conduct collaborative learning experiences at all? On the one hand, is it not the conflict that sometimes brings about an opportunity to learn from each other, as with Ulli and Johnny? Moreover, if teachers have a duty of care towards every student in a class, is it fair towards a student to expose him/her to group-work? Questions of fairness, of an Ethic of Care and of our responsibility towards teaching for life seem to clash.

REVIEW OF THE CHAPTER

The discourse phases of the dilemma unit were distributed between phases of individual reflection and comprised comparison of individual opinions in groups, collaborative preparations and presentations of posters, and a plenary discussion. Arguments in both classes indicated that there was critical thinking as well as critical reflection involved. It appears to me that perhaps the group discourse had caused some individuals to reflect critically on their own opinions after being confronted with conflicting opinions which led to some strong emotions in some students. This could indicate that the group-work and the confrontation with other opinions might be 'the' centrepiece of the moral learning experience during a dilemma unit. As one of the students said, 'You normally never get to hear what other people are thinking.' Making compromises, learning to negotiate, and to deal with other opinions were important learning opportunities provided by the collaborative learning experience. Dilemma units might therefore provide an arena for social and emotional learning (see Chapter 11), apart from rational decision making

However, the experiences of the collaborative learning phases seemed to have been different for Irene's and Sandra's students. In Irene's class, only one student criticised the group composition and the poster presentations. Others reported not only conflicts during the group work but also how these conflicts were resolved through either finding a common solution (consensus) or integrating different points of view (compromise). Some raised issues of maintaining a voice and daring to speak one's opinion in a group. Some interviewees focused on the benefits of the exchange of opinions. In Sandra's class, there were several critical voices – critical of group-work in general and of the group-constellations. In Irene's class, I observed good group-interactions and an intense final discussion. In Sandra's class, group-work appeared almost perfect on the outside, apart from Ulli and Johnny's conflict – no noise.

Could it be that Sandra's class worked so 'perfectly well' (on the outside) because they did not really interact due to the complex group-dynamics? On the inside however, Sandra's students, such as Ulli, rejected the group-work because they found it difficult to collaborate as a team. This might have been due to their strong individualism or it might have been preferable to them to strive for unanimity rather than for quality decisions, leading to groupthink. Additionally, authentic self-disclosure presupposes a climate where one can feel safe. If this climate is non-existent, students might feel reluctant to engage in group-work (Borchers, 1999b). I believe that this was largely the case in Sandra's class. Yet another perspective on Sandra's 'reluctant collaborative learners' could be, as Bruffee points out: sometimes students resist collaborative learning because "social engagement can be hard work." And it seems to require skills such as tact, responsive listening, willingness to compromise and negotiation skills that some of these students might not yet have developed (Bruffee, 1993)

301

In the light of the difficulties should we not 'just forget about it and get on with life'? On the other hand, should we not, given the apparent social difficulties of these 'individual agents', actually reinforce our attempts to give them more opportunities to practice collaborative work? Yet as I pointed out earlier the question remains – is it ultimately commensurable with an Ethic of Care to force students to speak about themselves in public (in the group) if they are not prepared to do this voluntarily? There appears to be a dilemma for the curriculum planner: could it be that the discourse we are trying to promote is sometimes potentially immoral?

Whilst the final discussion did not work very well in Sandra's class, it was very intense in Irene's class. Other students reported an emotional rollercoaster the discussion caused in them. So-called 'problem students' can potentially be a source of great frustration in group-work situations. However, in Irene's and Sandra's classes this was not the case. Johnny, as one of the problem-students in Sandra's class, contributed considerably to the learning processes in his group. Problem students might not only contribute positively to the discourse, like Alex, or through provocative comments, like Alois, but also through dissent, like Johnny. We might conclude therefore, that so-called 'problem students' should not be a reason for not engaging in collaborative learning. Just the opposite: this type of learning might provide an avenue for them to engage in the discourse on science.

The teachers played the roles of referees during the plenary discussions and 'social organisers' during the small group discussions. Irene experienced her role as demanding. Sandra admitted to being lost for words occasionally. Unlike Silver, who restricted his 'suggestions' to what a teacher 'should do', I think Bruffee's comment brings the challenging role of the teacher to the point,

> *"The nitty-gritty of this process of social organisation can look trivial on the page. But it adds up to fairly sophisticated expertise that includes some familiarity with the research on 'group dynamics', some forethought, some sensitivity to social situations and relationships, a somewhat better-than-average understanding of what is being taught, and self-control"* *(Bruffee, 1993).*

For a final discussion of the findings in this chapter, please see Chapter 11.

Chapter 10

Filling in the gaps: emergent findings

'You don't have to sit all the time, there are interruptions, you can have your own opinion, you can talk without being reprimanded, you can discuss, the teacher is not just talking about something you're not interested in but about something that's based on history. (U4p75-76)

INTRODUCTION

Given that, during the data analysis, I did not look for pre-existing categories but regarded all 'utterances of equal value', the result was that I had more findings than the original research questions required. These emergent findings appear to provide valuable information about some aspects of the dilemma approach that have gone largely unnoticed by much of the literature I have reviewed over the past few years. From an integral perspective, we might say that whilst quantitative research in the area of moral education has yielded certain valuable insights, this qualitative study has complemented earlier findings with insights that were formerly unavailable, thereby filling in the gaps. Therefore, this chapter has the purpose of presenting emergent findings that may complement the overall picture of what it was like to teach and to learn during dilemma units. The reader might notice that some themes appear to be more pronounced in one class than in the other. With regard to the epistemic status of the findings, I would like to add that the degree of generalisability of the data varies within the cases and from factor to factor. In this chapter, I am drawing primarily on student and teacher interview data. The chapter is organised in four parts – each part has several sections:

Part 1: External factors influencing the dilemma experience

- Section 1: Storytelling versus story-reading
- Section 2: Facilitating versus instructing
- Section 3: Time

Part 2: Ethics as a part of the curriculum

- Section 1: Ethics as part of science education
- Section 2: Ethics and other subjects

Part 3: Students' learning experiences and outcomes

- Section 1: A valuable experience?
- Section 2: Learning through dilemmas
- Section 3: Students' suggestions for improvement

Part 4: Teachers' impressions of the dilemma units

- Section 1: Irene
- Section 2: Sandra
- Section 3: Other teachers outside of the project

Book Antiqua was used for the narrators voice. Arial Narrow was used for researcher commentaries in 2003, summaries and reviews. Courier was used for students' post hoc commentaries and Tahoma illustrates teachers' post hoc perspectives. As in Chapter 7, 8 and 9, verbatim interview quotes are referenced as follows: initial of the pseudonym of the interviewee, followed by reference number and paragraph number (e.g., F23p2) to allow for the audit trail.

PART 1: EXTERNAL FACTORS INFLUENCING THE DILEMMA EXPERIENCE

Section 1: Storytelling versus story-reading: Which would you prefer?

During the Red Cross Project, a female board member of the Youth Red Cross who was also the director of a pedagogical academy criticised our curriculum development on the grounds that we suggested that it seemed to be more effective to tell the dilemma stories freely than to simply distribute paper-copies of the stories. She regarded our approach as an undue imposition on the teachers. Our suggestion was based on observations in the classroom. However, at the time, we did not have enough empirical evidence to support our claims, and we had to accept that we were not to suggest in the book that storytelling was in any way preferable to story-reading.

During this research study, I wanted to explore this phenomenon further. I asked students about their preferences, "Did you prefer that the teacher told the story or would it have been as good to read the story from paper copies?" Student responses yielded a number of foci that I present in the following section of the chapter. Overall, I can say that, with regard to the preference of storytelling to story-reading, there seemed to be great unanimity amongst the students - I was unable to find disconfirming evidence .

DILEMMA STORIES AS CONTEXT FOR IDENTIFICATION AND REFLECTION

Daniela said, she "…liked the storytelling because you can already think about it" (D10p74) And she added, "I think the idea is great." (D17p58) Gregor added a new perspective to Daniela's by recognising the stories as providing the necessary background for dilemma discourse, "It [the storytelling] is good because you need a context and if you

305

don't know that [context] you don't know what you should be discussing." (G7p24) Fatima, on the other hand, claimed that dilemma story telling was conducive to identifying with the story and/or the characters in the story, "If somebody is telling a story, one can imagine something…one can think oneself much better into a situation." (F12p16) This comment was also supported by Melinda, "One can much better imagine things than if one reads it only from transparency." (Me1p65)

DILEMMA STORIES FOCUS ATTENTION

For Melinda, one clear advantage of dilemma story telling seemed to be that it provoked focused attention by inviting students to listen actively, "I think that if she [the teacher] is telling the story more people will listen rather than when we read it from transparency." (Me1p65) Gregor arguing along a similar line of thought drew the logical conclusion that, "If somebody reads it out to you, you cannot <u>not</u> listen when everybody else does." (G8p27)

RESEARCHER COMMENTARY 2003

According to Gregor the stories provided a framework for dealing with the dilemma(s) whilst for Daniela they also promoted a reflection process. Melinda and Fatima both reported that the stories promote identification with another person as well as imagination. Reflection, imagination and identification with others were supposedly necessary for engagement with the dilemma and for creative decision-making (see also Chapter 9). Melinda and Gregor suggested that one advantage of storytelling was that it promoted attention by inviting students to listen to the teacher. On the other hand, I wonder if, given that storytelling does not often feature in mainstream curricula, some students might have been 'conditioned' to regard storytelling as something that is not 'really teaching' and therefore does not require their full attention – this might help to explain why some students in Irene's class chose to stay at home for the second unit, perhaps because 'they felt they were not actually 'learning anything'? I am aware that I am largely speculating here but I feel that it would be worthwhile exploring this issue further in future research.

DILEMMA STORYTELLING VERSUS READING

If a story is supposed to focus students' attention and get them to listen, an interest in listening to a story and a disinterest in reading as such seem to be one of the major allies of the teacher, as Fatima eloquently elaborated, "Nobody would be interested in that [reading the story] – it is much better anyway if one tells a story (F9p16)... it is just not so interesting when you're reading a story" (F10p16). And she added, "It is much more interesting like that, one actually listens" (F11p16). Her last comment supports what Gregor said earlier. Fatima's comment made me interested in why students expressed a disinterest in reading. Gregor tried to clarify this for me, "Nobody really reads because everybody is too lazy" (G8p27). Daniela, on the other hand, apparently experienced problems when she had to shift her focus and concentration from story-reading to thinking and vice versa, "Whilst you are listening to it, you can already start to form your own opinion rather than if you are reading it, then you have to concentrate on the reading and every time you think about a topic, you have to stop and re-start reading and so on. When you hear it then you can already make up your mind." (D10p74).

RESEARCHER COMMENTARY 2003

To me, this indicates that for some (more than we realise?) students the act of reading occupies much of their concentration capacity. To think and to read might become a task that uses up more time and intellectual effort than I believe many teachers, including myself, take into consideration. We, as teachers at secondary school level, seem to presume too often that reading and thinking happen simultaneously and effortlessly for kids of that age. Apparently, as Daniela's comments show, this might not be the case for every student in a classroom…Something to think about for future research!

DILEMMA STORIES AS TOOLS OF ENGAGEMENT

Ulli preferred storytelling because she experienced the story at a more personal level, "I like it [storytelling] better than reading it because it doesn't come across as well as when something's being told. And because she [Sandra] always does a good job at this… because she gets really engaged, it is more likely that you will get involved. If you read it only you will pick out a few keywords but if something is a long text like this one then I think it is better to use storytelling…" (U18p61) She elaborated further, "I think it is better to tell the story because there are feelings involved about how it is being told." (U17p61) The way a story is presented apparently affects students emotionally, and potentially influences their attitude, as Paul explained, "It would not have come across that well if one just throws up a transparency but if you tell it, then you convey it differently than if you just read it out aloud." (P16p58)… "Yes, if you look at people whilst you're telling a story it comes across much better than if she [Sandra] had just read it" (P17p62)

RESEARCHER COMMENTARY 2003

Apparently storytelling can 'reach' students because it also evokes emotions. The act of storytelling involves eye-contact, body-language and probably subtle details such as intonation, voice and storytelling style (engaged, tense, etc.) that support the 'underlying message'. These issues indicate to me that whilst it is seemingly 'safer' for teachers - in terms of not making themselves vulnerable in front of a class by telling (personal) stories - to distribute paper-copies of stories, many positive opportunities for learning and for connection between teacher, student and topic might be missed.

On the other hand, both approaches seem to have their drawbacks: through reading from paper-copies we might potentially 'lose' some students who are slow readers and who are more occupied with the act of reading than with reflection on the dilemma. Through storytelling, there is, of course, a danger that some students might not recognise it as 'teaching' and might drift off. Most of the students I interviewed argued that storytelling actually increases students' attention – although Alex, one of the 'problem students' in Irene's class, admitted that in the beginning he did not take it seriously and was only interested in having fun.

After her two dilemma units, I spoke to Irene about the issue of storytelling versus story-reading.

CONVERSATION WITH IRENE AFTER THE SECOND PART OF THE TREE DILEMMA

Lily (referring to the first round of interviews): They said that they really liked that you told the story freely. (I-FS2p72)

Irene: aha?...

Lily: They would not have appreciated it that much if it had come from an overhead projector or simply been distributed as photocopies. (I-FS2p76)

Irene: This is an old experience of mine as a teacher: if I want to get something across really well then I take the time to tell a story. Mostly stories from my travels where I can bring myself into the picture, and I get feedback on that in parent-teacher meetings that the kids take this home with them and continue to reflect on the issues, which is more or less 'the' characteristic of my teaching. Not hierarchical, chronological because there are always stories to tell, and yesterday during my Year 12 preparation class, I said to Nina, a student, that I am a bit fearful that we have not covered enough content – that was when she screamed, "Not enough? It is true that some of the classes looked more like 'idle chatter' but when I look at my notes now, there were so many key-words and concepts packed into that – I could never have learned that otherwise! (I-FS2p79)

SUMMARY OF SECTION 1 AND RESEARCHER PERSPECTIVE IN 2003

Students reportedly preferred storytelling to reading the stories. Reasons included that stories provided a context for identification, reflection, and a focus-point of attention. However, whilst some of the students described a 'struggle' with reading fluently and thinking simultaneously as a reason for their preference, other students reported laziness as a driving force. Some students appreciated having an opportunity to reflect on the story whilst it is being told.

It was very interesting for me to explore why students unanimously preferred storytelling to reading the stories. Reportedly, stories helped students focus their attention and helped them to identify with the dilemma situation and the characters in the story. Based on the presumption that the stories are 'primers' for the dilemma questions, evidence indicates that storytelling seems to be a more effective option (than having students read the stories) when it comes to presenting a dilemma to the students. Some students apparently have problems with reading the text, which might occupy part of their consciousness and distract them from focusing on the underlying message of the story.

Irene, the teacher, commented that she had had the experience earlier in her teaching that contents could be conveyed better if she told a story that in the ideal case also included herself. She claimed, quoting a Year 12 student, that through these little stories she had covered enormous amounts of content in a way that didn't 'feel like learning'.

Another issue that crystallised during the interviews was the students' thoughts about the teaching style. After several students had mentioned their preference for facilitation to traditional instruction, I deliberately explored the issue further with other students.

Section 2: Facilitating versus instructing

Students in Sandra's class appreciated the difference in the teaching style inasmuch as Sandra was facilitating rather than instructing. Interestingly enough, students in Irene's class did not mention the different teaching style.

Ulli pointed out the advantage of Sandra's moderation, "I think that some [students] would certainly have allowed themselves to be influenced by the opinion [Sandra's opinion] because they would have already heard one opinion. Without much reflection, they would have adopted the same opinion. I don't think it would have turned out as genuine in terms of individual feelings if s/he hears somebody else's opinion beforehand…like, 'This opinion is certainly better than mine!' " (U21p82) Ulli added, "I had great respect for the way how she [Sandra] was doing it. She certainly had made up her mind but she managed to convey it so that really everybody could voice their own opinion." (U33p82)

The crucial point for the students was the opportunity to voice their own ideas, as Julian explains, "If you're doing it [teaching a dilemma unit] you should not convey your own ethical opinion because everybody should get an opportunity to form their own. What you're saying, … like really [you should] explain everything how it really was and occasionally [you should] 'tease' someone if you think you don't agree because everybody has their own ethical ideas which simply cannot be ignored." (J16p65)

Maria supported this view, "I thought it was great that there was no manipulation involved" (M16p85) Daniela also problematised the influence of the teacher's opinion by saying, "I strongly appreciate this [non-manipulation] because like this everybody can form his/her own opinion. Because if, for example, the teacher says such

311

and such then many think, this is 'the' opinion I ought to
have too, and when the teacher does not convey his/her
opinion, then the student can have his/her own opinion and
not the teacher's opinion or the opinion of other students"
(D13p78)

SUMMARY OF SECTION 2 AND RESEARCHER COMMENTARY 2003

The student comments seem to answer some of the concerns voiced in the ongoing debate in moral education on instruction versus facilitation. Students apparently appreciated the opportunity to express their own opinions in a non-manipulative manner. The teacher seemed to be able to gain respect through this type of teaching. Julian seemed to argue that holding back your own perspective as a teacher is vital. If a teacher does not agree with an opinion, s/he has tools for 'teasing' the person in order to get him/her to reflect on their ideas, such as asking questions. Students were aware that some colleagues might simply adopt the teacher's opinion thinking that it was definitely better than their own, or that this was the opinion they ought to have too. For this reason it was also important, on the teacher's side, to recognise and accept individual differences in ethical thoughts. Summarising, students seem to have appreciated strongly the opportunity to form and to express their own opinions.

Section 3: Time

I expected student comments with regards to the length of the units because of the
difficulties we experienced in finishing one dilemma within a two-hour unit. In
fact it did not work out once.

Julian tried to express his dismay in a quite diplomatic manner, "It was
too drawn out! It was a bit too long" (J20p4-8) When I asked him,
"Where did we lose time?" He responded, "I think a little bit with
the story and also that we had to work out everything
individually - I mean you have to do this anyway but within a

group, you don't really have to present your own opinion that much - you can really spare yourself that." (J21p13)

Daniela on the other hand was more concerned about how the length of the dilemma unit should be adjusted to the topic, "I mean, it all depends strongly on the topic but, for example, for the topic 'violence' - this topic is so widespread I would take much more time." (D16p62)

Emma seemed frustrated about the interruptions too, "We should have continued to talk. It was pretty unsettling that the unit was so often interrupted, we would have needed more time, much more time in order to think ourselves back into it [the dilemma] (E17p3). Perhaps we should have taken a whole morning, enough time for everyone to get into it…(E18p6).

However, there was yet another time-related perspective voiced by Fatima. "The longer I listened to the story I found that my opinion changed (F57p43)... Later on at home I continued to think, 'Why doesn't she [Emma] have the same opinion as I do?' (F61p34)...Now as I know how the story went and I have heard the whole story, I am very enthusiastic because we have never done anything like this before at school." (F71p7).

RESEARCHER COMMENTARY 2003

Fatima's comment illustrates the time-dependency of the reflection on the dilemma: it apparently took time to 'sink in' and I think Fatima gave us a clear account of how her thinking developed over time.

Whilst time appeared to be a positive aspect with regard to the depth of the thinking, overall however, time was clearly the limiting factor. The discontinuity of the dilemma units was apparently seen as disturbing by many people involved. Whilst Julian suggested dropping the individual reflection phases in favour of group-work in order to save time, this did not seem to be in the interest of many of his class-mates, as I described in Chapter 9. Apparently there seemed to be a tension between the two extremes where people wanted to work in groups only versus students who would prefer to work only individually. This brings to the fore yet another dilemma for the teacher and curriculum-planner: whilst some students loathe group-work, others like Julian see the solution to the time problem in an <u>increased</u> proportion of group-work.

I asked Irene about her opinion on the 'time-issue'.

TEACHER COMMENTARY

<u>Irene</u>: I have to say, in principle, that the amount of time we used up was enormous - it was firstly those one and a half hours and then we continued from 2.15pm to 4.35pm and there were still some who did not run away. ...Yes I think this first part was incredibly long drawn out (I-FS2p57-59)

SUMMARY OF SECTION 3 AND RESEARCHER COMMENTARY 2003

Apparently Irene regarded it as a sign of positive engagement and interest that students did not 'give up' even though the units were too long. Furthermore, some students continued to discuss the dilemma after the unit was officially over (see Chapter 9).

Time appeared to be the limiting factor that constrained the dilemma experience considerably. The students reported their annoyance with the interruptions of the discussions. One student suggested favouring group-work instead of individual work. Given that a number of students expressed their dismay with group-work, I believe that this solution would not be acceptable in general. Irene was impressed that the students did not 'run away' even though the dilemma units were too long. Fatima mentioned another time-related issue: the time-dependency of the reflection process.

Given the ongoing discussion about whether or not ethics should be part of science education, and given the insecurity some teachers apparently have regarding the inclusion of ethics into the curriculum, I thought it would be interesting to explore what students as the recipients of such 'well meaning' intervention thought about the inclusion of ethics into science education.

PART 2: ETHICS AS A PART OF THE CURRICULUM

Section 1: Ethics in science education

I asked students, "<u>What do you think about the inclusion of ethics into science education?</u>"

When I asked Ulli, I was immediately confronted with a dilemma, formulated by her, "As long as it is voluntary, but I am not sure what everybody else thinks about integrating ethics into the science curriculum all the time. I think one should check who is for and who is against – I would do it but only as long as I'm interested." (U1p47-48)

RESEARCHER COMMENTARY 2003

The issue of voluntary involvement raises an important question – how can a teacher who regards ethics as an integral part of science teaching and learning include these topics but leave the participation voluntary. If we regard ethics as a basic component of scientific literacy can we dispense with it? On the other hand, if we make it compulsory – do we not risk losing some students because of disinterest?

BACK TO STUDENT COMMENTS

Not everybody thought ethics 'should' be a part of science education, "I do not find it good to have ethics as part of the [science] curriculum, rather as extra lessons like an ethics course." (M2p13)

RESEARCHER COMMENTARY 2003

Maria expresses apparently a perspective that ethics is not part of science and should therefore not be taught within science education. This is also well aligned with earlier comments of Maria's where she argued in favour of more science-content. She was, however, the only student who argued in favour of a separate 'ethics course'.

STUDENT COMMENTARY CONTINUED

Julian, on the other hand, made a comment that stands in stark contrast to Maria's statement, and that goes beyond the scope of what I would have expected of any student, "I believe that one should not restrict this type of teaching to natural sciences, sportsmen or piano players but that it is about human beings and does not depend on what they are doing." (J18p81)

Paul not only supports this view but develops the argument even further, "I believe that it cannot be reduced to the teaching of natural sciences. It is important for every area that there is some ethics education involved because this is basically the most important issue, isn't it? It is the life of our 'neighbour' that counts, isn't it? In real life, you also have to collaborate with others, you have to pay attention, and in this regard this is very important. It does not matter which profession one has. I mean in science we also have lab lessons, …you also have to be careful when we work in groups – therefore it is very important to do it. And if one [of the group] does not contribute and the whole group fails then this is also an ethical question – who is being held responsible for that, for example…" (P1p65-66)

In Irene's class there were obviously discussions about whether the Creative Branch of the school might have been a better place to implement the

316

ethics project as expressed by Melinda, "I am not sure why this project is implemented in the Natural Sciences Branch." (Me21p91) Emma, on the other hand, said that, "I think it really fits well into the Science Branch [see Chapter 3] although some people had thought it might fit better into the Creative Branch. I think you don't need to be creative to write down your own opinion – it is a really good project and I think it is important." (E27p45). And she added, "I think everybody needs that. I am not sure whether other classes do this as well but I think they should!" Damian, despite the language problems, conveyed that he thought ethics should be part of science education, "It is sometimes part of our life, how we live and so...how we live and decide, the environment and so... (Da8p89). Alex, one of the 'problem-students' said, "Yes! [it should be part of science education] because it has a lot to do with psychology – in the Languages [branch] you learn everything about languages, in the Creative Branch you learn how to act – no, I believe it fits better into the Natural Science Branch." (A24p100-107)

RESEARCHER COMMENTARY 2003

It was very interesting (and rewarding) to see some students, such as Julian, Paul and Alex, for example, express strong support for the inclusion of an ethics curriculum into science education. Whilst Maria was the only interviewee who said ethics should not be included into science education, Melinda was arguing that a different branch might have been a better choice. Maria's comment mirrors rather the traditional view of science as a value-free enterprise. I have to admit I was quite impressed that some students had realised the impact and importance of ethics on our lives and that a restriction to certain branches of the school was not an ideal solution.

SUMMARY OF SECTION 1

Ulli's demand that an inclusion of ethics, although good in principle, should only be on a voluntary basis presents a teacher who is convinced that ethics forms an integral part of science education with a dilemma. On the other hand, there was only one student who argued that it should be taught as a 'separate course'. In Irene's class there had apparently been a discussion about whether ethics should be included in the Natural Sciences Branch or rather in the Creative Branch. However, several students argued clearly for an inclusion of ethics into science education, stating that it should not be restricted to this subject. Several students had apparently reflected about the wider implications of ethics in our lives and thus argued for a general inclusion of ethics into the curriculum

Having established students' appreciation of the inclusion of ethics into science education, one important question for me was also whether or not students had (enough) opportunities to practice ethical reasoning and discourse or whether we were just imposing something that was already in place elsewhere.

Section 2: Ethics and other subjects

I asked the students, "Do you have opportunities in other subjects to discuss issues like that?"

Ulli responded, "In religious education, we have been talking about that for a few lessons but other issues about humans like human experiments etc., no – only in religious education." (U10p7-9). Paul supported this claim, " Really only in religious education but then again… no not really." (P18p140). Maria contended that they had some something vaguely similar, "…in religious education and as far as I know, in psychology next year." (M10p23-25)

SUMMARY OF SECTION 2 AND RESEARCHER COMMENTARY 2003

It was not surprising to me that religious educators tried to include ethical discourse in their teaching but this again raised the question for me about why ethical education should be restricted to students who subscribe to a particular religion and/or participate in religious education of a kind. In the current secular society it appears questionable that students have opportunities to discuss controversial issues in a safe environment outside their homes. It seems that curriculum developers worldwide have recognised this issue as problematic: the Austrian Curriculum Reform 99 tried to address this issue very clearly by including values and moral education in the overarching curriculum statement yet it seems as if there is not much happening outside the subjects where one would expect this type of education anyway (see Appendix 6 and also Chapter 1). In comparison, the Curriculum Council of Western Australia also dedicated a section of the overarching curriculum statement in the Curriculum Framework Document of Western Australia to values (Curriculum Council, 1998)

Whilst the previous chapters investigated the suitability of dilemma units for the teaching and learning of ethical issues, I regarded it as essential for the overall appreciation of the dilemma units to gain an insight into the students' and teachers' general impressions about the dilemma units.

PART 3: STUDENTS' LEARNING EXPERIENCES AND OUTCOMES

Section 1: A valuable experience?

I asked students, "Do you think the dilemma approach is a valuable method for teaching ethical issues? What did you think about it?" The responses varied from evaluative comments about the dilemma approach to critique of particular aspects of the dilemma teaching and learning.

Maria, to my great surprise, was slightly supportive of the dilemma units approach as such. However, she criticised the 'lack of information beforehand'. She said, "Yes, [I think it is a valuable method] but not directly the way we did it - first information, then discussions - what speaks for something, what against, what is being discussed in the media, what is already written in some conventions and only then discuss what we think about it." (M12p29) ...It was OK. Nothing new. In principle, something quite ordinary!" (M14p56-

57) Maria, added, "I cannot say that I did not feel good about it but you but for us it was a waste of time!" I asked her, "Why?" "Because these are issues we have to deal with anyway and not like this, in groups, especially in 'organised' groups, where we don't know each other, we don't like each other and together somehow...because if we want to talk we do that anyway! I personally would have preferred mathematics and physics lessons. And the content that now comes at a later time..."(M1p2-8)

RESEARCHER COMMENTARY 2003

Her last comment supports my suspicion that she was demanding more content orientation which is well aligned with the traditional view of science teaching and learning. Her criticism is partly justified - Irene and I both agree that this is particularly true for the Rainforest Dilemma (see Appendix 5). In that case it would have been better to provide more profound preparation with regard to the content to make it easier for the students to engage with the dilemma. On the other hand, I have to admit that I found Maria's criticism quite difficult to deal with in the interview. I really had to hold back on several occasions and not respond to her 'provocative' comments. On the other hand, it helped me enormously to find that she was the only student in her class who voiced condemning critique. And she was also the only one who would have preferred maths and physics lessons to the dilemma. I have come to understand that she was probably rejecting the authority person in me.

STUDENT COMMENTARY CONTINUED

Maria's statements stand in contrast to Daniela's comment who said, "[I liked] Actually everything. First of all, the story itself." (D20p5) Ulli's critique was more specific and was related to group-work as she had elaborated earlier, "I did not like the group work...in principle but apart from that I like everything. I can't think of anything negative to say, really!" (U28p55-58) She elaborated further, "Dilemma stories yes, but also only if I don't have to do something I don't like to do, for example, all that group-work where you have to discuss things – I don't really like to talk about what I am thinking. I think, if I don't have to tell all the time, how I see something then that's OK." (U1p47-48).

Julian commented, "I think it is very useful" (J17p93). Whilst Paul contended, "I believe it is quite useful because it is important to question issues and to enter situations prepared. That one is mentally prepared and considers consequences of something, for example. (P4p18). ...I have been thinking about this - that I have been in dilemma situations before and later on, if I get into a similar situation again - I might be prepared somehow. (P19p38) ...Yes, I do believe it is [useful] because I think that it is rather an education for life and in our schooling system there is virtually nothing apart from that. There is pure studying [only] and I believe that this is important. I mean there are non-compulsory subjects but nobody has the time for those." (P21p50)

Fatima, in Irene's class said, "It was really a great experience, the story and that and I hope that we will continue to do things like that." (F31p37) Emma elaborated on what she liked, "It was really good...especially that we had to write down our opinions individually." (E29p3&9) Whilst apparently for Emma it was the individual reflection phases that spoke to her, Gregor preferred the collaborative phases of the dilemma units, "I really liked the group-work and that we could hear other people's opinions." (G26p6) He added, "There wasn't really anything I did not like." (G27p21) Alex's pointed out that for him the discussion was what made the dilemma unit worthwhile. He said, "The discussion - I really liked that one." I asked him, "Why?" "I don't know for sure perhaps because I could voice my own opinion." " Is this not the case normally?" "No, that's not the case!" (A28p6-12)

SUMMARY OF SECTION 1

Maria was apparently advocating a more content-driven curriculum approach than I had in mind. However, her criticism appears to be warranted to some degree. Apart from that she apparently thought that the experience had been 'quite ordinary' which stands in stark contrast to Daniela's comment. Ulli contended that she liked the dilemma story, however, she did not like the group-work. Paul, on the other hand, seemed to have appreciated the dilemma units as an incentive to consider consequences of actions and as a mental preparation for future decision-making. Julian apparently regarded the dilemma unit as a unique opportunity to learn for life – something that was missing from the mainstream curriculum. Fatima had experienced the dilemma unit as 'great'. Whilst for Emma individual reflection had been the most appealing aspect, Gregor thought the same about the collaborative phases. For Alex, one of the so-called problem students, it appeared that the discussion opened an avenue for him, as I had suspected earlier, to participate in the class discourse in a productive manner. I wonder if, in case this is potentially a way of including students who do not normally participate positively in the classroom discourse, we should include plenary discussions more often in science education in order to provide an opportunity for those students. Summarising, I can say that most of the interviewed students experienced the dilemma units as useful and positive. Only one student voiced sharp criticism. For several students group-work was something they would rather have excluded from the dilemma units whilst, for others, group-work was what they really appreciated.

Section 2: Learning through dilemmas

When I asked students, "What was your experience of the learning in the dilemma unit like?" and "What did you think you have learned from the dilemma units?" Ulli gave me a detailed account of what the dilemma learning experience was like for her:

THE DILEMMA LEARNING PROCESS AS EXPERIENCED BY ULLI

When I asked Ulli, "How would you describe the experience?" She replied without hesitation, " Thrilling - you need to apply your intuition (U15p34). I believe that you can keep things in mind much better [like this] than learning everything only theoretically. Through discussing and listening to others it is certain that something is learned much faster as if you only quickly touch an issue during a lesson. If different topics were packed into those dilemma stories one could recall much more! Animal protection, for example, don't just say, "Let's protect the animals!" But I think that normally teaching [=curriculum] is often much too slack, in its organisation. There are some positive changes noticeable but school is for many first and foremost stress, pressure - if you do something like that, like these dilemma stories, I mean, there is also fun involved! Not in terms of making fun but that you are not only required to sit still and being talked to because not enough of that is being done at school…. (U3p73). …You don't have to sit all the time, there are interruptions, you can have your own opinion, you can talk without being reprimanded, you can discuss, the teacher is not just talking something you're not interested in but something that's based on history - it is easier to recall something like that if you like what you hear. If something is packed into a story you have to think it through, you can memorise things much better (U4p75-76). If I have to think myself into it and I have to assess the advantages and the disadvantages - you somehow learn from this (U9p28).

RESEARCHER COMMENTARY 2003

Ulli apparently appreciated especially the dilemma stories as a means of dealing with topics in detail. She also pointed out that the stories apparently helped create an appealing atmosphere that also involved fun, thereby counteracting school stress and routine. She explained further that a teaching approach involving various activities that require students to change their seats and focus is a pleasant feature; being allowed to voice one's opinion and to talk to each other without being reprimanded is another. She contended that one might learn better if "you hear it wrapped up in a story". She also suggests that the identification with others and with situations helps students to learn from the experience.

FEELINGS INVOLVED IN DILEMMA LEARNING

Reading the literature, I have become aware of the ongoing discussion about whether or not feelings and emotion should be included in the discourse of moral education. Interested in this aspect, I asked students, <u>"How did the reflection and the decision-making phase feel like?</u>

As described in Chapter 10 in detail, Ulli experienced strong feelings, especially anger, during her conflict with Johnny. Paul experienced the dilemma situation quite differently, "Somehow so hopeless, you feel desperate and you don't know what to do (P7p34)." Daniela contended that, "It was very difficult because there is always the possibility for a mistake and to the make a right decision – it is a funny feeling somehow to make a decision (D21p21)." Daniela added, "This is a weird feeling if you know that you can do something wrong" (D23p25). Fatima described her feelings, "It was weird, in the beginning I was so happy and then I sort of had a feeling as if I was 'contracting' myself inside." (F77p53) The discussion was the point where Emma's equanimity was challenged, "Well when it went on to the discussion, it became really hefty occasionally and well, ...'What shall I say now?' This really affected my feelings. There were highs and there were lows – it was always different!" (E29p30)

RESEARCHER COMMENTARY 2003

It appears that the decision-making process resulted in a range of feelings for some students. To me, this is evidence that students' engagement with the dilemma was profound – probably more than if a student had made a disconnected, rational statement. However, for researchers, feelings are 'messy' and their effect cannot be easily measured and categorised – perhaps this is the reason why feelings have been regarded rather as a nuisance than as a positive side-effect.

LEARNING ABOUT SELF

Some students reported insights about themselves initiated by the dilemma unit. Daniela, for example, found out about her own difficulty in dealing with different opinions, "I simply have to learn to accept that other people have different opinions. I think that I can really take this with me" (D3p49)....And she added, "One gets to learn about one's own characteristics!" (D19p70)." Ulli contended that she too had to learn how to respect other opinions, "That I [always] respect other people's opinion and that I don't draw premature conclusions – I mean that was clear to me somehow but rather to try and do the right thing during the dilemma units." (U27p45)

Emma contended that the dilemma learning experience contributed to, "...one's self-confidence especially if you see that there are a few people who share your opinion. And when you can say, 'This is not how I see it!' then you become more open towards other opinions as well. Because sitting in a circle it is much better to be confronted with this than being confronted with it and not being prepared for it." (E28p48)

325

On the other hand, Emma reported that, "…[I have learned] to attach greater value to some things and perhaps also to let go easier of some things…and to engage with all of that [the controversial issues]."

RESEARCHER COMMENTARY 2003

Whilst Daniela and Ulli were struggling with their ability to accept other opinions and to fully respect them, Emma experienced the dilemma units as an arena for boosting her self-confidence: if you see that you're not the only one in the class with a particular opinion, this is apparently very reassuring. Emma's comment regarding the value of things mirrors the results of critical self-reflection – she could not have arrived at this response without critically assessing her own beliefs.

LEARNING ABOUT OTHERS

For Ulli the learning experience not only involved learning about herself but also about others in class and about issues in the stories, "I have learned about the opinions of others, that you must discuss an issue and that my opinion is not always the only right one and that with issues like that you should take them seriously and not trying to have fun (U2p39) And she added, "[I have learned] from the story how different people are – because one of them stayed behind and the other one left. Also about questions of conscience – one of them supposedly had a bad conscience and the other one might have continued with his work because of his dream,… very self-centred, and one notices how people are, how they do not care as long as it is their dream." (U30p37)

Daniela elaborated that she had learned, "…very much, [about] class community, to accept other people's opinions, even if it's

326

difficult for me – obviously not everybody has the same opinion as I. (D3p49)

In Irene's class, students also appreciated the opportunity to 'get to know the others better' or to improve the class community. When I asked Gregor whether he felt he had learned anything, he replied, "Oh yes! You get to know your classmates much better because you can see what their opinions are and how they react to certain things. In general, I think that one gets to know each other much better through discussion and group-work." (G24p48) I asked further, "You discovered that others have opinions different to yours – do you think this insight can help you in any way later in life?" Gregor answered, "Yes, I think so because if I have done this already once then I know approximately how people are going to react. If you take part in a discussion or in a presentation, you often don't know how to react in the beginning because you just don't know what to do!" (G25p65-66)

Gregor apparently thought he was learning for life to some degree at least. Melinda also supported this when she said, "Yes, because you learn from this for life." So I asked further, "What? What do you think you have learned?" "About how to solve problems collaboratively, how to interact with others and how to argue and so… (Me28p83-86)… I have realized that there are many different opinions about one issue." (Me 29p56)

RESEARCHER COMMENTARY 2003

Ulli's comment reminded me of Fatima's insight about her friend Emma who did not share the same opinions all the time which proved to be an important insight for Fatima (see Chapter 9). For Ulli it seems, the 'fact' that people seem different and that her opinion was not always the 'right' one might have provided her with some food for thought. Daniela apparently also became acutely aware of other people's opinions. Both Gregor and Melinda argued that they felt that they might have learned something they could use later in life – for Gregor it was knowledge about how other people might react whilst for Melinda it was rather related to collaborative problem-solving. Both Ulli and Melinda had gained insights about the fact that there are different opinions. I think that this insight is an important one with regard to adolescent development – apparently the dilemma units confronted the students with opinions different from their own which might affect self-centredness thereby perhaps leading to critical self-reflection and thus potentially to moral learning.

BACK TO STUDENT COMMENTS

Julian, on the other hand, contended that he had learned that other opinions cannot simply be changed by will, "You cannot radically change somebody's opinion. The only thing you can do is to point out [a perspective] so that the other can pick out the best for him" (J6p69). Damian in Irene's class had a similar perspective to offer, "If somebody has an opinion...no, I cannot simply tell him to stop having this opinion." (Da6p26)

RESEARCHER COMMENT 2003

For Julian and for Damian it seemed to have became obvious that you cannot change a person's opinion if you do not like it but you have to use argumentation to try and convince the other person. This is a very important learning outcome with regard to how one views learning in general. These two students show an insight that is often lacking in adult discourse and which addresses directly the debate about values instruction versus dialogical approaches.

LEARNING HOW TO APPROACH CONTROVERSIAL ISSUES

Julian elaborated on how the dilemma learning might help him in future dealings with controversial issues, "I am not sure as to how to put this...always approach issues critically, for example, rumours,... but not in a way that is spiteful...[instead] always

328

asking what's behind something and asking questions if there is the opportunity for that (J9p89). Maria responded along a similar line of argument when I asked her, "Do you think you can take something with you from this dilemma unit?" "Yes, sure, to reconsider new things all the time, to recombine, to re-arrange something that has not yet fit in … it simply fills gaps (M11p95-99). Paul supported Julian's and Maria's comments by saying, "…that you have to question everything, to reflect on everything and carefully evaluate and look carefully [so] that you can better decide, because in life there are always decisions like these. Issues that are difficult, where somebody can be harmed, or simply that you have to take care of others (P6p54).

RESEARCHER COMMENTARY 2003

The above student comments seem to illustrate well that students learned to reflect critically and to ask questions without taking anything for granted. Whilst Maria's comment points rather in the direction of a restrictive critical thinking, Paul seemed to be aware that future decisions in real life might also involve ethical questions that involve other people's wellbeing. Julian promoted critical questioning of everything – I believe that these examples point towards budding ethical and political awareness.

STUDENT COMMENTARY CONTINUED

In Irene's class there were several comments that indicated that the dilemma units had an effect on students' attitude towards plants. Damian, for example, argued that he had learned that, "…you should not simply cut down trees – you hurt their feelings!" (Da11p6) Fatima indicated that, "I am sure that when I go out into the woods I will now think differently [about plants]." (F69p50)

SUMMARY OF SECTION 2 AND RESEARCHER COMMENTARY 2003

Applying one's intuition (i.e., emotional thinking), thinking rationally and critically, as well as reflecting critically on the self and on others seemed to be some of the key-ingredients of the dilemma learning process.

Ulli elaborated on the effects of the dilemma stories as a tool for learning and pointed out that they apparently created an atmosphere that was conducive to learning by allowing students to talk to each other and by offering a variety of activities instead of traditional teacher instruction only. She argued also that one might learn better from stories because they supported one's identification with others. Some students reported strong feelings involved in the decision-making process.

Other students apparently learned about themselves, about their difficulties with accepting other opinions, with abstaining from drawing premature conclusions, or with too great an attachment to particular objects. As Daniela expressed it, simply learning about one's own characteristics. Another student experienced the dilemma units as an opportunity to boost one's self-confidence in the light of other people's approval of one's opinion. These comments are pointing towards an engagement in critical self-reflection.

Other student comments focused on what they had learned about others. For some students, it had been an important insight to realise that there were so many different opinions and so many different 'people'. This might be interpreted as a step towards increased tolerance and towards seeing oneself increasingly in 'relation to others'. Especially in Irene's class, comments were focusing on the class community and how one could get to know each other better through group-work and discussion. Some students reported having learned for life by learning about collaborative problem solving, social interactions, and other people's reactions. At least two students became aware that it is not easy to change other students' opinions and that you can only use argumentation to convince others.

Other reported learning outcomes included an awareness of the need to approach controversial issues with a critical mind and, by practicing the art of critical thinking and of critical reflection, thereby taking over responsibility for one's decisions. This points also in the direction of a budding ethical and political awareness. In Irene's class, some students also reported changed attitude towards plants.

330

Students not only voiced praise or criticisms they also suggested ideas on how to improve the dilemma teaching

Section 3: Students' suggestions for improvement

As one might expect, there were several themes dominated students' suggestions, ranging from the frequency of dilemma units to group-issues, from topic-related issues to time-related issues. I asked students, " How often do you think (if at all) it might be useful to have dilemma units?" I was surprised to find agreement amongst the interviewees that it should be implemented on a regular basis. There were differences with regard to the length and the number of units during the school year.

FREQUENCY OF DILEMMA UNITS

"Every two or three months a unit...yes I do think so," Maria stated and she added, "So that it is regularly brought back into consciousness for those people who do not think by themselves" (M5p45-49) Ulli argued also in favour but cautioned, "Not as long as this was, but perhaps once a month for two hours in the afternoon, perhaps." She added, "I would support the idea of doing it regularly one afternoon per month. If it was being done every week, it would not be fun any longer..." (U27p69-70) Julian seemd to support Ulli's comment, "I think it cannot harm [to do this more often]. As long as it is not every week." (J19p85) Daniela emphasised the importance of repetition within limits, "Well, this depends very much on the topic...yes, on and off, so that people are forced to think, but one should not do it too often." (D26p60-66)

THE GROUP ISSUE RE-VISITED

Students raised the 'group issue' quite often in the form of suggestions, Paul indicated that in his view groups inhibit the formation of one's own opinion and should therefore be avoided. "...[I would suggest] that it is not so group-oriented … I think it should be more focused on individual work but groups…well I don't know!" (P14p22). This stands in stark contrast to Julian who suggested earlier on about having group-work only instead of individual reflection time.

STORY TOPICS RE-VISITED

Some students in Sandra's class were concerned about the topics of the stories, "[A story that is more meaningful to us...] some dilemma perhaps, some situation where we have to make a decision …because with our government, this is once again a right-wing government. It is difficult to say – [we should] not [say], this [a story like the Rocket Dilemma] won't happen again! Quite easily there can be a similar situation again..." (P20p46) Ulli argued that, "More general topics should be included, like for example Human Rights – so that one really has to deal with it and not just like, "Human Rights rarara" but that it [the issue] is somehow packed into stories like these so that one really has to identify with them, what would it be like in that situation and how would one act." (U27p69-70) Daniela argued along a similar line, "...for the longer term you have to choose different topics so that students' thinking is promoted. I think the idea is great." (D17p58) Daniela apparently regarded the dilemma approach as such as a good idea as long as the topics varied regularly and remained relevant to the students,

TIME-PROBLEM RE-VISITED

If one wants to implement dilemma units, one needs to make sure, "... that you really take more time, perhaps for a whole day or so, without many interruptions. Not so spread out over days because then you have 'internalised' the issue and you don't have to repeat everything that was done the previous time but you can do it all at once." (D18p9) Daniela's statement summarises well the necessity of planning dilemma units - better than I did - with regard to time in order to avoid unnecessary repetition and loss of interest. With regard to the time problem, Paul suggested sacrificing periods from other subjects in favour of dilemma units, "I believe that there should be less subjects and I think that art and music are really not so important. I think one could take one hour from there and perhaps use it." (P22p50)

SUMMARY OF SECTION 3 AND RESEARCHER COMMENTARY 2003

Ulli raised the issue of saturation with dilemma units indicating that well-meaning teachers should avoid an overload which might result in an aversion to the whole dilemma approach. The conclusion I would like to draw from this statement is that introducing dilemma classes on a regular basis is good as long as classes are not too close together which leads us to the topic of frequency: suggestions ranged from one month to three months. I presume Ulli's suggestion about once per month for two hours sounds quite reasonable. However, the teacher or curriculum developer is once again confronted with a dilemma. Students seemed to say, "Dilemmas, yes, please but not too often! And voluntary!" The group-issue was re-visited with Paul arguing for less group-work and Julian promoting more group-work. There were also suggestions with regard to topics: Paul was complaining about the topic earlier when he said that he could not identify with the goals of the main character in the story (see Chapter 7). He apparently suggested drawing topics from contemporary issues only. Ulli argued that other topics such as Human Rights should be included also. I cannot fully agree with that because the topics need to be relevant for science education. Other topics could be covered by other subject areas. Daniela wished for a variety of topics that would promote students' thinking. I agree up to the point where topics leave the 'wide arena' of science education. In this case, I believe that other subjects should cover those topics. Students also pointed towards possible improvements with regard to time-management which included suggestions to drop particular subjects such as art which of course is out of question in a largely compulsory curriculum like the Austrian one. The conclusion to draw here is rather to work on the length of the dilemma units.

PART 4: TEACHERS' IMPRESSIONS OF THE DILEMMA UNITS

After the dilemma units I interviewed Irene to find out about her general impression of the dilemma units and her plans for the future use of her experiences.

Section 1: Irene

Lily: Do you think that what we have just done is useful to achieve the personal ethical goal you mentioned to me last time (see Chapter 3)?

Irene: I think that this is a topic they have engaged with in much greater depth than usually so I believe that the [learning] effect will be stronger. From my perspective – knowing exactly what I have done with them [the students] I can always come back to that and make connections! This is how I imagine the future development [of the dilemmas] – whether or not it will really turn out like that – I cannot tell yet. And whether or not I will include this in the future more often....but I am certain that it is something I will always be able to re-connect to. (I-FS2p209-210)

Irene (continued): I have promised them that this is a long-term project and I have announced the project as such to them. Firstly I can relate my teaching to any of these stories and secondly I believe that it is simply useful. It is not necessary that we use up ten hours per dilemma unit but they [the students] will get faster too. This really speaks to me perhaps because I like to tell stories in any case. (I-FS2p84) I believe that I will also be able to connect to topics such as human biology, resources...information about contagious diseases the rainforest – I would like to use this [approach] throughout the upper school level with them. Because I can clearly see that this is a globalisation issue – the more we travel the more they travel – the greater the problems. (I-FS2p85) ...I will certainly go back and ask them, "Can you remember...? This is a similar situation to the one we discussed then – this depends on the perspective, and there are always several perspectives ...I have to accept them all.

Lily: Did you feel that the students worked better over time?

Irene: I believe they were faster and also more prepared to deal with the content. Perhaps because the students were better focused and because they knew what was expected of them. (I-FS3p4)

Lily: Why do you think this was the case?

Irene: Practice and perhaps also the insight of the students that it was beneficial to talk to each other, to reflect on the issues, reflect individually, have an opinion, something they like to do, and I believe that it is something really important. I am sure that this played a major role. (I-FS3P11-16)

Section 2: Sandra

Together with my supervisor, Peter, who was present during Sandra's plenary discussion phase, I interviewed Sandra after 'her' dilemma unit was finished.

Peter: Did the dilemma stories have an impact on your thinking?

Sandra: I just realised that for me it is very hard to decide what is right or wrong

Lily: The dilemma stories and the discussion – do you think there are some transferable skills?

Sandra: I don't know but I hope so.

Peter: What are the skills you might have transferred?

<u>Sandra</u>: I would hope that individuals have started to think about what they are doing and that they are a part of a greater system and see that everything has consequences.

<u>Peter</u>: You think they will develop a sense of ethical responsibility for their actions and their inactions as well?

<u>Sandra</u>: Yes! (S-FS4-p28-36)

<u>Peter</u>: Has this been the first dilemma-story you have taught? After this - one will there be another one?

<u>Sandra</u>: I am not sure…(laughing)

SUMMARY OF SECTIONS 1 AND 2, AND RESEARCHER COMMENTARY 2003

Whilst Irene had 'big plans' for connecting her future teaching to the dilemma units throughout the upper school level, Sandra – probably still under the impression of the rather 'slow' plenary discussion in her class – was not so sure whether she would use dilemma stories again nor whether she would write some herself. However, she had the hope for her students that they had perhaps gained an idea of the meaning of ethical responsibility, and that individuals might have started to think about the consequences of their actions. Irene noticed that over time students worked better in a more focused manner and were more prepared to take in the issues. She planned for the future to continue to use storytelling in her teaching and to point out dilemma situations when they occurred.

I think both teachers were aware that a one-month project is unlikely to 'change the world' but both were hoping it had had some effect. In order for it to have a broader effect, it would have been necessary to ensure that this type of teaching continues over the next few years. However, neither of the teachers 'vowed' to continue to work in that direction.

Section 3: Other teachers outside of the project

However, there were several very positive outcomes school-wide that included other teachers as well. There was interest from other teacher colleagues who were keen on finding out how the dilemma units worked – the religious education teacher of Irene's class and one of the chemistry teachers of the school.

The German teacher of Irene's class, for example, picked up on the issue of the tree dilemma and suggested the students could use their experiences during the dilemma unit for a German test that required them to discuss a 'conflict'. The students told me that they were positively impressed how well they could use what they had 'learned' during the dilemma units for their work in German.

Another positive aspect was that I received positive feedback from Josef, Irene's co-teacher who had witnessed parts of the dilemma units. He involved me in the following conversation:

CONVERSATION WITH JOSEF DURING IRENE'S TREE DILEMMA

<u>Josef</u>: What are you doing in your project?

I try to explain to him about what I am doing and why and how. Josef asks me whether he may read the story.

<u>Josef</u>: This story sends shivers down my spine when I read it – we have to be especially careful with our son because he has got two of these 'birth-trees'! I really like the idea of all this! I mean I am doing this also in my teaching - I always try to address dilemmas!
<u>Lily</u>: Yes, I have also always tried to include this in my teaching but I have experienced the fact that there are no materials for science-teaching as extremely unsatisfactory! I did not have the feeling that I could really 'touch' the students enough!
<u>Josef</u>: I wonder how one could find out about whether the students learn something from all this or not?

I try to explain my view of this problem by referring to constructivism as a referent for teaching, the changed role of a teacher within this framework, and the idea that learning can only be initiated by the teacher: the learning itself has to be done by the student.

<u>Josef</u>: Makes sense!

And he continues to film with the video-camera.

RESEARCHER COMMENTARY 2003

I have known Josef for a few years now and I know that he is not a gullible person. I interpret his genuine interest in my project and in the teaching and learning with dilemmas as very positive. Talking to other teachers about the project was also a good opportunity for me to reflect on the project and its implementation. Josef's probing about how could we know that students learned something was very helpful.

A few days after Irene's Tree dilemma, Josef surprised me with an unexpected plight. I would like to add a brief <u>vignette</u> about that scene.

<u>AFTERLUDE: JOSEF IN DILEMMA MOOD – 23.5.2000</u>

Bell rings...
Josef rushes in, "I need your tree-story, quickly!" I want to know why he is in such a desperate 'need for a dilemma in his life'. He has not got much time for explanations, "I have told you that I liked how the story worked out with Irene´s class the other day, and just then I realised that I could use this story with my grade 6 students – fits in perfectly well!" I try to give him the "How-To-Teach-a-Dilemma-Unit" lecture compressed in two minutes but he is probably too much in a hurry to take anything in. I ask, "When do you need it for?" "NOW! Actually for the unit after this one!"....
After two hours he comes back...
"Quickly, quickly explain to me again how it works – I need it NOW!" So I explain to him about the organisation of groups and the importance of time for self-reflection. "I see!" Suddenly he says with a panic-stricken look on his face, "What I´ll have to tell this story freely? Are you serious? I haven´t got the time to learn that!" Ingrid standing next to us adds knowingly and with a broad grin on her face, "Of course you´ll have to learn the story first. What did you think – you´d escape? No way! Everyone has to be able to tell the story freely!"
The next few minutes Josef spends sitting at a table, 'studying' for his performance as a dilemma facilitator.
I meet him later in the corridor, "It worked really well!", he tells me with a radiant smile on his face. "I have never thought of using this stuff for my teaching but it works out so well! Amazing! Thanks so much!"

RESEARCHER COMMENTARY 2003

Josef's positive feedback was very important for me because he was not one of the participating teachers and was not introduced to 'dilemma teaching', like Sandra and Irene. I asked him why he had not participated in the first place (see Chapter 3), and he admitted to not fully understanding at the time what it was all about because he had not read the announcement thoroughly and he could not imagine how the dilemma approach would benefit his teaching. His (final) enthusiasm was indeed very rewarding.

REVIEW OF THE CHAPTER

Exploring student preferences with regard to storytelling versus story-reading, all interviewees indicated they preferred the stories to be told. Reasons given included that storytelling provided a context for identification and reflection, promoted attention and engagement. Some students referred to a lack of interest in reading as well to difficulties in dividing one's attention between reading and reflecting on the dilemma. Irene found that stories always supported her science teaching and that she deliberately made use of his pedagogical tool as often as possible. Facilitating versus instructing was another issue raised by students in Sandra's class. They expressed their appreciation of the non-manipulative approach that allowed them to form and express their own opinions freely. Several students explained that the teacher's opinion would have been too influential and too disturbing. However, students appeared aware that some opinions were better than others and suggested the teacher uses 'teasing' with questions as a method.

Time was the limiting factor. For the future, improvement of the time management of dilemma units needs to be a key-factor to ensure satisfaction with the units. 'Should ethics be a part of the curriculum?' was another question that I explored with the students. Most interviewees contended that ethics should not only be part of the science curriculum but also should be integrated into other subjects. Only one student would have preferred a separate ethics course.

Overall, impressions of teachers and students yielded a wide range of issues. All interviewees contended that they regarded dilemma units as a valuable tool for teaching ethical issues. However, there were conflicting ideas as to whether the participation should be voluntary, and whether there should be more group-work instead of individual reflection or the other way round. Some students regarded this type of learning as a preparation for life. Other students apparently liked the stories best, whilst others were moved by the discussions. Hearing other opinions and learning more about colleagues seemed to be experienced positively. Some students explained that their experiences included strong feelings. Students also apparently appreciated the various activities and that they were not required to listen only to what the teacher said.

Students' perspectives about learning through dilemmas included issues related to learning about oneself, learning about others, learning how to approach controversial issues, learning that

340

one cannot simply change others' opinions – one needs to use other means. Students' suggestions for improvement included ideas regarding the frequency of dilemma units, groups, story-topics, and time-related issues.

Teachers' impressions of the dilemma units focused on the future use of dilemma stories, on the 'improved' student performance over time, and the hope that students had started to think about their own responsibilities and the consequences of their actions. I also presented my interactions with Josef, Irene's co-teacher, who became so 'convinced' by his observations of the Tree Dilemma that he trialled it with his own students after a mini-crash course – successfully, he claimed.

Chapter 11

Using dilemma stories for optimising the conditions of the teaching of and the learning about controversial, ethical issues in relation to science

Some opinions from BBC News TALKING POINT on whether or not schools should be teaching science ethics:

Science deals with facts. Ethics and philosophy are just a load of individual opinions, which vary wildly depending on what language you speak, where you were born and where you live, your sex and your social status. They are not suitable subjects for expending mental effort on except as a form of casual relaxation (Liam).

The consideration of the implications of science has now become unavoidable. Every pupil will have to deal with an increasingly scientific society as adults. In this case it seems fair to try and equip them with the means to deal with complex ethical issues...Ethics has become an intrinsic part of science so why not of science education as well? (Matthew) (BBC News TALKING POINT, 2001).

INTRODUCTION

The purpose of this chapter is to revisit the various stations along the research journey, to summarise the insights gained from the research, to draw conclusions from the findings and to attempt to give recommendations for the use of dilemma stories in science education as well as for future research in this area. The chapter is organised in three parts:

- Part 1: briefly elucidates the background of the study. In this part of the chapter, I summarise the background information of the research study. I

342

discuss the research context (see Chapter 3), followed by a brief overview of the research methodology (see Chapter 2, 4 & 6) and the development of the Ethics in Science curriculum (see Chapter 5 & 6).

- Part 2: explores what conditions need to be established to optimise the teaching of and learning about controversial, ethical issues in and around science in relation to the dilemma stories. I have used the 'emerged' research questions (see Chapter 1) as a scaffold to structure Part 2 of this chapter. Part 2 is organised in seven sections and around seven pedagogical dilemmas.

- Part 3: provides a summary of the whole study, conclusions for future applications and suggestions for further research in this area.

PART 1: BACKGROUND OF THE STUDY

Research context

The research was conducted at a non-denominational, co-educational, public senior high school in Graz, Austria. The school forms part of an alliance of several schools situated in the western suburbs of Graz. Due to my role as a former teacher, as the parent of a former student, and as a colleague of the participating teachers, I had experienced the school first-hand and was familiar with the context. In Chapter 3, I discussed in detail the particularities of the Austrian schooling system including issues such as the organisation of the school year, assessment issues, etc. Furthermore, I compared the Schulverbund Graz West - an alliance of several trial schools for a 'new' middle-school model - to the traditional Austrian schooling system and included a description of the organisation of the Schulverbund Graz West. During the fieldwork, I collaborated with two teachers and their classes: Irene and 'Form 5A' (Year 9) as well as with Sandra and 'Form

6A' (Year 10). The student population of the two classes consisted of commuters who travelled to school from the country as well as students who lived in the city. From a cultural and social perspective, there were several differences between the two classes: Form 5A, Irene's class, was multicultural whilst Sandra's class, Form 6A, consisted exclusively of 'native' Austrians (with one exception!). Many students in Irene's class had German as a second language. There was also a variety of religious denominations in Irene's class: Catholic, Lutheran, Muslim, and Buddhist. When I compare the philosophical background of both teachers, Irene seems to promote a philosophy of respect for life whilst Sandra seems to emphasise to her students the importance of reflecting on the consequences of one's actions.

Research methodology

The research methodology was distributed in strategic places throughout the thesis: In Chapter 2, I presented my thesis as an interpretive case study and gave an overview of the overall methodology and grounded the research in the 7th Moment of qualitative research, integral philosophy and critical constructivism (Kincheloe, 1998; Lincoln & Denzin, 2000; Taylor, 1998; Wilber, 1998, 2000). I portrayed my study as a 'bricolage' drawing from ethnography, feminism, hermeneutic phenomenology and biographical research. Chapter 6, my second methodology chapter, is strategically located before the findings chapter, and serves to present issues related to the fieldwork, data-generation and data-analysis. In Chapter 4, I presented the methodology relevant to autobiographical research. In Chapter 5, I discussed methodological issues related to the planning and implementation of the Ethics in Science curriculum: I introduced the reader to 'my life as a curriculum developer before the thesis': at that time I was involved in a curriculum development project that was initiated by the Austrian Youth Red Cross in order to produce curriculum materials for the then impending

Curriculum Reform 99. Whilst the curriculum development during the Red Cross Project was based on Kohlberg's work and on radical constructivism, in this study (see Chapter 6) I adopted a more integral perspective on moral education as suggested by Haynes (1998). In addition, I adopted the concept of the 'separate', the 'connected' and the 'constructed knower' as suggested by Belenky et al. (1997). As a framework for moral learning, I chose the Theory of Transformative Learning as suggested by Mezirow (1991) who combined critical reflection and critical constructivism.

In the next part of the chapter, I explore the conditions that seem to be necessary for engaging students during a dilemma unit.

PART 2: CONDITIONS FOR OPTIMISING STUDENT ENGAGEMENT DURING A DILEMMA UNIT IN RELATION TO THE DILEMMA STORIES

Background

In Chapters 7, 8, and 9, I presented scenes from the implementation of the dilemma stories in the classroom from my viewpoint as a participant observer, and discussed these examples from the Ethics in Science project by bringing together teachers', students' and my own perspectives at the time and at present. I tried to engage the reader by weaving together classroom observation, vignettes and commentaries in order to provide a 'colourful', lively impression of the 'Lebenswelt' at that moment interwoven with my interpretations of the events.

When I revisited the data, I noticed that there were a number of so-called 'contradictory' findings which may be expected if one draws from a number of sources. In Chapter 2, I quoted Slattery (1995) who said that traditionally in the West there is a tendency to believe that two opposites cannot coexist which is why often one pole of the bifurcation is eliminated to avoid ambiguity. However, instead of using the traditional elimination strategy, I have adopted an epistemology of ambiguity and an integral perspective in this study (Pallas, 2001;

Wilber, 1995). The integral perspective allows me to approach the two apparently contradictory poles through the application of integral vision which is a dialectical view in a Hegelian sense: the synthesis of two contradictory poles is the departure point for a higher level of understanding. Instead of discarding valuable information, one creates a whole that provides a much richer context to learn from than if one takes a (limited) part for the whole. Thus, in the case of this thesis, I would like to use the term 'pedagogical dilemmas' for the seemingly contradictory sets of findings. I call them dilemmas because they confront the educator with a choice between apparently mutually exclusive alternatives. The dilemmas are 'pedagogical' because they relate to the teaching and learning in a dilemma unit and affect our choice as to whether or not we as educators want to use a dilemma teaching approach for teaching ethics in science education. Pedagogical dilemmas bring to the fore what teachers and curriculum planners might encounter if they were to use dilemma stories in their classrooms.

In the following section of the chapter, I explore the suitability of dilemma stories for engaging students in a dilemma situation.

Section 1: The dilemma stories

In this part of the chapter, I summarise and discuss the significance and implications of the findings with regard to the following research questions:

- How well are dilemma stories suited for optimising the conditions of the teaching of and the learning about controversial, ethical issues in relation to science?
- How can we ensure appropriateness of the curriculum materials (i.e. the dilemma stories) with regard to the age of the students?
- Storytelling as a teaching method versus story-reading – does it really matter?

SUITABILITY OF DILEMMA STORIES AS A PEDAGOGICAL TOOL FOR INTRODUCING STUDENTS TO CONTROVERSIAL ISSUES IN SCIENCE

Overall, students seem to have regarded the dilemma stories as a suitable way of introducing them to a dilemma. The stories seemed to foster students' identification with the story characters and their situations, thereby evoking their imagination and emotions, and raising students' attention levels (see Chapter 7). Some students mentioned concerns such as a disinterest in the topic, a too high level of complexity of the storyline, and lack of age-appropriateness of the stories, as potential obstacles to student engagement with the stories. Students' lack of engagement resulted in high noise-levels, unproductive commentaries, and a reported lack of interest particularly during the introductory session of the Tree Dilemma which was apparently not as well received as I had hoped for. The turning point appeared to be a personal story Irene told that not only seemed to change her storytelling style but also students' levels of engagement. The Rainforest Dilemma was partly successful and partly not: some students experienced it as too difficult and too complex. They claimed to not feel engaged and seemed to not really see the dilemma(s) in the story, which indicates to me that the story was probably not age-appropriate for them. My classroom observations during the second dilemma unit indicated that students appeared less involved and somehow 'tired'. Reasons for this could have been the short interval between the two dilemma units (leading to 'dilemma-overload') and/or that the story was too complex for the age group. Students might have been overwhelmed because their knowledge base was not yet sufficient. This, of course, points towards the need for better preparation of students prior to dilemma units.

These findings lead us to the formulation of a pedagogical dilemma with regard to the appropriateness of the dilemma stories:

PEDAGOGICAL DILEMMA 1: WRITING ENGAGING DILEMMA STORIES – ENGAGING FOR WHOM?

The dilemma units in Irene's and in Sandra's classes have illustrated a potential pedagogical dilemma with dilemma stories: on the one hand, a teacher may choose a particular story because s/he regards it as presenting an engaging dilemma for the students but it might not actually engage them. On the other hand, students may sometimes experience a dilemma story as engaging whereas the teacher may consider it to be too simplistic. This research indicates also that, amongst students of the same age-group, some may 'see' the dilemma in a story whilst others may not. In dilemma teaching, non-engagement of students at the outset can have important repercussions for subsequent stages of the dilemma unit, especially for individual reflection, group-discourse, poster-presentations, plenary discussions, etc. Engaging as many students as early as possible may be vital for the success of these aspects of the dilemma learning process.

This pedagogical dilemma has led me to re-visit the research question:

- How can we ensure appropriateness of curriculum materials with regard to the age of the students?

In preparing the dilemma stories, I tried to address this issue by relying on Irene's and Sandra's familiarity with their classes. I stayed in close email contact with both teachers in order to write the 'right' stories, suitable for the age-group of their students. I relied heavily on the teachers' knowledge of the kids and on their professional experience. Scharf suggested that when writing your own dilemmas you should first get to know your students, then find out which topics seem especially pressing (Scharf, 1978). However, this research suggests that good knowledge of a class may not guarantee a good enough answer to this problem. This has highlighted to me probably <u>the</u> single most crucial problem of planning the dilemma teaching approach: No matter how careful our planning, when we develop curriculum materials for teaching ethics in science classrooms it may be difficult to meet 'everybody's taste'.

However, this study has indicated also that <u>one</u> way of helping to ensure a good level of student engagement during the initial phase of the dilemma unit may be for the teacher to tell the story freely instead of having students read from an overhead transparency or a photocopy.

STORYTELLING VERSUS STORY-READING

The findings revealed that students generally preferred storytelling by the teacher rather than their own reading of the stories. Reportedly, stories helped students to better focus their attention and to better identify with the dilemma situation and the characters in the story. Storytelling also seemed to provide a context for student reflection and to promote student attention and engagement. Some students pointed out that storytelling conveyed much more than reading because of issues related to body language, intonation, voice. Given that the stories are 'primers' for the dilemma questions, it was interesting to find that storytelling seems to be the more effective option when it comes to presenting a dilemma to the students. Some of the students described a 'struggle' with reading fluently and thinking simultaneously. Whilst some students explained their preference for listening as laziness, others students referred to a lack of interest in reading. However, some students cherished the opportunity to already reflect on the story whilst it was being told.

THE FINDINGS IN LIGHT OF THE LITERATURE

Lickona informs us that literature is a good vehicle for introducing moral education into the curriculum (Lickona, 1991). However, given that it may be difficult to write the 'right' dilemma stories, should we not give up the stories approach altogether and simply teach ethics as a series of propositions that might be discussed with the students? Murray addresses this question when he says that, "We learn through stories as children." And he adds, "Even the most committed devotee of analytical rigour must admit that most people, most of time, learn most of what they know about morality from narratives of one kind or another..." He explains further that some people who favour the teaching of ethics through propositions might argue that "...people are simply too dense to grasp, remember, or learn how to use propositions as such, so we must fall back on stories as heuristic devices" (Murray, 1997, pp. 6-7). At times when we encounter moral disagreement, we need to rely on what we know about morality and, Murray argues, some of our most reliable knowledge in such cases comes from the images or stories we have recorded in our memory: "Moral justification often consists of tracing the thread that ties the case now under scrutiny back to the image or narratives on the tapestry we know well and confidently" (Murray, 1997 pp. 14-15). Leming (quoting Vitz) argues along a similar line when he suggests that children's understanding of moral issues is interpersonal, emotional, imaginistic and story-like. Children therefore ought to experience moral development through narrative (Leming, 2000). Perhaps this is why religious leaders of the world, be they Jesus Christ or Buddha, chose stories as a tool to get across the meaning of their teachings. Based on Murray (quoting Nussbaum), we might argue that stories are not only a tool in moral education but are an essential element in moral understanding itself (Murray, 1997). This notion sits well with Narvaez's (quoting Bruner) suggestion that moral reasoning might perhaps actually combine 'propositional' thought (logical thinking independent of context) and narrative thought (contextualised thinking) (Narvaez, 2001) which would mean that dilemma stories might be a good way of teaching ethics after all. If, as Murray, Nussbaum and Narvaez argue so convincingly, stories really form the very core of moral reasoning, why is it that some students experience a dilemma as a dilemma whilst others of the same age-group do not?

One possible explanation comes from Narvaez (2001, 2002) who has studied students' comprehension of moral texts based on Cognitive Schema Theory (CST) which is commonly used in reading research. The theory, according to Narvaez, is based in constructivism by assuming that readers construct meaning from the text using their prior knowledge. She suggests that previous knowledge comes in the form of general knowledge structures – schemas. These schemas appear to be means to understand a text and seem to affect how a reader comprehends a text. A schema may be activated in a reader's mind by a single word or event in the text. The level of previous knowledge distinguishes experts from non-experts in a domain.

Applied to moral education, Narvaez informs us that several previous studies have suggested that differences in moral schema activation affect the comprehension of moral texts. In her own study she argues adamantly against the widespread adult belief that in a good story the children will understand what the adult wants them to understand. She proposes that readers comprehend what fits with their schemas and will remember the text by what made sense and what was meaningful to them: when a text conflicts with previous understandings, the reader's knowledge is likely to prevail unless the reader becomes dissatisfied with the level of explanation his/her knowledge provides. Thus, a student might understand a text differently from the teacher's intention and only if the student him/herself decides to change his/her schema might change occur (Narvaez, 2001).

In her paper 'Does reading moral stories build character', she adds another perspective: reading (in the case of this study it is rather listening to stories being told) involves theme-comprehension. A theme can be understood as a pattern among other story components in a form that is abstracted from the specific story context. A theme is the point of a story. In the case of the Ethics in Science curriculum, we could argue that the moral dilemmas in the stories represent themes in this sense. If students are to understand the dilemma as a dilemma they must therefore be able to extract the theme(s) from the text of the dilemma stories. Narvaez (2002) informs us that extracting a theme does not automatically accompany reading. Even if it is purposefully intended, children have a difficult time extracting a theme (p. 162). Even adults do at times. Narvaez concludes that the ability to extract a theme appears to be a developmental process and, regardless of the length of the intervention, there may be developmental hurdles that prevent children from comprehending an author's theme until sufficient developmental structures are in place (Narvaez, 2002, pp.166-167). Summarising, she points out that , "Much is unknown about how students extract general themes and how and why they fail."

I have to admit I found this conclusion reassuring even though it does not help much with developing more age-appropriate materials and thus with answering the research question. However, it appears that, apart from non-matching schemas and problems with extracting themes from the dilemma stories, the difficulties some students had reported with regard to the stories (e.g., Rainforest Dilemma) might also have been related to issues, such as the complexity of the story, the setting, the characters, the story theme, length and the level of vocabulary (Hedberg & Westby, 1993). These are issues that can be attended to when writing curriculum materials, and might be important factors that we need to get right when we want to engage students.

Another more recent explanation for why some students might not have understood the dilemma is offered by a theory that was developed originally by the American psychologist Clare Graves and elaborated further by Beck and Cowan: The Theory of 'Spiral Dynamics'. This theory elucidates human consciousness development from the point of view of 'ᵛmemes', each of which can be understood as a worldview, as a value system, as a level of psychological existence, as a belief structure, as an organising principle, as a way of thinking, and as a mode of living (Beck & Cowan, 1996). This theory offers some interesting aspects that might be applicable to moral education. In science education, Nancy Davis presented this theory as part of her work with practising teachers at the Annual International Conferences of the National Association Research for Science Teaching (Davis, 2003). Beck and Cowan (1996) distinguish eight core ᵛmemes in a two-tier model and colour-code them. The first tier includes Beige-Green followed by the second tier Yellow-Turquoise:

TIER ONE

<u>Beige</u>: staying alive through innate sensory equipment

<u>Purple</u>: blood relationships and mysticism in a magical, scary world

<u>Red</u>: enforce power over self, others, and nature through exploitive independence

<u>Blue</u>: absolute belief in one right way and obedience to authority

<u>Orange</u>: possibility thinking focused on making things better for oneself

<u>Green</u>: wellbeing of people and building consensus get highest priority

TIER TWO

<u>Yellow</u>: flexible adaptation to change through connected, big-picture views

<u>Turquoise</u>: attention to whole-earth dynamics and macro-level actions

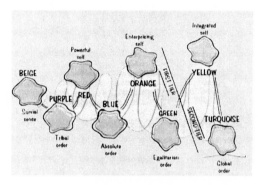

Figure 14: The developmental spiral (Beck & Cowan, 1996)

ᵛmemes mark stages of our development, however, these are not stages in a linear hierarchy but much rather situated along a developmental curve that has the shape of a spiral (see Figure 14). However, ᵛmemes determine our thinking, our decision-making and it is especially in this regard that the theory might be useful for moral learning. A particular ᵛmeme results in a particular way of thinking which determines what is relevant to us at a particular time of our development. The first of the two tiers is characterised by 'intolerance' towards the 'lower' ᵛmemes, whilst from yellow onwards, thinking becomes more inclusive and people understand that 'lower' ᵛmemes represent necessary stages of development everybody has to go through. This is a defining insight: there is no possibility to skip a level.

Applied to the dilemma approach this might mean that students could be on different ᵛmeme levels in their development, and might explain why some experience a dilemma as a dilemma whilst others cannot see it as a dilemma. Combining the Cognitive Schema Theory with the Theory of Spiral Dynamics, I would like to argue that perhaps a ᵛmeme is characterised by typical schemas that serve as organising cognitive structures. Students might thus interpret a dilemma story according to their ᵛmeme and its intrinsic schemas. This might result in some students who have the necessary moral schemas available to them being capable of making sense of a dilemma whilst others who (still) lack these predispositions might find it difficult to experience a dilemma as a dilemma.

Summarising, stories seem to have intrinsic value for moral education by providing not only a tool but also by forming part of moral understanding. The Cognitive Schema Theory in combination with the Theory of Spiral Dynamics seem to offer a plausible explanation for why some students do not experience a dilemma as a dilemma. In the next section of the chapter I explore these differences in thinking further.

Section 2: Individual reflection

In this section of the chapter, I summarise the findings in relation to the following research question (see Chapter 8):

- How well are dilemma stories suited to initiate 'thinking' in the individual student during the individual reflection phases of the dilemma units?

Student portfolio notes seemed to reveal different levels of reflective engagement with the dilemma when students were 'thinking' about the dilemmas and the solutions thereof: whilst some student commentaries indicated that students

354

might have been reflecting in a personal, critical manner that was oriented inwards (critical self reflection) others seemed to have preferred critical thinking that is, per definition, oriented outwards (Belenky et al., 1997). Again others appear to have used both – critical thinking for assessing and evaluating the dilemma problem - and critical self reflection as a means to check our past experiences, values and attitudes with a view to solving the problem. The latter students might perhaps fall into the category of the 'constructed knowers' (Belenky et al., 1997). The findings made me wonder whether I was actually looking at a developmental process – the ability to engage in critical thinking probably develops before critical self-reflection. This might be why some students use critical thinking exclusively, whilst others use both.

However, I had some concerns about the authenticity of students' thinking with regard to genuine individual work: during classroom observations in Irene's class, I had noted that a high number of students were talking to each other whilst they were supposed to be working individually. To be honest, the individual reflection phase during the first dilemma unit was, in my view, rather characterised by chaotic cooperation than by contemplative introspection. Partly, this might have been due to the crammed classroom situation where students could not easily find a private spot. On the other hand, I observed students quite openly copying their neighbours' work. There appeared to be a lack of student engagement during the individual reflection phase. According to the student interviews, possible reasons for the lack of student engagement might include: a disinterest in the story, feeling overwhelmed by a 'new' task, language-difficulties, and/or a lack of agency because decision-making might have been at odds with the experiences in the students' own 'Lebenswelt'. In contrast, there was no chaos in Sandra's class. To be precise, there was little interaction at all amongst students. Individual students appeared very task-oriented. Sandra's class was almost uni-cultural Austrian with no language difficulties. Some student statements and the (lack of) classroom interactions seem to express a tendency towards agency in Sandra's class whilst Irene's class appeared to be more focused on community

(Wilber, 1997). The exploration of the potential inauthenticity of student portfolio-notes resulted in the formulation of yet another pedagogical dilemma.

PEDAGOGICAL DILEMMA 2: CHAOTIC COOPERATION VERSUS CONTEMPLATIVE INTROSPECTION: THE (IN)AUTHENTICITY OF STUDENT PORTFOLIO-NOTES

Several students confirmed my suspicions and reported potential inauthenticity of student comments during the interviews. They mentioned fear of making a wrong decision as a possible reason, potential peer pressure was another. I was wondering whether fear of being assessed by the teacher, despite the teachers' reassurances, might have been another reason. One apparent case of inauthenticity was Melinda's portfolio: by comparing interview data and portfolio-notes I realised that Melinda had said the exact opposite in the interview of what she had written in her portfolio. This was really 'food for thought' and I came across yet another pedagogical dilemma related to the use of a dilemma teaching approach:

- Does it make sense at all to engage the students in individual reflection if their arguments potentially do not reflect authentic statements at all?

For the teacher this question is crucial as the students' portfolio-notes can serve as a tool for assessment. On the other hand, the findings indicate that some students appeared to have engaged in individual reflection and thus potentially in a learning process. Whilst it appears to make sense to include individual reflection phases in a dilemma unit as a primer for the plenary discussion, the question ultimately rests with the educator as to whether or not individual reflection should be used for assessment purposes. I am aware that my data present only a small data set, however, I believe it would be worthwhile for moral educators to investigate further the authenticity issue on a larger scale because if what my data suggest is more widespread then the value of measuring student morality levels before and after an intervention becomes a highly questionable practice.

ASSESSMENT USING STUDENT PORTFOLIOS

During the planning of the Ethics in Science curriculum the issue of assessment was raised by the teachers. This led me to formulate the following research question:

- How do we assess this type of learning?

The teachers and I agreed that portfolios might be the best choice. However, during the data-analysis it turned out that assessment on the basis of student portfolio notes was not as easy as expected: as pointed out above, the question of potential inauthenticity of student comments diminished the value of student portfolio notes for assessment purposes. Why should we assess something that is not the student's original work or something that s/he wrote only because s/he thinks this is what we want to read or something s/he thought would minimise peer-pressure in the group? I therefore doubt the value of serious assessment of these portfolios. Whilst portfolios still seemed to be the best assessment tool, I believe that this is another area that deserves more attention in future research.

SEPARATE AND CONNECTED KNOWERS

In relation to the above findings, it was also interesting to find that apparently some students were separate knowers with a focus on critical thinking and on agency, whilst other students appeared to be connected knowers with a focus on community (see Chapter 8). Interestingly enough, the data indicate that separate knowers seemed to be more common in Sandra's class which on the other hand appeared to be suffering from the effects of individualists and isolated groups. In Irene's class, there seemed to be a number of connected knowers. This seems to coincide well with the observation that community seemed to be an important focus. It is also interesting to note that the distinction separate-connected knowers appeared not to be gender-specific: Maria, for example, in Sandra's class seemed to be a separate knower whilst Alex and Damian, from Irene's class, appeared to be connected knowers (Belenky et al., 1997).The presence of students with varying dispositions towards thinking and knowing brings to the fore the need to ground the teaching approach to moral education in an integral ethical framework, such as the one suggested by Haynes (1998) which allows for an Ethic of Justice, an Ethic of Care and Ethic of Consequences to merrily co-exist.

FINDINGS IN LIGHT OF THE LITERATURE

Much of the moral education literature is based on the exploration of moral reasoning which is defined as the way non-adult learners explain their choices with regard to dilemmas. Critical analytical thinking appears to be advantaged when one wants to score high on the morality development scales. In Chapter 7, I introduced the Theory of Transformative Learning which has been developed within the domain of adult education. I pointed out the specific role of critical reflection and its potential for moral learning. If Mezirow is right and a change of our attitudes and values as a result of transformational learning is dependent on our ability for critical self reflection (Mezirow, 1991), then we must ask the question: Why does moral education of non-adult learners not put the same emphasis on the development of critical self-reflection? Why does this seem to be the domain of adult education only? Should we not also provide opportunities for our students to develop and engage in critical self-reflection? I mentioned earlier in this section that I have been wondering whether I was looking at a developmental process when I stated that some students appeared to be able to reason at a critical level whilst others used critical reflection as well.

Brookfield (1998) reviewed a number of papers and summarised the process by which adults become critically reflective about the moral assumptions, beliefs and values which they have assimilated during childhood and adolescence. Becoming critically reflective involves assessing the accuracy and validity of moral norms for the context of adult life. He informs us further that critical self-reflection is, in the view of the authors of the reviewed papers, a process that, by definition, is not generally observable in childhood. Critical reflection on moral issues can occur only as adults pass through experiences in their interpersonal, working and political lives which are characterised by breadth, depth, diversity and intensity. This breadth only comes with time (Brookfield, 1998, pp. 7-8). These assumptions are based largely on the belief that adults have more experience because they are older and therefore better equipped to make moral choices based on critical self-reflection. Brookfield, however, continues to argue that the simple equation of chronology and richness of experience is empirically unproven, "There is not attested evidence to prove that sticking around on the planet long enough to reach adult age always confers a corresponding capacity to learn from experience" (p. 3). Brookfield seems to argue that the simple fact that adults have lived longer than children does not make them necessarily more moral persons. If the capability of critical reflection is the defining issue whether or not one can engage in self-directed moral learning through transformative learning then my findings seem to indicate that the limitation of the critical reflection ability to adults appears too narrow and unwarranted: Some students in my study, despite their young age, appeared capable of engaging in critical reflection. As mentioned earlier these students also appeared to be able to use critical thinking. It appears to be the case therefore that critical thinking may be a prerequisite of critical reflection. This might explain why some other students seemingly used critical thinking only. These findings also appear to sit well with critical constructivism as a theory for learning (see Chapter 5).

Based on the findings, I would therefore like to suggest that at least some adolescents (of the age-group 15-16) appear to be capable of engagement in critical reflection, in Mezirow's sense. How, we may ask, would critical self-reflection help them with moral learning? We employ meaning schemes and perspectives to assign significance to events that shape fundamentally how we experience them (Mezirow, 1991). Brookfield argues that following a trigger-event (which can be an ethical dilemma) the moral learner undergoes a period of self-scrutiny and appraisal of new assumptions, explanations, roles, values, beliefs and behaviours in the light of a changed way of thinking and acting that makes sense or fits the disorienting dilemma. However, Mezirow argued (1991) that this new perspective is in the beginning still partial, tentative and fragile and needs to be confirmed through a series of incremental repetitions. Comparing the Theory of Transformative Learning with the Cognitive Schema Theory I mentioned earlier in the chapter (Narvaez, 2001, 2002), I find many commonalities: schemas or meaning schemes seem to determine how we make sense of an experience. Applied to the dilemma approach, the two theories seem to explain quite well how students' existing schemas or meaning schemes affect their engagement in moral learning. Not having the 'right' schemas available might explain why some students did not engage well during the individual reflection phase.

As mentioned earlier in this section, it appeared to be the case that some students were separate knowers whilst others were connected knowers (Belenky et al., 1997) With regard to these different modes of knowing and thinking, I found the Theory of Spiral Dynamics interesting in this regard: Beck and Cowan (1996) explain that ᵛmemes 'zig-zag' in a wave-like manner between a selfish and a selfless focus throughout human development: Whilst beige, red, orange, and yellow ᵛmemes represent a selfish focus, purple, blue, green and turquoise ᵛmemes have a selfless focus. They explain that these waves of self-centredness and communal engagement are related to our changing life-conditions: sometimes we are required to focus on the self whilst at other times we need to focus more on the community around us (Beck & Cowan, 1996). This relates well to what Wilber suggested in terms of 'agency' and 'communion' (Wilber, 1997). With regard to the findings, I would suggest that some students appear to have been at a particular ᵛmeme level that was focused on the 'I', as expressed through a focus on agency and being a separate knower (potentially on a red ᵛmeme level) whilst others appeared to be rather focusing on the 'we' as expressed through connected knowing and a focus on communion. These students might have been on a purple or blue level of development. Whilst I presume that, given their age, a purple ᵛmeme level is more likely, it is possible that the life-experiences of some of these students – war, slavery, orphanage, migration and living in a foreign country as a refugee, sometimes without parents – might have contributed to a higher level of development and personal maturity. Although during this study, I did not engage in ᵛmeme-analysis, which would have involved further in-depth interviews, I can see the potential benefit of exploring the relationship of ᵛmemes to moral learning through future research.

Section 3: Discourse phases

In this section of the chapter, I summarise the findings in relation to the following research question:

- Do dilemma stories have the potential to initiate discourse that can potentially lead to moral learning?

From the participant-observer's point of view, I formed the impression that the dilemma stories were a good starting point for discourse that might lead to moral learning. The discussion about whether or not a plant's life is as valuable as a human's or an animal's life, for example, involved students in reflecting on our different attitudes towards plants and animals and led to clashes of different opinions. During the interviews, many students reported that they enjoyed the dilemma approach because it gave them an opportunity to hear other people's opinions, as well as to learn more about and from their colleagues (see Chapter 8), which sits well with Vygotsy's notion of the Zone of Proximal Development (Tappan, 1998; Vygotsky, 1978).

    The discourse phases of the dilemma unit were distributed between phases of individual reflection and involved comparison of individual opinions in groups, collaborative preparations and presentations of posters, and a plenary discussion. As elaborated earlier, critical thinking and critical self-reflection were thinking modes applied during the individual reflection phases. Video-analysis of student comments during the discourse phases and interview data in relation to the discourse phases revealed that critical thinking as well as critical self reflection were applied by the students. It appears that perhaps the group discourse had caused some individuals to reflect critically on their own opinions after being confronted with conflicting opinions that apparently led to some strong emotions in some students. To me this indicates that, in a dilemma unit, the group-work and the confrontation with other opinions might be 'the' centrepiece of the moral learning experience. Making compromises, learning to negotiate and to deal with other opinions, seem to have been important learning opportunities provided by the collaborative learning experience in the small-group situation.

Based on the findings, I believe that dilemma stories can potentially promote discourse that can perhaps lead to moral learning. These findings give rise to the assumption that dilemma units could provide an arena for practicing not only rational decision making (as suggested so often in the literature) but also for social and emotional learning (see Chapter 10). However, it appears not always to be 'an easy ride' for students nor for teachers: There were apparently some concerns with regard to group-work and group-dynamics that I would like to elaborate on in the next section of the chapter.

GROUP-DYNAMICS IN THE TWO CLASSES

As elaborated in Chapter 9, there appeared to be several differences between Sandra's and Irene's classes. Irene had a multicultural class of around thirty students - all of whom arevery lively and socially active. Sandra's class on the other hand, was much smaller, almost 'unicultural' and organised in cliques. Irene's students were discussing enthusiastically (even after class) whilst in Sandra's class, there seemed to be a very limited number of discussants only. Social interaction in Sandra's class seemed to be largely limited to established groups, until Sandra mixed the groups, whilst in Irene's class cliques seemed less pronounced. Overall, Sandra's class appeared to be more task-oriented and 'efficient' than Irene's class which, on the other hand, demonstrated a stronger focus on mutual support and care. Some students, however, expressed concerns, particularly in Sandra's class, with regard to the group-processes surrounding the discourse that might have resulted in a dominance of a few opinions and might not have reflected the actual thinking of all the group-members.

CONCERNS ABOUT GROUP-WORK

It seems that group-processes were a determining factor in how students experienced the discourse phases. For students, this part of the dilemma unit required the practice of social skills and social intelligence in order to participate actively in the discourse. Some students reported conflicts during the group-work but also how they apparently solved these conflicts through either consensus or compromise. Others raised issues of maintaining a voice and daring to speak one's opinion in a group. In Sandra's class, several students appeared to be critical of group-work in general and of the group-constellations in particular. Whilst group-work in Sandra's class appeared almost 'perfect' on the outside (apart from Ulli's and Johnny's conflict), at a closer look problematic issues such as peer-pressure and group-think seemed to emerge. Some students seemed to feel that speaking about themselves and their values 'exposed' them to their classmates and enhanced their 'vulnerability'. This led me to the formulation of a third pedagogical dilemma with regard to the dilemma teaching approach.

PEDAGOGICAL DILEMMA 3: GOOD INTENTION VERSUS UNETHICAL IMPOSITION – AN (IM)MORAL DISCOURSE?

As discussed earlier, for some students classroom discourse seemed to provide valuable learning opportunities. However, in the light of the above difficulties, yet another pedagogical dilemma seemed to emerge:

- Is it not ultimately incommensurable with an Ethic of Care to 'force' students to speak about themselves in public (in the group) when they are not prepared to do this voluntarily?

- Can it be that some students are likely to deliberately write or say 'just anything' in order to protect themselves from potential peer-criticism and peer-pressure?

- Under these circumstances, does it make good pedagogical sense to expose them to a discourse situation about values at all?

- Could the discourse we are trying to promote actually be potentially 'immoral' – at least for some students?

- If this is the case - should we not simply forget about using classroom discourse on values and get on with life if there is the slightest possibility for an unintentional, unethical act on the side of the educator?

- On the other hand we might argue that, given the apparent social difficulties of some of these 'individual agents' (see Sandra's class), should we not actually reinforce our attempts to give them more opportunities to practice collaborative work?

FINDINGS IN LIGHT OF THE LITERATURE

Given that the main problems during the discourse phases were related to self-disclosure and group-work I re-visited the literature. In Chapter 4 when I was discussing literature on autobiography, I presented the Johari-window as a tool for interpreting interpersonal communication. The size of the window-panels suggests how 'open' we are towards our environment. The Private Self panel contains what we know about ourselves but do not communicate to others – reasons for non-communication of our private self include fear and insecurity (Augsburg College, n. d.; Yen, 1999). According to Coulter, teachers are often in danger of not respecting the privacy of their students well enough. He argues that children need the protection of privacy to form their own identities (Coulter, 2002). According to Borchers (1999b), authentic self-disclosure presupposes a climate where one can feel safe. If this is not the case, students might feel reluctant to engage in group-work.

This may have been the case in Sandra's class. Yet another perspective on Sandra's 'reluctant collaborative learners' could be that sometimes students resist collaborative learning because social engagement can be hard work that requires skills such as tact, responsive listening, and willingness to compromise and negotiation skills that some of these students might not yet have developed (Bruffee, 1993). Brookfield explains that some adults experience self-disclosure in a 'seating-circle' as a mandated disclosure because they feel an implicit or explicit pressure from peers or the teacher to say something, anything, whether or not they feel ready to speak (Brookfield, 1998). How much greater might the pressure be for some students in the more 'intimate' environment of an 'artificial' group?

Problems in the groups might also have been related to the different types of thinking that appeared to exist. Napier and Gershenfeld (1999) explain that some 'clashes' are grounded in perceived incompatibilities between rational thinkers and intuitive thinkers. They argue that whilst most of us are comfortable to think within the whole spectrum, sometimes individuals focus their thinking on one end of the spectrum, resulting in extremes. Intuitive individuals are usually referred to as free-spirited, able to think out of the box, whilst other individuals feel most comfortable with orderly, rational, linear thinking for whom logical thought provides intellectual stimulation. To rational thinkers intuitive thinkers appear to be disorganised, undisciplined, and overly emotional, whilst intuitive thinkers might regard their rational counterparts as rigid, inflexible, and tied to what is known. Thus, in groups with representatives of both camps present collisions can be caused by these perceptions (Napier & Gershenfeld, 1999). Again, it seems that our existing schemas that organise our thinking determine how we perceive others (Narvaez, 2001, 2002). However, a skilled facilitator who is aware that there are different thinkers in a group will provide opportunities for both rational problem-solving as well as intuitive problem solving. Rational problem-solving involves steps such as: problem identification, problem diagnosis, generation of alternatives, selecting solutions, implementation, evaluation and adjustment. Intuitive decision-making involves methods for becoming 'unstuck' such as brainstorming. Thus for future use of the dilemma approach, teachers as facilitators might want to include opportunities for both paths – the rational and the intuitive.

Conflict arises also when people have different values and beliefs that clash at some level (Napier & Gershenfeld, 1999). During the dilemma units, especially during the discourse phases, there are plenty of opportunities for practising not only rational but also social and emotional skills. It appears obvious that collaborative decision-making requires the rational problem-solving skills as outlined above. However, social skills are required also for solving conflicts and negotiating a consensus, as I elaborated in Chapter 9. Goleman, in his book 'Emotional Intelligence', elaborated on the connection between social and emotional learning. He developed a 'self-science' curriculum with learning outcomes such as: improved self-perception (being able to recognise one's own feelings), the ability to make personal decisions, to deal with emotions, the ability to reduce stress, to develop empathy and communication skills, the ability to open oneself up to others, the ability to gain an insight into one's own thought-patterns and reactions, self-acceptance, the ability to take over personal responsibility for one's actions, self-security, ability to deal with group-dynamics and conflict-resolution. All of these learning outcomes are grounded in the 'acquisition' of not only cognitive abilities but also emotional and communicative (social) abilities. The ability to develop empathy is vital if one deals with others. It depends strongly on the ability to think oneself into another person (Day, 2002; Goleman, 1997). Emotional feelings in combination with reason seem to determine moral action (Winston, 1999). The promotion of empathy, compassion and caring in students relates well to an Ethic of Care which is characterised by six core-virtues:

366

acquaintance, mindfulness, moral imagining, solidarity, tolerance, and self-care (Gregory, 2000; Noddings, 1984; Verducci, 2000; Zigler, 1998).

At this point, I would like bring in Buddhism as a referent because it has influenced my thinking at least during the last stages of the thesis: in Buddhism compassion is <u>the</u> central theme next to enlightenment and determines ethical behaviour and thinking. Through training the mind, one aims at developing 'boddhichitta' which is a 'mind of compassion' encompassing all living beings by recognising and taking on their suffering. In order to develop boddhichitta one must eliminate self-cherishing and self-grasping which are regarded as the sources of all suffering. This mind of compassion is regarded as being of highest importance if one is ever to go down the path to enlightenment. Given that Buddhists have been practising this type of training the mind for over two thousand years, one has to admit that recognising the importance of issues such as compassion and care, emotional and social intelligence, are not exactly new (Gyatso, 1988, 1990).

Summarising, I can say that many of the above learning outcomes appear to be promoted by a dilemma teaching approach: Students seem not only required to get to know themselves, their own values and thought-patterns, but also to develop empathy by putting themselves into somebody else's shoes. Communication skills apparently form an integral part of the dilemma teaching approach. This insight seems to be especially important given the apparent difficulties students apparently experienced during the group-discourse phases. The resulting conflicts might, amongst other issues, have been related to different values as well as to clashes between different types of thinkers.

<u>Section 4</u>: Should ethics be taught as part of science education at all?

This new research question emerged during the interviews. As discussed in detail in Chapter 10, I was surprised to find that despite a few criticisms regarding the teaching approach, there appeared to be strong agreement amongst the student interviewees that dilemma units should be implemented on a regular basis within science education. With one exception, students adamantly rejected the idea of a separate ethics course – if it was to be implemented then it should be implemented within science. Theorists, such as Allchin (1998; 1999a; 1999b; 2001), Patry (2000), Bowers (1993; 2002), Jones and Zucker (1986) and more recently Haste (1999), Scott (1998), Smith (1998), and Kolsto (2001), who are concerned with the teaching of ethical issues in science education, might be pleased to find that students themselves are in favour of including ethics in science. Furthermore, some students pointed out that the teaching of ethics should not be restricted only to science but that all subjects and all professions need some of it (see Chapter 10 & 5). These outcomes sit well with the mandate of the new Austrian curriculum document (see Chapter 5) which states that ethics should be taught as part of all subjects.

However, there were differences of opinion about the desired length and the number of dilemma units during the school year, ranging from once a month to once every three months. Students raised the issue of 'saturation with dilemma units' by implying that teachers should avoid dilemma overload. Concluding, we might say that including ethics classes on a regular basis within science education seemed to be regarded worthwhile by the students, however, it may be important for teachers to be cautious about the frequency. This presents curriculum developers and teachers with yet another pedagogical dilemma with regard to the frequency of dilemma units:

PEDAGOGICAL DILEMMA 4: ETHICS IN SCIENCE YES BUT NOT TOO OFTEN - (IN)FREQUENCY OF DILEMMA UNITS

This dilemma clearly leaves us with the question: how often is too often? It appears from the findings that once per month might be a good option. Ultimately this is a dilemma the educator will have to reflect on. Deciding on the frequency, however, appears to be an important issue if we want to keep students interested and engaged and avoid dilemma-overload. The findings seem to indicate also that a separate ethics course outside the context of science education or other subjects is not on the students' wish-list.

Section 5: Teachers' skills

Both teachers appeared to be quite enthusiastic about their participation in the study and both received a short introduction into the teaching of dilemma units. Neither of them apparently anticipated potential problems with their roles as facilitators and/or moderators of class discussion – after all they were teaching in their classrooms every day. However, both teachers admitted to struggling with the unfamiliar demands of a dilemma approach that, I believe now, we all probably underestimated.

According to Strauss, teachers play several roles when they act as storytellers, practising skills such as creating beginnings to draw students into the story, using their voices wisely by deliberating applying rhythm, intonation, loudness, etc., as tools. Furthermore, storytelling requires skills that include using one's body-language to illustrate the flow of the story. This is when storytelling becomes a visual and a musical art (Strauss, 1996).

In my study, teachers claimed to have played the roles of referees during the plenary discussions, 'social organisers' during the small group discussions, support-persons and communication facilitators during the reflection and discourse phases. These roles involved skills such as organising groups, providing optimal conditions for individual reflection, recognising problems and intervening when necessary, and dealing with group-conflict and conflict-resolution in case students are unable to 'sort it out themselves'.

Irene reportedly experienced her role as demanding. She admitted to finding it difficult not to judge student comments but to accept whatever comes up. Irene appeared also challenged that sometimes the factual knowledge of the students was simply 'wrong': this was when she reportedly felt she <u>had</u> to intervene.

During my observations, I also found that sometimes Irene did not appear to give instructions clearly enough, thereby causing delays and confusion on the student side. She might have let herself be distracted by individual students. Organising groups appeared to be another issue that Irene found difficult to deal with – she seemingly solved it by developing a sophisticated system of group-constellations which turned out to be good for the overall student engagement and for the organising teacher but unpleasant from the students' point of view – they apparently would have preferred to stay with their friends. Sandra, on the other hand, seemed to have learned from Irene's problems and thus had planned ahead for group-organisation. She reported being lost for words occasionally and being unsure as to when to intervene, especially in conflict situations, such as the argument between Ulli and Johnny (see Chapter 9) where she seemed to have decided to let them sort it out themselves.

Comparing the two teachers as storytellers, both teachers apparently did their best trying to tell the stories freely. However, this did not necessarily mean they were not struggling with the 'new' teaching style. It appears that they were 'better' storytellers when they could identify with the story (Rex, Murnen, Hobbs, & McEachen, 2002): that is when their own values coincided with the dilemma story. Irene normally is a 'natural' at storytelling and uses stories all the time in her teaching: she realised during the project that stories had always supported her science teaching and that she deliberately made use of this pedagogical tool as often as possible. During the first part of the tree-dilemma session, however, Irene appeared to be 'struggling' with the storytelling-style, and with the apparent 'simplicity' of the dilemma story. The students might have intuitively sensed her discomfort, which Fatima expressed as [the story was] 'told like in an animation'.

However, when Irene finally added in a personal story in combination with the presentation of the 'underlying' dilemma, the dilemma unit itself seemed to take a positive turn by evoking personal involvement in the students, as documented in Chapters 8 and 9. This enhanced engagement apparently resulted in an increased focus for some students which might have led to greater participation in the class activities. Sandra, on the other hand, appeared quite apprehensive with regard to storytelling before the dilemma unit. During the unit, however, she seemed to be quite confident in her role as a storyteller and added a very personal story. Irene used her voice as a tool quite successfully whilst Sandra's voice was very low and often difficult to hear.

STUDENT EXPERIENCES OF FACILITATION VERSUS INSTRUCTION

Student comments in Sandra's class raised another research question:

- How did students experience the 'changed' teaching style of facilitating instead of instruction?

It was interesting to find that all interviewees were apparently positively surprised and seem to have appreciated the teacher's non-imposition of her own values onto them. They stated that it was possible to come forward with their own ideas only because of Sandra's restraint from imposing her own opinions. However, Sandra's facilitating task was not without problems: at the beginning of the plenary discussion, Sandra virtually stopped moderating as if she apparently hoped the discussion would unfold by itself. Instead of keeping the discussion going by asking questions, there appeared to be no initiative from her, resulting in long moments of deafening silence. Sandra finally told a very personal story that sparked off the discussion and apparently brought her back into a facilitator's role. However, the discussion in her class never 'really took off' and remained slow and tenacious.

Summarising, I might say that the teaching of dilemma units appears not to be as easy as it looks, and even experienced teachers, like Irene, might struggle, if they are unfamiliar with the 'new' teaching style. In Chapter 9, I quoted Bruffee who emphasised that there is much know-how involved with regard to group-dynamics and sensitivity to social situations and relationships (Bruffee, 1993). I have to admit that I underestimated the level of skills involved. It is likely that, due to my own additional training as a communication facilitator, I naively presumed that every (experienced) teacher is able to ' just do it'. This could be due to the obliviousness of the 'expert' to the struggles of a newcomer (Narvaez, 2001). However, the findings made it clear to me that teachers' enthusiasm might not be enough to equip them for this type of teaching. This points out to me yet another pedagogical dilemma with regard to teacher skills:

PEDAGOGICAL DILEMMA 5: GOOD INTENTIONS VERSUS SOUND TEACHER SKILLS – DO WE REALLY NEED ALL THESE SKILLS?

Despite the enthusiasm teachers may bring to this type of teaching, potential problems with regard to facilitation of the group processes and storytelling may still occur. This leads to the question:

- Should teachers who are inexperienced with this type of teaching use a dilemma teaching approach at all?

The skills I am thinking of are primarily skills for facilitating collaborative learning, dealing with group-conflict, organising groups, etc. A lack of these skills may lead to teachers becoming frustrated and perhaps even dismissing of the whole dilemma teaching approach. On the other hand, teachers can be introduced to this type of teaching and learning as part of professional development. The resulting improved interpersonal communication skills might benefit their teaching in general.

FINDINGS IN LIGHT OF THE LITERATURE

Storytelling can potentially provide teachers with an opportunity to construct themselves as 'successful academic performers' and as a 'social actor' (Rex et al., 2002, p. 765). For teachers, a prerequisite to leading ethical discussions seems to be a balancing-act between two seemingly irreconcilable qualities – keeping the lesson focused on a values conflict, yet at the same time permitting the discussion to have some of the features of spontaneous conversations (Clare, Gallimore, & Patthey-Chavez, 1996, p. 325). Moral educators have often taken for granted the teacher's role and discussion leading skills. Given that many teaching approaches to moral education rely on teacher-led discussions there seems to be a serious problem. Oser supports my interpretation, as pointed out earlier in this section of the chapter: It takes more than good intentions to engage students in complex moral issues in the ways that theory and research indicate (Clare et al., 1996; Oser, 1992). Another issue Mattox pointed out was, "It appears that in order to use the Kohlberg approach to the best advantage, teachers should have their own emotional houses in order" (Mattox, 1975, p. 23). This is an important observation because it has implications for professional development in this area: it might be necessary for professional development that prepares teachers for the teaching of ethical issues to include opportunities that allow teachers to reflect critically on their own motivations, assumptions, beliefs and values before engaging students in going down that path. During this thesis research, I attempted to engage in this higher order learning by writing a critical autobiography (see Chapter 4) in which I explored my identity (Palmer, 1998) through critical reflective practice (Brookfield, 1995). This experience led not only to enhanced awareness of my personal practical knowledge as a teacher and researcher (Connelly & Clandinin, 1988) but also to a perspective transformation (Mezirow, 1991).

Section 6: Problem students

So-called 'problem students' can potentially be a source of great frustration in every classroom situation and in group-work situations in particular. Irene had reportedly been apprehensive about her two students, Alex and Alois, because in her experience they could have created chaos during the dilemma unit. Alex, who apparently became 'converted' during Irene's personal story, chose to participate in a productive manner for the remainder of the dilemma unit. Alois did not create havoc because he appeared to be closely supervised by the teacher. During the final plenary discussion, Alex and Alois appeared to be amongst the best discussants: whilst Alex contributed many valuable statements, Alois kept the discussion going by making provocative comments that 'set off' the other class-members. It seems that the dilemma story approach, especially the discussion phase, might have provided an arena for Alex and Alois to participate in the discourse even though initially they seemingly had different agendas. Johnny, as one of the problem-students in Sandra's class, contributed indirectly to the learning processes in his group. He seemed to contribute through dissent, apparently forcing the others in his group to reflect on their own thinking. We might conclude, therefore, that the presence of so-called 'problem students' should not be as a reason for not engaging students in collaborative learning and moral discussion. Actually, this type of learning might provide an avenue for 'problem students' to engage in the discourse on science.

PEDAGOGICAL DILEMMA 6: POTENTIAL TROUBLEMAKERS VERSUS PEACE OF MIND - DO 'PROBLEM STUDENTS' ALWAYS EQUAL CHAOS?

On the one hand, dilemma units can potentially be 'undermined' by disturbances of so-called 'problem students'. This might be a reason for the teacher not to use dilemma units, especially if s/he wants to retain her peace of mind and a healthy level of equanimity. On the other hand, it appears that the dilemma story approach to teaching ethics may have the potential to get on board those students who normally do not contribute positively to the classroom science discourse. Unfortunately, I have not been able to locate relevant literature on this issue, so I have to rely on my observations and interpretations.

Section 7: Time

Time was the limiting factor. In both classes, the dilemma teaching and learning seemed to have suffered from too many interruptions due to unfortunate time-tabling as well as (perhaps) the stories being too long. Given that the Ethics in Science Project was required to fit in with the usual time-tabling, we 'squeezed' the dilemma unit into double-periods (of 100 minutes) resulting in the unfortunate situation of the dilemma units not being completed in a single time period. Teachers, students, and I seemed to experience the lack of continuity as very disturbing. Time-requirements were seemingly related to the 'culture' in the individual classes': Irene's multicultural class needed (much) more time than Sandra's so-called 'native' Austrian class. In the future, I would thus cut back on the length of the stories and attempt to achieve better time-tabling, such as a whole morning or afternoon, in order to be able to finish a dilemma unit in one sitting. This has led me to the formulation of another pedagogical dilemma

PEDAGOGICAL DILEMMA 7: DILEMMA UNIT TIME-REQUIREMENTS VERSUS TEACHER TIME – HOW MANY HOURS ARE THERE IN A DAY?

On the one hand, dilemma units take time. On the other hand, if a teacher wants to use dilemma stories s/he needs to plan well in advance with regard to time-tabling, integration of other subjects, and with regard to the topic of the story, in order for the dilemma unit to work out. Given that a lack of time appears to be the prevalent problem for teachers in general, the logistical effort involved in organising a dilemma unit might scare away teachers from using this teaching method in their classrooms. Adapting the number of dilemma situations in a particular story might be a possibility for fitting the units to the circumstances.

PART 3: CONCLUSIONS AND IMPLICATIONS

Re-visiting the basic research question:

- Can we optimise the conditions of the teaching of and the learning about controversial, ethical issues in relation to science by using dilemma stories?

The findings indicate that dilemma stories can potentially contribute to the improvement of the conditions for ethical teaching and learning by providing opportunities for practicing rational, social and emotional learning. Despite these apparently generally positive outcomes, I have identified seven pedagogical dilemmas that may potentially affect teaching and learning during a dilemma unit. The pedagogical dilemmas address the issues of: the authenticity of students' comments, moral discourse, time and frequency, 'problem' students, teachers' skills, and the appropriateness of the stories. These issues may open a forum for further discussion and further research, and provide clues on what to take into consideration when an educator plans to use a dilemma teaching approach in a science classroom.

The implications of the findings are that I would make sure that the stories are not too long and not too complex. I would ensure that students and teachers enter the dilemma teaching approach well prepared that is: students have received the relevant factual information beforehand, whilst teachers have engaged in professional development.

SUGGESTIONS FOR FURTHER RESEARCH

Several questions have remained unanswered and may therefore provide a starting point for future research:

- How <u>do</u> we ensure age-appropriateness of the dilemma stories?
- How do we ensure that individual students do not provide inauthentic reasoning in their portfolio-notes?
- How do we ensure that individual students can feel safe enough in a group-work situation to discuss their ideas with other students?
- What is the ideal frequency of using dilemma units in science classrooms without producing dilemma-overload?
- How can teachers be encouraged to undergo professional development before using a dilemma teaching approach?
- To what extent can a dilemma teaching approach provide an avenue for 'problem-students' to engage in the discourse on science?
- Is it reasonable to expect teachers to use their valuable time for planning well ahead and for logistical issues such as organising time-tabling?

If I could do it all over again, I would explore in depth moral education and moral development in the light of integral psychology and the Theory of Spiral Dynamics (Beck & Cowan, 1996; Wilber, 1999).

WITH HINDSIGHT - A CONCLUDING NOTE…

EMAIL FROM IRENE (17. 3. 2003):

Regarding this new curriculum document [the new Austrian Curriculum document for the lower school levels], I have to say that I know about it, however, it was never really implemented. At our school, we do not even have a print-out of the document. It was mandated [by the education department?] that it was up to the teachers to obtain the information from the world-wide web. However, when I think about it – up to recently approximately 100 teachers were sharing one computer – I am asking myself, how we were supposed to do this. The federal government does not support private internet-connections financially which means that only very few colleagues have been informed.

I am going to ask around tomorrow about the extent to which other teachers are informed about this Curriculum Reform 99, whether we do have a print-out somewhere. I personally remember very clearly that the innovations did not sit well with my curriculum. However, this was not really necessary either because we [in the Schulverbund Graz West] work in an autonomous system anyway and have to write and submit our own curricula.

I have to admit that Irene's email had a thoroughly sobering effect on me because it confirmed what Ulrike Unterbrunner (see Chapter 1) had suggested: the Curriculum Reform 99 which was the foundation of the development and implementation of the Ethics in Science curriculum was a 'flop' – it never really happened. Knowing about the potential for innovation, this is disappointing. I might like to add: thank God I received this email at this late stage of my thesis research – however, I still felt like crying. Irene also informed me that she had not (despite good intentions) implemented another dilemma unit – there was no time! However, I believe that this study nevertheless provides some insights and I hope they might be useful for other science educators as well.

List of References

Adler, P. A., & Adler, P. (1994). Observational techniques. In N. K. Denzin & Y. S. Lincoln (Eds.), *Handbook of qualitative research* (pp. 377-392). Thousand Oaks, CA: Sage Publications.

Afonso, E. (2002). *Rethinking science teacher education in Mozambique.* Unpublished Master's Report, Curtin University of Technology, Perth, WA.

Allchin, D. (1998). Values in science and in science education. In B. J. Fraser & K. G. Tobin (Eds.), *International handbook of science education* (pp. 1083-1092). Dordrecht, NL: Kluwer Academic Publishers.

Allchin, D. (1999). Science gone to seed? *Science and Education, 8*, 63-66.

Allchin, D. (1999). Values in science: An educational perspective. *Science and Education, 8*, 1-12.

Allchin, D. (2001). Values in science: An educational perspective. In F. Bevilacqua, E. Giannetto & M. R. Matthews (Eds.), *Science education and culture* (pp. 185-196). Dordrecht, NL: Kluwer Academic Publishers.

Anderson, L. W., & Krathwohl, D. (Eds.). (2001). *A taxonomy for learning, teaching, and assessing: A revision of Bloom's taxonomy of educational objectives.* New York, NY: Longman Publishers.

Arbuthnot, J. B., & Faust, D. (1981). *Teaching moral reasoning: Theory and Practice.* New York, NY: Harper & Row Publishers.

Atherton, J. (2002). *Critical reflection.* Retrieved 13. 4. 2003, from http://www.staff.dmu.ac.uk/~jamesa/learning/critical1.htm

Atwater, M. (1996). Social constructivism: Infusion into the multicultural science education research agenda. *Science Teaching, 33*(8), 821-837.

Augsburg College. (n. d.). *The Johari Window: A graphic model of awareness in interpersonal relations.* Retrieved 26. 7. 2002, from http://www.augsburg.edu/education/edc210/johari.html

Bailin, S. (2002). Critical thinking and science education. *Science and Education, 11*, 361-375.

Barone, T. (2001a). *Touching eternity: The enduring outcomes of teaching.* New York, NY: Teacher College Press.

Barone, T. (2001b). Science, art, and the representations of educational researchers. *Educational Researcher, 30*(7), 24-28.

Barone, T., & Eisner, E. (1997). Arts-based educational research. In R. M. Jaeger (Ed.), *Complementary methods for research in education.* Washington, DC: American Educational Research Association.

Bastian, J. (1991). Werteerziehung [Values-education]. *Padagogik, 11.*

Battistich, V. (1999, November). *Toward a more adequate assessment of moral development.* Paper presented at the Annual Meeting of the Association for Moral Education, Minneapolis, MN.

Bauer, C. (1993). *Forderliche und hemmende Bedingungen fur Innovationsentwicklung: Einfuhrung der lernzielorientierten Leistungsbeurteilung. Warum war es so muhsam? [Supportive and impeding conditions for the development of innovations: The introduction of outcomes based assessment. Why has it been so tough?].* Graz, Austria: Schulverbund Graz West.

Bauer, C., Hofbauer, G., Kienzl, U., & Tasch, K. (1995). *Konferenzen anders gemacht: Erfahrungen, Uberlegungen, und Tips aus der Klusemannsstrasse und der Modellschule [Meetings conducted differently: Experiences, thoughts and suggestions of the Klusemannstrasse and the Modellschule].* Graz, Austria: Schulverbund Graz West.

BBC News TALKING POINT. (2001). *Should schools be teaching science ethics?* Retrieved 1. 10. 2002, from http://news.bbc.co.uk/2/hi/talking_point/1441265.stm

Bebeau, M. J., Rest, J. R., & Narvaez, D. (1999). Beyond the promise: A perspective on research in moral education. *Educational Researcher, 28*(4), 18-26.

Beck, D. E., & Cowan, C. C. (1996). *Spiral dynamics: Mastering values, leadership, and change.* Malden, MA: Blackwell Business Publishers.

Belenky, M. F., Clinchy, B. M., Goldberger, N. R., & Tarule, J. M. (1997). *Women's ways of knowing: The development of self, voice, and mind.* New York, NY: Basic Books.

Berger, P. L., & Luckmann, T. (1966). *The social construction of reality: A treatise in the sociology of knowledge.* London, UK: Penguin Books.

Berkowitz, M. W. (1985). The role of discussion in moral education. In M. W. Berkowitz & F. Oser (Eds.), *Moral education: Theory and application* (pp. 197-218). Hillsdale, NJ: Lawrence Erlbaum Associates Publishers.

Beyer, B. K. (1978). Conducting moral discussions in the classroom. In P. Scharf (Ed.), *Readings in moral education* (pp. 62-74). Minneapolis, MN: Winston Press.

Birkenbihl, M. (1997). *Train the trainer.* Landsberg am Lech, Germany: Verlag Moderne Industrie.

Blake, D. D. (1994). Revolution, revision or reversal: Genetics - ethics curriculum. *Science and Education, 3*, 373-391.

Borchers, T. (1999a). *Decision-making.* Retrieved 12. 9. 2001, from http://www.abacon.com/commstudies/groups/decision.html

Borchers, T. (1999b). *Self-disclosure.* Retrieved 12. 9. 2001, from http://www.abacon.com/commstudies/interpersonal/indisclosure.html

Borchers, T. (1999c). *Small group development.* Retrieved 12. 9. 2001, from http://www.abacon.com/commstudies/groups/devgroup.html

Borchers, T. (1999d). *Functions of interpersonal communication.* Retrieved 12. 9. 2001, from http://www.abacon.com/commstudies/interpersonal/infunctions.html

Borchers, T. (1999e). *Definition of a small group*. Retrieved 12. 9. 2001, from
   http://www.abacon.com/commstudies/groups/definition.html

Borchers, T. (1999f). *Roles in groups*. Retrieved 12. 9. 2001, from
   http://www.abacon.com/commstudies/groups/roles.html

Bowers, C. A. (1993). *Critical essays on education, modernity, and the recovery of the ecological imperative*. New York, NY: Teachers College Press.

Bowers, C. A. (2002). Toward a cultural and ecological understanding of curriculum. In J. Doll, W. E. & N. Gough (Eds.), *Curriculum visions* (Vol. 151, pp. 75-85). New York, NY: Peter Lang Publishers.

Brady, L. (1974). *Do we dare: A dilemma approach to moral development*. Sydney, NSW: Dymocks.

Brambring, J., Dobbelstein-Osthoff, P., Heckrath, E., Reinhardt, S., & Stiel, M. (1991). *Demokratisch urteilen und handeln [Judging and acting democratically]*. Soest, GER: Landesinstitut fur Schule und Weiterbildung.

Brookfield, S. D. (1995). *Becoming a critically reflective teacher*. San Francisco, CA: Jossey-Bass Publishers.

Brookfield, S. D. (1998). Understanding and facilitating moral learning in adults [Electronic version]. *Journal of Moral Education, 27*(3), 283-300.

Brookfield, S. D. (2000). The concept of critically reflective practice. In A. L. Wilson & E. R. Hayes (Eds.), *Handbook of adult and continuing education*. San Franscisco, CA: Jossey-Bass Publishers.

Brown, R. K. (1992). Max van Manen and pedagogical human science research. In W. F. Pinar & W. M. Reynolds (Eds.), *Understanding curriculum as phenomenological and deconstructed text* (pp. 44-63). New York, NY: Teachers College Press.

Brownfield, I. (1986). The moral reasoning of men and women when confronting hypothetical and real life dilemmas. In G. Sapp (Ed.), *Handbook of moral development*. Birmingham, AL: Religious Education Press.

Bruffee, K. A. (1993). *Collaborative learning*. Baltimore, MD: The Johns Hopkins University Press.

Bullough, R. V., & Pinnegar, S. (2001). Guidelines for quality in autobiographical forms of self-study research. *Educational researcher, 30*(3), 13-21.

Bundesministerium fur Bildung, W. u. K. (2000). *Neuer Lehrplan der AHS-Unterstufe*. Retrieved 18. 2. 2003, from http://www.bmbwk.gv.at

Clare, L., Gallimore, R., & Patthey-Chavez, G. G. (1996). Using moral dilemmas in childrens' literature as a vehicle for moral education and teaching reading comprehension. *Journal of Moral Education, 25*(3), 325-341.

Clark, D. (n.d.). *Critical reflection*. Retrieved 13. 4. 2003, from
   http://www.nwlink.com/~donclark/hrd/development/reflection.html

Cobern, W. W. (2000). *Everyday thoughts about nature: A worldview investigation of important concepts students use to make sense of nature with specific attention of science* (Vol. 9). Dordrecht, NL: Kluwer Academic Publishers.

Cobern, W. W., & Aikenhead, G. S. (1998). Cultural aspects of learning science. In B. J. Fraser & K. Tobin (Eds.), *International handbook of science education* (pp. 39-52). Dordrecht, NL: Kluwer Academic Publishers.

Cohen, L., Manion, L., & Morrison, K. (2000). *Research methods in education* (5th ed.). London, UK: Routledge Falmer Publishers.

Connelly, F. M., & Clandinin, D. J. (1988). *Teachers as curriculum planners: Narratives of experience.* New York, NY: Teachers College Press.

Cooper, T. J., Baturo, A. R., & Harris, E. L. (1998). Scholarly writing in mathematics and science education higher degree courses. In J. A. Malone, B. Atweh & J. R. Northfield (Eds.), *Research and supervision in mathematics and science education* (pp. 249-276). Mahwah, NJ: Lawrence Erlbaum Associates Publishers.

Coulter, D. (2002). Creating common and uncommon worlds: Using discourse ethics to decide public and private in classrooms. *Journal of Curriculum Studies, 34*(1), 25-42.

Cranton, P. (1994). *Understanding and promoting transformative learning: A guide for educators of adults.* San Francisco, CA: Jossey-Bass Publishers.

Cross, R. T., & Fensham, P. J. (Eds.). (2000). *Science and the citizen* (Vol. 41 (2)). Melbourne, VIC: Arena Publications.

Crotty, M. (1996). *Phenomenology and nursing research.* South Melbourne, VIC: Churchill Livingstone Publishers.

Cummings, R., Dyas, L., Maddux, C. D., & Kochman, A. (2001). Principled moral reasoning and behaviour of preservice teacher education students. *American Educational Research Journal, 38*(1), 143-158.

Curriculum Council. (1998). *Curriculum framework for kindergarten to year 12 education in Western Australia.* Osborne Park, WA: Curriculum Council.

Daleo, M. S. (1996). *Curriculum of love: Cultivating the spiritual nature of children.* Charlottesville, VA: Grace Publishing & Communications.

Damon, W. (Ed.). (1978). *Moral development.* San Francisco, CA: Jossey-Bass Publishers.

Davis, N. T. (2003, March). *Worldview of practising teachers and influences on planning inquiry teaching.* Paper presented at the Annual Conference of the National Association for Research in Science Teaching (NARST), Philadelphia.

Dawson, C. (2000). Selling snake oil: Must science educators continue to promise what they can't deliver? In R. T. Cross & P. J. Fensham (Eds.), *Science and the citizen* (Vol. 41 (2), pp. 121-132). Melbourne, VIC: Arena Publications.

Dawson, V. M. (1999). *Bioethics education in the science curriculum: Evaluation of strategies and meaningful implementation.* Unpublished dissertation, Curtin University of Technology, Perth, Australia.

Day, L. (2002). Putting yourself in other people's shoes: The use of Forum theatre to explore refugee and homeless issues in schools. *Journal of Moral Education, 31*(1), 21-34.

de Saint-Exupery, A. (1995). *The little prince* (T. V. F. Cuffe, Trans.). London, GB: Penguin Books.

Degenhart, M. A. B. (1986). The ethics of belief and education in science and morals. *Journal of Moral Education, 15*(2), 109-118.

Denzin, N. K. (1989). *Interpretive biography* (Vol. 17). Newbury Park, CA: Sage Publications.

Denzin, N. K., & Lincoln, Y. S. (1998). *Collecting and interpreting qualitative materials.* Thousand Oaks, CA: Sage Publications.

Denzin, N. K., & Lincoln, Y. S. (2000). *Handbook of qualitative research* (2nd ed.). Thousand Oaks, CA: Sage Publications.

Denzin, N. K., & Lincoln, Y. S. (2000). Introduction: The discipline and practice of qualitative research. In N. K. Denzin & Y. S. Lincoln (Eds.), *Handbook of qualitative research* (2nd ed., pp. 1-28). Thousand Oaks, CA: Sage Publications.

DeVries, R., & Zan, B. (1994). *Moral classrooms, moral children: Creating a constructivist atmosphere in early education.* New York, NY: Teachers College Press.

Dewey, J. (1944). *Democracy and education.* New York, NY: The Free Press.

Driver, R., Asoko, H., Leach, J., Mortimer, E., & Scott, P. (1994). Constructing scientific knowledge in the classroom. *Educational Researcher, 23*(7), 5-12.

Edel, L. (1984). *Writing lives: Principia Biographica.* New York, NY: W. W. Norton & Company Publishers.

Edwards, C. P., & Ramsey, P. G. (1986). *Promoting social and moral development in young children: Creative apporaches for the classroom.* New York, NY: Teachers College Press.

Eisenhart, M. (2000). Boundaries and selves in the making of 'science'. *Research in Science Education, 30*(1), 43-55.

Eisner, E. (1979). *The educational imagination: On the design and evaluation of school programs.* New York: Macmillan Publishers.

Ellis, C. (1997). Evocative autoethnography: Writing emotionally about our lives. In W. G. Tierney & Y. S. Lincoln (Eds.), *Representation and the text* (pp. 115-139). Albany, NY: State University of New York.

Ellis, C., & Bochner, A. P. (2000). Autoethnography, personal narrative, reflexivity: Researcher as subject. In N. K. Denzin & Y. S. Lincoln (Eds.), *Handbook of qualitative research* (2nd ed., pp. 733-768). Thousand Oaks, CA: Sage Publications.

Erickson, F. (1998). Qualitative research methods for science education. In B. J. Fraser & K. G. Tobin (Eds.), *International handbook of science education* (pp. 1155-1173). Dordrecht, NL: Kluwer Academic Publishers.

Erlandson, D. A., Harris, E. L., Skipper, B. L., & Allen, S. D. (1993). *Doing naturalistic inquiry: A guide to methods*. Newbury Park, CA: Sage Publications.

Ernest, P. (1995). The one and the many. In L. P. Steffe & J. Gale (Eds.), *Constructivism in education* (pp. 459-486). Hillsdale, NJ: Lawrence Erlbaum Associates Publishers.

Facione, P. A. (1996, 1998). *Critical thinking: What it is and why it counts*. Retrieved 13. 4. 2003, from http://www.calpress.com/critical.html

Feinberg, W., & Soltis, J. F. (1985). The hidden curriculum. In *School and society* (pp. 60-72). New York, NY: Teachers College Press.

Fine, M., Weis, L., Weseen, S., & Wong, L. (2000). For Whom? Qualitative research, representation, and social responsibilities. In N. K. Denzin & Y. S. Lincoln (Eds.), *Handbook of qualitative research* (2nd ed., pp. 107-131). Thousand Oaks, CA: Sage Publications.

Fontana, A., & Frey, J. H. (2000). The interview. In N. K. Denzin & Y. S. Lincoln (Eds.), *Handbook of qualitative research* (2 ed., pp. 645-672). Thousand Oaks, CA: Sage Publications.

Fraenkel, J. R. (1977). *How to teach about values: An analytic approach*. Englewood Cliffs, NJ: Prentice-Hall Publishers.

Frazer, M. J., & Kornhauser, A. (1986). *Ethics and social responsibility in science education*. Oxford, UK: Pergamon Press.

Freire, P. (1998). Cultural action and conscientization. *Harvard Educational Review, 68*(4).

Fuchs, E., & Frech, F. (1995). *Vom Teamteaching zur Teamarbeit: Ein Bericht aus der Praxis [From team-teaching to team-work: A report of the praxis]*. Graz, Austria: Schulverbund Graz West.

Gadamer, H. G. (1984). *Truth and method* (G. Barden & J. Cumming, Trans.). New York, NY: Crossroads Publishers.

Geelan, D. R. (1997). Epistemological anarchy and the many forms of constructivism. *Science and Education, 6*, 15-28.

Geelan, D. R., & Taylor, P. C. (2001). Writing our lived experience: Beyond the (pale) hermeneutic? *Electronic Journal of Science Education, 5*(4), Article 1.

Geertz, C. (1973). *The interpretation of culture*. New York, NY: Basic Books.

Geertz, C. (1983). *Local knowledge: Further essays in interpretive anthropology*. New York, NY: Basic Books.

Gergen, M. M., & Gergen, K. J. (2000). Qualitative inquiry: Tensions and transformations. In N. K. Denzin & Y. S. Lincoln (Eds.), *Handbook of qualitative research* (2nd ed., pp. 1025-1046). Thousand Oaks, CA: Sage Publications.

Gevisser, M., & Morris, M. (n.d.). *Manifesto on values*. Retrieved 4. 12. 2001, from http://education.pwv.gov.za/DoE_Sites/Curriculum/Values/manifesto_on_valu es.htm

Gilligan, C. (1982). *In a different voice: Psychological theory and women's development.* Cambridge, MA: Harvard University Press.

Gilligan, C., Ward, J. V., Taylor, J. M., & Bardige, B. (Eds.). (1988). *Mapping the moral domain.* Cambridge, MA: Harvard University Press.

Giroux, H. (1992). *Border crossings: Cultural workers and the politics of education.* New York, NY: Routledge Publishers.

Goleman, D. (1997). *Emotionale Intelligenz* (F. Griese, Trans.). Munchen, Germany: Deutscher Taschenbuch Verlag.

Good, R., & Shymansky, J. (2001). Nature-of-science literacy in benchmarks and standards: Post-modern/relativist or modern/realist? In F. Bevilacqua, E. Giannetto & M. R. Matthews (Eds.), *Science education and culture* (pp. 53-65). Dordrecht, NL: Kluwer Academic Publishers.

Goodin, R. E. (1993). Utility and the good. In P. Singer (Ed.), *A companion to ethics* (pp. 241-248). Oxford, UK: Blackwell Publishers.

Gregory, M. (2000). Care as a goal of democratic education. *Journal of Moral Education, 29*(4), 445-461.

Gribble, S. J., Rennie, L. J., Tyson, L., Milne, C. E., & Speering, W. (2000). Negotating values for the science curriculum: The need for dialogue and compromise. *Research in Science Education, 30*(2), 199-211.

Grumet, M. (1992). Existential and phenomenological foundations of autobiographical methods. In W. F. Pinar & W. M. Reynolds (Eds.), *Understanding curriculum as phenomenological and deconstructed text* (pp. 28-43). New York, NY: Teachers College Press.

Grundy, S. (1987). *Curriculum: Product or praxis?* London, UK: Falmer Press.

Gschweitl, R., Mattner-Begusch, B., Neumayr nee Settelmaier, E., & Schwetz, H. (1998). Neue Werte der Werterziehung: Anregende Lernumgebung zur Anbahnung uberdauernder Werthaltungen bei Jugendlichen [New values in values-education: Engaging learning environments for initiating values and attitudes in adolescents]. In O. Jugendrotkreuz (Ed.), *Gibt es nur einen Weg: Informations- und Unterrichtsmaterialien zur Friedenserziehung und Konfliktarbeit im Sinne der Genfer Abkommen und des Humanitaren Volkerrechts [Is there only one way: Information and curriculum materials for peace education and conflict work in the sense of the Geneva Convention and the Charta of Human Rights]* (Vol. 2, pp. 13-21). Vienna, Austria: OBV Pädagogischer Verlag.

Guba, E. G., & Lincoln, Y. S. (1989). *Fourth generation evaluation.* Newbury Park, CA: Sage Publications.

Gyatso, G. K. (1988). *Universal compassion.* London, UK: Tharpa Publications.

Gyatso, G. K. (1990). *Joyful path of good fortune.* Ulverston, UK: Tharpa Publications.

Halstead, J. M., & McLaughlin, T. H. (Eds.). (1999). *Education in morality*. London,UK: Routledge Publishers.

Halstead, J. M., & Taylor, M. J. (Eds.). (1996). *Values in education and education in values*. London, UK: Falmer Press.

Hargreaves, A., Earl, L., & Schmidt, M. (2002). Perspectives on alternative assessment reform. *Americal Educational Research Journal, 39*(1), 69-95.

Haste, H. (1998). Educating for an ecologically sustainable culture: Rethinking moral education, creativity, intelligence, and other modern orthodoxies [Electronic version]. *Journal of Moral Education, 27*(1), 107-109.

Hawley, R. C. (1974). *Value exploration through role-playing*. Amherst, MA: Education Research Associates.

Hawley, R. C., & Hawley, I. L. (1975). *Human values in the classroom: A handbook for teachers*. New York, NY: Hart Publishers.

Haydon, G. (1997). *Teaching about values*. London, UK: Cassell Publishers.

Haynes, F. (1998). *The ethical school*. London, UK: Routledge Publishers.

Hedberg, N. L., & Westby, C. E. (1993). *Analyzing storytelling skills: Theory to practice*. Tucson, AZ: Communication Skill Builders.

Heidegger, M. (1962). *Being and time* (J. Macquarrie & E. Robinson, Trans.). Oxford, UK: Blackwell Publishers.

Hempel, C. G. (1998). Science and human values. In E. D. Klemke, R. Hollinger, D. Wyss Rudge & A. D. Kline (Eds.), *Introductory readings in the philosophy of science* (pp. 499-514). New York: Prometheus Books.

Henderson, J. G. (2001). Deepening democratic curriculum work. *Educational Researcher, 30*(9), 18-21.

Hersh, R. H., Miller, J. P., & Fielding, G. D. (1980). *Models of moral education: An appraisal*. New York, NY: Longman Publishers.

Hersh, R. H., Pritchard Paolitto, D., & Reimer, J. (1979). *Promoting moral growth: From Piaget to Kohlberg*. New York, NY: Longman Publishers.

HGSE News. (2002). *Reconstructing Larry: Assessing the legacy of Lawrence Kohlberg*. Retrieved 2. 8. 2002, from http://www.gse.harvard.edu/news/features/larry10012000_page5.html

Hill, B. (1973). Implications for moral education of some current conceptions of education. *The Australian Journal of Education, 18*(3), 288-298.

Hill, B. (1993). *An education of value: Towards a value-framework for the school curriculum* (Monograph): Committee for the Review of the Queensland School Curriculum.

Hill, B. (1996, June). *Designing values curriculum*. Paper presented at the conference organised by West Australian National Professional Development Program Values Review Project, Perth, WA.

Hoff Sommers, C. (2000). *The war against boys*. Retrieved 5. 8. 2002, from
    http://www.theatlantic.com/issues/2000/05/sommers.htm

Hofmann, I. (1998). *Die Entwicklung des moralischen Urteilens nach Carol Gilligan*. Retrieved
    24. 8. 2002, from http://schulen.hagen.de/GSGE/ew/M05.html

Holstein, J. A., & Gubrium, J. F. (1994). Phenomenology, ethnomethodology, and
    interpretive practice. In N. K. Denzin & Y. S. Lincoln (Eds.), *Handbook of qualitative
    research* (pp. 262-285). Thousand Oaks, CA: Sage publications.

Hopferwieser, G. (1994). *Neue Mittelschule Schulverbund Graz West: Die
    Entstehungsgeschichte des Schulmodells [The new middle-school School Alliance Graz
    West: The history of the development of the school-model]*. Graz, Austria: Schulverbund
    Graz West.

Hudson, B. (2002). Holding complexity and searching for meaning: Teaching as reflective
    practice. *Journal of Curriculum Studies, 34*(1), 43-57.

Imel, S. (1998). *Transformative learning in adulthood*. Retrieved 30. 1, 2002, from
    http://www.ed.gov/databases/ERIC_Digests/ed423426.html

Infoplease.com. (2003). Retrieved 15. 4. 2003, from
    http://www.infoplease.com/ipd/A0723808.html

Ingall, C. K. (1997). *Metaphors, maps, and mirrors: Moral education in middle schools*.
    Greenwich, CT: Ablex Publishing Corporation.

Jarvis, C. (n. d.). *The Johari Window*. Retrieved 26. 7. 2002, from
    http://sol.brunel.ac.uk/~jarvis/bola/communications/johari.html

Johnston, J. (1995). Morals and ethics in science education: Where have they gone?
    Education in Science(163), 20-21.

Jones, C. (1976). The contributions of science to moral education. *Journal of Moral
    Education, 5*(3), 249-256.

Jones, R. L., & Zucker, A. (1986). Is science really value free? *Science Teacher, 53*(2), 38-41.

Kahn, P. (1999). *The human relationship with nature: Development and culture*. Cambridge,
    MA: MIT Press.

Kieffer, G. H. (1977). Ethics for the 'New Biology'. *American Biology Teacher, 39*(2), 80-104.

Kincheloe, J. L. (1998). Critical research in science education. In B. J. Fraser & K. G. Tobin
    (Eds.), *International handbook of science education* (pp. 1191-1205). Dordrecht, NL:
    Kluwer Publications.

Kirschenbaum, H. (1976). Clarifying values clarification: Some theoretical issues. In D.
    Purpel & R. Kevin (Eds.), *Moral education: It comes with the territory* (pp. 116-125).
    Berkeley, CA: McCutchan Publishers.

Kirste, B. (2001). *European Union*. Retrieved 8. 8. 2002, from http.//userpage.chemie.fu-
    berlin.de/adressen/eu.html

Klossowski, P. (1997). *Nietzsche and the vicious circle*. London, UK: The Athlone Press.

Kohlberg, L. (1980). Stages of moral development as a basis for moral education. In B. Munsey (Ed.), *Moral development, moral education, and Kohlberg: Basic issues in philosophy, religion, and education* (pp. 15-100). Birmingham, AL: Religious Education Press.

Kohlberg, L. (1984). *Essays on moral development: The psychology of moral development. The nature and validity of moral stages.* (Vol. 2). San Francisco, CA: Harper and Row Publishers.

Kohlberg, L. (1996). *Die Psychologie der Moralentwicklung.* Frankfurt am Main, Germany: Suhrkamp Verlag.

Kolsto, S. D. (2001). 'To trust or not to trust,...' - Pupils' ways of judging information encountered in a socio-scientific issue. *International Journal of Science Education, 23*(9), 877-901.

Konig, H., Krepelka, M., Messner, E., Schnelzer, W., Stauchner, E., & Weinberger, T. (1997). *Das Kooperationsmodell Schulverbund: Profil eines neuen Mittelstufentyps entwickelt und erprobt im Schulverbund Graz West von 1991-1997. Praxiserkenntinisse als Diskussionsgrundlage [The cooperation model school alliance: Profile of a new middleschool-type developed and trialled at the School Alliance Graz West from 1991-1997. Insights from practice as a basis for discussion].* Graz, Austria: Schulverbund Graz West.

Kramer, C. (n.d.). *Lawrence Kohlberg's stages of moral development.* Retrieved 24. 8. 2002, from http://www.xenodochy.org/ex/lists/moraldev.html

KU Eichstätt. (n.d.). *Schlüsselqualifikationen im Rahmen des Eichstätter Europastudiengangs.* Retrieved 8. 8. 2002, from http://www1.ku-eichstaett.de/Organe/didaktiken/did-f/schluesselqual/

Kvale, S. (1996). *Interviews.* London, UK: Sage Publications.

Lacey, H. (1999). Scientific understanding and the control of nature. *Science and Education, 8*, 13-35.

LaGrange College Education Department. (n.d.). *Critical thinking.* Retrieved 13. 4. 2003, from http://www.lgc.peachnet.edu/academic/educatn/Blooms/critical_thinking.htm

Lamb, A. (2001). *Critical and creative thinking.* Retrieved 13. 4. 2003, from http://eduscapes.com/tap/topic69.htm

Le Compte, M. D. (2000). Analyzing qualitative data. *Theory Into Practice, 39*(3), 146-154.

Lemin, M., Potts, H., & Welsford, P. (Eds.). (1994). *Values strategies for classroom teachers.* Hawthorn, VIC: Acer Publications.

Leming, J. S. (2000). Tell me a story: An evaluation of a literature-based character education programme. *Journal of Moral Education, 29*(4), 413-427.

Lemke, J. L. (1990). *Talking science: Language, learning and values.* Norwood, NJ: Ablex Publishers.

Lickona, T. (1991). Moral development in the elementary school classroom. In W. M. Kurtines & J. L. Gewirtz (Eds.), *Handbook of moral behaviour and development* (Vol. 3, pp. 143-162). Hillsdale, NJ: Lawrence Erlbaum Associates Publishers.

Lickona, T. (1992). *Educating for character: How our schools can teach respect and responsibility.* Riverdale, MD: Bantam Doubleday Dell Publishers.

Lincoln, Y. S. (1997). Self, subject, audience, text: Living at the edge, writing in the margins. In W. G. Tierney & Y. S. Lincoln (Eds.), *Representation and the text: Reframing the narrative voice* (pp. 37-55). Albany, NY: State University of New York.

Lincoln, Y. S., & Denzin, N. K. (2000). The seventh moment: Out of the past. In N. K. Denzin & Y. S. Lincoln (Eds.), *Handbook of qualitative research* (2nd ed., pp. 1047-1065). Thousand Oaks, CA: Sage Publications.

Lincoln, Y. S., & Guba, E. G. (2000). Paradigmatic controversies, contradictions, and emerging confluences. In N. K. Denzin & Y. S. Lincoln (Eds.), *Handbook of qualitative research* (2nd ed., pp. 163-188). Thousand Oaks, CA: Sage Publications.

Lind, G. (1987). Moral competence and education in democratic society. In G. Zecha & P. Weingartner (Eds.), *Conscience: An interdisciplinary approach* (pp. 37-43). Dordrecht, NL: Reidel Publishers.

Lind, G., Hartmann, H. A., & Wakenhut, R. (Eds.). (1985). *Moral devlopment and the social environment.* Chicago, IL: Precedent Publishers.

Macer, D. (1994b). *Introduction to bioethics.* Christchurch, NZ: Eubios Ethics Institute.

Marcus, G. E. (1994). What comes (just) after 'post'? A case of ethnography. In N. K. Denzin & Y. S. Lincoln (Eds.), *Handbook of qualitative research* (pp. 563-574). Thousand Oaks, CA: Sage Publications.

Marples, R. (Ed.). (1999). *The aims of education.* London, UK: Routledge Publishers.

Mattox, B. A. (1975). *Getting together: Dilemmas for the classroom based on Kohlberg's approach.* San Diego, CA: Pennant Publishers.

McInerney, J. D. (1986). Ethical values in biology education. In M. J. Frazer & A. Kornhauser (Eds.), *Ethics and social responsibility in science education* (Vol. 2, pp. 175-181). Oxford, UK: Pergamon Press.

McMullin, E. (1998). Values in science. In E. D. Klemke, R. Hollinger, D. Wyss Rudge & A. D. Kline (Eds.), *Introductory readings in the philosophy of science* (pp. 515-538). New York, NY: Prometheus Books.

McPhail, P. (1982). *Social and moral education* (Vol. 4). Oxford, UK: Basil Blackwell Publishers.

Mehlinger, H. (1986). Teacher training for moral education. In M. J. Frazer & A. Kornhauser (Eds.), *Ethics and social responsibility in science education* (Vol. 2, pp. 239-246). Oxford, UK: Pergamon Press.

Messner, E. (1995). *Lehrerrlnnen beschreiben ihre Arbeit in Unterricht und Schule: Innovationssteckbriefe fur einen padagogischen Markt [Teachers describe their work -*

teaching at school. Information on innovation for a pedagogical market]. Graz, Austria: Schulverbund Graz West.

Mezirow, J. (1991). *Transformative dimensions of adult learning*. San Francisco, CA: Jossey-Bass Publishers.

Michael, M. (1986). Science education and moral education. *Journal of Moral Education, 15*(2), 99-108.

Milne, C. E., & Taylor, P. C. (1998). Between a myth and a hard place: Situating school science in a climate of critical cultural reform. In W. W. Cobern (Ed.), *Socio-cultural perspectives on science education* (Vol. 4, pp. 25-48). Dordrecht, NL: Kluwer Academic Publishers.

Moustakas, C. (1994). *Phenomenological research methods*. Thousand Oaks, CA: Sage Publications.

Munsey, B. (Ed.). (1980). *Moral development, moral education, and Kohlberg: Basic issues in philosophy, religion, and education*. Birmingham, AL: Religious Education Press.

Murray, T. H. (1997). What do we mean by narrative ethics? In H. Lindemann Nelson (Ed.), *Stories and their limits: Narrative approaches to bioethics* (Vol. 3, pp. 3-17). New York, NY: Routledge Publishers.

Musgrave, P. W. (1978). *The moral curriculum: A sociological analysis*. London, UK: Methuen Publishers.

Naphtali, S. (2003). *Buddhism for mothers: A calm approach to caring for yourself and your children*. Crows Nest, NSW: Allen & Unwin Publishers.

Napier, R. W., & Gershenfeld, M. K. (1999). *Groups: Theory and practice* (6th ed.). Boston, MA: Houghton Mifflin Company.

Narvaez, D. (2001). Moral text comprehension: Implications for education and research. *Journal of Moral Education, 30*(1), 43-54.

Narvaez, D. (2002). Does reading moral stories build character? *Educational Psychology Review, 14*(2), 155-171.

Nash, R. J. (1997). *Answering the 'virtuecrats': A moral conversation on character education*. New York, NY: Teachers College Press.

Nevers, P., Gebhard, U., & Billmann-Mahecha, E. (1997). Patterns of reasoning exhibited by children and adolescents in response to moral dilemmas involving plants, animals and ecosystems [Electronic version]. *Journal of Moral Education, 26*(2), 169-182.

Noddings, N. (1984). *Caring: A feminine approach to ethics and moral education*. Berkeley, CA: University of California Press.

Nucci, L. (n.d.). *Moral development and moral education: An overview*. Retrieved 24. 8. 2002, from http://tigger.uic.edu/~lnucci/MoralEd/overview/html

Orr, D. W. (1992). *Ecological literacy: Eduation and the transition to a postmodern world*. Albany, NY: State University of New York Press.

Oser, F. (1992). Morality in professional action: A discourse approach for teaching. In F. Oser, A. Dick & J.-L. Patry (Eds.), *Effective and responsible teaching: The new synthesis* (pp. 109-125). San Francisco, CA: Jossey-Bass Publishers.

Oser, F., & Althof, W. (1992). *Moralische Selbstbestimmung. Modelle der Entwicklung und Erziehung im Wertebereich. Ein Lehrbuch [Moral self-determination: Models of development and education in the area of values. An instructional book].* Stuttgart, Germany: Klett-Cotta Verlag.

Pack, S. J. (1991). Character formation under capitalism: The downside of Smith's system of capitalism. In *Capitalism as a moral system: Adam Smith's critique of the free market economy*. Aldershot Hants, UK: Edward Elgar Publishers.

Packer, M. J., & Addison, R. B. (Eds.). (1989). *Entering the hermeneutic circle: Hermeneutic investigation in psychology.* Albany, NY: State University of New York Press.

Pädagogisches Institut Tirol. (n.d.). *Lehrplanerläuterungen.* Retrieved 8. 8. 2002, from http://www.pi-tirol.at/aps/Downloads/LP_Erlauterungen.pdf

Pallas, A. (2001). Preparing education doctoral students for epistemological diversity. *Educational Researcher, 30*(5), 6-11.

Palmer, P. L. (1998). *The courage to teach: Exploring the inner landscape of a teacher's life.* San Francisco, CA: Jossey-Bass Publishers.

Parker, W. C., Ninomiya, A., & Cogan, J. (1999). Educating world citizens: Toward multinational curriculum development. *American Educational Research Journal, 36*(2), 117-145.

Patry, J.-L. (2000, June). *Science is not value-free - neither in research, nor in school.* Paper presented at the International Conference on Values Education and Citizenship Education in the New Century, The Chinese University of Hong Kong.

Pelzmann, B., & Schiretz, G. (1996). *Der neue Gegenstand 'Okologie': Der autonome Lehrplan und seine Entstehung in der Praxis [The new subject 'ecology': The new autonomous curriculum and its development from a practical perspective].* Graz, Austria: Schulverbund Graz West.

Perry, W. G. (1970). *Forms of intellectual and ethical development in the college years: A scheme.* New York, NY: Holt, Rinehart & Winston Publishers.

Peters, R. S. (1981). *Moral development and moral education.* London, UK: Allen & Unwin Publishers.

Pettit, P. (1993). Consequentialism. In P. Singer (Ed.), *A companion to ethics* (pp. 230-240). Oxford, UK: Blackwell Publishers.

Piaget, J. (1977). *The moral judgement of the child.* Harmondsworth, UK: Penguin.

Pinar, W. F., Reynolds, W. M., Slattery, P., & Taubman, P. M. (1995/1996). *Understanding curriculum: An introduction to the study of historical and contemporary curriulum discourses* (Vol. 17). New York, NY: Peter Lang Publishers.

Pitt, J. C. (1990). The myth of science education. *Studies in Philosophy and Education, 10*, 7-17.

Poole, M. (1995). *Beliefs and values in science education. Developing science and technology education*. Bristol, UK: Open University Press.

Porter, N., & Taylor, N. (1972). *How to assess the moral reasoning of students: A teacher's guide to the use of Lawrence Kohlberg's stage-development method*. Toronto, CAN: Ontario Institue for Studies in Education.

Power, F. C., Higgins, A., & Kohlberg, L. (1989). *Lawrence Kohlberg's approach to moral education*. New York, NY: Columbia University Press.

Presno, V., & Presno, C. (1980). *The value realms: Activities for helping students develop values*. New York, NY: Teachers College Press.

Purpel, D. (1989). *The moral and spiritual crisis in education: A curriculum for justice and compassion in education*. Granby, MA: Bergin & Garvey Publishers.

Purpel, D., & Kevin, R. (1976). Moral education in the classroom: Some instructional issues. In D. Purpel & R. Kevin (Eds.), *Moral education: It comes with the territory*. Berkeley, CA: McCutchan Publications.

Reid, J.-A., Buckland, C., Clarke, C., & Mackay, I. (2000). *Critical reflection*. Retrieved 13. 4. 2003, from http://www.une.edu.au/tlc/alo/critical1.htm

Rex, L. A., Murnen, T. J., Hobbs, J., & McEachen, D. (2002). Teachers' pedagogical stories and the shaping of classroom participation: 'The dancer' and 'graveyard shift at the 7-11'. *American Educational Research Journal, 39*(3), 765-796.

Richardson, L. (1994). Writing: A method of inquiry. In N. K. Denzin & Y. S. Lincoln (Eds.), *Handbook of qualitative research*. Thousand Oaks, CA: Sage Publications.

Richardson, L. (2000). Writing: A method of inquiry. In N. K. Denzin & Y. S. Lincoln (Eds.), *Handbook of qualitative research* (2 ed., pp. 923-948). Thousand Oaks, CA: Sage Publications.

Rodriguez, A. J. (2000). Linking Bakhtin with feminist poststructuralism to unravel the allure of auto/biographies. *Research in Science Education, 30*(1), 13-21.

Rosegger, P. K. (2003). *The carpenter*. Retrieved 27. 5. 2003, from http://www.bruderhof.com/articles/Carpenter.htm

Roth, W.-M. (2000). Autobiography and science education: An introduction. *Research in Science Education, 30*(1), 1-12.

Roth, W.-M., & Bowen, G. M. (2000). Learning difficulties related to graphing: A hermeneutic phenomenological perspective. *Research in Science Education, 30*(1), 123-139.

Rudner, R. (1998). The scientist qua scientist makes value judgments. In E. D. Klemke, R. Hollinger, D. Wyss Rudge & A. D. Kline (Eds.), *Introductory readings in the philosophy of science* (pp. 492-498). New York, NY: Prometheus Books.

Ruggiero, V. R. (1997). *Thinking critically about ethical issues.* Mountain View, CA: Mayfield Publishing Company.

Scharf, P. (Ed.). (1978). *Readings in moral education.* Oak Grove, MN: Winston Press.

Schnelzer, W. (1994). *Zwei Jahre Versuchsarbeit in der Praxis: Erfahrungs berichte der Lehrerlnnen fur die Dokumentation 1992/93 [Two years of school-trial in praxis: Teachers' experiences for the documentation 1992/93].* Graz: Schulverbund Graz West.

Schubert, W. H. (1986). *Curriculum: Perspective, paradigm, and possibility.* New York, NY: Macmillan Publishing Company.

Scott, W., & Oulton, C. (1998). Environmental values education: An exploration of its role in the school curriculum. *Journal of Moral Education, 27*(2), 209-224.

Seidl, G. (1995). *Die Reise nach Waldau: Eine Beratering analysiert den kollegialen Erfahrungsaustausch mit einer befreundeten Schule [The journey to Waldau: An adviser analyses the collegial exchange with an associated school].* Graz, Austria: Schulverbund Graz West.

Settelmaier, E., & Taylor, P. C. (2001, December). *Ken Wilber's integral philosophy and educational research: Fleshing out the seventh moment (and beyond?).* Paper presented at the Annual Conference of the Australian Association for Research in Education (AARE), Fremantle, WA.

Sharma, S. R. (Ed.). (1999a). *Curriculum for moral education.* Delhi, India: Cosmo Publications.

Sharma, S. R. (Ed.). (1999b). *Teaching of moral education.* Delhi, India: Cosmo Publications.

Silldorf, W. (1997). *Alternative Lernformen: Eine Sammlung von ausgewahlten, bearbeiteten und praxiserprobten Lernspielen fur Deutsch [Alternative teaching practices: A collection of selected, evaluated and improved learning-games for the use in German].* Graz, Austria: Schulverbund Graz West.

Silver, M. (1976). *Values education.* Washington, DC: National Education Association of the United States.

Simmer-Brown, J. (1994). Commitment and openness: A contemplative approach to pluralism. In S. Glazer (Ed.), *The heart of learning* (pp. 97-112). New York, NY: Penguin Putnam Publishers.

Skolimowski, H. (1994). *The participatory mind: A new theory of knowledge and of the universe.* London, UK: Arkana Penguin Books.

Skovsmose, O. (1994). *Towards a philosophy of critical mathematics education* (Vol. 15). Dordrecht, NL: Kluwer Academic Publishers.

Slattery, P. (1995). *Curriculum development in the postmodern era.* New York,NY: Garland Publishing.

Smith, G. A. (1998). Earth in mind: On Education, environment, and the human prospect [Electronic version]. *Journal of Moral Education, 27*(1), 111-113.

Smith, H. (1992). *Forgotten truth: The common vision of the world's religions*. San Francisco, CA: HarperSanFrancisco Publishers.

Smith, R., & Standish, P. (Eds.). (1997). *Teaching right and wrong: Moral education in the balance*. Stoke on Trent, UK: Trentham Books.

Stein, D. (2000). *Teaching critical reflection*. Retrieved 13. 4. 2003, from http://ericacve.org/docgen.asp?tbl=mr&ID=98

Steiner, E., & Hitchcock, R. (1980). Teaching moral criticism in the sciences. *Viewpoints in Teaching and Learning, 56*(4), 63-73.

Stewart, D., & Mickunas, A. (1990). *Exploring phenomenology: A guide to the field and its literature*. Athens, OH: Ohio University Press.

Straughan, R. (1982). *Can we teach children to be good?* London, UK: John Allen & Unwin Publishers.

Strauss, S. (1996). *The passionate fact: Storytelling in natural history and cultural interpretation*. Golden, CO: Fulcrum Publishing.

Tan, S. K. (1997). Moral values and science teaching: A Malaysian school curriculum initiative. *Science and Education, 6*(6), 555-572.

Tappan, M. B. (1998). Moral education in the Zone of Proximal Development [Electronic version]. *Journal of Moral Education, 27*(2), 141-160.

Taylor, M. J. (Ed.). (1975). *Progress and problems in moral education*. Windsor, UK: NFER Publishing Company.

Taylor, P. C. (1998). Constructivism value added. In B. J. Fraser & K. Tobin (Eds.), *International handbook of science education* (pp. 1111-1123). Dordrecht, NL: Kluwer Academic Publishers.

Taylor, P. C., & Campbell-Williams, M. (1992, August). *Discourse towards balanced rationality in the high school mathematics classroom: Ideas from Habermas' Critical Theory*. Paper presented at the Sociological and Anthropological Perspectives Working Subgroup of the Seventh International Congress of Mathematics Educators (ICME-7), Quebec, CAN.

Taylor, P. C., & Timothy, J. T. (2000, April/May). *Experimental representation: A cross-cultural research alliance in a postmodern climate*. Paper presented at the Annual Conference of the National Association for Research in Science Teaching (NARST), New Orleans, LA.

Taylor, P. W. (1994). Respect for nature: A theory of environmental ethics. In L. Gruen & D. Jamieson (Eds.), *Reflecting on nature: Readings in environmental philosophy* (pp. 85-97). New York, NY: Oxford University Press.

Tobin, K. (2000). Becoming an urban science educator. *Research in Science Education, 30*(1), 89-106.

Tobin, K., & McRobbie, C. J. (1996). Cultural myths as constraints to the enacted science curriculum. *Science Education, 80*(2), 223-241.

Tobin, K., & Tippins, D. (1993). Constructivism as a referent for teaching and learning. In K. Tobins (Ed.), *Constructivism: The practice of constructivism in science education* (pp. 3-21). Hillsdale, NJ: Lawrence Erlbaum Associates Publishers.

Torney-Purta, J., & Hahn, C. H. (1988). Values education in the Western European tradition. In W. K. Cummings, S. Gopinathan & Y. Tomoda (Eds.), *The revival of values education in Asia and in the West* (pp. 31-57). Oxford, UK: Pergamon Press.

Torres, C. A. (2002). Globalisation, education, and citizenship: Solidarity versus markets? *American Educational Research Journal, 39*, 363-378.

Tronto, J. C. (1994). *Moral boundaries: A political argument for an ethic of care*. New York, NY: Routledge Publishers.

Van den Akker, J. (1998). The science curriculum: Between ideals and outcomes. In B. J. Fraser & K. G. Tobin (Eds.), *International handbook of science education* (Vol. 1, pp. 421-447). Dordrecht, NL: Kluwer Academic Publishers.

Van Maanen, J. (1988). *Tales of the field: On writing ethnography*. Chicago, IL: The University of Chicago Press.

van Manen, M. (1990). *Researching lived experience*. London, Ontario, CAN: State University of New York Press.

Vasquez-Levy, D. (2002). Bildung-centred didaktik: A framework for examining the educational potential of subject matter. *Journal of Curriculum Studies, 34*(1), 117-128.

Velasquez, M. G. (1998). *Business ethics: Concepts and cases* (4th ed.). Upper Saddle River, NJ: Prentice-Hall Publishers.

Verducci, S. (2000). A moral method? Thoughts on cultivating empathy through method acting [Electronic version]. *Journal of Moral Education, 29*(1), 87-99.

von Glasersfeld, E. (1990). An exposition of constructivism: Why some like it radical. In R. B. Davis, C. A. Maher & N. Noddings (Eds.), *Constructivist views on the teaching and learning of mathematics* (pp. 19-29). Reston, VA: The National Council of Teachers of Mathematics.

von Glasersfeld, E. (1995). A constructivist approach to teaching. In L. P. Steffe & J. Gale (Eds.), *Constructivism in education* (pp. 3-15). Hillsdale, NJ: Lawrence Erlbaum Associates Publishers.

Vygotsky, L. S. (Ed.). (1978). *Mind in society: The development of higher psychological processes*. Cambridge, MA: Harvard University Press.

Walker, G. H. (1997). *Critical thinking*. Retrieved 13. 4. 2003, from http://www.utc.edu/Teaching-Resource-Centre/critical.html

Walsch, N. D. (1998). *Conversations with God: An uncommon dialogue* (Vol. 3). London, UK: Hodder and Stoughton publishers.

Watzlawick, P. (Ed.). (1984). *The invented reality: How do we know what we believe we know? Contributions to constructivism*. New York, NY: Norton Publishers.

Wertsch, J. V., & Toma, C. (1995). Discourse and learning in the classroom: A sociocultural approach. In L. P. Steffe & J. Gale (Eds.), *Constructivism in education* (pp. 159-183). Hillsdale, NJ: Lawrence Erlbaum Associates Publishers.

West, D. (1996). *An introduction to continental philosophy.* Cambridge, UK: Polity Press.

Wheeler, K. A., & Bijur, A. P. (Eds.). (2000). *Education for a sustainable future.* New York, NY: Kluwer Academic/Plenum Publishers.

Wilber, K. (1995). *Sex, ecology and spirituality.* Boston, MA: Shambhala Publications.

Wilber, K. (1997). *The eye of the spirit.* Boston, MA: Shambhala Publications.

Wilber, K. (1998). *The marriage of sense and soul.* New York, NY: Broadway Books.

Wilber, K. (1999). Integral psychology. In *The collected works of Ken Wilber* (Vol. 4, pp. 423-626). Boston, MA: Shambhala Publications.

Wilber, K. (2000). *A theory of everything: An integrated vision for business, politics, science, and spirituality.* Boston, MA: Shambhala Publications.

Wilson, E. O. (2002). *The future of life.* New York, NY: Alfred A. Knopf.

Wilson, J. (1972). *Practical methods of moral education.* London, UK: Heinemann Educational Publishers.

Winston, J. (1999). Theorising drama as moral education. *Journal of Moral Education, 28*(4), 459-471.

Witz, K. G. (1996). Science with values and values for science. *Journal of Curriculum Studies, 28*(5), 597-612.

Yen, D. H. (1999). *Johari Window.* Retrieved 26. 7.v2002, from http://www.noogenesis.com/game_theory/johari/johari_window.html

Zeidler, D. (1984). Moral issues and social policy in science education: Closing the literacy gap. *Science Education, 68*(4), 411-419.

Zigler, R. L. (1998). The four domains of moral education: The contributions of Dewey, Alexander and Goleman to a comprehensive taxonomy [Electronic version]. *Journal of Moral Education, 27*(1), 19-33.

Appendices

Appendix 1	Letters of consent and information about the project
Appendix 2	Letters & emails & member-checking
Appendix 3	Emergent thesis structure
Appendix 4	Demographic data
Appendix 5	Dilemma stories - full text
Appendix 6	New Austrian curriculum document: The overarching curriculum statement
Appendix 7	Habermas' Human Interests
Appendix 8	Tales of the Field – excerpts from fieldnotes
Appendix 9	Interview structure
Appendix 10	Interviews coded in NVivo
Appendix 11	Poster-transcripts & video-transcripts
Appendix 12	Examples of student portfolio-notes
Appendix 13	Email attachment – STRAND: STSE and CASE STUDY GROUP Issues

Appendix 1

Letters of consent and information about the project

APPENDIX 1A

Sehr geehrte Eltern, Erziehende, liebe Schüler!

Ich bin eine in Österreich ausgebildetete AHS-Biologielehrerin und werde die, im Rahmen meiner Dissertation an der Curtin University of Technology in Perth, Westaustralien, nötigen Forschungsarbeiten, im Mai 2000 am BG / BRG Rosseggerstrasse bzw. der Neuen Mittelschule Graz West durchführen. Es geht in diesem Projekt um die **Vermittlung moralischer Werte im naturwissenschaftlichen Unterricht** – eine zentrale Forderung der Lehrplanreform 99. Die Klasse Ihres Kindes ist von ihrer Lehrerin ausgewählt worden, um mich bei meinem Forschungsvorhaben zu unterstützen. Die Lehrerin wird mittels Dilemmageschichten ethische Problembereiche in den Naturwissenschaften mit den Schülern bearbeiten. Ich werde als Beobachterin in der Klasse sein. Tonband- bzw. Videoaufnahmen vom Unterricht werden mich bei der Datensammlung unterstützen. Im Anschluß an den Unterricht werde ich einige Schüler bitten, mir für Interviews zur Verfügung zu stehen. Der "normale" Unterricht wird durch dieses Projekt so wenig als möglich gestört werden, da die Dilemmageschichten so gewählt wurden, daß sie zum jeweiligen Unterrichtsstoff passen.

Es ist wichtig zu betonen, daß die Anonymität der Beteiligten bewahrt wird. Die gewonnenen Daten, Video- bzw. Tonbandaufnahmen werden nur zu Forschungszwecken verwendet bzw. bei wissenschaftlichen Konferenzen unter Wahrung der Anonymität präsentiert. Jede/r TeilnehmerIn hat das Recht das Projekt vorzeitig zu verlassen, sollte er/sie dies wünschen – für diese Schüler werden dann andere Arrangements getroffen werden (müssen).

Ich ersuche Sie, die Eltern / Erziehenden, bzw. Euch, die Schüler mich bei meinem Forschungsvorhaben zu unterstützen. Den Ethikvorschriften meiner Universität entsprechend, habe ich Sie hiermit informiert und bedarf der Vollständigkeit halber nur noch Ihrer/Eurer Unterschrift. Sollten Sie noch genauere Informationen bezüglich des Projektes wünschen, ich werde ab 7. Mai in Österreich sein und vermutlich ab 9. Mai in der Schule erreichbar sein. Vielen Dank für Ihre/Eure Unterstützung im Voraus

Mag. Elisabeth Neumayr e.h.

_____ Bitte abtrennen und der Lehrerin weitergeben!_____

Ich / wir geben die Einstimmung für mein/unser
Kind...
am Dissertationsprojekt von Frau Mag. Elisabeth Neumayr mit dem Thema: "Moralerziehung im naturwissenschaftlichen Unterricht" teilzunehmen.

Unterschrift/en:...

Schüler/in: Ich ....werde am Dissertationsprojekt von Frau Mag. Elisabeth Neumayr mit dem Thema: "Moralerziehung im naturwissenschaftlichen Unterricht" teilnehmen.

Unterschrift:..
Elisabeth Neumayr

APPENDIX 1B

An die
Ko-Forscher i.e.  , und
am BG / BRG

Curtin University, 2.12.1999

RE – Forschungsvorhaben für Dissertation im Bereich Moralerziehung im naturwissenschftlichen Unterricht

Liebe Leute, Ko-Forscher, Kollegen und Freunde!

Ich habe mich sehr gefreut, als ich von Irene im letzten Email erfahren habe, dass Ihr bereit seid, bei meinem Dissertationsprojekt mitzuwirken. Ich habe ja bereits eine Kurzinformation zu Euch geschickt, gedenke aber nun, jeden von Euch einzeln mit dem Projekt bekannt zu machen. (Auf gut Deutsch – ich will Euch nicht dumm sterben lassen!).

Wie Ihr aus der beiliegenden Projektbeschreibung ersehen könnt, würde ich gerne meine Studie an Eurer Schule durchführen. Dafür gibt es mehrere Gründe:

- Ich kenne Euch persönlich, sowie die Bedingungen an dieser Schule, was meine Startbedingungen erleichtert! Außerdem wird mir diese Tatsache bei den Interviews eine grosse Hilfe sein!
- Ich weiß, dass diese Schule Neuem immer aufgeschlossen gegenüber steht
- Ich habe absichtlich eine koedukative, nicht konfessionelle öffentliche Schule gewählt, da ich der Meinung bin, dass konfessionelle Schulen von vornherein mehr Ethikunterricht betreiben als nicht-konfessionelle.
- Ich habe mich besonders gefreut, dass ich Euch als Ko-Forscher gewonnen habe – lauter Leute von denen ich weiß, dass sie sehr engagiert sind – da kann ja nur was Gutes rauskommen!

Nun denn zum Projekt selbst: ich habe für jeden von Euch eine Kopie der Projektkurzbeschreibung mitgeschickt, um Euch zu zeigen, worum's mir hauptsächlich geht!

Was bedeutet dies nun im Klartext für Euch:
- Ich bräuchte pro Lehrer eine Klasse! Nach Möglichkeit eine Klasse, die Ihr im Herbst auch noch haben werdet….
- Ich bräuchte Information über den Lehrstoff, den Ihr mit dieser Klasse gedenkt ungefähr Anfang Mai bis Ende Mai durchzumachen – ich weiss dies ist eine verdammt schwierige Bitte, aber notwendig, da ich praktisch für jede einzelne Klasse entsprechend dem Lehrstoff Dilemmageschichten verfassen muss. Ich möchte, dass der Inhalt der Geschichten so gut als möglich zum Lehrstoff paßt!
- Ich werde so Ende April, Anfang Mai bei Euch anrollen und werde mit Euch mal das Projekt durchbesprechen, die von Schwetz et al. entwickelte Unterrichtsmethode besprechen bzw. Euch kurz einführen, was ich in welchem Zusammenhang und warum machen will – wenn's Euch recht ist. Ich denke mir nur – Ihr sollt nicht das Gefühl haben, nicht ausreichend informiert worden zu sein! Also bitte scheut Euch nie zu fragen!!!!
- Jeder von Euch wird dann mit einer Dilemmageschichte plus der Methode bewaffnet auf die Klasse losgelassen. Ich werde mit Video- und Tonbandaufnahmegerät den Unterricht beobachten. Anschließend werde ich mit mehreren Schülern Interviews über ihre Eindrücke durchführen. Im Anschluß daran werde ich mit jedem von Euch ein längeres Interview durchführen, über Eure Eindrücke.
- Ich bitte Euch weiters ein "professionelles" Tagebuch zu führen, das Eure Eindrücke über Euren Unterricht, Eure Ideen, Verbesserungsvorschläge oder einfach nur Gedanken zum Thema hat. Dieses Tagebuch verbleibt bei Euch – ich würde Euch allerdings bitten, es mit zu den Interviews zu nehmen, da Ihr vielleicht das eine oder andere mit mir teilen wollt…(oder auch nicht!). Es soll dazu dienen, dass Ihr Euch Zeit nehmt und in Ruhe mal über einige Dinge nachdenkt, über die man im Alltagstrott kaum Zeit findet nachzudenken!…..
- Jede Klasse sollte mindestens einen Durchgang erleben, nach Möglichkeit aber zwei in dem Monat, wo ich bei Euch bin: einen am Anfang, den anderen am Ende….Ich bzw. Ihr brauche/t dafür eine Doppelstunde. Die Interviews müssen halt dann irgendwie eingeschoben werden…aber das läßt sich am besten vorort planen!
- Warum solltet Ihr die Klasse auch im Herbst weiterhin haben? Nun, eine Frage, die bei bisherigen Forschungsprojekten immer nur sehr mangelhaft abgedeckt wurde, ist diese: Hat sporadischer Moralunterricht irgendeinen Sinn? Kann man bei regelmäßiger Anwendung von Moraldilemmas eine tatsächliche Veränderung in der Grundhaltung der Schüler feststellen, eine, die dauerhaft ist? Nun, damit man dies feststellen kann, wäre es nötig, das die Schüler etwa jeden Monat einmal ein Moraldilemma durcharbeiten. Für Euch würde dies bedeuten, daß Ihr im Mai mit Euren Schülern zwei Dilemmas, nach Möglichkeit im Juni noch eines und dann erst wieder im September/Oktober eines, im November eines und im Dezember komme ich dann eh wieder selbst nach Österreich um "nach dem Rechten zu sehen"! Ich würde Euch mit den Dilemmageschichten versorgen, Ihr seid allerdings herzlichst

eingeladen, falls jemand von Euch Lust hat selbst zu schreiben, es selbst mal zu probieren. Ich habe vor, das Material, das im Rahmen dieses Projekts entsteht nach Möglichkeit in Buchform herauszubringen, was Euch natürlich auch zu Ko-Authoren machen würde (aber das ist noch Schnee von überübermorgen!!!!).

- Dies bringt mich zum nächsten ganz wichtigen Punkt: ein Schwerpunkt des Projekts ist es ja die Unterrichtsmethode von Schwetz et al. sorgfältig zu evaluieren und zu verbessern. Da Ihr in diesem Fall die Unterrichtenden seid, und ich schon gespannt bin auf Eure Verbesserungsvorschläge, werdet Ihr sozusagen nicht nur die "Beforschten" sein, sondern auch aktive Aktionsforscher......
- So hab' ich jetzt noch was vergessen? Ach ja, bevor ich bzw. Ihr mit den Dilemmas losstarte/t habe ich vor die moralischen Grundhaltungen der Schüler mit einem Fragebogen zu erfassen, sozusagen vor der Einwirkung des Werte- und Moralunterrichts.....

Ach ja: Direktion und Landesschulrat werden informiert und die Zustimmung der Beteiligten i.e. Ihr (jetzt!) , Eltern und Schüler (allerdings erst kurz davor!) eingeholt.
Es ist meine ethische Pflicht Euch auf folgende Punkte aufmerksam zu machen – mag zwar etwas übertrieben und nach "no-na" klingen – die Uni will's aber ausdrücklich so haben – nun so sei es:

- Ihr habt das Recht über das Projekt ausreichend informiert zu werden – ich hoffe, dass ich dies hiermit getan habe. Falls noch Unklarheiten bestehen, bitte zögert nicht nachzufragen, am besten via Email!
- Eure Anonymität bleibt gewahrt.
- Alle Daten inkl. Video- bzw. Tonbandaufnahmen werden , außer mit Eurer ausdrücklichen Erlaubnis nur zu Forschungszwecken bzw. eventuell bei Wissenschaftlichen Konferenzen präsentiert (nach erfolgter Nachfrage!).
- Jeder Teilnehmer hat die Möglichkeit vorzeitig aus dem Projekt auszusteigen (nach erfolgter Nachfrage!).
- Die Daten werden für fünf Jahre an der Curtin University of Technology aufbewahrt und dann vernichtet.

Ich ersuche Euch hiermit formell Eure Zustimmung zur Mitarbeit zu geben. Bitte füllt das Zustimmungsformular aus und schickt es mir bitte noch vor Weihnachten, wenn möglich zurück.

Viele Grüße

PS.: Sollten noch weitere Fragen offen sein, ich bin unter obiger Adresse, bzw. am Email: neumayr@ses.curtin.edu.au bzw. Unter folgenden Telefonnummern erreichbar: +8-9244 9495 bzw.
+8-9266 3593 (Uni)
ZUSTIMMUNGSERKLÄRUNG / LETTER OF CONSENT

Ich bin über folgende Punkte informiert worden:

- Ich habe das Recht über das Projekt ausreichend informiert zu werden – im Zweifelsfalle habe ich die Möglichkeit mich weiterzuinformieren.
- Meine Anonymität bleibt gewahrt.
- Alle Daten inkl. Video- bzw. Tonbandaufnahmen werden , außer mit meiner ausdrücklichen Erlaubnis nur zu Forschungszwecken verwendet bzw. eventuell bei Wissenschaftlichen Konferenzen präsentiert (nach erfolgter Nachfrage!).
- Ich habe die Möglichkeit vorzeitig aus dem Projekt auszusteigen, sollte ich dies wünschen.
- Die Daten werden für fünf Jahre an der Curtin University of Technology aufbewahrt und dann vernichtet.

Ich erkläre mich hiermit **bereit / nicht bereit** (Unzutreffendes bitte streichen) im Rahmen des Forschungsprojekts:"Towards Moral Education in Science Classrooms" mitzuarbeiten.

APPENDIX 1C

Elisabeth Neumayr

An die
Direktion des BG / BRG
Rosseggerstraße

Curtin University, 2.12.1999

RE – Forschungsvorhaben für Dissertation im Bereich Moralerziehung im naturwissenschftlichen Unterricht

Sehr geehrte Frau Direktor!

Wie Du aus der beiliegenden Projektbeschreibung ersehen kannst, würde ich gerne meine Studie an Deiner Schule durchführen. Dafür gibt es mehrere Gründe:

- Ich habe bereits mit mehreren Lehrern Kontakt aufgenommen, die bereit sind, an diesem Forschungsprojekt mitzuarbeiten (Roll, Höfert, Korak, Rautner)
- Ich kenne die Lehrer persönlich, sowie die Bedingungen an dieser Schule, was meine Startbedingungen erleichtert!
- Ich weiss, dass diese Schule Neuem immer aufgeschlossen gegenüber steht
- Ich habe absichtlich eine koedukative, nicht konfessionelle öffentliche Schule gewählt, da ich der Meinung bin, dass konfessionelle Schulen von vornherein mehr Ethikunterricht betreiben als nicht-konfessionelle.

Ich werde wahrscheinlich im April/Mai für einige Wochen auftauchen, die Lehrer in ihre Rolle als Co-Forscher einführen, den Unterricht beobachten, Video- und Tonbandaufnahmen machen, Interviews mit Lehrern und Schülern durchführen (siehe Projektbeschreibung!).

Ich werde natuerlich versuchen den Unterrichtsfluss moeglichst wenig zu beintraechtigen. Jede Klasse (pro Lehrer eine) sollte mindestens eine Dilemmaeinheit mitmachen koennen (eine Doppelstunde!). Nach Moeglichkeit, in Abhängigkeit von der Klassenverfügbarkeit, sollte jede Klasse noch einen zweiten Durchgang in diesem Monat durchmachen. Ich werde versuchen Interviews mit Schülern (zwischen drei bis fünf Schüler pro Klasse) so durchzuführen, dass diese möglichst wenig vom Unterricht versäumen. Die Interviews mit den Lehrern werden vorort vereinbart.

Schüler, Eltern und Lehrer, sowie der Landesschulrat werden informiert und die Zustimmung der Beteiligten eingeholt. Die Teilnehmer werden darauf aufmerksam gemacht, dass ihre Anonymität gewahrt wird, alle Daten, Video- bzw. Tonbandaufnahmen vertraulich und nur zu Forschungszwecken verwendet werden bzw. eventuell im Rahmen von wissenschaftlichen Konferenzen präsentiert werden. Jeder Teilnehmer hat die Möglichkeit vorzeitig aus dem Projekt auszusteigen, sollte er/sie dies wünschen. Die Daten werden für fünf Jahre an der Curtin University of Technology aufbewahrt und dann vernichtet.

Ich ersuche hiermit um die formelle Erlaubnis, mein Dissertations-Forschungsvorhaben am BG/ BRG Rosseggerstraße durchführen zu dürfen.
Vielen Dank im Voraus
Viele Grüße

PS.: Sollten noch weitere Fragen offen sein, ich bin unter obiger Adresse, bzw. am Email: neumayr@ses.curtin.edu.au bzw. Unter folgenden Telefonnummern erreichbar: ████████ bzw. ████████ (Uni)

402

APPENDIX 1D

Mag. rer,nat. Elisabeth Neumayr

An Herrn
Landesschulinspektor
Dr. Hinteregger
Landesschulrat für Steiermark
Körblergasse
A-8010 Graz

Curtin University, 2.12.1999

RE – Forschungsvorhaben für Dissertation im Bereich Moralerziehung im naturwissenschftlichen Unterricht

Sehr geehrter Herr Landesschulinspektor!

Ich bin Österreicherin mit Lehramt Biologie und Umweltkunde und befinde mich zur Zeit in Perth, Westaustralien, um ein Doktoratsstudium an der Curtin University of Technology im Bereich Science Education zu absolvieren. Mein Forschungsvorhaben wird einen Aufenthalt an einer der Schulen Ihres Zuständigkeitsbereichs beinhalten. Ich würde gerne meine Feldstudie am BG/BRG Klusemann-Strasse in Graz-Webling durchführen. Es gibt dafür mehrere Gründe:

- Ich habe an dieser Schule mein Unterrichtspraktikum absolviert
- Ich habe bereits mit mehreren Lehrern Kontakt aufgenommen, die bereit sind, an diesem Forschungsprojekt mitzuarbeiten
- Ich kenne die Lehrer sowie die Bedingungen an dieser Schule persönlich
- Ich weiss, dass diese Schule Neuem immer aufgeschlossen gegenüber steht
-

Ich werde wahrscheinlich im April/Mai für einige Wochen diese Schule besuchen, die Lehrer in ihre Rolle als Co-Forscher einführen, den Unterricht beobachten, Video- und Tonbandaufnahmen machen, Interviews mit Lehrern und Schülern durchführen (siehe Projektbeschreibung!).

Ich werde natürlich versuchen den Unterrichtsfluß möglichst wenig zu beinträchtigen. Jede Klasse (pro Lehrer eine) sollte mindestens eine Dilemmaeinheit mitmachen (eine Doppelstunde!). Nach Möglichkeit, in Abhängigkeit von der Klassenverfügbarkeit, sollte jede Klasse noch einen zweiten Durchgang in diesem Monat durchmachen. Ich werde versuchen Interviews mit Schülern (zwischen drei bis fünf Schüler pro Klasse) so durchzuführen, dass diese möglichst wenig vom Unterricht versäumen. Die Interviews mit den Lehrern werden vorort vereinbart.

Schüler, Eltern und Lehrer, sowie die Direktion werden informiert und die Zustimmung der Beteiligten eingeholt. Die Teilnehmer werden darauf aufmerksam gemacht, dass ihre Anonymität gewahrt wird, alle Daten, Video- bzw. Tonbandaufnahmen vertraulich und nur zu Forschungszwecken verwendet werden bzw. eventuell im Rahmen von wissenschaftlichen Konferenzen präsentiert werden. Jeder Teilnehmer hat die Möglichkeit vorzeitig aus dem Projekt auszusteigen, sollte er/sie dies wünschen. Die Daten werden für fünf Jahre an der Curtin University of Technology aufbewahrt und dann vernichtet.

Ich ersuche hiermit um die formelle, schriftliche Erlaubnis (wird von der Universität unbedingt verlangt!), mein Dissertations-Forschungsvorhaben am BG/ BRG Rosseggerstraße durchführen zu dürfen.

Beilage: Projektbeschreibung

Vielen Dank

PS.: Sollten noch weitere Fragen offen sein, ich bin unter obiger Adresse, bzw. am Email: neumayr@ses.curtin.edu.au bzw. Unter folgenden Telefonnummern erreichbar: ▮▮▮▮ bzw. ▮▮▮▮ (Uni)

BESTÄTIGUNG / PERMISSION

Ich bin über den Inhalt des Forschungsvorhabens informiert worden und

gebe / gebe nicht (Nicht Zutreffendes bitte streichen!) hiermit meine Erlaubnis, dass Frau Elisabeth Neumayr, ihr Forschungsvorhaben

am BG/ BRG Rosseggerstraße, Graz, Österreich, durchführen darf.

I have been informed about this research project and I hereby give/do not give permission to Mrs. Elisabeth Neumayr to conduct her

doctoral research at the BG/BRG Rosseggerstraße in Graz, Austria.

Appendix 1E Information for students

(Ad ANKÜNDIGUNGEN in den NAWI News!
Jugendlabor ▓▓▓▓▓ **Sandra**
Science Across the World Sabine
Forschungprojekt: Zusammenarbeit mit
Universitäten der Welt. ▓▓▓▓▓) **Irene**

WEGE AUS DEM Dilemma: Denke, entscheide, diskutiere!

NAWI SchülerInnen aus der 5A und 7A Klasse arbeiten an einem
Langzeitforschungsprojekt zum Thema **„Ethik im NAWI-Unterricht"**
mit der Universität Perth/Australien unter der Leitung von
Frau Mag. E. Neumayr mit. Dabei soll anhand von
„Dilemmageschichten", die auf den jeweiligen Unterrichtsinhalt
abgestimmt wurden /werden, eine ethisch-moralische
Auseinandersetzung mit einem Thema angeregt werden und ein
rasches Handeln in Entscheidungssituationen geübt werden.
Das Projekt läuft im Mai 2000 an, erste Erkenntnisse sind
bereits gewonnen. Die bearbeiteten Inhalte fließen nicht nur
in den Biologie- und Physikunterricht ein, sondern werden auch
in den Fächern Deutsch und Religion miteinbezogen.

Folgende Themenbereiche werden bearbeitet: Überbevölkerung,
Globalisierung, Umweltprobleme, Respekt vor dem Leben,
Wissenschaft als „neue Religion".
Betreuerinnen : ▓▓▓▓▓▓▓▓▓▓▓▓ ▓▓▓▓▓▓▓▓▓▓▓

Wir sind auf die Arbeit und die Ergebnisse schon sehr
gespannt.

PROJEKTBESCHREIBUNG

TITEL: *Towards Moral Education in the Science Classroom – a Phenomenological Study*

(Moralerziehung im naturwissenschaftlichen Unterricht – eine phänomenologische Studie)

Kurzbeschreibung:

Die vorliegende Studie wird zwei Hauptschwerpunkte haben:

1) eine Evaluierung der Anwendbarkeit und Effektivität der von Schwetz, Gschweitl, Mattner-Begusch und Neumayr 1998 erarbeiteten Methode für Wert- und Moralerziehung

2) die Erforschung der Effekte, die die Anwendung dieser Methode auf Lehrer sowie deren Schüler mit sich bringt

Hintergründe

1999 hat nicht nur für Australien sondern auch für Österreich eine grundlegende Lehrplanreform mit sich gebracht. In beiden Ländern wurde dabei großer Wert auf Werte- und Moralerziehung gelegt. Dies hat dazu geführt, dass viele Lehrer nun mit der Tatsache konfrontiert sind, "Werte und Moral" unterrichten zu müssen, ohne jedoch geeignetes Material bzw. Unterrichtsmethoden zur Verfügung zu haben. Auf dieser Grundlage beschloß das Österreichische Jugend-Rot-Kreuz im Jahr 1997 ein Projekt ins Leben zu rufen, dessen Hauptaufgabe es war, geeignetes Material zu erarbeiten, eine geeignete Unterrichtsmethode zu entwickeln, zu evaluieren und den Lehrern in Buchform zugänglich zu machen. Als Mitglied des Forschungsteams war ich direkt in der Planungs-, Anwendungs- und Evaluierungsphase dabei. Die Evaluierung erfolgte unter anderem am BG/BRG Klusemannstrasse, Graz-Webling, indem wir, die Mitglieder des Forschungsteams selbst unterrichteten und sozusagen die Klassen ("nur") zur Verfügung gestellt bekamen.

Außer der bereits erwähnten Unterrichtsmethode gibt es noch andere Vorschläge zum Werte- und Moralunterricht z.B. von Lind (1993) und Oser und Althof(1992).

Methodologischer Rahmen der Studie

Die im Rahmen des Rot-Kreuz-Projektes erarbeitete Unterrichtsmethode beruht im Wesentlichen auf den Arbeiten von Lawrence Kohlberg, der wiederum stark von Jean Piagts Arbeiten beeinflußt war. Das "moralische Lernen" selbst wird durch ein moralisches Dilemma, welches ein kognitives Disäquilibrium bewirkt, hervorgerufen. Dilemmageschichten sind durch einfache Sprache, welche persönliche Assoziationen

fördern soll, sowie durch ein oder mehrere moralische Dilemma gekennzeichnet. Sie haben ein offenes Ende und daher keine eindeutige Lösung. Die von uns entwickelte Unterrichtsmethode beruht auf konstruktivistischen Erkenntnissen, was bedeutet, dass die Tatsache, dass jeder Schüler sein eigenes Wissen konstruiert, in Betracht gezogen wird. Während die Geschichte erzählt wird, wird an geeigneten Stellen der Fluß der Geschichte unterbrochen, um Fragen an die Schüler zu stellen. Diese Fragen dienen dazu jeden Schüler persönlich "in das Dilemma hineinzuführen". Jeder Schüler überlegt zuerst für sich selbst, dann in Kleingruppen und schließlich im Plenum, welche Lösungen man anbieten könnte. Dilemmageschichten tragen wesentlich zur Entwicklung von Kommunikationsfähigkeit und Diskussionskultur bei.

Die Lehrerrolle ist vom konstruktivistischen Gesichtspunkt aus, die eines "facilitators", was man am besten so übersetzen kann: jemand, der (in diesem Fall) einen Denkprozess ermöglicht. Der Lehrer schafft die Rahmenbedingungen, die Lernen ermöglichen.

Diese Studie wird zwei Schwerpunkte haben:

1) Evaluierung der Unterrichtsmethode durch die am Forschungsprojekt beteiligten Lehrer. Die Lehrer selbst werden die Methode anwenden und sich als Aktionsforscher aktiv an der Verbesserung mitbeteiligen. Auch von der Schülerseite her werden mittels Fragebögen Meinungen eingeholt werden. Videoanalyse wird dazu dienen, das Gesamtbild abzurunden.

2) Eine phänomenologische Untersuchung der Erfahrungen welche Lehrer und Schüler mit Werte- und Moralerziehung haben. Es geht mir dabei vor allem um die Erforschung der "Ethischen Grundlage des naturwissenschaftlichen Unterrichts". Dieser Teil der Studie wird Interviews, das Führen eines "professionellen" Tagebuchs und eventuell Folgeinterviews beinhalten.

Theoretischer Rahmen der Studie

Diese Studie wird auf der Basis konstruktivistischer Erkenntnisse durchgeführt. Konstruktivismus dient als Grundlage für das Erstellen von Lehr-, Lern- und Lehr- bzw. Unterrichtsplanmodellen (Tobin, 1993). Ich werde mich vornehmlich an die Prinzipien des "kritischen Knostruktivismus" halten, der aus einer Kombination aus Konstruktivismustheorie und der "kritischen" Theorie von Jürgen Habermas (1972, 1984, 1990) entstanden ist und welcher eine ethische Basis für die diskursive Praxis der Wissens"konstruktion" darstellt. Zusätzlich kommt noch ein feministischer Ansatz zum Tragen.

Zielsetzungen der Studie

Der Hauptzweck dieser Studie liegt darin die Effekte der Anwendung des von Schwetz et al. (1998) vorgeschlagenen Unterrichtsansatzes auf Schüler und Lehrer zu erforschen. Dies führt zu folgenden Forschungsfragen:

- Welche Erfahrungen machen Lehrer und Schüler durch die Anwendung der oben genannten Unterrichtsmethode?

- Wie beschreiben die Lehrer die "ethische Grundlage" des naturwissenschaftlichen Unterrichts?

- Was denken die Lehrer über diese Methode hinsichtlich ihrer Anwendbarkeit, ihrer eigenen Kompetenz und ihres Selbstvertrauens?

- Kann Kohlbergs Theorie über Moralentwicklung beim Menschen, wenn sie auf der Basis des Konstruktivismus angewendet wird, bei regelmäßiger Anwendung ein wertvolles "Werkzeug" sein, um moralische Werte zu vermitteln? Kann sie daher signifikant zur Werte- und Moralerziehung beitragen?

Bedeutung der Studie

Die größte Bedeutung dieser Studie liegt in ihrer gesellschaftlichen Relevanz: es geht um die Förderung einer Ethik, die Respekt für die Würde des Menschen und für humanitäre Werte hochhält. Indem das Bewußtsein der Lehrer für ihre eigene ethische Unterrichtsgrundlage gehoben wird, ist es wahrscheinlich, daß die Lehrer die Wichtigkeit ihrer Rolle erkennen bei der Vermittlung von Wissen und von Fähigkeiten, die für eine sich verändernde Gesellschaft nötig sind. Naturwissenschaftlicher Unterricht ist aufgrund seiner Nähe zu traditioneller, positivistischer Forschung, welche "absolute" Wahrheiten propagiert, prädestiniert dafür, dass gerade in diesem Bereich ein moralisches Grundgerüst für den Unterricht entwickelt wird. Dieses kann Schülern dabei helfen, einander widersprechende "Wahrheitsansprüche" zu beurteilen. Diese Studie wird wesentlich zur Schaffung eines solchen moralischen Grundgerüsts innerhalb des naturwissenschaftlichen Unterrichts beitragen.

Appendix 2

Letters & emails & memberchecking

Appendix 2A: Setting up the project

Delivered-To: neumayr@ses.curtin.edu.au
From: ███████████████████████ *Irena*
To: "Elisabeth Neumayr" <neumayr@ses.curtin.edu.au>
Subject: Ideen2
Date: Thu, 20 Jan 2000 19:36:09 +0100
MIME-Version: 1.0
X-Priority: 3
X-MSMail-Priority: Normal
X-MimeOLE: Produced By Microsoft MimeOLE V4.72.2106.4

Hi, hast du gestern am 19.1.00 meinmail erhalten, weil ich unsicher bin, da ich ein remail erhalten
habe. Hier nun meine Vorschläge für die Themen: a) Bedeutung der Pflanzen für alle Lebewesen →die Fichl
b) Co2-Problematik.
c) Pandemien, Epidemien, (Virenund Bakterien -Verbreitung durch Globalisierung) --Prokaryonten als
Lebenskünstler. Gruß █████ *Irena*

Delivered-To: neumayr@ses.curtin.edu.au
From: ███████████████████████ *Irena*
To: "Elisabeth Neumayr" <neumayr@ses.curtin.edu.au>
Subject: Themenwahl
Date: Fri, 21 Jan 2000 07:53:32 +0100
MIME-Version: 1.0
X-Priority: 3
X-MSMail-Priority: Normal
X-MimeOLE: Produced By Microsoft MimeOLE V4.72.2106.4

Rippe wird langsam besser, kan seit 2 Tagen die Nacht wieder durchschlafen. Wo hast Du die
Herpesfreunde aufgetrieben, oder ist dies nur eine natürliche Reaktion auf die Summe deiner
Arbeitsbelastungen gepaart mit der sommerlichen Hitze? Es ist aber ausgesprochen unangenehm, hatte
auch einmal einen massiven Angriff.
Da du das mail vom 20. 1 nicht erhalten hast, teile ich dir mit: die gnannten Themen würden für meine
5. Klasse KV geeignet sein.besonders , weil es eine Multi-kulti Klasse ist: 12 verschiedene
Nationen./32 Schüler: bunt: d.h.von Ghana, Togo bis zur Mongolei. Im Moment arbeiten wir an den
Zellteilungsprozessen. Gruß █████ *Irena*

Delivered-To: neumayr@ses.curtin.edu.au
From: ███████████████████████ *Irena*
To: "Elisabeth Neumayr" <neumayr@ses.curtin.edu.au>
Subject: Dilemma 1
Date: Sat, 22 Jan 2000 19:10:40 +0100
MIME-Version: 1.0
X-Priority: 3
X-MSMail-Priority: Normal
X-MimeOLE: Produced By Microsoft MimeOLE V4.72.2106.4

Theresia   *Walter*
Meine Liebe, ich hoffe, daß dir die Antibiotika helfen und dich nicht zu sehr schwächen. Übrigens ████
und ████ haben mir eigentlich zugesagt mit dir Kontakt aufzunehmen. Sie werden nächste Woche die
Unterschrift bei mir abgeben, ich werde sie dir dann schicken, also schlecht schaut's nicht aus. █████
hat schon eine schulische e-mail aderse, nur sie kann damit noch nicht umgehen. Haben am Di vereinbart
einmal zu üben, hoffentlich fubktioniert diese blöde Schuladresse wenigstens bei ihr. -Wir steuern
nur wiedereinmal einem Semesterende zu, was mit Umengen an Prüfungen, Tests, Korekturen ua. verbunden
ist und die üblichen Sitzungen -daher ist unser timemanagement sehr beansprucht. Erwartest du von ████
auch eine Unterschrift? schönes weekend - ███████████ *Irena*

livered-To: neumayr@ses.curtin.edu.au
: "Elisabeth Neumayr" <neumayr@ses.curtin.edu.au>
bject: Dilemma 2
te: Tue, 25 Jan 2000 22:24:55 +0100
ME-Version: 1.0
Priority: 3
MSMail-Priority: Normal
MimeOLE: Produced By Microsoft MimeOLE V4.72.2106.4

, die Korrekturarbeiten , Tests, Laborberichte, Übungsmappen, und 3 FBA, die noch kaum im Entstehen
d, beschäftigen mich momentan außerordentlich, dazu die vielen Nachmittagseinheiten, so kam ich kaum
u deine Antwort zu lesen. Du bist ja trotz Krankeit sehr produktiv, im Grunde gefallen mir alle
ne Vorschläge. Ich überlege für welche Art ich mich entscheiden soll:
Wäre es nicht überlegenswert die Schüler in die Auswahl der Dilemmas miteinzubeziehen d.h. sie nach
er Kurzinfo wählen zu lassen?
Welche der Fragestellungen spricht 15 jährige besonders an?
In meiner MULTI-KULTI Klasse?. ist es günstig nach der Wertigkeit es Menschen in der DrittenWelt zu
gen, wenn einige meiner S aus solchen Ländern abstammen? oder gerade deswegen?
wenn ich sie fragen will, muß ich etwas warten, da sie momentan bei -20/-25°C in Kitzbühl auf
ikurs sind.
Dein Thema 1 Regenwalddilemma erscheint mir besonders komplex, dodaß ich befürchte, daß meine
blinge damit etwas überfordert sind.

anna ist auch in Sorge, sie befürchtet daß die Arbeit mit dir trtoz ihres Interesses daran, sehr
wendig wird. -will sehen wie sie sich daran beteiligt.
ke für den Hinweis ein Tagebuch zu schreiben . nehme mir kontinuierliche Notizen vor. Busi *Irene*

To: _____ *Irene*
From: neumayr@ses.curtin.edu.au (Elisabeth Neumayr)
Subject: Re: Dilemma 1

allo ____ *Irene*

anke fuer Deine prompte Antwort - bin immer noch "out of order" - heute kommt noch etwas Fieber dazu.
ie entzuendeten Stellen jucken nicht nur sondern tun manchmal sogar hoellisch weh! Nun, womit hab ich
das verdient - natuerlich gar nicht aber was soll man machen?

ei uns herrscht nach den sauheissen Tagen zwischen Weihnachten - bis nach Neujahr regnerisches (!!!)
etter mit heftigen Gewittern und Stuermen, die sich gewaschen haben. Peter nuetzt den heutigen kuehlen
ag um den Garten aufzuraeumen - was man hier nicht im Winter erledigen kann im Garten bleibt liegen
an kanns spaeter einfach nicht mehr tun - viel zu heiss!!!!!!....
ber die Hitze kommt bestimmt zurueck - noch was der Februar nicht da!!!
Walter Theresia
oll, wenn ____ und ____ auch mitmachen, wertet die Arbeit natuerlich auf!! Es ist schon Ok, wenn
hr die Unterschriften alle zusammen schickt - von ____ branch ich auch eine!.

ch hab ein wenig nachgedacht ueber Dein Prokaryontenthema. Moeglichkeiten waeren z.B

Ausbeutung des Regenwaldes unter dem Deckmaentelchen medizinischer Fortschritt versus Interessen der
inheimischen in diesen Gebieten. Monopolstellung der Pharmakonzerne gegen Ansprueche der Indigenen
oelker plus Schutz des regenwaldes im Allgemeinen!

ein ziemlich heisses Eisen waere das Dilemma, warum fuer die Erforschung bestimmter Krankheiten,
IDS Milliarden ausgegeben werden, waehrend fuer Krankheiten wie z.B. Grippe, die jaehrlich
undertausende Menschen das Leben kostet weltweit nur ein Bruchteil dieser Betraege eingesetzt wird.

Ein anderes moralisches Dilemma sehe ich in den Impfprogrammen der Weltgesundheitsorganisation in der
ritten Welt z.B. Kenia Gelbfieber - es wird nur dann z. B. ein Dorf (oder auch nur die Familie!)
urchgeimpft wenn einige Faelle nachweislich an Gelbfieber gestorben sind!!! - Vergleich mit den
mpfprogrammen bei uns - Ist ein Vergleich der Wertigkeit zwischen Menschen in der Dritten Welt und
ei uns zulaessig?

Ferntourismus vs. Einschleppung bislang unbekannter Krankheiten gegen die es keine oder kaum MIttel
ibt. Sollte die neuerworbene Mobilitaet zugunsten der allgemeinen Gesundheit eingeschraenkt werden -
der so aehnlich, muss ich erst fertig durchdenken!

a mir was DU von diesen Vorschlaegen grob haeltst! Hoffe bald von Dir zu hoeren...

. ussi Lily

Hallo ~~████~~, Irena

.....im Grunde gefallen mir alle deine Vorschläge.Ich überlege für welche Art ich mich entscheiden soll:
>1. Wäre es nicht überlegenswert die Schüler in die Auswahl der Dilemmas miteinzubeziehen d.h. sie nach einer Kurzinfo wählen zu lassen?

Wir brauchen ja ohnehin mehrere Dilemmas. Mehrere Moeglichkeiten waeren also notwendig!

>2. Welche der Fragestellungen spricht 15 jährige besonders an?
Du kennst die Schueler - es muss vor allem ein Dilemma sein, dass auch ein Dilemma fuer die Schhueler darstellt. Das ist der "crucial point"! Da DU Deine Schaefchen kennst, musst DU mir helfen. Ausserdem waren meine Vorschlaege soweit nur eine Hulkti-Pulti-Aktion damit ich Dir mal eine Idee gebe,was moeglich waere.....aber es gibt sicher noch andere Moeglichkeiten!

>3. In meiner MULTI-KULTI Klasse?. ist es günstig nach der Wertigkeit es Menschen in der DrittenWelt zu fragen, wenn einige meiner S aus solchen Ländern abstammen? oder gerade deswegen?
Es wird ja nicht die Wertigkeit dieser Menschen bezweifelt, es wird nur klar gemacht, dass in der rein wirtschaftlichen Welt dieser Teil der Welt oft durch die Finger schaut. So hab´ich das gemeint d.h. "eigentlich gerade deswegen"...

>4. wenn ich sie fragen will, muß ich etwas warten, da sie momentan bei -20/-25℃ in Kitzbühl auf Schikurs sind.
Ich bin mir nicht darueber klar, ob man sie bezueglich Themenauswahl zuviel fragen sollte - fragst DU sie bezueglich der Themen, die DU mit ihnen besprechen moechtest? Die DIlemmas sollten nur zu dem passen, was DU grob machst!

>5. Dein Thema 1: Regenwalddilemma erscheint mir besonders komplex, dodaß ich befürchte, daß meine Lieblinge damit etwas überfordert sind.
Haengt davon ab, wie´s geschrieben wird, aber ich kann ja mal eine Probefassung schreiben und DU beurteilst dann ob DU glaubst dass es zu hoch wird?
> Theresia
~~████████~~ ist auch in Sorge, sie befürchtet daß die Arbeit mit dir trotz ihres Interesses daran, sehr aufwendig wird. -will sehen wie sie sich daran beteiligt.

Mach´ihr mal klar, dass die Hauptarbeit nach wie vor bei mir liegt - ich schreibe die DIlemmas, sie muss nur ! unterrichten, was sie ohnehin machen wuerde, bekommt die UNterrichtsmethode geliefert....ich muss beobachten, Notizen machen etc. was fuer mich sicher mehr Arbeit bedeutet als fuer sie. Ihr Aufwand besteht hauptsaechlich darin mir fuer Interviews zur Verfuegung zu stehen, was kaum mehr als eine eineinhalb Stunden max. dauern wird (eines jeweils machen wir uebhaupt anfangen, jeweils eines nach der Durchfuehrung eines Dilemmas, eventuell falls notwendig noch eines, falls gewisse DInge unklar geblieben sind.) Ist das irgendwie klarer jetzt? Ausserdem, unser uns, hat sich ~~████~~ ja bis jetzt Theresia noch gar nicht beteilt weder aufwendig noch sonst wie....

>Danke für den Hinweis ein Tagebuch zu schreiben . nehme mir kontinuierliche Notizen vor.
Soll nicht in Mehrarbeit ausarten, aber z.B. solche Sachen wie anfaengliche Sorgen dass es zuviel Arbeit macht etc. ist im Nachhinein wertvolle Information! Und cih moechte natuerlich die Situation bei und fuer Euch so gut asl moeglich verfassen - ich moechte Euch wirklich gut gerecht werden und das schaffe ich nur, wenn ich mit Euch zusammenarbeiten kann, nachfragen kann etc. Sonst steht in der DIss womoeglich was drinnen, wo Ihr dann sagt, noe, also so haben wir das nicht gemeint, eigentlich ganz anders - das sollte nicht passieren. Ich werde auch wenn ich dann schreibe immer wieder drafts an Euch schicken mit der Bitte um Kommentar - soll wiederum nicht Mehrarbeit darstellen, sondern eher der Authentizitaet! Ausserdem ist das mehrmalige Aufeinanderabstimmen notwendige Routine in qualitativen Forschungsarbeiten - hier geht´s ja Gott sei Dank um die Menschen dahinter und nicht um blanke Zahlen- und Statistikspiele....

Also dann sei gegruesst
Lily

Delivered-To: neumayr@ses.curtin.edu.au
From: ▓▓▓▓▓▓▓▓▓▓▓▓▓▓▓ Irene
To: "Elisabeth Neumayr" <neumayr@ses.curtin.edu.au>
Subject: Dilemma3
Date: Fri, 28 Jan 2000 17:42:32 +0100
MIME-Version: 1.0
X-Priority: 3
X-MSMail-Priority: Normal
X-MimeOLE: Produced By Microsoft MimeOLE V4.72.2106.4

Theresia

Hallo, die Teletechnik stürzt mich doch jedesmal in neue Aufgaben. Wie bringe ich Deine Infos an
▓▓▓▓▓ , ausdrucken ist unmöglich, auf disc übertragen ging auch nicht , d.h. ich benötige wieder
fachliche Computerhilfe. ---geschafft: Job. wird dir sicherlich antworten und wie sie mir sagte, eigne
sich ihre 3. ph Kl für ein solches Projekt. du wirst ja sehen. ich vermute, sie hatte nur schrecklich
Angst vor der Auswertung von Fragebögen.
Wir sind nämlich noch in einem anderen Projekt stark involviert: Peer to peers für primäre
Drogenprophylaxe.(läuft über die gesamte Schule verteilt , macht einen enormen organisatrorischen
Aufwand, u. soll gerade in den nächsten Wochen neu konzipiert werden.
    1.. Schülerwahl: habe mich entschlossen meine Klasse zu informieren daß wir an einem solchen
mehrjährigen Projekt teilnehmen. lasse sie aber nicht wählen.---S, die nicht auf Schikurs sind,
bearbeiten bereits für ein Referat Ebola , Pest, Cholerea u.a.
    2.. Wie stehts mit deiner Lust zu einer Probefassung des Regenwaldthemas? wobei mir das Dil.
nat.Medizin / synthetischer Med. gefällt usw.
    3.. Im Stoff der 5.Kl bin ich gerade bei Mitose/Meiose und ihre Bedeutung und gehe dann auf das Them
: vom Einzeller zum Vielzeller -- sowie Zelldifferenzierung, Gewebe, Organe ein .Zur Info. :meine
Multikulti sind ungeheuer heterogen , 8 Mädchen, 24 Knaben, aber sehr herzlich, hilfsbereit , sozial
und schlampig., werden aber trotz Leistungsschwächen von allen KollegInnen sehr geschätzt. sicherlich
trennt sich langsam die Spreu vom Weizen, nicht so sehr, die Nicht-austrianer, als die austrians.
    4.. Scheue für dich keine Mehrarbeit, hoffe nur daß die Koll. alle dabei bleiben. Bussi ▓▓▓ Irene

Delivered-To: neumayr@ses.curtin.edu.au
From: ▓▓▓▓▓▓▓▓▓▓▓▓▓▓▓ Irene
To: "Elisabeth Neumayr" <neumayr@ses.curtin.edu.au>
Subject: Dilemma 4
Date: Wed, 2 Feb 2000 22:05:07 +0100
MIME-Version: 1.0
X-Priority: 3
X-MSMail-Priority: Normal
X-MimeOLE: Produced By Microsoft MimeOLE V4.72.2106.4

    Endlich, die Zeit rast dahin; Mo, ganztägig SAS- Projekt bei der Drogenstelle und am LSR, geht natürlich um
Fortsetzung der Projekte, und rechtlicher Absicherung, sowie Finanzierung: nervende Diskusionen ; täglich sitze ich bei
ien Korrekturen der FBAs (ca 5 Stunden täglich) ; Katze,ein Haustier! (Jenny)/ Dolly, was nun? (Daniela)/Traumatische
/erletzungen aus der Sicht eines Ersthelfers,(Gerald), leider arbeiten die Damen grauenhaft, was den Ausdruck und die
vissenschaftliche Auseinandersetzung mit dem Thema betrifft. Gerald dafür präsentiert mir nur lat. Volabeln ; alles sehr
nühsam . Gleichzeitig vertrete ich Tanja ständig, -- sie auf Kariereseminaren.- Direktorenstelle wird bald fällig, momentan
st sie nur professorisch - sieht nicht sehr gut aus. / habe aber meinen Regelunterricht trotzdem zu halten und unsere/meine
00 Blumen bedürfen intensiverer Pflege nach der Rippenpause und meinem halbamputierten Daumen (zerbrochenes
:eagenzglas im Waschbecken .....Schlachthofimpressionen!!!) Danke für deine techn, Nachhilfe, bin nur verwundert, daß
ein letzter Brief doppelt kam, wobei die 2. Hälfte mit eigenartigen Hiroglyphen ergänzt war. Raudi ist wiedereinmal sehr
rank, muß erst seine e-mail erfragen, damit ich ihn an Dich erinnere. Für heute keine Lust zum Überarbeiten deines
:riefes, wird schon wieder werden.! Gibts bei euch eigentlich auch Kelgelschnecken (CONIDAE) mein Paulchen
Ehemann sammelt nämich begeistert diese edlen Schönheiten der Meere.- Bis bald ▓▓▓ Irene

To: "Erich Fink" <e.fink@utanet.at>
From: neumayr@ses.curtin.edu.au (Elisabeth Neumayr)
Subject: Re: Dilemma3

>Hallo ▓▓▓▓,

die Teletechnik stürzt mich doch jedesmal in neue Aufgaben. Wie bringe ich Deine Infos an Johanna
,ausdrucken ist unmöglich
solange Dein Drucker funktioniert mit richtigem Durckertreiber sollte das problemlos gehen - ich drucke
ja auch die ganze Korrespondenz mit Euch aus!

, auf disc übertragen ging auch nicht , d.h. ich benötige wieder fachliche Computerhilfe. ---geschafft;
funktioniert unter "speichern als".... -erscheint dann als normales Word-file!

Joh. wird dir sicherlich antworten und wie sie mir sagte, eignet sich ihre 3. ph Kl für ein solches
Projekt. du wirst ja sehen. ich vermute, sie hatte nur schrecklich Angst vor der Auswertung von
Fragebögen.
Hat sie schon gemacht, obwohl sie von ihren Aengsten bezueglich Frageboegen nichts gesagt hat! Aber
selbst wenn ich Frageboegen mache, was ja noch nicht so ganz ausdiskutiert ist, sollten diese fuer Euch
keine Arbeit machen.

Welches Programm verwendest Du fuer Dein Email? Eine Moeglichkeit Mail an ▓▓▓▓ *Theresia* weiterzuschicken ist
"forward to" steht unter Nachricht (weiss nicht wie das jetzt auf Deutsch heisst!) aber Du markierst
mein Mail und gibst dann einfach Johannas Adresse als Empfaenger ein - dann wandert mein Mail auch an
Johanna weiter! Sollte problemlos funktionieren

>Wir sind nämlich noch in einem anderen Projekt stark involviert: Peer to peers für primäre
Drogenprophylaxe.(läuft über die gesamte Schule verteilt , macht einen enormen organisatrorischen
Aufwand, u. soll gerade in den nächsten Wochen neu konzipiert werden.

Klingt aber interessant!
> 1.. Schülerwahl: habe mich entschlossen meine Klasse zu informieren daß wir an einem solchen
mehrjärigen Projekt teilnehmen.
Das ist unbedingt notwendig! Kurz bevor ich anrausche, werde ich Euch Einverstaenndiserklaerungen
schicken, die die Kids sowie deren ELtern unterschreiben sollen - wieder mal eine Frage der Ethik.
Problem ist dabei natuerlich, was macht man wenn einer sagt er will nicht mitmachen?

lasse sie aber nicht wählen.---S, die nicht auf Schikurs sind, bearbeiten bereits für ein Referat
Ebola , Pest, Cholerea u.a.
> 2.. Wie stehts mit deiner Lust zu einer Probefassung des Regenwaldthemas? wobei mir das Dil.
nat.Medizin / synthetischer Med. gefällt usw.

Steht gut!
> 3.. Im Stoff der 5.Kl bin ich gerade bei Mitose/Meiose und ihre Bedeutung und gehe dann auf das
Thema : vom Einzeller zum Vielzeller -- sowie Zelldifferenzierung, Gewebe, Organe ein .
Waere Transplantation eine Moeglichkeit?

Zur Info. :meine Multikulti sind ungeheuer heterogen , 8 Mädchen, 24 Knaben, aber sehr herzlich,
hilfsbereit , sozial und schlampig., werden aber trotz Leistungsschwächen von allen KollegInnen sehr
geschätzt. sicherlich trennt sich langsam die Spreu vom Weizen, nicht so sehr, die Nicht-austrianer,
als die austrians.
Klingt gut!
> 4.. Scheue für dich keine Mehrarbeit, hoffe nur daß die Koll. alle dabei bleiben.
Sabine klingt sehr optimistisch und Johanna hat sich glaub´ich auch gerade einen Ruck gegeben - well
done!

. Bussi ▓▓▓ Irene

>>Delivered-To: neumayr@ses.curtin.edu.au
>>From: ███████████████████
>>To: "Elisabeth Neumayr" <neumayr@ses.curtin.edu.au>
>>Subject: Dilemma 5
>>Date: Thu, 10 Feb 2000 17:39:10 +0100
>>MIME-Version: 1.0
>>X-Priority: 3
>>X-MSMail-Priority: Normal
>>X-MimeOLE: Produced By Microsoft MimeOLE V4.72.2106.4
>>

>>Hi Lily! Was ist loss mit Dir ? Bin in Sorge, bist Du krank, weil ich
>>keine mails mehr von dir erhalten habe oder stimmt bei unserer Anlage
>>wieder etwas nicht. !! In der Schule ist der Teufel los, alle rennen nur
>>mehr mit rot umrandeten Augen herum, jeder ist korrekturgeplagt, und die
>>vielen Notenbesprechungen in den Teams nehmen auch unendlich viel Zeit in
>>Anspruch. Außerdem sind wir alle verpflichtet die täglichen
>>Spätnachrichten zu hören aufgrund der politischen Entwickung in Österreich
>>(FPÖ/ÖVP-Packt) und die Weltreaktionen darauf.. ..Mein Paulchen liegt mit
>>der Grippe und Vater mit einer Mageninfektion, und ich lebe noch!!!
>>wielange?
>>
>>Meine Bakterien/Virenreferate laufen jetzt an. Warte auf weitere
>>Instruktionen . Raudi ist seit 2 Tagen wieder an der Schule . Hastdu
>>Dilemma 4 erhalten? Bussi ███ *Irene*

Delivered-To: neumayr@ses.curtin.edu.au
From: ███████████████ *Irene*
To: "Elisabeth Neumayr" <neumayr@ses.curtin.edu.au>
Subject: Re ███████ *Theresia / Walter*
Date: Thu, 2 Mar 2000 15:33:53 +0100
MIME-Version: 1.0
X-Priority: 3
X-MSMail-Priority: Normal
X-MimeOLE: Produced By Microsoft MimeOLE V4.72.2106.4

Meine Liebe, bin trotz gerade genossener Ferien in Tirol ausgepowert, Morgen müsssen die 3 FBAs druck und pressfrisch in der Direktion abgegeben werden. Was tut man nicht alles, wenn Schüler nicht fertig werden?: man schreit ihnen Vorworte, Einleitungen und Nachworte, zusätzlich zur intensiven Lektorenarbeit. meine Augen tränen , mein Sitzfleisch ist überstrapaziert. So, zu deinem ausführlichen Brief. :

• attachements kann ich empfangen und ausdrucken
• *Walter*
• ███ wurde von mir ordentlich bearbeitet, hat schlechtes Gewissen, bekommt zur Einstimmung von mir deinen letz Brief und wird sich sicherlich melden, will eigentlich auch mitmachen, bei ihm mußt du nur immer um Drücker bleiben.
• *Theresia*
• ███: verausgabt sich bei der Organisation von SL- Seminaren steiermarkweit, hat 4. Kl als KV,BOBI- TAGE, und individuelle Betreuung der "werdenden Aussteiger" = HS-Abgänger. Sie macht sicher mit, bekommt soeben ein Internetanschluß zuhause, da der der Schule absulut unbrauchbar ist. (sie schafft ihn für DICH an)
•
• Schicke mir deine attachements, wenns geht,
•

Wie du siehst, besteht berechtigte Hoffung auf gute Zusammenarbeit. Bye,bye, bin schon wieder unterwegs zur ALKO u NAWI- Sitzung. Bussi ███ *Irene*

Von: Elisabeth Neumayr <neumayr@pop.ses.curtin.edu.au>
An: ~~████████████~~ Irene
Datum: Dienstag, 11. April 2000 09:50
Betreff: Re: Re ~~████████~~ Theresia / Walter

>Hi Lilly
>Arbeit frißt meine Zeit. Ständig in der Schule , vertrete wieder
Tanjá -Schülerinnenausschluß, Maturantenbeschwerden, Alkos ua.
>e-mail funktioniert gut, kann nur deine attachements noch nicht öffnen,
werde morgen abend Raudi fragen, nicht vorher, weil er bei Physikolympiade
ist.
>bin schon neugierig auf deine Dilemmas
Meine Lieblinge sind extrem leistungsschwach,--- 100 Frühwarnungen für 31
Schüler -toll!! hoffe, daß die Eltern zustimmen werden.
>melde mich sobald ich die Informationen gelesen habe
Werde Infobrief noch rechtzeitig austeilen. Einsammeln tue ich sie erst nach
Ostern . schicke dir die Teilnahmebestätigungen nicht, da du ja kommst. >
Videokamera ist selbstverständlich im Haus, muß sienur rechtzeitig
reservieren.
Was tust du in Amerika?Solltest du ein Quatrier benötigen, mußt du mir das
nur melden, bist herzlich willkommen. >Viele Bussis ~~████~~ Irene >

       To: ~~████████████████~~ Irene
     From: neumayr@ses.curtin.edu.au (Elisabeth Neumayr)
     Subject: Re: Dil 7

Hi Ingrid!
>>Arbeit frißt meine Zeit. Ständig in der Schule , vertrete wieder
>Tanjá -Schülerinnenausschluß, Maturantenbeschwerden, Alkos ua.
>>e-mail funktioniert gut, kann nur deine attachements noch nicht öffnen,
>werde morgen abend Raudi fragen, nicht vorher, weil er bei Physikolympiade
>ist.

ich hab mir schon gedacht dass du wiedermal voll im Stress bist.....

Um meine Attachments zu oeffnen:
1) mach Word auf
2) gehe auf open file
3) oeffna deinen attachment-folder (verwendest du Eudora als Emailprogram? Dann solltest du in Deinem
Programfolder einen Attachmentfolder haben, in welchem sich die files befinden sollten! ANsonsten such
die Files mit dem "Suche File" Befehl, dann weisst du auch wo sie drinnen sind - auf jeden Fall zuerst
Word aufmachen und dann das Attachment! Eigentlich ganz einfach!

>>bin schon neugierig auf deine Dilemmas
ich hab sie schon mehere Leute lesen lassen, den dazugehoerigen Senf habe ich eingearbeitet und hoffe
dass sie nun in verwendbarem Zustand sind...

>Meine Lieblinge sind extrem leistungsschwach,--- 100 Frühwarnungen für 31
>Schüler -toll!!
Na toll!
 hoffe, daß die Eltern zustimmen werden.
Ja das hoffe ich auch, aber da gibt es keinen Weg drumrum - ohne Erlaubnis keine Forschung -
Ethikvorschriften! Ist aber auch OK so!

>>melde mich sobald ich die Informationen gelesen habe
>Werde Infobrief noch rechtzeitig austeilen. Einsammeln tue ich sie erst nach
>Ostern .

Kriegst du die auch wieder zurueck?
 schicke dir die Teilnahmebestätigungen nicht, da du ja kommst. >
Ja klar!
>Videokamera ist selbstverständlich im Haus, muß sienur rechtzeitig
>reservieren.
Ja klar!
>Was tust du in Amerika?
Fahre auf zwei Konferenzen nach New Orleans, dann ein paar Tage nach New York und dann zu Euch!
Solltest du ein Quatrier benötigen, mußt du mir das
>nur melden, bist herzlich willkommen.

Vielen Dank fuer dein Angebot - bin diebezueglich in Lieboch versorgt - Gott sei Dank!

Hi Lily
Problem beim Attachementöffnen liegt in deinen verwendeten ! .,Kommas, oder
ähnlichem - einige Passagen schon gelesen, einiges noch in Hiroglyphenform.
bemühe mich weiter.
Möchtest du einen Elternabend veranstalten?, kann ihn organisieren.
Werde Deine Anweisungen befolgen.und mein Glück versuchen ., Habe
Zeitprobleme mit deiner Ankunft, sollt eigentlich mit einer 4.Kl auf eine
Projektwoche auf die Alm vom 8.- 12.5. / so müssen wir diese Veranstaltung
abblasen. sind aber gar nicht unglücklich darüber.
Werde dir gleich melden, wenn ich alles geöffnet habe.
Gruss und Kuss

▮▮▮ Irene

Meine Liebe, Vielleicht solltest Du mir die attachements tatsächlich nochmals schicken. Mit großem
Stolz berichte ich Dir, daß es mit gelungenist, den Elternbrief auszudrucken. Natürlich wäre ich
neugierig, was auf den restlichen 35 Seiten deiner Elternbriefinfo drauf und drinnen steht. Bis jetzt
mit all deinen lieben Anweisungen und der Hilfeleistung unserer "chefs" noch nicht mehr gelungen.
Spiele mich witer. Habe ja die Osterferien Zeit, außerdem kommt mein persönlicher Computerberater aus
Innsbruck (Neffe) zu den Osterfeiertagen. Irgendwie werden wir es schon schaffen.
Bezüglich Elternabend erhebt sich die Frage ob wir alle teilnehmenden Klassen zusammenfassen oder jede
einzeln. Für meine Klasse ,im spezeillen, muß ich ohnedies einen KA veranstalten, so könnte man den je
kombinieren. - mir erschiene Mittwoch oder Donnerstag abend günstig.
Mit meiner Absage der Almprojektwoche habe ich mehr Freunde als Feinde gewonnen, da diese Veranstaltung
von allen als sehr außer den Vereinbarungen den Hauses laufende Aktion interprediert wird, sodaß damit
eine eher positive Regelung getroffen wurde.
Morgen bin ich für 3 Tage in Grado beim Relaxen. Bussi ▮▮▮ Irene

Hallo Du,

bevor Du nach Grado abzischt - vielleicht kannst du mir sagen, welche Word - Version Du hast und ob
einen PC oder einen Mac benuetzt!

Tschuessi einstweilen Lily

Dann schick ich alles nochmal wenn ich weiss was du hast!

X-WM-Posted-At: topmail01; Mon, 31 May 99 15:30:11 +0100
Date: Mon, 31 May 1999 15:30:11 +0100

Irene

To: neumayr@ses.curtin.edu.au
X-EXP32-SerialNo: 00002711
Subject: Briefantwort.
Mime-Version: 1.0

Endlich, liebe Lilli! habe neue e-mail adress , leider hat die Schile große
server-problems, hoffe, daß nun alle Eionschränkungen beseitigt sind. Freue
mich über Deine Lebenszeichen. Bin begeistert über Dein neues Diss Thema.
Werde versuchen Dich zu unterstützen wie es in meiner Macht steht. Sind die
year 10`s unseren Erstklasslern im GYM entsprechend? Ich bin besonders
interssiert an der Frauenproblematik, bin neugierig was Du heraus finden
wirst. Selbstverständlich kann ich im nächsten Herbst Schüler für eine
Untersuchung auftreiben. Wieviele benötigst Du?. Werde voraussichtlich 2 erste
Klassen haben und eine 5. Klasse als KV. Auch werde ich mich auf die Such
nach Klusiunterlagen begeben und Dir hoffentlich welche schicken. Es wäre für
>mich nur wichtig zu wissen ob Du eher die organisatorischen Unterlagen, wie
z.B. Einführung von Teamteaching, Klassenschülerzahlen, Entwicklungsstrukturen
,Aufnahmebedingungen, oder eher päd, didaktische Unterlagen haben willst, wie
sie von Elgrid Messner erstellt worden sind. Nun hat Elgrid ja ein
Adoptivsöhnchen und ist in Karenz, wird aber von Christa Bauer
vertreten . Mit Christa verstehe ich mich sehr gut, sodaß ich sicherlich auch
neuere Ergebnisse unserer Arbeit auftreiben kann. Wie Du sicherlich weißt hat
dasFQS Qualitätssicherungsprojekt bei uns keine wesenlichen Ergebnisse
gebracht und wurde von uns Lehreren als unbrauchbar abgelehnt. Wohl aber
evaluieren wir weiter in der OST (Oberstufe) in den einzelnen Zweigen: NAWI,
KRA, IK(Sprache): ff: Bussi ▇ *Irene*

  Zu Deiner letzten Frage: LSI ist momentan Horst Lattinger

X-WM-Posted-At: topmail01; Mon, 31 May 99 15:47:36 +0100
Date: Mon, 31 May 1999 15:47:36 +0100
Sender: ▇▇▇ *Irene*
From: ▇▇▇
To: neumayr@ses.curtin.edu.au
X-EXP32-SerialNo: 00002711
Subject: Briefantwort
Mime-Version: 1.0

Hallo Lilli!
 Habe soeben ca 900 word gemailt, aber dieses Ungeheuer mag mich nicht. Unsere
server sind alle in Eimer! Tut mit leid, daß du erst heute von mir Nachricht
bekommst. 2.Brief fällt aus Zeitgründen kürzer aus. Schüler im Herbst
sicherlich auftreibbar. Habe 2 erste Klassen, und eine 5.Kl als Kv. Neuer LSI
= Host Lattinger werde Titel und Anschrift noch genau herausfinden.
Klusiunterlagen kann ich besorgen, wäre aber günstig genauers zu wissen-- eher
Organisatorisches, oder eher Pädagogisch - didaktisches? neue Koordinatorin
ist Christa Bauer
Beachte meien neue e-mail adress! Hoffe, daß diese nund funktioniert. bussi
▇▇▇ *Irene*

Dieses Mail wurde mit A-TOPMAIL versendet.
http://www.a-topmail.at

Delivered-To: neumayr@es.curtin.edu.au
From: ~~███████████████~~ *Irene*
To: "Elisabeth Neumayr" <neumayr@es.curtin.edu.au>
Subject: daheim
Date: Sun, 25 Jun 2000 21:17:09 +0200
MIME-Version: 1.0
X-Priority: 3
X-MSMail-Priority: Normal
X-MimeOLE: Produced By Microsoft MimeOLE V4.72.2106.4

Meine Liebe, wie oft denke ich an dich, leider bin ich nicht einmal dazugekommen meine e-mails
durchzusehen, seit deine Abreise war einiges los, organisatorisch und bürokratischer Mist., Die Matura
habe ich gut überstanden, dank der sogenannten Pfingstferien, die ich zum Arbeiten nützte;
Familienfest-20Leute , mit Schwesterchens Hilfe ein voller Erfolg, bei traumhaftem Wetter, eine
liebliche Nacht verbracht, die Übermüdung, die in mir steckt ist unbeschreiblich, dann Bau und
Gartenarbeit in Aflenz auf der Alm und im Tal- schriftliches erledigte ich dann des Nachts, wenn Vater
erschöpft schlief, dann in Graz noch die Einkocharbeiten : Erdbeeren, Kirschen, Himbeeren, und die
Rolls zur Pflege, außerdem meine alte Tante mit Lungenentzündung, und das alles bei 33-35°C, na ja, am
19, 20 wieder Matura von 7.30 - 21 Uhr ,und die übrigen schulischen Arbeiten. Seit 23 .vertrete ich
wieder ~~████~~ , weil sie in Bad Aussee bei der Matura ist, die 200 Blumentöpfe müssen für den Sommer
versorgt und rausgestellt werden, Mein Vater inzwischen auf Urlaub, Garten und Blumenpflege
selbstverständlich. - Meine "Sonderboys "bedürfen spezieller Diplomatie um sie in die nächste Klasse zu
bekommen, hoffe daß mir einige Manipulationen meiner KollegInnen gelingen.
Heute endlich Regen bei 12°C. *Sandra*
-----Zu Deinen Problemen: Werde ~~████~~ benachrichtigen aber erst im Juli da sie auf Nawiwochen sind
(Faak). Habe noch einige Unterlagen von meinen S bekommen, soll ich sie kopieren und schicken?.

      To: ~~█████████████████████~~ *Irene*
      From: neumayr@es.curtin.edu.au (Elisabeth Neumayr)
      Subject: Re: daheim

>Meine Liebe, wie oft denke ich an dich,.......
Thanks so much, good to hear!

> am 19, 20 wieder Matura von 7.30 - 21 Uhr ,und die übrigen schulischen Arbeiten. Seit 23 .vertrete
ich wieder Tanja , weil sie in Bad Aussee bei der Matura ist, die 200 Blumentöpfe müssen für den Sommer
versorgt und rausgestellt werden,.......
Hab´ ich´s mir doch gedacht!

> Meine "Sonderboys "bedürfen spezieller Diplomatie um sie in die nächste Klasse zu bekommen, hoffe daß
mir einige Manipulationen meiner KollegInnen gelingen.

Naja du hast ja auch nichts anderes zu tun....

>-----Zu Deinen Problemen: Werde Sabine benachrichtigen aber erst im Juli da sie auf Nawiwochen sind
(Faak).
Ist schon OK, nur vergessen sollte sie halt nicht, weil mir sonst die ganze demografische Beschreibung
ihrer Klasse fehlt! Ach ja, kannst du sie auch noch fragen, ob sie dazugekommen ist, Tagebuch zu
schreiben - vielleicht kann sie mir ja darueber berichten, wenn sie ihre Email im Griff hat!

Von wegen Tagebuch - von dir habe ich die zwei Seiten auch nicht mitgenommen - oder wolltest du sie mir
gar nicht geben? Weiss nicht mehr.....!

Next question - was ich noch vergessen hab´- ihr habt doch sicher irgendwo in der Schule eine Ausgabe
des ueberarbeiteten Lehrplans (99!) rumliegen - da muesste irgendwo eine Abteilung mit dem Grundlagen
drinnensein und darin muesste sich wiederum ein Abschnitt mit dem Thema Werteerziehung, Moralerziehung
etc befinden! Vielleicht findest du ja mal eine Mussestunde - haha! - und kannst mir die entsprechenden
Seiten kopieren - ich wollte das noch machen vor meiner Abreise, aber du weisst ja wie´s dann immer
staubt hinter mir!

Habe noch einige Unterlagen von meinen S bekommen, soll ich sie kopieren und schicken?.

Theresia

Delivered-To: neumayr@pop.ses.curtin.edu.au
Date: Fri, 28 Jan 2000 14:24:32 +0100 (MET)
From: ▓▓▓▓▓▓▓▓▓▓▓▓▓▓▓
To: neumayr@ses.curtin.edu.au
MIME-Version: 1.0
Subject: Forschungsvorhaben
X-Authenticated-Sender: #0002948599@gmx.net
X-Authenticated-IP: [193.170.222.18]
X-Flags: 0001

Liebe Lily!
Ich habe die Post gelesen, die Du an Ingrid geschickt hast. Du hast meine
Bedenken zerstreut. Ich bin gerne bereit mitzuarbeiten und werde meine
Einverständniserklärung ▓▓▓▓ zwecks gemeinsamer Post geben.
Genauere Informationen hätte ich noch gerne bezüglich des Tagebuches.
                                Mit lieben Grüßen   ▓▓▓▓▓ *Theresia*
Meine e-Mail-Adresse:▓▓▓▓▓▓▓▓▓▓

                    Irene

        To: ▓▓▓▓▓▓▓▓▓▓▓▓▓▓▓▓▓▓
      From: neumayr@ses.curtin.edu.au (Elisabeth Neumayr)
      Subject: Re: Forschungsvorhaben

Hallo ▓▓▓▓▓ *Theresia*

Gut von Dir zu hoeren!
Ich hab mir schon gedacht, dass Du womoeglich keinen Bock hast mit mir zusammenzuarbeiten, na Gott sei
Dank! Ich weiss dass ich mit ▓▓▓▓, ▓▓▓▓▓ und Dir (eventuell mit ▓▓▓▓▓▓) sicher Lehrer gewonnen
habe, die sich durch Ihren hohen persoenlichen Einsatz und vor allem dadurch auszeichnen, dass sie sich
was dabei denken, was sie machen!

>Ich habe die Post gelesen, die Du an ▓▓▓▓▓ geschickt hast. Du hast meine
>Bedenken zerstreut.
Mir ist klar dass ich mit meinem Forschungsvorhaben fuer Euch einen Mehraufwand inszeniere, aber bitte
glaube mir, dass ich versuchen werde diesen so klein als moeglich zu halten!

Ich bin gerne bereit mitzuarbeiten und werde meine
>Einverständniserklärung Ingrid zwecks gemeinsamer Post geben.

Cool!
>Genauere Informationen hätte ich noch gerne bezüglich des Tagebuches.

Nun denn, das Tagebuch ist eine ganz spezielle Sache: es soll vor allem Dir dazu dienen, Deine Gedanken
bezueglich des Projekts - Sorgen, Aengste und sonstige Hindernisse, natuerlich aber auch Deine
persoenliche und berufliche Weiterentwicklung (im Idealfall sollte ja jeder von uns was dazugelernt
haben am Schluss!) festzuhalten. Es hilft Dir Klarheit zu schaffen, ueber Dein eigenens Engagement,
aber auch ueber die positiven sowie negativen Aspekte des Projektverlaufs: Da ich Euch ja ab und an mal
interviewen werde, waere es natuerlich nuetzlich das Tagebuch dann mitzunehmen. Du kannst dann das, was
Du mit mir teilen moechtest, erzaehlen (sozusagen als Gedaechtnisstuetze). Grundsaetzlich ist das
Tagebuch aber eine private Sache - wenn Du nichts mit mir teilen moechtest, ist es auch Ok. Es
verbleibt auch nach Projektende bei Dir!

Klar genug, oder brauchst DU noch mehr Info?
Du waisst ja ich bin nur ein Email weg!

Viele Gruesse
Lily

Delivered-To: neumayr@ses.curtin.edu.au
From: ~~[redacted]~~ *Sandra*
To: "Neumayr Elisabeth" <neumayr@ses.curtin.edu.au>
Subject: Diss
Date: Tue, 4 Jan 2000 11:56:49 +0100
MIME-Version: 1.0
X-Priority: 3
X-MSMail-Priority: Normal
X-MimeOLE: Produced By Microsoft MimeOLE V5.00.2615.200

Liebe Lily!

Danke für die ausführliche Information zu deinem Forschungsvorhaben! Das klingt sehr spannend und ich freue mich schon drauf! Hab von Herbert Schwetz schon das Buch mit den Dilemmageschichten für's Rote Kreuz bekommen und auch den Film gesehen (ich arbeite mit ihm bzgl. Mathematik zusammen). Also: lustig, wie alles zusammenhängt!

Nun zu den Infos, die du brauchst:

Klasse:

Ich möchte das Projekt in der 6A-Klasse (Navi-Zweig) durchführen, in der ich Klassenvorständin bin. Ich habe dort Mathe, Physik und Physik-Labor.

Meine Motivation:

Wie du ja weißt, gibt es bei uns in der Oberstufe kein Soziales Lernen als eigenes Fach, so wie das in der Unterstufe der Fall ist. Das ist für mich ziemlich unbefriedigend, vor allem mit meinen Fächern finde ich wenig Gelegenheit, das im Unterricht zu integrieren.

Lehrstoff im Mai:

Im Prinzip wäre es sowohl in Physik, als auch in Mathe möglich, das Projekt durchzuführen. Nach genauer Überlegung scheint mir jedoch vom Inhalt her Mathe als geeigneter. In Physik hab ich noch Astronomie, Optik und Akustik am Programm, wobei die Reihenfolge egal ist.

Ich schlage dir also mal Mathe vor: da steht das Thema Wachstumsprozesse am Programm (mathematisch vor allem lineares und exponentielles Wachstum, Modellbildung). Dieses Thema möchte ich anhand einiger Artikel aus dem Club of Rome - Bericht "Grenzen des Wachstums" aufbereiten. Da sind also sicher geeignete Themen drin wie: Ressourcenknappheit, Umweltverschmutzung, Konsumverhalten, Nord-Süd-Konflikt,...

Falls du noch weitere Infos brauchst oder dir doch eines der Physik-Themen mehr liegt, laß es mich wissen!

Nun wünsche ich dir noch alles Liebe!

Liebe Grüße ~~[redacted]~~ *Sandra*

Delivered-To: neumayr@ses.curtin.edu.au
From: ~~[redacted]~~ *Sandra*
To: "Neumayr Elisabeth" <neumayr@ses.curtin.edu.au>
Subject: Dilemma
Date: Sun, 9 Jan 2000 10:50:27 +0100
MIME-Version: 1.0
X-Priority: 3
X-MSMail-Priority: Normal
X-MimeOLE: Produced By Microsoft MimeOLE V5.00.2615.200

Liebe Lily! Danke für dein mail! Das ist schon ein spannendes Kommunikationsmittel - ich staune immer wieder. Wüßte ich sonst, daß es in Australien so heiß ist, daß schon das Wasser rationiert werden muß? Wahrscheinlich nicht! Ja, du sagst es, Wasserknappheit ist für uns hier immer noch unvorstellbar! Du fragst, ob Herbert ALLES über die Sache mit den Dilemmageschichten erzählt hat. Das weiß ich natürlich nicht. Aber ich hab schon einiges mitgekriegt, daß das mit der Bezahlung und der Anerkennung der AutorInnen nicht so geklappt hat. Nun zu "unserem" Projekt: Ich hab da erstmal eine grundsätzliche Frage: Wäre es für dich denkbar, daß die Arbeit in der 6A z.B. mit einer Dilemmageschichte in Mathe beginnt, dann mal eine in Physik usw. - jenachdem wo's besser paßt. Ich habe bei dir rausgehört, daß du davon ausgehst, daß das in EINEM Fach passieren soll. Wenn das so ist, müssen wir uns natürlich überlegen, ob uns in Mathe genügend Anknüpfungspunkte einfallen. In Physik scheinen die Anknüpfungspunkte offensichtlicher. Außerdem hab ich da nicht soeinen Streß bezüglich Matura. Mir wäre es am angenehmsten, wenn das Projekt in beiden Fächern abwechselnd laufen könnte. Schreib mir bitte, wie du das siehst! Ich hab wegen MAthe ein bißchen recherchiert und da ist mir was Spannendes untergekommen: es gibt für australische Schulen eine Reihe von Heften von Mary Barnes, in denen sie für das Thema "Investigating Change" ein "gender-inclusive" Konzept verfolgt. Ich hab darüber in einer Didaktik-Zeitschrift einen Artikel gelesen und festgestellt, daß da viele Ideen für uns drinsein könnten. Unabhängig davon, ob wir nun Mathe nehmen bitte ich dich, mir diese Hefte zu besorgen (wenn's dir möglich ist)! Hier das genaue Zitat: Banes, M.: Investigating Change: An Introduction to calculus for australian schools.-Zehn SchülerInnenhefte (Units), Melbourne 1991 Nun hast du noch gefragt, welche Wünsche wir an dich haben bzgl. Einführung. Ich hab mit den anderen noch nicht Rücksprache gehalten, aber ich denke, daß sicher niemand mit den Grundidden des Konstruktivismus vertraut ist. Das ist sicher eine Voraussetzung, um den Sinn dieses Projekts zu verstehen. Hast du noch mitgekriegt, daß Herbert ein Video machen hat lassen? Ich finde das sehr gut und denke, es könnte bei der Einführung durch dich auch hilfreich sein. Toll wäre auch, wenn du mit uns eine Dilemmageschichte durcharbeiten könntest und uns so auch die Methoden näherbringst. Es ist immer leichter, was im Unterricht umzusetzen, das man "am eigenen Leib" erfahren hat. Wie gesagt: das sind jetzt nur meine Gedanken dazu - ich hab noch nicht mit ~~[redacted]~~ gesprochen. Liebe Grüße und Bussi von ~~[redacted]~~!

APPENDIX 2B: MEMBERCHECKING SANDRA'S CLASS

Hallo !

Ich habe eure Interviews ueber das Ethikprojekt 2000 interpretiert, und moechte dich aus Gruenden der Fairness bitten, zu checken, ob ich dich richtig interpretiert habe. Ausserdem moechte dich einige Fragen fragen.

Mir (Elke) hat der Lehransatz gut gefallen vor allem weil's um Menschen geht. Was ich nicht so gemocht habe war die Gruppenarbeit, da ich grundsaetzlich lieber alleine arbeite.

Waehrend der Gruppenarbeit bin ich mit ██ in Konflikt geraten, weil er eine voellig andere Meinung hatte als ich, die ich schwer zu akzeptieren fand. Ich habe mich geweigert, seine Meinung auf unser Poster zu schreiben, weil ich mich geaergert hab'. Ich habe versucht meinen Standpunkt klarzulegen und versucht ihn zu ueberzeugen davon, dass sein Standpunkt nicht in Ordnung ist, meiner Meinung nach. Er hat das dann auch eingesehen und seine Meinung geaendert, was mich persoenlich beruehrt hat....

- Wie denkst du heute ueber das Ethikprojekt 2000?

- Wie stehst du heute zu deinem Konflikt mit ██ ueber die Verdendung von Todeskandidaten fuer Menschenversuche?

Vielen Dank fuer deine Zeit und ich waere sehr dankbar, wenn du mir meine Fragen beantworten koenntest, da ich dich so fair als moeglich representieren moechte. Du kannst mir die Antwort entweder durch Frau Roll, die diese Rueckfrageboegen sammelt, oder per Email schicken:
Meine Emailadresse lautet:
E.Settelmaier@cc.curtin.edu.au

Hallo !

Ich habe eure Interviews ueber das Ethikprojekt 2000 interpretiert, und moechte dich aus Gruenden der Fairness bitten, zu checken, ob ich dich richtig interpretiert habe. Ausserdem moechte dich einige Fragen fragen.

In deinem Interview habe ich den Eindruck bekommen, dass du mal grundsaetzlich in Opposition warst und zumindest am Anfang den Eindruck erwecken wolltest, dass fuer dich nichts Positives dabei war (Dein Kommentar: Es war Zeitverschwendung, ich haette lieber Mathematik- und Physikstunden gehabt).
1. Habe ich dich richtig interpretiert dass du am Anfang sehr ablehnend warst?
2. Wenn ja, warum warst du so in Opposition?

Du sagst spaeter im Interview, dass es fuer dich vor allem schwierig war, weil du in zusammengestellten Gruppen nicht arbeiten wolltest. In Gruppen, wo du mit Leuten zusmamenwarst, die du "respektierst und magst", hast du es anscheinend gut gefunden, deine Meinung mit den anderen zu vergleichen.
1. Stimmt das?
2. Stimmt meine Interpretation, dass fuer dich die Gruppenzusammenstellung ein gewaltiger "Wohlfuehlfaktor" war, der sehr bestimmend fuer dich war?

Du sagst auch, dass die Grossgruppendiskussion interessant und spannend war
1. War das der Fall weil die zusammengestellten Gruppen in diesem Fall aufgeloest waren?

An einer Stelle sagst du:"Ich habe nach der Einheit noch ueber mein Bild von anderen Personen nachgedacht...."
- Kann es sein, dass du vor der Einheit eine andere Meinung ueber manche KlassenkameradInnen gehabt hast, die du dann zumindest neu ueberdacht hast?
- Du sagst am Schluss, dass du "ueber die Leute in der Klasse etwas gelernt" hast. Heisst das, dass du deine Meinung ueber manche Leute im Zuge dessen, was diese in der Diskussion gesagt haben, revidiert hast?

- Allgemein – was denkst du heute uber das Ethikprojekt 2000?

- Findest du immer noch, dass es "Zeitverschwendung" war?

Vielen Dank fuer deine Zeit und ich waere sehr dankbar, wenn du mir meine Fragen beantworten koenntest, da ich dich so fair als moeglich representieren moechte. Du kannst mir die Antwort entweder durch Frau Roll, die diese Rueckfrageboegen sammelt, oder per Email schicken:
Meine Emailadresse lautet: E.Settelmaier@cc.curtin.edu.au

Hallo ████!

Ich habe eure Interviews ueber das Ethikprojekt 2000 interpretiert, und moechte dich aus Gruenden der Fairness bitten, zu checken, ob ich dich richtig interpretiert habe. Ausserdem moechte dich einige Fragen fragen.

Auf meine Frage, ob so ein Dilemmaansatz grundsaetzlich eine gangbare Methode ist, ethische Fragen zu unterrichten, hast du geantwortet:

"Ja, es war sicher eine Moeglichkeit…wenn man's trotzdem macht, sollte man nicht seine eigene ethische Meinung weitergeben, weil jeder Mensch hat sich ja seine Meinung bilden koennen und das was man sagt, schon wirklich alles darlegen, wie's wirklich war und irgendwie hinbratzeln wenn man nicht einverstanden ist, weil es hat ja jeder seine eigenen ethischen Vorstellungen. Da kann ich das nicht so einfach weglassen…..

Meine Fragen:
1. Diese Methode war sicher EINE Moeglichkeit sowas zu unterrichten…..
   Was koenntest du dir sonst noch vorstellen?

2. Deine Aussage verstehe ich folgendermassen: Man sollte nicht "gezwungen" werden, seine Werte (ethische Meinung) oeffentlich darlegen zu muessen, da diese etwas sehr Privates sind, das jeder fuer sich selbst bildet. Wenn man's doch tut, dann kann's sein dass andere hinbratzeln weil sie eben andere Meinungen haben und das kann verletzend sein…???

3. Ist das, was du meinst oder bin ich voellig daneben?

4. Oder andere Interpreation desselben: Meinst du, dass ein Problem der Methode ist, dass man die eigenen Werte sozusagen oeffentlich klarstellen muss, wobei natuerlich jeder seine eigene Meinung hat, was man akzeptieren sollte?

5. Was denkst du heute ueber das Ethikprojekt 2000? Denkst du immer noch dass es an und fuer sich sinnvoll ist, falls nicht zu oft und nicht zu lang und dass es auch in anderen Gegenstaenden unterrichtet werden sollte?

Vielen Dank fuer deine Zeit und ich waere sehr dankbar, wenn du mir meine Fragen beantworten koenntest, da ich dich so fair als moeglich representieren moechte. Du kannst mir die Antwort entweder durch Frau Roll, die diese Rueckfrageboegen sammelt, oder per Email schicken:
Meine Emailadresse lautet:
E.Settelmaier@cc.curtin.edu.au

Hallo ████!

Ich habe eure Interviews ueber das Ethikprojekt 2000 interpretiert, und moechte dich aus Gruenden der Fairness bitten, zu checken, ob ich dich richtig interpretiert habe. Ausserdem moechte dich einige Fragen fragen.

Das Ethikprojekt hat mir ████ gut gefallen. Ich halte diesen Unterricht fuer wichtig, als ein "Training fuers Leben sozusagen". Was ich nicht so gemocht habe, war die Gruppenarbeit. Ich fand interesant zu hoeren, was die anderen so denken. Ich fand es schwierig mich in die Situation hineinzuversetzen.

Vielen Dank fuer deine Zeit und ich waere sehr dankbar, wenn du mir meine Fragen beantworten koenntest, da ich dich so fair als moeglich representieren moechte. Du kannst mir die Antwort entweder durch Frau Roll, die diese Rueckfrageboegen sammelt, oder per Email schicken:
Meine Emailadresse lautet:
E.Settelmaier@cc.curtin.edu.au

Hallo ██████!

Ich habe eure Interviews ueber das Ethikprojekt 2000 interpretiert, und moechte dich aus Gruenden der Fairness bitten, zu checken, ob ich dich richtig interpretiert habe. Ausserdem moechte dich einige Fragen fragen.

Mir ██████ hat das Projekt gut gefallen, vor allem die Diskussionsrunde. Bei meinen Entscheidungen war fuer mich vor allem wichtig, zu schauen wie meine Entscheidung die Zukunft beeinflusst. Es war ein seltsames Gefuehl fuer mich, eine Entscheidung treffen zu muessen die sich dann als falsch herausstellen kann. Ich fand es schwierig Meinungen zu akzeptieren, die meiner eigenen entgegenliefen.

- Frage: Was denkst du heute ueber das Ethikprojekt 2000?

- Wuerdest du immer noch sagen – es war gut und ich habe was daraus gelernt?

Vielen Dank fuer deine Zeit und ich waere sehr dankbar, wenn du mir meine Fragen beantworten koenntest, da ich dich so fair als moeglich representieren moechte. Du kannst mir die Antwort entweder durch Frau Roll, die diese Rueckfrageboegen sammelt, oder per Email schicken:
Meine Emailadresse lautet:
E.Settelmaier@cc.curtin.edu.au

Response from Daniela:

Sg Fr. Settelmaier
Ich habe ihnen meine Zeit gerne zur Verfügung gestellt. Sie haben meine Fragen ganz richtig interprediert:
1. ich denke noch immer positiv darüber, da auch andere Kinder in meinem damaligen Alter(17) etwas anders dazulernen können, und auch einmal zum Nachdenken angeregt werden. Vor allem ist es wichtig, dass sich Jugendliche eine eigene Meinung bilden können. Das liegt mir sehr am Herzen und kann so sicherlich gefördert werden.
2. Es war gut und ich lernte die Meinungen anderer voll und ganz zu akzeptieren, und sich ihre eigene Meinung über ein Thema bilden zu lassen.Ich denke auch sehr viel selber nach (mehr als früher) ; kann mir selbst über jedes Thema eine eigene Meinung bilden und bin nicht immer der Meinung wie andere.

Ich wünsche ihnen noch viel Erfolg für ihr Projekt.
Hochachtungsvoll ██████

APPENDIX 2C: MEMBERCHECKING IRENE'S CLASS

Hi Irene,

Waere es moeglich, dass du folgende Frage an ████████, ███████ und ██████ in deiner Klasse weiterleitest?

Liebe ████████, ███████ und ██████!

Lang lang ist's her - ich bin gerade am Fertigschreiben meiner Dissertation und habe noch einige Fragen bezueglich des Dilemmaunterrichts von vor drei Jahren...Ich wuerde mir sehr freuen wenn ihr mir behilflich sein koenntet. Vielleicht koennt ihr die Antwort per Email schicken, das waere am einfachsten:

- Wenn du an die beiden Dilemmaeinheiten zurueckdenkst (ich weiss es ist schon eine Weile her....:) !! Welche der beiden Geschichten hat dich mehr angesprochen und warum?
- Ich bin vor allem interessiert an: Interesse, Schwierigkeitsgrad, das Erzaehlen der Geschichte...
- War das Dilemma in der Geschichte ein Dilemma?

Vielen Dank im Voraus

Elisabeth Settelmaier (ex-Neumayr)

APPENDIX 2D: STUDENT MEMBER-CHECKING RELATED EMAILS WITH TEACHERS

----- Original Message -----
From: "Elisabeth Settelmaier" <E.Settelmaier@exchange.curtin.edu.au>
To: ███████████████████
Sent: Monday, May 06, 2002 8:07 AM
Subject: RE: Sandra interview- memberchecks

> Hi Lily
habe deinen Brief erhalten, werde heute versuchen die Schüler der 8a Klasse
zu informieren,,,wird nicht ganz so einfach sein, weil sie in dieser Woche
bei der Matura sitzen und ab dann nur mehr zu den unterschiedlichsten
Vorbereitungseinheiten erscheinen. ████ und ████ sind einfach zu
erreichen, da sie inzwischen in meiner Klasse sind. Mit ████ kann ich
irgendwie über ihren jüngeren Bruder in Kontakt treten. Werde mein
möglichstes tun. ████ ist schwer beschäftigt mit Akademie und Maturaklasse
und Schwangerschaft, werde ihre e-mail connections überprüfen, treffe sie
auch kaum, nicht einmal mehr bei unseren Teamsitzungen.
Wie du siehst habe ich deine attachements wunderbar öffnen können.
Wie sollst du die Antworten geschickt bekommen? Wenn ich sie einsammle, ev,
auf Diskette , könnte ich sie leicht als Anhang zurückmailen. Bis wann
brauchst du sie denn? Werde mein Glück versuchen. Bis bald Irene.

From: ██████████████████████
Sent: May 17, 2002 4:04 PM
Hi, übrigens hat Sandra deine Nachrichten auch erhalten und ausgedruckt den Schülern weitergegeben. d.h. eine ihrer
Adressen funktioniert.
Ich aber brauche noch die Fragen für Peter Landauer. auf seinem Brif ist nur die Bitte um Mithilfe gedruckt, keine
Statements, keine Fragen. Kannst du sie mir schicke? Hast du schon antworten erhalten? Hoffe sehr. Bussi Irene

From: ██████████████████████
Sent: 22. April 2002 2:45AM
Hi, du!
Meine Klasse ist bald fertig! Weiss nicht, ob sie noch zu irgendwas zu
motivieren sind! Bitte schick mir eventuelle Aufträge möglichst bald. Am
25.4. ist Beurteilungsschluss der 8. Klasse, dann schriftliche MAtura, dann
verläuft sich wahrscheinlich alles ziemlich rasch.
Ich krieg im August ein Baby, bin also auch schon am Absprung.
Wie geht´s dir? Wünsch dir alles Liebe
Bussi Sandra

----- Original Message -----
From: Elisabeth Settelmaier <E.Settelmaier@exchange.curtin.edu.au>
To: ████████████████████
Sent: Monday, April 08, 2002 12:31 PM
Subject: RE: Lebenszeichen
> Hi Sandra,>
> Was laeuft? Wann ist deine Klasse zur Matura dran? Ich muss denen naemlich
> noch einige Sachen zum Kommentieren schicken....>
> Bussi Lily

APPENDIX 2E: MEMBERCHECKING WITH TEACHERS

Email 7. 3. 2003

Irene,
Two more questions....

1) Mit der Regenwaldgeschichte - die war doch wirklich sehr dein Spezialgebiet und du hast alles sehr enthusiastisch unterrichtet - kann es sein dass die Schueler deinen Enthusiasmus nicht wirklich geteilt haben. Auf den Videos sieht man dass sie schneller sind und besser arbeiten als beim ersten Dilemma. Allerdings schauen alle ein bisschen apathisch drein In den Interviews haben einge gesagt dass das Thema zu schwierig war...

Was haeltst du davon?

2) Glaubst du, dass wir zwischen den beiden Dilemmaeinheiten laenger haetten warten sollen? Vielleicht waren sie einfach ueberfuettert?

Email 7. 3. 2003

Hallo Irene ,

Ich habe leider noch ein paar Fragen bezueglich der Diss - bin gerade am Fertigmachen:

>Hast du eigentlich nochmal ein Dilemma gemacht?

>Wuerdest du noch eines machen wenn du das Material haettest?

>Wie betrachtest du jetzt im Allgemeinen die Nuetzlichkeit von Dilemmageschichten fuer den Unterricht?

>Wo siehst du Schwachstellen?

>Was ist gut?
[Elisabeth Settelmaier]

Gruss und Kuss

Email 23.2. 2003

Lily

Was diese Lehrplanveränderung betrifft, bin ich zwar informiert, dass sie stattfand, aber nie wirklich in die Tat umgesetzt worden ist. Bei uns an der Schule gab es nicht einmal eine Ausdruck dieses Planes, man behauptete, daß der Lehrer in der sogenannten Holschuld sei und sich die Info aus dem Netz holen sollte. Wenn ich bedenke, daß wir bis vor wenigen Monaten für 100 Lehrer nur einen Computer besaßen, frage ich mich ,wie wir das anstellen hätten sollen, und ein persönlicher Netzugang wird vom Bund nicht bezahlt, d.h. dass nur wenige Kolleginnen wirklich informiert waren.

Werde morgen bei der Kollegenschaft nachfragen inwieweit es mit der Kenntnis über den 99 Lehrplan steht, oder ob ein Ausdruck doch irgendwo liegt. Ich persönlich weiß nur, dass mir die Änderungen, von denen ich wußte, überhaupt nich in den Unterrichtsplan gepasst haben. Das war auch nicht notwendig, weil wir ohnedies im autonomen System arbeiten, und unsere Lehrplän eigentlich selbst scheiben und einreichen müssen.

Dies wärs fürs erste. Bussi Irene

From: Elisabeth Settelmaier
To: █████████████████
Sent: Tuesday, May 28, 2002 6:05 AM
Subject: RE: Frage/ Lehrplan

Hallo,

Stress dich nicht mit scannen oder so, steck's nur in einen Umschlag und ab die Post - ich hab's dann in ungefaehr einer Woche, das ist bald genug!
<Wäre ja einmal etwas anderes, dir einen Brief per Post zu senden...fragt sich nur an welche Adresse?, ich habe jedenfalls keine „ aber Lily Settelmaiers "wird's in Perth nicht so viele geben...
Spass beisseite...
1. ich glaube ich habe mehr stress, wenn ich keinen stress mehr habe.
2. versuch dein Internetglück einmal mit folgender adresse: ... sie ist direkt vom Ministerium:
    www.bmbwk.gv.at
wenns klappt, melde es mir. Angeblich gibt es noch eine Adresse, wo man den Lehrplan nachfragen kann.
Hab's am Mittwoch nicht geschafft die Seiten zu kopieren...komme erst wieder am Mo 3.6. in die Schule .
Bis dahin wissen wir dann , ob ich sie schicken soll oder du schon alles weißt, was du wünschst.
Übrigens, wie geht es deinem ██████ gibt es ihn noch ? wenn ja....liebe grüße und alles gute zum Geburtstag...
hoffe daß sein schwer arbeitenden Weibchen nicht ganz darauf vergisst.
< Versuche Sandras Schüler zu finden, die dir hoffentlich auf deine Fragen eine Antwort geben,.... ist aber recht schwierig, da sie in der Vorbereitungszeit sind und es kaum zu eruieren ist, wann sie im Haus sind .
Bussi   Irene

----- Original Message -----
From: Elisabeth Settelmaier
To: █████████████████
Sent: Monday, May 27, 2002 5:09 AM
Subject: RE: Frage /Lehrplan

Danke fuer die Antowrten zu meinen fragen....

Bezueglich de Lehrplans...
<werde versuchen ihn so schnell als möglich zu kopieren und dann einzuscannen. Übrigens das BMUK hat einen eigene homepage, man muß nur die adresse kennen. werde sie morgen auftreiben, und über den Steir. Landesschulrat ist es auch üblich an die Lehrpläne heranzukommen. Hoffe, daß ich nicht vergessen werde die Unterlagen zu besorgen. Bis dann gute Nacht Irene

Email 23. 5. 2002

Hi, schön ,daß du Fragen hast , so kommen wir wenigstens zu einer Korrespndenz. Danke für ███ Check,
Hoffe, daß er bald darauf anntworten wird.

1. Öko wurde in den letzten Jahren von der Stundenverteilung her betrachtet etwas abgeändert. Ursprünglich waren dafür vorgesehen 4 Unterrrichtsstunden proWoche in den 1. und 2. Klassen, dann 3 ÖKO stunden /Woche in der 3. und 4. Kl, Es zeigte sich aber, daß wir mit dieser Verteilung nicht in der Lage waren den normalen Anforderungen des Lehrplans aus den RegelAHS gerecht zu werden, d.h. Geo-basiswissen der Topographie, sowie der Wirtschaftskunde sind nicht wirklich kombinierbar mit ökol./biologischen Inhalten, müßten aber abgedeckt werden. Daher die Änderung wie folgt: 1.KL: 2Stunden BIO + 2 Stunden Geo getrennt aber in beiden Fächern im Teamteaching = nur mehr heuer aus Spargründen der Regierung, 2.KL u. 3. KL= 3 ÖKOSTUNDEN und in der 4. Klasse BIO und Geo wieder getrennt.

Seit Sept. 2001 haben wir aber für die 3. +4. Kl ein Zusatzangebot, das die Schüler als Wahlpflichtfach wählen können: NAWEX: Nat.wiss. Experimentieren...wird sehr angenommen und macht allen sehr viel Freude, den Lehren aber ach Arbeit. (2 Ust: BIO Übungen: Praxis, 2 ust. CH- Übungen=3.KL, 2 Ust BIO-Übungen + 2 Ust PH Übungen = 4. KL)Wie du siehst haben wir Biologen uns wieder stark durchgesetzt. hurra! Leider war es aus administratorischen gründen nicht möglich eine Fächerübergreifende Einheit anzubieten. Wir sind aber sehr stolz auf dies Lösung und hoffen damit bessere , leistungswilligere Schüler aus der eigenen Anstalt in die OST zu bekommen. Damit haben wir nämlich momentan große Probleme.

Email 23. 9. 2001

In der Schule tat sich einiges. ███████ ist in unsere 1. dislozierte
Klasse nach Kallsdorf ausgewandert, ███████ hat die Administration
übernommen, ███████ kämpft tapfer gegen politische Windmühlen, Erfolg noch
nicht absehbar, aber auf grund der Eskalationen im letzten Jahr ist sie sehr
bemüht einen exakten Stil in den Betrieb zu bekommen auch mit allen
Hindernissen, die die Sparregierung in den Weg legt: kein Gled,
Klassenzahlen über 32, Haben eine neue 5.KL mit 36 Schülern und 5
Quereinsteigern, die das Labor nachholen müssen = 41 und 2 sind noch
angesagt. Daher ist es heuer viel ruhiger am Schulanfang gelaufen. Den
Stundenplan machen ███████ und ███████ und haben gleich zu Beginn für die
ersten3 Wochen einen Fulltimeplan aufgestellt, dann erst der Endplan. Unsere
NAWI Klasse 8 (Sandra)befindet sich in der Schweiz auf PH/CH Exkursion
Habe eine neue Probelehrerin, viele STunden , viele Pläne und die >Hoffnung
alles unter einenHut zu bekommen.
Wie gehts bei euch? Etwas mehr als ein Lebenszeichen erwarte ich mir
demnächst von Dir. Was macht deine Arbeit? Alles Liebe Irene

Email 22. 4. 2002 Sandra
Hi, du!
Meine Klasse ist bald fertig! Weiss nicht, ob sie noch zu irgendwas zu
motivieren sind! Bitte schick mir eventuelle Aufträge möglichst bald. Am
25.4. ist Beurteilungsschluss der 8. Klasse, dann schriftliche MAtura, dann
verläuft sich wahrscheinlich alles ziemlich rasch.
Ich krieg im August ein Baby, bin also auch schon am Absprung.
Wie geht´s dir? Wünsch dir alles Liebe
Bussi Sandra

----- Original Message -----
From: Elisabeth Settelmaier <E.Settelmaier@exchange.curtin.edu.au>
To: 'Sandra Höfert' <Sandra.hoefert@stsnet.at>
Sent: Monday, April 08, 2002 12:31 PM
Subject: RE: Lebenszeichen

> Hi Sandra,
>
> Was laeuft? Wann ist deine Klasse zur Matura dran? Ich muss denen naemlich

> noch einige Sachen zum Kommentieren schicken....
>
> Bussi Lily
>

Hi, Lily!
Ja, ich lebe noch!
 Ziemlich gut sogar!
Glaube, du brauchst noch was von mir!? Kannst mir auf die Sprünge helfen?
Ich bin da etwas schludrig, sorry!
Wie geht´s dir? Ist alles o.k., auch mit deiner "neuen Familie"? Wünsch´ dir
alles Liebe
Sandra

----- Original Message -----
From: Elisabeth Settelmaier <E.Neumayr@curtin.edu.au>
To: ▮▮▮▮▮▮▮ Sandra.hoefert@stsnet.al Sandra
Sent: Friday, September 21, 2001 4:19 AM
Subject: RE: Lebenszeichen

> Hallo ▮▮▮▮.
>
> Lebst du noch?
>
> Gruesse Lily
>

From: ▮▮▮▮▮▮▮▮▮▮
Sent: Thursday, 23 May 2002 2.19PM

Hi, schön ‚daß du Fragen hast , so kommen wir wenigstens zu einer Korrespndenz. Danke für Peters Check, Hoffe, daß er
bald darauf anntworten wird.
1. Öko wurde in den letzten Jahren von der Stundenverteilung her betrachtet etwas abgeändert. Ursprünglich waren dafür
vorgesehen 4 Unterrrichtsstunden proWoche in den 1. und 2. Klassen, dann 3 ÖKO stunden /Woche in der 3. und 4. Kl,
Es zeigte sich aber, daß wir mit dieser Verteilung nicht in der Lage waren den normalen Anforderungen des Lehrplans
aus den RegelAHS gerecht zu werden, d.h. Geo-basiswissen der Topographie, sowie der Wirtschaftskunde sind nicht
wirklich kombinierbar mit ökol./biologischen Inhalten, müßten aber abgedeckt werden. Daher die Änderung wie folgt:
1.KL: 2Stunden BIO + 2 Stunden Geo getrennt aber in beiden Fächern im Teamteaching = nur mehr heuer aus
Spargründen der Regierung, 2.KL u. 3. KL= 3 ÖKOSTUNDEN und in der 4. Klasse BIO und Geo wieder getrennt.
Seit Sept. 2001 haben wir aber für die 3. +4. Kl ein Zusatzangebot, das die Schüler als Wahlpflichtfach wählen können:
NAWEX: Nat.wiss. Experimentieren...wird sehr angenommen und macht allen sehr viel Freude, den Lehren aber ach
Arbeit. (2 Ust: BIO Übungen: Praxis, 2 ust. CH- Übungen=3.KL, 2 Ust BIO-Übungen + 2 Ust PH Übungen = 4. KL)Wie
du siehst haben wir Biologen uns wieder stark durchgesetzt. hurra! Leider war es aus administratorischen gründen nicht
möglich eine Fächerübergreifende Einheit anzubierten. Wir sind aber sehr stolz auf dies Lösung und hoffen damit bessere
, leistungswilligere Schüler aus der eigenen Anstalt in die OST zu bekommen. Damit haben wir nämlich momentan große
Probleme.
Irene

----- Original Message -----

From: Elisabeth Settelmaier

To: ▮▮▮▮▮▮▮▮▮▮

Sent: Monday, May 27, 2002 5:09 AM

Danke fuer die Antworten zu meinen fragen....

Bezueglich de Lehrplans...

<werde versuchen ihn so schnell als möglich zu kopieren und dann einzuscannen.

Übrigens das BMUK hat einen eigene homepage, man muß nur die adresse kennen. werde

sie morgen auftreiben, und über den Steir. Landesschulrat ist es auch üblich an die

Lehrpläne heranzukommen. Hoffe, daß ich nicht vergessen werde die Unterlagen zu

besorgen. Bis dann gute Nacht Irene

Wie geht's so?

>MAN VEGITIERT:

P.S: Pau hat um Versetzung in den Ruhestan angesucht , mit 1.9.2003 - noch kann ich es nicht glauben, daß wir alt werden!!

----- Original Message -----

From: Elisabeth Settelmaier

To: tinkerio@uta1002.at

Sent: Tuesday, May 28, 2002 6:05 AM

Subject: RE: Frage/ Lehrplan

Hallo,

Stress dich nicht mit scannen oder so, steck's nur in einen Umschlag und ab die Post - ich hab's dann in ungefaehr einer Woche, das ist bald genug!

<Wäre ja einmal etwas anderes, dir einen Brief per Post zu senden...fragt sich nur an welche

Adresse?, ich habe jedenfalls keine „ aber Lily Settelmaiers "wird's in Perth nicht so viele geben...

Spass beisseite...

1. ich glaube ich habe mehr stress, wenn ich keinen stress mehr habe.

2. versuch dein Internetglück einmal mit folgender adresse: ... sie ist direkt vom Ministerium:

www.bmbwk.gv.at

wenns klappt, melde es mir. Angeblich gibt es noch eine Adresse, wo man den Lehrplan nachfragen kann. Hab's am Mittwoch nicht geschafft die Seiten zu kopieren...komme erst wieder am Mo 3.6. in die Schule . Bis dahin wissen wir dann , ob ich sie schicken soll oder du schon alles weißt, was du wünschst.

< Versuche Sandras Schüler zu finden, die dir hoffentlich auf deine Fragen eine Antwort geben,... ist aber recht schwierig, da sie in der Vorbereitungszeit sind und es kaum zu eruieren ist, wann sie im Haus sind .

Bussi Irene.

----- Original Message -----

From: Elisabeth Settelmaier

To: linkerie@ruta1002.at

Sent: Monday, February 17, 2003 4:28 AM

Subject: RE:eine neue Frage/ Lehrplan

Hallo, Habe gehofft, daß wir uns nochmals sehen, was sichtlich nicht möglich war. Vater hat seine Gehirnoperation einigermaßen überstanden, mit viel Aufregeungen rundherum. Die chirurgische Versorgung war hevorragend. die medizinische aber eine Katastrophe, was dazu führte daß er durch eine neuerliche Felbehandlung eine Hepatitis bekam, die wiederum sein Immunsystem ausschaltete, was zu einer gewaltigen eitrigen Bronchitis führte und ihn gewaltig schwächte. So " misshandelt" haben wir ihn aus dem Spital heimgenommen um ihn wieder aufzupäppeln, was schon recht gut gelungen ist.
Mittlerweile war der Maturaball meiner Klasse eine voller Erfolg. Was sich aber in Lernleistungen noch nicht zeigt. Irgendwie werde ich sie schon zur Matura bringen, mit einigen Ausfällen.
Morgen gehts neue Semester los ... und damit viel Stress, was die Schulentwicklung anlangt.
Was diese Lehrplanveränderung betrifft, bin ich zwar informiert, dass sie stattfand, aber nie wirklich in die Tat umgesetzt worden ist. Bei uns an der Schule gab es nicht einmal eine Ausdruck dieses Planes, man behauptete, daß der Lehrer in der sogenannten Holschuld sei und sich die Info aus dem Netz holen sollte.
Wenn ich bedenke, daß wir bis vor wenigen Monaten für 100 Lehrer nur einen Computer besaßen, frage ich mich ,wie wir das anstellen hätten sollen, und ein persönlicher Netzgang wird vom Bund nicht bezahlt, d.h. dass nur wenige Kolleginnen wirklich informiert waren.
Werde morgen bei der Kollegenschaft nachfragen inwieweit es mit der Kenntnis über den 99 Lehrplan steht, oder ob ein Ausdruck doch irgendwo liegt. Ich persönlich weiß nur, dass mir die Änderungen, von denen ich wußte, überhaupt nich in den Unterrichtsplan gepasst haben. Das war auch nicht notwendig, weil wir ohnedies im autonomen System arbeiten, und unsere Lehrplän eigentlich selbst scheiben und einreichen müssen.
Dies wärs fürs erste. Bussi Irene.

From: Elisabeth Settelmaier
Sent: Friday, 7 March 2003 2:24PM

To: Erich Fink

RE:eine neue Frage/Lehrplan

Hallo Irene,

Ich habe leider noch ein paar Fragen bezueglich der Diss - bin gerade am Fertigmachen:

>Hast du eigentlich nochmal ein Dilemma gemacht?

>Wuerdest du noch eines machen wenn du das Material haettest?

>Wie betrachtest du jetzt im Allgemeinen die Nuetzlichkeit von Dilemmageschichten fuer den Unterricht?

>Wo siehst du Schwachstellen?

>Was ist gut?
[Elisabeth Settelmaier]

Gruss und Kuss Lily

From: Elisabeth Settelmaier
Sent: Friday, 7 March 2003 2:50PM
To: ████████
Irene,
Two more questions....
RE: eine neue Frage/Lehrplan

1) Mit der Regenwaldgeschichte - die war doch wirklich sehr dein Spezialgebiet und du hast alles sehr enthusiastisch unterrichtet - kann es sein dass die Schueler deinen Enthusiasmus nicht wirklich geteilt haben. Auf den Videos sieht man dass sie schneller sind und besser arbeiten als beim ersten Dilemma. Allerdings schauen alle ein bisschen apathisch drein In den Interviews haben einge gesagt dass das Thema zu schwierig war...

Was haeltst du davon?

2) Glaubst du, dass wir zwischen den beiden Dilemmaeinheiten laenger haetten warten sollen? Vielleicht waren sie einfach ueberfuettert?

APPENDIX 2F: OTHER EMAIL CORRESPONDENCE IN RELATION TO THESIS

From: Ulrike Unterbruner ████████████████
To: Elisabeth Settelmaier

Liebe Lily,

At 11:24 17.02.03 +0800, you wrote:
>Hallo Ulrike!
>Bin gerade dabei die Literatur die ich in Oesterreich fuer meine Diss
>gesammelt habe nochmals zu sichten und bin dabei auf eine Ungereimtheit
>gestossen, bei deren Aufklaerung du mir vielleicht behilflich sein kannst:
>
>Situation:
>Ich habe dir erzaehlt dass meine Diss eine Evaluirung einer
>Lehrplanentwicklung fuer Ethik im naturwissenschaftlichen Unterricht
>darstellt. Meiner Diss vorausgehend war ich 1998 in einem Rotkreuzprojekt
>involviert das die sogenannte Lehrplanreform 99 als Basis hatte. Ich
>erinnere mich bei unserem Gespraech im November machtest du eine Bemerkung
>dass diese Lehrplanreform nicht sehr erfolgreich war...
>
... "nicht erfolgreich" ist vielleicht der falsche Ausdruck. Wir
LehrplanautorInnen konnten uns gegen blödsinnige Änderungen im Bereich
Mensch und Gesundheit, die auf der politischen Ebene (Konservative Lobby mit
direktem WEg zum Ministersekretär) nachträglich durchgeführt worden sind,
nicht wehren.
Generell habe ich den Eindruck, dass viele HauptschullehrerInnen den LP 99
als positiv empfinden und die Chancen im Sinne inhaltlicher Autonomie gerne
nutzen. Etliche AHS-LehrerInnen - so meine konkreten Erfahrungen - weigern
sich immer noch, den LP 99 zur Kenntnis zu nehmen. Zu einem erheblichen Teil
ist das aber Resistenz gegen jedwede Innovation.

>Bei meinen Gespraechen in Schulen fand ich heraus dass alle Lehrer mit denen
>ich sprach nach wie vor das Lehrplandokument 1986 ! verwenden....

Der LP 99 ist nur für die 1. bis 4. Klasse gemacht worden, in der Ethik hast
du es ja mit Oberstufe zu tun, daraus erklärt sich diese Diskrepanz.
Mittlerweile wurde aber auch an einem neuen Oberstufen Lehrplan gearbeitet
(ich bin ja auch wieder dabei) und dieser wird voraussichtlich noch in
diesem Schuljahr verabschiedet werden. Somit ist dieser neue OstLP dann ab
dem Schuljahr 2004/05 für die 5. Klassen (aufsteigend) rechtskräftig.

>Am Web fand ich allerdings auf der Webseite des PI Tirols ein
>Lehrplandokument der Lehrplanreform 99 welches recht verschieden ist zu dem
>alten Dokument und in vielerlei Hinsicht eine Verbesserung und
>Neuformulierung darstellt.

Da weiß ich nicht, worum es sich handelt. Falls du Genaueres wissen willst,
teile mir mit, wo ich dieses Dokument finde.

>
>Meine Frage:
>Wie kommt es dass ein derartiges Dokument existiert jedoch nicht in Schulen
>verwendet wird? D.h. warum wurde dieses Dokument nicht verteilt? Warum
>muessen sich die Lehrer nicht an das spaetere Dokument halten?

s.o. Und weiters ist zu beachten, dass es auch schulautonome Lehrpläne gibt.
Schulen können solche beim Ministerium einreichen und genehmigen lassen.
Eine Ministerialrätin hat kürzlich erzählt, dass die Schulen in den letzten
Jahren davon relativ viel Gebrauch gemacht haben. Dies gilt z.B. für
Sprachenschwerpunkt, zusätzliche EDV-Stunden, Naturwissenschaften u.a.

Ich hoffe, das hilft dir weiter!
Liebe, himmelblaue und klirrend-kalte Wintergrueße, Ulrike

From ██████████████
Sent: Wedndesday, 4 July 2001 7:59AM
To: Elisabeth Neumayr
RE: hallo

Liebe Lily,
ich weiß wirklich nicht, was ich Dir über die Klasse schreiben soll -
es sind so unterschiedliche Typen drin. Einige sind sehr bemüht, es
fehlt ihnen an Möglichkeiten. Einige sind sehr begabt, die
interessierts halt nicht so sehr. Überrascht war ich von ihrer
Disziplin während der Projektwoche - so eine brave Klasse hatte ich
noch nie.
Schreib mir bitte, was Du konkret brauchst, ich versuche dann, darauf
einzugehen.
LG
████   Walter

Elisabeth Neumayr schrieb am 13.06.2001:
>From: Elisabeth Neumayr <E.Neumayr@curtin.edu.au>
>Date: Wed, 13 Jun 2001 14:20:05 +0800
>Subject: hallo!
>To: ██████████████████████████
>
>Hallo ████████Walter!
>
>Irene hat mir deine Emailadresse gegeben, da ich fuer meine Diss
>noch ein
>paar Auskuenfte von Lehrern brauche, die auch ihre Klasse die
>diesjaehrige
>6A unterrichten. Koenntest du mir ein paar Zeilen schreiben in denen
>du
>deine Eindruecke dieser Klasse kurz beschreibst?
>
>Vielen Dank
>Lily Neumayr

Appendix 3
Emergent thesis structure

APPENDIX 3A: January 2003
APPENDIX 3B: October 2003
APPENDIX 3C: July 2002

Appendix 3A

Thesis structure in January 2003			
Section I	Acknowledgments		
	Table of contents		
	List of Tables		
	List of Figures		
	Prologue		
	Abstract		
	Introduction	Chapter 1	
	Distributed Methodology	Methodological Interlude 1 (Qual. Research, Wilber?, Bricolage)	
Section II	Curriculum Development	Chapter 2 – Curriculum Theoretical Framework	
		Chapter 3 – Curriculum Metaphors	
Section III	Distributed Methodology	Methodological Interlude 2 (Fieldwork, res. Standards, ethical standards)	
	Research Context	Chapter 4 - Autobiography	
		Chapter 5 – School & Austrian Schooling System	
		Chapter 6 – Research Participants	
Section IV	Distributed Methodology	Methodological Interlude 3 – data-analysis	
	Results of data analysis	Chapter 7 - storytelling as experienced from different perspectives	
		Chapter 8 – individual decision-making process as experienced from different perspectives	
		Chapter 9 – moral discourse as experienced from different perspectives	
		Chapter 10 – summary, conclusion and implications	
Section VI	List of References		
	Appendices		

Appendix 3B

Thesis structure in October 2002		
Section I	Acknowledgments	
	Table of contents	
	List of Tables	
	List of Figures	
	Prologue	
	Abstract	
	Introduction	Chapter 1
	Distributed Methodology	Methodological Interlude 1 (Qual. Research, Wilber?, Bricolage)
Section II	Curriculum Development	Chapter 2 – Curriculum Theoretical Framework
		Chapter 3 – Curriculum Metaphors
Section III	Distributed Methodology	Methodological Interlude 2 (Fieldwork, res. Standards, ethical standards)
	Research Context	Chapter 4 - Autobiography
		Chapter 5 – School & Austrian Schooling System
		Chapter 6 – Research Participants
Section IV	Distributed Methodology	Methodological Interlude 3 – data-analysis
	Results of data analysis	Chapter 7 - Dilemma experience from researcher perspective
		Chapter 8 – student experience: The decision-making process
		Chapter 9 - student experience: External factors influencing the dilemma experience
		Chapter 10 - student experience: Evaluation of the curriculum implementation
		Chapter 11 – Dilemma experience from the teachers' perspective
Section V	Summary, Conclusions	Chapter 12
Section VI	List of References	Chapter 13?
	Appendices	

Appendix 3C
THESIS STRUCTURE IN JULY 2002

INTRODUCTION SECTION
- ➢ Chapter 1
  - ➢ Biographical account:critical events that led me to choose my thesis topic
  - ➢ The Red Cross Project: the theoretical background and literature, the teaching approach - make extensive use of the candidacy proposal

- ➢ Chapter 2
  - ➢ Theoretical framework guiding the research process (Wilber paper & seventh moment of qualitative research) and ethical guidelines

- • THE CASE STUDY SECTION (in the following methods are being discussed where appropriate i.e. at the beginning of each chapter and in greater detail in the appendix)

- ➢ Chapter 3: fieldwork
  - ➢ How and where the project was set up
  - ➢ Problems encountered etc.
  - ➢ Introduction to the Austrian schooling system
  - ➢ Introduction to the Schulverbund Graz West

Section FIELDWORK & CASES
- ➢ Chapter 4: CASE 1: Irene and her class, the 5A

- ➢ Chapter 5: the story of the "tree" dilemma
  - • My own account (autoethnography based on participant observation)
  - • Students' views single interviews
  - • Students' views (focus-group interview)
  - • Feedback and evaluation-sessions with Irene (action research?)

- ➢ Chapter 6: moral learning during this unit (discourse/analysis of video-data, audiotapes, hermeneutic analysis of students' notes and posters)

- ➢ Chapter 7: **CASE** 2: Sandra and her class, the 6A
- ➢ Chapter 8: the story of the "Rocketdilemma"
  - • My own account
  - • Feedback and evaluation-sessions with Sabine
  - • Students' views (single interviews)
  - • Students' views (focus-group interview)

- ➢ Chapter 9 – moral learning during this unit (discourse/analysis of video-data, audiotapes, hermeneutic analysis of students' notes and posters)

- ➢ Chapter 10: summary and comparison of the two cases – what have I (we) learned from all this?

- ➢ Chapter 11: Interpret results using relevant literature

Appendix 4
Demographic data

Appendix 4A: Irene's class

Country of Origin	First Language	Gender	Religious Denomination
Ghana	English/GSL	m	Lutheran Protestant
Togo	Kal/French/GSL	m	Islam
Austria	German	m	Catholic
Bosnia	Bosnian/GSL	f	Islam
Romania	Romanian/GSL	m	Greek Orthodox
Austria	German	m	Catholic
Austria	German	f	Catholic
Austria	German	m	Catholic
Austria	German	m	Catholic
Austria	German	f	Catholic
Bosnia	Bosnian/GSL	f	Islam
Austria	German	m	Catholic
Mongolia	MongolianGSL	m	Buddhist
Austria	German	m	Catholic
Austria	German	f	Catholic
Austria	German	f	Catholic
Austria	German	m	Catholic
Austria	German	f	Catholic
Iran	Persian/GSL	f	Islam
Austria	German	f	Catholic
Iran	Persian/GSL	m	Islam
Hungaria	Hungarian/GSL	f	Catholic
Austria	German	f	Catholic
Austria	German	m	Catholic
Austria	German	m	Catholic
Romania	Romanian/GSL	m	Greek Orthodox
Austria	German	f	Catholic
Austria	German	m	Catholic
Ghana	English/GSL	m	Lutheran Protestant

country of origin

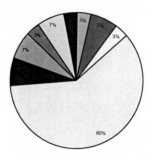

Countries of Origin

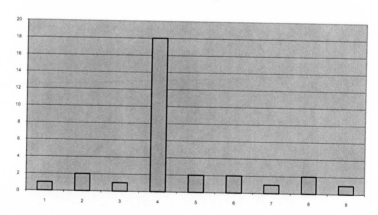

1 = Macedonia
2 = Ghana
3 = Togo
4 = Austria
5 = Bosnia
6 = Romania
7 = Mongolia
8 = Iran
9 = Hungary

Gender

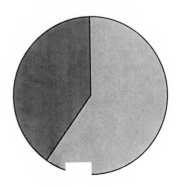

1 = Male
2 = Female

Gender

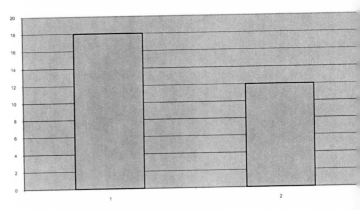

1 = Male

2 = Female

Religious denominations

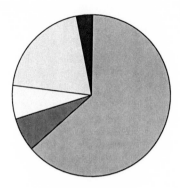

1 = Catholic
2 = Protestant
3 = Greek Orthodox
4 = Islam
5 = Buddhist

Religious denominations

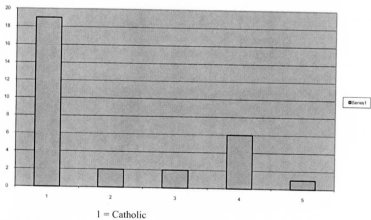

1 = Catholic
2 = Protestant
3 = Greek Orthodox
4 = Islam
5 = Buddhist

Appendix 4B: Sandra's class

Country of Origin	First Language	Gender	Religious Denomination
Austria	German	m	Not available
Austria	German	m	n/a
Austria	German	m	n/a
Austria	German	m	n/a
Austria	German	f	n/a
Austria	German	m	n/a
Austria	German	m	n/a
Austria	German	f	n/a
Austria	German	m	n/a
Austria	German	m	n/a
Austria	German	f	n/a
Bosnia	Bosnian/GSL	m	n/a
Austria	German	m	n/a
Austria	German	m	n/a
Austria	German	m	n/a
Austria	German	f	n/a
Austria	German	f	n/a
Austria	German	m	n/a
Austria	German	f	n/a
Austria	German	f	n/a
Austria	German	m	n/a
Austria	German	m	n/a
Austria	German	f	n/a

Country of Origin

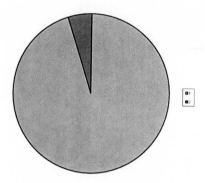

1 = Austrian
2 = Bosnian

Country of origin

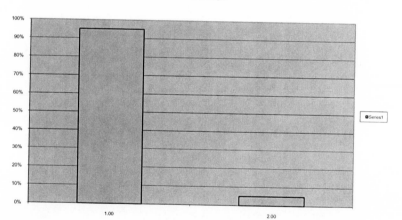

1 = Austrian
2 = Bosnian

Gender

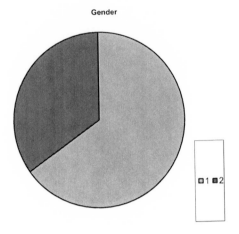

1 = Male
2 = Female

Gender

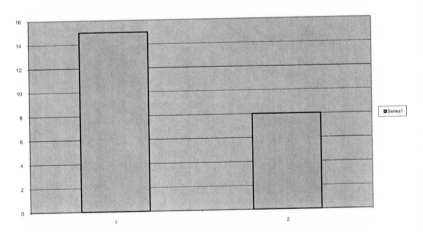

1 = Male
2 = Female

Appendix 5
Dilemma stories – full text

Appendix 5A: Tree Dilemma in German

Titel: Peters Fichte

Lehrplanthema: Botanik, Pflanzen als Lebewesen, der Wert des Lebens

Als Peter geboren wurde, bekamen seine Eltern zu seiner Geburt ein kleines Fichtenbäumchen geschenkt. Dieses Bäumchen wurde liebevollst im Vorgarten von Peters Elternhaus gepflanzt, damit man bei seinem Anblick immer an Peter Geburtstag erinnert würde. Alle Leute sagten, dass dieses kleine Bäumchen den kleinen Peter auf seinem weiteren Lebensweg begleiten werde.

Viele Jahre sind seitdem vergangen und Peter ist heute 33 Jahre alt. Er ist mit seinen 1,89 m Körpergröße recht groß geworden, doch seine Fichte überragt ihn bei weitem - sie ist ungefähr 12 m groß und ein stattlicher, gesunder Baum geworden.

In den letzten 33 Jahren hat sie eine Menge für die Familie getan: sie hat Wind und Wetter vom Haus ferngehalten, sie hat schädliches Kohlendioxid über ihre Nadeln aus der Luft aufgenommen und lebensnotwendigen Sauerstoff und Wasserdampf abgegeben. Damit hat sie die Luft für Peters Familie verbessert. Sie hat mit ihren Nadeln aber auch Staub und Schmutz aus der Luft aufgefangen, die dann beim nächsten Regen auf den Boden abgespült wurden. Sie hat damit die Luft für Peters Familie auch gereinigt. Mit ihren Wurzeln hat sie den Boden im Vorgarten gefestigt.

Das Rauschen der Äste bei starkem Wind ist manchmal richtig unheimlich. Ihre Äste sind mit vielen, vielen tausend dunkelgrünen spitzen Nadeln besetzt. Die jungen Triebe dagegen sind ganz weich und hellgrün. Der Duft ihrer Nadeln ist manchmal, vor allem bei Regen, betörend. Ihre rotbraune Rinde fühlt sich rauh an und wird von Peters Hund Racki als Massagebürste verwendet. Die dichten Äste bieten nämlich sowohl Racki als auch der Schildkröte Maxi ein perfektes Versteck, besonders im Sommer an heißen Tagen.

Peter Familie ist sehr stolz auf das Prachtexemplar von Fichte im Vorgarten. Peters Eltern leben mittlerweile alleine mit dem Großvater und dem Hund und Schildkröte im Haus. Die Kinder sind längst erwachsen und haben eigene Familien. Peters Eltern haben schon lange einen großen Wunsch. Sie spielen mit dem Gedanken ein Campingmobil zu kaufen, das sie sich bisher einfach nicht leisten konnten. Jetzt werden Prospekte und Annoncen in Zeitungen studiert. Endlich ist es so weit! Der langjährige Traum geht in Erfüllung. Ein Campingmobil wird angeschafft und die Freude ist riesengroß. Da kommt der Tag an dem das Campingmobil an seinen neuen Standplatz im Vorgarten von Peters Elternhaus Einzug hält. Doch Schreck!!! Es gibt ein Problem! Das Campingmobil paßt nicht an den dafür vorgesehenen Platz im Vorgarten. Es ist um einige Zentimeter zu lang und steht in die Straße hinaus. Da dies für die vorbeifahrenden Autofahrer unter Umständen eine Gefahr darstellen könnte, muß eine andere Lösung gesucht werden: **die Fichte muß weg!!!!!** Ein Profibaumumsäger soll sie am nächsten Sonntag umschneiden. Zuerst soll er die Äste abschneiden, dann soll er den Stamm absägen und zerhacken bis nur noch der Wurzelstock da ist. Doch auch dieser wird weichen müssen. Denn auch er ist im Weg. Peter erfährt, was mit seinem Baum geschehen soll. Er ist entsetzt.

> **Unterbrechung 1 - Dilemma 1:**

Stell´dir vor, du bist Peter: Welche Argumente würdest du zur Rettung deines Baumes anführen? Wie würdest du versuchen deine Eltern zu überzeugen? Begründe deine Argumente!

Fortsetzung der Geschichte:

Peter schlägt vor die Garteneinfahrt umzubauen, so dass man an der Fichte vorbei fahren könnte. Eine andere Möglichkeit wäre es einen Unterstellplatz zu mieten. In seiner äußersten Verzweiflung will sich Peter an die Fichte ketten, so wie dies Umweltorganisationen manchmal machen.

Stell dir vor du wärst Peters Eltern: welche Gegenargumente könntest du bringen, weshalb der Baum trotzdem geschnitten werden muß? Begründe Deine Argumente!

Fortsetzung der Geschichte:

Nach langer Diskussion einigen sich Peter und seine Eltern. Der Baum wird geschnitten. Doch dann wird Peter mit der folgenden Frage seiner Eltern konfrontiert: "Hör mal, wenn es dir so unangenehm ist, daß jemand anderer deinen Baum schneidet, warum schneidest du deinen Baum nicht selbst?"

➤ **Unterbrechung 2 - Dilemma 2:**

- Wenn du Peter wärst, wie würdest du dich entscheiden? Würdest du deinene eigenen Baum schneiden?

Begründe deine Argumente!

Fortsetzung der Geschichte:

Peter beschließt, daß es besser ist, wenn er schon den Baum nicht retten kann, den Baum selbst umzuschneiden.

➤ **Unterbrechung 2 - Dilemma 2:**

Was denkst du:

- Hat Peter eine richtige Entscheidung getroffen?
- War es fair seinem Baum gegenüber selbst die Axt anzulegen?
- Hat er seine Grundeinstellung, Tiere und Pflanzen schützen zu wollen, durch seine Entscheidung verletzt?

Warum glaubst Du fällt es Menschen leichter Pflanzen umzuschneiden, als z.B. ein Tier oder einen Menschen zu töten?

Appendix 5B: Tree Dilemma in English

Title: Peter's Tree

Curriculum: botany, plants as living beings, (value of) life

This is a story about life and death. In this case the
"victim" is tree - planted at the birth of a child, cut down
to provide room for a campervan…. (Almost) everyone will
agree with me that "life has value and needs to be
protected". BUT the basic question is - do we designate
different values to different forms of life? If yes why…?

When Peter was born, his parents received a little tree as a present, a baby fir. They planted
it in the front garden to celebrate the birth of their first-born child. People said that this tree
would accompany Peter through his life. He would always know that home is where the
tree is. Over the years a "relationship" developed between the boy, being very proud of
owning his own tree, and the tree – you could call it a spiritual relationship – the tree
became part of Peter. Both grew considerably over the years: Peter grew up to 6 feet in
height, but his tree has beaten him by far – after 35 years it has reached a height of
approximately 25 metres.

Over all these years the seemingly unmoving tree has done a lot in favour of Peter's
family:
It has protected the house from strong winds and rainstorms.
It has filtered the dust out of the air, cleaning the air they breathed.
During the process of photosynthesis, it has used carbon-dioxide and released oxygen
instead.
Its roots have helped to prevent soil erosion.

The sound of the branches at strong winds can be really spooky sometimes. The branches
are covered with thousands of dark-green needles, only the young branches are soft and of
a light green colour. The smell the fir releases especially after rainstorms is very strong.
The reddish brown bark feels rough when you touch it. The dense branches also offer a
perfect hide out for Racki the dog and Max the turtle. Peter spends a lot of time hiking and
climbing in the mountains, developing a great reverence for nature and life.

Of course the circumstances of Peter's family have changed too over the years: the kids
have all grown up, have got married and left home. So there are only Peter's parents and
his grandfather left in the house. For years his parents have had the dream of buying a
campervan, which would allow them to travel so much easier especially now as they have
retired. Up to now most of the money was spent either on repayments for the house or

invested into their children´s future. Now they can actually make their dream come true. They have spent some weeks browsing through brochures and visiting campervan dealers. Finally a decision is made. The van is bought and Peter´s father proudly tries to park it in the front garden.

BUT the campervan is too long protruding by a few centimetres into the street, which might cause a potential hazard to passing cars or cyclists, because the road is very narrow. There seems to be just one solution – **the tree has to go!** The spot where the tree is now would be perfectly suitable for a carport....

So they call Peter on the phone and tell him about their decision to get professional loggers in the next Saturday to have the tree felled.

Peter cannot believe his ears: his parents, who have planted this tree some thirty years ago for him, are now willing to have it cut down without hesitation, because of a campervan!! He cannot understand how and why anyone would fell a healthy, beautiful tree anyway. He tells them that he feels really hurt and that, if they proceed with their plans, they must be aware that they will sort of "unroot" him too! He has got the feeling that he will lose a part of himself.

- **Interruption 1 - Dilemma1:**

Imagine you are Peter – How would you try to convince your parents to let the fir-tree live? - Explain your answer!

Story continued: Peter suggests to change the driveway so that one could negotiate around the tree which would just about be possible. The other solution he has thought of, is to rent a garage nearby where they could park the campervan, if it is not in use.

- ➢ **Interruption 2 - Dilemma 2:**

Imagine you are Peter´s mother or father, how would you try to convince your obviously desperate son that the tree just has to go - Explain your answer!

Story continued: Peter´s parents decide to go ahead with their plans. Having the feeling, they should involve him into the decision making process, they suggest to him that, being an experienced mountaineer, he could climb up the tree himself and fell it piece by piece, if he feels so disturbed by the fact that strangers are to do this job.
So finally Peter is confronted with the decision whether to leave the cutting-down-job to strangers or do it himself. As a last attempt he brings up the argument:

"Have you ever thought about the fact that this tree is a living being?"

- **Interruption 3 - Dilemma 3:**

What do you think
- If you were Peter, would you go and cut the tree yourself, if it absolutely has to be done?
- Why do people tend to treat plants as if they were not living beings and "kill" them so much easier than animals or human being for example?

Does a materialistic wish like the one Peter´s parents have got justify the "killing" of any living being – even though it does not move, cry or scream? - Explain your responses!

Appendix 5C Rainforest Dilemma in German

Titel: Regenwalddilemma

Unterrichtsthema: Biologie / Viren und Bakterien; Mathematik / Wachstum

Zwei Wissenschaftler, die für eine pharmazeutische Firma arbeiten, werden nach Brasiliuen geschickt, um im Rahmen des Kampfes gegen einen Virus, der durch Europa und die USA wütet, in einem entlegenen Regenwaldgebiet Pflanzen zu beproben. Der Virus wurde durch Touristen, die zufällig damit im afrikanischen Regenwald in Kontakt kamen, verbreitet.

Anna ist eine junge Botanikerin und arbeitet für eine pharmazeutische Firma. Sie ist erst seit ein paar Monaten bei dieser Firma und ist sehr stolz darauf, daß ihr der Job in einem Projekt angeboten wurde, welcher sie in den brasilianischen Regenwald bringen wird. Diese Reise bedeutet für sie, daß die Firma ihre Fähigkeiten erkannt hat und sie, falls sie ihre Aufgabe gut erfüllt, mit einer Beförderung rechnen kann.

Ihr Mitreisender Bob ist der Projektleiter und ein leitender Wissenschaftler in der Firma. Ihre Aufgabe wird es sein, Pflanzen zu finden, welche einen Wirkstoff enthalten, der im Kampf gegen Virus X11 eingesetzt werden kann. Virus X11 hat sich innerhalb von wenigen Monaten von einer Quelle im afrikanischen Regenwald aus über die ganze nördliche Welthalbkugel verbreitet. Die ersten Opfer waren zwei Touristen, die nach ihrer Rückkehr nach Europa, Symptome von Multipler Sklerose zeigten. Der einzige Unterschied war, daß der körperliche Verfall viel rascher vor sich ging. Schließlich konnte der Virus X11 isoliert und als Verursacher festgestellt werden. Der Virus scheint sich durch direkten Kontakt mit Erkrankten zu verbreiten, ähnlich wie Grippe. Die Inkubationszeit betraegt 3 bis 6 Monate. Bis jetzt sind mehrere tausend Menschen an der Krankheit gestorben. Die Gesundheitsbehörden von fast allen betroffenen Ländern haben die Krankheit mittlerweile zur Epidemie erklärt und Leute angewiesen, bestimmte Vorsichtsmaßnahmen, wie z.B. den Kontakt mit Menschen außerhalb des Hauses einzuschränken, unbedingt zu befolgen. Die Vorsichtsmaßnahmen sind allerdings, bedingt durch die hohe Ansteckungsgefahr sehr eingeschränkt. Da der Virus ohne Vorwarnung zugeschlagen hat, sind keine Impfstoffe verfügbar bis jetzt. Außerdem gibt es große Probleme mit der Produktion eines Impfstoffes, da der Virus sehr rasch mutiert. Die Angst wächst überall. Während der Virus durch die nördliche Welt wütet, hat die Firma, für die Anna und Bob arbeiten, beschlossen, ihre Suche auf de brasilianischen Regenwald auszudehnen um ein Heilmittel gegen Virus X11 zu finden.

Kurz vor ihrer Abreise beginnt Anna sich nicht wohl zu fühlen - sie hat das Gefühl krank zu werden. Sie hat Fieber und ihre Nase läuft - eine Grippe kündigt sich an. Anna weiß, daß sie eher zuhause bleiben sollte und das Bett hüten, aber was würde dann aus ihrer Reise, ihrem Job und ihrer Beförderung werden?

Denk an eine Situation, in der Du unbedingt etwas tun wolltest und endlich hattest Du die Chance dazu....und plötzlich war da ein Grund, warum Du Deinen Wunsch in letzter Minute nicht erfüllen konntest......

Nun stell Dir vor Du wärest Anna, gerade dabei Deine Karriere aufzubauen, und plötzlich wirst Du krank kurz vor Deiner Abreise - wie würdest Du Dich entscheiden, zuhause bleiben und die Krankheit auskurieren oder ein paar Grippetabletten einnehmen und trotzdem losfahren?

Die Reise von Rio de Janeiro in das kleine Regenwalddorf dauert vier ganze Tage. Die letzten paar hundert Kolimeter bewältigen sie mit kleinen Booten und zu Fuß. Sie kommen in der Nacht an und schlafen die nächsten 24 Stunden durch, völlig erschöpft. Das erste das sie nach ihrem Erwachen tun ist mit den Eingeborenen in Kontakt zu kommen. Sie haben eine Übersetzer mit. Die Leute sind neugierig, freundlich und sehr hilfsbereit. Sie teilen ihr Wissen über die einheimischen Pflanzen gerne mit den beiden Forschern. Sie fuuhren Anna und Bob herum und erklären ihnen welche Pflanzen sie wofür verwenden, welche Teile und wie sie sie verarbeiten und aufbereiten. Anna und Bob ziehen viele Pflanzenproben welche sie in ihrem Feldlabor erstmals untersuchen. Jene Pflanzen, die erfolgversprechend aussehen, werden dann mitgenommen und im Hauptlabor der pharmazeutischen Firma analysiert. Kurz bevor die beiden wieder abreisen wollen, verliert Anna ihren Kampf gegen die Grippe und erkrankt sehr. Bob kümmert sich um sie. Die Eingeborenen bereiten einen Tee für sie zu, der das Fieber und die Kranheitssymptome rasch abklingen läßt. Bald fühlt sie sich besser und die beiden Forscher reisen nachhause.

Die Analysen ergeben, daß eine der Pflanzen eine Substanz enthält, die sehr wirksam im Kampf gegen Virus X11 erscheint. Es gibt nur ein Problem – die Substanz ist sehr instabil und muß an Ort und Stelle erst mal vorbehandelt werden, bevor sie nach Übersee verschifft werden kann. Dies wiederum bedeutet, daß die Firma Laborpersonal und –material in den Regenwald schicken muß. Der Aufwand scheint gerechtfertigt, da die Exklusivrechte für ein Heilmittel gegen Virus X11 große finanzielle Gewinne versprechen. Um diese Rechte auch exklusiv zu halten, hat die Firma mit der Regierung abgeschlossen, welcher ihr das alleinige Nutzungsrecht dieses Regenwaldgebietes für die nächsten fünf Jahre zusichert.

Als Anna und Bob in das Dorf zurückkehren, um alles für die Ankunft der Laborangestellten vorzubereiten, finden sie, daß etwa die Hälfte der Dorfbewohner in der Zwischenzeit an Grippe gestorben ist. Anna fühlt sich sehr schlecht, als ihr klar wird, daß sie es war, die einen Grippevirus zu den Eingeborenen eingeschleppt hat.

Anna fühlt sich schuldig, da ihre Entscheidung ihre Karriere zu verfolgen, sie trotz der Krankheitssymptome nach Brasilien hat fahren lassen. Dies hat bekanntlich vielen Eingeborenen das Leben gekostet.

- Was denkst du darüber – ist Anna "schuldig" am Tod dieser Menschen?
- Was denkst du über folgende Situation – während Forscher nach einem Heilmittel im Kampf gegen einen Virus suchen, der zuhause viele Menschen tötet, bringen sie andere, "fremde" Keime zu Menschen, die noch nie zuvor

damit Kontakt hatten. Rechtfertigt die Epidemie zuhause, dass andere Kranheiten bei den Eingeborenen eingeschleppt werden?

- Fernreisen sind mittlerweile ein wichtiger Bestandteil unseres modernen Lebens geworden. Dies bringt ein Problem mit sich – Krankheitskeime reisen mit uns – entweder sind wir es, die Krankheiten in andere Gebiete der Welt verschleppen, wo sie vorher noch nicht waren, oder wir bringen Keime aus anderen Welteilen nachhause.....Was denkst – wie koennten diese Nachteile des Massentourismus eingeschraenkt werden?

Damit die Produktion des Heilmittels anlaufen kann, müssen zuerst Bauarbeiter und Baumaschinen mit Hubschraubern eingeflogen werden, Laborgebäude errichtet, Bäume gefällt und Straßen gebaut werden. Am Anfang beobachten die Eingeborenen das Schauspiel mit großem Interesse, kurze Zeit später werden ihre Hütten abgerissen und am Dorfrand wieder aufgebaut.

Das Dorf und der umliegende Regenwald haben sich drastisch verändert: stat dichtem Wald, gibt es Baumstümpfe. Die Strassen stellen Narben dar, wo die rote Erde aufgerissen wurde. Wenn es regnet, verwandeln sie sich in tiefen Schlamm....

Die Bauarbeiter haben für sich selbst mittlerweile rostende Wellblechhütten gebaut, die sie vor dem Regen schützen sollen. Um das Leben hier am "Ende der Welt" etwas angenehmer zu gestalten, haben die Arbeiter Alkohol mitgebracht. Immer wieder bieten sie den Eingeborenen einen Schluck an und amüsieren sich köstlich, wenn diese dann betrunken werden....

➢ **Unterbrechung 3 – Dilemma 3:**

- Was denkst DU – wie könnte man vermeiden, daß die Eingeborenen dadurch leiden müssen (Verlust ihrer Kultur, Einschleppung von Krankheiten und Suchtmitteln,....), daß wir, die Bewohner der "entwickelten" Welt, etwas aus dem Regenwald nehmen, um es für uns zu nützen ?
- Wie könnte die Umweltzerstörung möglichst klein gehalten werden, wenn eine Vorproduktionsstätte schon an Ort und Stelle errichtet werden muß?

Die Stammesältesten kommen zu Anna und Bob, zu denen sie ein gutes Verhältnis hatten, bevor die Zivilisation Einzug hielt, in diesem entlegenen Teil der Welt, und fragen sie:
"Warum hat uns niemand gefragt, ob wir mit alldem einverstanden sind?"
"Warum hat uns niemand gefragt, ob wir soviele fremde Leute hier haben wollen?'
"Warum hat uns niemand gefragt, ob wir damit einverstanden sind, daß Pflanzen aus unserem Regenwald genommen werden?"
"Warum hat uns niemand gefragt, ob wir wollen, daß unsere Hütten an den Dorfrand verlegt werden?"
Anna und Bob verstehen die Sorgen der Leute, fühlen sich aber außerstande, etwas gegen die Probleme zu unternehmen. Sie haben nicht besonders viel Einfluß – die Entscheidungen werden viele tausend Kilometer weit weg getroffen. Sie diskutieren untereinander, wie sie den Dorfältesten sagen sollen, daß sie nichts ändern können an der Lage. Die Regierung des Landes hat der Firma bereits alle Rechte für die Nutzung des Regenwaldgebietes für die nächsten fünf Jahre zugesichert, was unter anderem die Eingeborenen des Rechts beraubt, gegen die Pläne Einspruch zu erheben.

> **Unterbechung 4 – Dilemma 4:**

Stell dir vor, du wärest Bob und / oder Anna – die Leute aus dem Regenwald haben dir vertraut und ihr Wissen mit dir geteilt. Sie sind an einer Kranheit gestorben die du mitgebracht hast.

Was denkst du:

> Sollte man den Eingeborenen die "ganze" Wahrheit über den Vertrag mit der Regierung sagen, welcher es für die Firma unnötig macht, um irgendetwas zu "bitten"?

> Ist es prinzipiellOK, daß "entwickelte" Länder im Regenwald (oder auch anderen bislang eher unerforschten Gebieten) Forschung betreiben, um Dinge zu finden, die unsere Lebensqualität steigern können?

> …über die traurige Tatsache, daß eingeborene Völker häufig ihrer Rechte beraubt werden, wenn es um "das Wohl aller" geht?

> Ist es prinzipiell in Ordnung, daß wir die Rohstoffe des Regenwaldes nützen ohne den Leuten, die dort leben etwas zurückzugeben?

> Falls Du denkst, wir sollten etwas zurückgeben, was könnte dies sein?

Erkläre und begründe Deine Antworten!

Appendix 5D: Rainforest Dilemma in English

Title: Rainforest Dilemma

Curriculum: biology / viruses and bacteria (but I think also suitable for) mathematics/ growth

Two scientists who work for a pharmaceutical company are being sent to Brazil in a remote rainforest area where they are supposed to take plant-samples in order to find a remedy against a virus which is rampaging through the developed world after having been spread from a source in the African rainforests through tourists who came in contact with it.

Anna is a young botanist and works for a pharmaceutical company. She has been with the company for only a few months so she feels very proud when she is being offered a job within a project which will bring her to the Brazilian Rainforest. This journey means for her that the company has recognised her abilities, and if she does a good job she might get promoted.

Bob, who will be travelling with her is a senior researcher and the project-leader. Their task is to find plants that may provide substances useful in the fight against Virus X11, a virus which has recently spread throughout the developed world within a few months, originating from a source in the African Rainforest. The first victims had been two tourists who shortly after arriving back home from their Africa trip started to show signs of disease similar to those of multiple sclerosis, with the degeneration proceeding much faster. The virus seems to be spread by direct contact with a sick person, similar to influenza. The incubation period is between 3 and 6 months. So far, several thousand people across Europe and the US have died, and the health authorities worldwide have finally decided to declare this an epidemic and advise people about possible precautions which in fact are very limited due to the nature of the virus. As the virus has hit without warning there are no vaccines readily available – it seems as if all efforts to produce a vaccine so far have been fruitless, as the virus seems to be mutating fast. Fear is growing everywhere.....

With the virus rampaging through the developed world, the company Bob and Anna are working for has decided to extend the search for a remedy against Virus X11 to the Brazilian Rainforest.

Shortly before their departure to Brazil, Anna starts to feel sick. She is running a temperature and has a runny nose. Somehow she feels that she should rather stay at home and stay in bed, but on the other hand she fears that this journey is a once in a lifetime chance to set up her career. Despite the warning signals from her body she takes off, hoping that flu-tablets will help.

Remember a situation where you really wanted to do something and suddenly there was the chance – and suddenly there was a reason why you potentially could not do it! Now imagine you were Anna, trying to set up a career – and suddenly you get sick shortly before you are planning to travel – How do you think you would decide – travel to Brazil despite feeling sick or rather stay at home?

The journey from Rio de Janeiro to the small village in the middle of the rainforest takes four whole days. The last few hundred kilometres they travel in small boats and on foot. They arrive at night-time and sleep for the next 24 hours, completely exhausted. The first thing they do after waking up is to get in contact with the local native tribe. They have a translator with them. The people are very friendly and curious, and willingly share their knowledge about the local plants with the two foreigners. They show them around and explain to them which plants they use for which purposes….. Anna and Bob take plant samples with them and perform some first analyses in their makeshift laboratory. They take more samples from plants which seem to provide interesting results. Shortly before they are to leave Anna finally loses her battle against the influenza which she has carried around with her all the time and gets seriously sick. Bob looks after her, supported by the Indian people who supply her with tea made from a local plant which relieves the symptoms and brings down the fever within a few days. Soon she feels better and strong enough to leave for home.

The analyses prove that one of the sampled plants has great potential for containing "the" substance needed to produce an effective drug to treat Virus X11. Laboratory tests at the site of the pharmaceutical company have shown promising results. There is just one problem – the essential chemical substance is very unstable and needs to be processed locally - that is, in the village, before this pre-product can finally be transported and manufactured overseas. This, in turn, means that the company has to send laboratory equipment as well as lab-technicians to the village. The effort seems well worthwhile as the exclusive rights for production and sale of "the" drug to treat X11 seem likely to yield big financial gains. To keep these rights exclusive the company has set up a contract with the Brazilian government which allows the company the right of use of the rainforest area surrounding the village for at least the next five years.

When they return to the village to prepare everything for the arrival of lab-personnel, they find that more than half of the villagers have died from influenza. Anna gets really upset, as she realises that it was she who carried the influenza-virus to the native people.

2 – Dilemma 2:

- Anna feels guilty because her wish to pursue her career and to go on this trip despite warning signs, cost the lives of many natives. Knowing about the fatal outcome of Anna's initial decision – do you think she is in one way or the other "guilty" of the death of so many Natives?

- What do you think about this situation: while looking for a cure for a virus which kills thousands of people at home, you bring other viruses and bacteria to people who would not have suffered from them without your visit.

- Travelling to exotic destinations has become an integral part of modern life. BUT there is always the danger of carrying germs with you when travelling: either you carry them to people living in remote areas who have never had contact with these germs before and which might be harmless to you OR you carry germs home with you which you contracted while travelling in foreign countries.
  From this point of view – how do you think these drawbacks of mass-tourism can be prevented?

Explain and justify your answers!

Story continued: In order to build a production-site for the new drug, trees have to be felled, houses and roads have to be built. This means that shortly after the (initial?) arrival of Anna and Bob in the village, construction-workers, building materials and machinery are being brought in by helicopter. In the beginning the natives watch with great interest what is happening to their village. Later their huts are being moved to the outside borders of the village.

Soon the village and the surrounding rainforest have lost any similarity with how they looked before: instead of lush forests, dead tree-stumps decorate the landscape. The newly built roads remind them of scars where the red earth has been torn open, and when it rains they turn into knee-deep mud. The construction workers have built for themselves shelters from corrugated iron which are supposed to protect them from the rain. Soon they start to rust in this climate. The workers have also brought with them alcohol supplies which are supposed to keep their spirits up in the middle of the forest. They offer drinks to the natives and make fun of them when they get drunk quickly…..

> **Interruption 3 – Dilemma 3:**

- How do you think it could be avoided that indigenous people have to suffer (from diseases, loss of cultural identity, destruction of their village-structure etc.) if we take things from the rainforest for our own good?
- How do you think the impact on the environment could be kept to a minimum if a pharmaceutical production-site has to be installed on-site?

Story continued: The elders of the tribe approach the two scientists and ask them," Why has nobody asked our consent for all this?" "Why has nobody asked us whether we want any foreign people here!" "Why has nobody asked us whether it is OK with us to take plants from our rainforest." "Why has nobody asked us whether we want our huts moved to the border of the village!" Bob and Ann feel embarrassed about everything the people say, because they feel that the natives are right. But of course there is the other problem that they do not have the power to change the situation much. The decisions are made overseas, thousands of kilometres away from the little village. So they discuss among each other about how to explain to the elders that there is nothing they can do. The government has already granted the rights of usage of the rainforest to the company for the next five years at least, thus preventing the natives from opposing the plans to go ahead with local production.

> ➤ **Interruption 4 – Dilemma 4:**

Imagine you are Bob and/or Anna - the people from the rainforest have trusted you, have shared their knowledge with you and have died from a disease which you carried to them.

- Do you think you should tell the natives the "whole truth" about the agreement between the government and the company which makes it "unnecessary" for the company to ask (!) anything from the Natives as the government already has granted it full rights?
- Do you think it is OK in principle for the "developed" countries to perform research in the rainforest in order to detect some well-hidden secrets which might help us to improve our (!) standard of living (enhance our health, etc.)?
- What do you think about the sad fact that "for the good of the rest of the world" indigenous people are stripped off their rights?
- Is it OK in principle to make use at all of the resources of the rainforest without giving anything back to the people who traditionally live there?
- If you think we should give something back to the people there – what do you think that might be?

Explain and justify your answers!

Appendix 5E: Rocket Dilemma in German

Titel: Das Raketendilemma - DIE REISE ZUM MOND

Die Geschichte ist über einen Wissenschaftler der von frühester Jugend an die Idee hat eine Rakete zu bauen, die bis zum Mond fliegen kann. Sie basiert grundsätzlich auf der Biographie von Werher von Braun, in dieser Geschichte Herbert von Bösenstein

"Mutter, werde ich einmal zum Mond fliegen?", fragt der kleine Bub seine Mutter, nachdem sie gerade die Gutenachtgeschichte über zwei Kinder die zum Mond fliegen beendet hat. Seine Mutter lächelt ihn an, streicht ihm übers Haar und sagt:"Ich glaube nicht, Herbert! Der Mensch hat bis jetzt noch keine Maschine erfunden, wie heißt es hier im Buch – eine Rakete! – mit der er zum Mond fliegen könnte. Ich glaube nicht, daß er das jemals schaffen wird!" "Ich werde es schaffen! Wenn ich erwachsen bin, baue ich eine Rakete, die zum Mond fliegen kann!" "Ja natürlich, mein Schatz, aber jetzt ist es Zeit zu schlafen. Ich lasse das Licht an für dich…" Herberts Mutter küßt seine Wange und verläßt den Raum. Herbert schaut sich noch einmal die Seite in seinem Buch an, wo die beiden Kinder in die Rakete einsteigen. Er sagt zu sich selbst:"Und ich werde einmal eine Rakete bauen!…."

Als Herbert älter wird sammelt er alles, was mit Raketen zu tun hat: Bücher, Bilder, Zeitungsausschnitte. An seinem zehnten Geburtstag bekommt er ein Buch mit dem Titel "Wie man eine Rakete baut" geschenkt. Er beginnt mit Experimenten im Garten seines Elternhauses. Viele seiner Schulkollegen denken, daß er etwas komisch ist, etwas sonderlich. Sie teilen seine Interessen nicht. Nur einige wenige Freunde finden es toll, bei den Experimenten mitzumachen. Sie diskutieren viele Stunden lang, warum manche Experimente schiefgegangen sind und entwickeln Pläne, wie man das Ganze verbessern könnte. Seine Eltern erkennen sein großes technisches Talent, denken aber immer noch, daß es sich dabei nur um eine Phase handelt. Obwohl sie der Meinung sind, daß ihr Sohn später mal Rechtsanwalt werden soll, unterstützen sie seine "Phase" finanziell. Dies bedeutet für sie keine Schwierigkeiten, da sie sehr reich sind.

An seinem letzten Schultag verkündet Herbert seinen Eltern, daß er nicht daran denke, Recht zu studieren, sondern zusammen mit seinem Freund Andreas technische Physik studieren wolle. Herbert's Vater ist außer sich: "Warum willst du Physik studieren? Da gibt's doch nichts mehr zu erforschen!" Herbert lächelt seinen Vater an und sagt:" Ich hab's dir doch schon gesagt – Ich werde mal eine Rakete bauen, die zum Mond fliegen kann!"

Auf der Universität werden Herberts und Andreas Talent bald von Professor Schubert erkannt, einem Spezialisten in Sachen Raketenbau. Beide werden Mitglieder im

Forschungsteam von Professor Schubert. Ihrer Karriere scheint nichts mehr im Wege zu stehen.

Doch von einem Tag zum anderen ändert sich die politische Situation: ein neues Regime übernimmt die Macht. Die neue Regierung stellt klar, daß in Zukunft nicht jedermann willkommen sein wird in diesem Land. Leute, die nicht mit der Politik der neuen Regierung einverstanden sind, oder Fremde, sogar Leute, deren Eltern oder Großeltern aus dem Ausland vor langer Zeit herkamen, sind nicht mehr willkommen. Viele Leute verlassen das Land. Doch nicht alle können das Land verlassen, da sie das Geld dazu nicht haben.

Auch Professor Schubert geht ins Ausland. Herbert und Andreas fürchten, daß die Forschungsgruppe ohne Schubert auseinanderfallen wird. Sie diskutieren, wie sich ihre Zukunft gestalten könnte und ob sie bleiben oder gehen sollen. Zu dieser Zeit werden Gerüchte laut, daß das neue Regime damit begonnen hat, Gefangenenlager einzurichten, wo alle diejenigen, die es noch nicht geschafft haben, sich ins Ausland abzusetzen, hingebracht werden. Manche sprechen von Folter, andere von Gaskammern. Niemand weiß Genaues. Viele Leute schenken den Gerüchten keinen Glauben – schließlich hat das Regime es geschafft, für alle Arbeitsplätze zu beschaffen und die Wirtschaft anzukurbeln – oder aber sie beschließen einfach über die Gerüchte hinwegzusehen.

Eines Tages werden Andreas und Herbert von einem Regierungsbeamten angesprochen. Der Beamte erzählt ihnen, daß der Staatsführer sehr beeindruckt sei von ihren Plänen eine Rakete zu bauen, die zum Mond fliegen kann. Er offeriert Herbert die Stelle, die Schubert innegehabt hatte, und Andreas die seines Assistenten. Er verspricht großartige Forschungsbedingungen und großzügige finanzielle Unterstützung, all das worauf Herbert und Andreas so lange schon gehofft hatten.

➢ Unterbrechung 1 – Dilemma 1:

Die neue Position als Forschungsteamleiter in Zusammenhang mit der finanziellen Unterstützung von der Regierung kann die Umsetzung von Herberts und Andreas Traum herbeiführen. Endlich könnten sie die Gelegenheit bekommen "ihre" Rakete zu bauen. Ihr Traum könnte wahr werden.

- Herbert und Andreas müssen eine Entscheidung treffen: Stell Dir vor, Du wärst Herbert – würdest Du das Angebot der Regierung annehmen? In welcher Weise würden die Gerüchte bezüglich Folter und Gefangenenlager Deine Entscheidung beeinflussen? Begründe Deine Erklärung!

Fortsetzung der Geschichte:

Herbert beschließt das Angebot anzunehmen und schafft es schließlich auch den widerstrebenden Andreas zu überzeugen. Er erklärt Andreas, daß sie so eine Gelegenheit "die Rakete zum Mond" zu bauen vielleicht nie wieder bekommen werden. Die beiden Forscher arbeiten Tag und Nacht um ihrem Ziel näher zu kommen, doch die Erfolge sind kläglich: die meisten Starts enden als Fehlversuche. Ein Regierungsbeamter erklärt ihnen, das der Staatsführer endlich Erfolge sehen wolle, und seine Geduld bereits überstrapaziert sei:" Das Land ist am Rande eines Krieges und wir brauchen diese Raketen, um Sprengsätze in die Städte des Feindes zu schießen!" "Ja aber da werden Zivilisten getötet!", ruft Andreas entsetzt aus. "Na klar," meint der Beamte,"darum geht es ja bei der ganzen Forschung hier, um Waffen!" Herbert, der nie im Sinne hatte, daß "seine" Raketen gegen Menschen eingesetzt werden sollen, fragt:"Was ist mit dem Mond? Wann werden wir Raketen bauen können, die zum Mond fliegen können?" "Später, später!", sagt der Beamte.

> ➤ Unterbrechung 2 – Dilemma 2:

Herbert ist zerrissen zwischen seinem Gewissen, welches ihm rät keine Raketen zu bauen, die für Kriegszwecke eingesetzt werden können und seiner Angst, daß er andrerseits womöglich nie wieder eine derartige Gelegenheit bekommen wird, "seine Rakete" zu bauen, und seinen Traum zu erfüllen.

- Herbert und Andreas erkennen plötzlich, daß sie keine freien Männer mehr sind. Sie haben die Wahl zwischen im Land zu bleiben und ihr Programm fortzusetzen oder das Land zu verlassen und womöglich ihren Traum aufgeben zu müssen. Stell' Dir vor, Du wärest Herbert, knapp vor der Erfüllung Deines Traumes – wie würdest Du entscheiden? Warum? Rechtfertige Deine Entscheidung!

Fortsetzung der Geschichte:

Andreas verläßt das Land – Herbert bleibt. Er versucht das Beste darauszumachen und versucht die unangenehmen Tatsachen zu ignorieren, um seinen Traum verwirklichen zu können. Die Regierung möchte Erfolge sehen und sie bekommt sie. Bald verlangt das Regime höhere Produktivität bei der Raketenerzeugung – Häftlinge aus den Gefangenenlagern werden als Arbeitskräfte herangezogen. Sie bekommen nicht genügend zu essen, viele sind krank und sterben durch die harte Arbeit. Die Arbeit mitten im Elend stumpft ab: Herbert beginnt in den Gefangenen immer mehr nur noch "Material" zu sehen, "Testmaterial". Er denkt immer noch an seinen Mondflug mit Menschen an Bord. Ihm ist klar, daß gewisse Probleme, die mit dem bemannten Mondflug auftreten könnten, nur durch Versuche mit Menschen geklärt bzw. minimiert werden können. Bald erhält er von der Regierung die Erlaubnis mit Häftlingen als Testmaterial zu experimentieren. Viele dieser "Versuchsmenschen" überleben nicht. Dennoch werden durch diese Versuche wichtige Erkenntnisse gesammelt für die bemannte Raumfahrt.

Heutzutage verkehren Spaceshuttles schon fast regelmäßig zwischen Erde und Weltall. Die Übertragung des Start bzw. der Landung eines Spaceshuttles im Fernsehen ist nach wie vor noch immer ein erhebender Moment.....

Hast Du schon jemals darüber nachgedacht, , um welchen Preis die Verwirklichung des uralten Traums der Menschheit vom Flug ins Weltall ermöglicht wurde?

- **Unterbrechung 3 – Schlußdilemma:**

Denke an Herbert und seinen Traum und welcher Preis dafür bezahlt werden mußte.....

Viele Wissenschaftler haben "große" Träume z.B. Idealmenschen zu erschaffen , Waffen zu bauen, die gefährlicher sind, als alles was man bisher gekannt hat etc. etc.....

- Wie weit soll wissenschaftliche Forschung gehen dürfen?
- Ist es unter gewissen Umständen angemessen, daß einige (in Herberts Fall Häftlinge) für das Wohl der ganzen Menschheit (z.B. den Traum von der Mondfahrt) geopfert werden? Warum? Erkläre Deine Antwort!

Appendix 5F: Rocket Dilemma in English

The story is about a scientist who has got this idea from early childhood onwards to build a rocket to fly to the moon. He spends most of his free time together with his friends experimenting in the backyard at first, in the local woods later. At the uni he meets one of the best teachers he could get and learns a great deal from him.

"Mother will I fly to the moon one day?" asks the little boy after his mother has finished reading a story from his favourite book to him, a book about two children flying to the moon. His mother smiles at him, runs her hand through his curly hair and says, "I don't think so, Herbert! Man has not yet built vehicles, what do they call them here "rockets", to fly to the moon and I can't think, he ever will!" "When I grow up, I will build a rocket which can fly to the moon." "Yes, my love, but now it's time to sleep. I leave the light on for you....." Herbert's mother kisses his cheek and leaves the room. Herbert looking at the picture in the book showing the little children entering the rocket, says to himself, "And I will build a rocket one day...."

As Herbert grows older he collects everything that has something to do with rockets, books, pictures, newspaper-articles. On his tenth birthday he gets a book with the title "How to build a rocket" He starts to experiment in his backyard. Many of his classmates do not share his passion and think he is queer, but some of his friends find interest in his idea. They spend hours discussing why certain experiments went wrong and develop plans on how to improve the set-up. His parents recognising his great technical talent and skills still think it is just a phase. Despite the fact that they want their son to become a lawyer one day, they support his ideas financially which is not a problem for them as they are quite wealthy.

On his last day at school he breaks the news to his parents that he does not intend to study Law, but that he and his best friend Andreas are going to study technical physics instead. Herbert's father is beside himself, "What do you want do study physics for?, he asks his son, "There is nothing left to be discovered!" Herbert smiles at his father and says, "I told you – I want to build a rocket which can fly to the moon ...."

At the university Herbert´s and Andreas´ talents are soon discovered by Professor Schubert who is a specialist in the area of rocket-research. Both become members of Schubert´s research team. Their careers seem to work out fine until.

From one day to the other the political situation in the country changes: a new regime takes over power. The new government makes it very clear that in the future not everybody will be welcome any more in this country. People who do not agree with the regime´s policies, foreigners who were not born in this country and people whose parents or grandparents came from different countries long time ago, are suddenly confronted with the situation that they have to leave (if they can, that is, if they have got the money to do so!).

Professor Schubert has to leave the country. Herbert and Andreas fearing that the research group will fall apart without Schubert spend long evenings discussing their future and whether they should leave the country or stay on. At this time rumours are spread that the new regime has started to establish prison camps for those who have not left yet. But as with everything, information is scarce and nobody really knows what is going on. Some sources speak of torture, others from gas-chambers. Many people do not believe the stories about the camps or prefer not to see the problem - after all the new government has given them jobs and improved the countries economy One day a government-official approaches Herbert and Andreas and offers them the great opportunity to run their own research group. He tells them that the countries´ new leader has been impressed by their plans to build a rocket which would fly to the moon. He promises substantial funding and explains to them that the new government is extremely interested in their research. He offers the position of team-leader to Herbert and the position of his assistant to Andreas.

➢ | Interruption 1 – Dilemma 1:|

The new position as a research-team-leader plus the funding from the government can ensure the realisation of Herbert´s and Andreas´ dream. Finally they could have the opportunity to build a rocket which can fly to the moon. Their dream might finally become true......

- Herbert and Andreas have to make a decision: Imagine you were Herbert – would you accept the government´s generous offer despite what the rumours say about prison-camps and gas-chambers? Explain your answer!

Story cont.: Herbert decides to take on the job-offer and he successfully convinces Andreas that despite the flaws of the new government this situation offers them the best possible opportunity to get closer to the realisation of their dream – the rocket to the moon. The two researchers work day and night to build rockets which can be successfully launched and will not fall back to the earth after a few hundred metres. Their experiments are not very successful at first. A government official tells them, "You must be aware that the countries leader is getting impatient about your little success. The country is on the brink of war. We need your rockets to carry explosives to the enemies´ cities!" "But then you are going to kill innocent civilians!" Andreas exclaims. The official smiles," Well, that´s what it´s all about...." Herbert who had never in mind that his rockets should harm anyone, asks, " But what about the moon? When will we build rockets to fly to the moon?" "Later, later!", the offical says.

> **Interruption 2 – Dilemma 2:**

Herbert is torn between his conscience which tells him not to build rockets which are suitable for war-purposes and his fear that otherwise he might not be able to fulfil his dream.

- Andreas and Herbert realise that they are no longer free men. They have got the choice between staying on and leaving the country. Imagine you were Herbert , how would you decide? Would you give up your dream ? Explain your answer!

```
He stays on again. The regime wants more and better results,
the production has to be increased. Prisoners from
concentration camps are being used as slaves. By that time he
has given up inhibitions about people's lives. "the idea" has
taken over his thinking! Facing problems which he cannot
solve without experimenting with humans , he even becomes
part of the man-torturing machinery himself.
```

Andreas leaves the country – Herbert stays on. He tries to make the best out of it by ignoring the ugly facts in favour of his work and his dream. The government wants to see successes. Finally his rockets fly. Soon the government demands higher productivity. Prisoners from concentration-camps are being used as labourers. They do not get enough food, most are weak and sick. Many die because of the hardships. Herbert starts to see these people as "material", as "non-human test-material". Soon he gets the government's permit to use prisoners as test-persons for his rocket research. As many of the experiments end unsuccessfully the "participants" die in due course.

After the war is over Herbert continues with his research. He has made great progress and finally he and his team manage to build a rocket suitable for the travel to the moon. The rocket carries men with them – a fact only made possible by the experiments using live humans! ….

Nowadays space-shuttles travel to and from space on an almost regular basis. Have you ever thought about the price which had to be paid to make this old dream of mankind possible?

> ➤ **Interruption3 – Final Dilemma3:**

Thinking of Herbert and his dream and the price which had to be paid for its fulfilment….

Many scientists have "great dreams" e.g. "building ideal human beings", "building weapons more dangerous than anything the world has ever seen before" etc. etc.

- How far should science be allowed to go?
- Is it acceptable under certain circumstances that some (in Herbert's case the prisoners) are being sacrificed for the good of the whole (humankind 's dream of flying to the moon)?
- Explain your answers!

Appendix 6

Bundesministerium fur Unterricht und Kunst (1998):
Austrian National Curriculum Document
Excerpt from The overarching curriculum statement

Appendix 6: The overarching curriculum statement (Excerpt)

4. AUFGABENBEREICHE DER SCHULE

Wissensvermittlung

Zur Vermittlung fundierten Wissens als zentraler Aufgabe der Schule sollen die Schülerinnen und Schüler im Sinne eines lebensbegleitenden Lernens zur selbstständigen, aktiven Aneignung, aber auch zu einer kritisch-prüfenden Auseinandersetzung mit dem verfügbaren Wissen befähigt und ermutigt werden.

Die Schülerinnen und Schüler sollen lernen, in altersadäquater Form Problemstellungen zu definieren, zu bearbeiten und ihren Erfolg dabei zu kontrollieren.

Kompetenzen

Eine so erworbene Sachkompetenz bedarf allerdings der Erweiterung und Ergänzung durch Selbst- und Sozialkompetenz. Die Entwicklung der eigenen Begabungen und Möglichkeiten, aber auch das Wissen um die eigenen Stärken und Schwächen sowie die Bereitschaft, sich selbst in neuen Situationen immer wieder kennen zu lernen und zu erproben, ist ebenso Ziel und Aufgabe des Lernens in der Schule wie die Fähigkeit und Bereitschaft, Verantwortung zu übernehmen, mit anderen zu kooperieren, Initiative zu entwickeln und an der Gestaltung des sozialen Lebens innerhalb und außerhalb der Schule mitzuwirken („dynamische Fähigkeiten").

Die Förderung solcher dynamischer Fähigkeiten soll die Schülerinnen und Schüler auf Situationen vorbereiten, zu deren Bewältigung abrufbares Wissen und erworbene Erfahrungen allein nicht ausreichen, sondern in denen Lösungswege aktuell entwickelt werden müssen.

Es ist wichtig, dass Schülerinnen und Schüler lernen, mit Sachthemen, mit sich selbst und mit anderen auf eine für alle Beteiligten konstruktive Weise umzugehen. Sie sollen Sachkompetenz, Selbstkompetenz und Sozialkompetenz in einem ausgewogenen Verhältnis entwickeln.

Religiös-ethisch-philosophische Bildungsdimension

Die Schülerinnen und Schüler stehen vor den Fragen nach Sinn und Ziel und ihrem Verlangen nach einem sinnerfüllten Leben in einer menschenwürdigen Zukunft. Bei der Suche nach Orientierung bieten Religionen und Weltanschauungen ihre Antworten und Erklärungsmuster für eine eigenständige Auseinandersetzung an. In den Unterrichtsgegenständen ist auf philosophische und religiöse Erklärungs- und Begründungsversuche über Ursprung und Sinn der eigenen Existenz und der Welt einzugehen. Junge Menschen sollen Angebote zum Erwerb von Urteils- und Entscheidungskompetenz erhalten, um ihr Leben sinnerfüllt zu gestalten. Orientierungen zur Lebensgestaltung und Hilfen zur Bewältigung von Alltags- und Grenzsituationen sollen die Schülerinnen und Schüler zu einem eigenständigen und sozial verantwortlichen Leben ermutigen. Die Achtung vor Menschen, die dabei unterschiedliche Wege gehen, soll gefördert werden. Diese Zielsetzungen bilden die Grundlage für eine fächerübergreifende und vernetzte Zusammenarbeit und vervollständigen damit die Beiträge der Unterrichtsgegenstände und Bildungsbereiche zur umfassenden Bildung der jungen Menschen.

5. BILDUNGSBEREICHE

Bildung ist mehr als die Summe des Wissens, das in den einzelnen Unterrichtsgegenständen erworben werden kann. Im Folgenden werden daher weitere Ziele der Allgemeinbildung in fünf Bildungsbereichen näher erläutert. Sie sind als Benennung wichtiger Segmente im Bildungsprozess zu verstehen und bilden ebenso wie die religiös-ethisch-philosophische Bildungsdimension eine Grundlage für die fächerverbindende und fächerübergreifende Zusammenarbeit. Die Bildungsbereiche bieten gemeinsam mit den Zielen in den Abschnitten "Aufgabenbereiche der Schule" und "Leitvorstellungen" den Bezugsrahmen für die Einordnung jener Beiträge, die die einzelnen Unterrichtsgegenstände für den gesamten schulischen Bildungsprozess zu leisten haben.

In den Bildungsbereichen sind auch jene Zielsetzungen enthalten, die von folgenden Unterrichtsprinzipien vertreten werden: Gesundheitserziehung, Erziehung zur Gleichstellung von Frauen und Männern, Medienerziehung, Musische Erziehung, Politische Bildung, Interkulturelles Lernen, Sexualerziehung, Lese- und Sprecherziehung, Umwelterziehung, Verkehrserziehung, Wirtschaftserziehung, Erziehung zur Anwendung neuer Technologien, Vorbereitung auf die Arbeits- und Berufswelt.

Bildungsbereich Sprache und Kommunikation

Ausdrucks-, Denk-, Kommunikations- und Handlungsfähigkeit sind in hohem Maße von der Sprachkompetenz abhängig. In jedem Unterrichtsgegenstand sind die Schülerinnen und Schüler mit und über Sprache – zB auch in Form von Bildsprache – zu befähigen, ihre kognitiven, emotionalen, sozialen und kreativen Kapazitäten zu nutzen und zu erweitern. Die Auseinandersetzung mit unterschiedlichen Sozialisationsbedingungen ermöglicht die

Einsicht, dass Weltsicht und Denkstrukturen in besonderer Weise sprachlich und kulturell geprägt sind.

Wenn die Begegnung mit anderen Kulturen und Generationen sowie die sprachliche und kulturelle Vielfalt in unserer eigenen Gesellschaft als bereichernd erfahren wird, ist auch ein Grundstein für Offenheit und gegenseitige Achtung gelegt.

Ein kritischer Umgang mit und eine konstruktive Nutzung von Medien sind zu fördern.

Bildungsbereich Mensch und Gesellschaft

Das Verständnis für gesellschaftliche (insbesondere politische, wirtschaftliche, rechtliche, soziale, ökologische, kulturelle) Zusammenhänge ist eine wichtige Voraussetzung für ein befriedigendes Leben und für eine konstruktive Mitarbeit an gesellschaftlichen Aufgaben.

Die Schülerinnen und Schüler sind zu einem verantwortungsbewussten Umgang mit sich selbst und mit anderen anzuleiten, insbesondere in den Bereichen Geschlecht, Sexualität und Partnerschaft. Sie sollen lernen, Ursachen und Auswirkungen von Rollenbildern, die den Geschlechtern zugeordnet werden, zu erkennen und kritisch zu prüfen.

Die Verflochtenheit des Einzelnen in vielfältige Formen von Gemeinschaft ist bewusst zu machen; Wertschätzung sich selbst und anderen gegenüber sowie Achtung vor den unterschiedlichen menschlichen Wegen der Sinnfindung sind zu fördern.

Es ist bewusst zu machen, dass gesellschaftliche Phänomene historisch bedingt und von Menschen geschaffen sind und dass es möglich und sinnvoll ist, auf gesellschaftliche Entwicklungen konstruktiv Einfluss zu nehmen. Aufgaben und Arbeitsweisen von gesellschaftlichen Institutionen und Interessengruppen sind zu vermitteln und mögliche Lösungen für Interessenskonflikte zu erarbeiten und abzuwägen.

Der Unterricht hat aktiv zu einer den Menschenrechten verpflichteten Demokratie beizutragen. Urteils- und Kritikfähigkeit sowie Entscheidungs- und Handlungskompetenzen sind zu fördern, sie sind für die Stabilität pluralistischer und demokratischer Gesellschaften entscheidend. Den Schülerinnen und Schülern ist in einer zunehmend internationalen Gesellschaft jene Weltoffenheit zu vermitteln, die vom Verständnis für die existenziellen Probleme der Menschheit und von Mitverantwortung getragen ist. Dabei sind Humanität, Solidarität, Toleranz, Frieden, Gerechtigkeit, Gleichberechtigung und Umweltbewusstsein handlungsleitende Werte.

Die Vorbereitung auf das private und öffentliche Leben (insbesondere die Arbeits- und Berufswelt) hat sich an wirtschaftlicher Leistungsfähigkeit, sozialem Zusammenhalt, einer für beide Geschlechter gleichen Partizipation und ökologischer Nachhaltigkeit zu orientieren. Dabei sind auch Risiken und Chancen der neuen Technologien zu berücksichtigen.

Die Auseinandersetzung mit religiösen und philosophischen Erklärungs- und Begründungsversuchen über Ursprung und Sinn der eigenen Existenz und der Existenz der Welt ist eine wichtige Aufgabe der Schule.

Bildungsbereich Natur und Technik

Die Natur als Grundlage des menschlichen Lebens tritt in vielfältiger, auch technisch veränderter Gestalt in Erscheinung. Die Kenntnisse über die Wirkungszusammenhänge der Natur sind als Voraussetzung für einen bewussten Umgang und die Nutzung mit Hilfe der modernen Technik darzustellen.

Verständnis für Phänomene, Fragen und Problemstellungen aus den Bereichen Mathematik, Naturwissenschaft und Technik bilden die Grundlage für die Orientierung in der modernen, von Technologien geprägten Gesellschaft.

Der Unterricht hat daher grundlegendes Wissen, Entscheidungsfähigkeit und Handlungskompetenz zu vermitteln. Die Schülerinnen und Schüler sind zu befähigen, sich mit Wertvorstellungen und ethischen Fragen im Zusammenhang mit Natur und Technik sowie Mensch und Umwelt auseinander zu setzen. Als für die Analyse und Lösung von Problemen wesentliche Voraussetzungen sind Formalisierung, Modellbildung, Abstraktions- und Raumvorstellungsvermögen zu vermitteln.

Bildungsbereich Kreativität und Gestaltung

Gedanken und Gefühle verbal und nonverbal zum Ausdruck zu bringen, ist eine wesentliche Lebensform der Menschen. Den Schülerinnen und Schülern ist Gelegenheit zu geben, selbst Gestaltungserfahrungen zu machen und über Sinne führende Zugänge mit kognitiven Erkenntnissen zu verbinden. Dabei eröffnet sich für sie die Chance, individuelle Fähigkeiten zu entdecken und zu nutzen und sich mit den Ausdrucksformen ihrer Mitmenschen auseinander zu setzen. Daraus sollen sich Impulse für das Denken in Alternativen, für die Relativierung eigener Standpunkte, für die Entwicklung eines kritischen Kunstverständnisses und für die Anerkennung von Vielfalt als kultureller Qualität ergeben. Die kreativ-gestaltende Arbeit soll im Spannungsfeld von Selbstverwirklichung und sozialer Verantwortung als individuell bereichernd und gemeinschaftsstiftend erlebt werden.

Bildungsbereich Gesundheit und Bewegung

Unter Bewusstmachung der Verantwortung für den eigenen Körper ist körperliches, seelisches und soziales Wohlbefinden zu fördern. Die Schülerinnen und Schüler sind zu unterstützen, einen gesundheitsbewussten und gegenüber der Umwelt und Mitwelt verantwortlichen Lebensstil zu entwickeln. Im Sinne eines ganzheitlichen Gesundheitsbegriffs ist ein Beitrag zur gesundheits- und bewegungsfördernden Lebensgestaltung zu leisten.

Im Vordergrund stehen dabei die Förderung von motorischen und sensorischen Fähigkeiten, wobei den Schülerinnen und Schülern Kompetenz für eine bewegungsorientierte Gestaltung ihrer Freizeit auch im Hinblick auf einen späteren Ausgleich zur beruflichen Beanspruchung zu vermitteln ist. Durch die Auseinandersetzung mit Gesundheitsthemen wie Ernährung,

Sexualität, Suchtprävention, Stress ist sowohl das körperliche als auch das psychosoziale Wohlbefinden zu fördern.

Die Schülerinnen und Schüler sollen lernen, sich am Straßenverkehr sicher und unfallverhütend zu beteiligen, technische Haushaltseinrichtungen risikobewusst zu nutzen und gefährliche Stoffe verantwortungsbewusst einzusetzen und zu entsorgen.

Appendix 7

Habermas' Human Interests

Appendix 7: Habermas' Human Interests

Grundy draws on Habermas when she proposes to reflect on the three basic human interests that influence how knowledge is constructed (Grundy, 1987; Taylor & Campbell-Williams, 1992)

- Technical Interest has a basic orientation towards controlling and managing the environment. Grundy point out the predominance of this interest in most modern school curricula and in classroom practice. The result is a product oriented curriculum where knowledge is regarded as a commodity. A mechanistic skills-based view of teaching determines classroom practice.
- Practical Interest has an orientation towards understanding. In this view curriculum regards teachers and students as subjects concerned with meaning-making activities. The teacher becomes an interpreter of curriculum documents rather than a technical implementer. He/she is an active participant in decision making.
- Emancipatory Interest has an orientation towards autonomy and responsibility. Grundy identifies ideology as a set of ideas of a powerful group in a culture which dominate the perceptions and actions of the majority of less powerful members of the culture (Grundy, 1987). With regard to science and science education, I would like to identify the predominant ideology as that of scientism, the purely materialistic view of science that negates values, negates subjectivity and overemphasises science's objective nature, and it denies, as Wilber states, the "real" existence of "inner landscapes" (Wilber, 1997).

Appendix 8

Tales of the Field – excerpts from fieldnotes

APPENDIX 8A: FIELDWORK
APPENDIX 8B: CONVERSATION WITH 'J.'
APPENDIX 8C: DISAPPOINTMENT

Appendix 8A: Excerpt 1 – week1

7.5 – arrival in Vienna

8.5 – drive from Vienna to Graz, meeting with Irene, who keeps this day free for me which allows us to get started with the organisation of the project shortly after my arrival. We set up a preliminary timeframe. Irene is very keen on getting Sabine involved as soon as possible but as it soon turns out – due to different teaching duties (and other private duties!) I haven´t managed yet to get the two of them together in one place.

Irene starts by introducing her class to me using a class-list, informing me about the characteristics of her class which is really very special: students from 8 nations, 3 continents, 9 different mother-tongues and 5 different religions. Many of the students have had a turbulent past: one has been a child-slave, another one arrived in Austria as an unaccompanied juvenile refugee from Mongolia, two years ago without a word of German – by now he writes German tests without spelling-mistakes and is one of the best students in the class! Another one (half Austrian) was taken to South Africa by his mother, spent his childhood in slums and was finally put onto a plane to Austria just by himself. The authorities here put into an orphanage etc. In general the class is seen by colleagues as friendly, collaborative and having a good attitude toward work in class. Despite this the general academic outcomes are surprisingly low for some students (not necessarily the foreign students though!!).

Met Sabine afterwards in the staff-room. Decided to meet her on Tuesday in a nearby café.

9.5 – Meeting with Sabine
Introducing her to what I intend to do and why and how….
Great to see that she has got some knowledge about Constructivism - she has recently started to work for Prof. You know who? – Dr. Schwanz ehm Schwetz!
She seems to be keen on getting started, reveals to me later though that she had also enrolled for a seminar which she considers extremely important and therefore would appreciate, if I planned around her. This means for me that my initial time-frame starts to crumble. I feel disappointed and a bit set up because after all I have been in email-contact since last June, more or less to get things organised! Anyway – I have to be happy that she collaborates at all

10.5. – Joining Sabine in her class, the 6A, for a physics-lesson. She teaches both Mathematics and Physics in this class and combines the two successfully. Her class has got an interesting group-structure characterised by a group of leaders (girls!) and the ones who do not belong to this group!
After class Sabine does the same thing Irene has done before – she introduces her class to me using the class-list. In this case I find it easier to relate to the different people because I have seen them before. She too gives me a lot of background information about her class. Contrary to the other class this one consists mainly of Austrian students with fairly normal backgrounds. The main characteristics and differences lie rather in the social behaviour and backgrounds respectively

I personally find it more difficult to relate to Sabine than to Irene which certainly has something to do with the fact that I have known Irene for years and that she has a "motherly" attitude toward me. Sabine is about my age, maybe even a bit younger, a bit shy (maybe?). She is certainly very engaged and interested though! I also found it a bit difficult to relate to Sabine´s class. She introduced me shortly to the class but as I could not speak without a voice, it was difficult to build up a rapport. Have to do that next week!

11.5. meeting Irene´s class. The fact that I can relate better to Irene´s class might have 3 different reasons: 1) some of the students are former students of mine, of course eager to find out whether I would still recognise them 2) they are a very friendly class in general 3) Irene was having them work on worksheets while she was walking with me from desk to desk and introducing every student personally to me. Of course like that I got a chance to talk to single students on a very personal level.

Afternoon: meeting with Irene at her house, invitation for coffee plus first interview: general information about herself: reasons for becoming a science teacher, her teaching style, her duties, finally the ethical basis of her teaching and the reasons for collaborating in this project about moral education. Very fruitful! Was never really like an interview, more like an in-depth conversation!

12.5. transcribing of interview

13./14.5. Salzburg

Tales of the field – Week2

15.5. - units 1 and 2 – dilemma 1 with Irene´s class, the 5A. The teacher for Catholic religious education offers his class to us so that we can have two units. He also offers to record the class with the video-camera during the first unit which allows me to concentrate on the events in the classroom. Neither of us manages to get the camera to focus properly, so we decide to continue with the recording despite the problems. As it turns out later – a tiny little button had to be pressed and oh magic everything became focused again! – but before that I encountered other problems in addition to the lack of focus. Suddenly during the second unit the battery went flat and I had to use the audio-recorder instead which means that for parts of the teaching unit I have got video-data, but not for the rest. Problem with the audio-recording of course is, that the general noise-level is very high, and thus difficult to understand what single students say! Irene spends a lot of time at the beginning of class with administrative and general issues which costs a lot time which means in the end that we cannot finish the dilemma within two units (which isn´t a problem normally)…..

After the unit we talk about our impressions, what was good, bad, needs improvement and how etc…..also very fruitful! Some students come up with really interesting comments.

Interesting is also that only three of the students immediately understand the spiritual connection between the boy/man and the tree which his parents want to cut down: these are the two African students and the Mongolian (Buddhist) boy!

General problem with the story is that it seems very easy, very low-level up to the point where we had to stop, so many students might have got the impression that Irene was telling them (the grown-ups!) a baby-story. The really challenging parts would have come afterwards...we´ll see this afternoon, when we continue where we had stopped on Monday.....

Continued to interview Irene in greater detail about her ethical background, her experiences teaching this unit, her challenges, her role as a learner.

Afternoon: transcribing of interview-data and of our evaluation-meeting

16.5. – transcribing ctd.

17.5. – arrived at the school around 10, finished the transcriptions, printed them out. Met Irene later, had her read the texts plus two impressionist tales which I wrote immediately after meeting her class for the first time and the first dilemma-unit respectively. She liked it.

Had an interesting discussion afterwards when she said that she was a completely unsuitable person to "philosophise with her students"....took me a while to convince her that that what she´s doing with her class more or less all the time, at least every time when she tries to get them to reflect on certain issues and look at things critically, is a form of philosophising. I had the impression she was really proud of herself in the end!

Afternoon in the library: students would normally have three biology-lab-units, Mr. Krumpholz, a biology teacher who originally had decided not to participate in the project, joined us because he would normally be team-teaching with Irene. He decided to play the video-man. After a while he got so interested in the whole thing that he started to read the story and started commenting on what he thought about it all (I´ll write an extra account of that). I received a wonderful feedback of him which I really appreciate because he is known as a person who is very critical of new things. During these units the students dealt with the last two dilemmas of the tree-dilemma, worked together in groups of five, each group produced a poster and presented it to the whole class. Worked out pretty well. Following the last dilemma Irene summarised the contents of the posters and moderated a whole group discussion. As usual in the beginning it took a while until the discussion really took off but when it did, the students had to be reminded of the negotiated rules of communication several times because they got so excited that some of them even, stood up to make their points clear. One who couldn´t wait any longer took his skate-board, sat down on it and rolled right in the middle of the discussion-circle. Interestingly the main discussants were students who until then seemingly had been rather disinterested – all wrong, they had very well thought about the dilemmas and came up with really interesting arguments. I hope that the video and the audio-tape will yield good documentation. Haven´t had time yet to check the quality out. But it was really great – at the end of the third unit Irene had to finish the discussion more or less abruptly because the time was over but the students kept on discussing on their way out. Good to hear that the German teacher will pick up the story and the arguments and will have them work on essays!

General impression: Class very slow!!! When working on questions, no matter whether by themselves or in a group. Asked Irene whether they might be trying to make time but she thinks that they are always like that. Maybe this has to do with their multiculturality?

18.5. – Interviewed two students, one originally from Iran, the other one originally from Bosnia, both speak German fluently – general outcome – they liked it a lot!

19.5. – Interviewed 4 students. Problems with one of the African students – he finds it difficult to express himself in German, especially when it comes to feelings, later when we switch over to English I find out that he has got the same problems in English and I start to suspect that talking about feelings is something he is definitely not used to do (cultural?). I found Austrian students much more open in this regard, with regard to gender the girls were much more open than the boys. I interviewed three boys and three girls, 3 Austrians and three migrants. I chose the students according to their contributions during the units – those who showed a lot of engagement, one student who excelled at first by contributing only useless comments, but suddenly really took off when the discussion started. – the interview showed that he hadn´t taken the whole thing seriously in the beginning but had suddenly found it interesting and was really excited about the dilemmas and the way of teaching…..
I received very positive but also some negative comments mainly to do with the organisation of the groups: one girl didn´ t appreciate that after a while Irene chose to put the groups together instead of letting them choose – I explained this reason to her. Later she – a very intelligent but also highly critical student who is going through a phase of general opposition against everything! -- also asked me why I had chosen to do this in the Natural Sciences branch of the school – she seemed to be happy with my explanation afterwards.

20./21.5. weekend – transcription of interviews, posters, watched the video – worked out well after all!

Tales of the field – week3

22.5. – 2nd dilemma with Irene – Tells the story very lively and freely – after all the rainforest is her special topic of interest, so she can weave in personal stories and experiences – she does it really well. This time the class works really well, except for one student – the other ones seem to be interested, most comments are well thought through and show personal engagement. The girl who asked me critical questions during her interview was very collaborative and engaged during this unit.
As they know already how things work, they are much faster than last time.
Quite a number of students are absent (7)- normally this unit would be a Catholic Religion class, so many students of other denominations do not have to come to this unit – but Irene has told them quite clearly on Friday that they would have to come as this unit would be used for the project. After a while 4 students come along – Irene is pretty furious – they claim that they hadn´ t been aware that they were expected to come earlier etc…..
Sabine has told me this morning that she will have to postpone her first dilemma again!!!
Crisis! Considering the fact that one dilemma story takes at least three units with the students of this school, time seems to be running out for her class!
I cannot quite understand why this class (Irene´ s class takes so long for everything – maybe it is just this special class but maybe it´ s also to do with the fact that Irene had to get used to

this type of teaching, while for me this is the style I´m used to....like she felt really stressed out by moderating the discussion last week!

23.5. – Conversation with Karin, a chemistry-teacher. She asks me about my project and wants to know details. During the conversation she talks about some really interesting aspects of "her" ethics of teaching chemistry This is when I decide that it might be interesting to interview some other teachers as well who are not directly involved in this project.
Krumpi rushes in and asks me for the tree-story: he wants to try it out with his grade 6 students. I introduce him shortly to the HOW and WHY to use dilemma stories. Later he tells me – "It worked fabulously!"
I also contact Christa Bauer the coordinator of the Schulverbund Graz-West to get some publications about the Schulverbund. I find out that there is a series of publications written for the Department of Education and which includes topics such as Alternative Teaching Approaches, Social Learning, Organisation of the Schulverbund etc. etc. I pick out what I think might eb useful for my purposes. Christa is very interested in the whole project and wants to see "a class in action". She has promised to come to Irene´s class on the 25th!

24.5. – Interview with Sabine
Finally I get Sabine for an interview. The outcome is very promising. She has got a lot of interesting views is interested in Nature of Science, critical of the truth claims of science and mathematics.

Appendix 8B: Conversation with J.

„Was machst du eigentlich in deinem Projekt?"
Versuche zu erklären, worum´s mir geht, was ich mache, wie ich´s mache.
K. fragt mich ob er die Geschichte mal lesen kann.

„Wenn ich die Geschichte so lese, rieselt s mir ganz kalt über den Rücken – wir müssen besonders aufpassen, weil wir haben gleich zwei Geburtsbäumchen für unseren Sohn! Mir gefällt die ganze Sache wirklich gut."
„Ich mach´ das ja auch in meinem Unterricht – versuche solche Dilemmas anzusprechen!"
Lily: "Ich hab´ das auch immer versucht, hab´ es aber immer extrem unangenehm empfunden, dass ich nicht das Gefühl hatte, dies so unterrichten zu können, das ich die Schüler auch persönlich erreichen kann."
Krumpi: „Was mich interessieren würde ist, wie kann man feststellen, ob die Schüler auch was lernen, ob da irgendetwas hängen bleibt?"

Versuche anhand der Prinzipien des Konstruktivismus zu erklären, welche Rolle der Lehrer hat, wie der Schüler lernt und warum es eigentlich darauf ankommt einen Denkanstoß zu geben.

Nachdem K. einige Zeit gefilmt hat und die Schlussdiskussion losbricht – K.: „ Das funktioniert ja super!"

Appendix 8C: Theresia

Dealing with disappointment

Disappointment about the two colleagues who had promised to collaborate.
Theresia a very (!) engaged biology-teacher had promised to collaborate with me because she felt it was very important to deal with ethical issues in her science teaching, according to the first email she had sent to me. Her interest seemed to abate as soon as I had asked the teachers to write a journal regarding their role as a teacher and a learner within this project about moral education. I received an email which expressed her fears about the use of the journal in my research. I responded by explaining to her about the "hows and whys" regarding the use of journals. She replied to me telling that she felt reassured by what I had told her but still – after this email she stopped the correspondence altogether.

For some naïve reason I had thought that she would explain her reasons for her withdrawal to me when I would get to Austria – instead I found that she seemed to "avoid" me – might be a personal impression only. I have tried to talk with her not to accuse her or make her feel guilty but because I am interested in the reasons why she suddenly decided not to collaborate. So far she has always produced reasons why she could not possibly talk to me "now"!

Walter the physics teacher who conveyed to Irene obvious enthusiasm about participating in the project, never responded to my emails at all. After a while I had given up the illusion that he might still get involved. When I meet him now he does not even pretend that he has no time – he simply does not mention the project at all!

But maybe I just feel disappointed because I think I as a co-researcher would have handled the situation differently - I would have tried to explain the reasons as to why I could not or would not participate. But I as the researcher will finally have to accept that different people handle the same situation differently – sounds so clear from a rational point of view – still a source of disappointment from the emotional point of view.

Appendix 9

Interview structure

Appendix 9A: Interview structure group-interview
Fokusgruppeninterview

THEMA: MORALERZIEHUNG IM NATURWISSENSCHAFTLICHEN UNTERRICHT

Lehransatz

- Wie hat euch der Lehransatz (Dilemmageschichte, Unterbrechungen, Diskussionen) zur Moralerziehung gefallen. Was war gut?
- Was war verbesserungswürdig?
- Für wie sinnvoll hältst du Moralerziehung im Rahmen des naturwissenschaftlichen Unterrichts grundsätzlich?

Werteerziehung

- Was bedeutet der Begriff „Wert" für dich?
- Was hast du über die Werte deiner Mitschüler gelernt?
- Wie glaubst du, kannst du diese Erkenntnis in Deinem zukünftiges Leben anwenden?

Lehr und Lernziele: Kommunikation, Kompromissbereitschaft, kritisches Denken:
- Wie hast du die Einzelarbeit, das „Für-Sich-Selbst-Überlegen-Müssen", empfunden?
- Wie war es für dich in der Gruppe deine Meinungen, Deine Werte mit denen anderer zu vergleichen und zu diskutieren?
- Wie leicht war es für dich, unterschiedliche Meinungen/Werte anderer zu akzeptieren?
- In wieweit hat die Diskussion in der Gruppe deine eigene Meinung/Werte beeinflusst?
- Wie hast du die Dilemmasituation/Wertekonflikt erlebt?

- Was denkst du, wie gut...
-hast du deine Meinung vertreten können?
-ist deine Meinung von den Mitschülern akzeptiert worden?
-sind Konflikte gehandhabt worden?
-sind Kompromisse gefunden worden?

Deiner Meinung nach, wie sehr:

- Wird kritisches Denken gefördert?
- Wird Kompromissbereitschaft gefördert?
- Wird die Fähigkeit gefördert auf andere Leute einzugehen?

Lehrerrolle: Deine Meinung

- Mir war immer klar, was ich zu tun habe, wie der Arbeitsauftrag lautet?
- Die Geschichte war vom Ablauf her klar und nachvollziehbar?
- Die Lehrerin hat das Akzeptieren anderer Meinungen gefördert?
- Die Lehrerein hat uns auf problematische Bereiche hingewiesen?
- Die Lehrerin hat in der Diskussion (nach Möglichkeit) alle zu Wort kommen lassen?
- Die Lehrerin hat in der Diskussion mit gezielten Fragen die Diskussion am Laufen erhalten?

Appendix 9B: Interview structure single interviews

- Was war gut an diesem Lehransatz?
- Hat es etwas gegeben das du nicht gemocht hast?
- Wie gut war die Kooperation mit deinen Mitschülern?
- Wie sinnvoll, glaubst du, ist es diesen Lehransatz fur Ethikerziehung zu verwenden?
- Sollte Ethikerziehung Teil des natruwisenschaftlichen Unterrichts sein?

2nd interview:
- Wie hat dir der Unterricht diesmal gefallen?
- Was war gut/besser als letztes Mal?
- Was war schlechter?

Appendix 10

Interviews coded in NVivo

Appendix 10A: Example of a coded interview

·Gibt dir der Lehransatz grundsätzlich gefallen?
Also ich geb's ehrlich zu am Anfang hab' ich's echt blöd gefunden

·Warum?
Weiß nicht, es hat mich nicht so interessiert. Ich war nicht so ganz dabei und je länger ich das dann angehört hab', jetzt ich bin voll begeistert von der Geschichte gewesen. Am Anfang wie ich's gehört hab', hab' ich nur auf die Uhr geschaut, wann ist endlich die Stunde vorbei. Aber jetzt wo ich weiß worum's gegangen ist und die ganze Geschichte gehört hab', bin ich ganz begeistert, weil so was haben wir noch nie gemacht in der Schule. Es ist auch irgendwie in einer lustigen Form erzählt worden am Anfang. Es hat mir schon gefallen.

·Das war das am Anfang was dir das Gefühl gegeben hat, es ist fad?
Weil's schon angefangen hat mit Peter und es gibt einen Baum. Es war einfach nicht so interessant wie im Zeichentrickfilm wurde es erzählt, aber dann wie ich das alles gehört hab' und wie's abgelaufen ist, und ich geb's auch zu ich hab' mich vorher für Pflanzen nicht so interessiert. Mein Interesse ist dadurch etwas mehr geworden. Kommt mir vor. Kann auch sein dass ich mich dadurch etwas mehr geworden. Kommt mir Begeistert erzählt, was ich nicht jeden tag über die Schule mach'. Aber ich war schon begeistert.

·Wenn du jetzt so denkst wie's gelaufen ist, was würdest du daran ändern?
Es war schon gut, dass wir's alle gehört haben, aber es wäre vielleicht besser gewesen, wenn wir die Geschichte so in Kleingruppen gehört hätten und nachher dass wir's dann zusammen besprochen hätten, zuerst einmal in Kleingruppen, aber es wäre sicher mühsam gewesen jedem die Geschichte zu erzählen, in Kleingruppen erzählen und dann nachher in der Gruppe besprechen was jeder so davon haltet und nachher der ganzen Klasse präsentieren.

·Grundsätzlich wenn du dann denkst, die Fr. Kok hat's jetzt erzählt, man hätte ja auch noch andere Möglichkeiten, man könnt es z.B. ausstellen für jeden oder vorlesen...
Na, da hätte sowieso keiner Interesse es ist sowieso besser wenn man eine Geschichte selber erzählt. Zu lesen oder im Buch, ich mein' so ist es ja viel interessanter so. Wenn man ja zu. Wenn man's jemand erzählt kann man sich irgendwas vorstellen. Wenn man's liest ist es nicht so interessant. Wenn man's erzählt kann man sich viel besser in die Situation hineinversetzen. Ist vielleicht ein bisschen interessanter. Für mich jedenfalls war's halt so!

·Weil wir jetzt gerade davon reden sich in eine Situation hineinversetzen Ihr seid ja praktisch immer gebeten worden, euch in die Situation hineinzuversetzen. Wie hast du das empfunden?
Am Anfang war's so schwer weil ich überhaupt kein Interesse gehabt hab', darum hab' ich mich nicht hineinversetzen können, aber dann, wie ich die Geschichte gehört hab' immer länger es war nicht so leicht. Trotzdem ich hab' mich nicht so wohl gefühlt.

·Offensichtlich ist nun zurückgekommen, dass jeder seine eigene Meinung hat wie war das jetzt für dich das rauszufinden?
Am Anfang war' s schon eine bisschen anstrengend überall mitzuhören und so und bei manchen Sachen hab' ich auch damit übereingestimmt, aber sonst, es war. Ich hab' oft aufgezeigt und bin auch oft drangekommen, aber es war schwer, weil man sich nicht ganz so richtig durchsetzen. Es ist eine große Klasse. Es hat jeder seine Meinung, auch wenn' s manchmal nicht wichtig ist, aber es ist halt schwer, sich manchmal durchzusetzen. Wenn man sagt es ist zehn gegen zehn, aber wenn ich jetzt eine bin, die eine völlig andere Meinung hat es ist auch das erste mal dass unsere klasse bei so was mitmacht, so richtig das auch mitgefühlt hat, weil, ich persönlich hab' unsere Klasse noch nie so erlebt. Dass jeder so gespannt zugehört hat, dass mich so gewundert, weil es ist eigentlich ja eine vollaute Klasse.

·Dworauf führst du das zurück?
Jo, überhaupt, in Mathe z.B.

·Dwas glaubst du das diesmal anders war?
Ich weiß es selber nicht. Am Anfang hab' ich jeden angeschaut, ganz lang sogar, und hab' gesehen, dass jeder ganz interessiert zuhört, aber ich glaub' ich war am Anfang die einzige, die am Anfang nicht so interessiert war, an der Geschichte. Je länger ich' s dann angehört dann, ich weiß nicht, dass ich so schnell dann eine andere Meinung gehabt hab'?! Wie ich schon gehört hab', der Peter" und ,der Baum" Die Frau Roll hat das auch so lustig erzählt und es war so macht' s einem auch Spaß zu lernen. Es war wirklich toll!

·Dwas würdest du sagen, wie sinnvoll ist es, so was, praktisch so eine Wertediskussion, nachdenken über eigene Werte gerade im naturwissenschaftlichen Unterricht durchzuführen? Weil ich kann mir vorstellen, das z.B. in Fächern wie Religion, man so was viel öfter macht.

Ich finde es schon sinnvoll und wir das glaub' ich ja auch noch weiterhin verfolgen und in Bio machen wir das ja sowieso auch noch weiter. Ich denke mir, so kann sich jeder auch einiges merken. Ich glaub', das kann jetzt nicht so schnell jeder vergessen. Jeder wird das in Erinnerung behalten.

·Dglaubst du, dass es so was wie Nachwirkungen geben könnt?
Ja schon! Wenn ich jetzt im Wald bin im Wald bin ich werde sicher anders denken. jetzt nach der Geschichte. 100 Prozent bin ich mir sicher!

Wenn du da jetzt ein bisschen konkreter wirst bei den Nachwirkungen, was könnten z.B. solche Nachwirkungen sein?
Ich persönlich hab' mich bei der Geschichte auch wohlgefühlt und einerseits auch nicht! Es war so komisch am Anfang war ich so glücklich und nachher hab' ich mich irgendwie so zusammenziehen müssen. So ein Gefühl hab' ich nicht gehabt in der Schule. Einerseits war ich eh ganz super, aber dann hab' ich gemerkt, dass je länger ich die Geschichte anhöre, es geht um einen Baum, aber das ist schon einiges, das ist schon viel, das ist was ganz Grosses,...weiß nicht...so ein Gefühl hab' ich noch nie gehabt, so richtig! Und ich hatte mir nie gedacht, dass wir so was im naturwissenschaftlichen Zweig machen....

·□Ist das was ihr im Unterricht öfters macht? Wo ihr z.B. konkret gebeten werdet über etwas persönlich nachzudenken, oder eure eigene Meinung kundzutun?

□Je schon. Aber wenn ich jetzt an den Peter denk' - ich hätt' s genauso schwer gehabt es war wirklich eine schwere Entscheidung. obwohl es sagt jeder so leicht, das war nur ein Baum. Wenn man die ganze Geschichte gehört hätte, dann ist es nicht so leicht. auch wenn' s nur ein Baum ist ∟nein es ist wirklich nicht so leicht! Es ist schwer nachher zu denken, was würde ich machen? Und dort wo wir unsere eigene Meinung hinschreiben haben müssen, da hab' ich mir auch so schwer getan wenn ich der Peter war', was hätte ich gemacht?

□Ihr seid ja im Anschluss an dieses Einzelnachdenken gebeten worden, mit anderen Leuten zu vergleichen. Wie war das für dich? Für mich war das sehr schwer, weil wir haben uns ein paar mal gestritten. Das ist normal nie der Fall, dass was wirklich so heftig...Es haben viele gesagt, es geht ja nur um einen Baum. Was streitet ihr darum, aber ich hab'...ich weiß nicht, es war so als ob ich das alles mitgemacht hätte und da hab' ich nicht mit anhören können, weil wir haben immer zum Streiten anfangen müssen. es war nicht leicht, weil jeder hat was anderes gesagt und einer hat gesagt: .Man kann doch den Baum einfach wegschneiden!' aber ich weiß nicht. ich war nicht der Meinung

·□Du weißt welche Meinung du selbst hast, aber gerade solche Dinge spricht man ja an und für sich in normalen Gesprachen nicht so an. Die kommen eigentlich nicht so zur Sprache d.h. man vergleicht relativ selten, seine Werte mit jenen der anderen. Wie war das jetzt für dich raus zu finden, dass z.B. andere Leute die du gut kennst, vielleicht eine ganz andere Meinung gehabt haben?

Manchmal war' s überraschend und manchmal war' s auch enttäuschend. Wenn ich daran denk' dass meine beste Freundin eine ganz andere Meinung gehabt hat als ich. obwohl ich sie solange kenn' und es hört sich fast so an bisschen lächerlich an ich war entäuscht, dass sie das geschrieben hat, dass sie den Baum eigentlich wegschneiden würde. Da war ich wirklich überrascht und hab' gedacht:.He, das gibt' s ja nicht?!' Und das hab' ich ihr auch nicht gesagt...trotzdem, ich weiß nicht, manchmal war auch nicht so richtig ernst genommen und haben irgendetwas hingeschrieben. Es ist auch nicht leicht, sich in die Situation hineinzuversetzen, wenn' s einen interessiert und so, wird das auch gehen

·□Diese Situation, die du gerade angesprochen hast, du sagst, du warst enttäuscht oder überrascht hat diese Situation zum Umdenken geführt manchmal?

Ja schon. Nicht so. Aber dann daheim, es hat schon immer wieder Moment gegeben, wo ich daran gedacht hab':.Warum hat sie nicht das Gleiche wie ich?' Gefragt hab' ich nicht. Aber ich denk' schon manchmal darüber nach jetzt auch, obwohl' s jetzt ja nur von gestern ist, aber trotzdem, das gibt' s ja nicht, es hat jeder verschieden Meinungen das ist klar. aber jetzt denkt man warum? Vielleicht hat derjenige oder diejenige eine gute Begründung. aber ich selber hab' die Begründung nicht gefunden...

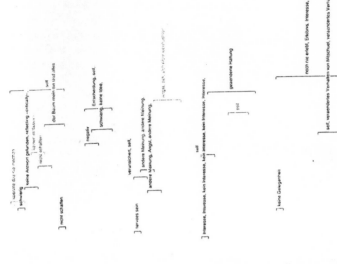

·Wenn du jetzt sagst, du hast dich zusammenziehen müssen, wenn du an das denkst, in welchen Situationen ist das aufgetreten?
Genau wo die Frage war: „Wenn du Peter wärst, würdest du den Baum selber schneiden?" Also ich könnte das nie machen! Es war nicht besonders schön ich hab' auch sehr lange überlegen müssen und trotzdem hab' ich's nicht geschafft die zu beantworten, weil ich würde sogar nicht einmal jemand anderen dranlassen an den Baum. Ich würd' es auch selber nicht schaffen! Sicher nicht. Da bin ich mir sicher, weil der Baum muss für mich ja mein ein und alles sein irgendwie, wenn ich dem 35 oder 33 Jahre großgeworden bin? Dann würd' ich's auch nicht über's Herz bringen.

·Die Situation die du gerade beschrieben hast war praktisch immer dann, wenn du an ein moralisches Dilemma gekommen bist ich empfinde eine negative Ja, genau. Das war immer so immer war es eigentlich konzentrieren können. Es war Entscheidung ich hab' mich nicht so richtig konzentrieren können. Es war so schwer und mir ist nichts eingefallen dabei. ich hab' mir gedacht: . ich hab' mir gedacht ich steh' vor was Gott was für einer Entscheidung.

·Wie hast du das jetzt ganz persönlich empfunden, welche Gefühle hat das in dir ausgelöst?
ich war so nervös am Anfang beim Schreiben. Ich hab' da herumgefragt: „Was schreibt's denn ihr? Was schreibt's denn ihr?" Es hat mir eh nichts gebracht weil es hat jeder seine eigene Meinung gehabt. Es war nicht ein schönes Gefühl, wenn man nicht weiß was man jetzt machen soll und da herumfragen muss so als ob man vor einer Prüfung steht und nichts kann! So hab' ich mich gefühlt! Genauso!

·In solche Situationen kommt man oft im Leben! Was glaubst du, kannst du aus dem ganzen mitnehmen für dein Leben?
ich war früher überhaupt nicht so auf Pflanzen, auf „Gieß' jetzt die Blumen!" oder „Geh' in den Garten!", aber jetzt, jetzt hör' ich schon. mehr zu und so und das mach' ich jetzt auch. Durch die Geschichte hab' ich ein anderes Gefühl am Anfang war's überhaupt nicht so, aber jetzt gestern noch die drei Stunden die haben auch...jetzt ist's ganz anderes Gefühl, für mich persönlich positiv, dass ich jetzt mehr darauf achte und da schau' ich jetzt schon mehr! Das heißt jetzt nicht: „Oh ich geh' auf die Wiese jetzt nicht!" Ich achte jetzt schon mehr drauf

·Wenn du jetzt an die zusammenarbeit mit den anderen denkst habt' ihr so in Unterricht Gelegenheit solche Dinge zu diskutieren?
Eben nicht. das ist ja so schade. ich hab' das so noch nie gemacht. also nur so spontan, so kurz oder so aber nicht so ein Thema. nicht so richtig und jetzt wo wir's gemacht haben hat jeder auch interesse, dass weiterhin solche Themen bearbeitet werden wie das es war einfach ein richtiges Erlebnis. Ich glaub' das war nicht nur ich es war, die kein Interesse gezeigt glaub' eigentlich nicht dass nur ich es war, die kein Interesse gezeigt hat. das waren mehrere v.a. der Sascha der ist normalerweise nicht so, dass er so interessiert ist. der ist wirklich....das hab' ich so super gefunden

·Über hat sich ja bei der Diskussion dann voll mitbeteiligt
Ja der ist normalerweise nicht so!

·Wenn du das ganze als Moralerziehung siehst für wie wichtig hältst du

dass das im naturwissenschaftlichen Unterricht praktiziert wird?
Ja, ich halt's schon für wichtig, nicht nur für die 5. wahrscheinlich
kann man das für die 6. und für die 7. Klasse auch noch brauchen. Wer
weiß, vielleicht kann ich ja auch für die 8. irgendeine Arbeit darüber
schreiben! Muss ja nicht nur sein, dass ich's jetzt brauch' und ich muss
ja nicht nur das beschreiben ich kann dann ja auch meine eigenen Gefühle
beschreiben z.B. es muss ja nicht sein, dass ich die ganze Geschichte
noch einmal aufschreib'. kann ja auch andere Dinge schreiben, die mir so
nahe stehen von dem....

·□Für wichtig hältst du es dass es überhaupt unterrichtet wird?
Ja ich halte das schon für wichtig. Also ich denke schon dass ich das
noch weiter brauchen werde. Nicht nur in der 5., ich denke schon, dass
ich in der 8. auch noch drüber schreiben kann.

·□Sonst noch irgendetwas, das du mir mitteilen möchtest?
Nein, es war wirklich ein Supererlebnis, so die Geschichte und ich hoffe
wir werden noch weiterhin solche Sachen machen.

·□Danke!

selt, Erlebnis, future,

selt, selt,

selt

selt

wichtig fuer Zukunft, unquotierbare,

Appendix 10B: Coding report

NVivo revision 2.0.161   Licensee: smec-203-1

Project: Fichte 22   User: Administrator   Date: 2/08/2003 - 2:50:30 PM
DOCUMENT CODING REPORT

Document: interview Fatima 1
Created: 14/06/2001 - 6:10:55 PM
Modified:22/06/2001 - 5:05:01 PM
Description:

18.5.2000

Nodes in Set: All Nodes
Node 1 of 179   (1 13 1) /learning experience/learning process/learning
Passage 1 of 1   Section 1.1, Para 47, 154 chars.

47: Ich denke mir, so kann sich jeder auch einiges merken. Ich glaub', das kann jetzt nicht so schnell jeder vergessen. Jeder wird das in Erinnerung behalten.

Node 2 of 179   (1 13 1 3) /learning experience/learning process/learning/forgetting
Passage 1 of 1   Section 1.1, Para 47, 154 chars.

47: Ich denke mir, so kann sich jeder auch einiges merken. Ich glaub', das kann jetzt nicht so schnell jeder vergessen. Jeder wird das in Erinnerung behalten.

Node 3 of 179   (1 13 4) /learning experience/learning process/listen to others
Passage 1 of 1   Section 1.1, Para 37, 66 chars.

37: Am Anfang war' s schon ein bisschen anstrengend überall mitzuhören

---

Node 4 of 179   (1 13 5) /learning experience/learning process/compare with others
Passage 1 of 1   Section 1.1, Para 34, 42 chars.

34: Warum hat sie nicht das Gleiche wie ich?"

Node 5 of 179   (1 13 6) /learning experience/learning process/observe~watch others

43: Am Anfang hab´ ich jeden angeschaut, ganz lang sogar, und hab´ gesehen, dass jeder ganz interessiert zuhört,

---

Node 6 of 179   (1 13 6 1) /learning experience/learning process/observe~watch others/veraendertes Verhalten
von Mitschuel

68: der Sascha, der ist normalerweise nicht so, dass er so interessiert ist, der ist wirklich....das hab´ ich so super gefunden

---

71: Ja der ist normalerweise nicht so!

Node 7 of 179   (1 13 6 2) /learning experience/learning process/observe~watch others/Interesse

7: Weiß´ nicht, es hat mich nicht so interessiert.

10: Weil´ s schon angefangen hat mit Peter und es gibt einen Baum. Es war einfach nicht so interessant

---

10: ich hab´ mich vorher für Pflanzen nicht so interessiert. Mein Interesse ist dadurch etwas mehr geworden, kommt mir vor.

16: da hätte sowieso keiner Interesse es ist sowieso besser wenn man eine Geschichte selber erzählt. Zu lesen oder im Buch

---

16: so ist es ja viel interessanter, so hört man ja zu

16: Wenn man´ s liest ist es nicht so interessant.

20: Am Anfang war´ s so schwer weil ich überhaupt kein Interesse gehabt hab

---

30: Es ist auch nicht leicht, sich in die Situation hineinzuversetzen, wenn´ s einen interessiert und so, wird das auch gehen

43: Am Anfang hab´ ich jeden angeschaut, ganz lang sogar, und hab´ gesehen, dass jeder ganz interessiert zuhört,

43: ich glaub´ ich war am Anfang die einzige, die am Anfang nicht so interessiert war, an der Geschichte

65: Ich war früher überhaupt nicht so auf Pflanzen,

68: Eben nicht, das ist ja so schade. Ich hab´ das so noch nie gemacht, also nur so spontan, so kurz oder so aber nicht so ein Thema, nicht so richtig und jetzt wo wir´ s gemacht haben hat jeder auch Interesse, dass weiterhin solche Themen bearbeitet werden wie das. Es war einfach ein richtiges Erlebnis. Ich glaub´ das war nicht nur ich am Anfang, ich glaub´ eigentlich nicht dass nut ich es war, die kein Interesse gezeigt hat, das waren mehrere v.a. der Sascha, der ist normalerweise nicht so, dass er so interessiert ist, der ist wirklich....das hab´ ich so super gefunden

Node 8 of 179   (1 13 6 2 1) /learning experience/learning process/observe~watch others/Interesse/kein Interesse

7: Weiß´ nicht, es hat mich nicht so interessiert.

10: Weil´ s schon angefangen hat mit Peter und es gibt einen Baum. Es war einfach nicht so interessant

10: ich hab´ mich vorher für Pflanzen nicht so interessiert.

16: da hätte sowieso keiner Interesse es ist sowieso besser wenn man eine Geschichte selber erzählt. Zu lesen oder im Buch

16: Wenn man´ s liest ist es nicht so interessant.

20: Am Anfang war´ s so schwer weil ich überhaupt kein Interesse gehabt hab

---

43: ich glaub´ ich war am Anfang die einzige, die am Anfang nicht so interessiert war, an der Geschichte

---

65: Ich war früher überhaupt nicht so auf Pflanzen,

68: Eben nicht, das ist ja so schade. Ich hab´ das so noch nie gemacht, also nur so spontan, so kurz oder so aber nicht so ein Thema, nicht so richtig und jetzt wo wir´ s gemacht haben hat jeder auch Interesse, dass weiterhin solche Themen bearbeitet werden wie das. Es war einfach ein richtiges Erlebnis. Ich glaub´ das war nicht nur ich am Anfang, ich glaub´ eigentlich nicht dass nut ich es war, die kein Interesse gezeigt hat, das waren mehrere v.a. der Sascha, der ist normalerweise nicht so, dass er so interessiert ist, der ist wirklich....das hab´ ich so super gefunden

---

34: aber dann daheim, es hat schon immer wieder Moment gegeben, wo ich daran gedacht hab´

34: aber ich denk´ schon manchmal darüber nach jetzt auch,

56: ich hab´ auch sehr lange überlegen müssen und trotzdem hab´ ich s nicht geschafft die zu beantworten,

---

16: sich irgendwas vorstellen.

30: Es ist auch nicht leicht, sich in die Situation hineinzuversetzen, wenn´ s einen interessiert und so, wird das auch gehen

---

Node 12 of 179   (1   13   13   2   10   3) /learning   experience/learning   process/decisionmaking/reflecting ~critically~/sich hineinversetzen koennen/sich hineinversetzen

Passage 1 of 6   Section 1.1, Para 16, 79 chars.

16: Wenn man´ s erzählt kann man sich viel besser in die Situation hineinversetzen.

Passage 2 of 6   Section 1.1, Para 20, 123 chars.

20: Am Anfang war´ s so schwer weil ich überhaupt kein Interesse gehabt hab´, darum hab´ ich mich nicht hineinversetzen können,

---

Passage 3 of 6   Section 1.1, Para 23, 34 chars.

23: wenn ich jetzt an den Peter denk´

Passage 4 of 6   Section 1.1, Para 23, 205 chars.

23: Es ist schwer nachher zu denken, was würde ich machen? Und dort wo wir unsere eigene Meinung hinschreiben haben müssen, da hab´ ich mir auch so schwer getan wenn ich der Peter wär´, was hätte ich gemacht?

Passage 5 of 6   Section 1.1, Para 26, 48 chars.

26: es war so als ob ich das alles mitgemacht hätte

Passage 6 of 6   Section 1.1, Para 30, 121 chars.

30: Es ist auch nicht leicht, sich in die Situation hineinzuversetzen, wenn´ s einen interessiert und so, wird das auch gehen

---

Node 13 of 179   (1   13   13   2   12) /learning   experience/learning   process/decisionmaking/reflecting ~critically~/nach dem Grund fragen

Passage 1 of 1   Section 1.1, Para 34, 79 chars.

34: es hat jeder verschieden Meinungen das ist klar, aber jetzt denkt man warum?

Node 14 of 179   (1 13 13 4 1) /learning experience/learning process/decisionmaking/Schwierigkeit/schwierig

Passage 1 of 10   Section 1.1, Para 23, 113 chars.

23: wenn ich jetzt an den Peter denk´ - ich hätt´ s genauso schwer gehabt es war wirklich eine schwere Entscheidung,

---

Passage 2 of 10   Section 1.1, Para 23, 59 chars.

23: dann ist es nicht so leicht auch wenn´s nur ein Baum ist

Passage 3 of 10   Section 1.1, Para 23, 151 chars.

23: Und dort wo wir unsere eigene Meinung hinschreiben haben müssen, da hab´ ich mir auch so schwer getan wenn ich der Peter wär´, was hätte ich gemacht?

Passage 4 of 10   Section 1.1, Para 26, 22 chars.

26: es war nicht so leicht

Passage 5 of 10   Section 1.1, Para 30, 121 chars.

30: Es ist auch nicht leicht, sich in die Situation hineinzuversetzen, wenn´s einen interessiert und so, wird das auch gehen

---

Passage 6 of 10   Section 1.1, Para 37, 66 chars.

37: Am Anfang war´s schon ein bisschen anstrengend überall mitzuhören

---

Passage 7 of 10   Section 1.1, Para 37, 128 chars.

37: Ich hab´ oft aufgezeigt und bin auch oft drangekommen, aber es war schwer, weil man kann sich nicht ganz so richtig durchsetzen.

Passage 8 of 10   Section 1.1, Para 37, 122 chars.

37: Es hat jeder seine Meinung, auch wenn´s manchmal nicht wichtig ist, aber es ist halt schwer, sich manchmal durchzusetzen.

Passage 9 of 10   Section 1.1, Para 56, 28 chars.

56: Es war nicht besonders schön

Passage 10 of 10   Section 1.1, Para 59, 151 chars.

59: Es war so schwer und mir ist nichts eingefallen dabei. Ich hab´ mir gedacht: „ ich hab´ mir gedacht ich steh´ vor weiß Gott was für einer Entscheidung.

Node 15 of 179   (1 13 13 4 2) /learning experience/learning process/decisionmaking/Schwierigkeit/muehsam
Passage 1 of 1   Section 1.1, Para 13, 200 chars.

13: es wäre sicher mühsam gewesen jedem die Geschichte zu erzählen, in Kleingruppen erzählen und dann nachher in der Gruppe besprechen was jeder so davon haltet und nachher der ganzen Klasse präsentieren.

Passage 1 of 2   Section 1.1, Para 23, 113 chars.

23: wenn ich jetzt an den Peter denk´ - ich hätt´ s genauso schwer gehabt es war wirklich eine schwere Entscheidung,

Passage 2 of 2   Section 1.1, Para 59, 273 chars.

59: Das war immer so immer war es eigentlich eine negative Entscheidung ich hab´ mich nicht so richtig konzentrieren können.Es war so schwer und mir ist nichts eingefallen dabei. Ich hab´ mir gedacht: „ ich hab´ mir gedacht ich steh´ vor weiß Gott was für einer Entscheidung.

Passage 1 of 1   Section 1.1, Para 59, 122 chars.

59: Das war immer so immer war es eigentlich eine negative Entscheidung ich hab´ mich nicht so richtig konzentrieren können.

Passage 1 of 1   Section 1.1, Para 59, 151 chars.

59: Es war so schwer und mir ist nichts eingefallen dabei. Ich hab´ mir gedacht: „ ich hab´ mir gedacht ich steh´ vor weiß Gott was für einer Entscheidung.

Passage 1 of 1   Section 1.1, Para 56, 102 chars.

56: ich hab´ auch sehr lange überlegen müssen und trotzdem hab´ ich s nicht geschafft die zu beantworten,

Passage 1 of 1   Section 1.1, Para 34, 53 chars.

34: aber ich selber hab´ die Begründung nicht gefunden...

34: Vielleicht hat derjenige oder diejenige eine gute Begründung,

---

56: Genau wo die Frage war: „Wenn du Peter wärst, würdest du den Baum selber schneiden?" Also ich könnte das nie machen!

56: Ich würd´ es auch selber nicht schaffen! Sicher nicht. Da bin ich mir sicher,

---

56: Dann würd´ ich ´s auch nicht über´ s Herz bringen.

26: Für mich war das sehr schwer, weil wir haben uns ein paar mal gestritten. Das ist normal nie der Fall, dass war wirklich so heftig...Es haben viele gesagt, es geht ja nur um einen Baum, was streitet ihr darum, aber ich hab´.., es war so als ob ich das alles mitgemacht hätte und da hab´ ich...ich weiß nicht, es war nicht so leicht, ich hab´ , das einfach nicht mit anhören können, weil wir haben immer zum Streiten anfangen müssen, es war nicht leicht jeder hat was anderes gesagt und einer hat gesagt: „Man kann doch den Baum einfach wegschneiden!" aber ich weiß nicht, ich war nicht der Meinung

---

26: Für mich war das sehr schwer, weil wir haben uns ein paar mal gestritten. Das ist normal nie der Fall, dass war wirklich so heftig...Es haben viele gesagt, es geht ja nur um einen Baum, was streitet ihr darum, aber ich hab´.., es war so als ob ich das alles mitgemacht hätte und da hab´ ich...ich weiß nicht, es war nicht so leicht, ich hab´ , das einfach nicht mit anhören können, weil wir haben immer zum Streiten anfangen müssen, es war nicht leicht jeder hat was anderes gesagt und einer hat gesagt: „Man kann doch den Baum einfach wegschneiden!" aber ich weiß nicht, ich war nicht der Meinung

Passage 1 of 3   Section 1.1, Para 37, 128 chars.

37: Ich hab' oft aufgezeigt und bin auch oft drangekommen, aber es war schwer, weil man kann sich nicht ganz so richtig durchsetzen.

Passage 2 of 3   Section 1.1, Para 37, 122 chars.

37: Es hat jeder seine Meinung, auch wenn' s manchmal nicht wichtig ist, aber es ist halt schwer, sich manchmal durchzusetzen.

Passage 3 of 3   Section 1.1, Para 37, 102 chars.

37: Wenn man sagt es ist zehn gegen zehn, aber wenn ich jetzt eine bin, die eine völlig andere Meinung hat

Passage 1 of 3   Section 1.1, Para 26, 131 chars.

26: Für mich war das sehr schwer, weil wir haben uns ein paar mal gestritten. Das ist normal nie der Fall, dass war wirklich so heftig.

Passage 2 of 3   Section 1.1, Para 26, 76 chars.

26: Es haben viele gesagt, es geht ja nur um einen Baum, was streitet ihr darum,

Passage 3 of 3   Section 1.1, Para 26, 49 chars.

26: weil wir haben immer zum Streiten anfangen müssen

Passage 1 of 1   Section 1.1, Para 7, 80 chars.

7: Aber jetzt wo ich weiß worum' s gegangen ist und die ganze Geschichte gehört hab

Passage 1 of 1   Section 1.1, Para 53, 132 chars.

53: je länger ich die Geschichte anhöre es geht um einen Baum, aber das ist schon einiges, das ist schon viel, das ist was ganz Grosses

(1 13 17 12) /learning experience/learning process/meaningmaking~/nach dem Grund fragen
Section 1.1, Para 34, 28 chars.

34: aber jetzt denkt man warum?

(1 13 17 13) /learning experience/learning process/meaningmaking~/Verstehen
Section 1.1, Para 7, 80 chars.

7: Aber jetzt wo ich weiß worum´ s gegangen ist und die ganze Geschichte gehört hab

(1 13 17 13 1) /learning experience/learning process/meaningmaking~/Verstehen/Bedeutung
Section 1.1, Para 53, 132 chars.

53: je länger ich die Geschichte anhöre es geht um einen Baum, aber das ist schon einiges, das ist schon viel, das ist was ganz Grosses

(1 14 1) /learning experience/dilemmastoryapproach/Interesse
Section 1.1, Para 7, 48 chars.

7: Weiß´ nicht, es hat mich nicht so interessiert.

Section 1.1, Para 10, 99 chars.

10: Weil´ s schon angefangen hat mit Peter und es gibt einen Baum. Es war einfach nicht so interessant

Section 1.1, Para 10, 120 chars.

10: ich hab´ mich vorher für Pflanzen nicht so interessiert. Mein Interesse ist dadurch etwas mehr geworden, kommt mir vor.

Section 1.1, Para 16, 119 chars.

16: da hätte sowieso keiner Interesse es ist sowieso besser wenn man eine Geschichte selber erzählt. Zu lesen oder im Buch

Section 1.1, Para 16, 50 chars.

16: so ist es ja viel interessanter, so hört man ja zu

Section 1.1, Para 16, 47 chars.

16: Wenn man´ s liest ist es nicht so interessant.

20: Am Anfang war´ s so schwer weil ich überhaupt kein Interesse gehabt hab

30: Es ist auch nicht leicht, sich in die Situation hineinzuversetzen, wenn´ s einen interessiert und so, wird das auch gehen

43: Am Anfang hab´ ich jeden angeschaut, ganz lang sogar, und hab´ gesehen, dass jeder ganz interessiert zuhört,

43: ich glaub´ ich war am Anfang die einzige, die am Anfang nicht so interessiert war, an der Geschichte

65: Ich war früher überhaupt nicht so auf Pflanzen,

68: Eben nicht, das ist ja so schade. Ich hab´ das so noch nie gemacht, also nur so spontan, so kurz oder so aber nicht so ein Thema, nicht so richtig und jetzt wo wir´ s gemacht haben hat jeder auch Interesse, dass weiterhin solche Themen bearbeitet werden wie das. Es war einfach ein richtiges Erlebnis. Ich glaub´ das war nicht nur ich am Anfang, ich glaub´ eigentlich nicht dass nut ich es war, die kein Interesse gezeigt hat, das waren mehrere v.a. der Sascha, der ist normalerweise nicht so, dass er so interessiert ist, der ist wirklich....das hab´ ich so super gefunden

7: Weiß´ nicht, es hat mich nicht so interessiert.

10: Weil´ s schon angefangen hat mit Peter und es gibt einen Baum. Es war einfach nicht so interessant

10: ich hab´ mich vorher für Pflanzen nicht so interessiert.

16: da hätte sowieso keiner Interesse es ist sowieso besser wenn man eine Geschichte selber erzählt. Zu lesen oder im Buch

---

Passage 5 of 9   Section 1.1, Para 16, 47 chars.

16: Wenn man´ s liest ist es nicht so interessant.

Passage 6 of 9   Section 1.1, Para 20, 71 chars.

20: Am Anfang war´ s so schwer weil ich überhaupt kein Interesse gehabt hab

---

Passage 7 of 9   Section 1.1, Para 43, 100 chars.

43: ich glaub´ ich war am Anfang die einzige, die am Anfang nicht so interessiert war, an der Geschichte

---

Passage 8 of 9   Section 1.1, Para 65, 47 chars.

65: Ich war früher überhaupt nicht so auf Pflanzen,

Passage 9 of 9   Section 1.1, Para 68, 574 chars.

68: Eben nicht, das ist ja so schade. Ich hab´ das so noch nie gemacht, also nur so spontan, so kurz oder so aber nicht so ein Thema, nicht so richtig und jetzt wo wir´ s gemacht haben hat jeder auch Interesse, dass weiterhin solche Themen bearbeitet werden wie das. Es war einfach ein richtiges Erlebnis. Ich glaub´ das war nicht nur ich am Anfang, ich glaub´ eigentlich nicht dass nut ich es war, die kein Interesse gezeigt hat, das waren mehrere v.a. der Sascha, der ist normalerweise nicht so, dass er so interessiert ist, der ist wirklich....das hab´ ich so super gefunden

---

Node 35 of 179   (1 14 2) /learning experience/dilemmastoryapproach/Langeweile
Passage 1 of 2   Section 1.1, Para 7, 104 chars.

7: Am Anfang wie ich´ s gehört hab´, hab´ ich nur auf die Uhr geschaut, wann ist endlich die Stunde vorbei.

Passage 2 of 2   Section 1.1, Para 10, 99 chars.

10: Weil´ s schon angefangen hat mit Peter und es gibt einen Baum. Es war einfach nicht so interessant

---

Node 36 of 179   (1 14 3) /learning experience/dilemmastoryapproach/Erlebnis
Passage 1 of 2   Section 1.1, Para 68, 574 chars.

68: Eben nicht, das ist ja so schade. Ich hab´ das so noch nie gemacht, also nur so spontan, so kurz oder so aber nicht so ein Thema, nicht so richtig und jetzt wo wir´ s gemacht haben hat jeder auch Interesse, dass weiterhin solche Themen bearbeitet werden wie das. Es war einfach ein richtiges Erlebnis. Ich glaub´ das war nicht nur ich am Anfang, ich glaub´ eigentlich nicht dass nut ich es war, die kein Interesse gezeigt hat, das waren mehrere v.a. der Sascha, der ist normalerweise nicht so, dass er so interessiert ist, der ist wirklich....das hab´ ich so super gefunden

80: ar wirklich ein Supererlebnis, so die Geschichte und ich hoffe wir werden noch weiterhin solche Sachen machen.

37: Dass jeder so gespannt zugehört hat, dass hat mich so gewundert, weil es ist eigentlich ja eine volllaute Klasse.

26: Das ist normal nie der Fall, dass war wirklich so heftig.

7: weil so was haben wir noch nie gemacht in der Schule.

30: Manchmal war´s überraschend und manchmal war´s auch enttäuschend.

30: Da war ich wirklich überrascht und hab´ gedacht: „He, das gibt´s ja nicht?!"

30: Und das hab´ ich ihr auch nicht gesagt, aber trotzdem, ich weiß nicht, manchmal war ich ganz überrascht und enttäuscht.

37: Dass jeder so gespannt zugehört hat, dass hat mich so gewundert, weil es ist eigentlich ja eine volllaute Klasse.

53: Und ich hätte mir nie gedacht, dass wir so was im naturwissenschaftlichen Zweig machen.

7: lustigen

43: Die Frau Roll hat das auch so lustig erzählt und es war so macht´ s einem auch Spaß zu lernen.

7: jetzt ich bin voll begeistert von der Geschichte gewesen

7: bin ich ganz begeistert,

10: ich hab´ daheim voll begeistert erzählt, was ich nicht jeden tag über die Schule mach´. Aber ich war schon begeistert.

43: Es war wirklich toll!

7: Es ist auch irgendwie in einer lustigen Form erzählt worden am Anfang.

10: wie im Zeichentrickfilm wurde es erzählt,

13: es wäre vielleicht besser gewesen, wenn wir die Geschichte so in Kleingruppen gehört hätten und nachher dass wir´ s dann zusammen besprochen hätten

---

16: es ist sowieso besser wenn man eine Geschichte selber erzählt.

4: Also ich geb´ s ehrlich zu am Anfang hab´ ich´ s echt blöd gefunden

---

13: Es war schon gut, dass wir´ s alle gehört haben,

30: manche haben´ s auch nicht so richtig ernst genommen und haben irgendetwas hingeschrieben.

16: Wenn man´ s erzählt kann man sich viel besser in die Situation hineinversetzen. Ist vielleicht ein bisschen interessanter. Für mich jedenfalls war´ s halt so!

30:   ich war enttäuscht, dass sie das geschrieben hat, dass sie den Baum eigentlich wegschneiden würde. Da war ich wirklich überrascht und hab´ gedacht: „He, das gibt´ s ja nicht?!"

30: Und das hab´ ich ihr auch nicht gesagt, aber trotzdem, ich weiß nicht, manchmal war ich ganz überrascht und enttäuscht.

74: Muss ja nicht nur sein, dass ich´ s jetzt brauch´ und ich muss ja nicht nur das beschreiben ich kann dann ja auch meine eigenen Gefühle beschreiben z.B. es muss ja nicht sein, dass ich die ganze Geschichte noch einmal aufschreib´, kann ja auch andere Dinge schreiben, die mir so nahe stehen von dem....

77: Ja ich halte das schon für wichtig. Also ich denke schon dass ich das noch weiter brauchen werde. Nicht nur in der 5., ich denke schon, dass ich in der 8. auch noch drüber schreiben kann.

7: es hat mich nicht so interessiert.

10: Kann auch sein dass ich mich täusch´ aber ich hab´ daheim voll begeistert erzählt, was ich nicht jeden tag über die Schule mach´. Aber ich war schon begeistert.

16: Für mich jedenfalls war´ s halt so

23: Ja schon. Aber wenn ich jetzt an den Peter denk´ - ich hätt´ s genauso schwer gehabt es war wirklich eine schwere Entscheidung,

---

26: Für mich war das sehr schwer, weil wir haben uns ein paar mal gestritten.

37: Ich hab´ oft aufgezeigt und bin auch oft drangekommen, aber es war schwer, weil man kann sich nicht ganz so richtig durchsetzen. Es ist eine große Klasse.

37: Wenn man sagt es ist zehn gegen zehn, aber wenn ich jetzt eine bin, die eine völlig andere Meinung hat

---

37: ich persönlich hab´ unsere Klasse noch nie so erlebt.

37: Dass jeder so gespannt zugehört hat, dass hat mich so gewundert, weil es ist eigentlich ja eine volllaute Klasse.

42: ·   Was glaubst du das diesmal anders war?

43: Ich weiß es selber nicht. Am Anfang hab´ ich jeden angeschaut, ganz lang sogar, und hab´ gesehen, dass jeder ganz interessiert zuhört, aber ich glaub´ ich war am Anfang die einzige, die am Anfang nicht so interessiert war, an der Geschichte. Je länger ich´s dann angehört dann, ich weiß nicht, dass ich so schnell dann eine andere Meinung gehabt hab´?!

47: Ich finde es schon sinnvoll und wir das glaub´ ich ja auch noch weiterhin verfolgen und in Bio machen wir das ja sowieso auch noch weiter. Ich denke mir, so kann sich jeder auch einiges merken. Ich glaub´, das kann jetzt nicht so schnell jeder vergessen

53: Ich persönlich hab´ mich bei der Geschichte auch wohlgefühlt und einerseits auch nicht! Es war so komisch am Anfang war ich so glücklich und nachher hab´ ich mich irgendwie so zusammenziehen

53: So ein Gefühl hab´ ich nicht gehabt in der Schule. Einerseits war ich eh ganz super, aber dann hab´ ich gemerkt, dass je länger ich die Geschichte anhöre es geht um einen Baum, aber das ist schon einiges, das ist schon viel, das ist was ganz Grosses,...weiß nicht...so ein Gefühl hab´ ich noch nie gehabt, so richtig! Und ich hätte mir nie gedacht, dass wir so was im naturwissenschaftlichen Zweig machen....

56: „Wenn du Peter wärst, würdest du den Baum selber schneiden?" Also ich könnte das nie machen! Es war nicht besonders schön ich hab´ auch sehr lange überlegen müssen und trotzdem hab´ ich s nicht geschafft die zu beantworten, weil ich würde sogar nicht einmal jemand anderen dranlassen an den Baum. Ich würd´ es auch selber nicht schaffen! Sicher nicht. Da bin ich mir sicher, weil der Baum muss für mich ja mein ein und alles sein irgendwie, wenn ich dem 35 oder 33 Jahre großgeworden bin? Dann würd´ ich´s auch nicht über´s Herz bringen.

59: Das war immer so immer war es eigentlich eine negative Entscheidung ich hab´ mich nicht so richtig konzentrieren können.Es war so schwer und mir ist nichts eingefallen dabei. Ich hab´ mir gedacht: „ ich hab´ mir gedacht ich steh´ vor weiß Gott was für einer Entscheidung.

62: Ich war so nervös am Anfang beim Schreiben. Ich hab´ da herumgefragt: „Was schreibt´s denn ihr?"

62: Es war nicht ein schönes Gefühl, wenn man nicht weiß was man jetzt machen soll und da herumfragen muss so als ob man vor einer Prüfung steht und nichts kann! So hab´ ich mich gefühlt! Genauso!

Passage 18 of 23   Section 1.1, Para 65, 78 chars.

65: Ich war früher überhaupt nicht so auf Pflanzen, auf „Gieß´ jetzt die Blumen!"

Passage 19 of 23   Section 1.1, Para 65, 132 chars.

65: jetzt ist´ s ganz anderes Gefühl, für mich persönlich positiv, dass ich jetzt mehr darauf achte und da schau´ ich jetzt schon mehr!

Passage 20 of 23   Section 1.1, Para 68, 125 chars.

68: . der Sascha, der ist normalerweise nicht so, dass er so interessiert ist, der ist wirklich....das hab´ ich so super gefunden

Passage 21 of 23   Section 1.1, Para 74, 526 chars.

74: Ja, ich halt´ s schon für wichtig, nicht nur für die 5. wahrscheinlich kann man das für die 6. und für die 7. Klasse auch noch brauchen. Wer weiß, vielleicht kann ich ja sogar in der 8. irgendeine Arbeit darüber schreiben! Muss ja nicht nur sein, dass ich´ s jetzt brauch´ und ich muss ja nicht nur das beschreiben ich kann dann ja auch meine eigenen Gefühle beschreiben z.B. es muss ja nicht sein, dass ich die ganze Geschichte noch einmal aufschreib´, kann ja auch andere Dinge schreiben, die mir so nahe stehen von dem....

Passage 22 of 23   Section 1.1, Para 77, 187 chars.

77: Ja ich halte das schon für wichtig. Also ich denke schon dass ich das noch weiter brauchen werde. Nicht nur in der 5., ich denke schon, dass ich in der 8. auch noch drüber schreiben kann.

Passage 23 of 23   Section 1.1, Para 80, 114 chars.

80: es war wirklich ein Supererlebnis, so die Geschichte und ich hoffe wir werden noch weiterhin solche Sachen machen.

Node 50 of 179   (2 3 3 3 1) /self and others/self/meinung/eigene/eigene Meinung
Passage 1 of 3   Section 1.1, Para 23, 151 chars.

23: Und dort wo wir unsere eigene Meinung hinschreiben haben müssen, da hab´ ich mir auch so schwer getan wenn ich der Peter wär´, was hätte ich gemacht?

Passage 2 of 3   Section 1.1, Para 37, 62 chars.

37: so und bei manchen Sachen hab´ ich auch damit übereingestimmt,

Passage 3 of 3   Section 1.1, Para 37, 122 chars.

37: Es hat jeder seine Meinung, auch wenn´ s manchmal nicht wichtig ist, aber es ist halt schwer, sich manchmal durchzusetzen.

Node 51 of 179   (2 3 3 3 4) /self and others/self/meinung/eigene/Meinung geaendert

Passage 1 of 2   Section 1.1, Para 43, 113 chars.

43: Je länger ich´ s dann angehört dann, ich weiß nicht, dass ich so schnell dann eine andere Meinung gehabt hab´?!

Passage 2 of 2   Section 1.1, Para 50, 87 chars.

50: Wenn ich jetzt im Wald bin ich werde sicher anders denken, jetzt nach der Geschichte.

Node 52 of 179   (2 3 3 4 2) /self and others/self/meinung/andere/andere Meinung

Passage 1 of 8   Section 1.1, Para 26, 29 chars.

26: jeder hat was anderes gesagt

Passage 2 of 8   Section 1.1, Para 26, 93 chars.

26: „Man kann doch den Baum einfach wegschneiden!" aber ich weiß nicht, ich war nicht der Meinung

Passage 3 of 8   Section 1.1, Para 30, 66 chars.

30: meine beste Freundin eine ganz andere Meinung gehabt hat als ich,

Passage 4 of 8   Section 1.1, Para 34, 130 chars.

34: aber dann daheim, es hat schon immer wieder Moment gegeben, wo ich daran gedacht hab´: „ Warum hat sie nicht das Gleiche wie ich?

Passage 5 of 8   Section 1.1, Para 34, 50 chars.

34: es hat jeder verschieden Meinungen das ist klar,

Passage 6 of 8   Section 1.1, Para 37, 102 chars.

37: Wenn man sagt es ist zehn gegen zehn, aber wenn ich jetzt eine bin, die eine völlig andere Meinung hat

Passage 7 of 8   Section 1.1, Para 62, 79 chars.

62: Es hat mir eh nichts gebracht weil es hat eh jeder seine eigene Meinung gehabt.

62: Ich hab´ sowieso ein ganz anderes Gefühl gehabt!

23: das war nur ein Baum.

23: dann ist es nicht so leicht auch wenn´ s nur ein Baum ist

---

26: „Man kann doch den Baum einfach wegschneiden!

65: jetzt hör´ ich schon mehr zu und so und das mach´ ich jetzt auch. Durch die Geschichte hab´ ich ein anderes Gefühl am Anfang war´ s überhaupt nicht so, aber jetzt gestern noch die drei Stunden die haben such...jetzt ist´ s ganz anderes Gefühl, für mich persönlich positiv, dass ich jetzt mehr darauf achte und da schau´ ich jetzt schon mehr! Das heißt jetzt nicht: „Oh ich geh´ auf die Wiese jetzt nicht!" Ich achte jetzt schon mehr drauf

---

56: weil der Baum muss für mich ja mein ein und alles sein irgendwie, wenn ich dem 35 oder 33 Jahre großgeworden bin?

56: weil ich würde sogar nicht einmal jemand anderen dranlassen an den Baum.

53: nachher hab´ ich mich irgendwie so zusammenziehen müssen.

53: So ein Gefühl hab´ ich nicht gehabt in der Schule.

53: so ein Gefühl hab´ ich noch nie gehabt, so richtig!

53: Es war so komisch am Anfang war ich so glücklich

53: Ich persönlich hab´ mich bei der Geschichte auch wohlgefühlt und einerseits auch nicht!

20: wie ich die Geschichte gehört hab´ immer länger es war nicht so leicht. Trotzdem ich hab´ mich nicht so wohl gefühlt.

53: Ich persönlich hab´ mich bei der Geschichte auch wohlgefühlt und einerseits auch nicht!

62: Es war nicht ein schönes Gefühl, wenn man nicht weiß was man jetzt machen soll und da herumfragen muss so als ob man vor einer Prüfung steht und nichts kann! So hab´ ich mich gefühlt! Genauso!

26: ich hab´ , das einfach nicht mit anhören können,

62: Ich hab´ da herumgefragt: „Was schreibt´ s denn ihr? Was schreibt´ s denn ihr?"

(2 3 15 6) /self and others/self/feelings/Enttaeuschung
Section 1.1, Para 30, 67 chars.

30: Manchmal war´ s überraschend und manchmal war´ s auch enttäuschend.

Section 1.1, Para 30, 79 chars.

30: dass sie das geschrieben hat, dass sie den Baum eigentlich wegschneiden würde.

(2 3 15 6 1) /self and others/self/feelings/Enttaeuschung/nicht darueber gesprochen
Section 1.1, Para 30, 119 chars.

30: Und das hab´ ich ihr auch nicht gesagt, aber trotzdem, ich weiß nicht, manchmal war ich ganz überrascht und enttäuscht.

Section 1.1, Para 34, 24 chars.

34: Gefragt hab´ ich nicht,

(2 3 15 6 7) /self and others/self/feelings/Enttaeuschung/jemanden kennen
Section 1.1, Para 30, 28 chars.

30: obwohl ich sie solange kenn´

(2 3 15 7) /self and others/self/feelings/nervoes sein
Section 1.1, Para 62, 34 chars.

62: o nervös am Anfang beim Schreiben.

(2 3 15 8) /self and others/self/feelings/Angst
Section 1.1, Para 62, 48 chars.

62: Ich hab´ sowieso ein ganz anderes Gefühl gehabt!

Section 1.1, Para 62, 193 chars.

62: Es war nicht ein schönes Gefühl, wenn man nicht weiß was man jetzt machen soll und da herumfragen muss so als ob man vor einer Prüfung steht und nichts kann! So hab´ ich mich gefühlt! Genauso!

37: Es ist eine große Klasse.

37: ich persönlich hab´ unsere Klasse noch nie so erlebt.

37: Dass jeder so gespannt zugehört hat, dass hat mich so gewundert, weil es ist eigentlich ja eine volllaute Klasse.

37: Am Anfang war´ s schon ein bisschen anstrengend überall mitzuhören

---

34: Warum hat sie nicht das Gleiche wie ich?"

43: Am Anfang hab´ ich jeden angeschaut, ganz lang sogar, und hab´ gesehen, dass jeder ganz interessiert zuhört,

---

Node 72 of 179   (2 5 1 1 2 6 1) /self and others/others/Klasse/relationship/communication/observe~watch others/veraendertes Verhalten von Mitschuel

Passage 1 of 2   Section 1.1, Para 68, 124 chars.

68: der Sascha, der ist normalerweise nicht so, dass er so interessiert ist, der ist wirklich....das hab´ ich so super gefunden

---

71: Ja der ist normalerweise nicht so!

Passage 1 of 12   Section 1.1, Para 7, 48 chars.

7: Weiß´ nicht, es hat mich nicht so interessiert.

Passage 2 of 12   Section 1.1, Para 10, 99 chars.

10: Weil´ s schon angefangen hat mit Peter und es gibt einen Baum. Es war einfach nicht so interessant

---

Passage 3 of 12   Section 1.1, Para 10, 120 chars.

10: ich hab´ mich vorher für Pflanzen nicht so interessiert. Mein Interesse ist dadurch etwas mehr geworden, kommt mir vor.

Passage 4 of 12   Section 1.1, Para 16, 119 chars.

16: da hätte sowieso keiner Interesse es ist sowieso besser wenn man eine Geschichte selber erzählt. Zu lesen oder im Buch

---

Passage 5 of 12   Section 1.1, Para 16, 50 chars.

16: so ist es ja viel interessanter, so hört man ja zu

Passage 6 of 12   Section 1.1, Para 16, 47 chars.

16: Wenn man´ s liest ist es nicht so interessant.

Passage 7 of 12   Section 1.1, Para 20, 71 chars.

20: Am Anfang war´ s so schwer weil ich überhaupt kein Interesse gehabt hab

---

Passage 8 of 12   Section 1.1, Para 30, 121 chars.

30: Es ist auch nicht leicht, sich in die Situation hineinzuversetzen, wenn´ s einen interessiert und so, wird das auch gehen

---

Passage 9 of 12   Section 1.1, Para 43, 108 chars.

43: Am Anfang hab´ ich jeden angeschaut, ganz lang sogar, und hab´ gesehen, dass jeder ganz interessiert zuhört,

---

Passage 10 of 12   Section 1.1, Para 43, 100 chars.

43: ich glaub´ ich war am Anfang die einzige, die am Anfang nicht so interessiert war, an der Geschichte

---

Passage 11 of 12   Section 1.1, Para 65, 47 chars.

65: Ich war früher überhaupt nicht so auf Pflanzen,

68: Eben nicht, das ist ja so schade. Ich hab' das so noch nie gemacht, also nur so spontan, so kurz oder so aber nicht so ein Thema, nicht so richtig und jetzt wo wir' s gemacht haben hat jeder auch Interesse, dass weiterhin solche Themen bearbeitet werden wie das. Es war einfach ein richtiges Erlebnis. Ich glaub' das war nicht nur ich am Anfang, ich glaub' eigentlich nicht dass nut ich es war, die kein Interesse gezeigt hat, das waren mehrere v.a. der Sascha, der ist normalerweise nicht so, dass er so interessiert ist, der ist wirklich....das hab' ich so super gefunden

Node 74 of 179   (2 5 1 1 2 6 2 1) /self and others/others/Klasse/relationship/communication/observe~watch others/Interesse/kein Interesse

7: Weiß' nicht, es hat mich nicht so interessiert.

10: Weil' s schon angefangen hat mit Peter und es gibt einen Baum. Es war einfach nicht so interessant

10: ich hab' mich vorher für Pflanzen nicht so interessiert.

16: da hätte sowieso keiner Interesse es ist sowieso besser wenn man eine Geschichte selber erzählt. Zu lesen oder im Buch

16: Wenn man' s liest ist es nicht so interessant.

20: Am Anfang war' s so schwer weil ich überhaupt kein Interesse gehabt hab

43: ich glaub' ich war am Anfang die einzige, die am Anfang nicht so interessiert war, an der Geschichte

65: Ich war früher überhaupt nicht so auf Pflanzen,

68: Eben nicht, das ist ja so schade. Ich hab´ das so noch nie gemacht, also nur so spontan, so kurz oder so aber nicht so ein Thema, nicht so richtig und jetzt wo wir´ s gemacht haben hat jeder auch Interesse, dass weiterhin solche Themen bearbeitet werden wie das. Es war einfach ein richtiges Erlebnis. Ich glaub´ das war nicht nur ich am Anfang, ich glaub´ eigentlich nicht dass nut ich es war, die kein Interesse gezeigt hat, das waren mehrere v.a. der Sascha, der ist normalerweise nicht so, dass er so interessiert ist, der ist wirklich....das hab´ ich so super gefunden

---

Node 75 of 179   (2 5 1 1 2 7) /self and others/others/Klasse/relationship/communication/sich durchsetzen
Passage 1 of 3   Section 1.1, Para 37, 128 chars.

37: Ich hab´ oft aufgezeigt und bin auch oft drangekommen, aber es war schwer, weil man kann sich nicht ganz so richtig durchsetzen.

Passage 2 of 3   Section 1.1, Para 37, 122 chars.

37: Es hat jeder seine Meinung, auch wenn´ s manchmal nicht wichtig ist, aber es ist halt schwer, sich manchmal durchzusetzen.

Passage 3 of 3   Section 1.1, Para 37, 102 chars.

37: Wenn man sagt es ist zehn gegen zehn, aber wenn ich jetzt eine bin, die eine völlig andere Meinung hat

---

Node 76 of 179   (2 5 1 1 2 8) /self and others/others/Klasse/relationship/communication/argueing with others
Passage 1 of 3   Section 1.1, Para 26, 131 chars.

26: Für mich war das sehr schwer, weil wir haben uns ein paar mal gestritten. Das ist normal nie der Fall, dass war wirklich so heftig.

Passage 2 of 3   Section 1.1, Para 26, 76 chars.

26: Es haben viele gesagt, es geht ja nur um einen Baum, was streitet ihr darum,

---

Passage 3 of 3   Section 1.1, Para 26, 49 chars.

26: weil wir haben immer zum Streiten anfangen müssen

Node 77 of 179   (2 5 1 1 2 10 1) /self and others/others/Klasse/relationship/communication/being empathic/sich was vorstellen
Passage 1 of 1   Section 1.1, Para 16, 27 chars.

16: sich irgendwas vorstellen.

Passage 1 of 1   Section 1.1, Para 30, 121 chars.

30: Es ist auch nicht leicht, sich in die Situation hineinzuversetzen, wenn´ s einen interessiert und so, wird das auch gehen

---

Passage 1 of 6   Section 1.1, Para 16, 79 chars.

16: Wenn man´ s erzählt kann man sich viel besser in die Situation hineinversetzen.

Passage 2 of 6   Section 1.1, Para 20, 123 chars.

20: Am Anfang war´ s so schwer weil ich überhaupt kein Interesse gehabt hab´, darum hab´ ich mich nicht hineinversetzen können,

---

Passage 3 of 6   Section 1.1, Para 23, 34 chars.

23: wenn ich jetzt an den Peter denk´

Passage 4 of 6   Section 1.1, Para 23, 205 chars.

23: Es ist schwer nachher zu denken, was würde ich machen? Und dort wo wir unsere eigene Meinung hinschreiben haben müssen, da hab´ ich mir auch so schwer getan wenn ich der Peter wär´, was hätte ich gemacht?

Passage 5 of 6   Section 1.1, Para 26, 48 chars.

26: es war so als ob ich das alles mitgemacht hätte

Passage 6 of 6   Section 1.1, Para 30, 121 chars.

30: Es ist auch nicht leicht, sich in die Situation hineinzuversetzen, wenn´ s einen interessiert und so, wird das auch gehen

---

Passage 1 of 3   Section 1.1, Para 30, 99 chars.

30: ich war enttäuscht, dass sie das geschrieben hat, dass sie den Baum eigentlich wegschneiden würde.

Passage 2 of 3   Section 1.1, Para 30, 120 chars.

30: Und das hab´ ich ihr auch nicht gesagt, aber trotzdem, ich weiß nicht, manchmal war ich ganz überrascht und enttäuscht.

34: aber dann daheim, es hat schon immer wieder Moment gegeben, wo ich daran gedacht hab´: „ Warum hat sie nicht das Gleiche wie ich?

30: Und das hab´ ich ihr auch nicht gesagt, aber trotzdem, ich weiß nicht, manchmal war ich ganz überrascht und enttäuscht.

34: Gefragt hab´ ich nicht,

30: obwohl ich sie solange kenn´

37: Es hat jeder seine Meinung, auch wenn´s manchmal nicht wichtig ist, aber es ist halt schwer, sich manchmal durchzusetzen.

37: so und bei manchen Sachen hab´ ich auch damit übereingestimmt,

23: Und dort wo wir unsere eigene Meinung hinschreiben haben müssen, da hab´ ich mir auch so schwer getan wenn ich der Peter wär´, was hätte ich gemacht?

43: Je länger ich´ s dann angehört dann, ich weiß nicht, dass ich so schnell dann eine andere Meinung gehabt hab´?!

50: Wenn ich jetzt im Wald bin ich werde sicher anders denken, jetzt nach der Geschichte.

26: aber ich weiß nicht, ich war nicht der Meinung

30: meine beste Freundin eine ganz andere Meinung gehabt hat als ich,

34: es hat jeder verschieden Meinungen das ist klar,

37: Wenn man sagt es ist zehn gegen zehn, aber wenn ich jetzt eine bin, die eine völlig andere Meinung hat

62: Es hat mir eh nichts gebracht weil es hat eh jeder seine eigene Meinung gehabt.

62: Ich hab´ sowieso ein ganz anderes Gefühl gehabt!

26: jeder hat was anderes gesagt

23: das war nur ein Baum.

23: dann ist es nicht so leicht auch wenn´ s nur ein Baum ist

26: „Man kann doch den Baum einfach wegschneiden!

68: der Sascha, der ist normalerweise nicht so, dass er so interessiert ist, der ist wirklich....das hab´ ich so super gefunden

71: Ja der ist normalerweise nicht so!

4: Also ich geb´ s ehrlich zu am Anfang hab´ ich´ s echt blöd gefunden

10: Weil´ s schon angefangen hat mit Peter und es gibt einen Baum.

10: Kann auch sein dass ich mich täusch´ aber ich hab´ daheim voll begeistert erzählt, was ich nicht jeden tag über die Schule mach´.

20: Am Anfang war´ s so schwer weil ich überhaupt kein Interesse gehabt hab´, darum hab´ ich mich nicht hineinversetzen können, aber dann, wie ich die Geschichte gehört hab´ immer länger es war nicht so leicht.

30: Manchmal war´ s überraschend und manchmal war´ s auch enttäuschend.

37: Am Anfang war´ s schon ein bisschen anstrengend überall mitzuhören und so und bei manchen Sachen hab´ ich auch damit übereingestimmt, aber sonst, es war.

53: Es war so komisch am Anfang war ich so glücklich und nachher hab´ ich mich irgendwie so zusammenziehen müssen.

68: Eben nicht, das ist ja so schade.

26: Das ist normal nie der Fall, dass war wirklich so heftig.

53: So ein Gefühl hab´ ich nicht gehabt in der Schule.

53: so ein Gefühl hab´ ich noch nie gehabt, so richtig!

37: ich persönlich hab´ unsere Klasse noch nie so erlebt.

68: Eben nicht, das ist ja so schade. Ich hab´ das so noch nie gemacht, also nur so spontan, so kurz oder so aber nicht so ein Thema, nicht so richtig und jetzt wo wir´ s gemacht haben hat jeder auch Interesse, dass weiterhin solche Themen bearbeitet werden wie das. Es war einfach ein richtiges Erlebnis. Ich glaub´ das war nicht nur ich am Anfang, ich glaub´ eigentlich nicht dass nut ich es war, die kein Interesse gezeigt hat, das waren mehrere v.a. der Sascha, der ist normalerweise nicht so, dass er so interessiert ist, der ist wirklich....das hab´ ich so super gefunden

7: Aber jetzt wo ich weiß worum´ s gegangen ist und die ganze Geschichte gehört hab´, bin ich ganz begeistert, weil so was haben wir noch nie gemacht in der Schule.

50: Wenn ich jetzt im Wald bin ich werde sicher anders denken, jetzt nach der Geschichte. 100 Prozent bin ich mir sicher!

80: es war wirklich ein Supererlebnis, so die Geschichte und ich hoffe wir werden noch weiterhin solche Sachen machen.

47: wir das glaub´ ich ja auch noch weiterhin verfolgen und in Bio machen wir das ja sowieso auch noch weiter.

74: It´ s schon für wichtig, nicht nur für die 5. wahrscheinlich kann man das für die 6. und für die 7. Klasse auch noch brauchen. Wer weiß, vielleicht kann ich ja sogar in der 8. irgendeine Arbeit darüber schreiben! Muss ja nicht nur sein, dass ich´ s jetzt brauch´ und ich muss ja nicht nur das beschreiben ich kann dann ja auch meine eigenen Gefühle beschreiben z.B. es muss ja nicht sein, dass ich die ganze Geschichte noch einmal aufschreib´, kann ja auch andere Dinge schreiben, die mir so nahe stehen von dem....

75:

76: ·   Für wichtig hältst du es dass es überhaupt unterrichtet wird?

77: Ja ich halte das schon für wichtig. Also ich denke schon dass ich das noch weiter brauchen werde. Nicht nur in der 5., ich denke schon, dass ich in der 8. auch noch drüber schreiben kann.

10: ich hab´ daheim voll begeistert erzählt, was ich nicht jeden tag über die Schule mach´.

34: aber dann daheim, es hat schon immer wieder Moment gegeben, wo ich daran gedacht hab': „ Warum hat sie nicht das Gleiche wie ich?

Node 101 of 179   (4 1) /space/Spatiality

Passage 1 of 2   Section 1.1, Para 10, 88 chars.

10: ich hab´ daheim voll begeistert erzählt, was ich nicht jeden tag über die Schule mach´.

Passage 2 of 2   Section 1.1, Para 34, 85 chars.

34: aber dann daheim, es hat schon immer wieder Moment gegeben, wo ich daran gedacht hab´

Node 102 of 179   (5 1) /evaluation/sinnvoll

Passage 1 of 1   Section 1.1, Para 47, 27 chars.

47: Ich finde es schon sinnvoll

Node 103 of 179   (5 8) /evaluation/importance

Passage 1 of 1   Section 1.1, Paras 74 to 77, 779 chars.

74: Ja, ich halt´ s schon für wichtig, nicht nur für die 5. wahrscheinlich kann man das für die 6. und für die 7. Klasse auch noch brauchen. Wer weiß, vielleicht kann ich ja sogar in der 8. irgendeine Arbeit darüber schreiben! Muss ja nicht nur sein, dass ich´ s jetzt brauch´ und ich muss ja nicht nur das beschreiben ich kann dann ja auch meine eigenen Gefühle beschreiben z.B. es muss ja nicht sein, dass ich die ganze Geschichte noch einmal aufschreib´, kann ja auch andere Dinge schreiben, die mir so nahe stehen von dem....

75:

76: ·   Für wichtig hältst du es dass es überhaupt unterrichtet wird?

77: Ja ich halte das schon für wichtig. Also ich denke schon dass ich das noch weiter brauchen werde. Nicht nur in der 5., ich denke schon, dass ich in der 8. auch noch drüber schreiben kann.

Node 104 of 179   (6 1) /Search Results/Single Text Lookup

Passage 1 of 1   Section 1.1, Para 26, 6 chars.

26: heftig

No other nodes in this set

code this document.

Appendix 10C: List of Nodes

NVivo revision 2.0.161   Licensee: smec-203-1

Project: Fichte 22   User: Administrator   Date: 2/08/2003 - 2:57:10 PM
NODE LISTING

Nodes in Set: All Nodes
Created: 6/07/2001 - 3:16:01 PM
Modified:6/07/2001 - 3:16:01 PM
Number of Nodes: 179

1   meaning of ethics for you~
2   (1) /learning experience
3   (1 13) /learning experience/learning process
4   (1 13 1) /learning experience/learning process/learning
5   (1 13 1 3) /learning experience/learning process/learning/forgetting
6   (1 13 2) /learning experience/learning process/imagination
7   (1 13 3) /learning experience/learning process/respect
8   (1 13 4) /learning experience/learning process/listen to others
9   (1 13 5) /learning experience/learning process/compare with others
10   (1 13 6) /learning experience/learning process/observe~watch others
11   (1 13 6 1) /learning experience/learning process/observe~watch others/veraendertes Verhalten von
Mitschuel
12   (1 13 6 2) /learning experience/learning process/observe~watch others/Interesse
13   (1 13 6 2 1) /learning experience/learning process/observe~watch others/Interesse/kein Interesse
14   (1 13 7) /learning experience/learning process/collaboration
15   (1 13 8) /learning experience/learning process/accepting othe opinions
16   (1 13 9) /learning experience/learning process/concentration
17   (1 13 13) /learning experience/learning process/decisionmaking
18   (1 13 13 2) /learning experience/learning process/decisionmaking/reflecting ~critically~
19   (1 13 13 2 10) /learning experience/learning process/decisionmaking/reflecting ~critically~/sich
hineinversetzen koennen
20   (1 13 13 2 10 1) /learning experience/learning process/decisionmaking/reflecting ~critically~/sich
hineinversetzen koennen/sich was vorstellen
21   (1 13 13 2 10 2) /learning experience/learning process/decisionmaking/reflecting ~critically~/sich
hineinversetzen koennen/funktionieren
22   (1 13 13 2 10 3) /learning experience/learning process/decisionmaking/reflecting ~critically~/sich
hineinversetzen koennen/sich hineinversetzen
23   (1 13 13 2 12) /learning experience/learning process/decisionmaking/reflecting ~critically~/nach dem
Grund fragen
24   (1 13 13 2 15) /learning experience/learning process/decisionmaking/reflecting
~critically~/Selbsterkenntnis
25   (1 13 13 4) /learning experience/learning process/decisionmaking/Schwierigkeit
26   (1 13 13 4 1) /learning experience/learning process/decisionmaking/Schwierigkeit/schwierig
27   (1 13 13 4 2) /learning experience/learning process/decisionmaking/Schwierigkeit/muehsam
28   (1 13 13 5) /learning experience/learning process/decisionmaking/Entscheidung
29   (1 13 13 5 1) /learning experience/learning process/decisionmaking/Entscheidung/Entscheidung
30   (1 13 13 5 2) /learning experience/learning process/decisionmaking/Entscheidung/negativ
31   (1 13 13 5 3) /learning experience/learning process/decisionmaking/Entscheidung/keine Idee
32   (1 13 13 5 4) /learning experience/learning process/decisionmaking/Entscheidung/keine Antwort
gefunden
33   (1 13 13 5 5) /learning experience/learning process/decisionmaking/Entscheidung/keine Begruendung
gefunden
34   (1 13 13 5 6) /learning experience/learning process/decisionmaking/Entscheidung/~gute, schlechte
Begruendung~
35   (1 13 13 5 7) /learning experience/learning process/decisionmaking/Entscheidung/koennte das nie
machen
36   (1 13 13 5 8) /learning experience/learning process/decisionmaking/Entscheidung/nicht schaffen
37   (1 13 13 5 9) /learning experience/learning process/decisionmaking/Entscheidung/nicht gewusst was tun

Appendix 11
Poster-transcripts & video transcripts

Appendix 11A: Examples poster-transcripts

Posters 5A, Dilemma 1 Irene, 18.5.2000:

Gruppe A:
- Wenn es sein müsste, würde ich ihn selbst abschneiden, denn ich würde nicht wollen, dass ihn irgendjemand abschneidet.
- Ich würde ein kleines Stück Krone behalten und einsetzen, damit die Schildkröte einen Schatten hat
- Wenn die Eltern unbedingt wollen, dass der Baum geschnitten werden muss, würde ich das schon selbst machen.
- Ich schneide den Baum nicht selber, auf den ich mein leben lang aufgepasst habe. Aber er wird geschnitten.
- Ich würde den Baum selbst schneiden, weil damit könnte ich der Abhängigkeit ein Ende setzen.

Gruppe B:
- Ich würde den Baum selbst fällen, da er ja sowieso gefällt werden muss und das eine Gelegenheit zum Verabschieden ist.
- Andrerseits wäre es schmerzhaft für mich, den Baum selbst zu fällen, da er praktisch ein Teil von mir ist
- Ich glaube, ich könnte den Baum nicht fällen, da ich nicht die Verantwortung für den zerstörten Lebensraum übernehmen könnte
- Ich kann ihn nicht selber fällen, da es mir sehr wehtun würde, einen Teil von mir abzuschneiden.

Gruppe C: selber schneiden
- Ich bin geistig mit ihm verbunden
- Weil ich ein Andenken haben möchte
- Weil ich mir noch einmal Erinnerungen durch den Kopf gehen lassen kann.

Nicht selber schneiden:
- Ich bringe es nicht über´ s Herz ihn selbst zu schneiden
- Weil ich Gefühle für ihn habe
- Weil ich nicht selbst dafür verantwortlich sein möchte

Gruppe D:
- Nein, ich würde meinen eigenen Baum niemals schneiden. Ich bin mit ihm aufgewachsen und außerdem habe ich ihm viel persönliches anvertraut.
- Wahrscheinlich würde ich ihn schneiden, denn bevor ich einen anderen Menschen, der keine Verbindung zu dem Baum hat, schneiden lasse, schneide ich ihn selbst.
- Ihr habt ihn eingepflanzt also fällt ihn auch

Gemeinsame Lösung:
- Wir würden es nicht über´ s Herz bringen den Baum zu fällen, weil er ein Teil von uns ist.

Es war eine wilde Diskussion, aber trotzdem konnten wir uns nicht einigen!

Gruppe E: Anfangs gab es Unstimmigkeiten über den Ausgang der Geschichte
Selber schneiden
- Bevor jemand den Baum fällt, der nicht weiß was dieser baum Peter bedeutet hat
- Am liebsten persönlich verabschieden

Schneiden lassen
- Es würde Peter viel zu sehr verletzen
- Er hätte Schuldgefühle, dass er dafür verantwortlich ist, dass der Baum gefällt wurde

Gruppe F:
- Fritz: ich würde den Baum nicht umschneiden, weil ein Teil meiner Jugend drinnen steckt

- Arna: Ich würde den Baum auch nicht umschneiden, weil es so wäre, als ob ich meinen besten Freund töte
- Paul: Ich würde den Baum umschneiden, weil er schon lange gedient hat. Dagegen würde ich einen neuen Baum anpflanzen
- Patrick: Ich würde den Baum umschneiden, weil ich meinen Eltern damit einen gefallen tue.

Appendix 11B: Examples video transcripts

Rainforest Dilemma

In the library

1 period Monday morning – many students are absent. Normally for no Catholic students this would be a free period. Irene is furious because she told them that they had to come to school because this was part of the ethics project. Irene introduces the new dilemma and tells the story freely.
Quiet - the students look rather bored – bad timing. Even those students who were full of praise last time.
She relates the story to Multiple Sclerosis. And one of the students Jacquie tells about an auntie who shares this problem.
Irene tells the story of a nephew who started to get MS at the early age of 28.

In the story the virus X12 causes MS like symptoms in a very short time.
Students are very quiet this time.

Alois tries to collaborate a little bit better this time – at least as much as he can. He is still the noisiest student of all.

1st dilemma:

Imelda: I would not risk my health for my career.If I am feeling bad then I cannot work properly and this is bad for my career as well.
Fatima: I would go because perhaps once I'm there I will feel much better.
Alex: argues that travelling with the flu is a bad idea because the virus might mutate and become even more infectious.

One student comes in late.

Students look overwhelmed. Story too complicated? Perhaps for an older age-group after all? Irene races through the dilemma. Group-work works well, especially the exchange of ideas. They are faster than last time but less involved.

Groups of three quickly present their results.
Some arguments include:
Melinda: People should go travelling only in very good health
Alex: Problem with travelling is that people also bring diseases home like Malaria.
Igor: One should get information about the country and try to find out not only which diseases one might get but also which diseases one might carry there.
Irene continues the story about the company tries to establish a production plant in the middle of the rainforest.
Groebacher: Does this pay off for the company at all to put so much effort into this project?

Irene explains shortly that if a company manages to produce a medicine against a disease and they are the first ones they can claim a monopoly and everyone who want the medicine has to pay them.

Bell rings. Dilemma unit has to be continued on Thursday in the first period.

In the biology lab (1st period)

Posterpreparation

One group have not prepared what they should haave prepared and they still have no idea what they are supposed to do. Finally after Irene has explained it several times, the group becomes a little bit more active.

Irene re-introduces dilemma situation, forms groups of four. The biology lab is absolutely unsuitable for this purpose. Tables that cannot be moved and that make group work extremely difficult.

Irene asks the students to prepare the posters in a way that dil 3 & 4 are written on the poster.
Alois keeps a relatively low profile but within his group he tries once again to be the clown.

Pretty hopeless filming! !
Groups do discuss their dilemmas but it is a drag. Cannot understand any comments on the video-tape because of the background noise in the bio lab much more echoing.

The religious education teacher comes in and students greet him. He walks around the room and reads posters.

Poster presentation

Jaquie, Emma, Fatima, Anna, volunteer as first group.

Emma: One should not travel everywhere and destroy other cultures. One should accept local religions and cultures and not try to impose one's own culture on others.

Irene tells from her own experiences in the rainforest. She tells the story of the transport of a huge crane into a remote area in the Brasilian rainforest that she had a chance to witness herself. Reason for this case was that in this particular area there were a few endemic plants – she explains what endemic means and that this actually goes together well with the story. Similar background.

Next group: Imelda. Melinda, Karin and Juergen.

Another interruption. Bell rings we still have not finished. Have to move class? Irene has one more period that day – the 6th period!!!

Irene has to make many announcements being the class teacher.

3rd attempt to finish the unit. In the library again: rest of the posters being presented and the discussion is initiated.

4th dilemma introduced.
Irene: Locals ask the two researchers: Why has nobody bothered to ask us whether the plants can be taken from our rainforest? But as a researcher you are powerless. Irene explains the higher politics of globalisation. Asks the students to reflect first by themselves.

Alois: It does not really matter whether or not the company bothers about asking the locals – it is going to happen anyway. It's always about money and after all the government can decide about everything.

Fatima: The government is only interested in the money, they are not interested in the people at all.

Youssi: …Something new is not always good!

Most students are in a better mood now – more social interactions. Some students argue that it is not OK to treat indigenous people as if they were wroth less than we are. The discussion works but only because Irene constantly asks students about their opinions. Some students are obviously close to falling asleep.

Alois: I think it's OK [to like the company did] as long as the locals get some compensation for their property – huts for example, new huts.

Irene is better this time. She is much more like her usual self. She is involved and moderates the discussion very well.

Aminou: He thinks that it is OK to perform research in rainforests because the locals might eventually need the medicine too.

Irene: But perhaps they cannot afford it then.

Aminou thinks hard: Shruggs his shoulders. Irene asks the students to finish off th last two questions in their portfolio.

Irene speaks about the dilemma question, where Anna and Bob have to consider the personal loss of trust and friendship with the local tribe.

Daniel: This is not a question of friendship only – it is a question of basic human rights.

Imelda & Georg: The people of the rainforest they live of the rainforest
One student: I might try to plant the plant somewhere else.

Irene; Biologically perhaps not so easy. Georg is very involved this time.

Plantations?

Georg: Those people are happy with what they have – we always want more and more. This is why I suggest that we try to breed these plants.

Last two questions remain unanswered.

Appendix 12

Examples of student portfolio-notes

Peters Fichte - Dilemma

> **Unterbrechung 1 - Dilemma 1:**

Stell dir vor, du bist Peter: Welche Argumente würdest du zur Rettung deines Baumes anführen?

Wie würdest du versuchen deine Eltern zu überzeugen?

Begründe deine Argumente!

- Wenn ihr den Baum fällt, dann fehlt ein Teil von mir.
- Ich habe eine Verbundenheit mit dem Baum.
- Ihr könnt doch nicht einfach wegen so einem Wohnmobile den Baum fällen.
- Stellt das Wohnmobil woandershin.
- Wenn der Baum weg ist, wo sollen dann die Tiere hin?
- Man muss ja nicht gleich den ganzen Baum fällen. Man kann ja einfach ein paar Äste weg schneiden.

> **Unterbrechung 2 - Dilemma 2:**

- Stell dir vor du wärst Peters Eltern: welche Gegenargumente könntest du bringen, weshalb der Baum trotzdem geschnitten werden muß?

Begründe Deine Argumente!

- Wir haben uns schon so lange so ein Wohnmobil gewünscht!
- Du hast eh die Fotos von dem Baum.
- Wir können einen neuen Baum weiter hinten anpflanzen.

Appendix 12 A

Du kommst ja so wie so fast nicht mehr zu
uns, also wird es auch keinen Unterschied machen
ob der Baum jetzt steht oder nicht.
• Das Wohnmobil hat so viel gekostet + man
kann es nicht mehr zurück geben.
• Wenn das Wohnmobil nicht unter einem Dach
steht wird es viel schneller kaputt.

Shit happens

Herbert und Andreas müssen eine Entscheidung treffen:
Stelle Dir vor, Du wärst Herbert - würdest Du das Angebot der Regierung
annehmen? In welcher Weise würden die Gerüchte bezüglich Folter und
Gefangenenlager Deine Entscheidung beeinflussen?

*würde ich es annehmen (was ich nicht glaube)
würde ich versuchen herauszufinden, was
an den Gerüchten wahr ist. Würde ich herausfinde
das diese wahr sind, würde ich meine Sachen
packen u. Prof. Schubert hinterher reisen und meine
Arbeiten mit ihm fortsetzen.*

→ *Wenn Gerüchte wahr wären, würden wir das
Land verlassen und unsere Arbeiten wo
anders fortsetzen.*

Herbert und Andreas erkennen plötzlich, daß sie keine freien Menschen mehr
sind. Sie haben die Wahl zwischen im Land zu bleiben und ihr Programm
fortzusetzen oder das Land zu verlassen und womöglich ihren Traum aufgeben
zu müssen. Stell dir vor, Du wärest Herbert, knapp vor der Erfüllung deines
Traumes - wie würdest du entscheiden?
Warum? Rechtfertige Deine Entscheidung!

*Ich würde weggehen! Einen Traum vergißt
man nicht. Herbert u. Andreas sollten weggehen,
ich würde. Wenn ich schon so lange an meinem
Traum arbeite und dann weggehen würde,
würde ich Prof. Schubert suchen, der Bestimmt
auch weiter gearbeitet hat.*

→ *Weggehen. Traum versuchen zu verwirklichen.*

Appendix 12B

Denke an Herbert und seinen Traum und welcher Preis dafür bezahlt werden mußte....

Wieviele WissenschaftlerInnen haben „große" Träume - z.B. den genetischen Code von Menschen manipulieren zu können, Gegenstände oder Menschen zu beamen, Kernfusion zu ermöglichen, etc., etc. ...

- Wie weit soll wissenschaftliche Forschung gehen dürfen?
- Ist es unter gewissen Umständen angemessen, daß einige (in Herberts Fall Häftlinge) für das Wohl der ganzen Menschheit geopfert werden? Warum? Begründe Deine Antwort!

→ Soweit, daß niemand sterben muß, außer er will für die Wissenschaft sterben.

→ Nein, nicht wenn sie unfreiwillig sterben müssen. Für das "Wohl" der Menschheit sollte niemand sterben! denn auch der, der stirbt, ist ein Teil der Menschheit. Es sollte niemand für irgendwen geopfert werden.

Appendix 13

Email attachment – tNARST distribution list

Dana Zeidler (2002)

Appendix 13

❑ The group discussed several potential ways that nature of science could facilitate moral reasoning and discourse in science education. For example, such " habits of mind" as curiosity, skepticism, and openness to new ideas are clearly related to both nature of science and moral reasoning. One individual said he teaches his high school physics students the concept that there are consequences, both good and bad, for knowledge they will gain in his class. Thus, there is a clear and necessary link between the skill and knowledge we teach students and moral and ethical reasoning.

❑ The group came to the conclusion that moral/ethical reasoning was related to both the application of scientific knowledge (e.g., STS type curricular emphases) as well as embedded within the subject matter itself. Both were viewed as important, with the latter being more complex and difficult for students to understand.

❑ There was agreement that teachers need a strong subject matter background if they are to teach nature of science and/or address moral/ethical reasoning. Without a strong background in subject matter, misconceptions would occur not only relative to subject matter, but also with respect to nature of science and moral/ethical reasoning relative to science.

❑ One interesting discussion thread developed regarding the relationship between decision-making on socio-scientific issues and understandings of nature of science. Randy discussed the results of his research, which compared the decision-making nature of science experts and non-experts. It turned out that both groups used similar reasoning patterns and reached similar decisions, despite their divergent views of science epistemology. Values, moral reasoning and personal experience all played a greater role in their decision-making than did their understandings of the nature of science.

❑ This lead to a discussion of the implications of these results. For one, just because people with expert knowledge of nature of science did not naturally use this knowledge in decision-making does not mean that they shouldn't. Perhaps they would reach "better" decisions if they were explicitly taught how to integrate their knowledge of nature of science into their decision-making processes.

❑ On the other hand, if the experts used values and moral reasoning in their decision-making, then perhaps some type of explicit instruction on values and moral reasoning would be the way to go. The group felt that it would be a mistake to try to teach (indoctrinate?) students with particular values. We agreed that metacognition was central to addressing these issues in public schools. Nature of science instruction can be described as the process of teaching students to think *about* science. Similarly, moral reasoning instruction involves teaching students to think about reasoning. Both types of instruction involve metacognition, which involves a set of high-level thinking skills that must be explicitly taught. Teaching students to think about how they think could segue nicely into the topics of thinking about science (NOS) and reasoning (moral reasoning).

❑ All of this begs the question of what is appropriate to teach when. Winchester wrote that introducing the tentativeness of scientific knowledge too early may lead to the unintended consequence of students throwing out the baby with the bath water. Fouad reminded us of Perry's work, which indicates that even college students do not tolerate ambiguity well. The challenge is to create methods and activities (including discourse on controversial issues) that are developmentally appropriate. The group agreed that this is a fruitful area for research.

❑ The issue of developmental appropriateness raised some interesting discussion. In particular, we considered whether certain topics should be considered developmental inappropriate or was the developmental appropriateness standard best applied to the depth of attention within a topical area.

❑ The group also considered whether students' inability to deal with ambiguity was something they learned or something that is inherent to humans. Again, this represented an area that the group viewed as an important area of research.

Overall, the group clearly supported the view that moral/ethical reasoning was important to the development of scientific literacy and that moral/ethical reasoning was intimately related to nature of science.

AND: Classroom Discourse Issues

discussion began with defining Moral reasoning and habits of mind.
ong the related topics were:
vancement of technology-genome project;
w much class discussion focuses on other than science issues;
ivacy issues-science can make more intrusions into lives;
te process (drug testing in schools);
iscourse-student empowerment and developmental issues;
internet discussions-argumentation during science reasoning;
the notion that science is devoid of democratic processes; and
the reasoning process-related to the role of parental input.

We have morally mature students in our classrooms; however, many science
teachers are not prepared to deal with moral and ethical issues. The
social context in which discourse occurs by students would mean that as
adults (i.e., teachers) we have to gain access to students' discourse.
Students will not always share their discourse with adults and/or adults
do not always understand the nature of student discourse. One possible way
to address student discourse is to create a caring community. Many
problems seem to arise based on the scale of schools -- small elementary
schools where students are known by name and face, increased sizes of
middle schools and increase high schools lead to the phenomenon of down
'facelessness' in our schools. We must engage in community building to
break down such 'facelessness'.

Our conversation then led us to discuss ethical/moral dilemmas and how do
we go about engaging our students and teachers in reasoning. Several
strategies were mentioned--debate, role playing scenarios, situations that
bring out emotions, character, and so forth.
In many instances in today's society, there is a conflict between what is
advocated v. context of our students' lives.

In many people's minds, there are two ways in which science is viewed:
science as fluid v. science is authoritarian a power differentially a
compelling reason for peer discourse. Science explanations are viewed as
appropriate, not as wrong or right. Students come to sophisticated
understandings more easily through peer discourse than through individual
reasoning alone. In these settings, the teacher can be an
agent/provocateur for critical thinking and moral reasoning.

There are also disparities in the way in which debate or discourse is
viewed in the science community and the education community: science v.
science education, where science is culture of discourse and science
education has little debate about science (tell me the answer v.
development/negotiate meaning of science).

The most important rationale for moral reasoning is that our students and
teachers bring society into classroom and the classroom is part of our
society.

Certain issues prevailed at our group's discussion --all related to
Strand: Cultural Issues:

-the whole issue of accessibility of science education and scientific literacy as being a moral imperative

-the issue that science must touch people more personally--once students leave formal schooling too many of them have little contact with science--therefore making connections with science during school and after schooling is an important issue

--we think it unfortunate that the tradition is to teach science in "moral vacuum"--thus making those connections more difficult to make for most students

--we were reminded of Okhee Lee's model of "cultural congruence" and that by explicitly promoting such a model we can do a better job of seeing how different components such as student AND teacher belief systems and cultural backgrounds can come into play before, during and after classroom teaching and learning experiences (someone contrasted this was the work of Roberta Barba--but I can't remember who and exactly what she said)

--We struggled a bit with just what our role is in preparing teachers with regard to moral and ethical reasoning--but we know we need to be more explicit than is currently the trend

--We made the point that there is a difference between teaching in a value-free environment and one that is value-fair (the one we prefer)--that is acknowledging that values must be respected and not ignored or discouraged from being exhibited when in fact a topic is value-laden

--Klaus brought up the issue that kids must be FREE enough to "absorb" and that one way to touch their values related to science is by respect and kindness

--We all pondered and doubted that there were currently any fifth grade books (science or otherwise) with any moral dimension whatever--when in fact there might be a way to promote awareness of that dimension of living.

--Randy asked us to think about working with preservice teachers and the issue of "fairness" when it comes to their notion of accessibility with the mentally challenged students. (e.g. Do we spend any time in our preservice programs dealing with the moral and ethical dimensions of teaching challenged students and THEIR "cultural congruence" as well as their accessibility to science education?

--That led us to discuss the need for teachers to be able to really weed out what needs to be achieved versus what specially challenged students might need and ask the question--should we add social to our moral and ethical dimensions? If so, is there a way to make all science learning look more alike--when in fact we, know it is going on in many different ways?

so solicited help from folks to come up with additional
ples of good case studies for ethical dilemmas in science
ing--as I turned out to have practically no science preservice
nts last semester. I am still searching for the paper where I
d down some of their ideas. I think I will call upon my group
mail to rekindle that discussion and refresh me on some of the
s that turned up. For example, the ethical dimensions of
erative group work--how selected, how assessed, etc.

STRAND: STSE and CASE STUDY GROUP Issues

general, the group was very supportive of STSE education, and the use of case studies in science education, as
e way of accomplishing some of the goals espoused by advocates of STSE education. Comments included:
- we cannot separate ethics from science or science from ethics.
- STSE is an extension of personal and social ethics.
- traditional STSE education (or perhaps STSE education as currently practiced by and large) only
  "points out" ethical dilemmas or controversy, but does not necessarily go beyond. Many felt that STSE
  is marginalized in the curriculum and in practice. It is not enough that curriculum documents (such as
  those in Canada) *identify* STSE as science education objectives/outcomes or expectations.

Case studies seemed to be a way of making STSE accessible and doable. Case study features include:
- an element of risk
- content in the making (contextualized – content is embedded in context)
- each case is different
- multi-disciplinary nature

This group spent considerable time discussing the challenges of STSE education and case study work. Challenges
included:
- assessment
- issue of ethics – whose ethics? Where and how do we position ourselves along the continuum i.e.
  indoctrination to relativism??
- moral reasoning – educators often feel ill-equipped in this area. Few have access to moral reasoning
  frameworks or structures that would be helpful in developing curriculum experiences for students
  around controversial issues or case studies.
- "informed" decision making – again, how do we teach about decision-making, what does "informed'
  really mean? What is the role of 'resolution' in the context of issues-based science curriculum?
- cultural congruence? Issues of cultural diversity, cultural values, beliefs, and norms
- the notion of 'habits of mind' found in many curriculum documents and policy papers - what does
  'habits of mind' look like? What does this phrase imply?
- teaching in a 'value-care' way (as opposed to a 'value -free' way)

Many felt the need to develop an on-going community of science educators interested in STSE, case studies etc.
The notion of in-service as a long-term professional development activity seemed critical (as opposed to one-shot
workshops that are usually deemed to be ineffective).